The Second Book of Samuel

THE NEW INTERNATIONAL COMMENTARY
ON THE
OLD TESTAMENT

General Editors

The Second Book of SAMUEL

David Toshio Tsumura

William B. Eerdmans Publishing Company
Grand Rapids, Michigan

Wm. B. Eerdmans Publishing Co.
4035 Park East Court SE, Grand Rapids, Michigan 49546
www.eerdmans.com

Published 2019
Printed in the United States of America

32 31 30 29 28 27 26 25   3 4 5 6 7 8 9 10

ISBN 978-0-8028-7096-4

Library of Congress Cataloging-in-Publication Data

A catalog record for this book is available from the Library of Congress.

For Susan and our six grandchildren,
Yuuki, Motoki, Yoshiki, Misaki, Kiho, and Shinya

Contents

General Editor's Preface

Long ago St. Paul wrote: "I planted, Apollos watered, but God gave the growth" (1 Cor. 3:6 NRSV). He was right: ministry indeed requires a team effort—the collective labors of many skilled hands and minds. Someone digs up the dirt and drops in seed, while others water the ground to nourish seedlings to growth. The same team effort over time has brought this commentary series to its position of prominence today. Professor E. J. Young "planted" it nearly fifty years ago, enlisting its first contributors and himself writing its first published volumes. Professor R. K. Harrison "watered" it, signing on other scholars and wisely editing everyone's finished products. As General Editor, I now tend their planting, and, true to Paul's words, through four decades God has indeed graciously "[given] the growth."

Today the New International Commentary on the Old Testament enjoys a wide readership of scholars, priests, pastors, rabbis, and other serious Bible students. Thousands of readers across the religious spectrum and in countless countries consult its volumes in their ongoing preaching, teaching, and research. They warmly welcome the publication of each new volume and eagerly await its eventual transformation from an emerging "series" into a complete commentary "set." But as humanity experiences a new century of history, an era commonly called "postmodern," what kind of commentary series is NICOT? What distinguishes it from other similarly well-established series?

Its volumes aim to publish biblical scholarship of the highest quality. Each contributor writes as an expert, both in the biblical text itself and in the relevant scholarly literature, and each commentary conveys the results of wide reading and careful, mature reflection. Ultimately, its spirit is eclectic, each contributor gleaning interpretive insights from any useful source, whatever its religious or philosophical viewpoint, and integrating them into his or her interpretation of a biblical book. The series draws on recent methodological innovations in biblical scholarship: for example, canon criticism, the so-called new literary criticism, reader-response theories, and sensitivity to gender-based and ethnic readings. NICOT volumes also aim to be irenic in tone, summarizing and critiquing influential views with fairness while defending their own. Its list of contributors includes male and female scholars from a number of Christian faith-groups. The diversity of contributors and their freedom to draw on all relevant methodologies give the entire series an exciting and enriching variety.

What truly distinguishes this series, however, is that it speaks from within that interpretive tradition known as evangelicalism. Evangelicalism is an informal movement within Protestantism that cuts across traditional denominational lines. Its heart and soul is the conviction that the Bible is God's inspired Word, written by gifted human writers, through which God calls humanity to enjoy a loving personal relationship with its Creator and Savior. True to that tradition, NICOT volumes do not treat the Old Testament as just an ancient literary artifact on a par with the *Iliad* or *Gilgamesh.* They are not literary autopsies of ancient parchment cadavers but rigorous, reverent wrestlings with wonderfully human writings through which the living God speaks his powerful Word. NICOT delicately balances "criticism" (i.e., the use of standard critical methodologies) with humble respect, admiration, and even affection for the biblical text. As an evangelical commentary, it pays particular attention to the text's literary features, theological themes, and implications for the life of faith today.

Ultimately, NICOT aims to serve women and men of faith who desire to hear God's voice afresh through the Old Testament. With gratitude to God for two marvelous gifts—the Scriptures themselves and keen-minded scholars to explain their message—I welcome readers of all kinds to savor the good fruit of this series.

Robert L. Hubbard Jr.

Author's Preface

This volume on 2 Samuel is the second and concluding volume of my commentary on 1–2 Samuel. When the late Professor R. K. Harrison invited me, a Semitic philologist who is not a native English speaker, to write an English commentary on 1–2 Samuel for this commentary series, he expected and encouraged me to deal with the difficult Hebrew text philologically.[1] He and I agreed to let the stories themselves give theological teachings and devotional insights. The most important matter was to decide the text on which my commentary should be based, for good comments on a wrong text will not help the readers to understand the original meaning.

Therefore, here, as in *The First Book of Samuel,* I concentrate on pursuing the meaning that the original author or authors[2] intended to convey to their audience, in my view readers of the early Divided Monarchy, possibly of the late tenth century B.C. or a little later, not readers of the Persian era of the sixth century B.C. as is often advocated in recent scholarly literature.

1. I had had no acquaintance with Professor Harrison, but he had read my detailed exegetical article on Hab. 3 ("Ugaritic Poetry and Habakkuk 3," *TynB* 40 [1988] 24-48) and asked me to contribute a commentary on 1–2 Samuel. I was trained in Hebrew exegesis and had published articles such as "Janus Parallelism in Hab. III 4," *VT* 54 (2004) 124-28 (reprinted in the special issue *Vetus Testamentum IOSOT* [*2013*] 113-16), but I was not a specialist of the history of ancient Israel.

2. Of course, this is a hypothetical "original" author or authors. In this commentary, my primary concern is the text itself, not the reception of the Books of Samuel in postbiblical times, though I did not ignore its reception by the NT authors. For recent treatments of the reception history of 1–2 Samuel, see W. Dietrich (ed.), *The Books of Samuel: Stories, History, Reception History* (BETL 284; Leuven: Peeters, 2016), as well as W. Dietrich, *Samuel* (BKAT; Neukirchen-Vluyn: Neukirchener, 2011-2015). For a history of the interpretation of a biblical book, see K. Greenwood (ed.), *Since the Beginning: Interpreting Genesis 1 and 2 through the Ages* (Grand Rapids: Baker Academic, 2018).

I am grateful for the critical attention my *The First Book of Samuel* has received, and I remain convinced of the basic correctness of my approach. For example, I still believe that many, if not all, MT texts can be supported as against the LXX as *lectio difficilior.* I have suggested taking a different linguistic approach rather than changing the text as a solution to those rather difficult problems since 1998.[3] Also, my approach does not use the consensus view of the Deuteronomistic redaction of the books of Samuel.[4] I am still convinced that in literary and linguistic studies, a synchronic reading should have a priority over a diachronic one and that a diachronic approach and a historical, or spatio-temporal, approach should not be confused. Finally, some critics cite as a major weakness of my commentary its lack of extended treatment of the literary aspects of the text. I am certainly aware of the importance of the literary aspects of the text but, in my view, a commentary on any book which has many textual problems first needs to fix the text on which the literary analysis is to be based. It is my hope that literary critics will use this commentary to do such a *dialogical* and *intertextual* analysis based on a solid Hebrew text. See Introduction (below) on *intertextuality* and my treatment of the story of the wise woman of Tekoa in 2 Sam. 14.[5]

Over a quarter century has passed since 1990 when I began this project. In that year I shifted my area of research from ANE and linguistic studies to biblical studies and became a full-time teacher of Old Testament at Japan Bible Seminary. Since I had been trained in poetic texts in both Hebrew and Ugaritic, I wanted to write on a poetic book. I chose the short poetic book Habakkuk as my research area to prepare myself to write a major commentary on Psalms or Job. So, when Professor Harrison asked me to write a commentary on the historical books 1–2 Samuel, I was a little reluctant to accept this invitation. But several people, especially Professor Cyrus H. Gordon, my mentor, encouraged me to accept it. After some research, I realized that my training in Canaanite religion and culture as well as in Semitic philology, especially Ugaritic, might contribute to clarifying some difficult exegetical problems. Besides, the fifteen years of teaching general and Semitic linguistics at University of Tsukuba had prepared me in dealing with the textual prob-

3. Paper read at Oslo International Organization for the Study of the Old Testament Meeting, published as D. T. Tsumura, "Scribal Errors or Phonetic Spellings? Samuel as an Aural Text," *VT* 49 (1999) 390-411; also Tsumura, "Textual Corruptions, or Linguistic Phenomena? The Cases in 2 Samuel (MT)," *VT* 64 (2014) 135-45.

4. See D. T. Tsumura, "Temporal Consistency and Narrative Cohesion in 2Sam 7,8-11," in Dietrich, *The Books of Samuel*, pp. 385-92.

5. For an evaluation of my commentary, *The First Book of Samuel*, from the linguistic side, especially from the discourse grammatical point of view, see F. Polak, *HS* 49 (2008) 352-55.

lems of Samuel linguistically, so I accepted. The commentary on 1 Samuel was completed finally in 2007.

I would like to thank Professor A. R. Millard for reading an earlier version of this volume. The series editor Professor R. L. Hubbard has waited patiently with an encouraging spirit for the past two decades. He has read my manuscript and given me constructive suggestions; Dr. A. Knapp has been most helpful in the practical editorial matters. I thank them for their help. My wife Susan, an MIT-trained linguist, has been a good companion in this strenuous scholarly and spiritual journey. To her, I dedicate this book with love and thanks.

בְּכָל־דְּרָכֶיךָ דָעֵהוּ וְהוּא יְיַשֵּׁר אֹרְחֹתֶיךָ׃ (Prov. 3:6)

Abbreviations

*	*(Semitic verbal root) or *(Proto Semitic form) or *(hypothetical form). These forms are not written in italics.
AASF	Annales Academiae Scientiarum Fennicae
AB	Anchor Bible
ABD	D. N. Freedman (ed.), *The Anchor Bible Dictionary.* 6 vols. New York: Doubleday, 1992.
ABRL	Anchor Bible Reference Library
AbrN	*Abr-Nahrain*
ABS	Archaeology and Biblical Studies
acc.	accusative
ACW	average column width
adj.	adjective
adv.	adverb, adverbial
AdvPh	adverbial phrase
AfO	*Archiv für Orientforschung*
AGE	K. Tallqvist, *Akkadische Götterepitheta* (SO 7). Helsinki: Societas Orientalis Fennica, 1938.
AHw	W. von Soden, *Akkadisches Handwörterbuch.* Wiesbaden: Otto Harrassowitz, 1965-1981.
AI	Y. Aharoni, *Arad Inscriptions* (JDS). Jerusalem: Israel Exploration Society, 1981.
AJBA	*Australian Journal of Biblical Archaeology*
AJBI	*Annual of the Japanese Biblical Institute*
AJSL	*American Journal of Semitic Languages*
Akk.	Akkadian
AKM	Abhandlungen für die Kunde des Morgenlandes
ALW	average letter width

AnBi	Analecta Biblica
Andersen	F. I. Andersen, *The Sentence in Biblical Hebrew*. The Hague: Mouton, 1974.
ANE	ancient Near East
ANEP	J. B. Pritchard (ed.), *The Ancient Near East in Pictures Relating to the Old Testament*. Princeton: Princeton University Press, 1954, 1968.
ANET	J. B. Pritchard (ed.), *The Ancient Near Eastern Texts Relating to the Old Testament*. 3rd edition. Princeton: Princeton University Press, 1969.
AnOr	Analecta Orientalia
Ant.	Josephus, *Antiquities of the Jews*
AOAT	Alter Orient und Altes Testament
AOS	American Oriental Series
AOTC	Apollos Old Testament Commentary
ARM	Archives royales de Mari
AS	Assyriological Studies (University of Chicago)
ATD	Das Alte Testament Deutsch
ATDa	Acta Theologica Danica
ATSAT	Arbeiten zu Text und Sprache im Alten Testament
AuOr	*Aula Orientalis*
AusBR	*Australian Biblical Review*
AUSS	*Andrews University Seminary Studies*
B-L	H. Bauer and P. Leander, *Historische Grammatik der Hebräischen Sprache des Alten Testaments*. Hildesheim: G. Olms, 1962 [orig. 1922].
BA	*Biblical Archaeologist*
BAR	*Biblical Archaeology Review*
BASOR	*Bulletin of the American Schools of Oriental Research*
BBR	*Bulletin for Biblical Research*
BDB	F. Brown, S. R. Driver, and C. A. Briggs, *A Hebrew and English Lexicon of the Old Testament*. Oxford: Clarendon Press, 1907.
BEATAJ	Beiträge zur Erforschung des Alten Testaments und des Antiken Judentums
BeO	Bibbia e Oriente
Berg.	G. Bergsträsser, *Hebräische Grammatik*. I/II. Hildesheim: Georg Olms, 1962 [orig. 1918].
BHDL	R. D. Bergen (ed.), *Biblical Hebrew and Discourse Linguistics*. Dallas: Summer Institute of Linguistics, 1994.
BHK	Biblia Hebraica Kittel
BHQ	Biblia Hebraica Quinta
BHS	Biblia Hebraica Stuttgartensia

Bib	*Biblica*
BibInt	*Biblical Interpretation*
Biella	J. C. Biella, *Dictionary of Old South Arabic: Sabaean Dialect* (HSS 25). Chico: Scholars Press, 1982.
BIOSCS	*Bulletin of the International Organization for Septuagint and Cognate Studies*
BIS	Biblical Interpretation Series
BKAT	Biblischer Kommentar Altes Testament
BL	*Book List*
BLS	Bible and Literature Series
BMECCJ	*Bulletin of the Middle Eastern Culture Center in Japan*
BMSAES	*British Museum Studies in Ancient Egyptian and Sudan*
BN	*Biblische Notizen*
BO	*Bibliotheca Orientalis*
BR	*Bible Review*
BS	*Bibliotheca Sacra*
BT	*The Bible Translator*
BTB	*Biblical Theology Bulletin*
BToday	*Bible Today*
BWANT	Beiträge zur Wissenschaft vom Alten und Neuen Testament
BZ	*Biblische Zeitschrift*
BZAW	Beihefte zur *ZAW*
CAD	*The Assyrian Dictionary of the Oriental Institute of the University of Chicago*. Chicago: The Oriental Institute of the University of Chicago, 1956–2006.
CAT	Commentaire de l'Ancien Testament
CB	C. H. Gordon, *The Common Background of Greek and Hebrew Civilizations.* New York: W. W. Norton, 1965.
CB	Coniectanea Biblica
CBA	Y. Aharoni, M. Avi-Yonah, A. F. Rainey, and Z. Safrai, *The Carta Bible Atlas*. 4th ed. Jerusalem: Carta, 2002.
CBC	Cambridge Bible Commentary
CBL	Colloquium Biblicum Lovaniense
CBQ	*Catholic Biblical Quarterly*
CH	*Code of Hammurabi*
CHANE	Culture and History of the Ancient Near East
CML	G. R. Driver, *Canaanite Myths and Legends.* Edinburgh: T. & T. Clark, 1956.
CML2	J. C. L. Gibson, *Canaanite Myths and Legends.* New ed. Edinburgh: T. & T. Clark, 1978.
cons.	consecutive
COT	Commentaar op het Oude Testament

CPTOT	J. Barr, *Comparative Philology and the Text of the Old Testament.* Oxford: Clarendon Press, 1968.
CRB	*Cahiers de la Revue Biblique*
CS	W. W. Hallo (ed.), *The Context of Scripture.* Vol. I: *Canonical Compositions from the Biblical World.* Leiden: E. J. Brill, 1997; Vol. II: *Monumental Inscriptions from the Biblical World.* Leiden: E. J. Brill, 2000; Vol. III: *Archival Documents from the Biblical World.* Leiden: E. J. Brill, 2002.
cstr.	construct state
CTCA	A. Herdner, *Corpus des tablettes en cunéiformes alphabétiques.* Paris: Impr. Nationale, 1963.
CTL	Cambridge Textbooks in Linguistics
DAH	G. A. Rendsburg, *Diglossia in Ancient Hebrew* (AOS 72). New Haven: American Oriental Society, 1990.
Davidson	A. B. Davidson, *An Introductory Hebrew Grammar*. 26th edition. Edinburgh: T. & T. Clark, 1966.
DBSup	Supplément au Dictionnaire de la Bible
DCH	D. J. A. Clines (ed.), *The Dictionary of Classical Hebrew.* 9 vols. Sheffield: Sheffield Phoenix Press, 1993-2014.
DDD	K. van der Toorn, B. Becking and P. W. van der Horst, *Dictionary of Deities and Demons in the Bible.* Leiden: E. J. Brill, 1995.
DJD	Discoveries in the Judaean Desert
DJPA	M. Sokoloff, *A Dictionary of Jewish Palestinian Aramaic of the Byzantine Period.* Ramat-Gan: Bar Ilan University Press, 1990.
DN	Divine Name
DNWSI	J. Hoftijzer and K. Jongeling, *Dictionary of the North-West Semitic Inscriptions.* Leiden: E. J. Brill, 1995.
DOSA	J. C. Biella, *Dictionary of Old South Arabic: Sabaean Dialect* (HSS 25). Chico, CA: Scholars Press, 1982.
DOTT	D. W. Thomas (ed.), *Documents from Old Testament Times.* New York: Harper & Row, 1958.
DSS	Dead Sea Scroll
DULAT	G. del Olmo Lete and J. Sanmartín, *A Dictionary of the Ugaritic Language in the Alphabetic Tradition* (HbO 112). Translated by W. G. E. Watson. Leiden: E. J. Brill, 2003.
EA	*El-Amarna tablets*
EB	*Études bibliques*
EBC	Expositor's Bible Commentary
EEC	Evangelical Exegetical Commentary
EHLL	G. Khan (ed.), *Encyclopedia of Hebrew Language and Linguistics.* Leiden: E. J. Brill, 2013.
EI	*Eretz Israel*

EQ	*Evangelical Quarterly*
ET	English translation
ETL	*Ephemerides Theologicae Lovanienses*
EvT	*Evangelische Theologie*
Exeg	*Exegetica: Studies in Biblical Exegesis.* Hamura, Tokyo: Biblical Exegesis Study Group in Japan.
ExTi	*Expository Times*
FB	Forschung zur Bibel
fem.	feminine
FOTL	Forms of Old Testament Literature
GB	F. Buhl, *Wilhelm Gesenius hebräisches und aramäisches Handwörterbuch über das Alte Testament.* 17th ed. Berlin: Springer, 1915.
Gibson	J. C. L. Gibson, *Davidson's Introductory Hebrew Grammar: Syntax.* 4th edition. Edinburgh: T. & T. Clark, 1994.
GKC	E. Kautszch and A. E. Cowley, *Gesenius' Hebrew Grammar.* Second English edition. Oxford: Clarendon Press, 1910.
GMD	R. Meyer and H. Donner, *Wilhelm Gesenius hebräisches und aramäisches Handwörterbuch über das Alte Testament.* 18th ed. Berlin: Springer, 1987.
GN	geographical name
GVG	Carl Brockelmann, *Grundriss der vergleichenden Grammatik der semitischen Sprachen.* 2 vols. Hildesheim: G. Olms, 1966 [orig. 1908 and 1913].
HAHE	J. Renz and W. Röllig, *Handbuch der althebräischen Epigraphik, I.* Darmstadt: Wissenschaftliche Buchgesellschaft, 1995.
HAL	L. Koehler, W. Baumgartner, and J. J. Stamm, *Hebräisches und aramäisches Lexikon zum Alten Testament.* 3rd ed. Leiden: E. J. Brill, 1967-2004.
HALOT	L. Koehler and W. Baumgartner, *The Hebrew and Aramaic Lexicon of the Old Testament.* Trans. by M. E. J. Richardson. Leiden: E. J. Brill, 1994-2000.
HAR	*Hebrew Annual Review*
HAT	Handbuch zum Alten Testament
HbO	Handbuch der Orientalistik
Hi.	Hiphil
Hišt.	Hištaphal
Hit.	Hithpael
HKAT	Handkommentar zum Alten Testament
HS	*Hebrew Studies*
HSAT	Die heilige Schrift des Alten Testaments
HSM	Harvard Semitic Monographs

HSS	Harvard Semitic Studies
HTR	*Harvard Theological Review*
HUCA	*Hebrew Union College Annual*
HUS	W. G. E. Watson and N. Wyatt (eds.), *Handbook of Ugaritic Studies* (HbO 39). Leiden: E. J. Brill, 1999.
IASH	Israel Academy of Sciences and Humanities
IB	*The Interpreter's Bible*
IBD	*The Illustrated Bible Dictionary*. 3 vols. 1980.
ICC	International Critical Commentary
IDB	*The Interpreter's Dictionary of the Bible*
IDBSup	*Supplement to IDB*
IEJ	*Israel Exploration Journal*
Iliad 1-12	Homer, *Iliad I*: Books 1-12. With an English translation by A. T. Murray, revised by William F. Wyatt. 2nd ed. LCL 170. Cambridge, Mass.: Harvard University Press, 1999.
Iliad 13-24	Homer, *Iliad II*: Books 13-24. With an English translation by A. T. Murray. LCL 171. Cambridge, Mass.: Harvard University Press, 1925 [repr. 1985].
inf	infinitive
inf. abs.	infinitive absolute
Int	*Interpretation*
IOS	Israel Oriental Studies
IOSCS	International Organization for Septuagint and Cognate Studies
IOSOT	International Organization for the Study of Old Testament
IrBS	Irish Biblical Studies
ISBE	G. W. Bromiley (ed.), *The International Standard Bible Encyclopedia*. 4 vols. Grand Rapids: Eerdmans, 1979-1988.
ITC	International Theological Commentary
J-M	P. Joüon and T. Muraoka, *A Grammar of Biblical Hebrew*. Part One: Orthography and Phonetics. Part Two: Morphology. Part Three: Syntax (Subsidia Biblica 14/I-II). Rome: Editrice Pontificio Istituto Biblico, 1991.
JAAR	*Journal of the American Academy of Religion*
JANES	*Journal of the Ancient Near Eastern Society*
JAOS	*Journal of the American Oriental Society*
Jastrow	M. Jastrow, *A Dictionary of the Targumim, the Talmud Babli and Yerushalmi, and the Midrashic Literature*. New York: Pardes, 1950.
JBL	*Journal of Biblical Literature*
JBQ	*The Jewish Bible Quarterly*
JCS	*Journal of Cuneiform Studies*
JDS	Judean Desert Studies

JETS	*Journal of the Evangelical Theological Society*
JHNES	Johns Hopkins Near Eastern Studies
JHS	*Journal of Hebrew Scriptures*
JJS	*Journal of Jewish Studies*
JNES	*Journal of Near Eastern Studies*
JNSL	*Journal of Northwest Semitic Languages*
JPOS	*Journal of the Palestine Oriental Society*
JPS	Jewish Publication Society
JQR	*Jewish Quarterly Review*
JRAS	*Journal of the Royal Asiatic Society*
JSOT	*Journal for the Study of the Old Testament*
JSOTSS	Journal for the Study of the Old Testament Supplement Series
JSS	*Journal of Semitic Studies*
JTS	*Journal of Theological Studies*
K.	Ketib
KAI	H. Donner and W. Röllig, *Kanaanäische und aramäische Inschriften*. 3 vols. Wiesbaden: Otto Harrassowitz, 1962, 1964, 1973.
KAT	Kommentar zum Alten Testament
KHCAT	Kurzer Hand-Commentar zum Alten Testament
KJV	King James Version
König	E. König, *Stilistik, Rhetorik, Poetik in Bezug auf die biblische Litteratur*. Leipzig: Theodor Weicher, 1900.
KTU	M. Dietrich, O. Loretz, and J. Sanmartín, *Die keilalphabetischen Texte aus Ugarit* (AOAT 24). Neukirchen-Vluyn: Neukirchener, 1976.
Lambdin	T. O. Lambdin, *Introduction to Biblical Hebrew*. London: Darton, Longman & Todd, 1973.
Lane	E. W. Lane, *An Arabic-English Lexicon*. London: William and Norgate, 1863 [repr. 1968].
LAPO	Littératures anciennes du Proche-Orient
LB	Late Bronze Age
LBH	Late Biblical Hebrew
Lesh	*Leshonenu*
LHBOTS	Library of Hebrew Bible/Old Testament Studies
lit.	literally
LSAWS	Lingusitic Studies in Ancient West Semitic
LXX	Septuaginta
LXX^{A}	Septuagint Codex Alexandrinus
LXX^{B}	Septuagint Codex Vaticanus
LXX^{L}	Septuagint Lucianic Manuscripts
MB	Middle Bronze Age
MR	Map Reference, based on *Student Map Manual: Historical Geography of the Bible Lands*. Jerusalem: Pictorial Archive (Near

	Eastern History) Est. Distributed by Grand Rapids: Zondervan, 1980. E.g., [MR 169-123] = Map Reference to Bethlehem according to the Grid [EW-NS].
MT	Masoretic Text
N	noun
NAB	New American Bible
NABU	*Nouvelles Assyriologiques Brèves et Utilitaires*
NAC	New American Commentary
NASB	New American Standard Bible
NB	Neo-Babylonian
NBD	I. H. Marshall, J. I. Packer, D. J. Wiseman, A. R. Millard (eds.), *New Bible Dictionary.* 3rd ed. Downers Grove, IL: InterVarsity Press, 1996.
NCB	New Century Bible
NDBT	T. D. Alexander and B. S. Rosner (eds.), *New Dictionary of Biblical Theology*. Leicester: Inter-Varsity Press, 2000.
NEA	*Near Eastern Archaeology*
NEAEHL	E. Stern (ed.), *The New Encyclopedia of Archaeological Excavations in the Holy Land.* 4 vols. Jerusalem: Israel Exploration Society; Jerusalem: Carta, 1993; Vol. 5. Jerusalem: Israel Exploration Society, 2008.
NEB	New English Bible
neg.	negative
Ni.	Niphal
NIBCOT	New International Biblical Commentary on the Old Testament
NICOT	New International Commentary on the Old Testament
NIDOTTE	W. A. VanGemeren (ed.), *The New International Dictionary of Old Testament Theology and Exegesis.* Grand Rapids: Zondervan, 1996.
NIV	New International Version
NIVAC	New International Version Application Commentary
NJB	New Jerusalem Bible
NJPS(V)	New Jewish Publication Society (Version)
NKJB	New King James Bible
NovT	*Novum Testamentum*
NP	noun phrase
NRSV	New Revised Standard Version
NRT	*Nouvelle Revue Théologique*
O	object
OBO	Orbis Biblicus et Orientalis
OEANE	E. M. Meyers (ed.), *The Oxford Encyclopedia of Archaeology in the Near East.* 5 vols. Oxford: Oxford University Press, 1997.

OL	Old Latin
OLA	Orientalia Lovaniensia Analecta
OLZ	*Orientalistische Literaturzeitung*
Or	*Orientalia*
OTA	*Old Testament Abstracts*
OTE	Old Testament Essays
OTG	Old Testament Guides
OTL	Old Testament Library
OTS	Oudtestamentische Studiën
OTWSA	Die Ou-Testamentiese Werkgemeenskap in Suid-Afrika
p	person
P	predicate
PBA	Proceedings of the British Academy
PEQ	*Palestine Exploration Quarterly*
pf.	perfect
PFES	Publications of the Finnish Exegetical Society
PHA	K. L. Younger, Jr., *A Political History of the Arameans: From Their Origins to the End of Their Polities* (ABS 13). Atlanta: SBL Press, 2016.
PLMU	C. H. Gordon, "Poetic Legends and Myths from Ugarit," *Berytus* 25 (1977) 5–133.
PN	personal name
$PN_{1, 2, 3}$	personal name 1, 2, 3
POS	Pretoria Oriental Series
POTT	D. J. Wiseman (ed.), *Peoples of Old Testament Times.* Oxford: Clarendon Press, 1973.
POTW	A. J. Hoerth, G. L. Mattingly, and E. M. Yamauchi (eds.), *Peoples of the Old Testament World.* Grand Rapids: Baker, 1994.
prepPh	prepositional phrase
pron.	pronoun
ptc.	participle
PTU	F. Gröndahl, *Die Personennamen der Texte aus Ugarit* (SP 1). Rome: Pontifical Biblical Institute, 1967.
Q.	Qere
qtl	perfect
RA	*Revue d'assyriologie et d'archéologie orientale*
RB	*Revue Biblique*
RBDSS	E. D. Herbert, *Reconstructing Biblical Dead Sea Scrolls: A New Method Applied to the Reconstruction of* 4QSam^{a} (STDJ 22). Leiden: E. J. Brill, 1997.
RBL	*Review of Biblical Literature*
REB	Revised English Bible

RelCl	relative clause
RIM	The Royal Inscriptions of Mesopotamia Project. Toronto
RlA	*Reallexikon der Assyriologie*
RQ	*Revue de Qumran*
RSO	Revista degli Studi Orientali
RSP	L. R. Fisher (ed.), *Ras Shamra Parallels.* Vol. 1 (AnOr 49). Rome: Pontifical Biblical Institute, 1972; vol. 2 (AnOr 50), 1975; S. Rummel (ed.), *Ras Shamra Parallels.* Vol. 3 (AnOr 51), 1981.
RSR	*Religious Studies Review*
RSV	Revised Standard Version
S	subject
SAA	State Archives of Assyria
SAAB	*State Archives of Assyria Bulletin*
SAAS	State Archives of Assyria Studies
SAOC	Studies in Ancient Oriental Civilization
SB	A. F. Rainey and R. S. Notley, *The Sacred Bridge: Carta's Atlas of the Biblical World.* Jerusalem: Carta, 2006.
SBLBES	Society of Biblical Literature Biblical Encyclopedia Series
SBLDS	Society of Biblical Literature Dissertation Series
SBLMS	Society of Biblical Literature, Monograph Series
SBTS	Sources for Biblical and Theological Study
SEL	Studi epigrafici e linguistici sul vicino Oriente Antico
SFSHJ	South Florida Studies in the History of Judaism
sg.	singular
SHBC	Smyth & Helwys Bible Commentary
SHCANE	Studies in the History and Culture of the Ancient Near East
SIL	Summer Institute of Linguistics
SJOT	*Scandinavian Journal of the Old Testament*
SLOCG	E. Lipiński, *Semitic Languages: Outline of a Comparative Grammar* (OLA 80). Leuven: Uitgeverij Peeters, 1997.
SP	Studia Pohl
SSI	J. C. L. Gibson, *Textbook of Syrian Semitic Inscriptions.* I-III. Oxford: Clarendon Press, 1971-1982.
SSN	Studia Semitica Neerlandica
ST	Studia Theologica
STDJ	Studies on the Texts of the Desert of Judah
StOr	Studia Orientalia
Syr.	Syriac
Targ.	Targum(im)
TDOT	G. J. Botterweck and H. Ringgren (eds.), *Theological Dictionary of the Old Testament.* 16 vols. Grand Rapids: Eerdmans, 1974-2018.
temp-ph	temporal phrase

THAT	*Theologisches Handwörterbuch zum Alten Testament*. 2 vols. Munich: Chr. Kaiser, 1971-1976.
TICP	Travaux de l'Institut Catholique de Paris
Tiq. soph.	Tiqqun sopherim ("corrections of scribes")
TLZ	*Theologische Literaturzeitung*
TO	A. Caquot, M. Sznycer, and A. Herdner, *Textes ougaritiques I: Mythes et legendes* (LAPO 7). Paris: Cerf, 1974.
TOTC	Tyndale Old Testament Commentaries
TR	*Theologische Rundschau*
TrinJ	*Trinity Journal*
TWAT	*Theologisches Wörterbuch zum Alten Testament*. 10 vols. Stuttgart: W. Kohlhammer, 1970-2016.
TWOT	R. L. Harris, G. L. Archer, Jr., and B. K. Waltke (eds.), *Theological Wordbook of the Old Testament*. 2 vols. Chicago: Moody Press, 1980.
TynB	*Tyndale Bulletin*
TZ	*Theologische Zeitschrift*
UBL	Ugaritisch-Biblische Literatur
UCOP	University of Cambridge Oriental Publications
UF	*Ugarit-Forschungen*
Ug.	Ugaritic
Ug	Ugaritica
UMM	University Museum Monograph
UnSemQ	*Union Seminary Quarterly Review*
UT	C. H. Gordon, *Ugaritic Textbook* (AnOr 38). Rome: Pontificium Institutum Biblicum, 1965.
UTS	Supplement to C. H. Gordon, *UT*.
UVST	J. Huehnergard, *Ugaritic Vocabulary in Syllabic Transcription* (HSS 32). Atlanta: Scholars Press, 1987.
V	verb
V1, V2	verb 1, verb 2
Vi	intransitive verb
VigChr	*Vigiliae Christianae*
VP	verb/verbal phrase
Vt	transitive verb
VT	*Vetus Testamentum*
VTS	Vetus Testamentum Supplement Series
w	simple waw (w›)
W-O	B. K. Waltke and M. O'Connor, *An Introduction to Biblical Hebrew Syntax*. Winona Lake, Ind.: Eisenbrauns, 1990.
Watson	W. G. E. Watson, *Classical Hebrew Poetry: A Guide to Its Techniques* (JSOTSS 26). Sheffield: JSOT Press, 1984.

wayhy	*waw* consecutive + Qal "imperfect" 3 m.s. *hyh ("to be")
wayqtl	*waw* consecutive + "imperfect" *(yqtl)*
WBC	Word Biblical Commentary
weqtl	*waw* + perfect (*qtl*)
Williams	R. J. Williams, *Hebrew Syntax: An Outline*. 2nd ed. Toronto: University of Toronto, 1976.
WMANT	Wissenschaftliche Monographien zum Alten und Neuen Testaments
WO	*Die Welt des Orients*
WTJ	*Westminster Theological Journal*
yqtl	imperfect
ZA	*Zeitschrift für Assyriologie*
ZAH	*Zeitschrift für Althebräistik*
ZAW	*Zeitschrift für die alttestamentliche Wissenschaft*
ZDMG	*Zeitschrift der Deutschen Morgenländischen Gesellschaft*
ZDMGSup	Supplement to Zeitschrift der Deutschen Morgenländischen Gesellschaft
ZDPV	*Zeitschrift des Deutschen Palästina-Vereins*
ZKT	*Zeitschrift für katholische Theologie*

Introduction

I. TEXTUAL CRITICISM

A. METHOD OF TEXTUAL RECONSTRUCTION IN DJD (2005)

Although the three Samuel scrolls from Cave 4, namely 4QSam[a], 4QSam[b], and 4QSam[c], have been known and partly studied by F. M. Cross and his pupils since their discovery in 1952,[1] they were not made fully available to the public until 1991 when the facsimile edition was published. In 1993 the Brill microfiche edition also was published.[2] However, it was only in 2005 that Cross and his colleagues published their belated detailed study of the scrolls as a volume in the Discoveries in the Judaean Desert series.[3]

The basic question regarding these Qumran biblical texts is still whether one should take these three groups of fragments as originally having constituted three independent scrolls, in view of the fact that 4QSam[b] and especially 4QSam[c] are very fragmentary. Moreover, quite recently, R. G. Kratz brought up the highly serious question of whether 4QSam[a] was a biblical manuscript (*Bibelhandschrift*) or a midrashic document.[4]

1. See "Introduction" of Tsumura, I, pp. 4-5. Cf. S. Pisano, *Additions or Omissions in the Books of Samuel: The Significant Pluses and Minuses in the Massoretic, LXX and Qumran Texts* (OBO 57; Göttingen: Vandenhoeck & Ruprecht; Freiburg: Universitätsverlag, 1984).

2. E. Tov (ed.), *The Dead Sea Scrolls on Microfiche: A Comprehensive Facsimile Edition of the Texts from the Judean Desert*, 2 vols. (Leiden: E. J. Brill, 1993).

3. F. M. Cross et al., *Qumran Cave 4*. XII: *1–2 Samuel* (DJD 17; Oxford: Clarendon Press, 2005).

4. R. G. Kratz, "Bibelhandschrift oder Midrasch? Zum Verhältnis von Text- und Liter-

For the most comprehensive survey of the Samuel studies of recent years, see W. Dietrich, "Von den ersten Königen Israels: Forschung an den Samuelbüchern im neuen Jahrtausend," *TR* 77 (2012) 135-70, 263-316, 401-25.

In 1997, I briefly compared Cross and Parry's method of reconstructing the broken parts of the text of 4QSam[b] with the reconstruction of 4QSam[a] by E. D. Herbert.[5] While the former simply gives *ad hoc* remarks such as "spacing requires," "the reconstruction required by the limited space," "there is no room," and "this line is long," the latter provides more objective criteria for reconstructing the text.[6] Herbert calculates the average column widths (ACW) and the average letter widths (ALW)[7] for 4QSam[a] and uses these to check whether a suggested reconstruction is likely.

Despite Herbert's significant contributions to the method for reconstructing 4QSam[a], Cross and his school ignored it in their most recent study in DJD. For example, like McCarter, II (1984), DJD reconstructs *h'lwhym* after *ḥesed* in 2 Sam. 2:5, thus reading [*ḥesed h'lwhym hz*]*h* and gives a comment similar to McCarter's:[8] "Space considerations suggest that 4QSam[a] had a text that conflated the readings of MT and LXX[A]."[9] However, Herbert had already demonstrated that this reconstruction was "unlikely" because the insertion of *h'lwhym* "would increase the reconstructed width of 2a [the section a of line 2] to 31.2mm, 11% above the section a average."[10] They should have at least responded to Herbert's view.

To cite another example, in 2 Sam. 21:5, McCarter translates *klh ʿlynw wyrdpnw* "set himself against us and persecuted us", based on LXX[B], for he thinks that the MT *klnw,* "exterminated us," is "impossible and obviously defective." Moreover, he reads *'šr dmh lhšmydnw* "who meant to eradicate us," in place of MT *'šr dmh lnw w(!)nšmdnw,* following Wellhausen, who takes *lnw wnšmdnw* as a "corruption of *lhšmydnw*,"[11] Cross et al. also take this position and reconstruct the relevant text as *klh ʿlynw wyrdpnw w dmh lhšmydnw.*[12]

---

argeschichte in den Samuelbüchern im Licht der Handschrift 4Q51 (4QSam[a])," in Dietrich, *The Books of Samuel*, pp. 153-80.

5. F. M. Cross and D. W. Parry, "A Preliminary Edition of a Fragment of 4QSam[b] (4Q52)," *BASOR* 306 (1997) 63-74; E. D. Herbert, *Reconstructing Biblical Dead Sea Scrolls: A New Method Applied to the Reconstruction of* 4QSam[a] (STDJ 22; Leiden: E. J. Brill, 1997) [=*RBDSS*].

6. See D. T. Tsumura, review of *Reconstructing Biblical Dead Sea Scrolls*, by Edward D. Herbert, *JETS* 43 (2000) 315-16.

7. The calculation of the length of the line is based on Herbert's Table 1, which lists individual ALW (millimeters) of the Hebrew letters in 4QSam[a] as follows:

א = 2.35, ב = 2.09, ג = 1.88, ד = 2.19, ה = 2.53, ו = 1.23, ז = 1.20, ח = 2.30, ט = 3.01, י = 1.49, כ = 1.81, ך = 1.97, ל = 1.73, מ = 2.17, ם = 2.93, נ = 1.25, ן = 0.99, ס = 2.95, ע = 2.48, פ = 1.50, ף = 2.16, צ = 2.36, ץ = 2.29, ק = 3.10, ר = 2.11, ש = 3.47, ת = 2.25, *Space* = 1.32, *Average* = 1.88.

8. McCarter, II, p. 82.

9. DJD 17, p. 106.

10. Herbert, *RBDSS*, p. 100.

11. McCarter, II, p. 438.

12. DJD 17, p. 177.

However, according to Herbert,[13] the reconstruction suggested by McCarter and Cross, et al., would not fit in the lacunae of 4QSam^a^. Herbert notes that the average column width (ACW) of the line is 101.3 ~ 110.6mm, and is never more than 117.6mm, so if 4QSam^a^ read *klh ʿlynw* in place of the MT's *klnw*, "the reconstructed width would increase by 9.6mm [more than any other column]."

Furthermore, if the line ended with *wyrdpnw* instead of MT's *wʾšr*, as reconstructed by Fincke, who follows McCarter and Cross et al., the total length of the line (117.71mm) would go beyond the maximum. Hence, Fincke's handwritten reconstruction of the Hebrew text[14] gives the wrong impression to the reader about the real length of the line. Because the total width of the reconstructed line is calculated as 117.71mm, which is longer than any other line in that column, it is misleading for Fincke to draw that line as if it were shorter than lines 20 and 25.[15]

B. RELATIONSHIP AMONG MT, LXX, AND DSS

In his review of my *The First Book of Samuel* in *RBL* (Dec. 2007), R. W. Klein claimed that I ignored "the fact that many of the LXX readings have been confirmed as based on an alternate Hebrew *Vorlage* by the three Samuel manuscripts from Qumran Cave 4." However, this is just one side of "the fact." Sometimes the MT readings are supported by DSS against the LXX as in 2 Sam. 3:28-29, 14:26, etc., while on the other hand at times the MT is supported by the LXX against 4QSam[a] as in 5:6. Moreover, both LXX[BAL] and 4QSam[a] wrongly supply the name "Mephibosheth" before the MT *son of Saul* in 4:1. Furthermore, we have cases such as 6:17, where although the MT and the LXX are supported by 4QSam[a], McCarter suggests omitting it as textually "secondary." For details, see the comments on the relevant passages.

13. Herbert, *RBDSS*, p. 183.

14. A. Fincke, *The Samuel Scroll from Qumran: 4QSam[a] Restored and Compared to the Septuagint and 4QSam[c]* (STDJ 43; Leiden: E. J. Brill, 2001), p. 322.

15. A handwritten text is often influenced by the reading of the original text by other scholars. Before presenting handwritten copies, one should check the photograph, preferably several photos, if not the original. See the problem of reading the Ugaritic text *KTU* 1.23, line 64, discussed in D. T. Tsumura, "Revisiting the 'Seven' Good Gods of Fertility in Ugarit: Is Albright's Emendation of *KTU* 1.23:64 correct?" *UF* 39 (2008) 629-41; see P. Bordreuil and D. Pardee, *A Manual of Ugaritic.* (LSAWS 3; Winona Lake, Ind.: Eisenbrauns, 2009), p. 103, for a handwritten text.

C. "PHONETIC SPELLING" — THE PHONETIC REALITY BEHIND THE SCRIPTS

In my studies I have suggested that some MT readings usually considered "corrupt" are in fact not corruptions but "phonetic spellings."[16] This troubles some traditional textual critics,[17] who are concerned more with formal features such as the shape of scripts and dittography or haplography. In other words, they are interested in how the scripts of the text were written or "copied" rather than what is actually involved phonetically behind the scripts.

To understand the phonetic reality behind the spellings of ancient literatures, it is useful to study the way ancient scribes or authors misspelled. In my study of misspellings in Ugaritic cuneiform texts,[18] I dealt with the phenomena of vowel *sandhi*,[19] loss and addition of signs, i.e., "loss of ʾ," "loss of *r*, *l*, *m*, *n*" and "addition of *q*," etc. These examples show that there is a definite tendency for a scribe, even a trained copyist, to make mistakes by writing phonetic reality into a written text. The fact is that these misspellings are often caused by phonetic reasons.

To cite an example from our text, it is often said that Bedan (1 Sam. 12:11) is a "corruption" from Baraq, but I have suggested that Bedan could be a phonetic realization of the original form Baraq.[20] In any case, those "corrupt" MT readings are usually *lectio difficilior*, hence likely more original (according to the traditional text-critical principle). One should note that phonetic spellings are attested in more than just a "few forms" (Klein) and often argue against the scribal error theory. In 1–2 Samuel phonetic spellings can be seen in the following verses:[21]

16. See Tsumura, I, pp. 9-10; also Tsumura, "Scribal Errors or Phonetic Spellings?," pp. 390-411.

17. E.g., R. W. Klein: *RBL* (December 2007); see also Klein, *1 Samuel*, pp. xxv-xxviii; his revised edition (2000), p. xl.

18. D. T. Tsumura, "'Misspellings' in Cuneiform Alphabetic Texts from Ugarit: Some Cases of Loss or Addition of Signs," in *Writing and Ancient Near Eastern Society: Papers in Honour of Alan R. Millard*, ed. P. Bienkowski, C. Mee, and E. Slater (LHBOTS 426; London: T. & T. Clark International, 2005), pp. 143-53.

19. See D. T. Tsumura, "Vowel *sandhi* in Ugaritic," in *Near Eastern Studies Dedicated to H. I. H. Prince Takahito Mikasa on the Occasion of His Seventy-Fifth Birthday* (Wiesbaden: Otto Harrasowitz, 1991), 427-35; Tsumura, "Vowel *sandhi* in Biblical Hebrew," *ZAW* 109 (1997) 575-88.

20. D. T. Tsumura, "Bedan, a Copyist's Error?" *VT* 45 (1995) 122-23.

21. See the "Index of Subjects" in Tsumura, I, p. 664; also p. 10 n. 41 and the index for this volume. For a detailed discussion on some examples in 2 Samuel, see Tsumura, "Textual Corruptions, or Linguistic Phenomena?," 135-45. An awareness of phonetic variation has been lacking in textual criticism. An eminent OT textual critic once told me that terms such as "*sandhi*" had never been part of his vocabulary.

1 Sam. 1:17, 28; 4:19; 6:12; 7:12; 10:7; 12:11; 14:27, 32, 47; 15:9; 17:31; 18:1, 29; 20:2, 30; 22:18; 25:8; 27:8; 30:5; etc.

2 Sam. 3:1, 8; 4:6; 5:2, 13; 7:7; 8:8; 11:24; 13:16; 14:19; 18:3, 12; 19:13; 20:5, 9, 14; 21:9, 12, 16; 22:6, 8, 27, 36, 40, 46; 23:8, 9, 20, 21, 29, 31, etc.

II. LITERARY AND HISTORICAL CRITICISM

A. PRINCIPLE OF SYNCHRONIC PRIORITY

Any theory of literary composition, however attractive, should be solidly based on a literary and linguistic reading of the text itself. In principle, a diachronic approach to a biblical text should be preceded by a synchronic study of the text as it is, for it is an axiom of textual and linguistic investigation that one should first read a text synchronically,[22] taking note of any linguistic and textual variants and apparent discrepancies, and only after that proceed to go behind the text and examine those *synchronic irregularities*, diachronically. In historical linguistics, it is the established understanding that "both synchronic irregularity and cross-language resemblance can only be explained by reference to earlier language states and to the systematic nature of language change."[23]

One might say that both the "traditional" historical-critical approach and the recent synchronic-only intertextuality approach seem to ignore this basic principle of *synchronic priority* in literary study. It was F. de Saussure in his *Cours de linguistique générale*, published posthumously in 1916,[24] who first distinguished between synchronic and diachronic approaches in linguistic research and put priority on synchronic investigation over diachronic. "He saw the history of a language as a succession of synchronic states, each a complete system *où tout se tient* and therefore definable only in terms of the relationships existing between its various opposing ele-

22. At the beginning of the introduction to his recent, thorough Samuel commentary, W. Dietrich discusses "Synchrone Aspekte" and then "Diachrone Aspekte"; see *Samuel 1-12*, pp. 1*-58*. It is noteworthy that more than half of the introduction is taken up by the discussions of "Handlungsbogen," "Strukturierung," "Charakterzeichnung," "Perspektivik," "Stilmittel" and "Gottesbilder." Only ten pages are used for the description of the Redaktionsgeschichte.

23. T. Bynon, *Historical Linguistics* (CTL; Cambridge: Cambridge University Press, 1977), p. 22.

24. F. de Saussure, *Cours de linguistique générale*, ed. C. Bally and A. Sechehaye, with the collaboration of A. Riedlinger (Lausanne: Payot, 1916; repr. 1964 [trans. W. Baskin, *Course in General Linguistics*, Glasgow: Fontana/Collins, 1977]), 114ff..

ments."[25] Yet, Saussure did not emphasize the synchronic approach at the expense of the diachronic approach. He simply distinguished between them and established the principle of the priority of the synchronic. The recent emphasis on the synchronic-only approach is an overreaction to the diachronic-only approach, and in cases it even seems to advocate getting rid of the spatio-temporal, that is, the historical, approach.

B. INTERTEXTUALITY

The synchronic-only literary approach is exemplified by the tendency to emphasize "intertextuality" in narrative criticism. For example, L. L. Lyke[26] wrote a book on the dialogue between King David and the wise woman of Tekoa in 2 Sam. 14 from his "post-modern reading sensibilities," finding his methodological bases in David Stern's works on the ambiguity of the Midrashic *meshalim* and Mikhail Bakhtin's notion of "dialogization," that is, "the inter-relationships and dialogue between various aspects of a composite narrative."[27]

As the events in the woman's *mashal* do not correspond at all closely to those leading to the current situation, in this work, Lyke pays close attention to "its verbal, motivic, and thematic particularities" for a clearer understanding of its significance, since, he thinks, "the narrative represents . . . a complex accumulation of overlapping biblical topoi, each of which must be interpreted within its present as well as traditionary context."[28] Thus, Lyke compares the fratricide of 2 Sam. 14:6 with that of Gen. 4:8 and notes "resonance" between them. Then, using the latter text as "a lens by which to view the episodes of sibling rivalry in Genesis," he moves on to the ancient Jewish traditions, which believed, for example, that Cain was the son of Sammael and that "each of major stories of sibling rivalry in Genesis is associated with Pesach" (p. 37). Several criticisms are in order:

25. Bynon, *Historical Linguistics*, p. 1 n. 1. See the commentary on 2 Sam. 7 for a concrete example of this problem.

26. D. T. Tsumura, review of *King David with the Wise Woman of Tekoa*, by Larry L. Lyke, *Themelios* 24:3 (1999) 48-49.

27. For recent studies in Bakhtin's theory and biblical scholarship, see R. Polzin, *Samuel and the Deuteronomist: A Literary Study of the Deuteronomic History Part Two; 1 Samuel* (Bloomington: Indiana University Press, 1989); B. Green, *Mikhail Bakhtin and Biblical Scholarship: An Introduction* (Semeia Studies 38; Atlanta: Society of Biblical Literature, 2000); K. Bodner, *David Observed: A King in the Eyes of His Court* (Hebrew Bible Monographs 5; Sheffield: Sheffield Phoenix Press, 2005), pp. 38-66.

28. L. L. Lyke, *King David with the Wise Woman of Tekoa: The Resonance of Tradition in Parabolic Narrative* (JSOTSS 255; Sheffield: Sheffield Academic Press, 1997), p. 12.

1. It is a tautology to assume "the multivocal and polysemous quality" of the text on the basis of the ambiguity of its "multiple voices" (p. 20). Just as the meaning of a polysemous word is decided by its use in a particular context, so the meaning of a *mashal* is to be determined by its particular context. One should distinguish carefully between the author's intended ambiguity and the postmodern reader's inability to decide the text and its meaning.[29] Critics should be aware of the danger of the word-association game and avoid it as much as possible in order to place their readings on a solid basis.[30]
2. Any given narrow constituent element (e.g., "two sons") can be found in any corpus of ancient Near Eastern wisdom literature. When we narrow down the size of the element and broaden its context, we risk *level skipping*, looking for a wider — intermediate — context while ignoring its immediate context. What is available from the ancient Near East, especially in Israel, is often too limited to make a definite judgment. This lack of availability rather than the author's intention could be the cause of the ambiguity or indeterminateness for the (post-)modern reader.[31]
3. For any comparison, difference is more important than similarity, for comparison is meaningful only when similar items are compared discriminately.[32] An overemphasis on similarities is disastrous to intertextual study. It is not enough just to trace various parallels with other traditions in the Hebrew Bible for understanding a *mashal*. What is needed is the competence to read the biblical *mashal* in its original cultural and historical setting, the ancient Near East, and to notice its uniqueness.[33]

29. E.g., see below on *hml'kym* in 2 Sam. 11:1.

30. An extreme case of such word association may be recognized, e.g., in J. S. Ackerman's association between Absalom's story and Abraham's story in terms of "the hair"; see J. S. Ackerman, "Knowing Good and Evil: A Literary Analysis of the Court History in 2 Samuel 9-20 and 1 Kings 1-2," *JBL* 109 (1990) 50. See below on 2 Sam. 18:9-10.

31. See also P. D. Miscall, *1 Samuel: A Literary Reading* (Bloomington: Indiana University Press, 1986).

32. See A. Gibson, *A Biblical Semantic Logic: A Preliminary Analysis* (Oxford: Blackwell, 1981); D. T. Tsumura, "Ugaritic Poetry and Habakkuk 3," *TynB* 40 (1989) 24-48; Tsumura, "Rediscovery of the Ancient Near East and Its Implications for Genesis 1-2" in *Since the Beginning: Interpreting Genesis 1 and 2 through the Ages*, ed. K. Greenwood (Grand Rapids: Baker Academic, 2018), pp. 215-38.

33. See, Tsumura, I, pp. 22-23.

C. CHARACTERS AND CHARACTERIZATIONS[34]

One of the characteristics of the new literary criticism is a focus on characters and characterization in narratives. Interpretation of a story can certainly be dependent on an assessment of the characters in the story. Besides the major characters such as Samuel, Saul, and David,[35] the recent emphasis on minor characters in the Books of Samuel is noteworthy. For example, U. Simon deals with the role of minor characters in narrative[36] while other authors have focused on the roles of a specific character such as Eliab, Joab, or Abigail. These character studies certainly disclose the biblical views on various aspects of the complexity of human reality such as interpersonal relationships, family affairs, suffering, pain, and death as well as happiness and sorrow.

Those minor characters are of great interest in themselves, yet, it should be noted that the author/narrator deals with those minor characters mainly in their relationship with major characters such as David,[37] Saul, and Samuel. For example, Jonathan is characterized as the person who stands in opposition to Saul, his father, in their relationships with David. The story of "Amnon and Tamar" (2 Sam. 13:1-22) is intentionally placed in a wider context, where Absalom is the major dramatis personae, that is, in the "Story of Absalom's Revolt" (13:1-20:26). Yet, the *entire* section is around David and his relationship with his son Absalom. This is the same in the case of Joab,[38] whose relationship with his masters, first David and later Solomon, played a significant role in the history of the united monarchy.

The attitude toward the literary analysis of the Books of Samuel hinges on how one treats the *entire* 1–2 Samuel.[39] Is 1–2 Samuel a collection of various stories about particular dramatis personae? Not so. Even a part of 1–2 Samuel

34. A new project has been proposed by K. Bodner and B. Johnson: *Characters and Characterization in Samuel–Kings.* See also Dietrich, *1 Samuel 1-12*, pp. 8*-14* on "Charakterzeichung."

35. See Tsumura, I, pp. 19-23 on a "Holistic Literary Approach."

36. U. Simon, "Appendix: Minor Characters in Biblical Narrative" in *Reading Prophetic Narratives* (Bloomington: Indiana University Press, 1997), 263-69.

37. On the recent characterization of David either as a pious hero or as "a man of blood," see D. A. Bosworth, "Evaluating King David: Old Problems and Recent Scholarship," *CBQ* 68 (2006) 191-210.

38. M. A. Eschelbach, *Has Joab Foiled David? A Literary Study of the Importance of Joab's Character in Relation to David* (Studies in Biblical Literature 76; New York: Peter Lang, 2005).

39. Concerning reading 1 Samuel literarily, Miscall says: "Reading is unending, incessant, because we must read 1 Samuel again if someone were to ask, what is 1 Samuel about?" (*1 Samuel: A Literary Reading*, p. 185.) From the biblical viewpoint, one may rather ask what the *entire* 1–2 Samuel is talking about.

is not worthy to be called David's biography.[40] The author/editor's concern is rather how God, the Lord of history, guides history through his human agents so that his divine purpose of saving his people may be fulfilled through the human agency of the messiah king, at a particular place of worship, that is, Zion: for example, Ps. 132.[41] Such character studies are most profitable when controlled by a spatio-temporal reality of individual circumstances, either cultural or historical.

D. DATE AND AUTHORSHIP

In my commentary on 1 Samuel I suggested tentatively that the final editors of 1–2 Samuel "probably worked around a time not later than the late tenth century, that is, the early period of Rehoboam's reign"[42] in the light of 1 Sam. 27:6, *Therefore Ziklag has belonged to the kings of Judah to this day.* B. Halpern states that "the picture of the central Negev in Samuel fits the 10th-century evidence, but that of no later time."[43] According to him, "the connection through Shishaq's list to the archaeology of the Negev" allows us to place 2 Samuel "no later than the 9th century, since the text reflects memories of the 10th century."[44] Since Shishaq conquered the area in 925 B.C., the comment of 1 Sam. 27:6 is unlikely even for the ninth century.

Moreover, as Halpern accepts based on the recent archaeological findings, "large parts of our information on the United Monarchy [in 2 Sam. 8] stem from roughly contemporary sources."[45] The concept of eternal dynasty or kingship as expressed in 2 Sam. 7 is not late; it had been expressed not only in the Ugaritic mythological text of the Baal Cycle (*KTU* 1.2 IV 10) but also in a letter from Alashia to the Ugaritic king (RS 18.113A+B). Laato notes that Assyrian royal building inscriptions from the second millennium onward rather support "the possibility that the idea of an eternal dynasty played an important role in Israelite royal ideology already during the time that David

40. One should note that there exists a structural difficulty in reconstructing David's biography from the books of Samuel, for they were not written for that purpose. For example, depending on their view of the last four chapters of 2 Samuel the result would be very different among the scholars. For a recent effort to this purpose, see S. L. McKenzie, *King David: A Biography* (Oxford: Oxford University Press, 2000).

41. See below on ch. 6 and its relationship with Ps. 132.

42. Tsumura, I, p. 32.

43. B. Halpern, *David's Secret Demons: Messiah, Murderer, Traitor, King* (Grand Rapids: Eerdmans, 2001), pp. 225-26.

44. Halpern, *David's Secret Demons*, p. 69.

45. Halpern, *David's Secret Demons*, p. 226.

planned to build a Temple for Yhwh."[46] This too supports the possibility that 2 Sam. 7 came from the era of the united monarchy.[47]

In the light of the above, my opinion in the previous volume that 1–2 Samuel was composed during the earliest period of the divided monarchy still holds, though this does not exclude the possibility that the books were slightly modernized in the following generation, that is, during the ninth century.[48] It is reasonable that the official history of the founder of a dynasty would have been written during the third generation; in the case of Davidic dynasty, at the time of Rehoboam during the tenth century.

E. GENRE AND STYLE

In discussing the historiography of 1–2 Samuel, Noth's hypothesis of Deuteronomistic history (DH) and historian(s) (DTR) is still influential among the mainline biblical critics, though his hypothesis has been variously modified since.[49] However, I believe that one must ask what *kind* of history (or narrative) the Books of Samuel are. In other words, one should not ignore the question of which genre[50] 1–2 Samuel belongs to.

Traditionally, 1–2 Samuel was placed between Judges and Kings in the Former Prophets. Yet, one might ask if 1–2 Samuel indeed belongs to the same genre as Judges or 1–2 Kings. One may take the whole of Judges through Kings as narrative prose. However, stylistically, while Judges is written in a more or less epic style, Kings is written in an annalistic style, Samuel is in an intermediate position, exhibiting both epic elements and annalistic features.

In comparison with Chronicles, Samuel is not so much an annalistic history as an epic-like story. For example, while in Chronicles David is introduced as the seventh son (1 Chr. 2:15), in the story of David's election (1 Sam.

46. A. Laato, *A Star Is Rising: The Historical Development of the Old Testament Royal Ideology and the Rise of the Jewish Messianic Expectations* (Atlanta: Scholars Press, 1997), p. 40.

47. See below the commentary on 2 Sam. 7.

48. M. Garsiel thinks that 1–2 Samuel was written "not much later than the ninth century BCE," though he posits that the book experienced four stages of editorial process including the final Deuteronomistic "light editing" during the Babylonian exile. See M. Garsiel, "The Book of Samuel: Its Composition, Structure and Significance as a Historiographical Source," *JHS* 10 (2010) 34; Garsiel, "The Valley of Elah Battle and the Duel of David with Goliath: Between History and Artistic Theological Historiography," in *Homeland and Exile: Biblical and Ancient Near Eastern Studies in Honour of Bustenay Oded*, ed. G. Galil, M. Geller, and A. Millard (VTS 130; Leiden: E. J. Brill, 2009), 404-10.

49. E.g., Jobling, Polzin, and van Seters. See Tsumura, I, pp. 16-19.

50. See D. G. Firth, *1 & 2 Samuel* (AOTC 8; Nottingham: InterVarsity, 2009), pp. 19-22 on "genre and purpose."

16) he is certainly presented as the eighth son of Jesse, who summoned David after he *made seven of his sons pass before Samuel.* It may be that one of David's brothers had died young, hence David being treated as the seventh, though he was actually the eighth son of Jesse.[51] However, it is noteworthy that Samuel mentions by name only the three oldest sons (1 Sam. 17:13). If we compare the x // x+1 number parallelism of the Canaanite epic tradition, David could be the seventh and, at the same time, the eighth son.[52] Such usage of numbers is not uncommon in a poetic parallelism as in "three, yes four" (Amos 1:3, 6, etc.; Prov. 30:15, 18, 21), "seven, yes eight" (Mic. 5:5; Eccl. 11:2), and "eighth, yes one of the seven" (Rev. 17:11).[53] Thus, in the epic-like story in Samuel, it should not be strange that David is described as the seventh, and at the same time, the eighth son.[54]

Another example of the epic style is the way the narrator of Samuel conveys that Saul was king only for a short time, ignoring at which age he became king and how long (1 Sam. 13:1).[55] In the narrator's mind, Saul was already rejected by God and is described as being king only *for two years* — *two* is the smallest numeral in Biblical Hebrew. An annalistic record like Kings would be interested in his age of accession and exactly how long he stayed on the royal throne. On the other hand, Judges is a collection of more epic-like stories, and thus uses round numbers for the periods of individual judges.[56]

Modern or postmodern narrative critics tend to be concerned only with the macrostructure of narrative discourse and ignore these individual "genre and style" characteristics. One should be mindful of the varieties of genres even in narrative discourse. This tendency may be in keeping with the idea of the so-called Deuteronomistic historian(s), which led/misled scholars to seek a macrostructure and historiography for the whole of Joshua through

51. Kalimi thinks that the Chronicler listed "seven" sons for Jesse in contrast to "four/ eight" sons in the book of Samuel. See I. Kalimi, "The View of Jerusalem in the Ethnographical Introduction of Chronicles (1 Chr 1–9)," *Bib* 83 (2002) 557 n.7. Also, S. Japhet, *I–II Chronicles: A Commentary* (OTL; Louisville: Westminster John Knox, 1993), p. 71, thinks it possible "that the numbers in I Sam. 16 (and 17) were guided by the literary pattern of 7+1, and that it is Chronicles which preserves the more original information."

52. See on 1 Sam. 16 in Tsumura, I, pp. 420-21.

53. Note also that seven was an ideal number in the biblical world. Especially, "seven sons" was the ideal number for a family to have. On this theme, see Tsumura, I, p. 145.

54. See also the commentary on 2 Sam. 24:13 (*seven years of famine*), whose Chronicle counterpart has "three years of famine." The phrase *seven years of famine* reflects an epic style. Cf. Japhet, p. 380.

55. See Tsumura, I, pp. 331-33.

56. Note C. H. Gordon's view who, comparing David's elegy in 2 Sam. 1:17-27 with the thirteenth-century Ugaritic epic of Aqhat, posits the origin of Hebrew historiography in the epic traditions that reached their height under David. See my comment in *The First Book of Samuel*, p. 32.

2 Kings — this went hand in hand with holistic approaches — even to the point of ignoring the differences among individual constituents. It is now *again* the time to be concerned with the uniqueness of individual constituents, that is, Judges, Samuel, and Kings, rather than with the universal aspects of the whole.

III. DISCOURSE STRUCTURE

I discussed discourse grammar in *The First Book of Samuel*,[57] but a few more notes might help the reader to understand this linguistic phenomenon.

Discourse grammar looks at how various grammatical phenomena as sentence structure and forms are used for guiding a discourse. In Longacre's groundbreaking study of the story of Joseph,[58] he points out that in general sentences with verb-initial *wayqtl* forms normally present the main-line of the story. However, as Longacre himself accepted, not every *wayqtl* points to the main-line discourse.

1. *initial* waw *vs. sequential* waw

For clarification, I would like to make the following distinction. That is, every *wayqtl* followed by a stated subject initiates a new discourse unit (subparagraph); hence that *waw* is initial. On the other hand, every *wayqtl* without a stated subject within a subparagraph carries on the previous EVENT and that *waw* is hence sequential.[59]

2. wayqtl *as SETTING and/or TERMINUS*

Though a *wayqtl* clause normally describes the EVENT of the narrative discourse, it sometimes appears in the SETTING, especially when a *wayqtl* form is used with an impersonal subject (e.g., 11:27; 24:1, 4) or with a plural verb with a non–dramatis persona as its subject. Also, when the verb is a movement verb, the *wayqtl* form might be indicating TRANSITION (e.g., 4:5; 12:1) rather than the EVENT.

3. weqtl *as a procedural discourse*

When a *weqtl* form follows a sequence of *wayqtl* forms, that *weqtl* clause is a PROCEDURAL discourse rather than NARRATIVE discourse. While in

57. For the basic principle of discourse grammar, see Tsumura, I, pp. 49-55.

58. R. E. Longacre, *Joseph: A Story of Divine Providence: A Text Theoretical and Textlinguistic Analysis of Genesis 37 and 39-48* (Winona Lake, Ind.: Eisenbrauns, 1989).

59. D. T. Tsumura, *The Earth and the Waters in Genesis 1 and 2: A Linguistic Analysis* (JSOTSS 83; Sheffield: Sheffield Academic Press, 1989), p. 119 n.9.

the latter the verbal form *wayqtl* describes WHAT happens, in the former the verbal form *weqtl* describes HOW it happens (e.g., 2 Sam. 7).[60]

4. *dialogue pattern*

In the Hebrew narrative, there seems to exist a pattern for a dialogue between two persons. For example, as in the following case,

A says to B:
He says:
He says:
B says to A:

For the second and the third, no stated subject is needed. However, for the fourth, the speaker is normally specified, in this case, "B." For example, in 1 Sam. 3:16-18:[61]

Eli called Samuel:
And he said:
And he said:
And Samuel told him.

With this in mind, one can easily note in 2 Sam. 18:23 the phrase ("And he said") should be supplied according to this dialogue pattern in Hebrew conversation.[62]

60. See D. T. Tsumura, "Tense and Aspect of Hebrew Verbs in II Samuel 7:8-16 — from the Point of View of Discourse Grammar," *VT* 60 (2010) 641-54. For a further treatment of this topic, see Tsumura, "Temporal Consistency," pp. 385-92.

61. See Tsumura, I, p. 181; also pp. 268, 270, 421, 435, 500, 615, and index (p. 659).

62. For very intricate features of conversation, see V. H. Matthews, *More Than Meets the Ear: Discovering the Hidden Contexts of Old Testament Conversations* (Grand Rapids: Eerdmans, 2008) and my review in *JAOS* 130 (2010), 324-25; also F. H. Polak, "Speaker, Addressee, and Positioning: Dialogue Structure and Pragmatics in Biblical Narrative," in *Interested Readers: Essays on the Hebrew Bible in Honor of David J. A. Clines*, ed. K. Aitken, J. M. S. Clines, and C. M. Maier (Atlanta: Society of Biblical Literature, 2013), pp. 359-72.

IV. LITERARY STRUCTURE AND MESSAGE

A. THE LITERARY STRUCTURE OF 1–2 SAMUEL

I. Prologue (1 Sam. 1:1–7:17): "Story of Samuel" — with the Embedded "Story of the Ark of God"
II. Transition to the Monarchy (1 Sam. 8:1-22)
III. "Story of Saul" (1 Sam. 9:1–15:35)
IV. "Story of Saul and David" (1 Sam. 16:1–31:13)
V. "Story of King David" (2 Sam. 1:1–20:26)
  i. Story of David's Reign (1:1–12:31)
    A. Death of Saul (1:1-27)
    B. King David (2:1–5:5)
    C. Jerusalem, the City of David (5:6-25)
    D. Zion, the Place of Worship (6:1-23)
    E. "Davidic Covenant": Eternal Throne (7:1-29)
    F. Catalogue of David's Military Activities (8:1-18)
    G. Mephibosheth (9:1-13)
    H. Israel-Ammon War (10:1–12:31)
      1, [A]. Beginning of Israel-Ammon War (10:1-19)
      2, [X]. David and Bathsheba (11:1–12:25)
      3, [B]. End of Israel-Ammon War (12:26-31)
  ii. Story of Absalom's Revolt (13:1–20:26)
    A. Absalom the Rebel (13:1–14:33)
    B. Absalom's Rebellion (15:1–20:22)
    C. David's Officers (20:23-26)
VI. Epilogues (2 Sam. 21:1–24:25)
    A. Famine and the Death of Saul's Sons (21:1-14)
    B. Philistine War (21:15-22)
    X.[63] Song of David (22:1-51) = Ps. 18
    X'. Last Words of David (23:1-7)
    B'. David's Heroes (23:8-39)
    A'. Census and the Lord's Anger (24:1-25)

B. THE MESSAGE OF 1–2 SAMUEL

The message of a piece of literature is usually built into its literary structure; hence we should start by observing how it is written in order to appreciate what is written there.

63. For the ABXX'B'A' pattern, see the commentary on Epilogue in 2 Sam. 21-24.

The message of the literary structure of 1–2 Samuel is how Yahweh, the Lord of history, through the human institution of monarchy guides his covenant people providentially in various aspects of life by his gracious and sovereign hands. Hence, the main concerns of the author(s) are the relationship between divine sovereignty and human institutions as well as the relation between God's providential guidance and human responsibility. As we noted in the first volume, Rom. 8:28 well summarizes the divine dealings of the people of his covenant: "And we know that for those who love God all things work together for good, for those who are called according to his purpose." (ESV)

Thus, the Books of Samuel are not a biography of particular persons, not even of King David himself. Certainly, characters such as Samuel, Saul, and David, are the main characters (dramatis personae) in the narrative and many subsidiary persons such as Hannah, Eli, Jonathan, Eliab, Abigail, Abner, Joab, Ish-bosheth, Mephibosheth, Bathsheba, and Absalom come and go along with these main characters. And, hence, recent emphasis[64] on the personal features of such *minor* characters in their relation to the main dramatis personae may help us to understand the character or complex personality of David as the human messiah.[65] On the other hand, it may mislead the readers into concentrating on a nonsubstantial subject or theme of the books.

These books are a *historical* narrative of God's salvation *history*, which conveys how the Lord of *history* advanced the divine plan of salvation a few more steps, including one *big* step in the Davidic covenant, which eventually would be fulfilled in the life and death of Jesus Christ, the Messiah, the heir of David (see Matt. 1:1) in *history*. Despite the serious failures of David, Yahweh, the Lord of the universe, works his plan of salvation, establishing his grace and his faithfulness (Ps. 89; see below on "Themes and Theology"), regardless of faithlessness on the side of his people.

Human Desires and Divine Plans

One theme that runs through 1–2 Samuel is that of human desires and divine plans.

i. Hannah

At the beginning of Samuel, Hannah desired to have a boy, so she promised if she were given one she would dedicate him to the Lord. However, God made her position greater than she could have expected; she would eventually become the mother of the king-maker, though she probably did not live to know that.

64. See above (p. 8 n. 34) for the project proposed by Bodner and Johnson.

65. E.g., see Bodner, *David Observed*, pp. 10-24, on Eliab.

ii. Saul
Although Saul did not start off desiring to be a king, he exerted himself to meet the people's expectation as "the longing of all Israel" (1 Sam. 9:20), that is, "the hope of Israel," and so became concerned with what the people thought of him rather than what the Lord wanted him to do. Fearing the people's reaction to him, he neglected fearing the Lord and obeying his word (chs. 13 and 15).

iii. David
David desired to build a house for the Lord, but the Lord did not allow it (2 Sam. 7). God's plan was to establish the Davidic throne eternally (7:16).

First Chronicles 22:8 and 28:3 explain that David was not allowed to build a temple because he had waged great wars and shed much blood before the Lord. However, through David's sin in carrying out the census in 2 Sam. 24, God led him to purchase the threshing floor of Araunah the Jebusite, where Solomon was later to build the temple.

Thus, God's plan of salvation continues despite the various phases of human desires. God is the one who proceeds with his plan and purpose by his holy sovereignty and by his grace.

V. EXEGESIS AND THEOLOGY

One of the criticisms of my commentary on 1 Samuel was that it lacks theological depth and does not pay attention to the "biblical narrative's literary contours." For example, S. Chapman says that the "fatal problems" in my approach are my presumptions "that history is the primary bearer of theological significance and that the narrative of Samuel is to be read for the ways in which it makes that history transparent." By such an appeal to history, Chapman holds, "the rich subtlety of the biblical narrative is streamlined in order to favor the 'history-likeness' of its plot."[66]

But I would argue that Chapman's subjective literary narrative approach is reading into the narrative what is not there. For example, having given up an appeal to history, Chapman sees "rhetorical strategy" in such a text like 1 Sam. 13:8 that says Saul went to Gilgal and waited seven days. According to him, Saul's apparent delay in following through on Samuel's commission in 10:8 is "a narrative device employed to lead the reader/hearer to forget the matter of Samuel's commission, for a little while, until it returns front and

66. S. B. Chapman, *1 Samuel as Christian Scripture: A Theological Commentary* (Grand Rapids: Eerdmans, 2016), pp. 234-35.

center in 1 Sam. 13."[67] Chapman holds that such a "narrative forgetting" is a device "to increase the reader's sympathy with Saul."[68]

Reading 1 Sam. 9-12 synchronically, however, it is most reasonable to assume that Saul went to Gilgal more than once between 10:8 and chapter 13. Certainly he was there, with Samuel, to be installed officially as a king (11:15). Moreover, the theme of waiting for seven days during religious rites is nothing peculiar. Often, a ritual waiting on God lasted seven days.[69] What is required of an exegete is an ability to read the text as it is, and an understanding of the common sense in the ancient Near Eastern religio-cultural milieu.

The importance of grammar in grasping the meaning and purpose of a narrative is also illustrated by the problem of whether to interpret the preposition *ʿal*, as "against" or "on" in 2 Sam. 14:1. See the commentary on that verse.[70] Another passage where philological analysis greatly influences the meaning of the narrative is 1 Sam. 1:5 on *ʾappāyim* (lit. "two noses").[71] Again, a theological understanding of one of the most important chapters in these books, 2 Sam. 7, depends on the grammatical analysis of the text itself. That is, (1) the tense of *weqtl* in vv. 9b-11b vs. 18b-19 as "poetic prose"; (2) the *speaker-oriented* particle *ʿal-kēn* and the vertical grammar of parallelism (AXX'B) in v. 22; (3) the exegetical solution of *crux interpretum* in v. 23; (4) the two different senses of the root *pdh in the light of Ugaritic economic texts. See the commentaries on the passages in 2 Sam. 7.

67. Chapman, *1 Samuel as Christian Scripture*, pp. 122-23.

68. See Tsumura, I, p. 21 n. 91 on the use of Sternberg's theory of "gapping" by a historian such as V. P. Long. See the commentary on 1 Sam. 13:9 (Tsumura, I, pp. 344-45).

69. The Hebrew term *mōʿēd* in this context is not "the time appointed by Samuel" (so, Miscall, *1 Samuel: A Literary Reading*, p. 84); it rather refers to the annual festival, to which Samuel was supposed to come. Note Samuel visited Bethel, Gilgal, and Mizpah yearly to *judge Israel at all these places* (1 Sam. 7:16). See Tsumura, I, pp. 343-45.

70. An example where the misunderstanding of the meaning of preposition *ʿal* affected the subsequent interpretation of the text is 2 Ki. 23:29. There the preposition *ʿal* was long, e.g., translated as "against," since Egypt had long been an enemy of the Assyrians (e.g., Vulgate and KJV). However, the Babylonian Chronicles have clarified the historical situation at that time (see A. Millard, "The Babylonian Chronicle," in *CS*, I, p. 467-68). The Assyrians asked for help from Egypt, for their capital city Nineveh was already destroyed in 612 B.C. and they wanted to reestablish their country against the Babylonians with the help of the Egyptians. The Pharaoh Neco *went up to the king of Assyria*, not to fight "against" the king of Assyria.

71. See Tsumura, I, p. 111 n. 40.

VI. THEMES AND THEOLOGY

A. DAVID'S THRONE AND HIS HEIR

Two important themes in 2 Samuel are David's *throne* and his *heir*,[72] which are especially dealt with in Yahweh's promise to David in 2 Sam. 7, just as David's heir (*zeraʿ*) and throne (*kissēʾ*) are the two main themes of Ps. 89:4 (also 29, 36). These two are expressed in Ps. 132 by the dual elections of David's heir (v. 11; see 2 Sam. 7) and of Zion (v. 13; see 2 Sam. 6; 1 Chr. 13; 15-16).

The theme of David's *throne* is carried on by the subsequent prophetic literatures, for example, *kissēʾ Dāwīd* in Isa. 9:7, while the theme of David's *heir* is seen in such passages as those concerning David's "branch" (*ṣemaḥ*) in Isa. 4:2; Jer. 23:5; 33:15; Zech. 3:8; 6:12; "shoot" (*ḥōṭer*) — "sprout" (*nēṣer*) in Isa. 11:1 (cf. Rev. 5:5; 22:16). In the messianic context "the house of David" (*bêt Dāwîd*) will carry on both "throne" and "heir" themes, for the term "house" refers to Davidic dynasty, that is, his "heir" on his "throne"; see "the throne of David" (Luke 1:32), "the house of David" (1:69).

B. DAVIDIC COVENANT

There is no doubt that the Davidic covenant[73] (2 Sam. 7) is the central theme of 2 Samuel, even of the entire Old Testament. It is certainly the turning point in the divine plan of salvation, as is reflected in the phrase *Jesus Christ, the son of David, the son of Abraham* (Matt. 1:1) where David, the prototype of messiah, God's anointed, is placed in the midpoint between Abraham (Gen. 17; cf. 12) and Jesus. The Lord promises[74] David that he will make a dynasty (lit. *house*; v. 11b) for him, by raising his *offspring* after him and by establishing the eternal kingdom and the throne of his offspring (vv. 12-13) so that David's *throne* might be *established for ever* (v. 16). This *throne* will be given to Jesus the Messiah, David's *offspring* who "will reign over the house of Jacob forever" and of whose "kingdom there will be no end" (Luke 1:33).

The theology of 2 Samuel, therefore, is about God's character in his dealings with his people, especially with his chosen individuals, with grace (*ḥesed*) for the sake of his plan and purpose. Because he is faithful to his covenant, in particular to his promise to Abraham (Gen. 12:1-3), God graciously

72. For the synonymous word pair of *seed/heir* (*zeraʿ*) and *name* (*šēm*), see the commentary on 1 Sam. 24:21; also for the Mesopotamian expression, *kingdom – name – seed*, see Tsumura, I, pp. 128 & 573.

73. See the introductory section to 2 Sam. 7.

74. Yahweh's promise begins with v. 11b; see the commentary of 7:11b-16.

deals with David in the same way in order that the plan of salvation be further fulfilled and finally completed in the life and death of his son Jesus Christ, the Messiah (2 Sam. 7:11b-16).

VII. PURPOSE OF 2 SAMUEL

In the previous volume on 1 Samuel, I noted that the purpose of that book is twofold:

(1) to explain the meaning of the establishment of the monarchy in Israel;
(2) to show how the Lord prepared David to sit on the royal throne after Saul.

The first purpose continues. However, the purpose of 2 Samuel is not only to explain the meaning of the Israelite monarchy as a political institution but also to show how God led King David's life specifically despite his grave sins against God in order to keep his promise to provide heirs, finally the heir, to establish his eternal dynasty.

In chapter 7 David, the prototype of messiah, the Lord's anointed, is granted the divine promise that his kingdom and the throne on which his heir will sit and rule will be established forever. With this Davidic covenant, the divine plan of salvation moves a big step forward since the promise to Abraham a thousand years earlier.

It is noteworthy that in the last words of David (2 Sam. 23:2-7) near the end of the book we find a reference to the "eternal covenant" (*b*ᵉ*rît ʿôlām*) that the Lord made with David (v. 5). Exactly because of this "eternal covenant" of God's faithfulness or grace (*ḥesed*), his son Jesus the Messiah died a sacrificial death for human sin in order to redeem human beings.

The final chapter, chapter 24, points to the place of worship where David's son would build the temple for the true King at the royal city of Zion, Jerusalem. However, just as the establishment of the human institution of monarchy sidetracked the covenant people away from the true King, in the same way, Solomon's Temple would lead the people to look at the physical temple and lead them away from the real presence of God throughout the history of ancient Israel.

Salvation is the recovery of the human fellowship with the holy God. Humans were created as the image of God for two purposes: (1) to worship the Creator; (2) to rule over other creatures as God's agent, his vice-regent (Gen. 1:26-27). The true recovery will come in the person of the true Messiah. Thus 1–2 Samuel ends with a hint of the preparation for the temple worship, which is a prototype of the true worship of the Sovereign God through His son Jesus Christ, the true Messiah.

VIII. OUTLINE OF 2 SAMUEL

V. "Story of King David" (2 Sam. 1:1–20:26)

Story of David's Reign (1:1–12:31)

- A. Death of Saul (1:1-27)
  1. Report of Saul's Death (1:1-16)
     - a. The Amalekite's Report (1:1-10)
     - b. David's Response (1:11-12)
     - c. Death of the Amalekite (1:13-16)
  2. David's Elegy for Saul and Jonathan (1:17-27)
     - a. Title (1:17-18)
     - b. Elegy (1:19-27)
- B. King David (2:1–5:5)
  1. David, the King of Judah (2:1-11)
     - a. David to Hebron (2:1-4a)
     - b. David and Jabesh-gilead (2:4b-7)
     - c. Ishbosheth in Mahanaim (2:8-11)
  2. Abner and Joab (2:12-32)
     - a. Helkath-hazzurim (2:12-16)
     - b. Death of Asahel (2:17-23)
     - c. Abner and Joab (2:24-32)
  3. Death of Abner (3:1-39)
     - a. House of Saul and House of David (3:1)
     - x. Sons of David in Hebron (3:2-5)
     - b. House of Saul and House of David (3:6)
     - c. Abner and Ishbosheth (3:7-11)
     - d. Abner Sends Messengers to David (3:12-16)
     - e. Abner Meets David at Hebron (3:17-21)
     - f. Joab Murders Abner (3:22-30)
     - g. Abner's Burial and David's Lament (3:31-39)
  4. Death of Ishbosheth (4:1-12)
     - a. Murder of Ishbosheth (4:1-3)
     - b. Note on Mephibosheth, Jonathan's Son (4:4)
     - c. Continuation of the Murder of Ishbosheth (4:5-7)
     - d. David Kills Rechab and Baanah (4:8-12)
  5. David, the King of Israel (5:1-5)

C. Jerusalem, the City of David (5:6-25)
    1. Royal City of Jerusalem (5:6-10)
    2. Royal Palace (5:11-12)
    3. Royal Family (5:13-16)
    4. Victories over the Philistines (5:17-25)
        a. David's First Victory (5:17-21)
        b. David's Second Victory (5:22-25)
D. Zion, the Place of Worship (6:1-23)
    1. Transfer of the Ark to Jerusalem (6:1-19)
        a. From the House of Abinadab (6:1-5)
        b. Perez-uzzah (6:6-11)
        c. From the House of Obed-edom (6:12-19)
    2. Michal and David (6:20-23)
E. "Davidic Covenant": Eternal Throne (7:1-29)
    1. The Lord's Promise (7:1-17)
        a. David's Desire (7:1-3)
        b. The Lord Sends Nathan to David (7:4-7)
        c. The Lord's Message to David (7:8-17)
    2. David's Prayer (7:18-29)
F. Catalogue of David's Military Activities (8:1-18)
    1. David's Military Activities (8:1-14)
    2. David's Officials (8:15-18)
G. Mephibosheth (9:1-13)
    1. David's Kindness for Jonathan's Sake (9:1)
    2. The King and Ziba (9:2-5)
    3. David and Mephibosheth (9:6-8)
    4. The King and Ziba (9:9-11)
    5. Mephibosheth at the King's Table (9:12-13)
H. Israel-Ammon War (10:1–12:31)
    1 [A]. Beginning of the Israel-Ammon War (10:1-19)
        a. David's Envoys to Ammon (10:1-5)
        b. War between Ammon and Israel (10:6-19)
            (1) Ammonites Hire the Arameans (10:6-8)
            (2) Joab and Abishai (10:9-14)
            (3) David's Victories over the Arameans (10:15-19)
    2 [X]. David and Bathsheba (11:1–12:25)
        a. Bathsheba, the Wife of Uriah (11:1–27)
            (1) Ammonite War of David (11:1)
            (2) Bathsheba, Wife of Uriah11: (2-5)
            (3) David and Uriah (11:6-15)
            (4) Death of Uriah (11:16-21)
            (5) Report of Uriah's Death (11:22-25)

(6) Bathsheba Becomes David's Wife (11:26-27)
b. "You Are the Man!" (12:1-15a)
(1) Nathan's Parable (12:1-6)
(2) The Lord's Message to David (12:7-12)
(3) David's Repentance (12:13-15a)
c. Death of David's Son and Birth of Solomon (12:15b-25)
3 [B]. End of Israel-Ammon War (12:26-31)

Story of Absalom's Revolt (13:1–20:26)
A. Absalom the Rebel (13:1–14:33)
1. Amnon and Tamar (13:1-22)
a. Absalom's Sister Tamar (13:1-2)
b. Jonadab's Advice (13:3-7)
c. Tamar Goes to Amnon's house (13:8-14)
d. Amnon Hates Tamar (13:15-18)
e. Absalom the Brother of Tamar (13:19-22)
2. Absalom's Vengeance and Escape (13:23-39)
a. Absalom's Invitation to Amnon (13:23-27)
b. Murder of Amnon (13:28-33)
c. Absalom Flees to Geshur (13:34-39)
3. Return of Absalom (14:1-33)
a. Wise Woman of Tekoa (14:1-20)
(1) David's Mind on Absalom (14:1)
(2) Joab Sends a Wise Woman of Tekoa (14:2-3)
(3) Two Sons in the Field (14:4-7)
(4) The King's Banished One (14:8-14)
(5) The Woman's Concern about Her and Her Son (14:15-17)
(6) Your Servant Joab Commanded Me (14:18-20)
b. Absalom Returns to Jerusalem (14:21-24)
c. David Receives Absalom (14:25-33)
B. Absalom's Rebellion (15:1-20:22)
1. Absalom's Conspiracy (15:1-12)
2. David's Escape from Jerusalem (15:13–16:14)
a. David Leaves the Palace (15:13-18)
b. Ittai (15:19-22)
c. David Crosses the Kidron (15:23)
d. Zadok with the Ark (15:24-29)
e. David Goes Up to the Mount of Olives (15:30-31)
f. Hushai (15:32-37)
g. Ziba (16:1-4)
h. Shimei (16:5-14)

3. Ahithophel and Hushai (16:15–17:23)
    a. Hushai Comes to Absalom (16:15-19)
    b. Ahithophel's Advice (16:20–17:4)
    c. Hushai's Advice (17:5-14)
    d. Hushai Warns David (17:15-23)
4. David Arrives at Mahanaim (17:24-29)
5. Absalom's Death (18:1–19:8)
    a. The King's Order (18:1-5)
    b. Absalom Killed (18:6-17)
    x. Absalom's Pillar (18:18)
    c. Man of Tidings (18:19-23)
    d. David Informed of Absalom's Death (18:24-32)
    e. David Mourns for Absalom (18:33–19:8)
6. David's Return to Jerusalem (19:9-43)
    a. Israel's Tribes and Judah (19:9-15)
    x. TRANSITION (19:16-18a)
    b. Shimei (19:18b-23)
    c. Mephibosheth (19:24-30)
    d. Barzillai (19:31-39)
    e. Men of Israel (19:40-43)
7. Sheba's Revolt (20:1-22)
    a. Sheba Son of Bichri (20:1-2)
    x. David's Ten Concubines (20:3)
    b. Joab Kills Amasa (20:4-14)
    c. Death of Sheba (20:15-22)

C. David's Officers (20:23-26)

VI. Epilogue (2 Sam. 21:1–24:25)
A. Famine for Three Years (21:1-14)
B. Philistine Wars (21:15-22)
X. Song of David (22:1-51) = Ps. 18
X'. The Last Words of David (23:1-7)
B'. David's Heroes (23:8-39)
A'. Census and the Lord's Anger (24:1-25)

IX. BIBLIOGRAPHY

Ackerman, J. S. "Knowing Good and Evil: A Literary Analysis of the Court History in 2 Samuel 9-20 and 1 Kings 1-2." *JBL* 109 (1990) 41-60.

Aharoni, Y. *Arad Inscriptions* (JDS). Jerusalem: Israel Exploration Society, 1981.

Aharoni, Y., M. Avi-Yonah, A. F. Rainey, and Z. Safrai. *The Carta Bible Atlas*. 4th ed. Jerusalem: Carta, 2002.
Ahituv, S. *Echoes from the Past: Hebrew and Cognate Inscriptions from the Biblical Period*. Jerusalem: Carta, 2008.
Alter, R. *The David Story: A Translation with Commentary of 1 and 2 Samuel*. New York: W. W. Norton, 2000.
Althann, R. "The Meaning of ארבעים שנה in 2 Sam 15,7." *Bib* 73 (1992) 248-52.
Andersen, F. I. *The Sentence in Biblical Hebrew*. The Hague: Mouton, 1974.
Andersen, F. I., and D. N. Freedman. "Another Look at 4QSam^{b}." *RQ* 14 (1989) 7-29.
Anderson, A. A. *2 Samuel* (WBC 11). Dallas: Word Books, 1989.
Armerding, C. E. "Were David's Sons Really Priests?" In *Current Issues in Biblical and Patristic Interpretation. Studies in Honor of Merrill C. Tenney*, ed. G. F. Hawthorne, pp. 75-86. Grand Rapids: Eerdmans, 1975.
Arnold, B. T. *1 and 2 Samuel* (NIVAC). Grand Rapids: Zondervan, 2003.
Artzi, P., and A. Malamat. "The Great King: A Preeminent Royal Title in Cuneiform Sources and the Bible." In *The Tablet and the Scroll: Near Eastern Studies in Honor of William W. Hallo*, ed. D. Snell and D. Weisberg, pp. 28-38. Bethesda, Md.: CDL Press, 1993.
Auld, G. *I and II Samuel* (OTL). Louisville: Westminster John Knox, 2011.
Avigad, N. "New Light on the Na'ar Seals." In *Magnalia Dei: The Mighty Acts of God; Essays on the Bible and Archaeology in Memory of G. Ernest Wright*, ed. W. E. Lemke, F. M. Cross, and P. D. Miller, pp. 294-300. New York: Doubleday, 1976.
Avigad, N., and B. Sass. *Corpus of West Semitic Stamp Seals*. Jerusalem: Israel Academy of Sciences and Humanities, 1997.
Avioz, M. "Nathan's Prophecy in II Sam 7 and in I Chr 17: Text, Context, and Meaning." *ZAW* 116 (2004) 542-54.
Baker, D. W. "Further Examples of the *wāw* explicativum." *VT* 30 (1980) 129-36.
Baldwin, J. G. *1–2 Samuel* (TOTC). Leicester: InterVarsity, 1988.
Bar-Efrat, S. *Narrative Art in the Bible* (JSOTSS 70). Sheffield: JSOT Press, 1989.
———. "Some Observations on the Analysis of Structure in Biblical Narrative." *VT* 30 (1980) 154-73.
Barthélemy, D. *Critique Textuelle de l'Ancien Testament I* (OBO 50/1). Fribourg: Éditions Universitaires; Göttingen: Vandenhoeck & Ruprecht, 1982.
Ben-Barak, Z. "The Legal Background to the Restoration of Michal to David." In *Studies in the Historical Books of the Old Testament* (VTS 30), ed. J. S. Emerton, pp. 15-29. Leiden: E. J. Brill, 1979.
Bergen, R. D. *1, 2 Samuel* (NAC 7). Nashville: Broadman & Holman, 1996.
———, ed. *Biblical Hebrew and Discourse Linguistics*. Dallas: Summer Institute of Linguistics, 1994.

Biella, J. C. *Dictionary of Old South Arabic: Sabaean Dialect* (HSS 25). Chico, Calif.: Scholars Press, 1982.

Biran, A., and J. Naveh. "An Aramaic Stela Fragment from Tel Dan." *IEJ* 43 (1993) 81-98.

———. "The Tel Dan Inscription: A New Fragment." *IEJ* 45 (1995) 1-18.

Birch, B. C. "The First and Second Books of Samuel: Introduction, Commentary, and Reflections." In *The New Interpreter's Bible*, vol. II, ed. L. E. Keck et al., pp. 947-1383. Nashville: Abingdon, 1998.

Bloch-Smith, E. M. "The Cult of the Dead in Judah: Interpreting the Material Remains." *JBL* 111 (1992) 213-24.

Block, D. I. "Empowered by the Spirit of God: The Holy Spirit in the Historiographic Writings of the Old Testament." *Southern Baptist Journal of Theology* 1 (1997) 42-61.

Bodine, W. R., ed. *Discourse Analysis of Biblical Literature: What It Is and What It Offers* (Semeia Studies). Atlanta: Scholars Press, 1995.

———, ed. *Linguistics and Biblical Hebrew*. Winona Lake, Ind.: Eisenbrauns, 1992.

Bodner, K. *David Observed: A King in the Eyes of His Court* (Hebrew Bible Monographs 5). Sheffield: Sheffield Phoenix Press, 2005, 2008.

———. *1 Samuel: A Narrative Commentary* (Hebrew Bible Monographs 19). Sheffield: Sheffield Phoenix Press, 2009.

Booij, Th. "Psalm 132: Zion's Well-Being." *Bib* 90 (2009) 75-83.

Bordreuil, P., and D. Pardee, *A Manual of Ugaritic* (LSAWS 3). Winona Lake, Ind.: Eisenbrauns, 2009.

Brichto, H. C. "Kin, Cult, Land and Afterlife — A Biblical Complex." *HUCA* 44 (1973) 1-54.

Broshi, M., and A. Yardeni. "On netinim and False Prophets." In *Studies in Honor of Jonas C. Greenfield*, ed. Ziony Zevit, S. Gitin and M. Sokoloff, pp. 29-37. Winona Lake, Ind.: Eisenbrauns, 1995.

Brueggemann, W. "1 Samuel 1: A Sense of a Beginning." *ZAW* 102 (1990) 33-48.

———. *First and Second Samuel* (Interpretation: A Bible Commentary for Teaching and Preaching). Louisville: John Knox, 1990.

Bryce, T. "The 'Eternal Treaty' from the Hittite Perspective." *BMSAES* 6 (2006) 1-11.

Bynon, T. *Historical Linguistics* (CTL). Cambridge: Cambridge University Press, 1977.

Caird, G. B. "The First and Second Books of Samuel." in *IB*, vol. 2, pp. 853-1176. Nashville: Abington, 1953.

Callaham, S. N. *Modality and the Biblical Hebrew Infinitive Absolute* (AKM 71). Wiesbaden: Otto Harrassowitz, 2010.

Campbell, A. F. *1 Samuel* (FOTL 8). Grand Rapids: Eerdmans, 2005.

———. *The Ark Narrative (1 Sam 4-6; 2 Sam 6). A Form-Critical and Traditio-Historical Study* (SBLDS 16). Missoula, Mont.: Scholars Press, 1975.

Caquot, A., and P. D. Robert. *Les Livres de Samuel* (CAT VI). Geneva: Labor et Fides, 1994.

Cartledge, T. W. *1 & 2 Samuel* (SHBC). Macon, Ga.: Smyth & Helwys, 2001.

Ceresko, A. R. "The Identity of 'the Blind and the Lame' *('iwwēr ûpisséaḥ)* in 2 Samuel 5:8b." *CBQ* 63 (2001) 23-30.

Chapman, S. B. *1 Samuel as Christian Scripture: A Theological Commentary*. Grand Rapids: Eerdmans, 2016.

Chavel, S. "Compository and Creativity in 2 Samuel 21:1-14." *JBL* 122 (2003) 23-52.

Childs, B. S. "Psalm Titles and Midrashic Exegesis." *JSS* 16 (1971) 137-50.

Claasen, W. T. "Speaker-oriented Functions of *kî* in Biblical Hebrew." *JNSL* 11 (1983) 29-46.

Cohen, C. "Literary and Philological Aspects of Biblical Hebrew (BH) צרעת." *Korot* 21 (2011-2012) 255-91.

Conroy, C. *1–2 Samuel, 1–2 Kings with an Excursus on Davidic Dynasty and Holy City Zion* (Old Testament Message 6). Wilmington, Del.: Michael Glazier, 1983.

———. *Absalom Absalom! Narrative and Language in 2 Sam 13-20* (AnBi 81). Rome: Pontifical Biblical Institute, 1978.

Cooper, A. M. "The Life and Times of King David According to the Book of Psalms." In *The Poet and the Historian: Essays in Literary and Historical Biblical Criticism* (HSS 26), ed. R. E. Friedman, pp. 117-31. Chico, Calif.: Scholars Press, 1983.

Craigie, P. C. *Psalms 1-50* (WBC 19). Waco, Tex.: Word Books, 1983.

———. *Ugarit and the Old Testament*. Grand Rapids: Eerdmans, 1983.

Cross, F. M. *Canaanite Myth and Hebrew Epic: Essays in the History of the Religion of Israel*. Cambridge, Mass.: Harvard University Press, 1973.

Cross, F. M., and D. W. Parry. "A Preliminary Edition of a Fragment of 4QSam[b] (4Q52)." *BASOR* 306 (1997) 63-74.

Cross, F. M., D. W. Parry, R. J. Saley, and E. Ulrich. *Qumran Cave 4*.XII: *1–2 Samuel* (DJD 17). Oxford: Clarendon Press, 2005.

Dahood, M. J., *Psalms I* (AB 16). Garden City, N.Y.: Doubleday, 1965.

Davies, E. W. "Inheritance Rights and the Hebrew Levirate Marriage. Part 1." *VT* 31 (1981) 138-44.

Dawson, D. A. *Text-Linguistics and Biblical Hebrew* (JSOTSS 177). Sheffield: Sheffield Academic Press, 1994.

De Regt, L. J. "The Order of Participants in Compound Clausal Elements in the Pentateuch and Earlier Prophets: Syntax, Convention or Rhetoric?" In *Literary Structure and Rhetorical Strategies in the Hebrew Bible*, ed. L. J. de Regt, J. de Waard, and J. P. Fokkelman, pp. 79-100. Assen: Van Gorcum, 1996.

De Ward, E. F. "Mourning Customs in 1, 2 Samuel." *JJS* 23 (1972), 1-27, 145-66.

Dietrich, W., ed. *The Books of Samuel: Stories, History, Reception History* (BETL 284). Leuven: Peters, 2016.

———. *The Early Monarchy in Israel: The Tenth Century B.C.E.* (SBLBES 3). Atlanta: Society of Biblical Literature, 2007.

———. *Samuel* (BKAT). Neukirchen-Vluyn: Neukirchener, 2011-2015.

Dion, P. E. *Les Araméens à l'Âge du Fer.* Paris: J. Gabalda, 1997.

Dobbs-Allsopp, F. W. "Ingressive *qwm* in Biblical Hebrew." *ZAH* 8 (1995) 31-54.

Driver, G. R. "Hebrew Notes." *ZAW* 52 (1934) 51-56.

Driver, S. R. *Notes on the Hebrew Text and the Topography of the Books of Samuel.* Oxford: Clarendon Press, 1913.

Edenburg, C. "David, the Great King, King of the Four Quarters: Structure and Signification in the Catalogue of David's Conquests (2 Samuel 8:1-4, 1 Chronicles 18:1-13)." In *Raising Up a Faithful Exegete: Essays in Honor of Richard D. Nelson*, ed. K. L. Noll and B. Schramm, pp. 159-75. Winona Lake, Ind.: Eisenbrauns, 2010.

Ehrlich, C. S. *The Philistines in Transition: A History from ca. 1000-730 BCE* (SHCANE 10). Leiden: E. J. Brill, 1996.

Eichrodt, W. *Theology of the Old Testament* (OTL). Vol. I. London: SCM Press, 1961.

Endo, Y. *The Verbal System of Classical Hebrew in the Joseph Story: An Approach from Discourse Analysis* (SSN 32). Assen: Van Gorcum, 1996.

Eschelbach, M. A. *Has Joab Foiled David?: A Literary Study of the Importance of Joab's Character in Relation to David* (Studies in Biblical Literature 76). New York: Peter Lang, 2005.

Eskenazi, T. C. "A Literary Approach to Chronicler's Ark Narrative in 1 Chronicles 13-16." In *Fortunate the Eyes That See: Essays in Honor of David Noel Freedman in Celebration of His Seventieth Birthday*, ed. A. B. Beck et al., pp. 258-74. Grand Rapids: Eerdmans, 1995.

Eskhult, M. *Studies in Verbal Aspect and Narrative Technique in Biblical Hebrew Prose* (Studia Semitica Upsaliensia 12). Uppsala: Acta Universitatis Upsaliensis, 1990.

Eslinger, L. *House of God or House of David: The Rhetoric of 2 Samuel 7* (JSOTSS 164). Sheffield: Sheffield Academic Press, 1994.

Evans, M. J. *1 and 2 Samuel* (NIBCOT 6). Peabody, Mass.: Hendrickson, 2000.

Faust, A. "Did Eilat Mazar Find David's Palace?" *BAR* 38.5 (September/October 2012) 47-52, 70.

Fensham, F. C. "The Treaty between Israel and the Gibeonites." *BA* 27 (1964) 96-100.

Fincke, A. *The Samuel Scroll from Qumran: 4QSam*[a] *Restored and Compared to the Septuagint and 4QSam*[c] (STDJ 43) Leiden: E. J. Brill, 2001.

Firth, D. G. *1 & 2 Samuel* (AOTC 8). Nottingham: InterVarsity, 2009.

Fishbane, M. *Biblical Interpretation in Ancient Israel.* Oxford: Clarendon Press, 1985.

Flanagan, J. W. "Court History or Succession Document? A Study of 2 Sam 9-20 and 1 Kings 1-2." *JBL* 91 (1972) 172-81.

Fleming, D. E. *The Legacy of Israel in Judah's Bible: History, Politics, and the Reinscribing of Tradition.* Cambridge: Cambridge University Press, 2012.

Fokkelman, J. P. *Narrative Art and Poetry in the Books of Samuel: A Full Interpretation Based on Stylistic and Structural Analyses.* Vol. I: *King David (II Sam. 9-20 & I Kings 1-2)* (SSN 20). Assen: Van Gorcum, 1981.

———. *Narrative Art and Poetry in the Books of Samuel.* Vol. II: *The Crossing Fates (I Sam. 13-31 & II Sam. 1)* (SSN 23). Assen: Van Gorcum, 1986.

———. *Narrative Art and Poetry in the Books of Samuel.* Vol. III: *Throne and City (II Sam. 2-8 & 21-24)* (SSN 27). Assen: Van Gorcum, 1990.

Ford, J. N. "The 'Living Rephaim' of Ugarit: Quick or Defunct?" *UF* 24 (1992) 73-101.

Freedman, D. N. "On the Death of Abner." In *Love and Death in the Ancient Near East. Essays in Honor of M. H. Pope*, ed. J. H. Marks and R. M. Good, pp. 125-27. Guilford, Conn.: Four Quarters, 1987.

———. "Psalm 113 and the Song of Hannah." *EI* 14 (H. L. Ginsberg Volume) (1978), pp. 56*-69*.

Garsiel, M. "The Book of Samuel: Its Composition, Structure and Significance as a Historiographical Source." *JHS* 10 (2010) 1-42.

———. "David's Warfare Against the Philistines in the Vicinity of Jerusalem (2 Sam 5,17-25; 1 Chron 14,8-16)." In *Studies in Historical Geography and Biblical Historiography Presented to Zecharia Kallai*, ed. G. Galil and M. Weinfeld (VTS 81), pp. 150-64. Leiden: E. J. Brill, 2000.

———. "The Story of David and Bathsheba: A Different Approach." *CBQ* 55 (1993) 244-62.

———. "The Valley of Elah Battle and the Duel of David with Goliath: Between History and Artistic Theological Historiography." In *Homeland and Exile: Biblical and Ancient Near Eastern Studies in Honour of Bustenay Oded*, ed. G. Falil, M. Geller, and A. Millard (VTS 130), pp. 391–426. Leiden: E. J. Brill, 2009.

———. "The Water Retrieval Mission of David's Three Warriors and Its Relationship to the Battle of the Valley of Refaim." In *Teshurot LaAvishur: Studies in the Bible and the Ancient Near East, in Hebrew and Semitic Languages; Festschrift Presented to Prof. Yitzhak Avishur on the Occasion of His 65th Birthday*, ed. M. Heltzer and M. Malul, pp. 51*-62*. Tel Aviv: Archaeological Center Publications, 2004.

———. "Word Play and Puns as a Rhetorical Device in the Book of Samuel." In *Puns and Pundits: Word Play in the Hebrew Bible and Ancient Near Eastern Literature*, ed. S. B. Noegel, pp. 181-204. Bethesda, Md.: CDL Press, 2000.

Geoghegan, J. C. "Israelite Sheepshearing and David's Rise to Power." *Bib* 87 (2006) 55-63.

George, A. R. *The Babylonian Gilgamesh Epic: Introduction, Critical Edition and Cuneiform Texts*, Vol. I. Oxford: Oxford University Press, 2003.

Gevirtz, S. *Patterns in the Early Poetry of Israel* (SAOC 32). Chicago: University of Chicago Press, 1963, 1973.

Gibson, A. *A Biblical Semantic Logic: A Preliminary Analysis*. Oxford: Blackwell, 1981.

Gilmour, R. "Who Captured Jerusalem? Reading Historiography and/or Collective Memory in Samuel." In *The Books of Samuel: Stories, History, Reception History*, ed. W. Dietrich (BETL 284), pp. 63-82. Leuven: Peters, 2016.

Gordon, C. H. "Build-up and Climax." In *Studies in Bible and the Ancient Near East Presented to Samuel E. Loewenstamm*, ed. Y. Avishur and J. Blau, pp. 29-34. Jerusalem: E. Rubinstein's, 1978.

———. *The Common Background of Greek and Hebrew Civilizations*. New York: W. W. Norton, 1965.

Gordon, C. H., and G. A. Rendsburg. *The Bible and the Ancient Near East*. 4th ed. New York: W. W. Norton, 1997.

Gordon, R. P. *I & II Samuel: A Commentary*. Exeter: Paternoster, 1986.

Grayson, A. K. "Assyrian Officials and Power in the Ninth and Eighth Centuries." *SAAB* 7 (1993) 19-52.

———. *Assyrian Rulers of the Early First Millennium* BC *II (858-745* BC*)* (Royal Inscriptions of Mesopotamia). Toronto: University of Toronto Press, 1996.

Green, B. *Mikhail Bakhtin and Biblical Scholarship: An Introduction* (Semeia Studies 38). Atlanta: Society of Biblical Literature, 2000.

Greenstein, E. L. "What Was the Book of Yashar?" *Maarav* 21 (2014) 25-35.

Greenwood, K. R. "Labor Pains: The Relationship Between David's Census and *Corveé* Labor." *BBR* 20 (2010) 467-78.

———, ed. *Since the Beginning: Interpreting Genesis 1 and 2 through the Ages*. Grand Rapids: Baker Academic, 2018.

Gunn, D. M. "From Jerusalem to the Jordan and Back: Symmetry in 2 Samuel xv-xx." *VT* 30 (1980) 109-113.

———. *The Story of King David: Genre and Interpretation* (JSOTSS 6). Sheffield: JSOT Press, 1978.

Haelewyck, J. C. "L'assassinat d'Ishbaal (2 Samuel IV 1–12)." *VT* 47 (1997) 145–53.

Hallo, W. W. "Proverbs Quoted in Epic." In *Lingering over Words: Studies in Ancient Near Eastern Literature in Honor of William L. Moran*, ed. J. Huehnergard and P. Steinkeller (HSS 37), pp. 203-17. Atlanta: Scholars Press, 1990.

Halpern, B. *David's Secret Demons: Messiah, Murderer, Traitor, King*. Grand Rapids: Eerdmans, 2001.

Harviainen, T. "Hushai the Archite, a Gentile in the King's Court (2 Sam. 16:18-19, 17:7-16)." *StOr* 55 (1984) 265-76.

Hatav, G. "The Infinitive Absolute and Topicalization of Events in Biblical Hebrew." In *Advances in Biblical Hebrew Linguistics: Data, Methods, and Analyses*, ed. A. Moshavi and T. Notarius (LSAWS 12), pp. 207-32. Winona Lake, Ind.: Eisenbrauns, 2017.

Hays, R. P. "A Problematic Spouse: A Text-Critical Examination of Merab's Place in 1 Samuel 18:17-19 and 2 Samuel 21:8." *ZAW* 129 (2017) 220-33.

Herbert, E. D. "2 Samuel V 6: An Interpretative Crux Reconsidered in the Light of 4QSam[a]." *VT* 44 (1994) 340-48.

———. *Reconstructing Biblical Dead Sea Scrolls: A New Method Applied to the Reconstruction of* 4QSam[a] (STDJ 22). Leiden: E. J. Brill, 1997.

Hertzberg, H. W. *I and II Samuel. A Commentary* (OTL). Philadelphia: Westminster, 1964 [orig. 1960].

Hester, D. C. *First and Second Samuel.* Louisville: Geneva, 2000.

Hill, A. E. "On David's 'Taking' and 'Leaving' Concubines (2 Samuel 5:13; 15:16)." *JBL* 125 (2006) 129-39.

Hobbs, T. R. "Reflections on Honor, Shame, and Covenant Relations." *JBL* 116 (1997) 501-3.

Hoffmeier, J. K. "What Is the Biblical Date for the Exodus? A Response to Bryant Wood." *JETS* 50 (2007) 235-47.

Hoffner, H. A., Jr. *1 & 2 Samuel* (EEC: Logos Edition). Bellingham, WA: Lexham Press, 2015.

———. "Propaganda and Political Justification in Hittite Historiography." In *Unity and Diversity: Essays in the History, Literature, and Religion of the Ancient Near East*, ed. H. Goedicke and J. J. M. Roberts, pp. 49-62. Baltimore: Johns Hopkins University Press, 1975.

———. "Symbols for Masculinity and Femininity: Their Use in Ancient Near Eastern Sympathetic Magic Rituals." *JBL* 85 (1966) 326-34.

Hoftijzer, J. "David and the Tekoite Woman." *VT* 20 (1970) 429-44.

Holloway, S. W. "Distaff, Crutch or Chain Gang: The Curse of the House of Joab in 2 Samuel III 29." *VT* 37 (1987) 370-75.

Homan, M. M. "Booths or Succoth? A Response to Yigael Yadin." *JBL* 118 (1999) 691-97.

Huehnergard, J. *An Introduction to Ugaritic.* Peabody, Mass.: Hendrickson, 2012.

———. *Ugaritic Vocabulary in Syllabic Transcription* (HSS 32). Atlanta: Scholars Press, 1987.

Hurvitz, A. "The Historical Quest for 'Ancient Israel' and the Linguistic Evidence of the Hebrew Bible: Some Methodological Observations." *VT* 47 (1997) 311-15.

Hutton, J. M. "'Abdi-Aširta, the Slave, the Dog': Self-Abasement and Invective in the Amarna Letters, the Lachish Letters, and 2 Sam 3:8." *ZAH* 15/16 (2002/2003) 2-18.

———. "Over the River and Through the Woods: Historical and Narrative Geography in 2 Samuel 18." In *The Books of Samuel: Stories, History, Reception History*, ed. W. Dietrich (BETL 284), pp. 105-27. Leuven: Peters, 2016.

Hutzli, J. "Role and Significance of Ancestors in the Books of Samuel." In *The Books of Samuel: Stories, History, Reception History*, ed. W. Dietrich (BETL 284), pp. 425-40. Leuven: Peters, 2016.

Ishida, T. *History and Historical Writing in Ancient Israel: Studies in Biblical Historiography* (SHCANE 16). Leiden: E. J. Brill, 1999.

———. "The Story of Abner's Murder: A Problem Posed by the Solomonic Apologist." *EI* 24 (Avraham Malamat Volume) (1993) 109*-13*.

Jackson, B. S. "Law in the Ninth Century: Jehoshaphat's 'Judicial Reform.'" In *Understanding of the History of Ancient Israel*, ed. H. G. M. Williamson (PBA 143), pp. 369-97. Oxford: Oxford University Press, 2007.

Janzen, D. "The Condemnation of David's 'Taking' in 2 Samuel 12:1-14." *JBL* 131 (2012) 209-20.

Japhet, S. *I–II Chronicles: A Commentary* (OTL). Louisville: Westminster John Knox, 1993.

Jenni, E. "'Schlagen' in 2. Sam 2,31 und in den historischen Büchern." *EI* 24 (Avraham Malamat Volume) (1993) 114*-18*.

Jobling, D. *1 Samuel* (Berit Olam). Collegeville, Minn.: Liturgical Press, 1998.

Käser, A. "Then David Wrote a Letter (2 Sam. 11:14) — He Himself or Was It His Secretary? A Study of the Criteria for Handling the 'Semantic Causative.'" *TynB* 65 (2014) 21-36.

Kalimi, I. "The Capture of Jerusalem in the Chronistic History." *VT* 52 (2002) 66-79.

———. "Reexamining 2 Samuel 10-12: Redaction History versus Compositional Unity." *CBQ* 78 (2016) 24-46.

———. "The View of Jerusalem in the Ethnographical Introduction of Chronicles (1 Chr 1-9)." *Bib* 83 (2002) 556-62.

Kasari, P. *Nathan's Promise in 2 Samuel 7 and Related Texts* (PFES 97). Helsinki: Finnish Exegetical Society, 2009.

Kaufmann, Y. *The Religion of Israel: From Its Beginnings to the Babylonian Exile.* Chicago: University of Chicago Press, 1960.

Kitchen, K. A. "Egypt and Israel During the First Millennium B.C." *Congress Volume: Jerusalem 1986*, ed. J. A. Emerton (VTS 40), pp. 107-23. Leiden: E. J. Brill, 1988.

———. *On the Reliability of the Old Testament.* Grand Rapids: Eerdmans, 2003.

Klein, R. W. *1 Samuel* (WBC 10). Waco, Tex.: Word Books, 1983.

———. *1 Samuel* (WBC 10). 2nd ed. Nashville: Thomas Nelson, 2000.

Klement, H. H. *2 Samuel 21-24: Context, Structure and Meaning in the Samuel Conclusion.* Frankfurt am Main: Peter Lang, 2000.

Kleven, T. "The Use of *ṣnr* in Ugaritic and 2 Samuel V 8: Hebrew Usage and Comparative Philology." *VT* 44 (1994) 195-204.

Korpel, M. C. A. *A Rift in the Clouds: Ugaritic and Hebrew Descriptions of the Divine* (UBL 8). Münster: Ugarit-Verlag, 1990.

Kratz, R. G. "Bibelhandschrift oder Midrasch? Zum Verhältnis von Text- und Literargeschichte in den Samuelbüchern im Licht der Handschrift 4Q51 (4QSam[a])." In *The Books of Samuel: Stories, History, Reception History*, ed. W. Dietrich (BETL 284), pp. 153-80. Leuven: Peters, 2016.

Kruse, H. "David's Covenant." *VT* 35 (1985) 139-64.

Laato, A. *A Star Is Rising: The Historical Development of the Old Testament Royal Ideology and the Rise of the Jewish Messianic Expectations*. Atlanta: Scholars Press, 1997.

———. "Second Samuel 7 and Ancient Near Eastern Royal Ideology." *CBQ* 59 (1997) 244-69.

Labuschagne, C. J. *The Incomparability of Yahweh in the Old Testament* (Pretoria Oriental Series 5). Leiden: E. J. Brill, 1966.

Layton, S. C. "The Steward in Ancient Israel: A Study of Hebrew *(ʾăšer) ʿal-habbayit* in Its Near Eastern Setting." *JBL* 109 (1990) 633-49.

Lemche, N. P. "Kings and Clients: On Loyalty between the Ruler and the Ruled in Ancient 'Israel.'" *Semeia* 66 (1995) 119-32.

Levenson, J. D., and B. Halpern, "The Political Import of David's Marriages." *JBL* 99 (1980) 507-18.

Levine, B. A. "'The Lord Your God Accept You' (2 Samuel 24:23): The Altar Erected by David on the Threshing Floor of Araunah." *EI* 24 (Avraham Malamat Volume) (1993) 122-29.

———. "The Semantics of Loss: Two Exercises in Biblical Hebrew Lexicography." In *Solving Riddles and Untying Knots: Biblical, Epigraphic, and Semitic Studies in Honor of Jonas C. Greenfield*, ed. Z. Zevit, S. Gitin, and M. Sokoloff, pp. 137-58. Winona Lake, Ind.: Eisenbrauns, 1995.

Levy, T. E., and M. Najjar, "Edom and Copper: The Emergence of Ancient Israel's Rival." *BAR* 32.4 (Jul/Aug 2006) 24-35, 70.

———. "New Iron Age Copper: Mine Fields Discovered in Southern Jordan." *NEA* 72 (2009) 98-101.

Lewis, T. J. *Cults of the Dead in Ancient Israel and Ugarit* (HSM 39). Atlanta: Scholars Press, 1989.

———. "The Ancestral Estate (נחלת אלהים) in 2 Samuel 14:16." *JBL* 110 (1991) 597-612.

Long, V. P., ed. *Israel's Past in Present Research: Essays on Ancient Israelite Historiography* (SBTS 7). Winona Lake, Ind.: Eisenbrauns, 1999.

Longacre, R. E. *Joseph: A Story of Divine Providence: A Text Theoretical and Textlinguistic Analysis of Genesis 37 and 39-48*. Winona Lake, Ind.: Eisenbrauns, 1989.

———. "*Weqatal* Forms in Biblical Hebrew Prose." In *Biblical Hebrew and Dis-*

course Linguistics, ed. R. D. Bergen, pp. 50-98. Dallas: Summer Institute of Linguistics, 1994.

Lyke, L. L. *King David with the Wise Woman of Tekoa: The Resonance of Tradition in Parabolic Narrative* (JSOTSS 255). Sheffield: Sheffield Academic Press, 1997.

MacDonald, N. *Not Bread Alone: The Uses of Food in the Old Testament.* Oxford: Oxford University Press, 2008.

Machinist, P. "The Transfer of Kingship: A Divine Turning." In *Fortunate the Eyes That See: Essays in Honor of David Noel Freedman in Celebration of His Seventieth Birthday*, ed. A. B. Beck et al., pp. 105-20. Grand Rapids: Eerdmans, 1995.

Maeir, A. M., S. J. Wimmer, A. Zukerman, and A. Demsky. "A Late Iron Age I/ Early Iron Age II Old Canaanite Inscription from Tell eṣ-Ṣâfī/Gath, Israel: Palaeography, Dating, and Historical-Cultural Significance." *BASOR* 351 (2008) 39-71.

Malamat, A. "Aspects of the Foreign Policies of David and Solomon." *JNES* 22 (1963) 1-17 [reprinted in A. Malamat, *History of Biblical Israel: Major Problems and Minor Issues* (Leiden: E. J. Brill, 2001), pp. 208-33].

———. "Doctrines of Causality in Biblical and Hittite Historiography: A Parallel." *VT* 5 (1955) 1-12.

———. "The Kingdom of David and Solomon in Its Contact with Egypt and Aram Naharaim." *BA* 21 (1958) 96-102.

———. *Mari and the Bible* (SHCANE 12). Leiden: E. J. Brill, 1998.

———. "Prophecy at Mari." In *"The Place Is Too Small for Us": The Israelite Prophets in Recent Scholarship*, ed. R. P. Gordon (SBTS 5), pp. 50-73 [orig. published in 1989]. Winona Lake, Ind.: Eisenbrauns, 1995.

Malul, M. *"Lᵉdabbēr baššelî* (2 Sam. 3:27) 'to Talk Peace.'" *JHS* 4 (2003) Article 8.

Margalith, O. "A Note on *šālîšîm*." *VT* 42 (1992) 266.

———. "Where Did the Philistines Come From?" *ZAW* 107 (1995) 101-9.

Marsman, H. J. *Women in Ugarit and Israel: Their Social and Religious Position in the Context of the Ancient Near East* (OTS 49). Leiden: E. J. Brill, 2003.

Martin, W. J. "'Dischronologized' Narrative in the Old Testament." In *Congress Volume Rome 1968*, ed. G. W. Anderson et al. (VTS 17), pp. 179-86. Leiden: E. J. Brill, 1969.

Mastéy, E. "A Linguistic Inquiry Solves an Ancient Crime: Re-examination of 2 Samuel 4:6." *VT* 61 (2011) 82-103.

Matthews, V. H. *More Than Meets the Ear: Discovering the Hidden Contexts of Old Testament Conversations.* Grand Rapids: Eerdmans, 2008.

Mattila, R. *The King's Magnates: A Study of the Highest Officials of the Neo-Assyrian Empire* (SAAS 11). Helsinki: Neo-Assyrian Text Corpus Project, 2000.

Mazar, B. *Biblical Israel: State and People.* Jerusalem: Magnes Press, 1992.

———. "King David's Scribe and the High Officialdom of the United Monarchy of Israel." In *The Early Biblical Period: Historical Studies*, ed. A. Ahituv and B. A. Levine, pp. 126-38. Jerusalem: Israel Exploration Society, 1986.

Mazar, E. "Jerusalem: 1. The City of David Visitors' Center." *NEAEHL* 5:1801.

———. *The Palace of King David: Excavations at the Summit of the City of David. Preliminary Report of Seasons 2005-2007*. Jerusalem: Shoham Academic Research and Publication, 2009.

Mazar, E., W. Horowitz, T. Oshima, and Y. Goren. "A Cuneiform Tablet from the Ophel in Jerusalem." *IEJ* 60 (2010) 4-21.

McCarter, P. K., Jr. *I Samuel: A New Translation with Introduction, Notes and Commentary* (AB 8). Garden City, N.Y.: Doubleday, 1980.

———. *II Samuel: A New Translation with Introduction, Notes and Commentary* (AB 9). Garden City, N.Y.: Doubleday, 1984.

McKenzie, S. L. *King David: A Biography*. Oxford: University Press, 2000.

Meier, S. A. *The Messenger in the Ancient Semitic World* (HSM 45). Atlanta: Scholars Press, 1988.

Melamed, E. Z. "Break-up of Stereotype Phrases as an Artistic Device in Biblical Poetry." In *Studies in the Bible*, ed. C. Rabin (Scripta Hierosolymitana 8), pp. 115-53. Jerusalem: Magnes Press, 1961.

Mettinger, T. N. D. *King and Messiah: The Civil and Sacral Legitimation of the Israelite Kings* (CB: Old Testament Series 8). Lund: C. W. K. Gleerup, 1976.

———. "'The Last Words of David': A Study of Structure and Meaning in II Samuel 23:1-7." *Svensk exegetisk Årsbok* 41/42 (1976/77), 147-56.

———. *Solomonic State Officials: A Study of the Civil Government Officials of the Israelite Monarchy* (CB: Old Testament Series 5). Lund: C. W. K. Gleerup, 1971.

Milgrom, J. *Leviticus 1-16: A New Translation with Introduction and Commentary* (AB 3). New York: Doubleday, 1991.

Millard, A. R. "Are There Anachronisms in the Books of Samuel?" In *Studies on the Text and Versions of the Hebrew Bible in Honour of Robert Gordon*, ed. G. Khan and D. Lipton (VTS 149), pp. 39-48. Leiden: E. J. Brill, 2012.

———. "King Solomon in His Ancient Context." In *Age of Solomon: Scholarship at the Turn of the Millennium*, ed. L. K. Handy (SHCANE 11), pp. 30-53. Leiden: E. J. Brill, 1997.

———. "King Solomon's Shields." In *Scripture and Other Artifacts: Essays on the Bible and Archaeology in Honor of Philip J. King*, ed. M. D. Coogan, J. C. Exum, and L. E. Stager, pp. 286-95. Louisville: Westminster John Knox, 1994.

———. "The Ostracon from the Days of David Found at Khirbet Qeryafa." *TynB* 62 (2011) 1-13.

Miller, P. D., and J. J. M. Roberts. *The Hand of the Lord: A Reassessment of the*

"Ark Narrative" of 1 Samuel (JHNES). Baltimore: Johns Hopkins University Press, 1977.
Miscall, P. *1 Samuel: A Literary Reading* (Indiana Studies in Biblical Literature). Bloomington: Indiana University Press, 1986.
———. "2 Samuel 24: A Meditation on Wrath, Guilt, and the King." *Shofar* 11 (1993) 65-79.
Mitchell, T. C. "The Music of the Old Testament Reconsidered." *PEQ* (1992) 124-43.
Muchiki, Y. *Egyptian Proper Names and Loanwords in North-West Semitic* (SBLDS 173). Atlanta: Society of Biblical Literature, 1999.
Mulder, M. J. "Un euphémisme dans 2 Sam. XII 14?" *VT* 18 (1968) 108-14.
Mullen, E. T., Jr. "The Divine Witness and the Davidic Royal Grant: Ps 89:37-38." *JBL* 102 (1983) 207-18.
Muraoka, T. "Philological Notes on the David-Bathsheba Story I." In *In the Shadow of Bezalel: Aramaic, Biblical, and Ancient Near Eastern Studies in Honor of Bezalel Porten*, ed. A. F. Botta (CHANE 60), pp. 289-304. Leiden: E. J. Brill, 2013.
———. "Philological Notes on the David-Bathsheba Story II." In *Sophia — Paideia: Sapienza e educazione (Sir 1,27); miscellanea di studi offerti in onore del prof. don Mario Cimosa*, ed. Gillian Bonney and Rafael Vicent, pp. 89-113. Rome: LAS, 2012.
———. "The Tripartite Nominal Clause Revisited." In *The Verbless Clause in Biblical Hebrew: Linguistic Approaches*, ed. C. L. Miller (LSAWS 1), pp. 187-213. Winona Lake, Ind.: Eisenbrauns, 1999.
Murray, D. F. "*mqwm* and the Future of Israel in 2 Samuel VII 10." *VT* 40 (1990) 298-320.
Na'aman, N. "Amasa the Asrielite (2 Samuel 17,25)." *Semitica* 57 (2015) 177-83.
———. "In Search of the Ancient Name of Khirbet Qeiyafa." *JHS* 8 (2008) 2-8.
———. "The List of David's Officers (*šālîšîm*)." *VT* 38 (1988) 71-79.
Naéh, S. "A New Suggestion Regarding 2 Samuel XXIII 7." *VT* 46 (1996) 260-65.
Nieh, H. "Ein unerkannter Text zur Nekromantie in Israel: Bemerkungen zum religionsgeschichtlichen Hintergrund von 2Sam 12, 16a." *UF* 23 (1991) 301-6.
O'Connor, M. "War and Rebel Chants in the Former Prophets." In *Fortunate the Eyes That See: Essays in Honor of David Noel Freedman in Celebration of His Seventieth Birthday*, ed. A. B. Beck et al., pp. 322-37. Grand Rapids: Eerdmans, 1995.
Olmo Lete, G. del. "David's Farewell Oracle (2 Samuel XXIII 1-7): A Literary Analysis." *VT* 34 (1984) 414-37.
Olmo Lete, G. del, and J. Sanmartín, *A Dictionary of the Ugaritic Language in the Alphabetic Tradition* (HbO 112). Translated and edited by W. G. E. Watson. Leiden: E. J. Brill, 2003.

Olyan, S. M. "Zadok's Origins and the Tribal Politics of David." *JBL* 101 (1982) 177-93.

———. "Honor, Shame, and Covenant Relations in Ancient Israel and Its Environment." *JBL* 115 (1996) 201-18.

Pardee, D. "An Overview of Ancient Hebrew Epistolography." *JBL* 97 (1978) 321-46.

Park, S.-M. S. "The Frustration of Wisdom: Wisdom, Counsel, and Divine Will in 2 Samuel 17:1-23." *JBL* 128 (2009) 453-67.

Parry, D. W. "The 'Word' or the 'Enemies' of the Lord? Revisiting the Euphemism in 2 Sam 12:14." In *Emanuel: Studies in Hebrew Bible, Septuagint and Dead Sea Scrolls in Honor of Emanuel Tov*, ed. S. M. Paul, R. A. Kraft, L. H. Schiffman, and W. W. Fields (VTS 94), pp. 367-78. Leiden: E. J. Brill, 2003.

Parunak, H. van Dyke. "Some Discourse Functions of Prophetic Quotation Formulas in Jeremiah." *BHDL* 489-519.

———. "Transitional Techniques in the Bible." *JBL* 102 (1983) 525-48.

Pisano, S. *Additions or Omissions in the Books of Samuel: The Significant Pluses and Minuses in the Massoretic, LXX and Qumran Texts* (OBO 57). Göttingen: Vandenhoeck & Ruprecht; Freiburg: Universitätsverlag, 1984.

Pitard, W. T. *Ancient Damascus.* Winona Lake, Ind.: Eisenbrauns, 1987.

Polak, F. H. "Conceptions of the Past and Sociocultural Grounding in the Books of Samuel." In *History, Memory, Hebrew Scriptures: A Festschrift for Ehud Ben Zvi*, ed. I. D. Wilson and D. V. Edelman, pp. 117-32. Winona Lake, Ind.: Eisenbrauns, 2015.

———. "Speaker, Addressee, and Positioning: Dialogue Structure and Pragmatics in Biblical Narrative." In *Interested Readers: Essays on the Hebrew Bible in Honor of David J. A. Clines*, ed. J. K. Aitken, J. M S. Clines, and C. M. Maier, pp. 359-72. Atlanta: Society of Biblical Literature, 2013.

Polzin, R. *Samuel and the Deuteronomist: A Literary Study of the Deuteronomic History; Part Two; 1 Samuel* (Indiana Studies in Biblical Literature). Bloomington: Indiana University Press, 1989.

Provan, I. W. "Ideologies, Literary and Critical: Reflections on Recent Writing on the History of Israel." *JBL* 114 (1995) 585-606.

Qimron, E. "The Lament of David over Abner." In *Birkat Shalom: Studies in the Bible, Ancient Near Eastern Literature, and Postbiblical Judaism Presented to Shalom M. Paul on the Occasion of His Seventieth Birthday*, ed. C. Cohen, V. A. Hurowitz, A. Hurvitz, Y. Muffs, B. Schwartz, and J. Tigay, vol. 1, pp. 143-47. Winona Lake, Ind.: Eisenbrauns, 2008.

Rahmouni, A. *Divine Epithets in the Ugaritic Alphabetic Texts* (HbO 93) Leiden: E. J. Brill, 2008.

Rainey, A. F., and R. S. Notley, *The Sacred Bridge: Carta's Atlas of the Biblical World.* Jerusalem: Carta, 2006.

Ravasco, A. "A Paleographical Note on 2Sam 19:10 in 4QSam^a." *RQ* 26 (2014) 461-66.

Reich, R., and E. Shukron. "Jerusalem: 2. The Gihon Spring and Eastern Slope of the City of David." *NEAEHL* 5:1801-7.

Rendsburg, G. A. "Confused Language as a Deliberate Literary Device in Biblical Hebrew Narrative." *JHS* 2 (1999) Article 6.

———. *Diglossia in Ancient Hebrew* (AOS 72). New Haven: American Oriental Society, 1990.

———. "The Internal Consistency and Historical Reliability of the Biblical Genealogies." *VT* 40 (1990) 185-206.

———. "The Northern Origin of 'The Last Words of David' (2 Sam 23,1-7)." *Bib* 69 (1988) 113-21.

Revell, E. J. "Concord with Compound Subjects and Related Uses of Pronouns." *VT* 43 (1993) 69-87.

Rezetko, R. *Source and Revision in the Narratives of David's Transfer of the Ark: Text, Language and Story in 2 Samuel 6 and 1 Chronicles 13, 15-16* (LHBOTS 470). New York: T. & T. Clark, 2007.

Ridout, G. "The Rape of Tamar: A Rhetorical Analysis of 2 Sam 13:1-22." In *Rhetorical Criticism: Essays in Honor of James Muilenburg*, ed. J. J. Jackson and M. Kessler, pp. 75-84. Pittsburgh: Pickwick Press, 1974.

Rofé, A. "4QSam^a in the Light of Historico-literary Criticism: The Case of 2 Sam 24 and 1 Chr 21." In *Biblische und Judaistische Studien: Festschrift für Paolo Sacchi*, ed. A. Vivian (Judentum und Umwelt 29), pp. 109-19. Frankfurt am Main: Peter Lang, 1990.

Rost, L. *The Succession to the Throne of David*. Sheffield: Almond, 1982.

Sakenfeld, K. D. *The Meaning of* Hesed *in the Hebrew Bible: A New Inquiry* (HSM 17). Missoula, Mont.: Scholars Press, 1978.

Sarna, N. M. "Psalm 89: A Study in Inner Biblical Exegesis." *Biblical and Other Studies* (Philip W. Lown Institute of Advanced Judaic Studies), pp. 29-46. Waltham, Mass.: Harvard University Press, 1963.

Saussure, F. de. *Cours de linguistique générale*, ed. C. Bally and A. Sechehaye, with the collaboration of A. Riedlinger. Lausanne: Payot, 1916. [Trans. W. Baskin, *Course in General Linguistics* (Glasgow: Fontana/Collins, 1977).]

Schipper, J. "Did David Overinterpret Nathan's Parable in 2 Samuel 12:1-6?" *JBL* 126 (2007) 383-91.

———. "Reconsidering the Imagery of Disability in 2 Samuel 5:8b." *CBQ* 67 (2005) 422-34.

———. "'Why Do You Still Speak of Your Affairs?': Polyphony in Mephibosheth's Exchanges with David in 2 Samuel." *VT* 54 (2004) 344-51.

Schley, D. G. "Joab and David: Ties of Blood and Power." In *History and Interpre-*

tation: Essays in Honour of John H. Hayes, ed. M. P. Graham, W. P. Brown, and J. K. Kuan (JSOTSS 173), pp. 90-105. Sheffield: JSOT Press, 1993.
———. "The *šālīšîm*: Officers or Special Three-man Squads?" *VT* 40 (1990) 321-26.
Schniedewind, W. M. *Society and the Promise to David: The Reception History of 2 Samuel 7:1-17*. New York: Oxford University Press, 1999.
———. "Tel Dan Stela: New Light on Aramaic and Jehu's Revolt." *BASOR* 302 (1996) 75-90.
Scurlock, J. "Oaths, Ancient Near East." In *The Encyclopedia of Ancient History*. John Wiley & Sons, 2012. https://doi.org/10.1002/9781444338386.wbeah01146
Segert, S. *A Basic Grammar of the Ugaritic Language: With Selected Texts and Glossary*. Berkeley: University of California Press, 1984.
Seow, C. L. *Myth, Drama, and the Politics of David's Dance* (HSM 44). Atlanta: Scholars Press, 1989.
Sergi, O. "The Composition of Nathan's Oracle to David (2 Samuel 7:1-17) as a Reflection of Royal Judahite Ideology." *JBL* 129 (2010) 261-79.
Simon, U. "The Poor Man's Ewe-Lamb. An Example of a Juridical Parable." *Bib* 48 (1967) 207-42.
———. *Reading Prophetic Narratives* (Indiana Studies in Biblical Literature). Bloomington: Indiana University Press, 1997.
Sivan, D. *A Grammar of the Ugaritic Language* (HbO 28). Leiden: E. J. Brill, 1997.
Smith, H. P. *A Critical and Exegetical Commentary on the Books of Samuel* (ICC). Edinburgh: T. & T. Clark, 1951.
Smith, M. S. "The Near Eastern Background of Solar Language for Yahweh." *JBL* 109 (1990) 29-39.
———. *Poetic Heroes: Literary Commemorations of Warriors and Warrior Culture in the Early Biblical World*. Grand Rapids: Eerdmans, 2014.
Stoebe, H. J. *Das zweite Buch Samuelis* (KAT 8.2). Gütersloh: Gütersloher Verlagshaus, 1994.
Stokes, R. E. "The Devil Made David Do It . . . Or *Did* He? The Nature, Identity, and Literary Origins of the *Satan* in 1 Chronicles 21:1." *JBL* 128 (2009) 91-106.
Talmon, S. "Double Readings in the Massoretic Text." *Textus* 1 (1960) 144-84.
Talstra, E. "Text Grammar and Hebrew Bible II: Syntax and Semantics." *BO* 39 (1982) 26-38.
Tidwell, N. L. "The Philistine Incursions into the Valley of Rephaim (2 Sam. V 17ff.)." In *Studies in the Historical Books of the Old Testament*, ed. J. A. Emerton (VTS 30), pp. 190-212. Leiden: E. J. Brill, 1979.
Toorn, K. van der. "Saul and the Rise of Israelite State Religion." *VT* 43 (1993) 519-42.
Toorn, K. van der, and C. Houtman, "David and the Ark." *JBL* 113 (1994) 209-31.

Tov, E., ed., *The Dead Sea Scrolls on Microfiche: A Comprehensive Facsimile Edition of the Texts from the Judean Desert*, 2 vols. Leiden: E. J. Brill, 1993.

Tromp, N. J. *Primitive Conceptions of Death and the Nether World in the Old Testament.* Rome: Pontifical Biblical Institute, 1969.

Tsumura, D. T. "Chaos and *Chaoskampf* in the Bible: Is 'Chaos' a Suitable Term to Describe Creation or Conflict in the Bible?" in *Conversations on Canaan and the Bible: Creation, Chaos, Monotheism, Yahwism*, ed. R. S. Watson and A. H. W. Curtis. Berlin: Walter de Gruyter, forthcoming.

———. "The 'Chaoskampf' Motif in Ugaritic and Hebrew Literatures."In *Le Royaume d'Ougarit de la Crète à l'Euphrate: Nouveaux axes de Recherche*, ed. J.- M. Michaud (Proche-Orient et Littérature Ougaritique II), pp. 473-99. Sherbrooke: GGC, 2007.

———. *Creation and Destruction: A Reappraisal of the* Chaoskampf *Theory in the Old Testament.* Winona Lake, Ind.: Eisenbrauns, 2005.

———. "The Creation Motif in Psalm 74:12-14? A Reappraisal of the Theory of the Dragon Myth." *JBL* 134 (2015) 547-55.

———. "The Family in the Historical Books." In *Family in the Bible*, ed. R. S. Hess and M. D. Carroll R., pp. 59-79. Grand Rapids: Baker Academic, 2003.

———. *The First Book of Samuel* (NICOT). Grand Rapids: Eerdmans, 2007.

———. "Hymns and Songs with Titles and Subscriptions in the Ancient Near East." *Exeg* 3 (1992) 1-7 [Japanese with an English summary].

———. "'Misspellings' in Cuneiform Alphabetic Texts from Ugarit: Some Cases of Loss or Addition of Signs." In *Writing and Ancient Near Eastern Society: Papers in Honour of Alan R. Millard* (LHBOTS 426), ed. P. Bienkowski, C. Mee, and E. Slater, pp. 143-53. London: T. & T. Clark International, 2005.

———. "The Problem of Childlessness in the Royal Epic of Ugarit." In *Monarchies and Socio-Religious Traditions in the Ancient Near East*, ed. T. Mikasa, pp. 11-20. Wiesbaden: Otto Harrassowitz, 1984.

———. "Revisiting the 'Seven' Good Gods of Fertility in Ugarit: Is Albright's Emendation of *KTU* 1.23:64 Correct? " *UF* 39 (2008) 629-41.

———. "Some Examples of Linguistic Variants in 1–2 Samuel." *Orient: Report of the Society for Near Eastern Studies in Japan* 38 (2003) 36-50.

———. "Speaker-oriented Connective Particle *'al-kēn* in 2 Sam 7:22." *JSS* [forthcoming].

———. "Temporal Consistency and Narrative Cohesion in 2Sam 7,8-11." In *The Books of Samuel: Stories, History, Reception History*, ed. W. Dietrich (BETL 284), pp. 385-92. Leuven: Peters, 2016.

———. "Tense and Aspect of Hebrew Verbs in II Samuel 7: 8-16 — from the Point of View of Discourse Grammar." *VT* 60 (2010) 641-54.

———. "Textual Corruptions, or Linguistic Phenomena? The Cases in 2 Samuel (MT)." *VT* 64 (2014) 135-45.

———. "Vertical Grammar of Biblical Hebrew Parallelism: The AXX'B Pattern in Tetracolons," *VT* 69 (2019) [in press].

———. "Vertical Grammar of Parallelism in Hebrew Poetry." *JBL* 128 (2019) 167-81.

Vanderhooft, D. "Dwelling Beneath the Sacred Place: A Proposal for Reading 2 Samuel 7:10." *JBL* 118 (1999) 625-33.

Van Seters, J. *The Biblical Saga of King David.* Winona Lake, Ind.: Eisenbrauns, 2009.

Vargon, S. "The Blind and the Lame." *VT* 46 (1996) 498-514.

Veijola, T. *Die ewige Dynastie: David und die Entstehung seiner Dynastie nach der deuteronomistischen Darstellung* (Annales Academiae Scientiarum Fennicae. Series B 193). Helsinki: Suomalainen Tiedeakatemia, 1975.

Walters, S. D. "Childless Michal, Mother of Five." In *The Tablet and the Scroll: Near Eastern Studies in Honor of William W. Hallo*, ed. M. Cohen, D. Snell, and D. Weisberg, pp. 290-96. Bethesda, Md.: CDL Press, 1993.

Watson, W. G. E. "Internal or Half-line Parallelism in Classical Hebrew Poetry." *VT* 39 (1989) 44-66.

———. "Internal Parallelism in Classical Hebrew Verse." *Bib* 66 (1985) 365-84.

Watson, W. G. E., and N. Wyatt, eds. *Handbook of Ugaritic Studies* (HdO 39). Leiden: E. J. Brill, 1999.

Weinfeld, M. "Divine Intervention in War in Ancient Israel and in the Ancient Near East." In *History, Historiography and Interpretation: Studies in Biblical and Cuneiform Literatures*, ed. H. Tadmor and M. Weinfeld, pp. 121-47. Jerusalem: Magnes Press, 1983.

Wendland, E. R. "Genre Criticism and the Psalms: What Discourse Typology Can Tell Us about the Text (with Special Reference to Psalm 31)." *BHDL* 374-414.

Westbrook, R. *Property and the Family in Biblical Law* (JSOTSS 113). Sheffield: JSOT Press, 1991.

Westermann, C. *Basic Forms of Prophetic Speech.* Louisville: Westminster John Knox, 1991.

Whitelam, K. *The Just King: Monarchical Judicial Authority in Ancient Israel* (JSOTSS 12). Sheffield: JSOT Press, 1979.

Wiseman, D. J. "'Is It Peace?' Covenant and Diplomacy." *VT* 32 (1982) 311-26.

Wright, D. P. "Music and Dance in 2 Samuel 6." *JBL* 121 (2002) 201-25.

Wright, J. W. "The Founding Father: The Structure of the Chronicler's David Narrative." *JBL* 117 (1998) 45-59.

Wyatt, N. "The Religion of Ugarit: An Overview." *HUS* 529-85.

Yadin, Y. "Some Aspects of the Strategy of Ahab and David." *Bib* 36 (1955) 332-51.

Young, T. "Psalm 18 and 2 Samuel 22: Two Versions of the Same Song." In *Seeking Out the Wisdom of the Ancients: Essays Offered to Honor Michael V. Fox on the Occasion of His Sixty-Fifth Birthday*, ed. R. L. Troxel, K. G. Friebel, and D. R. Magary, pp. 53-69. Winona Lake, Ind.: Eisenbrauns, 2005.

Youngblood, R. F. "1, 2 Samuel." In *The Expositor's Bible Commentary*, ed. F. E. Gaebelin, pp. 551-1104. Grand Rapids: Zondervan, 1992.

Younger, K. L., Jr. *A Political History of the Arameans: From Their Origins to the End of Their Polities* (ABS 13). Atlanta: SBL Press, 2016.

TEXT AND COMMENTARY

V. "STORY OF KING DAVID" (1:1–20:26)

STORY OF DAVID'S REIGN (1:1–12:31)

A. DEATH OF SAUL (1:1-27)

From here the history of the early Israelite monarchy moves into the second stage, the era of King David. The narrator first directs our attention to the end of Saul's life, his death and that of his sons at Mount Gilboa (1 Sam. 31). This episode emphasizes David's grief, especially as expressed in his elegy, but the deaths of the king and his heir are in fact a step toward David's kingship. Literarily and discourse grammatically, this section (a: 2 Sam. 1) functions as a LINK between the "Story of Saul and David" (A: 1 Sam. 16–31) and the "Story of King David" (B: 2 Sam. 1–20). In other words, the present section is "a" of the A/aB pattern ("transitional technique").[1]

Since not only Saul but his three sons died (though we are later informed that another son is alive), the question as to his successor is implicitly raised. But Saul's regalia are brought to David without his intervention, by a person acting completely on his own. The narrator presents the whole progress of events as the providential act of God.

1. Report of Saul's Death (1:1-16)

David in Ziklag hears of the death of Saul. But instead of rejoicing, he mourns and kills the man who claims to have killed Saul. His elegy (vv. 17-27) shows his deep personal grief over the deaths of both Saul and Jonathan.

a. The Amalekite's Report (1:1-10)

1 *After the death of Saul, when David had returned from attacking Amalek, David stayed in Ziklag for two days.*

2 *On the third day, a man came from the camp where Saul was,*[2] *with his clothes torn and with dirt on his head.*

When he came to David, he fell to the ground and bowed.[3]

1. See Tsumura, I, p. 14 and p. 53 (Introduction, VI.B).

2. Lit. "from the camp, from with Saul"; cf. "from Saul's camp" (McCarter, II, p. 56), but if so, we would rather expect *maḥănēh Šāʾûl*; cf. *maḥănēh Yiśrāʾēl* (2 Sam. 1:3).

3. Hišt. conjugation of *ḥwh*, as in Ugaritic; see Gordon, *UT*, §9.39; P. Bordreuil and

3 *And David said to him,*
"Where have you come from?"
And he said to him,
"I have escaped from the camp of Israel."
4 *And David said to him,*
"What happened?
Tell me!"
And he said,
"Because the people fled from the battle and many of the people fell and died.[4]
Saul and his son Jonathan are also dead."

5 *And David said to the young man who was telling him this,*
"How do you know that Saul and his son Jonathan are dead?"

Verse 1 follows after the events of 1 Sam. 30; David is back at home in Ziklag. In v. 4 the man, an Amalekite (v. 8), reports the events of 1 Sam. 31. Since he arrived on the third day after David's return to Ziklag, David had probably arrived home around the day that Saul died.

1 *After the death of Saul.* This way of beginning a new section is very common; verse 1a is a good example of a LINK between the previous two episodes (A: 1 Sam. 30 and 31) and the following one (B: 2 Sam. 1:1-16) in the pattern of A/aB, just as the entire chapter 1 (a) is a LINK between the "Story of Saul and David" (A) and the "Story of David" (B), as noted above.

This verse illustrates the multidimensional reality of life as against the monodimensional nature of linguistic description.[5] David had been back for two days after his attack on Amalek. During this time the Amalekite had been running from Gilboa to Ziklag. Since it probably would have taken him two full days to cover the distance — some 100-112 miles (160-180 km) — David probably had arrived in Ziklag around the day of the battle. The Amalekite must have taken Saul's diadem and armlet before "the next day" (1 Sam. 31:8), when the Philistines came to strip the slain.

The word order, *waw*+David *šāb* (pf.), signifies simultaneity; hence *when David had returned.* If it meant "After the death of Saul, David returned

D. Pardee, *A Manual of Ugaritic* (LSAWS 3; Winona Lake, Ind.: Eisenbrauns, 2009), p. 314; J. Huehnergard, *An Introduction to Ugaritic* (Peabody, Mass.: Hendrickson, 2012), pp. 66, 148.

4. 3 m.pl. McCarter (II, p. 56) takes the final *w* of *wymtw* as dittography of the *w* of the following *wgm*; thus he reads the verb as singular like the preceding verbs "fled" and "fell." However, the number of the successive verbs varies, depending on whether or not the narrator takes their agents as plural or collective.

5. See the discussion of the embedded story of the Witch of Endor (1 Sam. 28:3-25) in Tsumura, I, pp. 615-16; also pp. 63-64.

from" (NIV, Bergen),[6] the Hebrew sentence would have a different word order and structure such as *wayyāšob (*wayqtl*) *Dāwīd*.

Through all these details the narrator makes it clear that David was not involved in the death of Saul and his sons, especially Jonathan, even though he was a Philistine vassal at that time.

2 On the *third day*, a man comes running to Ziklag with the "good" news, which ends up causing the death of its bearer. On the similarity in narrative pattern between this episode and the messenger's reporting the defeat of Israel to Eli, see on 1 Sam. 4:12-17.[7] Torn clothes and dirt on one's head are expressions of extreme grief; see also 2 Sam. 13:19; 15:32 and the commentary on 1 Sam. 4:12.[8] If this man is lying (see below), his gestures *with his clothes torn and with dirt on his head* may have been planned "to lend dramatic weight to his story."[9]

3-4 First, David asks him where he came from. Then he asks: *What happened?* (lit. "what was the word/matter" = 1 Sam. 4:16). The man begins his answer with *'ăšer*; lit. "that."

It has been debated whether *'ăšer* here introduces a direct quotation[10] or indirect speech (JPS). However it is probably the first word in the direct speech, meaning "because," and exhibits some degree of hesitancy, as in 1 Sam. 15:20: "Because (*'ăšer*) I listened to the voice of the Lord, I went on the mission on which the Lord sent me." Like Saul, this man is reluctant to answer straightforwardly.[11] Hence, *because* is here not a matter of cause and effect; rather, it has a metalinguistic function, making an excuse for his answer, like a *speaker-oriented kî*, which explains the reason for the preceding words.[12]

6. R. D. Bergen, *1, 2 Samuel* (NAC 7; Nashville: Broadman & Holman, 1996), p. 285. Note that J. P. Fokkelman, *Narrative Art and Poetry in the Books of Samuel*, vol. II: *The Crossing Fates (I Sam. 13–31 & II Sam. 1)* (SSN 23; Assen: Van Gorcum, 1986), p. 592, takes both actions of David, i.e., *returned* and *stayed*, as "background," without giving due attention to the difference in the Hebrew verbal forms: pf. vs. *wayqtl*. For one thing, if the *wayqtl* were sequential to the preceding pf., the second stated subject "David" would be unnecessary; see Tsumura, I, pp. 51-52. Furthermore, it is most natural to take the *wayqtl* clause as the main clause after the temporal clause introduced by *wayhi*. Hence, "and David returned" should be taken as parenthetical, so "After the death of Saul, when David had returned. . ., David remained" (NRSV, ESV); "After the death of Saul — David had already returned from defeating the Amalekites — David stayed two days in Ziklag" (JPS). Fokkelman's comment "David's movement leads to rest, *šb* becomes *wyšb*" (*The Crossing Fates*, p. 631) is puzzling.

7. Tsumura, I, pp. 197-99.

8. Tsumura, I, pp. 197-98.

9. McCarter, II, p. 58.

10. McCarter, II, p. 58, following GKC, §157c; Driver, p. 97.

11. For the importance of sociolinguistic aspects of conversation see Matthews, *More Than Meets the Ear* and my review of it in *JAOS* 130 (2010) 324-25.

12. See Tsumura, I, pp. 48-49.

5 The term *young man* here refers particularly to a "young fighting man," that is, a soldier. For the broader meaning of *naʿar,* see the comments on 1 Sam. 9:3;[13] 2 Sam. 2:14; 19:17.

6 *And the young man who was telling him this said,*
"I happened to be on Mount Gilboa.
There was Saul leaning on his spear;
then the chariots and the cavalry were closing in on him.
7 *And he turned around and saw me and called to me.*
And I said,
'Here I am.'
8 *And he said to me,*
'Who are you?'
And I said[14] *to him,*
'I am an Amalekite.'
9 *And he said to me,*
'Stand by me and kill me,[15]
for anguish has seized me
because all my life is still within me.'
10 *So I stood by him and killed him,*
for I realized that he would not live after his falling.[16]
And I took the diadem that was on his head
and the armlet[17] *that was on his arm*
and brought them to my lord here."

6-10 This account of Saul's death contradicts that in 1 Sam. 31:3-5. There he fell on his own sword; here the Amalekite kills him. This discrepancy is most easily explained by assuming that the soldier lied in order to gain favor with David. Note also that in 2 Sam. 4:10 David does not say that the man had killed Saul, but just that he had brought the news.[18] Saul had destroyed most of the

13. Tsumura, p. 265.

14. So MT (Q.); cf. "he said" (K.).

15. For *kill me* (*ûmōtᵉtēnî*), see also vv. 10, 16. The Polel of *mwt,* "to die," means "to make a full end of" (*HALOT,* p. 562), that is, "to deliver the death blow" as in Judg. 9:54; 1 Sam. 14:13; 17:51.

16. The term *niplô* is Qal inf. of the *qitl*-type; see B-L, p. 368. Cf. *noplô* (1 Sam. 29:3).

17. For *and the armlet,* McCarter, with Wellhausen and Driver, reads *whṣʿdh* instead of the MT *wᵉʾeṣʿādāh,* as in the *wᵉhaṣṣᵉʿādôt* of Isa. 3:20, since the MT form, though it is an attested noun (Num. 31:50), lacks the article. However, it is not uncommon for an article to be omitted in direct speech, just as it is in poetry.

18. For a detailed discussion of "the unity of the account" and the "apologetic themes" of this episode, see McCarter, II, pp. 62-65.

Amalekites (1 Sam. 15), but as this man was the son of a sojourner (v. 13), it is not surprising he was in Israel.

6 For Mount Gilboa, see the commentary on 1 Sam. 28:4, 31:1.[19]

Chariots (*rekeb*; see on 1 Sam. 8:11)[20] were the most important weapons of the Philistine army, but were ineffective in the mountains. Saul had apparently retreated from the plains of Jezreel into the mountainous area of Gilboa to escape them, so the young man's report that *the chariots . . . were closing in on him* is probably a fictional embellishment.

The term *cavalry* (*baʿălê happārāšîm*) is literally "the owners of the horses/horsemen." Since this expression "is unparalleled," Wellhausen, followed by many scholars, omits *baʿălê* and takes *happārāšîm* as "horsemen." However, *pārāš* can mean either "military horse" or "horseman,"[21] and the LXX supports the MT's longer reading.[22] Thus, the MT phrase *baʿălê happārāšîm* as it stands most likely means *cavalry.*

8 It is surprising that the man confessed his background both to Saul, who had destroyed many of the Amalekites (1 Sam. 15), and to David, who had just come back from warring with them. The Amalekites are the archetypal plunderers in biblical tradition; see on 1 Sam. 14:48; 15:2.[23]

9 The term *šābāṣ* for *anguish* (so ESV) is a hapax legomenon, the exact sense of which is uncertain; cf. "convulsions" (NRSV), "the throes of death" (NIV, REB); see *HALOT*, p. 1402: a) "dizziness, trembling"; b) "weakness."

The word order of the expression *because all my life is still within me* (*kî-kol-ʿôd napšî bî*) is unusual; lit. "because all *still* of my life in me"; see Job 27:3 (BDB, p. 482). McCarter holds that two variant readings are combined here, *ky kl npšy by* and *ky ʿwd npšy by*, and that *kl* in the MT "must be read adverbially: 'yet still my life is wholly within me' (cf. GKC (2) §128e)." He translates: "yet there is life in me still," which reflects the second variant.[24] However, this unusual word order might be an example of the AXB pattern, in which X ("still") is inserted between AB ("all my life"), thus interrupting a normal sequence A-B while still modifying the phrase AB as a whole.[25]

10 The *diadem* and the *armlet* are the royal insignia; the former was an emblem worn on the forehead, given to the king at the time of his coronation (2 K. 11:12, etc.). The armlet is mentioned as an ornament in Num. 31:50.[26]

19. See Tsumura, I, pp. 620, 650.

20. Tsumura, I, pp. 256-57.

21. Note that in Hab. 1:8 the term *pārāšâw* means both "his horses" and "his horsemen"; see D. T. Tsumura, "Polysemy and Parallelism in Hab. 1,8-9," *ZAW* 120 (2008) 194-203.

22. McCarter, II, p. 57.

23. See Tsumura, I, pp. 383 and 389-90.

24. McCarter, II, p. 57.

25. See Introduction in Tsumura, I, pp. 60-61.

26. See J. Krecher, "Insignien," *RlA* 5 (1976-80), 109-14.

b. David's Response (1:11-12)

11 *And David seized his clothes and tore them; so did also all the men who were with him.*

12 *And they lamented and wept and fasted till evening over Saul and his son Jonathan and over the people of the Lord and over the house of Israel, for they fell by the sword.*

11-12 When David heard this man's report, he and all his men *lamented* (*spd; see on 1 Sam. 25:1),[27] by tearing their clothes (see above on v. 2) and fasting, a sign of mourning, as in 1 Sam. 31:13 and 2 Sam. 3:35. The *evening* was the end of the day; see Judg. 20:26 and 1 Sam. 14:24. The law often refers to uncleanness "till evening" (Lev. 11:24, etc.).

After this summary statement (v. 12), the story resumes the actual dialogue between David and the young man who brought this news.

c. Death of the Amalekite (1:13-16)

13 *And David said to the young man who was telling him this,*
"Where are you from?"
And he said,
"I am the son of a sojourner, an Amalekite."
14 *And David said to him,*
"How were you not afraid of extending your hand
to destroy the Lord's anointed?"
15 *And David called one of the servants and said,*
"Go near and strike him down!"
And he struck him, and he died.
16 *And David said to him,*
"Your blood be on your head!
For your mouth has testified against[28] you by saying
'I have killed the Lord's anointed.'"

13 When David asked the young man's background, he introduced himself as *a sojourner, the Amalekite*. The legal status of a "sojourner" (or "a resident alien") *gēr* was distinguished from that of a foreigner (*nēkār*). He had a special status both with privileges and with responsibilities. He was protected by the

27. Tsumura, I, pp. 574-75.
28. Lit. "answered in."

community law, but at the same time bound by legal obligations and penalties as described in Lev. 24:22; cf. 20:2; 24:16; etc.

14-16 One may wonder if the order of these verses is confused, seeing that v. 16 is addressed to one who died in v. 15. It may be that this section follows the AXB pattern, in which David's speech from v. 14 to v. 16 is interrupted by the insertion of v. 15. Such an insertion is not accidental, for *And David said to him* is repeated both in v. 14 and v. 16. It may be that David's words were deliberately given at the end of the section in order to emphasize this man's testimony that he *killed the Lord's anointed.*

14 As a sojourner who was subject to the laws of Israel, the Amalekite should have recognized the sanctity of Saul as his king — contrast Saul's armor-bearer (1 Sam. 31:4). David himself had earlier refrained from killing Saul, saying he was *the Lord's anointed*; see on 1 Sam. 24:6; 26:9;[29] also 2 Sam. 19:21 (MT 22).

16 The expression *Your blood be on your head* means that "you, not I, are responsible for your own death"; see Josh. 2:19; 1 K. 2:32-33, 37; Ezek. 33:4.

2. David's Elegy for Saul and Jonathan (1:17-27)

David's lament is a wonderful expression of public and personal grief. It expresses his heartfelt sorrow for the deaths of both Saul and Jonathan, for both the one who sought his life and the one who helped him with love and friendship. David accepts both of their relationships with him as God-given.

a. Title (1:17-18)

17 *And David chanted this elegy*[30] *for Saul and his son Jonathan:*[31]
18 *To teach the sons of Judah the bow. (It is written in the Book of Jashar.)*

17 This *elegy* (*qînāh*) is said to have been preserved in the *Book of Jashar*, a prebiblical written source that also included Josh. 10:12-13, and according to the Septuagint text, Solomon's poem in 1 K. 8:12-13.

Most modern translations interpret *the Bow* as the name of the lament's tune (NRSV, JPS, NIV, ESV, etc.), but this is pure speculation.[32] However, it

29. Tsumura, I, pp. 567, 600.
30. *qyn with a cognate accusative *qînāh.*
31. Lit. "chanted . . . and said."
32. Based on LXX[B, L], McCarter takes this "enigmatic" reference to *a bow* as "intrusive"

may be that *To teach the sons of Judah the bow* (*lᵉlammēd bᵉnê-Yᵉhûdāh qāšet*) is a heading referring to how this elegy was used, like the heading of Ps. 60, "A Miktam of David; for instruction." This elegy was possibly used in connection with military training in fighting with the bow and other weapons, as is suggested by the use of *miktam* in Pss. 16 and 56-59.[33] Certainly, Saul and Jonathan were ideal heroes who would be emulated by Israelite soldiers.

For the expression *chanted* an *elegy* (*qyn, Polel with a cognate accusative *qînāh*), see also 2 Sam. 3:33. Note that the motif of "the mourning for a dead hero by his surviving comrade" occurs in the *Odyssey* where Achilles mourns for Patroclus[34] as well as in the Gilgamesh epic (VIII 1-45) where Gilgamesh mourns for Enkidu.[35]

18 *wayyōʾmer* here has been interpreted in two ways:

(1) "And ordered (to do . . .)" as in the NIV and NRSV.

(2) "Saying," as a formula introducing the elegy itself like in 2 Sam. 22:2 (= Ps. 18 heading; see the commentary on that verse) and several Egyptian hymns and songs, which is how the NRSV takes it. Klostermann holds that "everything after *wayyōʾmer* must originally have been part of the poem."[36]

Another possibility, however, is that the verbal sequence "chanted . . . and said" is an example of the pattern, *verbal action*+ "and said," as mentioned in the Introduction of *The First Book of Samuel*.[37]

b. Elegy (1:19-27)

19 *"How the prince, O Israel, was slain on your high places;*
how the warriors have fallen!
20 *Tell it not*[38] *in Gath,*
bring not the tidings to the streets of Ashkelon,
lest the daughters of the Philistines rejoice,

---

and omits it, translating: "and said it should be taught to the people of Judah" (II, p. 67). REB also translates: "this dirge over them should be taught."

33. Gordon, *CB*, p. 264 n. 1. He surmises that "the meaning of this problematic term is 'a psalm for military training.'" For a recent treatment of the Book of Yashar, see E. L. Greenstein, "What was the Book of Yashar?" *Maarav* 21 (2014) 25-35.

34. See Gordon, *CB*, p. 71, also p. 65.

35. A. R. George, *The Babylonian Gilgamesh Epic: Introduction, Critical Edition and Cuneiform Texts*, Vol. I (Oxford: Oxford Univ. Press, 2003), pp. 651-55.

36. See McCarter, II, p. 67. Gevirtz even tries to reconstruct a bicolon after *wayyōʾmer*. See S. Gevirtz, *Patterns in the Early Poetry of Israel* (SAOC 32; Chicago: University of Chicago Press, 1963, 1973), pp. 73-76.

37. Tsumura, I, p. xii.

38. In this verse the negative particle *ʾal* is repeated.

lest the daughters of the uncircumcised exult!
21 *O mountains in Gilboa and fields of the heights,*
let there be no[39] *dew and no rain upon you!*
For there was defiled the shield of the warriors;
the shield of Saul was not anointed with oil.
22 *Without the blood of the slain, without the fat of the warriors,*
Jonathan's bow turned[40] *not*[41] *back*
and Saul's sword returned not empty.
23 *Saul and Jonathan, the beloved and charming,*
in life and in death they were not separated.
They were swifter than eagles; they were stronger than lions!
24 *O daughters of Israel, weep for Saul*
who dressed you in scarlet with luxuries,
who put a golden ornament over your cloth!
25 *How the warriors have fallen*
in the midst of the battle;
how Jonathan was slain on your high places!
26 *I grieve for you,*[42] *my brother Jonathan;*
you were so good to me.
Your love was wonderful[43] *to me,*
more than the love of women.
27 *How the warriors have fallen*
and perished, by the weapons of war!

The elegy itself, vv. 19-27, begins with a reference to Saul as "the prince" of Israel and ends by expressing David's very personal feelings toward his "brother" Jonathan. Literarily, it constitutes a unified whole with the repetition of key words and the refrain, as well as with a number of word pairs. It addresses first Israel, then the mountains of Gilboa, the daughters of Israel, his brother Jonathan, and finally it laments the fallen warriors Saul and Jonathan. The reverse of the order of the word pair from *Jonathan – Saul* (v. 22) to *Saul – Jonathan* (v. 23) indicates a change of emphasis. However, it ends with the refrain *How the warriors have fallen!* mourning both of them.

39. The negative particle *'al* is repeated.

40. The verb *turn* (*nāśôg*) is usually taken as Ni. pf. 3 m.s., but if so, Jonathan would be the subject, since *bow* is a feminine noun. One could take this as a colloquialism that ignores gender (see below on v. 24), but if we take *nāśôg* as an inf. abs., this incongruence disappears.

41. The negative particle *lō'* is repeated.

42. Lit. "to be depressed, worried" (*HALOT*, p. 1058).

43. The MT form *niplᵉ'atāh* for *was wonderful* is an "anomaly," but, as McCarter explains, this anomaly can be explained "by reference to the pattern of the final-*he* verbs, a category from which final-*'alep* verbs frequently borrowed forms (Driver; cf. GKC, §75oo)." (McCarter, II, p. 73.)

There is no reason to doubt Davidic authorship of this elegy, for the poem could hardly have been composed apart from the present context.[44]

19 *How the warriors have fallen!* (*'êk nāpᵉlû gibbôrîm*), repeated in v. 25 and the final v. 27, is the theme that echoes throughout the elegy. Verses 19 and 25 are an inverted distant parallelism that form an "envelope" (*inclusio*). That is, v. 19a ("the prince was . . . slain on your high places") is parallel to v. 25c ("Jonathan was slain on your high places"), while v. 19b ("How the warriors have fallen") is repeated in v. 25a. Though both v. 19b and v. 25a start with the word "how" (*'êk*), v. 19a and v. 25c do not. However, the parallelisms between v. 19a and b and v. 25a and c suggest that "how" is implied in all four lines.

Your high places, "your" meaning Israel, is in both verses 19 and 25, while *the prince* (*haṣṣᵉbî*) in v. 19, referring to Saul, is replaced by *Jonathan* in v. 25. *Prince* literally means "gazelle"; cf. the translations "your glory" (NIV; JPS; NRSV); "your beauty" (NASB). Designating notable people as cattle can be seen also in expressions such as Ug. "gazelle" (*ẓby*) // "bull" (*ṯr*) in the Keret Epic (*KTU* 1.15 IV 6-7, 17-18).[45]

The term *high place* (*bāmāh*) referred originally to "the swell of the rib cage of a human being or animal" and later to "back, flank" or "high place, ridge, hill-flank."[46] For the religious meaning of this term in the OT, see the commentary on 1 Sam. 9:12;[47] also see 2 Sam. 22:34.

20 Gath and Ashkelon were two major Philistine cities. For Gath, see the commentary on 1 Sam. 5:8; it is probably modern *Tel eṣ-Ṣâfī.*[48] For Ashkelon, see the commentary on 1 Sam. 6:17.[49] David cannot bear to think about the Philistine victory celebrations. Compare the Israelite women rejoicing in 1 Sam. 18:6-7.[50]

The first line *Do not tell it in Gath* seems to be too short; we would expect some phrase like "the streets of" (*ḥûṣōt*) before *Gath.* As it stands, the two lines are scanned as 2 [6] // 3 [11]. However, all the texts read *bgt.*

In this verse, the expression "the uncircumcised Philistine(s)," which appears in Judg. 14:3 and 1 Sam. 17:26, 36, is divided into a parallel word-pair,

44. See M. S. Smith, *Poetic Heroes: Literary Commemorations of Warriors and Warrior Culture in the Early Biblical World* (Grand Rapids: Eerdmans, 2014), p. 276: "the poem fits a tenth-century dating either in David's time or shortly thereafter."

45. *UT*, §19.1045; *DULAT*, pp. 1003, 930.

46. Vaughn, cited by McCarter, II, p. 75.

47. See Tsumura, I, pp. 292-93.

48. See Tsumura, I, pp. 209-10.

49. See Tsumura, I, p. 223.

50. See Tsumura, I, pp. 475-78. On women's singing victory songs, see H. J. Marsman, *Women in Ugarit and Israel* (OTS 49; Leiden: E. J. Brill, 2003), pp. 552-53.

the Philistines - the uncircumcised.[51] The word pair *rejoice* (*śmḥ*) - *exult* (*ʿlz*) also appears in Jer. 50:11; Zeph. 3:14.

21 The first half of this verse (21a)

> *hārê bagilbōaʿ*
> *ʾal-ṭal w^{e}ʾal-māṭār ʿălêkem*
> *ûśdê t^{e}rûmōt*

is usually translated as

> You mountains of Gilboa,
> let there be no dew or rain upon you,
> nor fields of offerings! (ESV)

The phrase *O mountains in Gilboa* (*hārê bagilbōaʿ*) is literally "mountains-of in Gilboa," with a cstr. noun followed by a prepPh; this is an unusual, but not impossible construction.[52] The third line *ûś^{e}dê t^{e}rûmōt* has been variously emended,[53] though it is generally agreed that it is part of the curse of drought. Instead of emending the text, however, or using the traditional interpretation "offerings" (BDB; cf. *HALOT*) for *t^{e}rûmōt*, I would suggest "heights," based on the verbal root *rwm, "to be exalted, be high" (also Freedman, Dahood, Shea, Firth, etc.).

Most translations take the first line as vocative and the second and third as a bicolon within a tricolon and supply a "nor" in the third line as parallel to "no dew or rain," as in ESV. However, such a scansion seems very awkward. It is more likely that *ś^{e}dê t^{e}rûmōt* "fields of heights"[54] in the third line is parallel to *mountains of Gilboa* in the first line and refers to the *fields* on Mt. Gilboa. It would possible to scan v. 21a as follows:

hārê bagilbōaʿ ʾal-ṭal	3 [7]	A x
w^{e}ʾal-māṭār ʿălêkem ûśdê t^{e}rûmōt	4 [12]	x' &B

However, since the parallelism between two lines would be rather unbalanced, it seems better to see here the AX&B pattern,

51. See E. Z. Melamed, "Break-up of Stereotype Phrases as an Artistic Device in Biblical Poetry," in *Studies in the Bible,* ed. C. Rabin (Scripta Hierosolymitana 8; Jerusalem: Magnes Press, 1961), pp. 115-53; D. T. Tsumura, "Literary Insertion (AXB Pattern) in Biblical Hebrew," *VT* 33 (1983) 468-82; Tsumura, "Vertical Grammar of Parallelism in Hebrew Poetry," *JBL* 128 (2009) 179-81; Tsumura, "Parallelism," *EHLL* 3:18.

52. "Cf. Isa. 9:2; etc. See GKC, §130a." (McCarter, II, p. 75)

53. See BDB, 929; McCarter, II, 70; *HAL*, 1220. See my "'O Mountains in Gilboa and Fields of the Heights' (2 Sam. 1:21a)," in *Festschrift for Prince Mikasa on the Occasion of His Eighty-Eighth Birthday* (Tokyo: Tosui Shobo, 2004), 514-21 (in Japanese).

54. See "lofty highlands" in Smith, *Poetic Heroes*, p. 272.

hārê bagilbōaʿ	A
ʾal-ṭal w^{e}ʾal-māṭār ʿălêkem	X
ûśdê t^{e}rûmōt	&B

where A&B (*mountains in Gilboa and fields of the heights*) are broken up by the insertion of X (*let there be no dew and no rain upon you*), for the purpose of slowing the movement.[55] In other words, the parallelism is underlyingly a well-balanced bicolon,

hārê bagilbōaʿ ûśdê t^{e}rûmōt	4 [11(?)] [A & B]
ʾal-ṭal w^{e}ʾal-māṭār ʿălêkem	3 [9] X

O mountains in Gilboa and fields of the heights,
let there be no dew and no rain upon you!

where the two juxtaposed phrases [A & B] (line 1) are broken up by the insertion of the expression [X] (line 2). Thus the underlying bicolon is well balanced: 4 (11) // 3 (9). With this, the enigmatic "and" in front of "fields of the heights" presents no problem either grammatically or semantically.

The expression *no dew and no rain* is virtually the same as the Ugaritic curse formula *bl ṭl bl rbb* "Let there be no dew /Let there be no rain" (*KTU* 1.19 I 44) pronounced by King Dan'il in the Aqhat Epic when he cursed the place where his crown prince was slain with "a sabbatical cycle of drought."[56] C. H. Gordon notes that it fits in with "the widespread idea that the slaying of a hero brings drought and famine on the scene of the tragedy. . .. The attitude and utterance of David . . . are plainly reflexes of the same tradition that gave rise to the Ugaritic Epic of Aqhat."[57]

For (v. 21b) functions as a *speaker-oriented* particle, which explains why David curses the mountains and fields.

The line *there was defiled the shield of the warriors* is paralleled by the next line, *the shield of Saul was not anointed with oil,* that is, "not in proper condition," as leather shields were treated with oil. The phrase *not anointed* does not refer to Saul, whom David repeatedly refers to as "anointed" (v. 16; also 1 Sam. 24:6, etc.). For *shield,* see also 2 Sam. 22:3. The two expressions, *was defiled* and *was not anointed with oil,* constitute the *A, not B* pattern, in

55. See D. T. Tsumura, "Coordination Interrupted, or Literary Insertion AX&B Pattern, in the Books of Samuel," in *Literary Structure and Rhetorical Strategies in the Hebrew Bible*, ed. L. J. de Regt, J. de Waard, and J. P. Fokkelman (Assen: Van Gorcum, 1996), pp. 117-32; also Tsumura, I, pp. 60-64.

56. Gordon, *PLMU*, pp. 21-22; Pardee, *CS*, I (1997), p. 351.

57. Gordon, *CB*, pp. 164f.

which an idea is expressed by a word and its "negated antonym"; the two lines constitute a chiasmus. The Ni. of this verb appears only here; "be defiled"; "is begrimed." For the practice of anointing leather shields in Mesopotamia, see Millard.[58]

McCarter reads *warriors* (MT) as "warrior" (sg.) + enclitic *mem* and interprets it as referring to Saul.[59] However, in v. 19 the plural noun "warriors" also appears in parallel to "prince," which refers to Saul. Hence, v. 19 and v. 21b form an *inclusio*, with the key terms in order of *abba*, i.e., "prince" (sg.) - "warriors" (pl.) // "warriors" (pl.) - "Saul" (sg.).

22 *Blood* and *fat* are often used as a word pair to refer to the whole of a sacrifice (e.g., Exod. 23:18; Isa. 1:11; Ezek. 39:19). For *Jonathan's bow*, see 1 Sam. 20:20. In this "internal parallelism"[60] of two short half-lines, two kinds of word pairs are used; one (*blood* - *fat*) is merismatic, the other is a breakup of the phrase "slain warriors." Hence, there is no need to emend *ḥălālîm* "the slain" to *ḥayyālim* "the valiant," as Gevirtz does.[61]

The second and the third lines constitute a synonymous parallelism, with *Jonathan's bow* and *Saul's sword* corresponding to each other.

The preposition *min* in the first line usually means "from," but it seems better to take is here as a privative, hence *without*. This would mean that the heroes' weapons did not *return empty*, i.e., without slaying enemy warriors.

23-27 After the positive description of Saul and Jonathan as *the beloved and charming* in v. 23, the reader / audience is commanded positively, for the first time, to "weep" for Saul (v. 24). Then, after the refrain *How the warriors have fallen* in v. 25, the focus switches from Saul to Jonathan. Note that the paired expression, *the prince* (= Saul) - *the warriors* (v. 19), is replaced by *the warriors* - *Jonathan* in a chiastic order in v. 25.

23 "Saul and Jonathan" reverses the order of v. 22. While the third line certainly constitutes an "internal parallelism," *They were swifter than eagles // they were stronger than lions!* the scansion in the first half of the verse poses a difficulty. The MT, followed by NASB and NIV, has the imbalanced parallelism: 2 (6) -3 (13) -2 (7).

Šā'ûl wîhônātān
hanne'ĕhābîm wᵉhannᵉʿîmīm bᵉḥayyêhem
ûbmôtām lō' niprādû

58. A. R. Millard, "Saul's Shield Not Anointed with Oil," *BASOR* 230 (1978) 70.

59. McCarter, II, p. 71.

60. See W. G. E. Watson, "Internal Parallelism in Classical Hebrew Verse," *Bib* 66 (1985) 365-84; Watson, "Internal or Half-line Parallelism in Classical Hebrew Poetry," *VT* 39 (1989) 44-66.

61. McCarter, II, p. 71.

Saul and Jonathan
in life they were loved and gracious,
and in death they were not parted. (NIV)

McCarter, after a long discussion of the LXX translators' problem, concludes that MT originally had the longer reading of the LXX, but it was shortened by haplography. So, he reconstructs and translates v. 23a as:

Saul and Jonathan! Beloved and charming!
They were not parted in life.
and in death they were not separated.[62]

However, NRSV and JPS apparently analyze the verse as follows:

Šā'ûl wîhônātān // hanne'ĕhābîm wehanne'îmīm
beḥayyêhem ûbmôtām lō' niprādû
minnešārîm qallû // mē'ărāyôt gābērû

This constitutes an elegant tricolon, which has two "internal parallelisms," one in the first line, the other in the third. The balance would be: 2-2 // 3 // 2-2; or (6)-(10) // (11) // (6)-(7). I believe this is a convincing analysis, so I translate it as above:

Saul and Jonathan, the beloved and charming,
in life and in death they were not separated.
They were swifter than eagles; they were stronger than lions!

The term *charming* (*ne'îmīm*; lit. "the good ones") is used here as a technical stock phrase for heroes (see on v. 26), as in Ugaritic *n'mm*. The phrase *in life and in death* is a *merismus*, which means "all the time." Since the Amalekite specified that "his son Jonathan" was dead, it appears that Saul continued to treat him as his heir. Apparently they were able to maintain a relationship, working together and eventually fighting and dying together for Israel.

24 The depiction of women wailing for the dead is common in Hebrew, Greek, and other literatures.[63] David addresses here the women in Saul's court, who had been treated luxuriously by Saul. *Scarlet* (*šānî*) cloth, made from the bodies of various kermes insects (Persian and Arabic *qirmiz* 'crimson' [*HALOT*]), was a sign of prosperity (Prov. 31:21).

62. McCarter, II, p. 72.
63. Gordon, *CB*, p. 168.

The root *'dn* of the term *luxuries* means primarily "to make abundant in water-supply" as with the case of "Eden" (Gen 2:8) and secondarily "to enrich, prosper, make luxuriant." The cognate term appears in the Aramaic section of the bilingual Aramaic-Akkadian inscription from Tell Fekheriye as *m'dn mt kln // muṭaḫḫidu kibrāti* "one who makes the whole land abundant in water-supply."[64]

"You" in the phrase "dressed you," is masculine (2 m.pl.), despite the clear feminine referents, while "your" in the phrase "your cloth" is feminine plural. For the use of masculine pronouns for feminine nouns, see GKC, §135o, which explains this "inaccuracy" as "probably passed from the colloquial language." This variation has been explained as an example of "gender neutralization," which is a characteristic of the spoken Hebrew dialect.[65]

25 Here, *warriors* is paired with *Jonathan*, while in v. 19 and v. 21 it is paired with "prince" = "Saul." The refrain *How the warriors have fallen* constitutes an *inclusio* with the first verse of this lament, and the order is chiastic.

By mentioning *Jonathan* here David "effectually connects the Jonathan 'afterthought,' as Talmon describes it, to the main body of the poem."[66]

26 The most personal grief is expressed in this verse, where David mourns his close friend.

The term *n'm* means "good" in a special way; this root appears in Samuel only in v. 23 (above) and 2 Sam. 23:1 (*the minstrel of the songs of Israel*) as an adjective, *nā'îm*. Jonathan's goodness to David was more than just human affection; Jonathan had been first attracted by David's brave fight against Goliath and his trust on the Lord of Hosts. The quality of David's faith was the same as that of Jonathan, who had expressed his complete trust on God in his attack on the Philistine garrison in 1 Sam. 14. Jonathan remained faithful to his covenant (see 1 Sam. 18:3; 20:8, 16, cf. 42) and even went and encouraged David in the wilderness of Horesh while David was hiding from Saul (23:15-18).

Jonathan's *love* (see on 1 Sam. 20:17) for David had not only "political overtones" (see McCarter on 20:17) but also refers to the warm personal intimacy between the two.[67]

27 The subject of the verbal pair, "to fall" and "to perish," is *the warriors*. The first half is the refrain, which has already appeared in verses 19 and 25.

Almost all translations take the parallel structure as a-b-c // b'-C' and so interpret "weapons" as the subject of *perished*. However, the analysis a-b-c // b'-D' seems to be better:

64. D. T. Tsumura, *Creation and Destruction: A Reappraisal of the* Chaoskampf *Theory in the Old Testament* (Winona Lake, Ind.: Eisenbrauns, 2005), pp. 116-17.

65. See Rendsburg, *DAH*, p. 44.

66. McCarter, II, p. 76.

67. Tsumura, I, p. 510.

'êk nāpᵉlû gibbôrîm	How have the warriors fallen
wayyō'bᵉdû kᵉlê milḥāmāh	and perished, by the weapons of war!

In the sequence [V1+V2] - AdvPh, the AdvPh can modify either V1 or V2. Therefore the phrase *kᵉlê milḥāmāh* can mean either "(along) with the weapons of war" or "by the weapons of war" and can modify either "fallen" or "perished." If it modifies "perish," the sentence means: "How the warriors fell and perished (along) with the weapons of war!" as in Ezek. 32:27a ("who went down to Sheol with their weapons of war"). However, the expression "to fall by the sword" is such a common one that it seems more likely that *by the weapons of war* in the second line modifies vertically[68] the verb *have . . . fallen* in the first line. [69]

B. KING DAVID (2:1–5:5)

Judah makes David their king, while Saul's general Abner seeks to restore Saul's kingdom under Saul's son Ishbosheth. However, during the struggle between the two kingdoms, Abner quarrels with Ishbosheth and decides to support David, but is killed by David's commander Joab. Later, Ishbosheth is killed by two of his own men. With no candidate for king in the house of Saul, all of Israel unites to anoint the hero David as king.

1. David, the King of Judah (2:1-11)

a. David to Hebron (2:1-4a)

David settles in Hebron, the central city of Judah, and there is crowned king of Judah. This is the first step toward the union of Judah and Israel under him.[70]

1 *Afterward David inquired of the LORD, saying*
"Shall I go up to one of the cities of Judah?"

68. For "vertical grammar of parallelism" see Tsumura, I, pp. 55-59; also, Tsumura, "Vertical Grammar of Parallelism," 167-81; Tsumura, "Verticality in Biblical Hebrew Parallelism," In *Advances in Biblical Hebrew Linguistics: Data, Methods, and Analyses*, ed. A. Moshavi and T. Notarius (LSAWS 12; Winona Lake, Ind.: Eisenbrauns, 2017), pp. 189-206.

69. See D. T. Tsumura, "An Exegetical Consideration on Hab 2:4a," *Tojo* 15 (1985) 1-26 (in Japanese).

70. See B. Mazar, "David's Reign in Hebron and the Conquest of Jerusalem," in *In the Time of Harvest: Essays in Honor of Abba Hillel Silver on the Occasion of His 70th Birthday*, ed. D. J. Silver (New York: Macmillan, 1963), pp. 235-44 [= B. Mazar, *Biblical Israel: State and People*, ed. S. Aḥituv (Jerusalem: Magnes Press, 1992), pp. 78-87].

And the LORD *said to him,*
"Go up!"
And David said,
"Where shall I go up to?"
and he said,
"To Hebron."

2 *And David went up there along with his two wives, Ahinoam the Jezreelite*[71] *and Abigail the widow*[72] *of Nabal the Carmelite.*

3 *As for his men who were with him, David brought them up, each with his household, and they dwelt in the cities of Hebron.*[73]

4a *And the men of Judah came and there anointed David as king over the house of Judah.*

1-3 With Saul no longer pursuing him and Ziklag burnt, David inquires of the Lord and moves to the Hebron area with his family and men.

1 The phrase *inquired of* (*š'l b-*) is also used in 1 Sam. 10:22; 14:37; 30:8; etc.[74] As in 23:2-4 and 10-12, David inquires of the Lord in two steps to make it certain that the Lord himself was guiding him; cf. 2 Sam. 5:19, 23. For the meaning of "to ask for," see on 1 Sam. 1:28.[75] We are not told how David inquired. Note that there might have been more than one method for inquiring of the Lord.[76]

For *Hebron* [M.R. 159103], see on 1 Sam. 30:31.[77] Hebron is the most important city of southern Judah. It was associated with Abraham (Gen. 13:18; 23:2; 25:10), was given to Caleb by Joshua (Josh. 14:13), and was a priestly city (Josh. 21:13).[78]

David would naturally have considered Hebron as a good place to establish his home base, away from the Philistines and against the Saulide kingdom. Strategically, it was located on a ridge just twenty-five to thirty-one miles (40-50 km) from Ziklag. Politically, it was near his hometown of Bethlehem, and his wives were from the area. Thus, he could unite Judah and other southern clans such as the Calebites, Kenazites, Kenites, and Jer-

71. The Hebrew spelling for *Jezreelite yizr*^{e}*ʿēlît* here is a *sandhi* spelling, without ʾ (א; cf. *yizr*^{e}*ʿēʾlît* יִזְרְעֵאלִית). See Tsumura, "Vowel *sandhi* in Biblical Hebrew," pp. 575-88.

72. Lit. "woman" or "wife." For this phrase, see the commentary on 3:3 below.

73. McCarter omits the phrase *in the cities of* [*b*^{e}*ʿārê*] *Hebron* with Syr. However, the term *ʿîr* sometimes refers to towns or villages in the vicinity of a city in passages as Deut. 3:5 ("unwalled villages"); see on 1 Sam. 6:18 Tsumura, I, p. 224.

74. See the Excursus on technical verbal expressions in Tsumura, I, pp. 617-18.

75. Tsumura, I, pp. 132-34.

76. See Tsumura, I, p. 298 on 1 Sam. 10:22, and pp. 378-80 on 14:40-41.

77. See Tsumura, I, p. 648.

78. See *ABD*, III, pp. 107-8.

ahmeelites (see 1 Sam. 30:29), and "probably the Cherethites in the western Negeb around Ziklag."[79]

But even though he may have already given thought to the matter, David inquires, "Where shall I go up to?" Perhaps this indicates his willingness to be led by the Lord's word.

2 Even before he became king, David had two wives, Ahinoam and Abigail (1 Sam. 25:42-43). For them, this is a homecoming. Ahinoam is from Jezreel, and Abigail from Carmel (25:43; 25:3). For Carmel, see the commentary on 1 Sam. 15:12.[80]

4a Judah apparently has decided that having a king is a good thing, but rather than seeking out a relative of Saul, they choose as king one of their own, the hero David, the chosen of the Lord (1 Sam. 16; 25:30). Even in Saul's time, Judah formed a separate part of the army (11:8; 15:4), so it was prepared to act independently from the rest of the country.

The phrase *men of Judah* (*ʾanšê Yᵉhûdāh*) probably refers to "the elders of Judah" (*ziqnê Yᵉhûdāh*) (1 Sam. 30:26), just like "the men of Israel" (8:22; cf. "the elders" in v. 4) and "all the men of Jabesh" (11:1; cf. v. 3) which refer to the elders. As McCarter notes, they are "the leading citizens of the towns of Judah and are empowered, it seems, to act officially on behalf of the people of Judah, who constitute, we must assume, some kind of organized and at least partially independent political body."[81]

David is here officially anointed as *a king over the house of Judah*. In 1 Sam. 16:1, 13 he was anointed by Samuel to become the future king over "Israel," which presumably included Judah, and now we have the first step in actualizing his monarchy. In this passage there is no mention of a prophet. Similarly, in 2 Sam. 5:3, the leaders of the people request David to become their king.

This is the first occurrence of the phrase *the house of Judah* in the Bible. Compare "the house of David" (*bêt dāwīd*) in 1 Sam. 20:16 and 2 Sam. 3:1, 6, as well as in the late-ninth-century Tell Dan inscription written in Aramaic, which is the earliest attested extrabiblical document that mentions the name David.[82]

79. *SB*, p. 159.

80. See Tsumura, I, p. 397.

81. McCarter, II, p. 84.

82. See Tsumura, I, pp. 25-26. For a detailed discussion, see A. Biran and J. Naveh, "An Aramaic Stela Fragment from Tel Dan," *IEJ* 43 (1993) 81-98; Biran and Naveh, "The Tel Dan Inscription: A New Fragment," *IEJ* 45 (1995) 1-18; W. M. Schniedewind, "Tel Dan Stela: New Light on Aramaic and Jehu's Revolt," *BASOR* 302 (1996) 75-90.

b. David and Jabesh-gilead (2:4b-7)

4b *When David was told*[83] *that*[84]
the men of Jabesh-gilead were those who[85] *buried Saul,*
5 [86]*David sent messengers to the men of Jabesh-gilead and said to them,*
"May you be blessed by the LORD!
For you did this loyal deed to your lord Saul
and buried him.
6 *And now, may the LORD do you a gracious and truthful deed.*
And I too shall do the same good to you
since you have done this deed.
7 *And now, let your hands be strong*[87]
and be brave,
for[88] *your lord Saul is dead*
and I am the one whom the house of Judah has anointed as king over them."

The deed of the men of Jabesh-gilead in rescuing the bodies of Saul and his sons from the Philistines and burying them was reported in 1 Sam. 31:11-13.[89] David here seems to be presenting himself as Saul's successor and to be suggesting that Jabesh-gilead enter into a treaty relationship with Judah. We are not told whether at this point he knows about Ishbosheth's survival. However, one gets the impression that David was not simply motivated by politics when he sent messengers to Jabesh-gilead. He was moved by their faithfulness toward their mutual lord and wanted to reward them with blessings from the Lord and deeds from himself.

5 The MT reading *'ăśîtem haḥesed hazzeh you did this loyal deed* should be retained. While LXX^B is missing at this point, the *Vorlage* of LXX^A seems to have been *ḥsd h'lhym* (the loyal deed of God).

83. Lit. "and they told David, saying."

84. Lit. "to say" (inf.); usually it is to be understood as introducing direct speech.

85. McCarter thinks that *those who* (*'ăšer*) "has been displaced in MT to follow 'Jabesh-gilead'" since LXX^B, he holds, reflects the original word order: "saying that the men of Jabesh-gilead buried Saul." MT is certainly unusual but not impossible; rather, it is an emphatic expression and should be retained as the *lectio difficilior*. Hence, ESV translates as "It was the men of Jabesh-gilead who buried Saul." For unusual word order such as unusual topicalization in 1–2 Samuel, see Tsumura, I, Introduction, V.A.

86. For the problem of the textual reconstruction of 4QSam^a in this verse, see the Introduction, I. Textual Criticism, 1. Method.

87. *teḥĕzaqnāh*; "take courage" (JPS) or "be encouraged," as in 2 Sam. 16:21; Judg. 7:11; Ezek. 22:14; Zech. 8:9, 13; cf. "steady" (McCarter, II, p. 85).

88. This particle *kî* is *speaker-oriented*, explaining why David said this.

89. See Tsumura, I, p. 655.

Generally speaking, a *loyal deed* involves "a responsible keeping of faith with another with whom one is in a relationship."[90] For this term, see also on 1 Sam. 15:6; 20:8; 2 Sam. 22:26; etc.[91]

6 The hendiadys a *gracious and truthful deed* (lit. "grace and truth" *ḥesed we'ĕmet*) appears again in 2 Sam. 15:19-20, where David during his escape from Absalom urges his faithful servant Ittai the Gittite to go back and stay with Absalom. He discharges Ittai's obligation to himself and blesses him using this phrase. According to Sakenfeld, by using a similar blessing, David is here suggesting that the political relationship between Jabesh-gilead and Saul was at an end, though, in the case of Ittai, David, the beneficiary of the obligation, discharges the obligation, while David has no right to discharge their responsibility to Saul.[92] However, he may be implying that by their good deed they have themselves discharged their responsibility to Saul and that "they are now free to establish a new formal relationship with David (rather than with Saul's descendants), which David offers and suggests that they do."[93] This point is made clear in the expression *And now, may the LORD . . . ! And I too.*

The Hebrew expression *'āśāh ṭôbāh* ("to do goodness"), like Akkadian *ṭābūta epēšu,*[94] may refer to the establishment of friendship, i.e., diplomatic amity, by treaty. However, while such a political aspect certainly existed in David's dealings with the people of Jabesh-gilead, David's word has a religious tone, centering more on the *gracious and truthful deed* of the Lord than on his own intentions.

7 The phrase *be brave* is literally "become sons of might" (also 2 Sam. 13:28). McCarter thinks that here David invites the men of Jabesh into his service because "sons of might" can be depended upon for loyal service.[95]

David gives two reasons: their lord Saul is now dead, and David has become king over the house of Judah. The second is certainly an invitation to accept him as king. But apparently they do not accept it, as Gilead becomes part of Ishbosheth's kingdom (v. 9).

c. Ishbosheth in Mahanaim (2:8-11)

8 *As for Abner son of Ner, the army commander who belonged to Saul, he had taken Ishbosheth son of Saul and brought him over to Mahanaim,*

90. K. D. Sakenfeld, *The Meaning of Hesed in the Hebrew Bible: A New Inquiry* (HSM 17; Missoula, Mont.: Scholars Press, 1978), p. 233; also pp. 40-42.
91. See also *NIDOTTE* #2874 (2:211-18).
92. Sakenfeld, *The Meaning of Hesed in the Hebrew Bible,* pp. 107-11.
93. Sakenfeld, *The Meaning of Hesed in the Hebrew Bible,* p. 111.
94. See *CAD,* Ṭ, 42.
95. McCarter, II, p. 85.

9 *And he made him king over Gilead, the Ashurites, and Jezreel, and over*[96] *Ephraim and Benjamin, namely*[97] *over Israel in its entirety.*

10 *— Ishbosheth son of Saul was forty years old when he became king over Israel and he ruled for two years. —*

But the house of Judah followed David.

11 *And the length of time*[98] *that David was king in Hebron over the house of Judah was seven years and six months.*

Abner tries to continue Saul's kingdom, even on a reduced scale. But from these verses and 3:6-11, it appears that Ishbosheth was little more than his puppet.

8 *As for Abner . . .*, which is the *casus pendens* (so "Now" [RSV], "Meanwhile" [NIV]), is the SETTING, introducing a new agent, Abner, with his background. The EVENT is vv. 8bf. where Abner's actions are described by the *wayqtl*s in the mainline of narrative discourse: *brought him . . . and made him king.*

For Abner, see the commentary on 1 Sam. 14:50.[99] He is probably Saul's uncle. The phrase *the army commander who belonged to Saul* means that he was Saul's commander-in-chief of the army; see 1 Sam. 12:9.

Ishbosheth appears as "Ishbaal" in the genealogies in 1 Chr. 8:33, 9:39. Since *Ishbosheth* probably means "Man-of-shame," the *bosheth* in Samuel is usually taken as be "a euphemistic substitution" for "baal" since the latter suggests the Canaanite god. Similarly, the name of Jonathan's son is given as Mephibosheth in 2 Sam. 4:4, etc. but as Meribaal in 1 Chr. 8:34 and 9:40, and Gideon is called Jerubbaal in Judg. 6:32 but Jerubbesheth in 2 Sam. 11:21. However, whether the *baal* in the names originally referred to Baal or simply meant "lord" is hotly debated.[100] Certainly, there is no reason why Saul should name his sons after the foreign god Baal, and there is no hint that he worshipped any god but the Lord. Therefore, it is often suggested that the "lord" in these names refers to the Lord, i.e., "Yahweh."[101] For the relationship with the Ishvi of 1 Sam. 14:49, see the commentary there.[102]

Mahanaim (modern Tell edh-Dhahab el-Gharbi [M.R. 214177]), a city near the Jabbok River (Nahr ez-Zerqa), was apparently the capital of Gilead. The fact that the capital had to be in Transjordan suggests the precariousness

96. *w*e*ʿal*; note that the first three GNs are preceded by *ʾel*, but the second three GNs by *ʿal*: lit. "and over [*ʿal*] Ephraim and over [*ʿal*] Benjamin and over [*ʿal*] Israel."

97. Taking *waw* as *explicative*, or "even" (NASB).

98. Lit. "the number of days."

99. See Tsumura, I, pp. 384-85.

100. See J. H. Tigay and A. R. Millard, "Seals and Seal Impressions," in *CS*, II, 199 n. 19.

101. For example, McCarter, II, pp. 86f.

102. Tsumura, I, p. 384.

of Ishbosheth's rule. Later David used the site as his base of operations during Absalom's revolt (2 Sam. 17:24–19:8).[103]

9 *Gilead* and *the Ashurites* and *Jezreel* refer to the northern and Transjordan part of the country, *Ephraim* and *Benjamin* to the central and main part. *Gilead* is "the tribal claims of Gad and Reuben, territory ruled by Saul after his victory over Nahash, king of the neighboring state of Ammon."[104]

Ashurites is a plural form of the gentilic noun, hence "people of Ashur"; cf. "Ashuri" (NIV). Their identity is unknown. Probably they have nothing to do with the tribe of Asher.[105] *Jezreel* is the area around modern Zer'in,[106] not the Jezreel of David's wife Ahinoam.

Ephraim refers to the Israelite heartland. *Benjamin* is the homeland of the house of Saul, centered on the ridge of hills between Jerusalem and Bethel.

JPS treats the last phrase as a summary: "over Gilead, the Ashurites, Jezreel, Ephraim, and Benjamin — over all Israel." However, since the MT clearly distinguishes the first three names from the second three by the use of two distinct prepositions, the phrase *Israel in its entirety* seems to restate "Ephraim and Benjamin" and to refer here only to the central part. Ishbosheth did not necessarily have real control over all this area, especially as the Philistines apparently were still in the Jezreel Valley (see 1 Sam. 31:7).

10-11 David apparently has decided that his allegiance to Saul as God's anointed king does not extend to Saul's descendants, as the rest of the section shows. Furthermore, in 2 Sam. 4:11 he just refers to Ishbosheth as a "righteous man," not as a king or an anointed one as he had referred to Saul (1 Sam. 24:6; 26:9; 2 Sam. 1:14).

Thus, for a time, there were two kings in the land of Israel. Ishbosheth reigned only two years, but David's reign as king of Judah at Hebron was *seven years and six months* (also 5:5). Probably it took some time after Ishbosheth's death for Israel to recognize David (5:1); the period may also include the time when David was king in Hebron over all Israel before capturing Jerusalem.

103. See D. V. Edelman, "Mahanaim," in *ABD*, IV, pp. 471-72; *CBA*, #98; also K. A. Kitchen, "Mahanaim," in *NBD*; J. M. Hutton, "Over the River and Through the Woods: Historical and Narrative Geography in 2 Samuel 18," in Dietrich, *The Books of Samuel*, pp. 108-11.

104. McCarter, II, p. 87.

105. D. E. Fleming, *The Legacy of Israel in Judah's Bible: History, Politics, and the Reinscribing of Tradition* (Cambridge: Cambridge University Press, 2012), p. 153 n. 23.

106. McCarter, II, p. 87.

2. Abner and Joab (2:12-32)

a. Helkath-hazzurim (2:12-16)

12 *And Abner son of Ner and the servants of Ishbosheth son of Saul marched out of Mahanaim toward Gibeon.*

13 *As for Joab son of Zeruiah and the servants of David, they marched out and encountered them together by the pool of Gibeon. One group stationed itself on this side of the pool; the other group, on that side of the pool.*

14 *And Abner said to Joab,*
"Let some of the young men arise
that they may have a contest before us!"
And Joab said,
"Let them arise!"

15 *And they arose and came across by number: twelve of Benjamin, that is,*[107] *of Ishbosheth son of Saul, and twelve of the servants of David.*

16 *And they seized each other's heads, with a sword at each other's sides, and fell together.*
— So the place was called[108] *Helkath-hazzurim which is in Gibeon. —*

12 Why did the hostilities begin at Gibeon? It is not unlikely that David was negotiating with the Gibeonites as he had attempted to do with Jabesh-gilead, since they harbored a deep resentment against Saul (2 Sam. 21:1-9). Ishbosheth's court, upset at David's overture to Jabesh-gilead, may have acted to prevent this union. Gibeon is the modern el-Jib (M.R. 167139), about 5 miles (8 km) northwest of Jerusalem.[109]

13 This section marks the first appearance of *Joab son of Zeruiah*, though Abishai was identified as his brother in 1 Sam. 26:6. Joab is commander over the army (2 Sam. 8:16) and appears frequently in 2 Samuel, often as a mover of events. He is eventually killed by Solomon's order (1 K. 2:34).[110] Since Abner knows him and his brothers well (vv. 20-22), he probably came to Saul's court soon after David's rise to prominence. He is one of the three sons — Joab, Abishai, and Asahel—of David's sister Zeruiah, and thus David's nephew (v. 18). Their father probably died young, as he had a grave in Bethlehem (v. 32) and it was unusual for a man to be known by his mother's name.

107. Taking *waw* as *explicative*.

108. Lit. "he called," used as an *impersonal* passive.

109. For the battle by the pool at Gibeon, see *CBA*, #99.

110. For Joab, see D. G. Schley, "Joab and David: Ties of Blood and Power," in *History and Interpretation: Essays in Honour of John H. Hayes*, ed. M. Patrick Graham, William P. Brown, and Jeffrey K. Kuan (JSOTSS 173; Sheffield: JSOT Press, 1993), pp. 90-105.

Zeruiah is not identified in Samuel, but according to 1 Chr. 2:16, she and Abigail, the mother of Amasa, were sisters of David and his brothers. Abigail is identified in 2 Sam. 17:25 as *the daughter of Nahash, sister of Zeruiah.* It appears that Abigail, and probably Zeruiah, were maternal half-sisters of David by an earlier marriage of their mother. The name *Joab* (*yôʾāb*) is probably a shortened form of the full spelling *yhwʾb* Yehoʾab, which appears in Arad 39:10.[111] The *pool of Gibeon,* also mentioned in Jer. 41:12, has been identified with the "Great Pool of Gibeon," the huge water system uncovered by J. B. Pritchard.[112]

14-16 Abner proposes a ritual military contest between the two groups. McCarter suggests that this contest was not considered simply a contest of skill, but one whose outcome would determine the divine will, following Fensham, who believes the issues of the divine will and the legitimation of kingship are implicitly present in this account.[113] While such contests might be a way of deciding the divine will about some things, it seems unlikely that Abner and Joab could decide the matter of the kingship on their own.

14 For the term *young men* (*nᵉʿārîm*), see the commentary on 1 Sam. 9:3.[114] It can be "a technical or semi-technical military term" like Ugaritic *nʿr*, and is "often used to refer to first-class fighting men."[115]

16 The connection of the name with the event is uncertain. McCarter translates the name *Helkath-hazzurim* (*ḥelqat haṣṣūrîm*) as "Flints' Field," explaining that the weapons used here were probably flint swords or knives (see *ḥarbôt ṣūrîm* "flint knives" in Josh. 5:2).[116] His view is hardly correct though, since the blades made during the tenth century B.C. were made of either bronze or iron.

The comment of v. 16b serves as the TERMINUS of the episode.[117]

b. Death of Asahel (2:17-23)

17 *The fighting was very*[118] *severe on that day.*
And Abner and the men of Israel were smitten before the servants of David.
18 *And three sons of Zeruiah — Joab, Abishai, and Asahel — were there.*
Now Asahel was fast on his legs like one of the gazelles that are in the field.

111. See Y. Aharoni, *AI,* p. 69.
112. See *ABD,* II, pp. 1011-13.
113. McCarter, II, p. 95.
114. Tsumura, I, p. 265.
115. A. F. Rainey, "Institutions: Family, Civil and Military," in *RSP* 2, p. 99.
116. McCarter, II, p. 96.
117. Tsumura, I, pp. 50-52.
118. Hebrew: *ʿad-mᵉʾōd.*

19 *And Asahel chased after Abner; he did not turn aside to go either to the right or to the left from chasing after Abner.*

20 *And Abner turned around and said,*
"Is it you, Asahel?"
And he said,
"Yes, it is."

21 *And Abner said to him,*
"Turn aside either to the right or to the left.
Seize one of the young men and take his spoil."[119]
But Asahel was not willing to turn away from him.

22 *And Abner again said to Asahel,*
"Turn away from me!
Why should I strike you down to the ground?
How could I raise my face to Joab, your elder brother?"

23 *And he refused to turn away.*
And Abner struck him in the belly with the butt of the spear.
And the spear came out of his back.
And he fell down there and died where he was.[120]
As for all who came to the place where Asahel fell and died, they stopped.

17 This transitional verse connects the first episode, the fight at Gibeon, with the second, the death of Asahel. After this episode, the enmity between the surviving sons of Zeruiah and Abner will be a major factor, until Joab finally assassinates Abner (2 Sam. 3:27) over this private matter.

18 *Abishai* is Joab's older brother and the eldest of the three sons of Zeruiah: in 1 Chr. 2:16 the order is "Abishai, Joab, and Asahel." He first appeared in 1 Sam. 26:6 when David asked him to go down with him into the camp of Saul.

Asahel is the youngest of the three. He was one of David's mighty warriors "among the thirty" (2 Sam. 23:24; 1 Chr. 11:26; 27:7). All three brothers favored direct, swift action, though Joab was also politically active.

19 The verb "to turn aside" (*nṭh) here and in v. 21 is different from the verb "to deviate" (*swr) in 2 K. 22:2, etc. While the former focuses on the goal, the latter focuses on the process. So, here the phrase *did not turn aside to go either to the right or to the left* emphasizes the goal of his chasing, that is, Abner. On the other hand, 2 Ki. 22:2 says that Josiah *did not deviate to the right or to the left*, away from the right path, i.e., *the way of his father David* (cf. 2 Chr. 34:2; Num. 20:17; Prov. 4:27).

119. Hebrew *ḥălīṣātô* = what is stripped off of him.

120. Lit. "under him"; "on the spot" (NIV, JPS, NASB); cf. "right there" (W-O, §11.2.15).

20 *Is it you, Asahel?* : lit. "are you here Asahel?" Muraoka enumerates five cases where the demonstrative *zeh* follows *'attāh*: Gen. 27:21, 24; 2 Sam. 2:20; 1 K. 18:7, 17. In all five cases "the speaker is attempting to reassure himself that he has correctly established the identity of the other party." Their context is "highly personal and characterized by a ring of immediacy, which is suitably expressed" by the deictic element "here" (*zeh*).[121]

23 Abner, an experienced warrior, apparently attacks Asahel, who is following immediately behind him, without reversing the direction of his spear, which would have given Asahel warning.

The Hebrew *wayhî* introduces the TOPIC of the sentence *As for all who came to the place where Asahel fell and died, they stopped*; see also 1 Sam. 11:11.[122]

c. Abner and Joab (2:24-32)

24 *And Joab and Abishai chased after Abner.*

As the sun set, these two[123] *came to the hill of Ammah, which is opposite Gia, by the way to the wilderness of Gibeon.*

25 *The Benjaminites gathered together behind Abner and became one band and took their stand on the top of one hill.*

26 *Then Abner called to Joab:*[124]

"Should a sword devour forever?
Don't you know
that bitterness will be in the end?
How long will it be until you command the people to turn away from pursuing their brothers?"

27 *Joab said,*

"As God lives!
If you had not spoken,
it would have been in the morning[125] *when the people would have given up*[126] *the pursuit of each other's brothers."*

28 *Then Joab blew the horn.*

All the people stopped; they no longer chased after Israel and they fought again no more.

121. T. Muraoka, "The Tripartite Nominal Clause Revisited," in *The Verbless Clause in Biblical Hebrew: Linguistic Approaches*, ed. Cynthia L. Miller (LSAWS 1; Winona Lake, Ind.: Eisenbrauns, 1999), p. 210.

122. Tsumura, I, p. 311.

123. Lit. "they" (independent pron.).

124. Lit. "called to . . . and said"; see Tsumura, I, p. xii.

125. Lit. "from the morning"; see BDB, p. 581b.

126. Ni. (reflexive); lit. "take oneself away (from following)."

29 *As for Abner and his men, they traveled in the Arabah all that night and crossed the Jordan and went all morning*[127] *and came to Mahanaim.*

30 *As for Joab, he returned from going after Abner and gathered all the people.*

There were missing from the servants of David nineteen men and Asahel.

31 *As for the servants of David, they struck*[128] *some of the Benjaminites who were among the men of Abner;*[129] *three hundred and sixty men died.*

32 *So they carried Asahel and buried him in the grave of his father, which is in Bethlehem.*

Joab and his men went all night.
Dawn broke[130] *on them in Hebron.*

24 *As the sun set* (*wᵉhaššemeš bā'āh*) is literally "and the sun was entering." In ancient thought, this "entering" is presumably into the netherworld. The noun *šemeš*, which is usually masculine in Hebrew, is here feminine and used idiomatically. See on 2 Sam. 12:11 and 1 Sam. 20:19.[131]

The location of *the hill of Ammah* is unknown. The relative clause *which is opposite Gia* modifies *the hill of Ammah*, while the phrase *by the way to the wilderness of Gibeon* is an adverbial phrase in the main clause which modifies the verb *came*, not *Gibeon*. For a similar syntax, see 1 Sam. 2:29; 2 Sam. 11:27; 13:16; 15:7.[132]

28-29 Here as in 2 Sam. 18:16 and 20:22, Joab uses a trumpet to summon an army to mark the end of fighting after a victory. *The Arabah* is the Jordan Valley rift (also 4:7).[133]

30 The word order of the compound subject *nineteen men and Asahel* is unusual, for most examples of the compound subject are of the "principal and adjunct" type, for example, "David and his men." According to Revell, the purpose of this unusual construction is seemingly to "draw attention to

127. So NASB; McCarter, II, p. 97, following W. R. Arnold, "The Meaning of *btrwn*," *AJSL* 28 (1911/12), 274-83; also "the whole forenoon" (NRSV); cf. "through the whole Bithron" (NIV); "through all of Bithron" (JPS). According to BDB, Bithron refers to the cleft, ravine, east of Jordan.

128. See E. Jenni, "'Schlagen' in 2. Sam 2,31 und in den historischen Büchern," *EI* 24 (Avraham Malamat Volume; 1993) 114*-18*.

129. McCarter reads the Hebrew of "among the men of Abner" as *m'nšy 'bnr* ("from the men of Abner"), based on 4QSam[a] and LXX. However, the MT *ûbᵉ'anšê 'abnēr* (lit. "and in the men of Abner"), with the *explicative waw* (also p. 67 n. 107 above), might be translated as *who were among the men of Abner*, or "i.e., from the men of Abner."

130. Hebrew *wayyē'ōr*. The *wayqt* form of ni. impf. 3 m.s. (of daybreak).

131. Tsumura, I, pp. 512-13.

132. See Tsumura, Introduction: V. Grammar and Syntax: B. Relative Clause Inserted into the Main Clause, of *The First Book of Samuel*, p. 48 n. 219.

133. *SB*, p. 40.

the singular component while showing that the person represented [here, Asahel] is not a significant actor in the immediately following context." Also "the unusual terminal position" of Asahel draws attention (i.e., "end focus") to the significance of his death.[134] See also the commentary on 3:22.

32 The way from Gibeon to Hebron passes through Bethlehem.

The movement verb *went* in the *wayqtl* form here signals the TERMINUS of the episode.

3. Death of Abner (3:1-39)

This chapter tells of the death of the most powerful character in the house of Saul. It is a continuation of the slow process by which David becomes king over all Israel.

Clearly, one of the concerns of the author is to show that David was not guilty of involvement in the deaths of Abner or Ishbosheth. In fact, the present section is the most "apologetic" in tone of the "Story of King David." However, as McCarter notes, "From the perspective of the larger narrative, the motivating force was Yahweh's will and his special favor for David." But this event took place by the "interplay of four human personalities," Ishbosheth, David, Abner, and Joab.[135]

a. House of Saul and House of David (3:1)

1 *And the war between the house of Saul and the house of David became prolonged. David was getting stronger and stronger, while the house of Saul was getting weaker and weaker.*

The first verse provides a new SETTING as well as a TRANSITION to the following episode, which begins with v. 6 after the insertion of the list of David's sons in vv. 2-5.

The MT *hammilḥāmāh ʾărukkāh* is here translated as *the war . . . prolonged*. However, if it is a phonetic spelling[136] for *hammilḥāmāh hāʾărukkāh*, the translation "a long war" (so, NRSV, NASB) might be better, though literally "*the* long war." The term *ʾărukkāh* is a *qatul* type adjective.[137]

134. E. J. Revell, "Concord with Compound Subjects and Related Uses of Pronouns," *VT* 43 (1993) 71-73, 80; also p. 63 n. 85.

135. McCarter, II, pp. 121f.

136. See Tsumura, "Scribal Errors or Phonetic Spellings?," pp. 390-411.

137. B-L, p. 467.

x. Sons of David in Hebron (3:2-5)

2 *Sons were born*[138] *to David in Hebron.*
His firstborn was Amnon by Ahinoam the Jezreelite;
3 *his second was Chileab by Abigail*[139] *the widow of Nabal the Carmelite;*
the third was Absalom the son of Maacah, daughter of Talmai, king of Geshur;
4 *the fourth was Adonijah, the son of Haggith;*
the fifth was Shephatiah son of Abital;
5 *the sixth was Ithream by Eglah the wife of David.*
These were born to David in Hebron.

This list of David's sons born in Hebron is an *inserted* paragraph, which interrupts the flow of narrative from v. 1 to v. 6. Its purpose may be to contrast David's flourishing house with the waning house of Saul. There is also a list of sons born in Jerusalem in 5:13-16, and a combined list in 1 Chr. 3:1-9.

Six sons of six wives and/or concubines are mentioned here. Besides these wives, he had also married Saul's daughter Michal (1 Sam. 18:27; 2 Sam. 3:12-16), and later married Bathsheba (11:27), and others (5:13), and he had at least ten concubines (15:16). Wives and concubines were a sign of a king's wealth; see especially the case of King Solomon (1 K. 11:3); cf. Song of Solomon 6:8.[140]

2 *Amnon* (*'amnôn*) is the major character in ch. 13. McCarter takes *'ămînôn* (13:20) as the correct vocalization, hence he uses "Aminon."[141] For *Ahinoam*, see the commentary on 1 Sam. 25:43.[142]

3 Chileab is never mentioned again, and David's fourth son Adonijah (v. 4) later claimed David's throne (1 K. 1:5), so it is presumed that Chileab died early. The phrase *widow of Nabal* is literally "woman, wife of Nabal"; see 2:2 and 1 Sam. 27:3; 30:5. Note that a woman could still be called the wife of her dead husband (Ruth 4:5, 10).

Absalom (*'abšālôm*) is the central character of 2 Sam. 13-19. It is certainly possible that this name as well as *Solomon* (*Šlmh*) contains the old Canaanite

138. MT (K.) *wyldw* [wayyull^{e}dû] (Qal pass.) "they were born," with *bānîm* "sons" as subject; cf. MT (Q.): *wayyiwwāl^{e}dû* (Ni.). Note that 4QSam^{a} *wywld* (Ni. impf., 3 m.s.) is singular as in Gen. 4:18; 46:20; and Num. 26:60. For ergativity in the Hebrew verb *yld, see Tsumura, I, p. 508 n. 46.

139. MT Q. (*'ăbîgayil*); cf. K. *'bygl* ['ăbîgal]. See Tsumura, I, p. 591 n. 81; also 2 Sam. 17:25.

140. Marsman, *Women in Ugarit and Israel*, pp. 377-78.

141. McCarter, II, p. 319.

142. Tsumura, I, p. 594.

divine name *Šlm*, which appears in the "official" pantheon list from ancient Ugarit.[143] However, the element *'ab* "father" may stand for God in *Absalom* and the other element *šālôm* may be simply the noun "peace."

Absalom's mother is Maacah of Geshur, "a small Aramaic state between Bashan and Hermon" (*HALOT*).[144] Absalom apparently named a daughter after her (1 K. 15:2, 13; 2 Chr. 11:20-22). *Talmai* is probably a non-Semitic PN (cf. Hurrian *tal(a)mi* "great").[145]

4-5 At the time of David's death *Adonijah* was his oldest surviving son; see 1 K. 1:5. *Shephatiah* is mentioned only here and in the genealogy in 1 Chr. 3:3. *Abital* (*'ăbîṭāl*) could mean "My father is *Ṭal*," and *Ṭal* may be a theophoric element";[146] cf. dṬalaya (RS 16.156:8, 17) and the name of Baal's daughter *Ṭly*.[147] *Ithream* also is mentioned only here and in 1 Chr. 3:3; it could mean "Remainder of *'m*."[148] *Eglah* as a proper noun occurs only here and in 1 Chr. 3:3.

These were born is a summary statement, which signals the TERMINUS of the present embedded discourse.

b. House of Saul and House of David (3:6)

6 *While the war was going on between the house of Saul and the house of David, it was Abner who was gaining*[149] *power in the house of Saul.*

6 The clause *While the war was going on between the house of Saul and the house of David* is a variation on v. 1, thus resuming the narrative flow after the interruption of vv. 2-5. It also serves as a transition to the following episode in which Abner is the major character.

The *hāyāh* + participle in *it was Abner who was gaining power* (*we'abnēr hāyāh mitḥazzēq*) gives emphasis to an action continuing from the *past*; see GKC, §116*r*.

143. See A. Cooper, "Divine Names and Epithets in the Ugaritic Texts," in *RSP* 3, p. 423.

144. See B. Mazar, "Geshur and Maacah," *JBL* 80 (1961) 18-21; Younger, *PHA*, pp. 204-19.

145. McCarter, II, p. 101.

146. F. B. Knutson, "Divine Names and Epithets in the Akkadian Texts," in *RSP* 3, p. 488.

147. *DULAT*, p. 889.

148. Knutson, "Divine Names and Epithets in the Akkadian Texts," p. 492.

149. The use of "inflected forms of היה (perfect, imperfect, imperative) plus the participle" is a common feature of Mishnaic Hebrew. G. A. Rendsburg holds that its appearance is "to be explained by the vernacular of the writers exerting its influence over the classical idiom" (G. A. Rendsburg, *DAH*, p. 146.); also see 2 Sam. 3:17, 10:5.

c. Abner and Ishbosheth (3:7-11)

Abner, after a quarrel with Ishbosheth, convinces the Israelite elders that they should go with David. However, he is killed by Joab. The author stresses repeatedly that David had not consented (vv. 21, 26, 28, 37), and, indeed, since Abner was plotting to make him king of Israel, it seems that he would have had nothing to gain from Abner's death.

7 *Now Saul had a concubine; her name was Rizpah daughter of Aia.*
And [Ishbosheth] said to Abner,
"Why have you gone in to the concubine of my father?"
8 *And Abner got very angry with the words of Ishbosheth and said,*
"Am I a dog's head which is for Judah?
Today I am loyal to the house of Saul your father,
that is to[150] *his kinsmen*[151] *and his friends.*
I did not deliver you[152] *into the hand of David.*
And yet today you charge me[153] *with guilt about the woman!*[154]
9 *May God do thus to Abner and thus again to him,*
if, as the LORD *swore to David, I do not do this for him:*
10 *to transfer the kingdom from the house of Saul*
and establish the throne of David over Israel and Judah
from Dan to Beersheba!"
11 *And he could no longer return any word to Abner because he was afraid of him.*

7 *Rizpah* was the concubine (*pîleges̆*) of Saul and had borne him two sons, Armoni and Mephibosheth (ch. 21:8-11).

Abner is here accused of lying with Saul's concubine Rizpah. Taking the king's wives seems to have been considered a prerogative of the throne (see 12:8; 16:21-22; 1 K. 2:22). However, it was a particular woman ("a concubine" in sg.), Rizpah, not an entire harem, who is referred to here. So, even if the accusation was true, it does not necessarily mean that Abner was trying to claim the kingship.

8 Dogs were unclean animals and considered insignificant, as in

150. The preposition *'el* is asyndetically connected to the preceding phrase *to the house of Saul* with an *explicative* force.

151. Lit. "brothers" (*'eḥâw*).

152. MT *himṣîtīkā*, Hi. pf. 1 c.s. of *mṣ', with a 2 m.s. object suffix, is a phonetic spelling without the etymological *aleph.*

153. Lit. "visit on me" (*pqd *'ālay*). For the pattern: *pqd + *'t*-NP + *'l*-NP, see Amos 3:2, 14; Hos. 1:4; 2:13; Exod. 20:5; 34:7; Deut. 5:9; etc. (+ 10×) — BDB, p. 823.

154. Lit. "the guilt of the woman" (*'ăwōn hā'iššāh*).

1 Sam. 17:43; 24:14; 2 Sam. 9:8; 2 K. 8:13; Eccl. 9:4. But, the significance of the phrase *a dog's head* (*rō'š keleb*) is not clear. Hutton says "head" is a case of a semantic borrowing from Akkadian *rēšu* "slave," and takes the phrase *rō'š keleb* not as a construct chain, but as appositive, translating "a slave, a dog."[155] Though attractive, the suggestion seems to be a little far-fetched.

9-10 This promise of the Lord is implied in 1 Sam. 15:28 and 16:13, and people in general also seem to have had knowledge of it (24:4; 25:30; 2 Sam. 3:18). Abner had heard about it, but probably had not particularly believed it, or decided that if the Lord would have David king, the Lord would crown him. However, now it gives him a good reason for deserting Ishbosheth. One need not assume here a prophetic or a later Deuteronomistic interpolation as some scholars often assume.

9 For the oath formula, *May God do thus to. . .*, see the commentary on 1 Sam. 3:17.[156] The third person is used for the speaker also in 1 Sam. 20:13 and in 25:22.

11 The phrase *return any word* (i.e., respond/answer/report; *lᵉhāšîb 'et-'abnēr dābār*) is the standard word order, in which the *internal object* is pushed back to after the external one (see Jer 9:3):[157] *šwb* + (*'et-*) NP + *dbr*; see 2 Sam. 24:13; 1 K. 2:30; 12:6, 16; 2 K. 22:9, 20; Prov. 27:11; 1 Chr. 21:12; 2 Chr. 34:16, 28. Even when a pronominal suffix is used instead of a NP, the word order is the same. Only 1 K. 12:9 (and the parallel in 2 Chr. 10:9) has the word order: [*šwb*+ *dbr*] + *'et* -NP. In later Hebrew, the word order [*šwb*+ *dbr*] + *l*-NP appears, e.g., 2 Chr. 10:6.

d. Abner Sends Messengers to David (3:12-16)

12 *And Abner sent messengers to David on his own behalf, saying,*
"Whose is the land?"
saying
"Make your covenant with me!
Here my hand is with you
to turn all Israel over to you."
13 *And he said,*
"Good!
I will make a covenant with you,
but one thing I am going to ask of you,

155. J. M. Hutton, "'Abdi-Aširta, the Slave, the Dog': Self-Abasement and Invective in the Amarna Letters, the Lachish Letters, and 2 Sam 3:8," *ZAH* 15/16 (2002/2003) 2-18.

156. Tsumura, I, p. 182.

157. D. T. Tsumura, "Niphal with an Internal Object in Hab 3, 9a," *JSS* 31 (1986) 11-16.

that is to say,[158]
you shall not see my face
unless you first bring Michal the daughter of Saul
when you come to see my face."

14 *Then David sent messengers to Ishbosheth son of Saul, saying,*
"Give me my wife Michal
whom I betrothed to myself for a hundred foreskins of the Philistines."

15 *So Ishbosheth sent and took her from her husband,*[159] *that is from Paltiel son of Laish.*

16 *But her husband went with her, weeping after her as far as Bahurim.*
Then Abner said to him,
"Go, return!"
And he returned.

12-13 David clearly does not mind taking the Israelite kingdom from Ishbosheth, and he stresses his closeness to Saul as Saul's son-in-law. David had legally paid the bridal price and never divorced Michal even though she remarried, so she is still legally his wife. David presumably expects Abner to support his argument when the matter is discussed in Ishbosheth's court.

12 The phrase *on his behalf* (K. *tḥtw*; Q. *taḥtâw*) has been interpreted variously; e.g., "in (David's) place," i.e., "where he was" = Hebron (see LXXL; NRSV) or "immediately" (JPS), based on LXX *parachrēma*. If it means "in Abner's stead," the expression is redundant, for a messenger by definition is a "representative" of the one who sent him; cf. "as his representatives" (McCarter). The best interpretation seems to be "on his behalf" (NIV; ESV), since Abner urges David to make a covenant with him, not with Ishbosheth.

13 David, recognizing Abner's leadership in the northern part of the country (i.e., *the land* in v. 12), agrees to *make a covenant with* Abner on the one condition that he bring *Michal the daughter of Saul* (see 1 Sam. 18:20-27)[160] back to David. To "see the face of," or to have an audience with, was a privilege as in 14:24, 32; Gen. 43:3.

David's request for Michal may have been in part political, but since he had Abner's support even without that, it may also have been personal.

14 It is surprising to see Ishbosheth's involvement, since Abner is negotiating to eliminate him. Noth thinks that David's marriage to Michal in 1 Sam. 18-19 is a later tradition and hence the present verse is secondary.

158. Heb. *lēʾmōr*; see "namely" (NASB).
159. Lit. "a man" (*ʾîš*).
160. Tsumura, I, pp. 481-88.

Thus he thinks that "Ishbosheth" in v. 15 should be corrected to "Abner." But there is no reason to reject the account of the early marriage. Ishbosheth's involvement would mean that even he recognized David's connection with the house of Saul. As David had paid the bride price, he could not refuse to return his wife to him. Note that this is not violating the law in Deut. 24:1-4, for David did not divorce Michal. Mesopotamian laws[161] permitted a husband who had been forced to leave the country to reclaim his former wife even if she had become the wife of another man.[162]

In 1 Sam. 18:25-27, the *hundred foreskins* were what Saul had demanded as a bride-price (*mōhar*) in v. 25, so the extra hundred (v. 27) were a gift.

15 *Paltiel son of Laish* is Michal's second husband; 1 Sam. 25:44 has the shorter hypocoristic name *Palti.*

16 The modern site of *Bahurim* is Râs eṭ-Ṭmîm, north of Mount Scopus, Jerusalem. It was a Benjamite village and the home of Shimei (2 Sam. 19:16) and Azmaveth (23:31); also see 17:18. Weisman interprets the name as meaning "warrior's village," that is, one inhabited by select warriors (see on 1 Sam. 24:2).[163]

e. Abner Meets David at Hebron (3:17-21)

17 *Now the word of Abner reached*[164] *the elders of Israel, saying,*
"Formerly[165] *you were seeking for David to be king over you.*
18 *Now then, do it!*
For the LORD *has spoken of David, saying,*
'By the hand of David my servant
I am about to save my people Israel
from the hand of the Philistines,
from the hand of all their enemies.'"
19 *And Abner also spoke to the Benjamites in person.*
And Abner also went to tell David at Hebron in person about everything that was good in the eyes of Israel and the whole house of Benjamin.
20 *And Abner came to David at Hebron with twenty men with him.*
And David made a feast for Abner and the men who were with him.

161. Z. Ben-Barak, "The Legal Background to the Restoration of Michal to David," in *Studies in the Historical Books of the Old Testament*, ed. J. A. Emerton (VTS 30; Leiden: E. J. Brill, 1979), pp. 15-29.

162. See McCarter, II, p. 115.

163. Z. Weisman, "The Nature and Background of *bāḥūr* in the Old Testament," *VT* 31 (1981) 450; Tsumura, I, p. 564.

164. Lit. "the word of Abner was with."

165. Lit. "as yesterday, as the third day."

21 *And Abner said to David,*
"Let me arise and go!
Let me gather all Israel to my lord the king
that they may make a covenant with you
and you may become king in whatever your soul desires."
And David sent Abner forth, and he went in peace.

17-19 The Israelites, even the members of Saul's own tribe of Benjamin, seem to think they are getting nowhere with Ishbosheth as king.

17 The *elders of Israel* (*ziqnê Yiśrā'ēl*; see the commentary on 1 Sam. 4:3[166] and also on 2 Sam. 2:4) were a group of senior tribal leaders who exercised jurisdiction on behalf of the people of Israel.

18 The designation of king as the *servant* of his god was widespread in the ancient Near East (e.g., in Ugarit, king Keret as "servant of El"; see *KTU* 1.15 II 19), so it cannot be regarded as distinctively Deuteronomistic as is often alleged.

19 The expression *good* has a special meaning in the context of a treaty. Thus, what was *good in the eyes of Israel* was "what David would be obliged to do to establish a covenant relationship with them."[167]

21 The phrase *he went in peace* (*hlk *bᵉšālôm*) is repeated in vv. 22 and 23, emphasizing David's innocence in Abner's death.

f. Joab Murders Abner (3:22-30)

22 *As for David's servants, when Joab came back from the raid, they brought back much plunder with them. But Abner was not with David at Hebron, for he had sent him forth and he had gone in peace.*

23 *When Joab and all the army that was with him came back, it was reported*[168] *to Joab,*
"Abner son of Ner came to the king.
And he sent him forth and he went in peace."
24 *And Joab came to the king and said,*
"What have you done?
Behold, Abner came to you.
Why did you send him forth and he has indeed gone?
25 *You know Abner son of Ner!*

166. Tsumura, I, pp. 190-92.

167. McCarter, II, p. 117. See W. L. Moran, "A Note on the Treaty Terminology of the Sefîre Stelas," *JNES* 22 (1963) 173-76.

168. Lit. "they reported": impersonal pl.

For it was to deceive you that he came,
to learn of your going out and your coming in
and to learn all that you are doing."

26 *And Joab went out from David and sent messengers after Abner, and they brought him back from Bor-hassirah. But David did not know.*

27 *And Abner returned to Hebron.*

And Joab drew him aside into the midst of the gate to speak with him privately, and there he struck him in the belly,[169] *and he died for the blood of Asael,*[170] *his brother.*

28 *And David heard afterward and said,*
"I and my kingdom are innocent before the LORD *forever*[171]
of the blood of Abner son of Ner.
29 *May it fall on the head of Joab and on*[172] *all his father's house!*[173]
May the house of Joab never lack one that has a discharge,
or one who has a skin disease or who holds a distaff,[174]
or one who falls by the sword or who is in need of bread!"

30 *Thus Joab and his brother Abishai murdered*[175] *Abner because he had put their brother Asael to death in the battle in Gibeon.*

169. Lit. "the belly"; adv. acc.

170. MT: *ʿăśāh-ʾēl*; cf. "Asahel" (NASB). Note that 4QSam[a] has *ʿśʾl*.

171. McCarter translates the phrase *ʿad-ʿôlām*, "now and forever," (II, p. 110) based on LXX[LMN], against 4QSam[a]. However, the posited *Vorlage* of LXX[LMN] as well as that of LXX[B], that is *mʿm yhwh mʿth wʿd ʿwlm*, could be a secondary expansion of the *mʿm yhwh ʿd ʿwlm* of the MT (also 4QSam[a]). On the other hand, he reads the MT phrase *mdmy, of* (lit. "from") *the blood of* as *wdm* with 4QSam[a], holding the first *m* of *mdmy* to be a dittography after *ʿwlm*. However, as noted above, the phrase *mdmy* goes well with the verb *are innocent*.

172. MT: *wᵉʾel*; cf. *wʿl* (4QSam[a]) and *καὶ ἐπί* (LXX). While LXX seems to reflect *wʿl*, "it is quite possible that a translator would also have translated ואל thus in the context." See Herbert, *RBDSS*, p. 112.

173. MT: *bêt ʾābîw* is supported by LXX; cf. *byt ywʾb* (4QSam[a]).

174. Also "who holds a spindle" (NRSV); "a male who handles the spindle" (JPS); *HALOT*, p. 933. McCarter follows the LXX *kratōn skytalēs* "the one who relies on sticks" and interprets the "sticks" as "crutches" based on the Phoenician *plkm* "crutches" in the Karatepe inscription (*KAI* 26A II 6), but Gibson translates this Phoenician term as "spindle" (Gibson, *SSI*, 3:59; McCarter, II, p. 118). Holloway suggested a new interpretation of *pelek* as "work-duty, corveé," but against this Layton supports the meaning "spindle" in the light of Phoenician and Ugaritic cognates. See S. W. Holloway, "Distaff, Crutch or Chain Gang: The Curse of the House of Joab in 2 Samuel III 29," *VT* 37 (1987) 370-75; S. C. Layton, "A Chain Gang in 2 Samuel iii 29? A Rejoinder," *VT* 39 (1989) 85. Hoftijzer and Jongeling (*DNWSI*, pp. 915-16) accept "spindle" for Phoenician *plk*.

175. McCarter reads *hārᵉgû lᵉ-* (*murdered*), as *ṣpnw l-* in the light of 4QSam[a], which he reads as [ ]*pnw l-* "had been lying for." However, Herbert, *RBDSS*, p. 112 rejects this reading of *p* in 4QSam[a] as "most unlikely" and reads *ʾ* instead. The construction could be an Aramaism, which is not necessarily a late phenomenon as is normally claimed.

22-30 Here, as later in 18:14 and 20:10, the motive for Joab's actions can be seen as concern for David's position (v. 25), concern for his own position (especially as David had not told him what was going on, v. 23), private vengeance (v. 30), or a mixture. We are not told what part Abishai played (vv. 30, 39), but he seems to have been a loyal supporter of his brother (see 10:9-12; 18:2; 20:6-10; also see on 8:13).[176]

22 The syntax of the first half of this verse, lit. "the servants of David and Joab came back (sg.)," is puzzling since normally the singular component of a compound subject is first,[177] but, in contrast to 2:30, the verb here is singular. McCarter amends the verb to plural, but he does not solve the problem of the unusual verb-final position of the following clause in the narrative *they brought back much plunder with them* (lit. "and much plunder with them they brought back"). Instead of emending the text, one could take the clause *and Joab came back from the raid* as parenthetical and the phrase *David's servants* as *casus pendens* (i.e., topicalization[178]) and translate as above.

23 Joab did not come back until after Abner left. One suspects that David had timed his meeting with Abner to avoid conflict between him and Joab.

25 The expression *your going out and your coming in* probably refers to military actions as in 1 Sam. 18:13. In other words, Joab claims Abner came as a spy.

26 *Bor-hassirah* is near modern Ṣîret el-Bellaʿ, an oasis about two and a half miles (4 km) north of Hebron. The narrator emphasizes again David's noninvolvement.

27 McCarter takes MT *ʾel-tôk haššaʿar* (*into the midst of the gate*) as a corruption of *ʾl yrk* (*haššaʿar*), which he thinks is reflected by LXX *ek plagiōn*, and translates "beside the gate." But the MT makes a good sense when the elaborate structure of a city-gate is taken into consideration; see also the commentary on 1 Sam. 9:18.[179]

The phrase *for the blood of Asael, Joab's brother* refers to the death of Asael in 2:18-23. Here, Joab exercises his duty as "the avenger of blood" (*gōʾēl haddām*, Num. 35:19, etc.) for the death of his brother Asael. However, it does not seem that this duty necessarily applied to those killed in battle. David says Joab avenged "in the time of peace for blood that had been shed in war" (1 K. 2:5). Besides, otherwise how could peace be made after a conflict?

176. On Abner's murder, see T. Ishida, "The Story of Abner's Murder: A Problem Posed by the Solomonic Apologist," *EI* 24 (Avraham Malamat Volume; 1993) 109*-13*.

177. See E. J. Revell, "Concord with Compound Subjects and Related Uses of Pronouns," pp. 80.

178. Tsumura, I, pp. 46-48.

179. Tsumura, I, pp. 276-77.

28 MT *mēʿīm YHWH* (lit. "from with the LORD"), so 4QSam[a],[180] is here translated as *before the LORD*, for the verb "to be innocent" (*nqy) is most likely to be in collocation with the phrase *of the blood*, lit. "bloods" (*middᵉmê*). The same phrase, *nqy + *min*, appears in Num. 32:22 as "to be free of obligation to the LORD."

29 The plural noun "bloods" *of Abner* (*dᵉmê ʾabnēr*) in the previous verse is the subject of the plural verb *fall on* (*yāhūlû*; lit. "whirl about"); cf. [yh]*wl* (sg.) in 4QSam[a].

The term *məṣōrāʿ* refers to various types of *skin disease*, not necessarily Hansen's disease,[181] though some modern translations keep the term "leprosy" (NIV11; also ESV; cf. "eruption" JPS). For a similar imprecation, see Deut. 28:27.[182] J. Milgrom has noted that some Akkadian curse formulas include the term *saḫaršubbû* ("scale disease"), which is one of the Akkadian semantic parallels to Hebrew *ṣāraʿat*.[183]

In this verse, all nominal forms are masc.sg., referring to male descendants of Joab. One who *holds a distaff* (*maḥăzîq bappelek*) is one forced to do the menial woman's work of spinning, a great comedown for the offspring of the mighty warrior Joab.

The vassal treaties of Esarhaddon in Akkadian have a comparable curse: "May all the gods called by name in this treaty spin you round like a spindle (*pilakki*), may they make you like a woman before your enemy" (616A-617).[184]

g. Abner's Burial and David's Lament (3:31-39)

31 *Then David said to Joab and to all the people who were with him,*
"Tear your clothes
and gird on sackcloth

180. See Herbert, *RBDSS*, p. 109.

181. See Gordon, *CB*, p. 220.

182. J. Milgrom holds that *ṣāraʿat* can "in no way be identified with leprosy"; see J. Milgrom, *Leviticus 1-16: A New Translation with Introduction and Commentary* (AB 3; New York: Doubleday, 1991), p. 775. For the most recent study of its etymology, see C. Cohen, "Literary and Philological Aspects of Biblical Hebrew (BH) צרעת," *Korot* 21 (2011-2012) 284-87. (Thanks to Prof. T. Muraoka, who called my attention to this article.)

183. Milgrom, *Leviticus 1-16*, p. 820; Cohen, "Literary and Philological Aspects of Biblical Hebrew (BH) צרעת," pp. 267-68.

184. D. J. Wiseman, "The Vassal-Treaties of Esarhaddon," *Iraq* 20 (1958) 76; see R. P. Gordon, *I & II Samuel: A Commentary* (Exeter: Paternoster, 1986), which alludes to this. Also, see H. A. Hoffner, "Symbols for Masculinity and Femininity: Their Use in Ancient Near Eastern Sympathetic Magic Rituals," *JBL* 85 (1966) 326-34, esp. pp. 329 and 332; Cohen, "Literary and Philological Aspects of Biblical Hebrew (BH) צרעת," pp. 287-91. See also Gordon, p. 220.

and lament before Abner."
As for king David, he was walking after the bier.
32 *They buried Abner in Hebron.*
And the king raised his voice and wept by[185] *the grave of Abner.*
All the people wept.
33 *And the king chanted an elegy for Abner, and he said,*
"Like a fool dies[186] *should Abner die?*
34 *Neither your hands nor your feet were bound;*
they were not put in fetters.
Like a falling before sons of injustice have you fallen?"
And all the people continued to weep over him.
35 *Then all the people came to have David to eat bread while it was still daytime.*
But David swore, saying,
"May God do thus to me and thus again,
if, before the sun sets, I taste bread or anything else!"
36 *Now all the people observed it and it was good in their eyes, just as everything the king did was good in the eyes of all the people.*
37 *And all the people and all Israel knew that day that it was not the king's will that Abner son of Ner be put to death.*
38 *And the king said to his servants,*
"Do you not know
that a prince and a great man fell this day in Israel?
39 *As for me, I am still weak today, though*[187] *anointed king,*
while these men, the sons of Zeruiah, are too wild for me.
May the LORD *reward the evildoer according to his evil!"*

31-39 Joab is apparently too important and useful for David to punish, so he does the best he can by cursing him and having a splendid funeral for Abner and making a show of publicly mourning and chanting a lament for him. This is the only funeral described in detail in the Old Testament.[188] As elsewhere, tearing clothes, wearing sackcloth, and fasting are features of mourning.

31 For tearing clothes as a mourning custom, see the commentary on 1 Sam. 4:12.[189] Note also that in the Ugaritic mythological text *KTU* 1.6 VI 14-15 the god El mourns Baal's death by pouring "dust" and "powder" on his head

185. Hebrew *'el-*, which is often interchangeable with *'al-*.

186. Lit. "Like a death of a fool."

187. Lit. "and"; as an *explicative waw*; see Davidson §136, cited by D. W. Baker, "Further Examples of the *waw explicativum*," *VT* 30 (1980) 135.

188. See E. F. de Ward, "Mourning Customs in 1, 2, Samuel," *JJS* 23 (1972) 1f.

189. Tsumura, I, pp. 197-98.

and covering himself with a loincloth. The origin of the custom of wearing *sackcloth* is not certain.[190] The term *lament* (*spd) appears also in 1 Sam. 25:1; 28:3; 2 Sam. 1:12; and 11:26, and it is distinct from *'bl, "to mourn," which appears in 1 Sam. 6:19. For mourning at Samuel's death, see the commentary on 1 Sam. 25:1.[191]

As for the phrase *lament before Abner*, Wensinck holds that it shows that "in funerary *mispēd* it was the corpse, or perhaps the departed spirit, which was addressed,"[192] but S. R. Driver takes the phrase as indicating that David preceded the bier in the procession. However, as de Ward notes, in the same verse, David was reported as *walking after the bier*.[193] Probably the procession was led by Joab, accompanied by his troops; the bier went next, and then David.

33 The verb *chanted an elegy* (*wayqōnēn*; *qyn, Polel) is here without a cognate accusative *qînāh*, unlike 2 Sam. 1:17. The *introductory* formula, "and he said," appears also in the superscript of Ps. 18 (= 2 Sam. 22:2) and several Egyptian hymns and songs with titles.[194] Hence, this may be a case of such a superscription.

34 According to the MT scansion, the second and third lines of the quadracolon elegy (vv. 33b-34c), i.e., vv. 34 a-b, are divided as follows:

yādekā lō'-'ăsūrôt	Your hands were not bound 2 (7)
wᵉraglệkā lō'-linḥuštayim huggāšû	your feet were not fettered 3 (12)

However, they are metrically unbalanced. Hence, McCarter, Freedman, A. A. Anderson[195] and Qimron[196] all add "by manacles" (*bzqym*) or "in chains" after the first clause, based on 4QSama, *bzqym*, to improve the balance within the parallelism. However, one can scan the lines like the BHS does as follows:

190. See de Ward, "Mourning Customs in 1, 2, Samuel," 10-15.

191. Tsumura, I, p. 574.

192. See de Ward, "Mourning Customs in 1, 2, Samuel," 16.

193. De Ward, "Mourning Customs in 1, 2, Samuel," 16 n. 92.

194. See D. T. Tsumura, "Hymns and Songs with Titles and Subscriptions in the Ancient Near East," *Exeg* 3 (1992) 2, which comments on 2 Sam. 22:2.

195. McCarter, II, p. 111; D. N. Freedman, "On the Death of Abner," in *Love and Death in the Ancient Near East. Essays in Honor of M. H. Pope*, ed. J. H. Marks and R. M. Good (Guilford, CT: Four Quarters, 1987), pp. 125-27; A. A. Anderson, *2 Samuel* (WBC 11; Dallas: Word Books, 1989), pp. 52, 54.

196. E. Qimron, "The Lament of David over Abner," in *Birkat Shalom: Studies in the Bible, Ancient Near Eastern Literature, and Postbiblical Judaism Presented to Shalom M. Paul on the Occasion of His Seventieth Birthday*, ed. C. Cohen et al. (Winona Lake, Ind: Eisenbrauns, 2008), I, pp. 143-47.

yādekā lō'-'ăsūrôt wᵉraglêkā	your hands were not bound and your feet;
lō'-linḥuštayim huggāšû[197]	they were not put in fetters.

The line *yādekā lō'-'ăsūrôt wᵉraglêkā* is an example of "interrupted coordination," the AX&B pattern in which A&B *your hands and your feet* (*yādekā wᵉraglêkā*) is interrupted by the insertion of X *were not bound* (*lō'-'ăsūrôt*) to mean "Neither your hands nor your feet were bound" like Ps. 11:5a ("The Lord tests the righteous and the wicked"; so NRSV, NASB).[198] In this understanding, the "and" of "and your feet" (so MT, 4QSam[a]) is necessary rather than being an additional conjunction; cf. "your feet" (McCarter).

One might take the interrogative *h-* in the first line (2 Sam. 3:33b) as modifying the fourth line (v. 34c) too; thus, "have you fallen?" // "should Abner die?" This four-line parallelism probably constitutes an AXYB pattern, in which the middle two lines are the *inserted bicolon* as in Ps. 17:1, Job 12:24-25.[199] Note that the inserted bicolon here has the *qinah* pattern (3:32), which is the most suitable for a lament; see 2 Sam. 18:33.

35 For the oath formula *May God do thus to me and thus again*, see on 1 Sam. 3:17; cf. "*ysp* — Hypocoristicon, '(DN) has added (a son to the family)' or '(DN) will reward' (2 Sam. 3:35, etc.)."[200]

37 The phrase *all Israel* means Abner's own countrymen. VanderKam suggests that David actually planned the murder, though the present narrative covers it up.[201] However, he seems to underestimate the importance of Joab, and it is hard to see what David would have gained at this point.

39 The formula *May the Lord reward* (*yᵉšallēm YHWH lᵉ-*) means that "God will repay good for good, and bad for bad"; also Prov. 25:22; Job 21:31; Ruth 2:20; and Arad 21:42 ("the Lord will give my master his due").[202] McCarter believes that 4QSam[a] skips from 2 Sam. 3:39a to 4:1, and so v. 39b in the MT and the ancient versions was "the pious addition of a scribe."[203] However, Herbert refutes McCarter's claim on the basis of "the two previously unidentified fragments" that he identifies as containing v. 39b. According to

197. Pu. "were brought near" (lit.); 4QSam[a] has *hg* [*y*]*š* (see Herbert, *RBDSS*, 113), not *hgš* (McCarter, II, p. 111).

198. See D. T. Tsumura, "Coordination Interrupted, or Literary Insertion AX&B Pattern, in the Books of Samuel," pp. 117-32; Tsumura, I, pp. 61-63.

199. Tsumura, I, p. 63. See also the commentary on 2 Sam. 7:22.

200. N. Avigad and B. Sass, *Corpus of West Semitic Stamp Seals* (Jerusalem: IASH, 1997), p. 504. Tsumura, I, pp. 181-82.

201. J. C. VanderKam, "Davidic Complicity in the Deaths of Abner and Eshbaal: A Historical and Redactional Study," *JBL* 99 (1980), 529-33 and 539.

202. Y. Aharoni, *AI*, p. 42.

203. McCarter, II, p. 112.

his reconstruction, only *qāšîm mimmennî* ("too hard for me") is lacking from 4QSam[a].[204]

4. Death of Ishbosheth (4:1-12)

Chapter 4 relates the death of Saul's son, the king Ishbosheth. It is stressed that David had no part in it. David now has no rival for the kingship of Israel.

a. Murder of Ishbosheth (4:1-3)

1 *When the son of Saul heard that Abner was dead in Hebron, he lost courage; all Israel was dismayed.*

2 *Now the son of Saul had two men, commanders of bands;*[205] *the name of the first was Baanah, the name of the second Rechab, sons of Rimmon the Beerothite from the tribe of Benjamin, for Beeroth is also considered part of*[206] *Benjamin.*

3 *— And the Beerothites had fled to Gittaim and have been sojourners to this day —.*

1 The *son of Saul* here is Ishbosheth. However, LXX[BAL] and 4QSam[a] have "Mephibosheth son of Saul," which is clearly a mistake for "Ishbosheth son of Saul."[207]

he lost courage is literally "both of his hands (fem. du.) sank down" (*wayyirpû yādâw*). As for the masculine verbal form *wayyirpû*, it may be explained as third-person common dual *yqtl* as in Zeph. 3:16; Neh. 6:9; 2 Chr. 15:7, though in Ugaritic almost all examples of third-person common dual *yqtl* are *tqtl(n)*.[208]

2-3 Beeroth, modern Khirbet el-Burj, is a few miles (km) south of Gibeon and one of a "tetrapolis" led by Gibeon that tricked Joshua into making a treaty with them (Josh. 9); see "Kiriath-jearim, Kephirah, Beeroth" (Ezra 2:25; Neh. 7:29).

The Beerothites, the original pre-Israelite inhabitants, probably fled *to Gittaim* (*gittāymāh*), according to Neh. 11:33 a city in Benjamin,[209] at the

204. Herbert, *RBDSS*, p. 114.

205. Lit. "there were two men . . . to the son of Saul." MT *ben-šā'ûl* cannot be the subject of the plural verb *hāyû*; it is to be taken as adverbial here.

206. Hebrew *'al*, lit. "on, by the side of."

207. See DJD 17, p. 116.

208. See *UT* §9.15; also D. Sivan, *A Grammar of the Ugaritic Language* (Leiden: E. J. Brill, 1997), pp. 119, 132, 136, 149, 151, 157, 165. See also on 1 Sam. 6:12 in Tsumura, I, p. 219 n. 42.

209. See D. A. Dorsey, "Beerothite," in *ABD*, I, pp. 646-47.

time Saul put the Gibeonites to death (2 Sam. 21:1-2). From the present verse it would seem that after that event, Benjaminites, including Rimmon and his family, came to live there. Joshua 18:25 counts it as part of Benjamin. If this is correct, it suggests that the incident of the Gibeonites occurred early in Saul's reign, since it is Rimmon, the father of Baanah and Rechab, who is described as *the Beerothite*. This passage thus stresses that those who killed Ishbosheth were from his own tribe, not partisans of David.

2 In the phrase *the name of the first*, the cardinal number "one" (*'eḥād*) is used as an ordinal, as in Gen. 1:5 ("day one" = "the first day"), in conjunction with the other ordinal number, "the second" (*haššēnî*).[210]

The terms *Beerothite* (*habbᵉ'erōtî*) and *Beeroth* (*bᵉ'ērôt*) in v. 2 appear in shorter, *sandhi* forms, *hbrty* (4QSam[a]) and *habbērōtî* (1 Chr. 11:39), which resulted from vowel *sandhi* after the loss of the intervocalic *'aleph*.[211] See also on 2 Sam. 23:37.

3 For the phrase *to this day*, see the commentary on 1 Sam. 8:8.[212] McCarter thinks that the sentence *for . . . to this day* is a later insertion. But, "for" (v. 2b) is a *speaker-oriented* particle that introduces a clause to explain the designation *the Beerothite*. Hence, only v. 3 is parenthetical. But its being parenthetical does not necessarily mean it is a later insertion.

Gittaim is Gath-rimmon (Josh. 19:45), not the Philistine Gath. It is located at or near modern Ramleh.[213]

b. Note on Mephibosheth, Jonathan's Son (4:4)

4 *Now, Jonathan son of Saul had a son who was crippled in his feet.*

He was five years old when the report of Saul and Jonathan came from Jezreel, and his nurse carried him and fled. When she was in a hurry to flee, he fell and became lame.

His name was Mephibosheth.

This verse interrupts the flow of discourse. However, the information about *Mephibosheth* (*mᵉpîbōšet*) is probably put here to show why there was no move to make him king after Ishbosheth's death—he was still a child, and he was *crippled*. He is further mentioned in 2 Samuel in ch. 9; 16:1-4; 19:24-30; and 21:7. On the relation with the name *Meribbaal* in 1 Chr. 8:34, see the commen-

210. See Tsumura, I, p. 108.

211. Tsumura, "Vowel *sandhi* in Biblical Hebrew," pp. 575-88.

212. Tsumura, I, p. 252.

213. *SB*, p. 116.

tary on 2 Sam. 2:8. Note that the Mephibosheth in 21:8 is a different person, the son of Saul and Rizpah.

c. Continuation of the Murder of Ishbosheth (4:5-7)

5 *Now the sons of Rimmon the Beerothite, Rechab and Baanah, went, and they came into the house of Ishbosheth in the heat of the day, while he was lying on his bed in midday*

6 *— hither they came, even to the middle of the house as takers of wheat — and struck him on the belly. Rechab and Baanah his brother escaped.*

7 *In this way,*[214] *they came into the house, while he was lying on his bed in his bedroom, and struck him and killed him and cut off his head; and they took his head and traveled the Arabah road all night.*

This section describes how *Rechab* and *Baanah* murdered Ishbosheth at *midday*. Many emendations of the text have been suggested, but a close look at the sequence of the verbal forms suggests that most of them are unnecessary.

Now the sons of Rimmon . . . went (v. 5a) is the *wayqtl* [*waw* cons. + impf] of a movement verb (*wayyēlᵉkû*) with a stated subject and so marks a TRANSITION of discourse; it is the SETTING for a new episode.[215] The second *wayqtl* (*wayyābōʾû* "and they came") in v. 5b is EVENT 1, which is continued in the next *wayqtl* (*wayyakkūhû* "and they struck him": EVENT 2) in v. 6b. This short episode terminates with a sentence with the *qtl* [pf.] verb "they escaped" (*nimlāṭû*).

The parenthetical sentence between the two *wayqtls*, *hither*[216] *they came, even to the middle of the house, as takers of wheat* (v. 6a), is a *procedural discourse*[217] ("how") with a verbal form of *qtl*,[218] which explains how these brothers entered, that is, "as takers of wheat," taking *lōqᵉḥê ḥiṭṭîm* adverbially rather as a subject.

With the expression *in this way, they came* (EVENT 1) in v. 7, the narrator's viewpoint[219] changes from that of one watching the brothers from afar

214. Lit. "And" (*explicative waw*).

215. See Tsumura, I, pp. 51-52; also the commentaries on 1 Sam. 18:5, 20:1. See Introduction, III.2 in this volume.

216. E. Mastéy, "A Linguistic Inquiry Solves an Ancient Crime: Re-examination of 2 Samuel 4:6," *VT* 61 (2011) 82-103, interprets this particle as "behold," reading *hinnēh*. But, such emendation of the text is unnecessary.

217. For "procedural discourse," see R. E. Longacre, "Weqatal Forms in Biblical Hebrew Prose," *BHDL*, pp. 50-98. See also the Excursus in 2 Sam. 7:8-16.

218. See D. T. Tsumura, "Tense and Aspect of Hebrew Verbs in II Samuel 7:8-16," pp. 641-54.

219. On the topic of viewpoint, see Tsumura, I, pp. 54-55.

("went"; v. 5a) to that of one who is inside the house and sees them come *into the house*, even into the bedroom! EVENT 2 ("they struck him") is repeated but with further actions, that is, "and killed him and cut off his head" and "took his head."

The above discussion on the discourse structure may be summarized as below:

SETTING
(5) Now . . . Rechab and Baanah went (*wayqtl*) . . .
EVENT 1 (what) they came (*wayqtl*) into the house . . .
SITUATION — he was lying (participle) . . .
PROCEDURE (how) (6) they came (*qtl*) . . .
EVENT 2 (what) they struck (*wayqtl*) him . . .
TERMINUS Rechab and Baanah escaped (*qtl*).

EVENT 1 (what) (7) In this way, they came (*wayqtl*) into the house . . .
SITUATION — he was lying (participle) . . .
EVENT 2 (what) they struck (*wayqtl*) him and killed (*wayqtl*) him and cut (*wayqtl*) off his head; and they took (*wayqtl*) his head
TERMINUS and went (*wayqtl*).

Some claim that v. 7 is a later rephrasing of the account of v. 6.[220] But it is reasonable to take it rather as an expansion of the previous verse. The repetitive style is due to its narrative nature, and the discourse structure of vv. 5-6 as noted above supports this interpretation. After recapitulating vv. 5-6, the narrator relates the further actions by the sequence of four *wayqtl*s after "struck": that is, *and killed him (wayqtl) and cut off (wayqtl) his head . . . took (wayqtl) his head and went (wayqtl) the Arabah road all night.* The final *wayqtl* of the movement verb, "and (they) went," marks TERMINUS of this episode.[221]

The *Arabah road* is the road along the Jordan Valley; see the commentary on 2 Sam. 2:29.

6 The *takers of wheat* (*lōqᵉḥê ḥiṭṭîm*) could be "buyers" of wheat (see Jastrow, p. 717). This suggests that they pretended to be purchasers[222] of wheat in order to gain entry into the house. The LXX reads, "The portress of the house had been gathering wheat; she had nodded and fallen asleep," and the vast majority of scholars accept Wellhausen's view that the LXX reflects the

220. E.g., J. C. Haelewyck, "L'assassinat d'Ishbaal (2 Samuel IV 1–12)," *VT* 47 (1997) 145–53.

221. See D. T. Tsumura, "Textual Corruptions, or Linguistic Phenomena?," pp. 142-45.

222. See "purchaser" in the Murabba'at texts, cited in *DCH*, 4:573a.

original version and the MT is corrupted from its original. McCarter assumes the MT derived its text through several degrees of "graphic confusion."[223] However, his emendation depends too much on the graphic similarity, that is, on the likeness of the shape of scripts.[224]

E. Mastéy made a detailed linguistic inquiry into this textual problem and supports the MT's originality.[225] He translates *lōq^{e}ḥê ḥiṭṭîm* as "grain robbers" without a reasonable lexical support and interprets the situation as follows: when the two brothers arrive at the house, "grain robbers" were "already inside" and had *struck* Ishbosheth. So, the brothers *escaped.* Later, they returned and *struck him and killed him* (v. 7). Thus, according to Mastéy, Ishbosheth was *struck* twice, once by the robbers and then by Rechab and Baanah.[226] Interesting though it may be, his interpretation is a little forced, for Rechab and Baanah would not have needed to strike Ishbosheth again, as he was presumably still lying on his bed, stricken, and all they would have needed to do was to "kill" him and "cut off" his head.

d. David Kills Rechab and Baanah (4:8-12)

8 *And they brought the head of Ishbosheth to David in Hebron and said to the king,*

"Here is the head of Ishbosheth, son of Saul, your enemy
who sought your life.
And the LORD has given my lord the king vengeance this day
on Saul and his offspring."

9 *And David answered Rechab and Baanah his brother, the sons of Rimmon the Beerothite:*[227]

"As the LORD lives,
who has redeemed my life from every danger!
10 *For the one who once told me,*
'Now Saul is dead!'
thought[228] *he was a bearer of good news,*
but I seized him and killed him in Ziklag,
the one to whom I was supposed to give reward for good news.

223. McCarter, II, pp. 125-26.

224. See Tsumura, "Scribal Errors or Phonetic Spellings?," pp. 390-411, on the possibility of explaining passages interpreted as "scribal errors" as phonetic spellings.

225. Mastéy, "A Linguistic Inquiry Solves an Ancient Crime," 83-90.

226. Mastéy, "A Linguistic Inquiry Solves an Ancient Crime," 96-97.

227. Lit., "answered . . . and said to them"; see 1 Sam. 20:32 [and said to him], and Tsumura, I, Introduction.

228. Lit., "in his eyes."

11 *How much more,*[229] *when wicked men have killed a righteous man*[230]
in his house on his bed!
And now, shall I not require his blood from your hand
and exterminate[231] *you from the land?"*

12 *And David commanded the young men, and they killed them and cut off their hands and feet and hung them by the pool in Hebron; but they took the head of Ishbosheth and buried it in the grave of Abner in Hebron.*

The stage changes from Ishbosheth's residence to David's court in Hebron. The verbal phrase *brought . . . to David* marks the TRANSITION to a new episode.

8 *Saul, your enemy, who sought your life.* It is true that Saul had sought David's life. However, despite that, David had already refused to kill Saul (1 Sam. 24:4-6; 26:8-9), and furthermore that did not give them an excuse to kill a "righteous man" (v. 11), even if he was Saul's son (see Deut. 24:16).

9 For the oath formula, *as the Lord lives,* see the commentary on 1 Sam. 14:39.[232] The full expression appears again in 1 K. 1:29. The Hebrew term *pdh ("redeem") was originally an economic term which means either (1) "to pay ransom to" (*pdh + *lᵉ*) or (2) "to release . . . from" (*pdh + *min*) like Ugaritic *pdy.*[233] Here, David acknowledges that it was *the Lord* who freed his *life from every danger.*

10-11 This refers to the incident in 2 Sam. 1:13-16. The Amalekite had at least given the excuse that Saul had requested his own death, but Ishbosheth's death was out-and-out murder. However, as noted earlier, David says nothing here about Ishbosheth as the Lord's anointed.

The term *bᵉśōrāh* means *reward for good news.*[234] In the MT, the particle *'et* is prefixed to an indefinite noun phrase *a righteous man* (*'et-'îš-ṣaddîq*), whose meaning is determined by the following phrases.[235] For the expression *require . . . from your hand* (*bqš + *miyyedkem*), see the commentary on 1 Sam. 20:16.[236]

229. Hebrew: *'ap kî*; see 1 Sam. 14:30; 21:5; 23:3; 2 Sam. 16:11; and Hab. 2:5.

230. Or "an innocent man" (NIV; McCarter).

231. Lit., "burn."

232. Tsumura, I, p. 377.

233. See *DULAT*, pp. 663-64; *HALOT*; also D. T. Tsumura, "The Incomparability of Israel the People of Yahweh," *Exeg* 14 (2003) 51-61 (Japanese with English summary). See also the commentary on 7:23.

234. BDB, 142f.: 1. "good tidings" (2 Ki. 7:9); 2. "tidings, news" (2 Sam. 18:20, 25, 27); 3. "reward for good tidings" (2 Sam. 4:10, 18:22).

235. GKC, §117d.

236. Tsumura, I, pp. 509-10.

12 Unlike the case of Joab, there is no problem with executing the killers of Ishbosheth. For hanging a body after death, see 2 Sam. 21:6-14; and Josh. 8:29; 10:26.

5. David, the King of Israel (5:1-5)

It is not stated how soon the events of chapter 5 followed upon those of chapter 4, though it could have been as much as five and a half years (see on 2 Sam. 2:10-11). Presumably the deaths of Abner and Ishbosheth caused a shock among David's supporters in the north (3:19) and caused them to put off accepting David as king immediately. Some of the shock seems to have remained at the time this account was written. David apparently just bided his time, waiting for the elders of Israel to decide they wanted him as king.

1 *And all the tribes of Israel came to David at Hebron and said,*
"Here, we are your bone and flesh!
2 *Even formerly,*
when Saul was king over us,
it was you who brought Israel in and out.
And the LORD said to you,
'You yourself shall shepherd my people Israel;
you yourself shall become a prince over Israel!'"
3 *Thus all the elders of Israel came to the king at Hebron.*
And King David made covenant with them at Hebron before the LORD,
and they anointed David as king over Israel.

4 *David was thirty years old when he became king; for forty years he ruled.*
5 *In Hebron he ruled over Judah seven years and six months; in Jerusalem he ruled thirty-three years over all Israel and Judah.*

1-5 Finally, David is accepted and anointed as king over the entire house of Israel. First messengers from *all the tribes* come and ask him to become king, then the elders of Israel come themselves. David makes a covenant with them as representatives of the nation, and they anoint him king over Israel (cf. 1 Sam. 10:25; 11:15). David is one of them (see Deut. 17:15), he is a proven military leader, and he is the chosen of the Lord.

1 The particle *hinneh* (*Here*) is contrasted with *formerly*, which refers to David's former leadership in Israel. *We are your bone and flesh* (*'aṣmᵉkā ûbᵉśārᵉkā*), i.e., "your own flesh and blood" (NIV, JPS). Even though there was a distinct division between Judah and the rest of Israel, they still recognize each other as kin (similarly, "brothers" in 2 Sam. 2:26-27).

2 The expression, "to go out and in," refers to the activity of a soldier in battle; see the commentary on 2 Sam. 3:25 and 1 Sam. 18:13.[237] The causative (Hi.) *brought . . . in and out* here connotes David's leadership in battle. The K. of the MT *hāyîtāh mwṣy' whmby 't-yśr'l*, translated here as *who brought Israel in and out*, is probably a phonetic spelling of *hāyîtā hammôṣî' wᵉhammēbî' 'et-Yiśrā'ēl*, as in the Q.[238]

Budde and Eissfeldt[239] take the expression *the LORD said to you* as part of the oracle that Doeg claimed Ahimelech gave David in 1 Sam. 22:10. On the other hand, McCarter thinks that this statement is added by the Deuteronomistic writer, based on its similarity with Nathan's speech in 2 Sam. 7, which he takes to be a Deuteronomistic insertion.[240] However, I would disagree that Nathan's speech has been Deuteronomistically revised. See the commentary on 2 Sam. 7.

3 *Thus all the elders of Israel came.* Hertzberg holds that the representatives who came to David in v. 1 came again in this verse, but most commentators see here "independent accounts of a single event, redactionally combined."[241] However, it seems best to understand that *all the tribes* in vv. 1b-2 means messengers of the tribes, and that having received David's positive response, *all the elders of Israel* came in person to make covenant with David and anoint him as *a king over Israel.*

On anointing, see the commentaries on 1 Sam. 9:16; 16:13.[242] The covenant probably involved promises on both sides; cf. 10:25. Now, at last, the entire people of Israel, the covenant community, accept David as their representative, i.e., the anointed king of both Judah and Israel. It was probably more than ten years since he was anointed before his father and brothers in 1 Sam. 16. The account in 1 Chr. 11:3 adds the phrase "according to the word of the LORD by Samuel."

4-5 4QSamᵃ lacks these verses, as do 1 Chr. 11:3 and Josephus.[243] McCarter thinks, with Barthélemy, that these verses were suppressed "in one textual tradition because of the inexact correspondence of the years of David's reign given in vv. 4 (40) and 5 (7 1/2 + 33)." However, as rounding off reign years was normal, this would hardly have been considered a problem. Compare this verse and 2:11, which give "seven years and six months," with 1 K. 2:11 and 1 Chr. 29:27, which give "seven years." Also, this would not explain why his age is not given in the latter passages.

237. Tsumura, I, p. 480.

238. For "phonetic spellings," see Tsumura, "Scribal Errors or Phonetic Spellings?," pp. 390-411.

239. O. Eissfeldt, *Die Komposition der Samuelisbücher* (Leipzig: Hinrich, 1931), 27.

240. McCarter, II, p. 132.

241. McCarter, II, p. 131.

242. Tsumura, I, pp. 274-75, 423-25.

243. See Herbert, *RBDSS*, p. 118.

4 It is often explained that the numbers *thirty . . . forty* are round numbers, hence not accurate. Solomon's reign is also given as 40 years (see 1 K. 11:42), while Eli's judgship lasted 40 years (1 Sam. 4:18). David's life span is the ideal number "30+40" = 70; see Ps. 90:10. The narrator here may have used the number 40 as a symbolic figure for a full and ideal length of generation, just as 480 years in 1 K. 6:1 possibly stands for twelve generations.[244] However, at least in David's case, the number 40 is not necessarily symbolic, for the number 40 is the sum of 7 years (or 7 years and 6 months) and 33 years. A round number is not always "unhistorical." The age of the David we see in 1 K. 1 could easily have been around 70.

C. JERUSALEM, THE CITY OF DAVID (5:6-25)

1. The Royal City of Jerusalem (5:6-10)

6 *And the king and his men went to Jerusalem, to the Jebusites, the inhabitants of the land, and they*[245] *spoke to David, saying,*
"You cannot come in here.
For even[246] *the blind and lame will surely turn you away."*
thinking, "David cannot come in here."
7 *And David captured the stronghold of Zion, that is the City of David.*
8 *And David said on that day,*
"Whoever strikes the Jebusites,
let him strike down[247] *the 'lame and blind,'*
those hated by[248] *the soul of David,*

244. See K. A. Kitchen, "The Exodus" in *ABD*, 2, pp. 700-708; J. K. Hoffmeier, "What Is the Biblical Date for the Exodus? A Response to Bryant Wood," *JETS* 50 (2007) 225-47. Hoffmeier notes that "no Egyptian pharaoh in 3000 years of recorded history ruled 40 years" and that "only two early Assyrian kings are allotted approximately 40 years in recently published eponym lists from Kultepe." It is certainly true that some of the biblical forty years are symbolic.

245. Taking the Hebrew text with singular forms (*haybûsî yôšēb hā'āreṣ*) as collective. Or, perhaps "the Jebusite, the ruler . . . he," as W. G. E. Watson, "David Ousts the City Ruler of Jebus," *VT* 20 (1970) 501-2 suggested.

246. The MT *kî 'im* is reflected in Syriac, Vulgate, and Targum; cf. "even" (NRSV; JPS; NIV); "but" (NASB). However, 4QSam^a, and probably the LXX, has only *ky*. Herbert supports the MT reading: "A limiting or contrasting sense is sufficiently unnatural at this point that it is not easy to understand how *'im* could have been added later if it had not been originally present," though he interprets it as having "the force of strengthened *ky*" ("2 Samuel v 6: An Interpretative Crux Reconsidered in the Light of 4QSam^a," *VT* 44 [1994], 342, 348).

247. Heb. *w^{e}yigga'*; *waw*+jussive; cf. *yg'* (4QSam^a), without *waw*.

248. *ś^{e}nū'ê*; following Q. Cf. *śn'h* (4QSam^a) with *nepeš* as the subject: "David's soul hated"; so McCarter, II, p. 140: "for David hates."

by means of the water tunnel."
Therefore it is said,
"The 'blind and lame' shall not enter the palace."[249]
9 *And David lived in the stronghold and called it the City of David.*
And David built a wall around it from the Millo and inward.
10 *And David became greater and greater, for the* LORD *God of hosts was with him.*

The account of the Davidic kingdom of Israel starts with the capture of Jerusalem, a city on the boundary between Judah and Benjamin. It had not been controlled by any tribe, and thus both symbolically and geographically it was better suited to be the capital of all Israel than Hebron, which is in central Judah.[250]

Jerusalem was the "Salem" of Melchizedek (Gen. 14:18). Its history goes back to the third millennium, and it had been fortified since the Middle Bronze Age, that is, the first half of the second millennium B.C.[251] In the second half of the millennium it was one of the Canaanite city-states under the influence of Egypt. Among the fourteenth-century Amarna letters are several letters to the Pharaoh from the king of Jerusalem.[252] A tiny fragment of an Akkadian tablet from the same period was recently found in a fill taken from the Ophel area, between the Old City's southern wall and the City of David, which has been excavated by Eilat Mazar of Hebrew University. Jerusalem was evidently a major Canaanite city-state during the Late Bronze Age.[253]

The *Jebusites* are among the Canaanites listed in Gen. 10:16 and, broadly speaking, are considered to be among the Amorites (Josh. 10:5). The city was too strong to be conquered at the time of Joshua (15:63; Judg. 1:21). The Jebusite city, the city of Zion, was located on the western slope of the Kidron Valley above the city's water source, the spring of Gihon. An extensive network of water tunnels has been excavated. The *water tunnel* through which David's men entered the city was probably one of these. Most likely, it was a Canaanite tunnel (see below) that connects with the shaft now known as "Warren's Shaft," which was dug directly over the water channel near the spring. The Hebrew does not specify going "up" the shaft, however, just going *through*. It should be noted that not all scholars accept that the attack involved the water tunnels, as discussed below.

249. So NIV; cf. "the House" (JPS); "the Lord's house" (REB); "the temple" (McCarter, II, p. 140; also Herbert, "2 Samuel V 6," p. 347); *eis oikon kuriou* (LXX).

250. See *CBA*, #100.

251. See B. Mazar, *Biblical Israel: State and People* (Jerusalem: Magnes Press, 1992), pp. 88-99; also P. J. King, "Jerusalem," *ABD*, III, 747-67.

252. *SB*, pp. 85-86.

253. See E. Mazar, W. Horowitz, T. Oshima, and Y. Goren, "A Cuneiform Tablet from the Ophel in Jerusalem," *IEJ* 60 (2010) 4-21.

According to 1 Chr. 11:6, Joab led the attack and was therefore made David's chief commander. See also the commentary on 1 Sam. 17:54.[254] The author of Samuel intentionally focuses on David (see 2 Sam. 5:8) and credits him with the deeds of his men. As R. Gilmour comments, "Samuel is concerned with the glory of David in his capacity and abilities as king, while Chronicles emphasizes the unity of David's kingdom as he leads 'all' Israel."[255]

6 Various interpretations have been suggested for the significance of *the blind and lame* here. McCarter summarizes them into three groups: (1) "the city is so strong that its blind and lame citizens will suffice to drive off David" — by Josephus, Kimchi, Caird, McKane, Hertzberg, Ravenna; (2) they are "instruments or at least reminders of the sanctions to be imposed if David violates the oath and enters the city" — by Heller, Yadin, Brunet; (3) it refers to "those among David's troops who are like blind and lame men in the presence of the impregnable fortress"—Stoebe.[256] The first interpretation fits the context best, especially considering v. 8.[257] For the uses of "blind" and "lame" in proverbial sayings, Hallo notes two similar proverbs: "In the city of the lame, the halt is courier" (a Sumerian proverb); "In the market place of the blind they call the one-eyed man (their) leader" (a Rabbinic saying).[258] In both these sayings, the blind and the lame are the weakest of society.

The phrase *surely turn you away* (*hĕsîrᵉkā*), in a 3 m.s., pf. form, has been taken as suffering from problems of both number and tense.[259] Hence Wellhausen and S. R. Driver emend the text to *yᵉsîrūkā*, while others support the rendering "except you take away the blind and the lame" (KJV, RV) either by emendation (Klostermann) or by taking the verb as an infinitive construct with suffix (Stoebe). Herbert takes this perfect tense as past, thus translating "Surely the blind and the lame have turned you aside saying, 'David will not

254. Tsumura, I, pp. 468-69.

255. R. Gilmour, "Who Captured Jerusalem? Reading Historiography and/or Collective Memory in Samuel," in Dietrich, *The Books of Samuel*, p. 68. For Chronicles' accounts, see I. Kalimi, "The Capture of Jerusalem in the Chronistic History," *VT* 52 (2002) 66-79.

256. McCarter, II, p. 138.

257. See S. Vargon, "The Blind and the Lame," *VT* 46 (1996) 498-514.

258. W. W. Hallo, "Proverbs Quoted in Epic," in *Lingering over Words: Studies in Ancient Near Eastern Literature in Honor of William L. Moran*, ed. J. Huehnergard and P. Steinkeller (Atlanta: Scholars Press, 1990), pp. 207-8.

259. For the textual history of this expression in various versions, including the LXX and 4QSam[a], see Herbert, "2 Samuel V 6," pp. 344f; also see Introduction, I.B (p. 3 above). Note also that on v. 8 McCarter translates the MT verb *hĕsîrᵉkā* (*swr) as "had incited (*swt) them," reading the Hebrew "original" as *hsytw*, based on 4QSam[a] and LXX ἀντέστησαν; he explains the MT *hsyrk* as "the result of graphic confusion of *-t(w)* and *-rk*." However, Herbert has reexamined the Qumran manuscript and suggests rather that the reading in the 4QSam[a] is *hsyt(whw)*, and holds that the LXX (both LXX[B] *antestēsan* and LXX[L] *apestēsan*) support the MT against 4QSam[a]. See Herbert, *RBDSS*, pp. 118-19.

enter here.'"[260] But, the perfect of MT verbal form can be explained as *perfect of certainty* and the singular as collective.

If one considers the last clause as the narrator's comment on the Jebusites' thoughts, it is not superfluous.[261] They issue their challenge to David because they are confident in the strength of their fortress.

7 The *stronghold of Zion . . . the City of David*, which is the pre-Israelite city, is located at the southeast corner of later Jerusalem. The name *Zion* appears here for the first time in the Bible. The exact meaning of the name is not certain, but based on Arabic etymologies it may mean "a fortress located on a ridge."[262] The east wall of the Jebusite city has been excavated; it had been fortified since the Middle Bronze Age. The *City of David* has been excavated by E. Mazar, who claims that a part of David's palace has been found (see below).[263]

8 It was unnecessary to repeat the subject *David*, as it is clear from the context, but discourse-grammatically, the stated subject for the narrative tense *wayqtl* signals a new subparagraph.[264] The phrase *Whoever strikes the Jebusites* (*kol-makkēh yᵉbûsî*, lit. "as for all those who strike a Jebusite") is a *casus pendens*, that is, a topicalization, so appears before the *waw*+jussive.[265]

The next phrase is *wᵉyiggaʿ baṣṣinnôr wᵉʾet-happisḥîm wᵉʾet-haʿiwrîm* (lit. "and let him strike down in/by the water tunnel and the lame and the blind"). The syntax is difficult. It is often translated something like "he should reach the water shaft and strike down the lame and the blind." The verb is *ngʿ "to touch, strike down." It often takes the preposition *b-* before its object: e.g., Gen. 3:3; Exod. 19:12; Lev. 5:2; 1 Sam. 6:9; 2 Sam. 14:10; 23:7. The next word *ṣinnôr* probably means something like "water tunnel" (see below). As the water tunnel was probably the weakest point in the city's defenses, taking *ṣinnôr* with the preposition *b-* as the object of the verb appears to be reasonable. However, then what do you do with *wᵉʾet-happisḥîm wᵉʾet-haʿiwrîm* (the lame and the blind)? The verb *ngʿ itself does not imply upward motion, as crawling up a tunnel. The present context rather requires the phrase "the lame

260. Herbert, "2 Samuel V 6," p. 348.

261. Herbert, "2 Samuel V 6," p. 344.

262. W. H. Mare, *ABD*, VI, p. 1096.

263. See E. Mazar, "Jerusalem: 1. The City of David Visitors' Center," *NEAEHL* 5:1801; E. Mazar, *The Palace of King David: Excavations at the Summit of the City of David. Preliminary Report of Seasons 2005-2007* (Jerusalem: Shoham Academic Research and Publication, 2009). While E. Mazar claims that it was David who built the Large Stone Structure, A. Faust holds that the structure was likely built by the Jebusites in the Iron Age I and reused by David; see A. Faust, "Did Eilat Mazar Find David's Palace?" *BAR* 38.5 (Sept/Oct 2012) 47-52, 70. (A. Millard called this article to my attention.)

264. See Introduction, III.1 (above).

265. See Introduction of Tsumura, I on "Unusual Topicalization" (V.A).

and blind" to be the object, even though it does not have the preposition *b-*. If it is correct, the phrase *baṣṣinnôr* should be taken adverbially *by means of the water tunnel*: lit. "in/by" or "through" the water tunnel. (McCarter claims that 4QSam[a] is "damaged at this point (*b* [])," but the entire phrase *by means of the water tunnel* [*baṣṣinnôr*] is clearly attested there.)[266]

As for the word *ṣinnôr*, its occurrence in Ps. 42:8 ("waterfalls" [ESV]) makes it highly probable it is some kind of waterway into the city.[267] It is usually interpreted as some kind of water pipe ("spout, duct" in Jastrow, p. 1291; "canal, pipe" in Mishnaic Hebrew; see BDB, p. 857; compare also "[water]pipe" in Ugaritic text *KTU* 4.370:45), and many modern commentators identify this particular pipe with a vertical shaft known as the Warren's Shaft on the southeastern slope of the City of David.

While some scholars rejected the meaning of *ṣinnôr* as a pipe on the basis of philological arguments by such scholars as Albright and Yadin, Kleven again supported the identification with "some type of water-shaft"[268] and noted Gill's recent geological investigation (1991) of Warren's Shaft, which suggests that "ancient (Jebusite) Jerusalem could be entered from at least two extramural points on the eastern hillside: the cave of Gihon and the upper tunnel of Warren's Shaft Installation."[269] Recently, however, R. Reich[270] on the basis of the large stone structures the Spring Tower and the Pool Tower excavated during 1995-2004, has proposed the theory that there were three water systems in the old "City of David": (1) Hezekiah's tunnel; (2) the Siloam channel; (3) a Middle Bronze Age shaft above the eighteenth century B.C. pool. In view of a newly discovered horizontal tunnel from MB II, Mazar's suggestion that the *ṣinnôr* here is the horizontal tunnel connected to Warren's shaft is being taken seriously again.[271]

Note that the phrase *the 'lame and blind'* (*wᵉʾet-happisḥîm wᵉʾet-haʿiwrîm*; lit. "and the lame and the blind") as a whole serves as the object of the verb *strike down*; the initial *waw* is pleonastic; cf. "those 'lame and blind'" (NIV). David is here echoing the Jebusites' words in v. 6. Hence, it probably does not mean David hates those who are literally lame or blind, but that he is referring to the self-confident Jebusites who attempted to keep him out.

266. See Herbert, *RBDSS*, p. 119.

267. T. Kleven, "The Use of *ṣnr* in Ugaritic and 2 Samuel V 8: Hebrew Usage and Comparative Philology," *VT* 44 (1994) 198.

268. Kleven, "The Use of *ṣnr* in Ugaritic and 2 Samuel V 8," p. 203.

269. *Science* 254 (1991) 1470, cited by Kleven, "The Use of *ṣnr* in Ugaritic and 2 Samuel V 8," p. 203.

270. R. Reich and E. Shukron, "Jerusalem: 2. The Gihon Spring and Eastern Slope of the City of David," *NEAEHL* 5:1801-2.

271. B. Mazar, *The Mountain of the Lord* (Garden City, N.Y.: Doubleday,1975), pp. 168-69, cited by Kleven, "The Use of *ṣnr* in Ugaritic and 2 Samuel V 8," pp. 203 and 198 n. 14.

Therefore (*ʿal-kēn*) is a *speaker-oriented* particle, which provides an explanatory note from the perspective of the speaker, not an editorial comment by a later redactor.[272] It introduces a sentence that is on a level of discourse different from the preceding speech of David, hence followed by *it is said* (lit. "they say").[273]

Here, the expression *the blind and the lame* is used sarcastically (see *it is said*) to refer to the Jebusites in general. "House" can mean either "temple" or "palace."[274] And as there is no biblical prohibition against the blind and the lame entering the temple for worship, the prohibition probably means that the Jebusites may not enter David's *palace* even as his subjects.

McCarter has a very complicated view of vv. 6-8. He interprets v. 6 as "for the blind and the lame had incited them," explaining it as a later gloss to explain v. 8. In v. 8, he translates *wᵉyiggaʿ baṣṣinnôr* as "strike at the windpipe," and interprets it to mean to deliver a fatal blow, as David hated having mutilated people, which was related to the prohibition of men with defects serving as priests (Lev. 21:17-21). But there is no biblical prohibition against the blind and the lame entering the temple for worship. Besides, the verbal phrase is never used with a noun for a body part in the literal sense, "to strike s.o. on (a part of body)"; cf. *haḥayil ʾăšer-nāgaʿ ʾĕlōhîm bᵉlibbām* (1 Sam. 10:26) "warriors whose hearts God had touched" (NRSV). Other suggestions for the meaning of *ṣinnôr* are "with a dagger" (LXX; *en paraksiphidi*), "joint" (Albright), "phallus" (Glück), etc.[275] As the water tunnel interpretation makes sense linguistically and contextually, such interpretations are unnecessary.

9 David called the Jebusite stronghold *the City of David*. Another example of the renaming of a captured city in the ancient Near East is that of the Assyrian king Shalmaneser III (858-824 B.C.) who captured Til-Barsip and renamed it Kār-Shalmaneser.[276]

What David built (*wayyiben dāwīd*) is probably *a wall*, though the MT omits the object by the literary device of *brachylogy* (see below); cf. "He

272. See the commentary on 7:22.

273. Note that this *speaker-oriented* particle (*ʿal-kēn*) is often not followed by a term for the speech-act (i.e., "I say" or "they say"), as in 1 Sam. 5:5; 2 Sam. 7:22; etc.

274. See p. 95 n. 249 (above). A. R. Ceresko, "The Identity of 'the Blind and the Lame' (*ʿiwwēr ûpisséaḥ*) in 2 Samuel 5:8b," *CBQ* 63 (2001) 23-30; J. Schipper, "Reconsidering the Imagery of Disability in 2 Samuel 5:8b," *CBQ* 67 (2005) 422-34.

275. For a detailed survey of the history of interpretation of this term, see Kleven, "The Use of *ṣnr* in Ugaritic and 2 Samuel V 8," pp. 195-97.

276. A. K. Grayson, *Assyrian Rulers of the Early First Millennium BC II (858-745 BC)* (RIM 3; Toronto: University of Toronto Press, 1996), p. 19, line 34. I am grateful to A. Millard for bringing this reference to my attention. He also informed me that although the Assyrian king Sargon II (721-705) founded a new capital and named it Dur-sharrukin, he did not capture the city, for legal deeds show he bought the property.

built up the area" (NIV); "David built the city" (NRSV). McCarter translates "He built a city," following 4QSam[a]. His view that MT has *dwd* ("David") instead of *'yr* ("city") "by graphic confusion"[277] is not convincing. Rather, the threefold repetition of the post-*wayqtl* subject ("David") in vv. 9-10 is a rhetorical device.

Brachylogy is omission of an understood word such as the direct object of a transitive verb.[278] Hebrew often omits "messenger(s)" after "send," as in 2 Sam. 10:5. Similarly in English, though not in all languages, one can say "I am reading," without specifying an object.

The Millo (*millô'*) is literally "the fill," some kind of rampart, perhaps the Jebusite terracing found in the excavations in the "G section" on the eastern slope of the City of David. Solomon later rebuilt it (1 K. 9:15, 24).[279]

10 Some scholars think the long story of David's ascent to the throne of Israel ends with the description *And David became greater and greater*,[280] while others consider 2 Sam. 7 to be the conclusion to the story of David's rise (*hdr).[281] However, it seems unlikely that the story ended either here or with chapter 7.[282] For one thing, a catalogue of David's victories over the neighboring nations follows immediately in ch. 8.

The LORD . . . was with him is the theological leitmotif of Samuel; see 1 Sam. 16:18; 18:12, 14, 28; and 2 Sam. 7:9. For *the LORD God of hosts* (*YHWH 'ĕlōhê ṣᵉbā'ôt*), usually *YHWH ṣᵉbā'ôt*, see the commentary on 1 Sam. 1:3.[283]

2. The Royal Palace (5:11-12)

11 *And Hiram*[284] *the king of Tyre sent messengers to David with cedar logs*[285] *and carpenters and stonemasons,*[286] *and they built a house for David.*

277. McCarter, II, p. 136.

278. See Tsumura, I, Introduction VII.D.

279. See also N. Na'aman, "The Interchange Between Bible and Archaeology: The Case of David's Palace and the Millo," *BAR* 40.1 (Jan/Feb 2014) 57-61; https://www.biblicalarchaeology.org/daily/biblical-sites-places/jerusalem/king-davids-palace-and-the-millo/?mqsc=E3726793.

280. See J. H. Grønbaek, *Die Geschichte vom Aufstieg Davids (1. Sam. 15 - 2. Sam. 5): Tradition und Komposition* (Acta Theologica Danica 10; Copenhagen: Prostant apud Munksgaard, 1971), pp. 29-35.

281. See T. N. D. Mettinger, *King and Messiah: The Civil and Sacral Legitimation of the Israelite Kings* (CB: Old Testament Series 8; Lund: C. W. K. Gleerup, 1976), pp. 41-45.

282. See Tsumura, I, pp. 13-14.

283. Tsumura, I, pp. 109-10.

284. *ḥîrām*; cf. Q. *ḥûrām* (K. *ḥyrm*) in 1 Chr. 14:1.

285. *'ăṣê 'ărāzîm*; so NIV; JPS. See 2 Sam. 7:2.

286. *ḥārāšê 'eben qîr*; cf. *ḥārāšê qîr* (1 Chr. 14:1); also 4QSam[a].

12 *And David knew that the LORD had established him as a king over Israel and that he had exalted his kingdom for the sake of his people Israel.*

In 2006, Eilat Mazar identified the Large Stone Structure at the south of the Temple Mount with the tenth-century remains of King David's palace, built by the Phoenicians. G. Barkai calls Mazar's findings unprecedented. "She has for the first time after more than 150 years of archaeology in Jerusalem discovered a massive public building dating back to the 10th century B.C.E."[287]

11 *Hiram* the *king of Tyre* was a contemporary of David and Solomon and is mentioned in 1 K. 5 as a friend of Solomon who provides the cedars to build the temple, just as he here provides David with cedars to build his house (see "a house of cedars" in 2 Sam. 7:2). Tyre, the Iron Age capital of the Phoenicians, was a trading empire, and it was in its interest to keep the inland trade routes open to its merchants, especially those routes through Israel to Egypt.

According to Josephus, the fourth year of Solomon's reign (1 K. 6:1), when he began to build the temple of the Lord, corresponds to either the eleventh or twelfth year of Hiram's reign. If this is correct, the present event would have occurred during the late part of David's forty-year reign.

The cedars of Lebanon, which have now all but disappeared, were famous throughout the Near East. There are Assyrian reliefs showing men cutting them down and transporting them to Nineveh.

12 The expression *established . . . kingdom* anticipates that of 2 Sam. 7:12. Some claim that since the language is "dynastic," it is a Deuteronomistic addition and postexilic. However, in my view, dynastic language does not necessarily make something a postexilic Deuteronomistic addition.[288]

3. The Royal Family (5:13-16)

13 *And David again took concubines and wives in Jerusalem after he came from Hebron.*
And sons and daughters were born to David again.
14 *These are the names of those who were born to him in Jerusalem:*
Shammua and Shobab,
Nathan and Solomon,[289]

287. For a detailed description of the Large Stone Structure, see Mazar, *The Palace of King David*, pp. 47-65. But see also p. 97 n. 263 above.

288. See Laato, *A Star Is Rising*; also the commentary on 2 Sam. 7.

289. For the name *Solomon*, see the commentary on 12:24. McCarter, II, p. 147 holds that "space considerations" suggest that in 4QSam[a] "his sons" (*bnyw*) appeared before *those*

15 *Ibhar and Elishua and Nepheg and Japhia,*
16 *Elishama and Eliada and Eliphelet.*

13-16 This is a summary statement about David's kingship in Jerusalem (cf. 3:2-5); it does not mean these eleven sons were all born before v. 17. *These are* (*w^{e}’ēlleh*) in v. 14 is a formula introducing a list of names.[290] The birth of *Solomon* is mentioned in 12:24. None of the other sons are mentioned in the narratives, but according to 1 Chr. 3:5, the first four were children of Bathsheba. The parallel passages 1 Chr. 3:5-8 and 14:4-7 list two more sons between Elishua and Nepheg ("Eliphelet" and "Nogah") for a total of thirteen sons. Comparison with 4QSam^{a} suggests that the two names might have been omitted in the Samuel MT.[291] *Nathan* was an ancestor of Jesus (Luke 3:31; cf. Matt. 1:6).

13 The MT *in Jerusalem* (*mîrûšālaim;* cf. *bîrûšālaim* in 1 Chr. 14:3) has been translated as "from Jerusalem" (NASB, McCarter) like *eks Ierousalēm* (LXX), which is indeed the normal reading. However, it would seem that here is a phonetic spelling derived from the normal *bîrûšālaim* ("in Jerusalem") as the result of a progressive total assimilation at a word boundary:[292] thus,

w^{e}nāšîm bîrûšālaim → w^{e}nāšîm mîrûšālaim

If it meant "from Jerusalem," the Hebrew form *min-y^{e}rûšālaim* or a variant form *mērûšālaim* would be expected. So, if it is correct, the MT is not a copyist's error, that is, an error that arose in the process of scribal practice, but simply a phonetic variant that already existed at the time of the LXX.[293]

15-16 *Elishua* (*’ĕlîšûa‘*) and *Eliada* (*’elyādā‘*) are the variant forms of "Elishama" (*’ĕlîšāmā‘*) in 1 Chr. 3:6 and "Beeliada" (*b^{e}‘elyādā‘*) in 1 Chr. 14:7. While the former variation can be explained phonetically, i.e., *am – uw*, both consonants being bilabial, the latter is a variant designation of deity, i.e., "god" (*’ēl*) for "master" (*b^{e}‘el*), perhaps related to the aversion to the word *ba‘al* seen also elsewhere in Samuel; see commentary on 2:8.

---

who were born (*hayyillōdîm*). However, based on the calculation of the reconstructed width, Herbert rejects McCarter's reconstruction as incorrect. See Herbert, *RBDSS*, p. 120.

290. See D. T. Tsumura, "List and Narrative in I Samuel 6, 17-18a in the Light of Ugaritic Economic Texts," *ZAW* 113 (2001) 353-69.

291. The space seems to allow to reconstruct these two names in the lacuna of 4QSam^{a}: see Herbert, *RBDSS*, p. 120; also McCarter, II, p. 148.

292. See Tsumura, "Scribal Errors or Phonetic Spellings?" 401.

293. Tsumura, "Textual Corruptions, or Linguistic Phenomena?," p. 137.

4. Victories over the Philistines (5:17-25)

a. David's First Victory (5:17-21)

17 *And the Philistines heard that David had been anointed*[294] *as a king over Israel.*

And all the Philistines came up to seek David.
And David heard and went down to the stronghold.
18 *As for the Philistines, they came and spread out in the Valley of Rephaim.*
19 *And David inquired of the LORD,*
"Shall I go up against the Philistines?
Will you give them into my hand?"
And the LORD said to David,
"Go up!
For I shall indeed give the Philistines into your hand."
20 *And David came to Baal-perazim.*
And David defeated them there and said,
"The LORD has broken out upon my enemies before me
like an outburst of water."
Therefore he called the name of that place Baal-perazim.
21 *And they abandoned their idols there.*
And David and his men carried them off.

17-21 Until now the Philistines may have considered that David was still a vassal to some extent (1 Sam. 27); at least they must have been happy about his struggle with Ishbosheth. However, when David becomes king over *Israel,* that is, both Israel and Judah, and even captures Jerusalem, they realize he is a threat.

17 *Went down to the stronghold* (*hammᵉṣûdāh*). This is sometimes explained to refer to a stronghold in the direction of the Philistine country, for one usually "goes up" to Zion. Hence some scholars hold that this *stronghold* may be that of Adullam (see 1 Sam. 22:1; 2 Sam. 23:13) and David *went down* from Hebron where he was anointed (5:3); and from there was told to "go up" to the Valley of Rephaim in v. 19.[295] However, the fact that the Philistines came to the Valley of Rephaim, the valley leading toward Jerusalem from the southwest, surely implies David was in Jerusalem, not in Hebron.

Garsiel convincingly argues that "the Philistines would not have concentrated such extensive forces merely to engage in punitive expeditions and lay fields waste."[296] Certainly, David's going down to *the stronghold* of Adullam

294. Lit. "they had anointed David"; 3 m.pl. impersonal usage for a passive meaning.
295. McCarter, II, p. 153; R. P. Gordon, p. 229.
296. See M. Garsiel, "David's Warfare Against the Philistines in the Vicinity of Je-

would not make sense when the Philistines *came up* to kill him. The expression *David . . . went down to the stronghold* would make sense topographically if the stronghold refers to the original Jebusite citadel in Jerusalem, which is surrounded by the hills. David must have been at some higher point toward the top of a hill that was outside of *the stronghold*.[297]

18 *And they spread out* (cf. "raided" *wayyipšᵉṭû* in 1 Chr. 14:9). The Philistines "spread out" also in Judg. 15:9 in order to capture Samson. The Philistines came up to this valley, probably by way of the Valley of Sorek, in order to cut the lines of communication between David's newly united dominions.[298]

20 "Baal" in *Baal-perazim* (*Ba'al-pᵉrāṣîm*) could be a common noun meaning "lord," which seems how it is interpreted here; see on 2 Sam. 2:8. McCarter explains it as a sanctuary on or near Mount Perazim (Isa. 28:21). If David is marching north from Adullam, as McCarter holds, the location would be on "the southern or western border" of the Valley of Rephaim.[299] However, if the stronghold is that of Zion as suggested above, David would *go up* (v. 19) to the higher location of Baal-perazim, which Garsiel identifies with Mount Abu Tor, near the modern railway station in Jerusalem.[300]

The verbal root *prṣ in the phrase *kᵉpereṣ māyim* (*like an outburst of water*; so McCarter) frequently refers to breaking through a wall; e.g., 2 K. 14:13; also Amos 4:3; Neh. 4:3; 6:1. The expression was probably an old metaphor; it must have been idiomatic even before David; thus, the war is here described by a language of flood; just as a flood can be described by the language of war;[301] see also Nah. 1:8.[302]

21 This verse is a reversal of 1 Sam. 4:11, where the Philistines carried off the ark. However, the fate of these idols is very different from that of the ark in 1 Sam. 4-6. According to 1 Chr. 14:12 David had the idols burnt. *Their idols* (*'ăṣabbêhem*) here should be compared with "their gods" (*'ĕlōhêhem*) in the Chronicles passage; also LXX. Carrying off the gods of a defeated enemy was normal; see the commentary on 1 Sam. 5:1.[303]

---

rusalem (2 Sam 5,17-25; 1 Chron 14,8-16)," in *Studies in Historical Geography and Biblical Historiography Presented to Zecharia Kallai*, ed. G. Galil and M. Weinfeld (VTS 81; Leiden: E. J. Brill, 2000), pp. 156-57.

297. However, 2 Sam. 23:13 refers to the cave of Adullam where David was. So, it is most likely that the term "stronghold" in that passage (v. 14) refers to the cave of Adullam or the place near it, not the stronghold of Jerusalem, namely, Zion.

298. Garsiel, "David's Warfare Against the Philistines," p. 154. For the historical geography, see *SB*, p. 160.

299. McCarter, II, p. 154.

300. Garsiel, "David's Warfare Against the Philistines," p. 160.

301. See Tsumura, *Creation and Destruction*, pp. 182-95.

302. D. T. Tsumura, "Janus Parallelism in Nah 1:8," *JBL* 102 (1983) 109-111.

303. Tsumura, I, p. 203.

b. David's Second Victory (5:22-25)

22 *Again the Philistines came up and spread out in the Valley of Rephaim.*
23 *And David inquired of the LORD and he said,*
"You shall not go up.
Go around to their back
and come to them in front of balsam-trees.[304]
24 *When you hear the sound of marching*[305]
in the tops of the balsam-trees,
then act with decision,[306]
for then the LORD will have gone out[307] *before you*
to strike the camp of the Philistines."
25 *And David did so according as the LORD commanded him and defeated*
the Philistines from Geba up to Gezer.

22-25 It may be that the *sound of marching* in the trees frightened the Philistines (cf. 2 K. 7:6-7). Another possibility is that David was able to use the sound as cover for his attack.[308] By this victory, David drove the Philistines out of the central hill country area. For Geba, see the commentary on 1 Sam. 13:16.[309]

The expulsion of the Philistines *up to Gezer* (2 Sam. 5:25) made it possible for David to have access to the ark of the Lord in the Gibeonite city of Kiriath-jearim, where it was currently residing; see 1 Sam. 7:1.

22 Divine inquiry was often made in two stages; see the commentary on 2 Sam. 2:1. Note the repetition of phrases in vv. 17-21 and in vv. 22-25.

McCarter asserts the antiquity of this account of a second battle; others think it is unauthentic or a variation on vv. 17-21. But Tidwell has demonstrated

304. Ancient versions suggest that *balsam-tree* (*b^{e}kāʾîm*) refers to some kind of tree; "*bakaʾ*-shrubs" (*HALOT*, p. 129).

305. McCarter alters the MT *ṣ^{e}ʿārāh* (*marching*) to *sʿrh* "wind" on the basis of LXX^{LMN}. He also takes MT *b^{e}rāʾšê* (*in the tops of*) as "a corruption" of *bʾšry* / *mʾšry* "in /from the asherahs," as supported by LXX "in/from the (sacred) groves," and proposes that the sound of the wind in these "asherahs," wooden cult objects, is a sign of Yahweh's presence. However, his emendation "is gratuitous and does not yield good sense in the context," as Emerton says; see J. Emerton, review of *II Samuel*, by P. K. McCarter, *VT* 35 (1985) 254. Also the LXX may mean "in the groves of the balsam trees," similar to the MT's *in the tops of the balsam-trees*, rather than McCarter's geographical interpretation: "in the asherahs of Bachaim" (McCarter, II, pp. 155-57).

306. See BDB: "cut, sharpen, decide."

307. Pf.; an example of the use of past tenses for future acts; see T. L. Fenton, "The Hebrew 'Tenses' in the Light of Ugaritic," in *Proceedings of the Fifth World Congress of Jewish Studies, Held in 1969*, vol. 4 (Jerusalem: World Union of Jewish Studies, 1973), p. 37.

308. I would like to thank my wife Susan for this suggestion.

309. Tsumura, I, p. 350.

that "the similarity in form is simply a reflection of the conventionalized nature of battle reports."[310] This may be literary "repetition" or "a build-up and climax"[311] based on two historical incidents that happened one after another within a short period. Certainly in a strategic location more than one battle can occur.

25 *Geba* (*geba'*); so NRSV; JPS; NASB; cf. "Gibeon" (NIV; McCarter), based on LXX and 1 Chr. 14:16. On the "Gibeah" – "Geba" – "Gibeon" identification, see the comments on 1 Sam. 9:2, 10:10 and 13:2.[312]

D. ZION, THE PLACE OF WORSHIP (6:1-23)

Jerusalem has become the political capital of the united Israel; now it becomes the religious center also. David brings the ark of the Lord of Hosts to Jerusalem from Baale-judah (that is, Kiriath Jearim), where it has been most of the time since the Philistines returned it in 1 Sam. 6, perhaps about twenty years ago.[313] Its arrival in Jerusalem is a climactic moment in the religious history of the Israelites, the covenant people. From now on the Lord would place his Name in Jerusalem.

For the Israelite people during the time of wandering in the wilderness the ark had been a symbol of presence of the Lord, especially of his presence in battle.

310. N. L. Tidwell, "The Philistine Incursions into the Valley of Rephaim (2 Sam. V 17ff.)," in Emerton, *Studies in the Historical Books of the Old Testament*, pp. 193-95, 206. For various views on the two parts, see McCarter, II, p. 155.

311. C. H. Gordon, "Build-up and Climax," in Y. Avishur and J. Blau (eds.), *Studies in Bible and the Ancient Near East Presented to Samuel E. Loewenstamm* (Jerusalem: E. Rubinstein, 1978), pp. 29-34.

312. Tsumura, I, pp. 263, 292, 334-35.

313. L. Rost and his followers take all or parts of 2 Sam. 6 as belonging to an originally independent "Ark Narrative" consisting generally of 1 Sam. 4:1b-7:1 + 2 Sam. 6. See A. F. Campbell, *The Ark Narrative (1 Sam 4-6; 2 Sam 6): A Form-Critical and Traditio-Historical Study* (SBLDS 16; Missoula, Mont.: Scholars Press, 1975), pp. 126-43, 169-74, and passim. However, others, as Schunck, Schicklberger, and Miller and Roberts, say 2 Sam. 6 must have had a different origin from the 1 Samuel ark narrative, in particular because of many differences in names (e.g., Kiriath-jearim vs. Baalah; Eleazar vs. Uzzah), style, and theme. See Tsumura, I, pp. 12-13; McCarter, II, pp. 182-84.

For recent studies of the ark narrative in 1 Chr. 13-16, see T. C. Eskenazi, "A Literary Approach to Chronicler's Ark Narrative in 1 Chronicles 13-16," in *Fortunate the Eyes That See: Essays in Honor of David Noel Freedman in Celebration of His Seventieth Birthday*, ed. A. B. Beck et al. (Grand Rapids: Eerdmans, 1995), pp. 258-74; J. W. Wright, "The Founding Father: The Structure of the Chronicler's David Narrative," *JBL* 117 (1998) 45-59; R. Rezetko, *Source and Revision in the Narratives of David's Transfer of the Ark: Text, Language and Story in 2 Samuel 6 and 1 Chronicles 13, 15-16* (LHBOTS 470; New York: T. & T. Clark, 2007).

> And whenever the ark set out, Moses said, "Arise, O LORD, and let your enemies be scattered, and let those who hate you flee before you."
>
> And when it rested, he said, "Return, O LORD, to the ten thousand thousands of Israel." (Num. 10:35-36)

It is mentioned several times in connection with battle (Num. 14:44; Josh. 6:4; 1 Sam. 4:3; 14:18). However, there is no mention of it in the account of David's international victories in 2 Sam. 8, though it does seem to have been taken on the campaign against Rabbah (11:1). David clearly rejected using the ark as a talisman against Absalom (15:25) as the Israelites apparently did against the Philistines (1 Sam. 4). The narrator, so David himself, seems to treat the ark as being not so much for a military purpose as for a religious purpose.

This section is placed between David's victories over the Philistines (2 Sam. 5:17-25) and Nathan's oracle to David (7:1-17). Only after his victories over the Philistines could David bring the ark to his royal city. The ark's arrival in Jerusalem can be seen as the fulfillment of statements like Deut. 12:5, 11. It had been taken from Shiloh into battle against the Philistines by the Shilonite priesthood, which had been rejected by the Lord (1 Sam. 2-5). The ark was captured by the Philistines, and eventually returned to Kiriath-jearim (chs. 5-6).

Certainly, the ark as the symbol of the holy presence of God would give the newly conquered royal city legitimacy as the holy city of the country, the national center for worship of the national god Yahweh. Ever since Sumerian times, a royal city, the very center of the realm, was never complete as such until the national temple was constructed. In this sense, bringing the holy ark into Jerusalem was a crucial event in the history of the monarchy in Israel.

Psalm 132 refers to David's earnest desire to transfer the ark from Ephrathah,[314] from "the fields of Jaar" (v. 6) into the "dwelling place" (v. 5), namely the "resting place" (v. 8) for the Lord in the royal city in order to make it the holy city (2 Sam. 6). "The fields of Jaar" most probably refers to Kiriath-jearim, i.e., Baalah of Judah.[315] One need not distinguish between "dwelling place" (Ps. 132:7: *miškᵉnôt*) and "resting place" (v. 8: *mᵉnûḥāh*) as if the former refers to the tabernacle and the latter to the temple (of Solomon). In this psalm vv. 11-12, the Lord's *covenant* with David is mentioned together with the key words such as "son" (v. 12; also, v. 11: lit. "your fruit

314. Ephrathah does not refer here to Bethlehem, the home of David as in Mic. 5:1. The word *ya'ar* in this verse refers to Kiriath-jearim.

315. For a detailed discussion on the relationship between Ps. 132 and 2 Sam. 6, see McCarter, II, pp. 176-78, and most recently, T. Booij, "Psalm 132: Zion's Well-Being," *Bib* 90 (2009) 75-83.

of the womb") and "throne," as in Ps. 89 ("heir" and "throne").[316] Thus, Ps. 132 refers to the election of David and of Zion, the events that are treated in chs. 6 and 7.

> 1 Remember, O Lord, in David's favor,
> all the hardships he endured,
> 2 how he swore to the Lord
> and vowed to the Mighty One of Jacob,
> 3 "I will not enter my house
> or get into my bed,
> 4 I will not give sleep to my eyes
> or slumber to my eyelids,
> 5 until I find a place for the Lord,
> a dwelling place for the Mighty One of Jacob."
>
> 6 Behold, we heard of it in Ephrathah;
> we found it in the fields of Jaar.
>
> 7 "Let us go to his dwelling place;
> let us worship at his footstool!"
>
> 8 Arise, O Lord, and go to your resting place,
> you and the ark of your might.
> 9 Let your priests be clothed with righteousness,
> and let your saints shout for joy.
> 10 For the sake of your servant David,
> do not turn away the face of your anointed one.
>
> 11 The Lord swore to David a sure oath
> from which he will not turn back:
> "One of the sons of your body
> I will set on your throne.
> 12 If your sons keep my covenant
> and my testimonies that I shall teach them,
> their sons also forever
> shall sit on your throne."
>
> 13 For the Lord has chosen Zion;
> he has desired it for his dwelling place:
> 14 "This is my resting place forever;

316. See the commentary on ch. 7.

here I will dwell, for I have desired it.
15 I will abundantly bless her provisions;
I will satisfy her poor with bread.
16 Her priests I will clothe with salvation,
and her saints will shout for joy.
17 There I will make a horn to sprout for David;
I have prepared a lamp for my anointed.
18 His enemies I will clothe with shame,
but on him his crown will shine."

1. Transfer of the Ark to Jerusalem (6:1-19)

The ark of the Lord has remained at Kiriath-jearim (see 1 Sam. 7:2) up until now, though there is mention of its being in the battle camp at the time of the Battle of Michmash (1 Sam. 14:18), and it was possibly at Nob for at least a while; see 1 Sam. 21:1; 22:19.[317] Now David proposes to bring the ark from *Baalah of Judah*, which was earlier called Kiriath-jearim (see 1 Chr. 13:6), into his royal city of Jerusalem. The procession is an elaborate one, including at least two priests and a throng of jubilant people and musicians (2 Sam. 6:5). However, as the procession draws near to Jerusalem, *Uzzah*, one of the officiating priests, is struck down by the Lord *for his irreverence* (v. 7).

Why does the Lord act so severely toward Uzzah and hence to David? Both of them had good intentions, but by bringing it on a cart, however new, like the Philistines who returned the ark to Israel (see 1 Sam. 6:7), they transgressed God's commandment, which required the Levites to carry the ark of God by poles (Exod. 25:14).

David, being afraid of the Lord, moves the ark of God to the house of Obed-edom for three months. Then, he resumes the procession with rejoicing and dancing accompanied by numerous sacrifices (2 Sam. 6:12-15). Finally the ark of the Lord is brought into the tent that David has prepared for it in Jerusalem.[318]

317. See Tsumura, I, p. 546.

318. See C. L. Seow, *Myth, Drama, and the Politics of David's Dance* (HSM 44; Atlanta: Scholars Press, 1989); K. van der Toorn and C. Houtman, "David and the Ark," *JBL* 113 (1994) 209-31; D. P. Wright, "Music and Dance in 2 Samuel 6," *JBL* 121 (2002) 201-25.

EXCURSUS: THE ORIGIN OF THE CULTIC PROCESSION IN 2 SAMUEL 6

The details of this passage presumably reflect ritual practices of the Jerusalem cult of the monarchical period — but which practices? There are several hypotheses:[319]

(1) It is based on an annual temple rite such as "the new year festival, the enthronement festival of Yahweh" (Mowinckel), "the festival which commemorated purely historical events, viz. the choice of Zion and election of David" (Kraus) or "a Canaanite coronation rite" (Porter).

(2) It is based on a ritual for transferring the ark, which has its parallel in the historical accounts in the annals of Assyrian kings (e.g., Esarhaddon and Assurbanipal), such as the one that refers to the return of Marduk to his city and temple after eleven years of exile in Assur.[320] However, here the ark is not returned to Shiloh, but taken to a new location.

(3) It is based on a ritual for bringing a god into a new royal city, as we see in the historical accounts of the introduction of the national god Assur to the new royal cities of Assyrian kings (e.g., Assurnasirpal II, Sargon II, Sennnacherib, and Esarhaddon).

The third view is the most reasonable for explaining the origin of the cultic procession described in this chapter. Like those Assyrian kings, David played the key role as the patron of the Jerusalem cult in introducing Yahweh to the new royal city.

a. From the House of Abinadab (6:1-5)

1 *And David again gathered*[321] *all the select men of Israel,*[322] *thirty*[323] *thousand.*

2 *And David arose and went with all the people who were with him to Baalah of Judah to bring up from there the ark of God, the name of which is called by the very name of the* LORD *of Hosts, who sits on the cherubim.*

319. See McCarter, II, pp. 178-82 for a detailed analysis of these hypotheses.

320. See P. D. Miller and J. J. M. Roberts, *The Hand of the Lord: A Reassessment of the "Ark Narrative" of 1 Samuel* (JHNES; Baltimore: Johns Hopkins University Press, 1977), pp. 16-17.

321. *wayyōsep* is probably a *phonetic spelling* of the expected form *wayye'ĕsōp* (2 Sam. 10:17, 12:29), though it is also possible to take it like other I-*yod* verbs; see the commentary on 1 Sam. 15:6 (see Tsumura, "Scribal Errors or Phonetic Spellings?," pp. 390-411; Tsumura, I, p. 392 n. 27).

322. *bᵉyiśrā'ēl*; lit. "in" / "from" (cf. LXX).

323. Cf. "seventy" in LXX.

3 *And they loaded the ark of God on a new cart and transported it from the house of Abinadab, which was on the hill. Uzzah and Ahio, the sons of Abinadab, were leading the new cart.*[324]

4 *As they transported it from the house of Abinadab, which was on the hill,*[325] *with the ark of God, Ahio was walking before the ark.*

5 *David and all the house of Israel were celebrating before the LORD with all the branches of fir trees, and with lyres, harps, tambours, sistrums, and cymbals.*

1-2 For *the ark* of the Lord, see the commentary on 1 Sam. 4:3.[326]

In 1 Sam. 7:1, the name of the city where the ark was kept is given as Kiriath-jearim; the fact that in David's time the name was *Baalah of Judah* suggests that 1 Sam. 4:1–7:2 belongs to a tradition from before David's time.

1 The term *selected men* (*bāḥur*) may be a technical term for "selected warriors," i.e., men chosen for warfare; see Judg. 20:15, 16, 34; 1 Sam. 26:2; also see 1 Sam. 24:2; 2 Sam. 10:9.

The Hebrew *'elep* can mean either "thousand" or the military unit *'elep*. See the commentary on 1 Sam. 4:2 and 6:19.[327]

2 *Baalah of Judah* (so NIV) is translated variously: e.g., "Baale-judah" (RSV; NASB); "Baalim of Judah" (JPS); cf. 4QSam[a] *b'lh hy' qr[yt y'rym 'šr] lYHWH.*[328] McCarter thinks that MT *ba'ălê y[e]hûdāh* is "probably a corrupt remnant of a reading like that of 4QSam[a]" and translates simply "Baalah," omitting "of Judah." But the MT is possibly either a *phonetic spelling* of "Baalah of Judah":

ba'ălāh y[e]hûdāh → ba'ălāy[e]hûdāh → ba'ălayhûdāh → ba'ălêhûdāh

or a form based on an older name *ba'lay, which experienced a *monothongization* of the diphthong: *ba'lay → *ba'ălê*.

ba'lay y[e]hûdāh → ba'ălay y[e]hûdāh → ba'ălê y[e]hûdāh

324. MT *hā'ăgālāh ḥădāšāh*, without article *ha-* for the adjective, may be a *sandhi* spelling as a result of the loss of an intervocalic *h*: *hā'ăgālāh ḥădāšāh ← hā'ăgālāhaḥădāšāh ← hā'ăgālāh haḥădāšāh*. See Tsumura, "Vowel *sandhi* in Biblical Hebrew," pp. 575-88.

325. The section *new. . . . As they transported it from the house of Abinadab, which was on the hill* (*ḥădāšāh . . . wayyiśśā'ūhû mibbêt 'ăbînādāb 'ăšer baggib'āh*) is lacking in the LXX and 4QSam[a]; see Herbert, *RBDSS*, p. 123.

326. Tsumura, I, pp. 190-92.

327. Tsumura, I, pp. 189-90, 226-27.

328. See Herbert, *RBDSS*, p. 254 [column 36]; but, cf. p. 121.

This was the later name of Kiriath-jearim; see "to Baalah [*baʿălātāh*], that is, to Kiriath-jearim, which belongs to Judah" (1 Chr. 13:6); also Josh. 15:9. For Kiriath-jearim, see the commentary on 1 Sam. 6:21.[329]

The ark of God (*'ărôn hā'ĕlōhîm*) is a visible sign of the presence of the Lord. See the commentary on 1 Sam. 3:3.[330] 1 Samuel 7:2 says that the ark was at Kiriath-jearim for twenty years.

The ark of God *is called by the name* (*niqrā' šēm . . . ʿālâw*); lit. "to which the name is called." See the commentary on 1 Sam. 1:3. The phrase *the LORD of Hosts who sits on the cherubim* is identical to that in 1 Sam. 4:4. This reminds one of the description of the ark in Exod. 25:18-20. For the phrase "the LORD of Hosts," see on 1 Sam. 1:3.[331]

3-4 They loaded (*rkb [Hi.]) the ark onto a *new cart*, that is, a ritually clean cart, as the Philistines did (1 Sam. 6:7). However, the Lord had commanded his people that it should be carried by the Levites; see Exod. 25:14-15; Num. 4:15; 7:9; Deut. 10:8; 31:9, 25; also Josh. 3:15 and 1 Chr. 15:2.

3 In Arad Inscription 1:6-7, *trkb* (Hi.) means not simply "to load" but "to transport" or "to send" objects on a wagon;[332] also "to load meal on to a donkey."[333] See the commentary on 1 Sam. 25:42.[334]

Abinadab was the father of the priests Uzzah and Ahio as well as Eleazar; see 1 Sam. 7:1. *Uzzah* (*ʿuzzā'*) and *Ahio* were probably brothers of *Eliazar* (*'elʿāzār*) in 7:1, though Uzzah and Eliazar may have been the same person, since it is phonetically possible that "Uzzah" (*ʿz*), a hypocoristicon of a theophoric name *ʿuzzî'ēl*, is a variation of "Eliazar" (*'lʿzr*), similar to the variants Uzziel (*ʿuzzî'ēl*) in 1 Chr. 25:4 and Azarel (*ʿăzar'ēl*) in 25:18 or King Uzziah (*ʿuzzîyāhû*; 2 K. 15:32-34; 2 Chr. 26:1) and Azariah (*ʿăzaryāh*; 2 K. 15:1). Note that a syllable- or word-final consonant */r/* may be dropped phonetically as in the cases of Ugaritic DN *kṯ* (*KTU* 1.3:VI:18) for *kṯr* and *ʿqš* (1.100:33-34) for *ʿqšr*.[335]

4 The order in which the names Uzzah and Ahio appear is that of the ABBA pattern: namely, "Uzzah and Ahio" (3) – "Ahio" (4) – "Uzzah" (6). There is no need to reconstruct "Uzza walking alongside the ark," as McCarter posits on the basis of LXX^L, before "and Ahio."[336]

5 The phrase *the house of Israel* here refers to all the tribes of Israel; it appears for the first time in Samuel in 1 Sam. 7:2. *Celebrating* (*m^eśaḥăqîm*)

329. Tsumura, I, p 228.
330. Tsumura, I, pp. 175-76.
331. Tsumura, I, pp. 109-10.
332. Y. Aharoni, *AI*, p. 13.
333. See *HALOT*, pp. 1230ff.
334. Tsumura, I, p. 594.
335. Tsumura, "'Misspellings' in Cuneiform Alphabetic Texts from Ugarit," pp. 143-53.
336. McCarter, II, p. 163.

or "making merry"; see 1 Sam. 18:7; cf. "dancing" (NRSV); "danced" (JPS), based on *paizontes* (LXX).

The phrase *before the LORD* (*lipnê YHWH*), as in Exod. 28:29; 2 Sam. 6:14; etc., means before the ark, which represents God's presence with his people. That it was not just an arbitrary symbol of his presence, but something that was not to be treated lightly is shown both in 1 Sam. 4:1-7:2 and in this passage. Note that *before the LORD* is a key phrase in Leviticus, referring to man's approach to the holy presence of God.

The phrase *with all the branches of fir trees* (*b*[e]*kōl ʿăṣê b*[e]*rôšîm*) has been interpreted in various ways.

(1) Traditionally, the phrase has been explained as referring to musical instruments made of fir wood. However, its relationship with the other instruments in v. 5b is not clear.
(2) Based on the archaeological evidence, it has been interpreted as referring to clappers made of fir wood.[337] But with this interpretation the phrase *b*[e]*kōl* "with/in all" does not make much sense.
(3) Some have emended the MT to *bkl ʿz wbšyrym*,[338] as "with all their might and with songs," following the reading of 1 Chr. 13:8, LXX, and 4QSam[a];[339] e.g., "with all their might, with songs" (NRSV; also NIV); "with all their might to the sound of singing" (REB); "with all their might, singing to the accompaniment of" (NJB).
(4) McCarter translates as "with sonorous instruments and songs," reading *bkly ʿz* (lit. "with instruments of might") *wbšyrym*; he also read *bkl ʿz* (v. 14) as *bkly ʿz*.[340]
(5) Seow draws our attention to an Akkadian cognate *burāšu* "crushed wood" and connects it with "wood shavings used in rituals, particularly in connection with the *akītu* festival."[341]

However, it may be that *ʿăṣê* here refers to *branches* rather than "trees," since it sometimes refers to a vine; see *dm ʿṣ*, "wine" (lit. "blood of the vine"), in Ugaritic. Certainly, the branches of the aromatic juniper trees would be most fitting in the context. One might compare these branches with those used in celebrating the king's procession into his royal city described in Matt. 21:8. Certainly, for David and the Israelite people, the

337. Wright, "Music and Dance in 2 Samuel 6," p. 205.

338. Wright, "Music and Dance in 2 Samuel 6," pp. 205-6.

339. *b*]*kwl ʿz* [*w*]*bšyrym*; see DJD 17, pp. 124 and 126.

340. McCarter, II, pp. 163-64.

341. Seow, *Myth, Drama, and the Politics of David's Dance*, p. 97 n. 51. See *CAD*, B, pp. 327-28.

procession of the ark into Jerusalem was the procession of the real king into his holy city.

Music is part of worship in most societies, and it was an important part of Israelite worship. The prophets in 1 Sam. 10:5 were accompanied by harp, tambourine, flute, and lyre. David sings God's praises in 2 Sam. 22:50, and in his old age he organized musicians to praise the Lord in the temple (1 Chr. 23:1-5). The psalms were composed to be sung, and there are many references to using instruments in worship, as in Pss. 71:22; 92 (heading); 149:1; and 150.

The lyre and the harp were the most common stringed instruments, and David was a skilled lyrist; see 1 Sam. 16:18. For *harp, tambourine, pipe, and lyre*, see the commentary on 1 Sam. 10:5.[342] The term *sistrums* (*mᵉnaʿanʿîm*) is a *hapax legomenon*. The Hebrew root *nwʿ "to shake" implies that this instrument has a "rapidly repeated movement."[343] While "castanets" (ESV) is a reasonable guess, it might also be a "sistrum," an instrument consisting of metal rings or disks shaken on rods. Mitchell follows Latin Vulg. *sistra*. The word for *cymbals* (*ṣelṣelîm*) has the variant form *mᵉṣiltayim* (= Ug. *mṣltm*) in 1 Chr. 13:8; 15:28. There were various types of *cymbals* in the ancient Near East. Some were several inches in diameter; some were hit while being held upright, like modern orchestral cymbals; in other cases, the two cymbals of the pair were held horizontally with rods, one above the other.

b. Perez-uzzah (6:6-11)

6 *And they came up to the threshing floor of Nacon.*[344]

And Uzzah reached out his hand to the ark of God and took hold of it, for the oxen almost let it fall.[345]

7 *And the anger of the* LORD *burned against Uzzah.*

And God struck him down on the spot[346] *for his irreverence, and he died there by*[347] *the ark of God.*

342. For the musical instruments of the OT, see T. C. Mitchell, "The Music of the Old Testament Reconsidered," *PEQ* (1992) 124-43.

343. Mitchell, "The Music of the Old Testament Reconsidered," p. 131.

344. MT *nākôn*: a place-name "Nacon" or a Ni. ptc. "certain." McCarter translates "Nodan," based on 4QSamᵃ, which he reads *nwdn*; see McCarter, II, p. 164. He thinks that LXXᴮ's *nōdab* and *kydn* (1 Chr. 13:9) is a corruption of the original *nōdan*. However, Herbert convincingly reads it as *nwrn* (*RBDSS*, p. 124). Thus, 4QSamᵃ "deviates from all witness."

345. 3 m.pl., with a collective singular noun, *habbāqār* "the oxen" as the subject.

346. So JPS; lit. "there."

347. Hebrew *ʿim* ; lit. "with."

8 *And David was angry because the LORD had burst forth with an outburst upon Uzzah, and that place is called*[348] *Perez-uzzah to this day.*

9 *And David was afraid of the LORD that day and said,*

"How can the ark of the LORD come to me?"

10 *David was unwilling to move the ark of the LORD toward himself,*[349] *toward the City of David.*

And David took it aside to the house of Obed-edom the Gittite.

11 *And the ark of the LORD stayed at the house of Obed-edom the Gittite for three months.*

And the LORD blessed Obed-edom and all his household.

6-11 The death of Uzzah resembles the outbreak against Beth-shemesh in 1 Sam. 6:19. The ark was not to be touched. Even though Uzzah's motive was clearly to prevent desecration, his fault was brought on by the earlier mistake in the mode of transport (see on vv. 3-4). In 1 Chr. 15:13 David states the outbreak was because the Levites did not carry the ark.

6-7 Tur-Sinai argues that the stories in 1 Sam. 6:19 and the present passage are "two versions of a single etiological legend." But, as McCarter holds, they could both be the "instances of the awesome power of Yahweh's ark." Both teach that "the transference of the ark from one place to another . . . was not a task to be taken lightly."[350]

6 The phrase *reached out his hand* is literally "sent," without any object. This is a phenomenon of *brachylogy*[351] of "hand," rather than due to the "haplography" (McCarter). Uzzah was probably following the ark, since Ahio was *walking before the ark* (v. 4).

7 The expression *for his irreverence* (*'al-haššal*) is translated variously: e.g., "because of his irreverent act" (NIV); "for his indiscretion" (JPS); cf. "because he reached out his hand to the ark" (NRSV).[352] Even a careless handling of the holy object could be a cause of the divine anger, for the priests were supposed to know how to transport the ark of God.

8-9 *David was angry* — lit. [nose][353] became hot for David — means David "became ill-humoured (in the face of Yahweh)" (see *HALOT*) as of Samuel in 1 Sam. 15:11. See "David was distressed" (JPS); "was vexed" (REB).

348. Hebrew *wayyiqrā'*, impersonal passive: "one called," i.e., "(it) is called." One may also take it as "David called."

349. Lit. "to him." Cf. "to be with him in the City of David" (NIV); "to his place in the City of David" (JPS); "into his care" (NRSV); "into the city of David with him" (NASB).

350. McCarter, II, pp. 169-70.

351. See Tsumura, I, pp. 64-65.

352. The meaning of the term is uncertain; see BDB, p. 1016; *HALOT*, p. 1502.

353. "Nose" is omitted in this idiom by *brachylogy*; see Tsumura, I, pp. 64-65.

While *the anger of the LORD* (v. 7) burned against Uzzah himself, David's anger was toward the situation in which the Lord's *anger* burned against Uzzah. Then, David *was afraid of the LORD* (v. 9), i.e., he literally feared the Lord for his awesomeness and fearfulness.

For the formula *to this day*, see the commentary on 1 Sam. 8:8.[354] The expression does not automatically make any particular verse Deuteronomistic, since the same expression occurs in 6:18b, which seems to be definitely pre-Davidic, and in 1 Sam. 27:6, which seems to have been written early in the divided monarchy.

10-11 Since David was unwilling to transfer the dangerous ark to his capital, he moved it to the house of *Obed-edom* (*ʿōbēd-ʾĕdôm*), who was a *Gittite*, a foreigner from Philistine Gath, where David had served as a mercenary (1 Sam. 27-30).

There are three theories as to the origin of this Gittite: (1) He may have been a follower of David from that time, just as Ittai and the six hundred Gittites (2 Sam. 15:18-22) may have been. (2) Later, in 1 Chr. 15 he is described as a Levite musician (v. 21) and doorkeeper (vv. 18, 24; also 26:15). His descendants are listed in 26:4-8. However, McCarter doubts that Obed-edom was a Levite, for his name contains a non-Yahwistic element; he analyzes the name as "servant of (the deity) Edom," following Albright.[355] (3) It is also possible that he was from another Gath, such as Gath-rimmon (Josh. 21:24-25). The first theory may be preferable to the other two.

c. From the House of Obed-edom (6:12-19)

12 *And King David was told,*
"The LORD blessed the house of Obed-edom
and all that belongs to him
because of the ark of God."
And David went and brought up the ark of God from the house of Obed-edom to the City of David with rejoicing.

13 *Whenever the bearers of the ark of the LORD advanced six paces, he sacrificed a bull and a fatling.*
14 *David was dancing with all (his) might before the LORD;*
and David was wearing a linen ephod.
15 *David and all the house of Israel were bringing up the ark of the LORD*
with shouting and the sound of the trumpet.

354. Tsumura, I, p. 252.
355. McCarter, II, p. 170.

16 *When the ark of the LORD was about to enter the city of David, Michal the daughter of Saul was looking down through the window. She saw King David leaping and dancing before the LORD and despised him in her heart.*

17 *And they brought the ark of the LORD and set it in its place in the midst of the tent that David had pitched for it.*

And David offered burnt offerings and peace offerings before the LORD.[356]
18 *And David finished offering the burnt offering and the peace offerings and blessed the people in the name of the LORD of hosts*
19 *and distributed to all the people, to all the multitude of Israel, to both men and women, individually, the following items:*

bread-cake	*one*
and date-cake	*one*
and raisin-cake	*one.*

And all the people went back, each to their own house.

This section, vv. 12-19, is rather a long episode, with a multilayered discourse structure. Noting the verbal forms in this unit, one can recognize here the movement of discourse, which is in parallel with the actual movement of the ark from the house of *Obed-edom* to Jerusalem.

The SETTING "And King David was told (passive)," is followed by a list of EVENTS, all of which have David as subject. After a parenthetical sentence about Michal (v. 16), there is a TRANSITION "And they brought . . . and set," and two more EVENTS with David as subject, then the TERMINUS, "And all the people went back."

13 This time the ark is carried properly. It seems that David sacrificed every *six steps*. Here LXX is unintelligibly divergent from MT.[357] 1 Chr. 15:26 preserves a different tradition: "And because God helped the Levites who were carrying the ark of the covenant of the LORD, they sacrificed seven bulls and seven rams."

Ancient Near Eastern literature refers to repeated sacrifices in relation to processions accompanying the transfer and installation of gods.[358] As for

356. McCarter takes *and peace offerings* as "secondary" since the word order in LXX follows that of MT "burnt offerings before the Lord and peace offerings," while Syr. has "before the Lord" at the end. However, this is another example of the "literary insertion" AX&B pattern in which the phrase *before the LORD* (*lipnê YHWH*) is inserted into the phrase "burnt offerings and peace offerings," while still modifying the phrase as a whole. See Tsumura, "Coordination Interrupted, or Literary Insertion AX&B Pattern, in the Books of Samuel," p. 122; and Tsumura, I, pp. 60-64.

357. See McCarter, II, p. 166.

358. Miller and Roberts, *The Hand of the Lord*, pp. 17, 96 n. 157.

the number of sacrificed animals, Solomon sacrificed a multitude of oxen and sheep during the dedication of the temple. David probably did not slaughter the animals himself, but this emphasizes that he was the central character in bringing the ark to Jerusalem. The purpose of sacrificing all along the way to Jerusalem is to appease the Lord's anger and please his God.

The expression *a bull and a fatling* could be a *hendiadys* meaning "a fatted bull."

14 For the term *dancing* (*mᵉkarkēr*), lit. "hopping, jumping," McCarter translates "strumming on a sonorous instrument,"[359] taking the verb *krr as referring to an activity of the fingers, like David's special skill in playing a lyre (1 Sam. 16:18). However, as the Ugaritic term *krkr* "to twist, twiddle"[360] suggests, this movement is concerned with more than his fingers. For the phrase *with all (his) might* (*bᵉkol-ʿōz*), see the commentary on v. 5 (above); cf. "on a sonorous instrument" (McCarter), based on LXX.

David's *linen ephod* (*ʾēpôd bād*) was a simple linen robe like that of the young Samuel (1 Sam. 2:18). He is scantily clad, without outer robes.

15 The phrase *David and all the house of Israel* (v. 5) is repeated. All the tribes of Israel join David in *bringing up the ark of the Lord* to the city. The *trumpet* (*šôpār*), literally "a horn," is an instrument made of a ram's horn, usually used for signaling.

16 When the ark of the Lord enters the city, his wife *Michal, the daughter of Saul* sees him *leaping and dancing*, and despises him for his unsuitable, unkingly behavior; see v. 20 (below).

The Hebrew for *when*, *wᵉhāyāh*, which is *waw*+pf. (*weqtl*) has been explained as "abnormal"; certainly, the normal form is *wayhî*. However, the use of this form signals that v. 16 is one step off the mainline narrative and gives the background information in an *embedded discourse*.[361]

For the motif of "the woman at the window," see Judg. 5:28 and 2 K. 9:30 as well as ivory plaques from Samaria, Arslan Tash, Nimrud, and Khorsabad.[362] The motif became a narrative convention in Hebrew literature for depicting a woman who is waiting for someone either with joyous expectation or anxious concern.

17 With the ark of the Lord *set . . . in the midst of the tent*, Jerusalem the royal city becomes the holy city of Zion, where the Lord's presence is

359. McCarter, II, p. 171.

360. *DULAT*, p. 455.

361. See Tsumura, I, p. 119 n. 84 on 1 Sam. 1:12. For the basic pattern of discourse analysis, see pp. 50-52. Also Longacre, "Weqatal Forms in Biblical Hebrew Prose," p. 88. See McCarter, II, p. 166 for de Boer's explanation ("The Perfect with *waw* in 2 Samuel 6:16" in *Selected Studies in Old Testament Exegesis*, ed. C. van Duin [OTS 27; Leiden: E. J. Brill, 1991], pp. 142-51).

362. See McCarter, II, 172; Seow, *Myth, Drama, and the Politics of David's Dance*, p. 129.

assured by the visible presence of the ark in the *tent*.[363] The *tent* corresponded to the tabernacle of Exod. 26. McCarter omits the phrase *in its place* (so LXX) as textually "secondary" with Syr. and 4QSam[a], as well as the shorter text in Josephus (*Ant.* 7.86) and 1 Chr. 16:1. However, as Herbert shows, the space considerations of 4QSam[a] rather support the inclusion of this phrase, thus supporting the MT and making McCarter's lengthy argument moot.[364]

Peace offerings (*šelāmîm*) are sacrifices offered to the deity and then eaten by the worshippers in his presence; see Deut. 27:7.

19 These gift items are listed in a list formula, as in 1 Sam. 6:17-18 and 25:18.[365] The term *date-cake* (*'ešpār*) appears only here and the parallel 1 Chr. 16:3. See *HALOT*, p. 97. The *raisin-cake* is a lump of dried compressed grapes, a nourishing and sustaining food; it also appears in Song 2:5.

2. Michal and David (6:20-23)

20 *And David returned to bless his house.*
And Michal the daughter of Saul came out to meet David and said,
"How the king of Israel distinguished himself today!
He uncovered himself today to the eyes of his servants' maids
as one of the rabble[366] *uncovers himself!"*
21 *And David said to Michal,*
"It was before the LORD,
who chose me above your father and above all his house
to appoint me ruler over the people of the LORD, over Israel;
I will celebrate before the LORD!
22 *I will be still more lightly esteemed than this*
and will be humiliated in my own eyes!
But by the maids whom you have mentioned,
by them I will be honored!
23 *And Michal the daughter of Saul had no child to the day of her death.*

20-23 This section is a kind of epilogue of the story of the transfer of the ark to Jerusalem. Michal is being sarcastic. She no doubt felt he should wear his royal robes as befitted a king, not just an ephod (v. 14). But David stresses that he was dressed simply *before the Lord*.

363. M. D. Fowler, "The Meaning of *lipne* YHWH in the Old Testament," *ZAW* 99 (1987) 389.

364. See Introduction, I.A of this book.

365. Tsumura, I, pp. 221-22, 583-84.

366. See *HALOT*.

20 *How . . . distinguished himself* (*kbd), i.e., "honored himself"; this is sharp sarcasm. Her aristocratic "tone" can be detected in the phrase "his servants' maids" which means all the young women of Israel.

The term *uncovered himself* (*niglāh*), or "revealed oneself," does not mean that he was bare, as he was wearing a linen ephod, but it was not what a king would wear in public. McCarter's translation "like some dancer" is based on LXX.

22 Some MT manuscripts read "in his [the Lord's] eyes" for *in my own eyes*, in which case it would mean David's humility before the Lord.

23 It is not clear whether Michal's childlessness was natural, with the suggestion that it was punishment for her attitude here, or whether David was no longer intimate with her.

E. "DAVIDIC COVENANT": THE ETERNAL THRONE (7:1-29)

Second Samuel 7, which announces the messianic promise, is a turning point in the history of salvation in the Bible. In Gen. 12:1-3 God promised Abr(ah)am to make of him *a great nation* (v. 2) and confirmed that *all the nations of the earth be blessed* through his *offspring* (22:18). This promise to Abraham was confirmed and made specific by the promise to David that the *offspring* of David will sit enthroned eternally (2 Sam. 7:12-16). Here the Lord promises to make one family, that of David, the representative of his people forever. There is nothing here to suggest that David deserved this favor; it is according to God's own heart (v. 21) that he promises David's descendants his *grace* (*or* "steadfast love" *ḥesed*) (v. 15).

Verses 8-17 are often described as the "Davidic covenant," even though the term "covenant" does not appear there. But in Ps. 89:3 this promise is described using the words, "I have made a covenant with my chosen one."[367] The term "covenant" (*b^e^rît*) appears several times in this psalm (vv. 3, 28, 34) and other key words from chapter 7 are also used: e.g., the word pairs "stead-

367. For the relationship between 2 Sam. 7 and Ps. 89, see, e.g., N. M. Sarna, "Psalm 89: A Study in Inner Biblical Exegesis," in *Text and Studies 1* (Philip W. Lown Institute of Advanced Judaic Studies; Waltham, Mass.: Harvard University Press, 1963), pp. 29-46; E. T. Mullen Jr., "The Divine Witness and the Davidic Royal Grant: Ps 89:37-38," *JBL* 102 (1983) 207-18; M. Fishbane, *Biblical Interpretation in Ancient Israel* (Oxford: Clarendon Press, 1985), pp. 466-67; M. E. Tate, *Psalms 51-100* (WBC 20; Dallas: Word Books, 1990), pp. 417-18; L. Eslinger, *House of God or House of David: The Rhetoric of 2 Samuel 7* (JSOTSS 164; Sheffield: Sheffield Academic Press, 1994); Laato, *A Star Is Rising*; Laato, "Second Samuel 7 and Ancient Near Eastern Royal Theology," *CBQ* 59 (1997) 244-69; W. M. Schniedewind, *Society and the Promise to David: The Reception History of 2 Samuel 7:1-17* (Oxford: Oxford University Press, 1999), pp. 41-42, 93-96, 111-14.

fast love" (*ḥesed*) – "faithfulness" (*'ĕmûnāh*) in vv. 1, 2, 24 and 33, "offspring" (*zera'*) – "throne" (*kissē'*) in vv. 4, 29 and 36, and "steadfast love" – "covenant" in v. 28.

> Ps. 89:1 I will sing of your steadfast love, O LORD, forever;
> with my mouth I will proclaim your faithfulness to all generations.
> 2 For I said,
> "Steadfast love will be built up forever;
> in the heavens you will establish your faithfulness."
> 3 You have said,
> "I have made **a covenant** with my chosen one;
> I have sworn to **David** my servant:
> 4 'I will establish your offspring forever,
> and build your throne for all generations.'" Selah
>
> Ps. 89:19 Of old you spoke in a vision to your godly one, and said:
> "I have granted help to one who is mighty;
> I have exalted one chosen from the people.
> 20 I have found **David**, my servant;
> with my holy oil I have anointed him,
> 21 so that my hand shall be established with him;
> my arm also shall strengthen him.
> . . .
> 24 My faithfulness and my steadfast love shall be with him,
> and in my name shall his horn be exalted.
>
> 28 My steadfast love I will keep for him forever,
> and my **covenant** will stand firm for him.
> 29 I will establish his offspring forever
> and his throne as the days of the heavens.
> 30 If his children forsake my law
> and do not walk according to my rules,
> 31 if they violate my statutes
> and do not keep my commandments,
> 32 then I will punish their transgression with the rod
> and their iniquity with stripes,
> 33 but I will not remove from him my steadfast love
> or be false to my faithfulness.
> 34 I will not violate my **covenant**
> or alter the **word** that went forth from my lips.
> 35 Once for all I have sworn by my holiness;
> I will not lie to **David**.

Verses 36-37 of this psalm should be treated as a quadracolon, a four line parallelism:

zar'o le'olam yihyeh
wekis'o kesemes negdi
keyareah yakkon 'olam
we'ed bassahaq ne'man

A His [David's] *heir*[368] shall be forever,
X His *throne* shall be, like the sun, before me;
X' like the moon, it shall be established forever,
B as the faithful witness on the clouds.[369]

Note that this fourline parallelism constitutes the AXX'B pattern, in which the middle two parallel lines (X//X') are inserted between A and B where A and B hold a vertical grammatical relationship, that is, "His heir shall be forever as the faithful witness on the clouds." This David's *heir* will be the "faithful witness" on the clouds. According to the Christian canonical understanding, this heir of David is the Messiah to come (see Rev. 3:14; 1:5).

The covenant was to be "forever" (2 Sam. 7:16; Ps. 89:36). The expression "eternal covenant" (*bᵉrît 'ôlām*) appears sixteen times in the whole Bible (e.g., Isa. 24:5; 55:3; 61:8; Jer. 32:40; 50:5; Ezek. 16:60; 37:26), in particular, in the "Last Words of David" (2 Sam. 23:5). However, the concept is not a late one, as illustrated by the Hittite use of the expression "eternal treaty" during the second millennium B.C.[370]

However, the "covenant" in 2 Sam. 7 did not specify the obligations of two parties like the Sinai covenant in Exod. 20-31, but was a one-sided promise, a *grant* or promise like the one to Abraham in Gen. 12:1-3; 15:18-21; and 17:1-21. David expresses his desire to build a house for the Lord. But the Lord does not approve, and instead states on his own initiative that he will establish David's house (i.e., dynasty) eternally, promising him an eternal throne: *And your house and your kingdom will endure forever before you; your throne will be established forever* (v. 16).

Psalm 132 says that on this occasion the Lord promised David with "a

368. See the commentary on 2 Sam. 23:4.

369. For the AXX'B pattern of this tetracolon (vv. 36-37), see the commentaries on 3:34, 7:22, etc. This "faithful witness in the skies/clouds" is neither Yahweh himself (as Veijola) nor "a lower divine member of Yahweh's heavenly court" (as Mullen) nor "the Davidic throne" (as Mosca). It is the Davidic "offspring" who is a faithful witness in the clouds. See above, Introduction, Themes and Theology of 2 Samuel.

370. T. Bryce, "The 'Eternal Treaty' from the Hittite Perspective," *BMSAES* 6 (2006) 1-11, http://www.thebritishmuseum.ac.uk/bmsaes/issue6/bryce.html.

sure oath"[371] that "one of the sons of your body I will set on your throne" (v. 11; 2 Sam. 7:12). This points to Solomon who would "sit on the throne of Israel" and build "the house for the name of the Lord" (1 K. 8:20), and eventually, to Jesus, the Messiah who will sit on the throne eternally (Luke 1:32-33). See Ps. 89:20-38; Isa. 55:3; Jer. 33:17, 20-22; 2 Chr. 13:5; 21:7; etc.

EXCURSUS: THEORIES OF THE LITERARY COMPOSITION OF 2 SAMUEL 7

It has usually been held among scholars that the entire chapter is most likely a product of the Deuteronomistic writing.[372] However, recently some have accepted that some of the material is derived from the preexilic, or pre-Deuteronomistic period, and one of the hotly debated issues is how much. For example, O. Sergi claims Nathan's oracle experienced three stages of composition and redaction:[373]

I. The Earliest Layer of the Oracle (vv. 1a, 2-3, 11b)
II. The Deuteronomistic Layer (vv. 1b, 4-6a, 8-9, 11a, 12-16)
III. The Post-Deuteronomistic Layer (vv. 6b-7, 10).

According to him, the first, pre-Deuteronomistic layer was written during the late ninth to early eighth centuries B.C. The oracle was positive in character, providing divine legitimacy to and focusing on the Davidic dynasty, rather than on the temple theme.

The second stage, undertaken by the Deuteronomist with his cultic interest, incorporated the theme of the temple into that of dynasty. Thus, Nathan's oracle was set as the founding text of the whole history of the Davidic monarchy. Sergi dates this redaction to the late seventh century, during Josiah's era.

At the final stage, vv. 6b-7 and 10 were inserted by the post-Deuteronomistic redactor (probably the Priestly writer) in the Persian period, who disregarded the importance of the dynasty in building the temple.

371. On the "oath" in the ancient Near East, see J. Scurlock, "Oaths, Ancient Near East," in *The Encyclopedia of Ancient History* (John Wiley & Sons, 2012). https://doi.org/10.1002/9781444338386.wbeah01146.

372. E.g., W. Dietrich, *The Early Monarchy in Israel: The Tenth Century B.C.E.* (SBLBES 3; Atlanta: Society of Biblical Literature, 2007), 20.

373. O. Sergi, "The Composition of Nathan's Oracle to David (2 Samuel 7:1-17) as a Reflection of Royal Judahite Ideology," *JBL* 129 (2010) 261-79.

Verses 1b and 11a are understood as belonging to the Deuteronomistic layer due to the fact that they both speak about "rest." And based on a conventional view of the verbal tense in Biblical Hebrew, it is normally held that *waYHWH hēnîaḥ-lô* in v. 1b refers to the Lord's PAST dealing with David ("the LORD had given him rest"), while *wahănîḥōtî lᵉkā* in v. 11a refers to the Lord's FUTURE dealing, i.e., his promise ("I will give you rest").[374] With this understanding, however, there is a problem in temporal consistency within the Deuteronomistic layer itself, that is, "had given" vs. "will give."

However, some recent developments in the study in the tense and aspect of Hebrew verbs, as well as discourse grammar, show that the discrepancy in the tense of Hebrew verbs that is used to argue for several different literary layers[375] in 2 Sam. 7, is not actually a discrepancy. See below and Excursus.

EXCURSUS: 2 SAMUEL 7 IN ITS ANCIENT NEAR EASTERN CONTEXT

Now, it is clear that the idea of eternal kingship had existed among countries neighboring Israel at least since the beginning of the second millennium B.C, as can be seen in the prologue to the Code of Hammurabi i.1-49, esp. i.26:

> When the august god Anu, king of the Anunnaku deities, and the god Enlil, lord of heaven and earth, who determines the destinies of the land, allotted supreme power over all peoples to the god Marduk, the firstborn son of the god Ea, exalted him among the Igigu deities, named the city of Babylon with its august name and made it supreme within the regions of the world, and established for him within it eternal kingship whose foundations are as fixed as heaven and earth.[376]

In the Late Bronze city-state Ugarit, the concept of *eternal kingship* was expressed in the mythological text of the Baal Cycle, *KTU* 1.2 IV 10:

> As for your enemy, O Baʿlu,
> as for your enemy, you'll smite (him),

374. Stoebe translates the same way, that is, as the future, though he takes the preceding verbs as denoting the past, i.e., "Ich bestimmte . . . und pflanzte"; H. J. Stoebe, *Das zweite Buch Samuelis* (KAT VIII.2; Gütersloh: Gütersloher Verlagshaus, 1994), p. 219.

375. E.g., see P. Kasari, *Nathan's Promise in 2 Samuel 7 and Related Texts* (PFES 97; Helsinki: Finnish Exegetical Society, 2009).

376. M. Roth, in *CS*, II, p. 336.

> you'll destroy your adversary.
> You'll take your eternal kingship (*mlk ʿlmk*),
> your sovereignty (that endures) from generation to generation.[377]

Furthermore, we find it referring to a human king in a letter sent from an official in Alashia (i.e., Cyprus) to the Ugaritic king (RS 18.113A+B):

> I do pronounce to Baʿlu-Ṣapuni, to Eternal Sun, to ʿAṯtartu, to ʿAnatu, to all the gods of Alashi[a] (prayers for) the splendor of (your) eternal kingship.[378]

The phrase *eternal king* (*mlk ʿlm*), used for the god El in Ugarit, also appears as the title of the deified king in *KTU* 1.108:1 and parallels.[379]

While the idea of eternal kingship is not necessarily the same as that of *eternal dynasty*, certainly any monarchic system desires that the dynastic succession last as long as possible, i.e., forever, and the idea of *eternal kingship* may be reasonably assumed as the basis of that of *eternal dynasty.* As Laato notes, Assyrian royal building inscriptions from the second millennium onward express the idea of an eternal dynasty, so it would not be surprising if the idea played an important role in Israelite royal ideology at the time of David.[380] It must be mentioned here that the concept of "eternity" in Assyria might mean "perpetuance" of the succession, hence "stability," while in the Bible it also refers to "future time" (see *HALOT*, II, p. 799).

The entire section of the historical narrative discourse (1-17) is structured as follows:

Historical Narrative: Yahweh's promise (vv. 1-17)
[Episode 1]
1a [SETTING 1]: Temp. clause (*When the king was living . . .*)
 1b — Embedded sentence (*the* Lord *had given him rest . . .*) —
2-3 [EVENT 1]: Dialog between the king and Nathan
[Episode 2]

377. D. Pardee, in *CS*, I, p. 248. See also S. Rummel, "Narrative Structures in the Ugaritic Texts," in *RSP* 3, p. 240.

378. D. Pardee, in *CS*, III, p. 104.

379. Also, *nmry mlk ʿlm* "Nimmureya (=Amenophis III), eternal king." 2.42:9; see *DULAT*, p. 159. Also see H.-P. Müller, "Malik," in *DDD*, p. 540. In the OT, the Lord is "the eternal king" (*melek ʿôlām*) in Jer. 10:10 and Ps. 10:16.

380. Laato, *A Star Is Rising*, p. 40.

4a [SETTING 2]: Temp. Clause (*In that night*)
4b-17 [EVENT 2]: *the word of the LORD came to Nathan* [Nathan spoke to David]
4b Formula: *saying*
5-16 — Embedded prophetic speeches [A: 5-7], [B: 8-16] —
17 TERMINUS of narrative discourse

1. The Lord's Promise (7:1-17)

a. David's Desire (7:1-3): [SETTING 1] – [EVENT 1]

1 *When the king was living*[381] *in his house, — the LORD had given him rest from all his enemies around —*
2 *the king said to Nathan the prophet,*
"See now,
I am living in a house of cedars,
while the ark of God is sitting in the midst of curtains!"
3 *And Nathan said to the king,*
"Now, do whatever is in your mind,
for the LORD is with you."

David's desire to build the temple for the Lord is apparently influenced by his current situation, that *the LORD had given him rest from all his enemies around.* In the ancient Near East, the building of temples could be best done in a time of peace and prosperity, as we can see in the opening statement of the Gudea Cylinders. R. E. Averbeck explains:

> The building of temples was closely associated with fertility, abundance, and prosperity in the ANE. The Gudea Cylinders open with a statement of general economic prosperity as the background for the call to build the temple. [The god] Enlil determined a good destiny for Lagash (Cyl. A i.1–4) leading to or consisting of the overflow of Enlil's heart (Cyl. A i.5–8) in the form of the seasonal flood of the Tigris river that fertilized the agricultural land of the Lagash region (Cyl. A i.9).[382]

David contrasts his own cedar house (see 5:11) with the tent that houses the ark (see 6:17). It was natural for a king to build a temple to honor his god.

381. The perfect of *yšb* often means "is living or sitting," "has been settled" in a stative or resultative sense; e.g., Ps. 1:1; 122:5; similarly Ps. 120:5 (*škn, gwr*).

382. R. E. Averbeck, "The Cylinders of Gudea (2.155)," in *CS*, II, p. 419, no. 4.

Nathan probably means his words *the LORD is with you* (7:3) as a general comment on David (see on v. 9) and gives his own opinion as David's counselor. However, that night he receives a specific revelation from God, which he delivers to David as a prophet, the messenger of God.

1 This verse introduces the key word of this chapter, namely *house*, which links it to the preceding narrative in 6:20-23, especially 20a; see the commentary on 6:20. In this initial context *the king* is not identified; only in v. 5, in the words of Yahweh the king is mentioned as *my servant David*. It may be that the narrator tries to emphasize the contrast between the earthly king and Yahweh who is enthroned in the heaven. Note the parallel passage in 1 Chr. 17:1, which begins with "David," thus, "When David was living in his house, David said to Nathan the prophet." The chronicler seems to emphasize the plain known fact that the king is David.

The sentence *the LORD had given him rest from all his enemies around* is absent from 1 Chr. 17:1.[383] It has long been pointed out that this half-verse (2 Sam. 7:1b) seems to contradict other passages, e.g., chapter 8, which gives a catalogue of David's victories, and Solomon's statement in 1 K. 5:3 that David could not build the temple because of warfare. However, "rest" could refer to a *temporary* warless situation, not necessarily complete victory over all his enemies. Moreover, the events of chs. 7 and 8 are not necessarily in chronological order and, as discussed below, the latter chapter describes David's victories thematically, not chronologically (see the commentary on 8:3-12). For v. 11b (*I have given you rest from all your enemies*), see below.

2 *Nathan the prophet* appears here for the first time; no background information is given for him. He plays an important role in the aftermath of the Bathsheba affair (2 Sam. 12) and in the dispute involving succession (1 K. 1). Two of the officials listed in 1 K. 4:5 are sons of Nathan. "The records of Nathan the prophet" are mentioned in 1 Chr. 29:29 and 2 Chr. 9:29. Nathan was most probably a prophet who took the role of counselor to the king at the royal court. On the "court prophets" in Israel and Mari, see the commentary on 1 Sam. 22:5.[384]

David's *house of cedars* (*bêt 'ărāzîm*) was a palace paneled with cedar like those in the Assyrian capitals (see the palace of Tiglathpileser I in Assur[385]), built by the craftsmen of Tyre with Lebanese cedars; see 2 Sam. 5:11. Here, the material of his house, *cedars* (plural for emphasis), is contrasted with that

383. For a detailed discussion on the differences between 2 Sam. 7 and 1 Chr. 17, see M. Avioz, "Nathan's Prophecy in II Sam 7 and in I Chr 17: Text, Context, and Meaning," *ZAW* 116 (2004) 542-54, esp. 549. See also Japhet, p. 328.

384. Tsumura, I, pp. 540-41. See also A. Malamat, "Intuitive Prophecy: A General Survey," in *Mari and the Bible* (SHCANE 12; Leiden: E. J. Brill, 1998), p. 67.

385. *CAD*, E, p. 276.

of the ark's dwelling, *the curtains* (Heb. sg.),[386] which is a *metonymy* for the tent (see 6:17). See v. 6 (below).

3 McCarter and others find it difficult to consider this verse and vv. 5-7 as the work of a single author for Nathan gives contradictory answers. Hence McCarter posits that "the positive tone of v. 3 represents the attitude of the author of the oldest stratum of our passage, upon which the negativity of vv. 5-7 was subsequently imposed."[387] However, it would not be contradictory for Nathan to give the advice "whatsoever" as David's counselor, but on the next day to convey the Lord's oracle as a prophet, i.e., a messenger, using the messenger formula: *Thus says the Lord.* One would have to wonder why the "author of the oldest passage" was positive about the matter. Certainly there is no indication anywhere that David *did* build a temple.

b. The Lord Sends Nathan to David (7:4-7)

4 *In that night the word of the Lord came to Nathan, saying,*
5 *"Go and say to my servant David:*
'Thus says the Lord,
Are you the one who will build me a house
as my dwelling place?
6 *For*[388] *I have not lived in a house*
from the day I brought up the Israelites from Egypt
until this day,
but have been moving about in a tent,
namely[389] *in a tabernacle!*
7 *Wherever I have moved about among all the sons of Israel,*
did I ever speak a word to one of the tribal leaders of Israel
whom I commanded to shepherd my people Israel saying,
"Why have you not built me a house of cedar?"

4 For the nocturnal revelation, see the commentary on 1 Sam. 3.[390] For the formula, *the word of the Lord came,* see on 1 Sam. 15:10.[391] Nathan here takes the role of a messenger-prophet.

386. See *HALOT*, p. 439.
387. For other views, see McCarter, II, pp. 196-97. Recently this view has been supported by O. Sergi, as noted above.
388. This is a *speaker-oriented kî*: the reason why I ask you this question. See n. 451 below.
389. The *waw* is here *explicative*.
390. Tsumura, I, pp. 171-80.
391. Tsumura, I, p. 395.

5 This same expression *Go and say lēk wᵉʾāmartā* appears also in Isa. 6:9 and 1 Chr. 17:4; its variant form *hālôk wᵉʾāmartā* appears in Isa. 38:5; Jer. 28:13; etc. The two prophetic speeches here (vv. 5b-7 and 8b-16) are introduced by virtually the same messenger formula: *Go and say to my servant David* (v. 5a) followed by *Thus says the LORD* (*kōh ʾāmar YHWH*) and *Now, thus you shall say to my servant David* (v. 8a) also followed by *Thus says the LORD*. *Thus says the LORD* is the quotation formula used by the prophets of the Lord.[392] Thus, these speeches (vv. 5-16) are embedded into the entire discourse structure of the historical narrative (vv. 1-17).

5-16 — Embedded prophetic speeches [A: 5-7] & [B: 8-16] —

[A] 5-7
Introductory Formulas (5a)
Messenger formula (5a1)
Go and say to my servant David:
Quotation formula (5a2): *Thus says the LORD*
Prophetic Speech (5b-7)
[B] 8-16
Introductory Formulas (8a)
Messenger formula (8a1)
Now, thus you shall say to my servant David:
Quotation formula (8a2): *Thus says the LORD of hosts*
Prophetic Speech (8b-16)

Since the designation of a king as a *servant* of a god is widespread in the ancient Near East,[393] it cannot be regarded as distinctively Deuteronomistic in Israel. In the Books of Samuel, it is only used here and in 3:18; in both passages the Lord is speaking of David. In other books God uses this expression for people like Moses, David, Isaiah, Eliakim, and Job.

In this speech, the Lord is concerned with the *house* (*bayit*). The term appears three times in the short first prophetic speech.

6 In v. 6 the Lord declares: *I have not lived in a house*. Kruse thinks that this statement is "anachronistic and historically erroneous," because the ark was in a house in Shiloh.[394] The shrine at Shiloh was called a house (*bêt*) or temple (*hêkāl*) and did have a door in 1 Sam. 1:7, 9; 3:3, 15 (see

392. C. Westermann, *Basic Forms of Prophetic Speech* (Louisville: Westminster John Knox, 1991); H. Van Dyke Parunak, "Some Discourse Functions of Prophetic Quotation Formulas in Jeremiah," *BHDL*, p. 505.

393. See R. de Vaux, *The Bible and the Ancient Near East* (Garden City, N.Y.: Doubleday, 1971), pp. 155-56.

394. H. Kruse, "David's Covenant," *VT* 35 (1985) 144.

the commentary on 1:7),[395] but even a tent could be called a "house" (see Ugaritic *bt*, Akkadian *bîtu*). As there is also a reference to the "entrance to the tent of meeting" (1 Sam. 2:22), it may be that some kind of permanent structure was built around the tent at Shiloh. Of course, the ark had been in the house *bêt* of Abinadab (6:3) for several decades, but that was a temporary expedient.

For *until this day*, see Tsumura, I, pp. 17-18.

7 McCarter interprets *the tribal leaders of Israel* (*šibṭê Yiśrāʾēl*) as "staff bearers" by positing a participle *šōbēṭ, of a denominative verb from *šēbeṭ* "staff." Others, in the light of 1 Chr. 17:6 (*šōpᵉṭê Yiśrāʾēl*) as well as the voicing of /p/ in an intervocalic position,[396] interpret *šibṭê* as "judges of" (cstr). Although the Lord did not appoint the leaders of "the tribes of Israel" to govern his people, one of the tribal leaders, often the "judge," was chosen to lead the people of the Lord from time to time. One may note that the root *špṭ means more broadly "to rule" or "to lead" in Hebrew and Ugaritic; see *HALOT*, pp. 1623-24; *UT*, 19.2727. It is possible to regard the term "scepter, staff" (*šēbeṭ*) as a metonymy for "the one who holds the scepter" (*tômēk šēbeṭ* in Amos 1:5). First Chronicles 17:6 interpreted the phrase "one of the staff-holders" as referring to "one of the judges": *šōpēṭ*.

One can well contrast here the Lord, who is content with a tent even when offered a house of cedars, with the god Baal in the Ugaritic mythological text *KTU* 1.3, who covets a house, and one bigger and better than those of the other gods. C. H. Gordon notes that here "the biblical reaction against Canaanite materialism is applied to God's attitude toward His own dwelling."[397]

c. The Lord's Message to David (7:8-17)

8 *"Now, thus you shall say to my servant David:*
'Thus says the LORD *of hosts,*
I am the one
who took you from the pasture,
from looking after the sheep,
to become prince over my people Israel
9 *and was with you wherever you went*
and cut off all your enemies from before you.

395. Tsumura, I, pp. 114-15.

396. For this phenomenon, see Tsumura, "Scribal Errors or Phonetic Spellings?," p. 406 and n. 79.

397. Gordon, *PLMU*, p. 75.

Thus I have made a great name for you,
like the name of the great men on the earth;
10 *I have provided a place for my people Israel*
and have planted them there
so that they may exist where they are[398]
and not tremble again,
and that wicked people may not afflict them any more
as formerly,
11 *that is, ever since*[399] *I appointed judges*
over my people Israel;
In consequence, I have given you rest from all your enemies.

And the LORD *tells you*
that, as for a house, the LORD *will make one for you!*
12 *When your days are full*
and you lie down with your fathers,
I will raise your offspring after you,
who will come out of your bowels,
and I will establish his kingdom.
13 *He is the one who will build a house for my name;*
and I will establish the throne of his kingdom forever.
14 *I will become a father to him;*
and he will become a son to me.
When he commits iniquity,
I will correct him with a rod of men
and with strokes of sons of man.
15 *But my grace will not depart from him*
as I withdrew it from Saul,
whom I withdrew from before you.
16 *And your house and your kingdom will endure*
forever before you;[400]
your throne will be established forever.'"

17 *In accordance with all these words, namely all this vision, so Nathan spoke to David.*

398. Lit. "(in) its place."

399. "That is, ever since" (*ûlmin-hayyôm 'ăšer*): cf. "from the time that" (NRSV); "ever since the time" (NIV). The *waw* here is *explicative*; see Wernberg-Møller, cited by Baker, "Further Examples of the *wāw explicativum*," p. 136.

400. Some Hebrew MSS and LXX have "before me" (so ESV, NIV), instead of "before you" (MT).

8-17 Nathan informs David that God will not let him build him a *house* (*bayit*); rather, God will build David a *house* (*bayit*), that is, a ruling dynasty. Here no reason is given for the refusal, but in 1 K. 5:3, Solomon says David was not able to build the temple (*bayit*) because of the warfare, and 1 Chr. 22:8 gives the reason in more detail, "You have shed much blood and have waged great wars . . . you have shed so much blood before me on the earth." This text appears to say that since David is a warrior and killed people, he was not allowed to build a house for Yahweh.

Of course any warrior king sheds the blood of enemies. But the phrase *before the LORD* here may add a liturgical connotation. Susan Tsumura orally called my attention to the fact that Saul's sons and grandsons were hung "before the Lord" (2 Sam. 21:6), the only case in the Bible where this phrase is used of killing, except for animal sacrifices. Could this be what is referred to? On the other hand, one should note that the *bloodguilt* in Leviticus and other places does not necessarily result from actually shedding the blood of others. Perhaps one of the events this refers to is the death of many of his people as a result of his taking the census in ch. 24. See commentary on that chapter.

There has been much confusion concerning what parts of this prophecy refer to the past, and what to the future. Hebrew verbs do not express tense in the same way English verbs do. Even though the verbal forms are the same, it seems that in vv. 9b-11a the Lord says what he *has* done — he has already cut off David's *enemies* (vv. 1, 9) and appointed a place for Israel — while in 11b-16 the LORD declares (v. 11b *the LORD tells you*) what he *will* do, that is, establish David's dynasty (*bayit*). See below.

8 For *looking after the sheep,* see the commentary on 1 Sam. 16:11-13;[401] this is not "following the sheep," for a shepherd would lead the flock, not follow it.

On *prince,* see the commentary on 1 Sam. 9:16.[402] This is the last occurrence of this term in Samuel. The title usually refers to the king-designate or crown prince. Though the title "prince" was not used in the account of David's anointing in 1 Sam. 16:11-13, David is referred to as "prince" by Samuel in 13:14 and by Abigail in 25:30.

9a For *I was with you* (see also v. 3), see the expression "The Lord was with David" in 1 Sam. 16:18; 17:37; 18:12, 14, 28; 20:13, as well as in 2 Sam. 5:10; 7:3. This is "the theological leitmotif" of the story of David's rise with Saul's rejection in the background; see the commentary on 1 Sam. 16:18.[403] However, there is no reason why one should regard this expression as exclusively

401. Tsumura, I, pp. 421-35.
402. Tsumura, I, pp. 274-75.
403. Tsumura, I, pp. 429-30.

Deuteronomistic;[404] it is a common expression which can be used for any person at any time; e.g., Gen. 26:3; 1 Sam. 3:19.

From context, the phrase *all your enemies* refers to those who stood in the way of David's kingship, including Saul and Ishbosheth. The phrase "all his enemies" occurs also in 22:1 (= Ps. 18:1).

9b-16 Until now the discourse has been using the narrative sequence of *qtl – wayqtl – wayqtl* ["I . . . took . . . and was with you . . . and cut off"] (8b-9a), but in v. 9b it suddenly changes to *weqtl – weqtl – weqtl.* Virtually all versions take these *weqtl* as "*waw* consecutive + perfect," hence "imperfect," and translate vv. 9b-11a as referring to the future, "and I will make for you a great name. . . . And I will appoint a place for my people Israel and will plant them . . . and I will give you rest from all your enemies" (NRSV).

Such an interpretation, however, leads to a contradiction between v. 11a ("and I will give you rest from all your enemies") and v. 1b ("the LORD had given him rest from all his enemies around him"). The KJV took v. 11a as PAST: "and have caused thee to rest." Though in the minority, several prominent modern scholars also hold the PAST tense interpretation. For example, A. A. Anderson translates as follows: "Thus I have given you peace from all your enemies."[405] But no explanation for this translation is given. The 1985 *Elberfelder Bibel* gives both as possibilities.[406]

Moreover, in 1 Chr. 17:1, which corresponds to 2 Sam. 7:1b, the statement "the Lord had given him rest" is omitted. Scholars such as McCarter and McKenzie take the promise of "rest" in v. 11a of the Samuel text as futuristic and explain that the contradictory statement of v. 1b is a marginal note and hence not original.[407] However, one should note that Chronicles fails to mention of "rest" not only in verse 1, but also in 1 Chr. 17:10a, the text parallel to Samuel's v. 11a, which reads, "And I will subdue all your enemies."

> *wahănîḥōtî lᵉkā mikkol-ʾōyᵉbêkā* (2 Sam. 7:11a) *nwḥ
> *wᵉhiknaʿtî ʾt-kol-ʾôyᵉbêkā* (1 Chr. 17:10a) *knʿ

I believe that Chronicles does not use the "rest" theme due to its different focus and perspective. While the Samuel passage focuses on the state of

404. So, F. M. Cross, *Canaanite Myth and Hebrew Epic: Essays in the History of the Religion of Israel* (Cambridge, Mass.: Harvard University Press, 1973), p. 252.

405. Anderson, *2 Samuel*, p. 110.

406. *Die Bibel: Elberfelder Übersetzung, revidierte Fassung* (Wuppertal: R. Brockhaus Verlag, 1985): "Und ich verschaffe dir Ruhe (oder *ich habe dir Ruhe verschafft*) vor all deinen Feinden."

407. See, e.g., McCarter, II, p. 191; McKenzie, *King David: A Biography*, p. 309 n. 27. See above for Sergi's view that v. 1b belongs to the Deuteronomistic layer, while v. 1a belongs to the earliest (original) layer.

"rest" (*nwḥ), that is, the result of the destructive action[408] (i.e., the "cutting off" *krt) against David's *enemies* (2 Sam. 7:9a; 1 Chr. 17:8a), the Chronicler emphasizes the act of destruction itself, i.e., "to subdue" (*knʿ). Therefore, the lack of the phrase "the Lord had given him rest" in Chronicles does not necessarily support the contention that the phrase in Samuel is not original.

Contextually, when we look at David's prayer of thanksgiving, in vv. 25-26 he says "as for the word that you have spoken concerning your servant and his house, confirm it forever. . .. As for the house of your servant David, may it be established before you!" This suggests that David considers the promise beginning not with v. 11a (giving rest), but only at v. 11b, where an imperfect verb *yaʿăśeh* ("he will make/build") expressing the future tense occurs and is continued by the series of *weqtl* forms (*wᵉšākabtā . . . wahăqîmōtî . . . wahăkînōtî . . . wᵉhōkaḥtîw . . . wᵉneʾman . . .*) in vv. 12-16. Also, in v. 11b the tense of *weqtl* is certainly present, hence *And the LORD tells you.*

Therefore, the verses before this announcement, vv. 8-11a, are most likely in the PAST tense.[409] Already several scholars have expressed an opinion that the context seems to require the past tense interpretation for vv. 9b-11a.[410] Murray in fact holds that v. 10 by the use of *waw*+pf. (*weqtl*) expresses "Yahweh's action on behalf of Israel toward a goal" which is fully realized by "the continuance of David's rule through that of his offspring."[411]

EXCURSUS: A DISCOURSE GRAMMATICAL POINT OF VIEW

The problem of verbal tense and aspect of the second message from the Lord to David in 2 Sam. 7:8b-16 should be dealt with from a discourse grammatical point of view. This episode seems to consist of several levels, or layers, of discourse:

Prophetic Speech (8b-16)

NARRATIVE (8b-9a)	PAST (*qtl - wayqtl*)
PROCEDURAL (9b-11aα)	(*weqtl - weqtl- weqtl*)
RESULT (11aβ)	(*weqtl*)
DECLARATIVE (11b)	PRESENT *performative* (*weqtl*):
PREDICTIVE (12-16)	FUTURE (*yqtl - weqtl*).

408. Similarly, the "rest" theme in Exod. 20:11 focuses on the state of "rest" (*nwḥ) after the creative action, while the end of the creative work itself is referred to by the term *šbt ("to cease") in Gen. 2:2-3. See D. T. Tsumura, "The Meaning of 'The LORD rested on the seventh day' (*wayyānaḥ bayyôm haššəbîʿî*)," *Exeg* 24 (2013) 37-48 (in Japanese with an English abstract).

409. Tsumura, "Tense and Aspect of Hebrew Verbs in II Samuel VII 8-16," pp. 641-54.

410. E.g., Kruse, "David's Covenant," p. 151; also Anderson, *2 Samuel*, p. 110.

411. D. F. Murray, "*mqwm* and the Future of Israel in 2 Samuel VII 10," *VT* 40 (1990) 318.

A detailed analysis of the tenses is as follows:

PAST:	8b-9a	took (pf.) - was (*wa*+impf.) - cut off (*wa*+impf.)
	9b-11aα	*making a great name for you* (*w*+pf.)
		providing a place for my people Israel (*w*+pf.)
		and *planting them there* (*w*+pf.)
		- they have existed
		- but they will not tremble
		- but they will not do again
	11aβ	*I have finally given (you) rest* (*w*+pf.)
PRESENT:	11b	And the Lord tells you (*w*+pf.)
		. . . the Lord will make (impf.)
FUTURE:	12-16	When . . . I will raise (*w*+pf.) your offspring

Note here that the tense is PAST up to v. 11aβ, though there seem to be two levels of discourse: i.e., the primary level (vv. 8-9a) with the narrative tense (*qtl + wayqtl - wayqtl*), and the secondary level (vv. 9b-11aβ) with *weqtl - weqtl - weqtl - weqtl*. The latter is a little off the mainline discourse and is what R. E. Longacre calls "a procedural discourse," explaining "how-it-was-done."[412]

The verbal sequence *wayqtl . . . weqtl* in a narrative discourse is not unique to this passage. A similar example occurs in 1 Sam. 17:38.

wayyalbēš Šā'ûl 'et-Dāwīd maddâw
w^{e}nātan qôba' n^{e}ḥōšet 'al-rō'šô wayyalbēš 'ōtô širyôn

Then Saul clothed David with his armor (WHAT),
putting a helmet of bronze on his head and *clothing* him with a coat of mail (HOW).[413]

Here the first *wayqtl* states WHAT Saul did to David (i.e., "And Saul clothed [*wayyalbēš*] David with his armor"), while the form *weqtl* and the following *wayqtl* explain HOW Saul put his armor on David (i.e., "He put [*w^{e}nātan*] a helmet . . . on him and clothed [*wayyalbēš*] him with a coat of mail"). The second *wayqtl* is simply sequential to the preceding *qtl* verb *nātan* within the procedural discourse.[414]

412. See the Introduction (III.3) of this book, as well as Section VI ("Discourse Analysis") in Tsumura, I, pp. 49-52. Also Longacre, "Weqatal Forms in Biblical Hebrew Prose," pp. 50-98; Longacre, *Joseph: A Story of Divine Providence*.

413. G. Rendsburg notes that normally the helmet would have been put on last, and explains the strange order as a deliberate literary device; "Confused Language as a Deliberate Literary Device in Biblical Hebrew Narrative," *JHS* 2 (1999) Article 6, pp. 12-13.

414. Also see 1 Sam. 1:4; 7:15-16; Job 1:5; etc.

The pattern of discourse, *wayqtl* (NARRATIVE) . . . *weqtl* (PROCEDURE), followed by a result clause *weqtl* (RESULT) can be noted in Jer. 37:15.[415] The first *weqtl* explains the PROCEDURE, while the second one explains the RESULT.[416]

In the light of the above, the primary level in 2 Sam. 7:8b-9a describes the Lord's past dealings ("what-happened") with David who became *prince* over the Lord's people *Israel*: the *qtl* verb, followed by two *wayqtl*s, referring to "a single and instantaneous action" (i.e., *took*):

> the Lord *took* David *from the pasture* . . . (see 1 Sam. 16)
> the Lord *was with* David *wherever* he *went* (see 1 Sam. 18)
> the Lord *cut off all* his *enemies from before* him (see 2 Sam. 22:1).

On the other hand, the secondary level describes the Lord's continuous dealings with David, i.e., *making, providing,* and *planting* (*weqtl* - *weqtl* - *weqtl* "how-it-was-done" in 2 Sam. 7:9b-11aα), from the time he became king, and *in consequence, I have given you rest* (*weqtl* in v. 11aβ).[417]

> the Lord has made a great name for David; (aorist in LXX *epoiēsa*)
> the Lord has provided a place for his people Israel; (future in LXX *thēsomai*)
> the Lord has planted them there; (aorist in LXX *kataphyteusō*)
> the Lord has given David rest from all his enemies. (future in LXX *anapausō*).

Then, in v. 11b, after the introductory phrase And the Lord tells you, Nathan delivers the Lord's message of his future dealings: he will make a house for David.

The section vv. 9b-11aβ therefore serves as a transition from the Lord's past dealings to his future dealings with David, that is, the divine promise in vv. 12-16. Thus, as Murray puts it, "the divinely-guided career of David is merely a part of Yahweh's wider plan for Israel; its full realization requires the continuance of David's rule through that of his offspring."[418]

---

415. For the result clause, see Tsumura, "Temporal Consistency," pp. 385-92.

416. Also Judg. 3:23; 7:13b; 2 K. 17:21b; 21:3-4 [= 2 Chr. 33:3-4]; 22:17.

417. See Tsumura, "Temporal Consistency," pp. 385-92. For other *wayqtl* . . . *weqtl* structures, see Exod. 39:3; Judg. 3:23; 1 Sam. 1:4; 17:35, 38; 2 Sam. 7:9; 12:16; 13:18, 19; 16:13; 21:9; 1 K. 14:27 [= 2 Chr. 12:10]; 18:4; 20:21; 2 K. 17:21; 23:4, 12, 15; Isa. 44:15; Jer. 37:15; Ezek. 25:12; 31:10; 35:13; 40:35; Amos 7:4; Job 1:5.

418. Murray, "*mqwm* and the Future of Israel in 2 Samuel VII 10," p. 318.

9b The phrase *a great name* (*šēm gādôl*) appears only here; but see 1 Sam. 12:22 on *šᵉmô haggādôl* "his great name." On the Lord's great fame, see Josh. 7:9; 1 K. 8:42; Jer. 44:26; Ezek. 36:23; 2 Chr. 6:32.

10 What is this *place* (*māqôm*)? McCarter thinks that it refers to a place of worship; not the land but the temple.[419] Similarly, Vanderhooft takes the term as referring to a "sacred place."[420] However, the phrase "to set a place" would idiomatically mean "to provide a place for someone/something to exist"; also Exod. 21:13; 1 Chr. 17:9; see "I have provided a place for the ark" (1 K. 8:21).[421] There are four verbs in v. 10, *nṭʿ* ("to plant"), *škn* ("to exist"), *rgz* ("to be disturbed") and *ʿnh* ("to afflict"), that grammatically can take *māqôm* as subject, or as object since the pronominal suffixes are 3 m.s. However, Murray made a detailed study of them and concluded that their appropriate subject, or object, is not *māqôm, but* "my people Israel" (hence "they" or "them"), and that the term *māqôm* refers to "land," not "shrine," in the light of the usages of the verbs "to plant" and "to exist."[422] Therefore it seems that these expressions refer to Israel's establishment in the promised land as the Lord's people.

In the light of the above, v. 10 seems to refer to the past actions of the Lord for his people (so Rost, Hertzberg, Loretz, etc.)[423] and has nothing to do with a promise of land during the exilic time as often advocated by scholars such as McCarter. Moreover, as Murray shows, this verse is "not reminiscent of the Deuteronomic *mqwm* formula either in structure, language, or thought."[424] According to him, "contrary to expectation, the temple as such is never directly and uniquely identified in the 'Deuteronomistic' allusions as the Deuteronomic *mqwm*. The clearest and most consistent substitute for the *hmqwm* of the formula is the city Jerusalem."[425]

Murray holds that in light of Exod. 21:13 and 1 K. 8:21, "the purpose Yahweh has in mind in 'establishing an appropriate place for Israel' is both permanence and security." "Israel's occupation of the land, long since a physical reality, has been beset by many hazards," but 2 Sam. 7:10 affirms that "through David (and his dynasty) Yahweh will transform that place of hazard into a place of safety, into a permanent haven of security for his people."[426]

419. See McCarter, II, pp. 202-3.

420. D. Vanderhooft, "Dwelling beneath the Sacred Place: A Proposal for Reading 2 Samuel 7:10," *JBL* 118 (1999) 625-33.

421. On Exod. 21:13 and 1 K. 8:21, see Murray, "*mqwm* and the future of Israel in 2 Samuel VII 10," pp. 314-17.

422. Murray, "*mqwm* and the Future of Israel in 2 Samuel VII 10," p. 306.

423. See Vanderhooft, "Dwelling beneath the Sacred Place," p. 626.

424. Murray, "*mqwm* and the Future of Israel in 2 Samuel VII 10," pp. 307ff.

425. Murray, "*mqwm* and the Future of Israel in 2 Samuel VII 10," p. 312.

426. Murray, "*mqwm* and the Future of Israel in 2 Samuel VII 10," pp. 318-19.

The phrase *sons of wickedness* (*bᵉnê-ʿawlāh*) refers to the wicked among the people of Israel; see on v. 11.

11 The phrase *I have given you rest* corresponds to v. 1; see above.[427]

The phrase *all your enemies* refers to David's domestic enemies such as the *sons of wickedness* (v. 10) as well as to foreign enemies such as the invading Philistines in ch. 5. David's defeat of the Philistines is given a summary statement in 8:1.

And the LORD tells you is *waw*+pf.; the perfect verb is "performative" and has the force of a solemn declaration, hence PRESENT. One should not see an "awkward" shift from first-person speech (vv. 8b-11a) to third-person speech here.[428] As in vv. 9b-11a, *waw* is simply a conjunctive here and not a *waw consecutive*, while *waw*+pfs. in vv. 12-16, which are consecutive to *the LORD will make* (impf.) of v. 11b, denote FUTURE (*I will raise, I will establish*, etc.).

David wants to build a physical *house* for the Lord (v. 5), but the Lord is rather concerned with David's *house* (dynasty). This is exactly what this chapter conveys: the Lord does not see as man sees (1 Sam. 16:7).[429] While David saw his own *house of cedars* (v. 2) and compared it with the tent shrine of the ark of God, the Lord reveals here his eternal plan of salvation that is to be realized through the agency of the Davidic dynasty.

12-13 *Offspring* (lit. "seed") and *throne* are paired words in Ps. 89:36. It is interesting to note that the phrase *the throne of his kingship* has a parallel expression in the Phoenician *ksʾ mlkh* "his royal throne" (*KAI* 1.2).[430] Note also *kussi šarrūtaka* "your royal throne" in El Amarna 34:52 and in Assyrian royal inscriptions.[431] For the combination of "kingdom," "name" and "seed" in the ANE, see the commentary on 1 Sam. 24:21 and on the meaning of the name "Samuel."[432]

A *house for my name* indicates the temple of the Lord, to be built by David's offspring Solomon, in which he puts his name, i.e., his presence itself.

14 The expression *I will become a father to him . . . he will become a son to me* denotes adoption.[433] *When he commits iniquity, he* can refer to any descendant of David who sits on the throne of David.

15 Here, God's dealing with David's *offspring* is contrasted with his dealing with Saul. For the general meaning of the term *ḥesed* (grace), see the commentary on 2:5.

427. On the theme of rest and the chosen place, see McCarter, II, p. 204. However, McCarter's emendation has been criticized by Murray, "*mqwm* and the Future of Israel in 2 Samuel VII 10," pp. 319-20.

428. *Pace* Sergi, "The Composition of Nathan's Oracle to David," pp. 263.

429. See Tsumura, I, p. 419.

430. See Laato, *A Star Is Rising*, p. 43.

431. *CAD*, K, pp. 591, 592 (Alan Millard called this to my attention).

432. Tsumura, I, pp. 128 and 573.

433. See Rainey, "Institutions: Family, Civil, and Military," p. 85.

16 The phrase *your house and your kingdom* is a *hendiadys* which can be translated "your royal house" (McCarter); see 1 Sam. 25:28 for "an enduring house" that refers to the Davidic dynasty. Note that the eternity of the Davidic throne is especially emphasized here with the final clause *your throne will be established forever*. Even if David's sons are like Saul and unworthy to sit on the throne of their father, the throne will not remain empty. A line of succession of David's throne is here promised, until the real son, the messiah, eventually comes.

2. David's Prayer (7:18-29)

18 *And King David came and sat before the LORD and said,*
"Who am I, O Lord GOD,
and what is my house,
that you should have brought me to this place?
19 *And this is yet a small matter in your sight, O Lord GOD,*
and you have spoken also of the house of your servant
about the distant future.
Is this the law for man,[434] *O Lord GOD?*
20 *And again what more shall David say to you?*
For you are the one who knows your servant, O Lord GOD!
21 *For the sake of your word and according to your heart*
you have done the whole of this great thing
to let your servant know it.

22 *Therefore [I say], you are great, O Lord GOD!*
For there is no one like you;
and there is no God besides you,
in all that we[435] *heard [about you] with our ears.*

23 *And who is like your people, like Israel,*
the only nation on the earth,
for whom angels went to pay ransom to make it a people[436]
and to put a name to it,
and to do for them[437] *the great and awesome things*

434. McCarter, II, p. 233, translates "and shown me the generation (lit. the turn of mankind to come)," reading *wtr'ny twr h'dm hm'lh*, based on 1 Chr. 17:17, following Ewald and Wellhausen. However, this emendation of the MT is not necessary, since the Hebrew makes good sense.

435. "We . . . our": 1 c.pl.; cf. 1 c.s. in other verses in the present section (vv. 18-29).

436. The phrase *to make it a people* is literally "as a people" (*lᵉʿām*).

437. So NRSV, JPS; see MT MSS; BHS apparatus; rather than Leningrad codex's "for you (pl.)"; cf. "for Thee" (NASB); McCarter simply omits it. Alter also thinks MT's "for you (pl.)"

for your (sg.) land in the presence of[438] *your people,*
whom you have released for yourself from Egypt,
that is, from the nation and its gods,[439]
24 *and have established*[440] *for yourself your people Israel*
to become your people forever,[441]
while you yourself, O LORD, have become their God?[442]
25 *Now, O LORD God,*
as for the word
that you have spoken concerning your servant and his house,
confirm it forever
and do as you have spoken
26 *that your name may be great forever, namely*[443]
'May the LORD of hosts be God over Israel!'
As for the house of your servant David,
may it be established before you!
27 *For you are the LORD of hosts, the God of Israel;*
you have revealed[444] *this to your servant, saying*
'A house I will build for you.'
Therefore your servant has found courage[445]
to pray this prayer to you.

28 *Now, O Lord GOD,*
you are God;
may your words be truth;
and you have spoken this good thing to your servant.
29 *Now, be pleased to bless the house of your servant*
to be forever before you!
For O Lord GOD, you yourself have spoken,
and by your blessing
may the house of your servant be blessed forever!"

---

problematic and translates "for them." But, does the unknown writer whom Alter assumes in v. 22 ("Therefore are You great, O LORD God . . .") appear here inadvertently? See R. Alter, *The David Story: A Translation with Commentary of 1 and 2 Samuel* (New York: W. W. Norton, 2000), p. 235.

438. Lit. "from the face of." See below.

439. LXX and 4QSam[a] read "tabernacles." This indicates the former's textual dependence on a *Vorlage* akin to the latter. See DJD 17, p. 130.

440. *waw*+impf., which is *sequential* to "you have redeemed" (pf.); cf. "For Thou hast established" (NASB); "For when you established" (McCarter).

441. Lit. "to you as a people forever" (*lᵉkā lᵉʿām ʿad-ʿôlām*).

442. Lit. "you have become God to them."

443. Lit. "saying."

444. Lit. "opened the ear of."

445. Lit. "his heart."

18-29 In this moving prayer David uses the phrase *O Lord GOD* (*'ădōnāy YHWH* [='*ĕlōhîm*]) seven times (vv. 18, 19x2, 20, 22, 28, 29), expressing his close intimacy with his God as *YHWH*. In vv. 22-23, the incomparability, hence the uniqueness, of the Lord and that of his people Israel are clearly described. The Lord is the only god who is truly God, and Israel is the Lord's people whom he has redeemed from Egypt and established for himself forever.

This prayer of David is not a psalm, but a prose prayer. However, when one analyzes it as poetry, one can see the existence of poetic parallelism. Hence, it is reasonable to describe the prose of this prayer as *poetic prose.*[446] Another example of poetic prose is the description of Eli's two sons in the prose of 1 Sam. 2:12-17.[447] Therefore, in the translation above, the sentences are divided according to their poetic parallelisms.

The outline of the prayer is as follows:

I. The Lord's Promise (vv. 18-21)
 The Lord's past dealings with David and his house (v. 18)
 The promise of the Lord's future dealings with his house (v. 19)
 David's being overwhelmed with the Lord's promise (vv. 20-21)
II. David's Confession: "You are great, O Lord God in all that" (v. 22a. . .c)
 The incomparability of the Lord (v. 22b)
 The incomparability of Israel (v. 23-24)
III. David's Supplication (vv. 25-29)
 Confirmation of the Lord's promise to David and his house (vv. 25-27)
  David's house (dynasty): "forever" (*'ad 'ôlām*)
  Yahweh's great name: "forever" (*'ad 'ôlām*)
 Prayer for the Lord's eternal blessing on David's house (vv. 28-29)
  The Lord's blessing: "forever" (*lᵉ'ôlām*)
  David's house: "forever" (*lᵉ'ôlām*)

18 The "movement" verb *came*, in the *wayqtl* form, signals a TRANSITION and change of viewpoint.[448] David, the human king, humbly *sat before the Lord* who is enthroned at the royal throne of the heavens. The rhetorical question *Who . . . and what . . . that . . . should?* conveys David's humility before the sovereign God with regard to himself and his house and expresses his unworthiness of God's guidance *to this place*, namely until this time.

446. For the subject "poetic prose," see Tsumura, I, pp. 59-60; and D. T. Tsumura, "Poetic Nature of the Hebrew Narrative Prose in I Samuel 2:12-17," in *Verse in Ancient Near Eastern Prose*, ed. J. C. de Moor and W. G. E. Watson (AOAT 42; Neukirchen-Vluyn: Neukirchener, 1993), pp. 293-304. For a poetic analysis of prose narrative in the Books of Samuel, see the commentary on 1 Sam. 2:12-17 (Tsumura, I, pp. 152-58).

447. See Tsumura, I, pp. 152-58.

448. See Tsumura, I, pp. 52 et passim (cf. p. 663 [index]).

19 *Is this the law for man, O Lord God?* "This is instruction for mankind" (ESV) or, "Is this your custom for mankind?" that is, "Is this your usual way of dealing with man?" (NIV). David expresses his amazement at the Lord's special treatment of him and his *house*, i.e., his dynasty, even *about the distant future.*

20-21 God *knows* David truly well as he is the one who called him, has been with him and has given him victories over his enemies as explained in vv. 8-9; see the commentary on 1 Sam. 2:3 for God's *true knowledge.*[449] Here, *you* (the independent pronoun *ʾattāh*) is emphasized, being placed before the verb "you know" (*yādaʿtā*), in contrast with *I* (*ʾānōkî*) in the rhetorical question *Who am I . . . ?* (v. 18).

Your word here means God's will and purpose; it is not necessarily referring to specific promises through prophets like Samuel. David is aware that God has revealed his will even to him: *to let your servant know.* God has *done all these great things* in harmony with his *word* and *heart.* Certainly, in God there is neither contradiction nor discrepancy between his thought, his word, and his conduct.

22 Alter claims that David "does not elsewhere speak in this elevated, liturgical, celebratory style," and suspects that in this passage "the influence of the presence of another writer might be plausible."[450] In fact, one can see the characteristics of poetic prose in the prayer. However, David was a noted poet, so he was certainly capable of speaking in an elevated style, and Alter's argument does not work.

The particle *ʿal-kēn* usually introduces a logical conclusion or consequence: "A *therefore* B." For example, verse 27

> You have revealed (*qtl*) this to your servant, saying
> 'A house I will build (*yqtl*) for you.'
> Therefore your servant has found (*qtl*) courage
> to pray this prayer to you.

In this verse, "therefore" (*ʿal-kēn*) indicates the result of the fact in the first half, that is, the Lord revealed, and therefore David found courage.

But, here in v. 22, *ʿal-kēn* does not indicate the result of the previous sentence: God's promise did not *make* him great; rather it showed David that he *was* great. In other words, it introduces a sentence on a different level from the preceding discourse in v. 21, giving a comment or explanatory note from the speaker's perspective; hence, "A *therefore I say* B" or "A is why *I say* B" or

449. Tsumura, I, pp. 144-45.
450. Alter, *The David Story*, p. 234.

"because of A, *I say* B." It is hinted that A is an indirect cause of B, but not a direct cause. Thus, it should be translated as follows:

> Therefore, [*I say*,] you are great (*qtl*), O Lord GOD.

This usage is *speaker-oriented* like *kî*.[451] For other examples of such a *speaker-oriented ʿal-kēn*, see Excursus (below).

For expressions of "comparative negation" such as *there is no one like you*, see the commentary on 1 Sam. 2:2.[452]

The phrase *there is no God besides you* juxtaposes the incomparability and uniqueness of the Lord, as Labuschagne notes:

> Through Yahweh's mighty deeds in history, in the history of His people (vss. 23f.) and in that of the house of David in particular (vss. 18b, 21), He showed Himself to be incomparable. This means primarily the exclusion of all rival gods, and therefore it is Yahweh who is God (cf. also vss. 26 and 28). From His imcomparability His uniqueness is logically deduced, for the former essentially implies the latter.[453]

See also Ps. 86:8-10; Deut. 4:34-35; etc. This is an explicit statement of monotheism; compare 1 Sam. 2:2.[454]

The grammatical structure of v. 22, however, is somewhat strange according to the traditional understanding of the prose grammar. A literal translation is:

> "Therefore, [*I say*,] you are great (*qtl*), O Lord GOD.
> For there is none like you and there is no God besides you
> *in* all (*bᵉkōl*) that we heard with our ears."

The last clause is usually translated as

> *according to* all that we have heard with our ears. (ESV)

or

> *as* we have heard with our own ears. (NIV; also JPS, REB)

451. See W. T. Claasen, "Speaker-oriented Functions of *ki* in Biblical Hebrew," *JNSL* 9 (1983) 29-46; Tsumura, I, pp. 48-49.

452. Tsumura, I, pp. 142-44.

453. C. J. Labuschagne, *The Incomparability of Yahweh in the Old Testament* (POS 5; Leiden: E. J. Brill, 1966), p. 119.

454. Tsumura, I, p. 143.

However, it is rather forced to translate the preposition b^{e} as "according to" or "as" in this context.

However, when the entire verse is regarded as a quadracolon, that is, a four-line parallelism, we can see that grammatically the fourth line depends on the first line *vertically*. So,

> You are great, O Lord God,
> in all that we heard with our ears.

In between the two lines, a synonymous bicolon is inserted that gives the reason why he says God is great, that is, "for there is no one like you, and there is no God besides you." Note that the particle "for" (*kî*) is *speaker-oriented.* Verse 22 thus constitutes a parallelistic structure of the AXX'B pattern,[455] or an "inserted bicolon" as in Amos 1:5; Ps. 9:7; 17:1; etc.[456]

Therefore [I say], you are great, O Lord God!	A
— For there is no one like you;	X
and there is no God besides you —	X'
in all that we heard [about you] with our ears.	B

EXCURSUS: "SPEAKER-ORIENTED *'AL-KĒN*"[457]

Speaker-oriented 'al-kēn can also be seen in several other passages. For example, 1 Sam. 5:5

> *'al-kēn lō'-yidr^{e}kû kōhănê Dāgôn w^{e}kol-habbā'îm bêt-Dāgôn 'al-miptan Dāgôn*
> *b^{e}'Ašdôd 'ad hayyôm hazzeh*
>
> *Therefore* the priests of Dagon and all who enter the house of Dagon do not tread on the threshold of Dagon in Ashdod to this day.

This is a comment by the narrator, which explains that the custom had come about because of the previous event. In other words, this comment is a *speaker-oriented* utterance.

455. See p. 122 n. 369 (above) for Ps. 89:36-37.

456. See Tsumura, I, pp. 60-64; also Tsumura, "Vertical Grammar of Biblical Hebrew Parallelism: The AXX'B Pattern in Tetracolons," *VT* 69 (2019), forthcoming.

457. Tsumura, "Speaker-oriented Connective Particle *'al-kēn* in 2 Sam 7:22," *JSS* (forthcoming).

It may be reasonable to think that an introductory phrase such as "they say" or "it is said" is omitted in the light of an example such as 1 Sam. 19:24b

ʿal-kēn yōʾmᵉrû hăgam Šāʾûl bannᵉbîʾîm
Thus they say, "Is Saul also among the prophets?"[458]

and 2 Sam. 5:8b

ʿal-kēn yōʾmᵉrû ʿiwwēr ûpissēaḥ lōʾ yābôʾ ʾel-habbāyit
Therefore it is said,[459] "The blind and the lame shall not come into the house."

In 1 Sam. 23:28b the verb "they called" follows *ʿal-kēn.*

ʿal-kēn qārᵉʾû lammāqôm hahûʾ selaʿ hammaḥlᵉqôt
Therefore they called that place the Rock of Escape.

There is also an example involving the similar particle *lākēn* in Gen 4:15, *lākēn kol-hōrēg Qayin šibʿātayim yuqqām*. The beginning of this verse is translated variously.

"Not so! If anyone kills Cain, vengeance shall be taken on him sevenfold." (ESV)
"I promise, if anyone kills Cain, sevenfold vengeance shall be taken on him." (JPS)

While ESV, NIV, and REB adopt the LXX's reading *ouch houtōs* ("Not so!"), JPS, taking *lākēn* like *ʿal-kēn,* translates "I promise," that is, God's performative utterance. I accept the latter interpretation and would translate as follows:

"Therefore, I say, anyone who kills Cain will suffer vengeance sevenfold."

We find a particularly clear case of this use of *ʿal-kēn* in Job 9:22b

ʾaḥat hîʾ ʿal-kēn ʾāmartî tām wᵉrāšāʿ hûʾ mᵉkalleh
It is all one; therefore I say (performative pf.),
'He destroys both the blameless and the wicked.' (ESV)

458. See 1 Sam. 10:12b.
459. See the commentary on 2 Sam. 5:8.

Here, Job introduces his utterance by "Therefore I say" in the *speaker-oriented* manner, with the performative perfect verb "I say."

In the light of these examples, one might better translate 2 Sam. 7:21, 22 as follows:

> Because of your promise . . . you have brought about all this
> greatness. . .,
> Therefore, *I say*, you are great, O Lord God.

In other words, what you have done causes me to say you are great.

---

23 This verse is notoriously difficult and has even been labeled by Pfeiffer as "the worst instance of illiterate inanity."[460] However, the best approach to any seemingly impossible text is to seek its plain meaning, the one that is grammatically and semantically the most natural.

After confirming the incomparability of the Lord in v. 22 with the expression *there is no one like you*, David turns his attention to the incomparability of Israel with the similar phrase *who is like your people, like Israel, the only nation on the earth* (see 1 Sam. 22:14, 26:15), describing the people Israel as *incomparable* among the nations of the world.[461] The phrase *gôy 'eḥād* (lit. "one nation") here probably means *the only nation* (see JPS: "a unique nation"); cf. "other nation" (McCarter, following the LXX, reads *'ḥr*). David is here referring to the Exodus events through which the Israelites became God's covenant people.

The next phrase says that *'ĕlōhîm went to pay ransom* for Israel, *to make it a people* (lit. "as a people"). What does this *'ĕlōhîm* refer to? The LXX translates it as "God," *ho theos*, and McCarter as "a god." The parallel passage in Chronicles (1 Chr. 17:21 *hālak hā'ĕlōhîm*) is clearly "God." However, since the verb *went* is plural, the subject *'ĕlōhîm* is better translated as "angels" or "divine beings," the agents of God, rather than as "God"; see "destroying angels" (Ps. 78:49).

The relative clause *for whom as a people angels went to pay ransom* means that God's agents, the angels, went to pay ransom so that Israel might be freed and become his people. And *to pay ransom for* means "to redeem." So, "whom God went to redeem to be his people" (ESV). Compare NASB's "redeem for Himself" (also see NIV), which is influenced by "for yourself" (NASB: "for Thyself") of the second half of the verse. The Israelite people were "slaves" of the Egyptians. In a sense God paid *ransom for* his people in order "to release

460. Cited by McCarter, II, p. 238.

461. For a detailed study of this verse, see Tsumura, "The Incomparability of Israel, the People of Yahweh," *Exeg* 14 (2003) 51-61 [Japanese with an English summary].

them from the Egyptians." It should be noted that in this verse the verb *pdh is used in two different meanings, namely (1) "to pay ransom for someone" and (2) "to release someone from." These exact two usages can be seen in two different passages from the Ugaritic legal text *KTU* 3.4. (See Excursus below).

The textual problem in verse 23a of *lākem*, "for you (pl.)" in the Leningrad codex, has long been noted. McCarter simply omits it. NRSV, JPS, etc. as well as BHS apparatus read "to them" *lāhem*. However, I would suggest it is possible to explain *lākem* as due to a scribe's phonetic misremembering of the sound [xem] as [hem] as he was copying the text, rather than a scribe's misreading of the text.

The second half of verse 23, is also problematic, especially with respect to the syntactic relationship of the prepositional phrase *mippᵉnê ʿammᵉkā* (lit. "from the face of your people"). Most modern translations follow the LXX and 1 Chronicles 17:21, which reads (*lᵉgārēš*), and translate either "by driving out before your people" (ESV) or "by driving out nations and their gods" (NIV; also, JPS, REB). NRSV even translates: "by driving out before his people nations and their gods?" giving up translating the rest of the verse.

Here, again, it might be useful to note the parallelistic structure of this *poetic prose*. In standard prose grammar, the relative clause, *ʾăšer pādîtā lᵉkā mimmiṣrayim* "whom you have released *for yourself*[462] from Egypt," would normally modify the immediately preceding word, namely "your people." However, given the poetic nature, it would seem more likely that *the only nation* (*gôy ʾeḥād*) in the second line is followed by *two* parallel relative clauses,

> "for whom angels went to pay ransom"

and

> "whom you have released for yourself from Egypt,"

so both clauses modify "the only nation." In this case, the prepositional phrase *mippᵉnê ʿammᵉkā* should be taken as a part of the preceding relative clause, namely, "for whom angels went to pay ransom . . . the great and awesome things for your land," and interpreted as meaning something like "in the presence of your people."[463]

The end of verse 23, the phrase *from the nation and its gods (gôyīm wē[ʾ]lōhâw)* is literally "nations and its gods." However, as "nations" is plural and "its" is singular, it is usually translated as "nations and their gods" (NRSV, NIV, NASB, JPS), taking the suffix to be plural, though the ESV and McCarter,

462. The context requires the translation *for yourself*; cf. "[to pay ransom] to him" (see Excursus, below).

463. The preposition *min* sometimes means "in front of" (*HALOT*, s.v. *pnh*, 5.c.i "in front of the enemy" (Ps 61:4; Lam 2:3). Cf. *miḥûṣ* "outside of" (Gen. 19:16; Deut. 23:12); *miqqedem* "in the east" (Gen. 3:24).

following the LXX (*ethnē*), translate both as singular, "a nation and its gods." However, keeping the MT intact, we would like to take the *mem* of *gôy-im* as an enclitic with an adverbial force (*from*) instead of as a plural suffix. This enclitic *mem* functions as X of the AXB pattern, in which X is inserted into the compound phrase "the nation and its gods" (A & B) and yet modifies the phrase as a whole (see Ps. 1:2 *yômām wālāylāh* "day and night").[464] Hence, we suggest the translation *from the nation and its gods*, with the *nation* referring to Egypt only.

24 The first word *watt^ekônēn*, being a *wayqtl*, is in sequence with the perfect verb *pādîtā* in the previous verse and so is a part of the relative clause, *whom you have redeemed*. Thus, v. 24 is a continuation of v. 23 where David confesses the incomparability of Israel using traditional covenant terms: Israel became *your people*, while the Lord became *their God*. Here, David reconfirms the special covenant relationship beween the incomparable *God* (v. 22) and his incomparable *people* (v. 23).

25-29 The third section (III) of David's prayer, verses 25-29, has the following elements:

1. Confirmation of the Lord's promise to David and his house (vv. 25-27)
   David's house (dynasty): "forever" (*'ad 'ôlām*)
   Lord's great name: "forever" (*'ad 'ôlām*)
2. Prayer for Lord's eternal blessing on David's house (vv. 28-29)
   Lord's blessing: "forever" (*l^e'ôlām*)
   David's house: "forever" (*l^e'ôlām*).

David asks first that the Lord's promise of an eternal dynasty be confirmed, and then, that the Lord's blessing be on his house (that is, dynasty "forever" [*l^e'ôlām*]).

27 With the expression *you are the LORD of hosts* David is confessing that the Lord is the Eternal King who is enthroned in heaven as the sovereign Lord. For the phrase *the LORD of hosts* (*YHWH ṣ^ebā'ôt*), see the commentary on 1 Sam. 1:3.[465]

28 The plural *words* of the expression *your words are truth* refers to the concrete and specific promises of God to David, while the *word* (vv. 21 and 25) refers to God's will and his deeds in general concerning David and his *house*.

29 *For O Lord GOD, you yourself have spoken* — this is David's grounds for asking God for his blessing. The expression *l^e'ôlām* "forever" appears only here (twice) in the entire Books of Samuel; cf. *'ad-'ôlām* that appears sixteen times; see Introduction. Alter summarizes the key words in David's prayer that function as formal rhetorical motifs as follows:[466]

464. For the AXB pattern, see Tsumura, I, pp. 60-64.

465. Tsumura, I, pp.109-11.

466. Alter, *The David Story*, p. 235.

"speak": the act of God's promise and continuing revelation;
"house": dynasty and palace but, in this speech, not temple;
"blessing": in the final sentence it occurs three times in three different forms;
"forever": the adverbial index of the permanence of God's promise.

EXCURSUS: RANSOMING AND REDEEMING[467]

In 2 Sam. 7:23 the verb *pdh appears twice, though with slightly different meanings:

1. "to pay ransom for" (v. 23a) [Israel] *for whom angels went to pay ransom to make it a people* (lit. "as a people")
2. "to release . . . from" (v. 23b) *you have released [it] for yourself from Egypt*

These exact two usages can be seen in two different passages in the Ugaritic legal text *KTU* 3.4.

1. "to pay ransom for" = "to redeem."

w pdyh[m] PN *mit ksp* "and PN paid ransom of one hundred silver for them" = "and PN redeemed them for one hundred (shekels of) silver" (3.4:12)[468]

The act of paying ransom for somebody is the act of redeeming that person. This common economic transaction is metaphorically used in the Bible for the saving act of redemption, in this passage, for the Lord's saving of Israel.

2. "to release . . . from" = "to redeem . . . from."

PN_1 *pdy* PN_2 . . . *b yd* PN_3

"PN_1 released PN_2 . . . from the power of PN_3" = "PN_1 redeemed PN_2 . . . from PN_3" (3.4:2)

467. Tsumura, "The Incomparability of Israel the People of Yahweh," 58-60.

468. *DULAT*, pp. 663-64. G. "to redeem, ransom"; cf. Heb. *pdh*, *HALOT*, pp. 911f.; for Akk., see *AHw*, p. 808; for Arabic, see Lane, pp. 2353f.; for Old South Arabic, see Biella, *DOSA*, p. 401.

In some contexts, the act of paying ransom for others is expressed as freeing someone from the control of others. This verse, 23b, is such a case where the verb is used with the preposition *min* "from." The same usage is attested in Deut. 7:8; 13:5; etc. as well as in Jer. 15:21; Hos. 13:14; and Ps. 49:15.[469]

F. CATALOGUE OF DAVID'S MILITARY VICTORIES (8:1-18)

Chapter 8 starts with a catalogue of David's victories (vv. 1-14), from the old enemies, the Philistines, to the Transjordan nations of Moab and Ammon, through the Syrian countries, and all the way to "the River," the Euphrates, and ends with a statement on his administration (vv. 15-18). It is not necessarily in chronological order with the rest of the book. The Ammon war of chapters 10-12 may have been the prelude to David's defeat in this chapter of the important kingdom of Zobah. Verse 13 has ties with the title to Psalm 60: "A mitkam of David; for instruction; when he strove with Aram-naharaim and with Aram-zobah [see v. 3], and when Joab on his return struck down twelve thousand of Edom in the Valley of Salt" (ESV). The older empires in Egypt and Mesopotamia were at a low point, which allowed David to take advantage of the international situation. The material in the chapter possibly comes from the earlier period of David's reign.

1. David's Military Activities (8:1-14)

The organizing principle in this section is not chronology, but geography, since it is "a catalogue of victories" that shows how under David the land extended its borders in four directions, i.e., from west (Philistia) to east (Moab) in vv. 1-2 and from north (Aram) to south (Edom) in vv. 3-8, 13-14,[470] to become a small empire extending from the Orontes to the River of Egypt. Nevertheless, David apparently did not assume the ancient Near Eastern title "the Great King" (*melek rab*).[471]

469. The verb *pdh is similar to *g'l (redeem) in meaning and usage. *g'l occurs in passages such as Mic. 4:10; Ps. 103:4; 106:10; and 107:2. The two are a word pair in passages like Jer. 31:11; Hos. 13:14; and Ps. 69:18.

470. Younger, *PHA*, p. 198. Younger notes the same pattern in 1 Chr. 18, i.e., from west to east in vv. 1-2 and from north to south in vv. 3-8, 12-13. See C. Edenburg, "David, the Great King, King of the Four Quarters: Structure and Signification in the Catalogue of David's Conquests (2 Samuel 8:1-4, 1 Chronicles 18:1-13)," in *Raising Up a Faithful Exegete: Essays in Honor of Richard D. Nelson*, ed. K. L. Noll and B. Schramm (Winona Lake, Ind.: Eisenbrauns, 2010), pp. 161-62.

471. See P. Artzi and A. Malamat, "The Great King: A Preeminent Royal Title in Cu-

1 *After this David defeated the Philistines and subdued them.*
And David took Metheg-ammah from the hand of the Philistines
2 *and defeated Moab and measured them with the measuring-cord, making them lie down on the ground, and measured two lots to put to death and one full lot to keep alive.*
And Moab became David's vassals[472] *who paid tribute.*
3 *And David defeated Hadadezer son of Rehob the king of Zobah, when he went to restore his rule*[473] *at the River.*[474]
4 *And David captured from him*[475] *1,700 horsemen with their horses and 20,000 foot soldiers.*
And David hamstrung all the chariot horses but left 100 chariot horses out of them.
5 *And Aram-Damascus came to help Hadadezer the king of Zobah.*
And David killed 22,000 men in Aram.
6 *And David put garrisons in Aram-Damascus.*
And Aram became David's vassals who paid tribute.
And the LORD gave David victory wherever he went.

7 *And David took the gold quivers that belonged to*[476] *the servants of Hadadezer and brought them to Jerusalem;*
8 *and from Betah and Berothai, cities of Hadadezer, King David took a very large amount of bronze.*
9 *And Toi the king of Hamath heard that David had defeated all the army of Hadadezer.*
10 *And Toi sent Joram his son to King David to greet him*[477] *and congratulate him, because he had fought against Hadadezer and defeated him — for Hadadezer had been a man who fought often with Toi*[478] *— and he brought silver articles and gold articles and bronze articles.*
11 *These too King David consecrated to the LORD, with the silver and gold that he had consecrated from all the nations he had subdued,*

---

neiform Sources and the Bible" in *The Tablet and the Scroll: Near Eastern Studies in Honor of William W. Hallo*, ed. M. E. Cohen, D. Snell, and D. Weisberg (Bethesda, Md.: CDL Press, 1993), p. 38.

472. Lit., "servants"; also v. 6 as well as 1 Sam. 27:12.

473. McCarter, II, pp. 247-48, reads "leave his stela," based on LXX, and comments: "the Euphrates was a boundary to which western kings aspired to march and leave a monument"; see the case of Thutmosis III.

474. I.e., the Euphrates (see MT, Q.); cf. "the Euphrates River" (NIV; JPS).

475. Heb. *mimmennû*; this phrase is missing in 4QSam[a].

476. So NIV; lit., "had been to" (*hāyû 'el*); or "were carried by" (NASB, NRSV, also JPS).

477. Lit., "to ask him of peace."

478. Lit., "a man of wars of/with Toi"; or "at war" (NASB).

12 *from Edom*[479] *and Moab and the sons of Ammon, and the Philistines and Amalek, as well as those from the spoil of Hadadezer son of Rehob, the king of Zobah.*

13 *And David made a name for himself*[480] *when he returned from defeating 18,000 Edomites in the Valley of Salt,*

14 *and put garrisons in Edom; in all Edom he put garrisons.*
And all Edom became servants to David.
And the LORD gave David victory wherever he went.

1 *Metheg-ammah* (*meteg hā'ammāh*) is otherwise unknown. Possibly, it refers to a type of land. The parallel text, 1 Chr. 18:1, has "Gath and its villages" (lit., her daughters), which, according to Rainey, probably refers to Gath-rimmon northwest of Gezer.[481] After the time of David, there are no references to battles with the Philistines until the time of Hezekiah (2 K. 18:8).[482]

2 When David was a fugitive from Saul's court he had asked the king of Moab to let his parents live at Mizpeh of Moab (1 Sam. 22:3). Though Saul was their common enemy at that time, Israel and Moab are now enemies, even though according to Ruth 4:13-17 David's great-grandmother was Moabite. For the historical geography, see *CBA*, #101.

The method of selecting prisoners of war for execution by the use of *the measuring-cord* (*ḥebel*) is not attested elsewhere. Note that the Akkadian cognate *eblu* "rope [of land]" (= 6 iku) is a unit of measurement for land.[483] The *full* (*m^{e}lō'*) is used almost like the numeral 1, as Ug. *ml'*, Nuzi Akk. (*ma-la* "1"), Heb. (only with measures); see "a full homer of wine" (Arad 2:5); "a full omer" (Exod. 16:32-33); "a full reed" (Ezek. 41:8).[484]

3-12 Zobah and Damscus were both in Syria ("Aram" in Hebrew). *Zobah* (see 10:6), situated on the eastern slope of the Anti-Lebanon mountain in the northern part of the Beqaa Valley (modern Lebanon), was the leading Aramean state at the time of David and before the rise of Damascus.

While one may take the present events as preceding the crucial affair with Bathsheba and Uriah in chapter 11,[485] the references in 10:6, 16 to *Zobah*

479. As in a number of MT MSS as well as LXX, Syr., 1 Chr. 18:11; cf. "Aram" (NASB; MT in BHS).

480. So NASB; or "became famous" (NIV); cf. "built a monument" (McCarter, II, pp. 245-46).

481. *SB*, p. 160.

482. On the "dark ages" of the Philistines after their defeat by David, see C. S. Ehrlich, *The Philistines in Transition: A History from ca. 1000-730 BCE* (SHCANE 10; Leiden: E. J. Brill, 1996).

483. See *RlA* 7 (1989), p. 480; D. T. Tsumura, "Exegetical Notes," *Exeg* 1 (1990) 26.

484. Gordon, *UT*, §19.1479; also *DULAT*, p. 546.

485. See *SB*, p. 160.

and *Hadadezer* suggest that the events of chs. 10-12 may chronologically be the prelude to v. 3. If so, after his disastrous defeat by David and the defection of his vassals (10:19) and the defeat of Ammon (12:31), Hadadezer went to the Euphrates to try to restore his power over his vassals, but was attacked on the way by David (8:3).

If so, the course of events might be summarized as follows:

1. Moab was conquered and became David's vassal (8:2).
2. The new Ammonite ruler Hanun insulted David's ambassadors; Hanun hired the Aramean soldiers; David sent Joab and Abishai with his army to fight with the Ammonites and the Arameans; the latter were defeated and fled, while the former *entered* the fortified city of Rabbah (10:1-14).
3. *Hadadezer* sent for all his vassals and associates among the Aramean kingdoms and tribes as far as the Euphrates. They assembled at Helam, where David defeated them. They then made *peace* with Israel and served them. *And the Arameans were afraid to help the Ammonites again* (10:15-19).
4. David sent the army under Joab to capture Rabbah (11:1; 12:26-31).
5. *Hadadezer* the king of Zobah went to restore his rule *at the River*; but David *defeated Hadadezer* and his associates; Toi the king of Hamath sent his son to congratulate David; King David consecrated various silver and gold articles to the Lord; David conquered the Edomites (8:3-14; see 1 Chr. 18:12-13).[486]

3 *Hadadezer son of Rehob* was the leader of the Aramean coalition that opposed David, according to 10:16. The phrase *son of Rehob* has been taken as evidence that Zobah was ruled by a dynasty from Beth-rehob; see 10:6. Malamat suggests that possibly Hadadezer ruled first in Beth-rehob and then combined it with Zobah.[487] He seems to have had enough influence to draw together Arameans even from *beyond the River*. Though his name does not appear in contemporary extrabiblical materials, "he has been provisionally identified with an unnamed Aramean king mentioned in Assyrian annals as having conquered certain territories on the upper Euphrates south of Carchemish in the time of the Assyrian monarch Ashurrabi II, a contemporary of David."[488]

486. On the conquest of Edom, see *CBA*, #103.

487. A. Malamat, "Aspects of the Foreign Policies of David and Solomon," *JNES* 22 (1963) 2-3 [repr. in Malamat, *History of Biblical Israel: Major Problems and Minor Issues* (CHANE 7; Leiden: E. J. Brill, 2001), pp. 208-33]. See also Younger, *PHA*, p. 201.

488. A. Malamat, "The Kingdom of David and Solomon in Its Contact with Egypt and Aram Naharaim," *BA* 21 (1958) 101-2; see McCarter, II, p. 248.

The subject of the phrase *when he went to restore his rule* (*bᵉlektô lᵉhāšîb yādô*), lit., "in his going to bring back his hand (i.e., power, rule)," is ambiguous, but JPS, REB, and NJB clearly identify it as Hadadezer.[489] McCarter, on the other hand, says that if it was Hadadezer who marched to the Euphrates, "he would hardly have encountered David on the way since Israel was south of Zobah and the Euphrates north." However, the text does not suggest that Hadadezer had "encountered" David on the way. Rather, it seems that David took the initiative and went and attacked and *defeated* Hadadezer. As mentioned above, it is possible this event occurred after those in 10:15-19, where David's victories over the Arameans are described.

4 Having captured chariot horses, David apparently decided to experiment with a small chariot force. It is not clear why he would hamstring the other horses. It may have been to keep them from falling into enemy hands, or it may have been in response to the warning in Deut. 17:16 that the king must not acquire many horses for himself. The hamstrung horses could presumably have been used as farm or pack horses. In Josh. 11:6-9, the Lord tells Joshua to hamstring captured horses and burn captured chariots, and Joshua obeys.

For the MT phrase *1,700 horsemen* (*pārāšîm*), the translation "a thousand of his chariots, seven thousand charioteers" (NIV; also McCarter), has been suggested based on the LXX. McCarter assumes that MT experienced a haplography and a subsequent "imperfect attempt to correct the damage."[490] Yet, the combination of 1,000 chariots and 7,000 charioteers seems rather unbalanced. The view of Ap-Thomas that the original figures were 1,000 chariots, 700 cavalrymen, and 20,000 foot soldiers sounds more reasonable.[491] It may be, however, that the term *pārāšîm*, which can mean either "(military) horses" or "horsemen" (see Hab. 1:8)[492] and is parallel here with the *foot soldiers*, refers to a horse and rider as a pair. On the other hand, the Hebrew term *hārekeb*, which is literally "the chariot," here clearly means chariot *horses*, since most were *hamstrung* (*ʿqr; see Josh. 11:6, 9). Thus David probably kept the 1,700 riding horses and 100 of the chariot horses unstrung, for cavalry would be useful in a mountainous area like Judah, while chariots would not. For the possibility of Hebrew *ʾelep* as a military unit, see the commentary on 1 Sam. 4:2.[493]

5-6 At the time of David, *Zobah* (see v. 3) overshadowed *Aram-Damascus* among the small Aramean states. After the events of chapter 10,

489. See Younger, *PHA*, pp. 196-97.

490. McCarter, II, p. 244.

491. D. R. Ap-Thomas, "A Numerical Poser," *JNES* 2 (1943) 198-200.

492. Tsumura, "Polysemy and Parallelism in Hab 1,8-9," pp. 194-203.

493. Tsumura, I, p. 189.

Aram was defeated and became *David's vassals.*[494] Putting *garrisons* in Aram indicates a formal Israelite presence there; see the commentary on 1 Sam. 10:5.[495]

The comment *and the LORD gave David victory wherever he went* is a summary statement concerning the Lord's dealing with David. McCarter thinks that the notice is premature at this point, having arisen here accidentally as it is repeated in v. 14. However, this phrase marks the end of each of the two sections, vv. 1-6 and vv. 7-14, of this somewhat dull, list-like[496] description.

7-8 Here the second part of this catalogue of David's victories begins. *The gold šilṭê* have been interpreted as "gold shields" (NRSV, NIV, JPS, etc.), but this has no etymological support. The term *šeleṭ* probably means "quiver" or "bow case" in the light of Aramaic. Akkadian *šalṭu* "bow-and-arrow case," which appears only in Neo-Assyrian and Neo-Babylonian texts, is possibly an Aramaic loanword.[497]

Some versions (4QSam^a, LXX, OL, Josephus, *Ant.* 7.106) have a longer text that mentions that Shoshenq, king of Egypt, later took these gold quivers. These texts, except the first, as well as 1 Chr. 18:8, also mention that Solomon used the bronze mentioned here to make the bronze sea and pillars and utensils for the temple. But, the shorter text of MT probably stands closer to the primitive text.[498]

Betah (*Beṭaḥ*): so NASB, NRSV, JPS; cf. "Tebah" (NIV, McCarter), following Syr, LXX^L; cf. 1 Chr. 18:8 "Tibhath" (*Ṭibḥat*). McCarter identifies Tebah with a city in the Beqaa south of modern Ḥoms. It is mentioned in the Amarna archive as *ṭu-bi-ḫi* (EA 179:15 et passim) as well as in Papyrus Anastasi I, 19:1 as *du-bi-ḫi.*[499] It is possible that Tebah is a metathesis[500] of the original form *biṭḥ- of the segolate *Betah*: *ṭebaḥ* < *ṭibḥ-* < *biṭḥ-*.

Berothai is attested as modern Bereitan, a few miles south of Ras Ba'albek, the site of Cun, in the Beqaa Valley. Cun appears in the synoptic parallel to the present passage in 1 Chr. 18:8. McCarter thinks that all three cities,

494. See W. T. Pitard, *Ancient Damascus* (Winona Lake, Ind.: Eisenbrauns, 1987), pp. 87-95; P. E. Dion, *Les Araméens à l'Âge du Fer: Histoire politique et structures sociales* (Paris: J. Gabalda, 1997). For the most recent and comprehensive study of *Aram-Damascus*, see Younger, *PHA*, pp. 549-654.

495. Tsumura, I, p. 286.

496. For the list and the list-like description, see Tsumura, I, pp. 350-51, etc.

497. *CAD* Š/1, pp. 271-72; *AHw*, p. 1147. For the meaning "bow cases," see R. Borger "Die Waffenträger des Königs Darius: Ein Beitrag zur alttestamentlichen Exegese und zur semitischen Lexikographie," *VT* 22 (1972) 393. For a detailed description, see *HALOT*, p. 1522.

498. See McCarter, II, p. 244.

499. *SB*, p. 72.

500. Tsumura, "Scribal Errors or Phonetic Spellings?," pp. 390-411, esp. 395-96.

Tebah, Berothai, and Cun, were principal cities in the kingdom of Zobah.[501] Berothah (Ezek. 47:16) may be a dialectical variant of *Berothai.*[502]

9 *Hamath* was on the middle Orontes River; it was the capital of a Neo-Hittite state that bordered Zobah on the north. It has been suggested that the name *Toi* (*Tōʿî*) is Hurrian.[503]

10-12 Toi, though he was not a formal ally of David, sent his son Joram with valuable gifts to David in order to establish an alliance between Israel and Hamath, in which Israel was the superior partner.[504] The expression, "to ask the peace," possibly marks the start of diplomatic negotiations. Toi's son *Joram* (*Yôrām*; LXX Ieddouran) is called *Hădôrām* (LXX Idouram) in 1 Chr. 18:10. Malamat suggests that Hadoram, which means "Haddu is exalted," took the second Yahwistic name "Joram" ("Yahweh is exalted") as an expression of loyalty to David.

The victory over Ammon is mentioned here, even though the Ammon war itself is described in chs. 11-12. David's victories are listed thematically rather than chronologically. See the commentary on 7:1.

The treasures later became part of Solomon's treasure and were used to build the temple or were placed in the temple treasury (1 Chr. 18:8; 1 K. 7:51).

13 *The Valley of Salt* (*gêʾ-melaḥ*) must have been in the Edomite territory south and east of the Dead Sea.[505] First Chronicles 18:12 states that Abishai son of Zeruiah killed the Edomites.[506] Here, the deeds of David's generals are ascribed to David, just as in Chronicles the deeds of Abishai's men are ascribed to Abishai. Joab seems to have led the campaign (title of Ps. 60); at this time, Hadad of the royal house of Edom escaped (1 K. 11:14-18).

14 *"And the LORD gave David victory wherever he went."* : = v. 6b ends the catalogue.

501. McCarter, II, p. 250.

502. *SB*, p. 17.

503. See McCarter, II, p. 250. Cf. "Tou" in LXX[BMN], OL and 1 Chr. 18:9 (*Tōʿû*).

504. Malamat, "The Kingdom of David and Solomon," 101; Malamat, "Aspects of the Foreign Policies of David and Solomon," 6; also see *SB*, p. 161.

505. For archaeological confirmation of tenth- to ninth-century B.C. Edomite history, see the most recent discovery of "King Solomon's mine" in Edom; T. E. Levy and M. Najjar, "Edom and Copper: The Emergence of Ancient Israel's Rival," *BAR* 32.4 (2006) 24-35, 70; Levy and Najjar, "New Iron Age Copper: Mine Fields Discovered in Southern Jordan," *NEA* 72.2 (2009) 98-101; T. E. Levy, M. Najjar, and E. Ben-Yosef, "The Iron Age Edom Lowlands Regional Archaeology Project: Research, Design, and Methodology," in *New Insights into the Iron Age Archaeology of Edom, Southern Jordan*, ed. T. E. Levy, M. Najjar, and E. Ben-Yosef (Los Angeles: UCLA Cotsen Institute of Archaeology Press, 2014), pp. 1-86.

506. For a detailed discussion of the several versions, see McCarter, II, p. 246.

2. David's Officials (8:15-18)

15 *And David ruled over all Israel.*
And David was doing justice and righteousness for all his people.
16 *Joab son of Zeruiah, army general;*
Jehoshaphat son of Ahilud, recorder;
17 *Zadok son of Ahitub and Ahimelech son of Abiathar, priests;*
Seraiah, scribe;
18 *Benaiah son of Jehoiada, Cherethites-Pelethites general;*
David's sons were priests.

15-18 This is a list of David's officials; see also the list in 20:23-26 and the similar list of Solomon's officials in 1 K. 4:1-6. It is paralleled in 1 Chr. 18:14-17.

15 Like the list in Kings, this one starts with the office of the king. It was the task of the king to establish *justice and righteousness* (*mišpāṭ ûṣdāqāh*; see 1 K. 10:9), following the Lord, who exercises "justice and righteousness"; see Isa. 33:5; Jer. 9:24; etc.[507]

16 For *Joab son of Zeruiah*, see the commentary on 2:13.

The term *army general* (*'al-haṣṣābā'*) is a case of the *nominalization* of the prepositional phrase "over the army."[508] It corresponds to *turtānu* "the field marshal" of the Neo-Assyrian royal court.[509]

Jehoshaphat son of Ahilud is listed as *recorder* in all three lists; he remained in office under Solomon. The offices of *recorder* and *scribe* (v. 17) were common in surrounding countries. The *recorder* (*mazkîr*) is an official in charge of public records. This term appears on a Moabite seal and has been translated as "the 'memorist', herald," but the title is not really understood.[510]

Some have asserted that the Davidic court administration was patterned specifically after the Egyptian model and render *mazkîr* as "remembrancer" (McCarter) or "herald" in the light of Egyptian *wḥmw* "speaker," whose duty was "to make reports to the king and transmit royal decrees."[511] But Mazar as well as the leading Egyptologists Kitchen and Redford reject the equation

507. For "social justice" in ancient Israel and in the ancient Near East, see M. Weinfeld, *Social Justice in Ancient Israel and in the Ancient Near East* (Jerusalem: Magnes Press, 1995).

508. For the phrase *that which was upon it* (1 Sam. 9:24), see Tsumura, I, p. 279.

509. See A. K. Grayson, "Assyrian Officials and Power in the Ninth and Eighth Centuries," *SAAB* 7 (1993) 21f.; R. Mattila, *The King's Magnates: A Study of the Highest Officials of the Neo-Assyrian Empire* (SAAS 11; Helsinki: Neo-Assyrian Text Corpus Project, 2000).

510. N. Avigad and B. Sass, *Corpus of West Semitic Stamp Seals* (Jerusalem: Israel Academy of Sciences and Humanities, 1997), p. 467 (No. 1011).

511. See McCarter, II, p. 255. This corresponds to *nāgir ekalli* "the palace herald," one of the Neo-Assyrian high officials. See also Grayson, "Assyrian Officials and Power in the Ninth and Eighth Centuries," p. 21f.

of this term with Egyptian *wḥmw*.[512] As Layton notes, every royal court had similar officials, and hence no direct dependence should be assumed between these two terms.[513] Mazar has suggested that David was influenced by the long history of Jerusalem as an independent city-state and must have learned from it and other conquered city-states about civil administrative systems.[514] The recent discovery outside Jerusalem's Old City wall of an Akkadian administrative tablet fragment with similarities to the Amarna letters would support the contention that in the fourteenth century B.C. Jerusalem had royal archives and hence a Late Bronze Age civil administrative system.[515] Technical terms such as *recorder* and *scribe* were probably derived from earlier Canaanite terms.

17 *Zadok* would help David during Absalom's rebellion (15:24-29; 17:15; 19:11). After David's death he continued to hold the office of high priest under Solomon (see 1 K. 2:35). The origin of Zadok has been hotly debated. Zadok's father *Ahitub* was probably not Ahitub, grandson of Eli (see 1 Sam. 14:3), as Eli does not appear in the genealogy in 1 Chr. 6:6; see also 1 K. 2:27.

Rowley's 1939 "Jebusite hypothesis," which is followed most recently by Rendsburg,[516] takes this PN as related to the DN *Ṣdq*, and concludes that the priest Zadok was originally associated with the Jerusalem cult of that god (see also Gray and Rosenberg). Cross criticizes Rowley's hypothesis and holds that the name is a hypocoristicon of DN-*ṣaduq*, "The god N is righteous," and is not connected with the DN *Ṣdq*.[517] According to 1 Chr. 6:3-8, Zadok was the descendant of Aaron's son Eleazar. Though this genealogy has been taken by Wellhausen and his followers[518] as "a sacerdotal fiction" to legitimize his line in postexilic times, Cross defends the authenticity of the Aaronid lineage of Zadok as a descendant of Aaron through a line other than the Shilonide priesthood.[519]

512. K. A. Kitchen, "Egypt and Israel During the First Millennium B.C.," *Congress Volume: Jerusalem 1986* (VTS 40; Leiden: E. J. Brill, 1988), pp. 113-24; and D. B. Redford, "Studies in Relations between Palestine and Egypt During the First Millennium B.C. I. The Taxation System of Solomon," in *Studies on the Ancient Palestinian World*, ed. J. W. Wevers and D. B. Redford (Toronto: University of Toronto Press, 1972), p. 144.

513. S. C. Layton, "The Steward in Ancient Israel: A Study of Hebrew *('ăšer) 'al-habbayit* in Its Near Eastern Setting," *JBL* 109 (1990) 646.

514. B. Mazar, "King David's Scribe and the High Officialdom of the United Monarchy of Israel," in *The Early Biblical Period: Historical Studies*, ed. A. Ahituv and B. A. Levine (Jerusalem: Israel Exploration Society, 1986), p. 128.

515. E. Mazar, "A Cuneiform Tablet from the Ophel in Jerusalem," pp. 4-21.

516. G. A. Rendsburg, "The Internal Consistency and Historical Reliability of the Biblical Genealogies," *VT* 40 (1990) 197.

517. Cooper, "Divine Names and Epithets in the Ugaritic Texts," p. 409.

518. Recently, Rendsburg, "The Internal Consistency and Historical Reliability of the Biblical Genealogies," p. 197.

519. F. M. Cross, *Canaanite Myth and Hebrew Epic: Essays in the History of the Religion*

This is the only reference to the priest *Ahimelech son of Abiathar*, except for the parallel passage in 1 Chr. 18:16. His father Abiathar was son of Ahimelech the priest at Nob and accompanied David in his wilderness days (1 Sam. 22:20; 23:6; and 30:7).[520] He worked with Zadok during Absalom's rebellion, but was banished for supporting Adonijah's attempt to become king (1 K. 2:26-27).

Abiathar is referred to as priest along with Zodak in the account of Absalom's rebellion (15:24-29; 17:15; 19:11), the list in 20:25, and in 1 K. 1-2, and there is no other reference to him having a son Ahimelech. Therefore it is possible that the MT *Ahimelech son of Abiathar* is a scribal mistake for "Abiathar son of Ahimelech" (Syr.; 1 Sam. 23:6; 30:7).[521] However, it is also possible that "Ahimelech" is the name of Abiathar's son as well as that of Abiathar's father, since naming a son after his grandfather was a common practice; see the commentary on 1 Sam. 14:3.[522] In this case, Abiathar may have retired early in David's reign from his position as one of the chief priests in favor of a son, as Zadok later did (1 K. 4:2), and later, when the son died or had some other problem, Abiathar resumed the position.

It is possible that the secretary *Seraiah* (*śᵉrāyāh*) is the same as the *Sheva* (*šᵉwāʾ* 20:25[Q.]) and *Shisha* (*šîšāʾ* 1 K. 4:3) of the other two lists, but this is not established. McCarter suggests "Shausha" as the original name, following 1 Chr. 18:16 (*šawšāʾ*) and LXX (Sousa, here and 2 Sam. 20:25). It may be that it was a foreign name, which would have been especially liable to variant spellings. Mazar thinks it might have been originally a Hurrian name, possibly *Šewe-šarri*, which is known from Nuzi documents.[523] Like the recorder, scribes existed in every royal court; David did not have to model his officer on the Egyptian example.[524]

18 *Benaiah*, whose name means "A builder/creator is Yah(u)," or "Yah(u) creates,"[525] was in charge of David's personal force of Cherethites and Pelethites. He was one of David's "mighty men" (23:20-22). Like Zadok, he supported Solomon against Adonijah, and under Solomon became commander of the whole army in place of Joab (1 K. 1-2, 4:4).

The *Cherethites and the Pelethites* (also 15:18; 20:7; 1 K. 1:38, 44) were foreigners who made up the king's bodyguard (cf. 1 Sam. 28:2). They probably

of Israel (Cambridge: Harvard University Press, 1973), pp. 207-15. See also S. Olyan, "Zadok's Origins and the Tribal Politics of David," *JBL* 101 (1982) 177-93.

520. See Tsumura, I, p. 547.

521. Gordon, p. 276.

522. See Tsumura, I, p. 358.

523. Mazar, "King David's Scribe and the High Officialdom of the United Monarchy of Israel," p. 134.

524. See Mazar, "King David's Scribe and the High Officialdom of the United Monarchy of Israel," pp. 131-33.

525. Knutson, "Divine Names and Epithets in the Akkadian Texts," p. 492.

came to Palestine with the migrations of the Sea Peoples. In Papyrus Anastasi I from the reign of Ramses II (1290-1224 B.C.), the *Sherden*, one of the Sea-Peoples, appear as a mercenary corps, since the Egyptians of the New Kingdom frequently conscripted soldiers from conquered nations into their combat units.[526] On the *Cherethites* as "Cretans," see 1 Sam. 30:14. "David and his successors used Cherethite and Pelethite troops for generations. Indeed, such Philistine and similar mercenaries, of Aegean origin, did much to spread 'Caphtorian' culture in Palestine and through-out the Levantine coast."[527]

David's sons were priests (kōhănîm). It is not known what their duties were, but obviously they were not important compared to those of the levitical priests Zadok and Abiathar and Ahimelech, who were concerned with the ark (15:24); the other lists do not mention them. Other translations have been suggested for "priests," such as "chief ministers" (NASB) and "royal advisers" (NIV). In 1 Chr. 18:17 they are said to be *ri'šōnîm*, which is translated as "chiefs" (NASB), "chief officials" (NRSV; NIV); "first ministers" (JPS). Most scholars agree that the titles in Chronicles and the ancient versions of the present verse are "interpretive paraphrases" of the MT by scribes who considered it impossible to have non-Levitical priests. But if the term does mean "priests," rather than "high-ranking officers" (see Kimchi) or "a minister of state" (Grotius), they may have been just chaplains for the rituals carried out in the royal family, like Ira the Jairite who was *a priest for David* (2 Sam. 20:26).[528] The priestly line and the royal line were essentially separate.

G. MEPHIBOSHETH (9:1-13)

In this chapter David showed "kindness" to Jonathan's son Mephibosheth, through whom Saul's line would flourish for generations (1 Chr. 8:34-40). This is in response to Jonathan's request expressed in 1 Sam. 20:15: "but you shall never cut off your kindness from my house, and never!" and Saul's similar request in 24:21-22. Kings often destroyed the family of their predecessor when there was a change of dynasty (2 K. 10, etc.).

526. See A. Malamat, "Military Rationing in Papyrus Anastasi I and the Bible," in *Mélanges bibliques rédigés en l'honneur de André Robert* (Paris: Bloud & Gay, 1956), p. 116 [reprinted in Malamat, *History of Biblical Israel*, pp. 353-61].

527. Gordon, *CB*, pp. 39-40.

528. See C. E. Armerding, "Were David's Sons Really Priests?" in *Current Issues in Biblical and Patristic Interpretation. Studies in Honor of Merrill C. Tenney*, ed. G. F. Hawthorne (Grand Rapids: Eerdmans, 1975), pp. 75-86; D. T. Tsumura, "Kings and Cults in Ancient Ugarit," in *Priests and Officials in the Ancient Near East: Papers of the Second Colloquium on the Ancient Near East; The City and Its Life Held at the Middle Eastern Culture Center in Japan (Mitaka, Tokyo), March 22-24, 1996*, ed. K. Watanabe (Heidelberg: C. Winter, 1999), pp. 215-38.

EXCURSUS: RELATIONSHIP OF 2 SAMUEL 9 TO 2 SAMUEL 21:1-14

Following Klostermann and others, McCarter thinks that the account of the execution of the seven sons and grandsons of Saul in 2 Sam. 21:1-14 probably originally preceded this chapter and the two were a unit, which he thinks displays "a literary and thematic completeness in itself." However, 21:7 says that David spared Mephibosheth because of the oath between David and Jonathan, so this theory must assume 21:7 is an interpolation.

McCarter, following Budde, thinks if all eight sons and grandsons of Saul had been alive, David would have known about the whereabouts of at least some of them. However, if he did not know the location or even the existence of Jonathan's son, certainly the most prominent descendant left, how would he have known where the sons of a concubine or a daughter were? It is likely that the two families went into hiding after Ishbosheth's death. Merab's children were still young at the time (cf. 1 Sam. 18:19 and 2 Sam. 5:4), and it would be natural for the sons of a concubine to be much younger than Saul's other sons, especially since Rizpah was probably still relatively young (3:7).

The entire section, vv. 1-13, constitutes a well-organized literary unit and can be analyzed as follows:

1. SETTING: David's desire to do kindness for Jonathan's sake (1)
2. Dialogue A: The king and Ziba (2-5)
3. Dialogue B: David and Mephibosheth (6-8)
4. Dialogue A: The king and Ziba (9-11)
5. TERMINUS: Mephibosheth at the king's table (12-13)

Some claim that v. 1 is a later editorial addition to the following section, but discourse grammatically, it is an apt introduction for the entire episode, providing a SETTING for the subsequent dialogues. The narrator carefully distinguishes the second dialogue, that between David and Mephibosheth, from the other two by using "David," instead of "the king." This literary structure shows that the central character of this episode is Mephibosheth.

1. David's Kindness for Jonathan's Sake (9:1)

1 *And David said,*
"Is there still anyone who is left of the house of Saul,
that I may show kindness to him for Jonathan's sake?"

1 Veijola takes this verse as "editorial" since it anticipates v. 3.[529] However, the construction, *wayyōʾmer* (*wayqtl*) + subject, often introduces a new episode, marking a SETTING for the subsequent EVENT, as in Gen. 7:1; 12:1; Exod. 12:1; Num. 26:1; Josh. 8:1; 1 Sam. 12:1; 15:1, 32; 16:1; 27:1; and 1 K. 17:1. David probably said this to his servants, who suggested summoning Ziba.

The phrase *show kindness* (*ʿśh + *ḥesed*; lit. "do kindness")[530] appears also in this chapter in vv. 3, 7. This *kindness* is based on David's covenant with Jonathan and its language is a direct reflection of that covenant; see the commentaries on 2:5 and on 1 Sam. 20:14-15.[531] The threefold repetition of the term emphasizes that this is David's motive.

2. The King and Ziba (9:2-5)

2 *Now there was a servant of the house of Saul; his name was Ziba, and he was called*[532] *to David.*

And the king said to him,
"Are you Ziba?"
and he said,
"Your servant."
3 *And the king said,*
"Is there not yet anyone of the house of Saul,
that I may show the kindness of God to him?"
And Ziba said to the king,
"There is still a son of Jonathan, crippled in both feet."
4 *And the king said to him,*
"Where is he?"
And Ziba said to the king,
"He is now in the house of Machir son of Ammiel, in Lo-debar."
5 *And King David sent and brought him from the house of Machir son of Ammiel, from Lo-debar.*

2 For Ziba, the *servant* (here the word is *ʿebed*) of Saul's house, see on v. 9; also 2 Sam. 16:1; 19:17.

3 For Mephibosheth's lameness, see 4:4; 19:26.

529. T. Veijola, *Die ewige Dynastie: David und die Entstehung seiner Dynastie nach der deuteronomistischen Darstellung* (Annales Academiae Scientiarum Fennicae, Series B 193; Helsinki: Suomalainen Tiedeakatemia, 1975), p. 87 n. 43.

530. On the term *ḥesed*, see Tsumura, I, p. 506. *NIDOTTE* #2874 (2, pp. 211-18).

531. See Tsumura, I, p. 509; McCarter, II, p. 260.

532. Lit. "they called him."

4 Abner and Ishbosheth had established a government after Saul's death in the Transjordanian city of Mahanaim, and Mephibosheth had probably been taken there during that time (2:8-9; 4:4). *Machir* in the present passage was probably a powerful man loyal to the house of Saul. When David fled from Absalom and came to Mahanaim, *Machir son of Ammiel* was among those who brought provisions to David and his group (17:27). The name *Ammiel* (*'ammî'ēl*) means either "My uncle is El"[533] or "God is my uncle." The exact location of *Lo-debar* is unknown, but it seems to have been in northern Transjordan (17:27). Various suggestions for identification of this city have been suggested, but none is decisive.[534]

The name *Machir* has a good pedigree in northern Gilead. In the biblical genealogies Machir was the firstborn son of Manasseh and the father of Gilead (Gen. 50:23; Num. 26:29; 36:1; Josh. 17:1). Moses gave the Makirites a part of Gilead, especially the territory between Mahanaim and the Yarmuk (Num. 32:40; Deut. 3:15; Josh. 13:31; etc.).

3. David and Mephibosheth (9:6-8)

6 *And Mephibosheth son of Jonathan son of Saul came to David and fell on his face and prostrated himself.*
And David said,
"Mephibosheth."
and he said,
"Here is your servant."
7 *And David said to him,*
"Do not be afraid,
for I will surely show kindness to you
for the sake of Jonathan your father
and return to you all the land of Saul your father.
As for you, you shall eat bread at my table regularly."
8 *And he prostrated himself and said,*
"What is your servant
that[535] *you should have regarded graciously*[536] *a dead dog like me?"*

533. Knutson, "Divine Names and Epithets in the Akkadian Texts," p. 491.

534. See D. V. Edelman, "Lo-Debar," *ABD*, 4, p. 345; *SB*, p. 152.

535. NIV, JPS, NRSV, NASB take this as a rhetorical question followed by *kî* of *result*: "What is . . . that you should?" Also Labuschagne, *The Incomparability of Yahweh in the Old Testament*, p. 24.

536. Heb. *pānîtā* (pf.), lit. "you turned to"; cf. "notice" (NIV); "regard for" (JPS); "look upon" (NRSV); "regard" (NASB).

6 For the name *Mephibosheth* and his genealogy, see the commentary on 4:4.

7 Note that the Hebrew word *'āb* is used to mean "father" (Jonathan) in one sentence and "grandfather" (Saul) in the next (cf. "grandfather" in LXX). This phenomenon can also be seen in some of the genealogies, as probably the one in 1 Sam. 9:1. Note that in a Sumerian text "Enlil's son, Ishkur" (Enmerkar and the Lord of Aratta 1.170) means Enlil's grandson.[537]

David had apparently taken control of Saul's property, but here promised to return it to Mephibosheth. C. H. Gordon notes that though David had taken the kingship from the house of Saul, he recognized the right of Saul's grandson to Saul's estate. This may be compared with the situation in *Odyssey* I:394-404, where Odysseus's son admits that though others might have the right to the kingship of Ithaca, he insists that he at least had the right to his father's house and slaves.[538]

The phrase *eat bread at my table* (also v. 10) means that Mephibosheth will have royal patronage and special favor; see 2 Sam. 19:28.[539] In 1 K. 2:7, David on his deathbed told Solomon to let the sons of Barzillai of Gilead eat at his table. The prophets of Baal and Asherah ate at Jezebel's table (1 K. 18:19), and King Jehoiachin ate regularly at the table of the king of Babylon (2 K. 25:27-30). In Ps. 23 the psalmist rejoices that the Lord is a gracious king ("shepherd") who sets him a place at his table and permits him to live in his house.[540]

8 *Dead dog* is a term of self-abasement here and in 1 Sam. 24:14; in 2 Sam. 16:9 it is used as a term of contempt. See the commentary on 1 Sam. 24:14.[541] Compare also 2 Sam. 3:8 "a dog's head of Judah."

4. The King and Ziba (9:9-11)

9 *And the king called Ziba, Saul's steward, and said to him,*
"All that belonged to Saul and all his house
I give[542] *to the son of your master.*
10 *You shall cultivate the land for him*
with your sons and your servants;
and you shall bring (its harvest)
so that your master's son may have a living.

537. T. Jacobsen, *CS*, I, p. 549, no. 10.

538. Gordon, *CB*, p. 240.

539. For eating at the king's table, see N. MacDonald, *Not Bread Alone: The Uses of Food in the Old Testament* (Oxford: Oxford University Press, 2008).

540. See Rainey, "Institutions: Family, Civil, and Military," p. 89.

541. Tsumura, I, p. 571.

542. Heb. *nātattî*; lit. "I gave"; this is a *performative* perfect. See Tsumura, I, p. 395, etc.

As for Mephibosheth your master's son,
he himself shall eat bread regularly at my table."

— Now Ziba had fifteen sons and twenty servants. —

11 *And Ziba said to the king,*
"According to all that my lord the king commands his servant
so your servant will do."
(and he said,)
"Now Mephibosheth is going to eat at my table
like one of the king's sons!"

9 *Ziba* is referred to in this verse as a *naʿar*, often translated as "young man," but as he had fifteen sons (v. 10) it probably meant "steward of an estate." See the commentary on 1 Sam. 1:24.[543] Some Hebrew and Ammonite seals have been found reading "*naʿar* of X."[544] Ziba had probably continued as steward in charge of Saul's land, but had paid the benefits of the estate to David or to someone David had assigned them to. But from now on he is supposed to pay the benefits to Mephibosheth.

10 The phrase *its harvest* is supplied here; the object noun, such as "produce, yield," of the verbal phrase *w*^{e}*hēbēʾtā* (*and you shall bring*) is presumably omitted by the phenomenon of *brachylogy*.

The phrase *have a living* translates the Hebrew phrase *hyh *l*^{e}-NP *leḥem waʾăkālô* (lit. "to have food and eat it"). McCarter thinks that since Mephibosheth himself will be supported at David's expense, the produce must be for Mephibosheth's dependents, hence he reads "You will bring food into your master's house for them to eat," based on the LXX^L.[545] On the other hand, Rainey sees in the MT "an administrative system under which royal courtiers were supported by income from their estates."[546] Food was not the only necessity. When the MT makes good sense both linguistically and from the social custom, it is unnecessary to emend it based on LXX. Mephibosheth himself will eat meals with David, but in general he will be supported by products of his land. Compare the NASB translation, "so that your master's grandson may have food; nevertheless Mephibosheth . . . shall eat at my table," which omits "and eat it" (*waʾăkālô*) after "have food."

543. Tsumura, I, pp. 131-32.

544. See N. Avigad, "New Light on the Naʿar Seals," in *Magnalia Dei: The Mighty Acts of God; Essays on the Bible and Archaeology in Memory of G. Ernest Wright*, ed. F. M. Cross, W. E. Lemke, and P. D. Miller (Garden City, N.Y.: Doubleday, 1976), 294-300.

545. McCarter, II, pp. 259, 262.

546. *SB*, p. 221.

Now Ziba had fifteen sons and twenty servants: this information is repeated in 19:17.

11 *"Now Mephibosheth is going to eat at my table like one of the king's sons!"* This is often taken as the narrator's comment: following the LXX.[547] However, the MT *'ōkēl*, which is a participle, means *is going to eat*, though the majority translate it as "ate" (NIV, NRSV, NASB, McCarter, with LXX), reading *y'kl* (MT[MSS], Vulg.). Also the MT *'al-šulḥānî*, which means *at my table* (so JPS), would be expected if we take the entire section as a dialogue: i.e., David said to Ziba (v. 9) — Ziba said to David (v. 11a) — David said to Ziba (v. 11b). Hence, we should supply the phrase *(and he said)* after Ziba's speech. Compare "at David's table" (NIV, NRSV, NASB, McCarter), following LXX^{BAMN}. The arrangement that David sets up for Mephibosheth is similar to that of at least David's older sons. Though the king's sons "ate at the king's table," some of them lived in their own houses in Jerusalem (13:7, 20) and had fields and agricultural lands of their own to support them (13:23; 14:30).

5. Mephibosheth at the King's Table (9:12-13)

12 *Now Mephibosheth had a young son; his son was Mica.*
And all who lived in the house of Ziba were servants to Mephibosheth.
13 *And Mephibosheth lived in Jerusalem, for he was eating regularly at the king's table; he was lame in both feet.*

12 *Mica* had multiple descendants (1 Chr. 8:34-35; 9:40-44). Thus, the house of Saul will be preserved under David's protection, as requested by Jonathan (1 Sam. 20:14-16) and Saul (24:21-22).

13 The narrator mentions again at the close of the narrative that Mephibosheth was *lame (pisseăḥ)*, while earlier in v. 3 Ziba introduced him as being *crippled in both feet.* This *inclusio* prepares us for 16:1-4 and 19:24-30.

H. THE ISRAEL-AMMON WAR (10:1–12:31)

The next three chapters are set against the background of the war with Ammon. As far as David's empire went, it led to his domination of the Syrian kingdoms (see 10:15-19; 8:3-12). However, more importantly to the biblical writer, it was the setting for David's great sin. Thus, from a literary structural

547. See McCarter, II, p. 259.

point of view, the story of the Ammonite war constitutes a "frame" for the story of David and Bathsheba in 11:1-12:25.[548]

As mentioned in the commentary on chapter 8, it is possible that these chapters occur chronologically prior to the events of 8:2-3.

1 [A]. The Beginning of the Israel-Ammon War (10:1-19)

a. David's Envoys to Ammon (10:1-5)

1 *Afterward the king of the Ammonites died,*
and his son Hanun became king in his place.
2 *And David said,*
"I will show kindness to Hanun son of Nahash,
just as his father showed kindness to me."
And David sent his servants with a message to console him concerning his father.
And David's servants came to the land of the Ammonites.
3 *And the leaders of the Ammonites said to Hanun their lord,*
"Do you think that David is honoring your father
because he has sent consolers to you?
Isn't it for the sake of searching the city,
to spy on it and overthrow it,
that David has sent his servants to you?"
4 *And Hanun took the servants of David and shaved off half of their beards and cut off their garments in half up to their buttocks and sent them away.*
5 *And David was informed and sent (messengers) to meet them, for the men were greatly humiliated.*
And the king said,
"Stay at Jericho until your beards grow,
and then return."

Like the previous episode in ch. 9, this chapter begins with David's concern toward a person to whom he felt he should do "kindness" (lit. do *ḥesed*). In the earlier case, his concern was toward the son of his best friend; in the present case, it is toward the son of his former ally.

1-2 Nahash was presumably the Nahash of 1 Sam. 11. There he was the

548. Against the redaction-history approach, I. Kalimi contends that 2 Sam. 10-12 has "a compositional unity embodied by its literary structures, methods, stylistic techniques, and theological framework." See I. Kalimi, "Reexamining 2 Samuel 10-12: Redaction History versus Compositional Unity," *CBQ* 78 (2016) 24-46.

enemy of Israel, but perhaps he became an ally of David as an enemy of Saul. The "kindness" (*ḥesed*) might refer to a specific act, or it could refer to their relation as allies. McCarter thinks it must refer to the gifts brought to David by his son Shobi during Absalom's rebellion (17:27),[549] but that passage does not say that Nahash sent him, and such an interpretation would certainly be completely at odds with the general understanding that Absalom's rebellion was long after the Ammon war. For the phrase "Nahash, king of the Ammonites" in 4QSam[a], see the commentary on 1 Sam. 11:1.[550]

3-5 David's good will is not accepted by the Ammonite leaders. It may be that the leaders of Ammon are alarmed by the representatives of the conqueror of Moab (8:2), the country directly south of them. (Compare Joab's reaction to Abner's visit in 3:25.) Hanun listens to their advice and humiliates Israel's official envoys, in effect breaking off diplomatic relations and declaring war against Israel.

Humiliation by shaving off half of the beard and by cutting off the garment in half up to the buttocks (see Isa. 20:4) was probably symbolic demasculization.

David shows his concern for his messengers, allowing them to stay in Jericho so they do not have to display their humiliation at court. *Jericho* is situated on the most direct road from the Ammonite capital city Rabbah to Jerusalem; the road crosses the river Jordan just north of the Dead Sea.

b. War between Ammon and Israel (10:6-19)

Some scholars such as Rost, Flanagan, and Gunn think that the Aramean war in vv. 6-19 is a secondary insertion and has nothing to do with David's conflict with the Ammonites. On the other hand, McCarter, following Hertzberg, takes chapter 10 as a unit, since the intervention of the Zobah coalition would be consistent with the interests of both parties in view of the growing Israelite threat.[551] The geography makes it natural for kings of Ammon to seek help from Aramean states to the north. In later Ammonite epigraphy, Aramean influence is clear.[552]

1) Ammon Hires the Arameans (10:6-8)

6 *And the Ammonites saw that they had become odious to David.*
And the Ammonites sent (messengers) and hired:

549. McCarter, II, p. 270.

550. See Tsumura, I, pp. 302-3.

551. McCarter, II, p. 271.

552. This was called to my attention by A. R. Millard. For the Aramean states, see Younger, *PHA*.

Aram Beth-rehob and Aram Zobah	*20,000 foot soldiers*
the king of Maacah	*1,000 men*
the men of Tob	*12,000 men.*

7 *And David heard of it and sent Joab and all the army, the mighty men.*
8 *And the Ammonites came out and deployed themselves for battle at the entrance of the gate, while the Arameans of Zobah and Rehob and the men of Tob and Maacah were by themselves in the field.*

6-8 The Ammonites realize David is about to attack and prepare by hiring armies from Aram (Syria). *Beth-rehob, Zobah, Maacah* and *Tob* were Syrian kingdoms in the northern Transjordan and the Beqaa Valley.[553] For the relationship of this passage with chapter 8, see on chapter 8. Hiring armies was not uncommon (2 K. 7:6). The numbers of troops are listed according to the usual list formula, which gives an item followed by the number of that item; see on 1 Sam. 6:17; 25:18.[554]

6 For the phrase *become odious to* (*nibʾăšû*), i.e., "be hated by,"[555] see the commentary on 1 Sam. 13:4;[556] the Ni. of this verb appears only in Samuel; cf. "had offended David" (McCarter). Olyan[557] explains it as a technical term for covenant violation; see also 2 Sam. 16:21. But 1 Sam. 13:4 is not a covenant violation.

As in vv. 5 and 16, the MT omits the understood object of the verb *sent*, that is "messengers," by *brachylogy*. First Chronicles 19:6-7 supplies the object of the verb *sent* as follows: "sent a thousand talents of silver" and adds other details about the Aramean armies.[558]

Beth-rehob refers to Rehob, near Lebo-hamath (Num 13:21; NRSV), which is said to mark the northern boundary of Canaan. It lay at the southern foot of Mount Hermon and the Anti-Lebanon range; see Judg. 18:28. Zobah was ruled by Hadadezer son of Rehob (8:3). The fact that Beth-rehob is mentioned here before *Zobah* may support Malamat's hypothesis that Zobah was ruled by a dynasty from Beth-rehob; see the commentary on 2 Sam. 8:3.

Maacah occupied the Golan, north of Gilead and south of Mount Hermon.[559] *Tob* was a small state in northern Transjordan (see Judg. 11:3, 5), usu-

553. See Younger, *PHA*, pp. 192-220.

554. Tsumura, I, pp. 222-23, 583-84.

555. See *HALOT*, p. 107.

556. Tsumura, I, p. 338.

557. S. M. Olyan, "Honor, Shame, and Covenant Relations in Ancient Israel and Its Environment," *JBL* 115 (1996) 213 n. 39.

558. According to McCarter, II, p. 268, this addition is attested in 4QSam[a], which reflects "a mixed text containing elements" from the MT of Samuel and Chronicles. He thus reconstructs 4QSam[a] on the basis of the Chronicles texts. See, however, Herbert's rejection of McCarter's reconstruction in *RBDSS*, pp. 136-37.

559. See Younger, *PHA*, pp. 213-19.

ally identified with modern et-Taiyibeh, ca. twelve miles (19.3 km) southeast of the Sea of Galilee.[560]

8 The *gate* is that of the city of Rabbah (11:1), the capital of Ammon. For the phrase *deployed themselves* (or "drew up"), see on 1 Sam. 4:2.[561]

2) Joab and Abishai (10:9-14)

9 *And Joab saw that the battlefronts were set against him both before and behind, and chose (men) from all the select men in Israel and drew up to meet Aram.*

10 *But the rest of the people he gave into the hand of Abishai his brother, who drew up to meet the Ammonites.*

11 *And he said,*
"If Aram is too strong for me,
you shall become my help;
but if the Ammonites are too strong for you,
I will go to help you.
12 *Be strong and behave courageously on behalf of our people*
and the cities of our God!
As for the LORD, he will do what is good in his eyes."

13 *And Joab, together with the people who were with him, drew near to battle against the Arameans, and they fled from before him.*

14 *As for the Ammonites, they saw that the Arameans had fled, and fled before Abishai and entered the city.*

And Joab returned from against the Ammonites and came to Jerusalem.

9-19 David's army under Joab is trapped between the Arameans and the Ammonites, but they defeat the Arameans and force them to leave. Joab returns to Jerusalem, but presumably Abishai stays, keeping up the siege against the Ammonites.

9 For *select men* (or "selected warriors"), see on 1 Sam. 24:2 [MT 3].[562] Presumably the hired Arameans would be more skilled than the ordinary Ammonite soldiers, so Joab takes the very best of the troops to meet them.

12 The phrase *the cities of our God* (*ʿārê ʾĕlōhênû*) has been emended variously, though all the textual witnesses support this reading. However, Giveon suggests the phrase may refer to "cities with venerable associations with Yahweh in southern Transjordan."[563] In fact, the expressions such as "Yahweh

560. See Younger, *PHA*, pp. 219-20.
561. Tsumura, I, p.189.
562. Tsumura, I, p. 564.
563. See McCarter, II, p. 272.

of Samaria" and "Yahweh of Teman" in the ninth century inscriptions from Kuntillet Ajrud[564] may support the idea of Yahweh's *cities* in Joab's speech. Of course, he could just mean Israelite cities.

3) David's Victories over the Arameans (10:15-19)

15 *And the Arameans saw that they had been defeated before Israel and gathered together.*

16 *And Hadadezer sent (messengers) and brought out the Arameans who were beyond the River, and they came to Helam, with Shobach the commander of Hadadezer's army before them.*

17 *And it was told to David, and he gathered all Israel and crossed the Jordan and came to Helam.*

And the Arameans drew up toward David and fought with him.

18 *And the Arameans fled from before Israel.*

And David killed out of the Arameans

700 charioteers;[565]

40,000 horsemen.

But Shobach the commander of their army he struck down, and he died there.

19 *And all the kings, the servants of Hadadezer, saw that they were defeated before Israel and made peace with Israel and served them.*

And the Arameans were afraid to help the Ammonites again.

Some scholars think these verses are secondary and refer to a different campaign, but this is not necessary. *Hadadezer* of Zobah (see 8:5) attacks again at *Helam*, but is again defeated.

16 The phrase *beyond the River* means "beyond the Euphrates." By the time of David, the Arameans were firmly established along the middle and upper Euphrates and in northwest Mesopotamia.[566] For *Hadadezer*, see the commentary on 8:3.

The exact location of *Helam* is unknown, but it is apparently some place in northern Transjordan. One possible identification is the town of Alema, modern ʿAlma, located about halfway between *Rabbah* (called Rabbath-

564. S. Aḥituv, *Echoes from the Past: Hebrew and Cognate Inscriptions from the Biblical Period* (Jerusalem: Carta, 2008), pp. 315, 320-21; also D. T. Tsumura, "Yahweh and His Asherah: Monotheism and Polytheism in Ancient Israel," *Kyuyaku-gaku Kenkyu* [= *Old Testament Studies*] 3 (2006) 1-15 (in Japanese).

565. Lit. "chariots."

566. See A. Malamat, "The Kingdom of David and Solomon in Its Contact with Egypt and Aram Naharaim," *BA* 21 (1958) 100 n. 19.

bene-ammon in 12:26) and Damascus.[567] The name is spelled *ḥêlām* in v. 16 and *ḥēlā(')m(āh)* in v. 17.

17 According to Yadin,[568] the best route for a military expedition into Transjordan would be to cross the Jordan at Adamah at the southern end of the Valley of Succoth. See Josh. 3:16 for Adam, where the water of the Jordan is said to have *piled up in a heap* when the Israelite people *passed over opposite Jericho*.

18 The term "Aram" is used here as a collective noun, standing for *the Arameans*, like "Edom" for "the Edomites" in Arad 24:20.

The adverbial phrase *out of the Arameans* governs both groups in the list formula, i.e., 700 charioteers and 40,000 horsemen; see on 1 Sam. 25:18.[569] For *commander*, see 1 Sam. 12:9.

19 Hadadezer's vassals *made peace with Israel*, i.e., they entered a state of nonhostility with Israel as opposed to a state of war, and *served* Israel. They thus exchanged Israelite for Aramean suzerainty. The expression itself does not necessarily denote "treaty or covenant status," despite McCarthy's assertion.[570] As Malamat argues,[571] David took over Hadadezer's realm not only territorially, but also structurally.

2 [X]. David and Bathsheba (11:1–12:25)

Chapters 11 and 12 relate the story of David and Bathsheba. It is embedded in the story of the Ammonite war of David, that is, between 11:1 and 12:26-31, which constitute a "frame," since "Joab - Rabbah" and "David - Jerusalem" in 11:1 correspond to 12:26-31, which begins with "Joab - Rabbah" and ends with "David – Jerusalem." At the same time, verse 1b ("Now David was staying at Jerusalem") functions as the SETTING for the following EVENT (v. 2). Thus, vv. 1-2 constitute an integral part of the present story, regardless of whether the narrator is emphasizing the contrast between Joab and David.

The story of "David and Bathsheba" is the "great turning point" of the entire story of David. As Alter says, "it seems as though the writer has pulled out all the stops of his remarkable narrative art in order to achieve a brilliant realization of this crucially pivotal episode."[572]

One may wonder why such a negative story is narrated during the account of the victorious battle against the Ammonites. This is because the

567. See *SB*, p. 161.
568. Y. Yadin, "Some Aspects of the Strategy of Ahab and David," *Bib* 36 (1955) 347-51.
569. Tsumura, I, pp. 583-84.
570. See D. J. Wiseman, "'Is It Peace?' Covenant and Diplomacy," *VT* 32 (1982) 313f.
571. A. Malamat, "Aspects of the Foreign Policies of David and Solomon," p.3.
572. Alter, *The David Story*, p. 249.

biblical narrator intends to convey a warning — even the most successful king like David may do evil *in the eyes of the LORD* (v. 27); in fact, just because of his success, both military and political, King David blinded himself spiritually in his relationship with the holy and sovereign God. Once he broke the tenth commandment in his heart, his outward actions escalate even to breaking the commandment against murder, thus

X: "You shall not covet." (Exod. 20:17)
VII: "You shall not commit adultery." (v. 14)
VI: "You shall not murder." (v. 13)

Only God's grace makes David realize how sinful he has been and allows him as a sinner to be accepted again by the holy sovereign Lord.

a. Bathsheba, the Wife of Uriah (11:1-27)

Bar-Efrat[573] notes that in the story of David and Bathsheba the opening and concluding parts of the narrative (vv. 2-5 and 26-27) move quickly, while the two sections in the middle of the narrative (vv. 6-15 and 18-25) move relatively slowly with a large amount of direct speech. Only the factual account of Uriah's death itself (vv. 16-17) moves quickly. So the narrative exhibits the following structure in terms of speed:

Quick	Bathsheba (11:2-5)	
Slow		Uriah (11:6-15)
Quick	Uriah (11:16-17)	
Slow		Uriah (11:18-25)
Quick	Bathsheba (11:26-27)	

David's misconduct is presented bluntly and without explanation, as if any hint of his motivation might mitigate his crime in the mind of the reader.[574]

McCarter holds that David here is the king "who *takes*" as in 1 Sam. 8:11-17 and hence he assumes that both passages belong to "the prophetic history that embraces the story of the origins of monarchy in Israel."[575]

573. S. Bar-Efrat, "Some Observations on the Analysis of Structure in Biblical Narrative," *VT* 30 (1980) 159-60.

574. M. Garsiel, "A Review of Recent Interpretations of the Story of David and Bathsheba: II Samuel 11," *Immanuel* 2 (1973) 20; Garsiel, "The Story of David and Bathsheba: A Different Approach," *CBQ* 55 (1993) 244-62.

575. McCarter, II, p. 290.

However, while in 1 Samuel the prophet describes the normal costs of a monarchy, which includes taking people as servants, it is clear from the story that taking an officer's wife was not one of the king's rights; see the commentary on 1 Sam. 8:11-17.[576] For the parallels between Nathan's speech in 2 Samuel 12 and Samuel's in 1 Samuel 15, see the commentary on 2 Sam. 12:7-12.

1) Ammonite War of David (11:1a)

1a *In the turn of the year, at the time when messengers go out, David sent Joab and his servants with him and all Israel, and they destroyed the Ammonites and besieged Rabbah.*

The phrase *t^{e}šûbat haššānāh* has been translated as "in the spring" (so NIV, NASB, Bergen), "in the spring of the year" (RSV, NRSV, ESV), "in the following spring of the year" (Anderson), or "the turn of the year" (JPS, REB, NJB; see LXX *epistrepsantos tou eniautou*). McCarter, like most modern translations, takes the subject of "go out" as "the kings" found in many versions (see below) and thinks that the phrase means a full year since the Aramean kings marched to the aid of the Ammonites in 10:6. He reasons that the definite article of "the kings" would refer to "specific kings." However, his translation is somewhat forced: "When the time of year at which the kings had marched out came around again, David sent off Joab."[577]

The various interpretations of this verse have been conveniently summarized by Bodner.[578] Most say the phrase refers to kings' military campaigning during the particular season of spring.[579] However, this interpretation requires that we take the subject of the verb "go out" as meaning "kings."

The subject in the MT Q. is the strange form *malkîm*. While the MT K.'s subject *hml'kym* unambiguously means "messengers," some manuscripts of the MT have *hmlkym* ("kings"), and "kings" appears in the LXX, OL, Targ., Vulg., and the parallel text 1 Chr. 20:1 (*hamm^{e}lākîm*), and many modern English versions translate it as such.

R. P. Gordon suggests that at some point an MT scribe may have added an *aleph* to the word for "kings" to make it mean "messengers" and thus salvage something for David's reputation as a war-lord.[580]

576. Tsumura, I, pp. 254-59.
577. McCarter, II, pp. 284-85.
578. Bodner, *David Observed*, pp. 80-81.
579. E.g., Anderson, pp. 152-53; Stoebe, II, p. 277; Bergen, p. 362.
580. R. P. Gordon, p. 252.

Bodner[581] and others hold that the term is intentionally ambiguous, meaning both "messengers" and "kings" and do not discuss whether the original reading was *ml'kym* or *mlkym.*

However, one can argue that the MT spelling *hml'kym*, with the *aleph*,[582] reflects the original reading. Since it means "messengers," not "kings," no ambiguity exists for this spelling. The issue is not whether the MT spelling is ambiguous—it is not—but whether the spelling found in some manuscripts without *aleph, hmlkym,* which normally means "kings," can refer to messengers.

As noted elsewhere, the spellings in 1–2 Samuel are often phonetic and the consonantal *aleph* is sometimes omitted. If this is the case here, we could explain the process thus:

messengers: *mal'ākîm — (*aleph* dropped)→ *malākîm
— (vowel reduction in the distant open syllable)→ *m^{e}lākîm : *mlkym*

(Note: the Hebrew form for "kings" cannot be *malkîm.*)[583]

If any ambiguity is involved in this passage, the form *mlkym* is the one that could mean "messengers" as well as "kings." We would like to take the simplest solution, taking the MT consonantal form, with *aleph*, as "messengers." The term *messenger* (*mal'āk*) certainly functions as a *Leitwort* in this chapter;[584] see vv. 1, 4, 19, 22, 23, and 25.

As for the phrase *turn of the year (t^{e}šûbat haššānāh)*, it might be compared with Ugaritic *nqpt 'd* (*KTU* 1.23:67) "turns (or yearly cycles) of time," which is in parallel with the phrase *šnt tmt* (*KTU* 1.23:66-67) "complete years."[585] The Hebrew phrase therefore would refer not so much to a particular season such as spring, as to the beginning of a new administrative year, when a ruler might send out messengers (MT: *hml'kym*) to every district of the country to check the current conditions, or, possibly to register its population (see 2 Sam. 24:2-9).

Even if the passage refers to "kings," however, it would be hard to see it as criticizing David for staying in Jerusalem. The king would have civic responsibilities, and it seems he did follow events in the field closely.

581. Bodner takes the chapter as a whole as having the tone of ambiguity and sees here an instance of intentional ambiguity; see Bodner, *David Observed*, pp. 5, 78-88.

582. J. P. Fokkelman, *Narrative Art and Poetry in the Books of Samuel: A Full Interpretation Based on Stylistic and Structural Analyses.* Vol. I: *King David (II Sam. 9-20 & I Kings 1-2)* (SSN 20; Assen: Van Gorcum, 1981), p. 50.

583. *Pace* Firth, p. 413.

584. Firth, p. 414. For messengers and their functions in the biblical world, see S. A. Meier, *The Messenger in the Ancient Semitic World* (HSM 45; Atlanta: Scholars Press, 1988).

585. See *DULAT*, pp. 641 and 871.

With the defeat of the Arameans, David is now free to concentrate on taking *Rabbah* (*the city* in 10:14; 11:16, 25; *Rabbah of the Ammonites* or *Rabbath-bene-ammon*).[586] Rabbah was situated about twenty-two miles (35 km) east of the Jordan. To get there from Jerusalem they had to descend more than 3281 feet (1000 meters) and, after crossing the Jordan river, ascend another 3281 feet (1000 meters).

2) Bathsheba, Wife of Uriah (11:1b-5)

1b *Now David was staying at Jerusalem.*

2 *One evening David arose from his bed and walked around on the roof of the royal palace and saw from the roof a woman bathing; the woman was very beautiful.*

3 *And David sent (someone) and made inquiry about the woman, and that one*[587] *said,*

"Isn't this Bathsheba daughter of Eliam,
the wife of Uriah the Hittite?"[588]

4 *And David sent messengers and took her and she came to him and he lay with her, who, on her part, had been purified from her uncleanness, and she returned to her house.*

5 *And the woman conceived and sent (a messenger) and told David:*[589]
"I am pregnant."

1b *Now David was staying at Jerusalem.* The focus is now on David who is *staying* (ptc. *yôšēb*) at ease at his royal palace in Jerusalem, in sharp contrast to *Joab and his servants* who are actively engaged in warfare. And David *saw a woman* and *took her* (see below on v. 4), just as Eve looked at the tree with the wrong intention and "took" its fruits (see Gen. 3:6). Certainly temptation comes and captures sinners when they are relaxed and not alert. Even if it does not lead to outward adultery, "everyone who looks at a woman with lustful intent has already committed adultery with her in his heart" (Matt. 5:28, ESV).

2 *One evening* (lit. "At the time of the evening"); why did he arise from

586. *SB*, p. 161; *ABD*, V, pp. 598-600; *HALOT*, p. 1178.

587. So, Firth, p. 412; lit. "and he said." This person who says cannot be David, for he *made inquiry*. For an impersonal use of the 3 m.s. verb instead of the more common 3 m.pl., see J-M, §155*b*.

588. 4QSam[a] has the phrase "armor-bearer of Joab" *n*]*wś' kly yw'b*[after *the Hittite*. This variant reading appears only in Josephus, *Ant.* 7.131. See DJD 17, pp. 138-39; Herbert, *RBDSS*, p. 140. Since no other version of Samuel has it, one wonders how significant such information is for the study of the text of 2 Samuel. See Bodner, *David Observed*, pp. 89-97.

589. For the translation *told . . . :* (lit. "told . . . and said"), see Introduction in Tsumura, I, p. xii.

his bed in the evening? David was relaxing at his house, without any sense of urgency and tension, while his soldiers were fighting the Ammonites.

The *royal palace* (lit. "house of the king") in the City of David has now been partly excavated; see the comments on 2 Sam. 5:7, 11-12.

McCarter takes *from the roof* as "secondary" since it appears after the verb "saw" in LXX^L while Syr. omits it. However, a word's inversion or omission in ancient translations is not evidence for its secondary origin. The word order [V-O (Rel. Cl.)-AdvPh] in MT *wayyar' 'iššāh rōḥeṣet mēʿal haggāg* is not abnormal in Hebrew;[590] see also v. 27 (below).

The woman is probably bathing to purify herself *from her uncleanness* (v. 4) after her period (Lev. 15:19-24). Thus it is clear that the child conceived in v. 5 was not Uriah's. *Beautiful* (*ṭôbat mar'eh*) is literally "good in appearance." Compared with the usual Hebrew adjective *yāpāh* for "beautiful" (as in 1 Sam. 25:3 where it is used of Abigail), the emphasis is rather on her looks.

3 The two elements of the name *Eliam* (*'ĕlîʿām*) are exchanged in Ammiel, the name given in 1 Chr. 3:5. Eliam the son of Ahithophel the Gilonite appears in 2 Sam. 23:34 among David's mighty men; he is apparently the son of David's counselor, Ahithophel the Gilonite (15:12), so it is often said that Bathsheba is Ahithophel's granddaughter. However, it is not certain that the Eliam in this list is her father.

Uriah the Hittite is also listed among David's top warriors, the "thirty," in 23:39. The name means "Yah is my light." While his Yahwistic name suggests that he was born in Israel, the designation "the Hittite" traces his family background to the Aramean population in the Neo-Hittite states,[591] i.e., the "hieroglyphic" Hittite states (ca. 1200 B.C. onward), at the time of David. Muraoka suspects that the repetition of *the Hittite* five more times in this story hints that the king may have behaved differently if Uriah had been an Israelite.[592] However, even if it helps explain his behavior, there is no hint that it excuses it.

Firth's guess that Uriah, David's elite warrior, "may have seemed to David to be the sort of threat he had been to Saul"[593] is rather farfetched and without support in the text.

4 Given the elaborate attempt David makes to cover up his adultery in vv. 6-13, it is hardly likely that he makes his intention clear when he summons Bathsheba. Probably he makes inquiry about the welfare of the family of his trusted officer during his absence, gives his wife the honor of a private inter-

590. For the construction, see Tsumura, I, p. 48.

591. See the commentary on 2 Sam. 8:9; also H. A. Hoffner Jr., *1 & 2 Samuel* (EEC; Bellingham, WA: Lexham Press, 2015), Introduction.

592. T. Muraoka, "Philological Notes on the David-Bathsheba Story I," in *In the Shadow of Bezalel: Aramaic, Biblical, and Ancient Near Eastern Studies in Honor of Bezalel Porten*, ed. A. F. Botta (CHANE 60; Leiden: E. J. Brill, 2013), p. 291.

593. Firth, p. 416.

view, even sending messengers (pl.) to invite her, and after his tragic death takes his widow under his protection as his own wife (v. 27).

The verb "to take" (*lqḥ) is used here as in 1 Sam. 8:11-17, where the king is said to take people's sons (v. 11), daughters (v. 13), agricultural properties (v. 14), and male and female servants (v. 16). Nevertheless, the idea of "taking" is not the same in both passages. Here, David took as a sexual partner a woman who he knew was married. His "taking" was the sin of adultery, initiated by covetousness in his heart; see Exod. 20:17; Hab. 1:6; 2:6.

and she came to him may imply that Bathsheba consented to lie with him.[594]

The circumstantial clause, *who, on her part, had been purified from . . .* (lit. "and she was purifying herself from . . ."), has the effect of slowing down a series of quick actions (*wayqtl*): "sent" - "took" - "came" - "lay" - "returned." Since it appears between "lay" and "returned," the question is whether this circumstantial clause denotes the condition of Bathsheba at the time of her intercourse with David or after it. The latter position is reflected in translations such as the NASB; it would refer to her uncleanness derived from intercourse with David (Lev. 15:18) and have nothing to do with her bathing in v. 2.

However, in the construction, *wayqtl* . . . [circumstantial cl.] . . . *wayqtl*, the circumstantial clause is usually subordinate to the preceding main clause; e.g., Judg. 4:21; 1 Sam. 22:9; 2 Sam. 4:7; 13:8; 1 K. 19:19; 20:12; 2 K. 2:18; 2 Chr. 22:9; 34:22; but cf. Gen. 18:8; 2 K. 2:23; 6:30. The MT punctuation with *atnah* at the end of the circumstantial clause also supports the former position.[595] So it would mean that at the time of her intercourse with David she had purified herself from her uncleanliness. Moreover, this makes good sense contextually. When David saw her bathing, she was probably cleansing herself after the impurity of menstruation (Lev. 15:19-24). Accordingly she knew the child she conceived was David's. Therefore, McCarter's translation: "It was the time of her purification" is somewhat forced. Since the Hebrew participle can have resultative aspect[596] as well as the durative aspect,[597] the clause should be rendered as above: she "had been purified from her uncleanness"; cf. "(She had purified herself from her uncleanness.)" (NIV).

3) David and Uriah (11:6-15)

6 *And David sent (a messenger) to Joab, (saying)*
"Send me Uriah the Hittite!"
And Joab sent Uriah to David.

594. Muraoka, "Philological Notes on the David-Bathsheba Story I," p. 293.
595. Driver, p. 289: "The *athnaḥ* is thus in its right place."
596. See J.-M. §121e.
597. See J.-M. §121c.

7 *And Uriah came to him.*

And David asked about the welfare of Joab and the welfare of the people and the situation of the war.

8 *And David said to Uriah,*
"Go down to your house
and wash your feet!"
And Uriah went out of the royal palace.
And the present from the king went out after him.

9 *And Uriah slept at the door of the royal palace with all the servants of his master; and he did not go down to his house.*

10 *And they told David, saying*
"Uriah did not go down to his house."
And David said to Uriah,
"Haven't you come from a journey?
Why didn't you go down to your house?"
11 *And Uriah said to David,*
"The ark and Israel and Judah are staying in booths.
And my lord Joab and the servants of my lord are camping on the front of the battlefield.[598]
As for me, shall I go to my house to eat and drink and to lie with my wife?
By your life and by the life of your soul,
I will never do this thing!"
12 *And David said to Uriah,*
"Stay here today, too.
And tomorrow I will let you go."
And Uriah stayed in Jerusalem that day and the next.
13 *And David called him,*
and he ate and drank before him,
and he made him drunk.
And he went out in the evening to lie on his bed with his lord's servants,
but to his house he did not go down.

14 *In the morning David wrote a letter to Joab and sent it by the hand of Uriah.*

15 *And he wrote in the letter,*
"Put[599] *Uriah in the front line of the severe fighting*
and withdraw from him,
and he will be struck and be dead."

598. Lit. "field."
599. Lit. "give" (*yhb).

6-13 The king had certain rights, but clearly adultery was not one of them, as David has to cover his deed up. Instead of repenting and trying to settle the matter openly, David tries to cover up his wrongdoing by making it appear that his child by Bathsheba is Uriah's.

David sends a messenger to Joab asking him to send Uriah, for the ostensible purpose of getting first-hand information about the military situation (v. 7).

David *said to Uriah* three times (vv. 8, 10, 12), thus escalating his attempt to cover up his transgression. The contrast in the moral and spiritual condition of the two men becomes sharper at each step.

8 The phrase *wash your feet* means "to refresh yourself," though it is possibly a euphemism for sexual intercourse.

For *present from the king*, McCarter holds that "with the weapon-bearers" (*bnśʾy hklym*) is more original than *maśʾat hammelek* found in the MT and others; he reconstructs 4QSam^a as [*wyṣʾ*] *ʿwryh b* [*nsʾy hklym*] to support his reading.[600] But McCarter's reconstruction is rejected by Herbert, since "the first letter of the word after אוריה is almost certainly a מ (as in SMT), and clearly not a ב (too tall for a ב, and possessing a sloping base line)."[601] So there is no reason to think 4QSam^a deviates from the MT.

9 Sexual intercourse was a source of ritual impurity (Exod. 19:15; Lev. 15:18) and so was avoided during a campaign, as is mentioned in 1 Sam. 21:5. Uriah considered himself still on duty, in contrast to David. For this, see Deut. 23:9. "Evil" in that passage refers to something "unseemly," or "improper" rather than morally evil. Certainly "excrement" (Deut. 23:13) is not morally evil, but like intercourse it does make one unclean.

11 Here as in 1 Sam. 4:4 and 14:18 the ark is taken on a military campaign.

One can see here a contrast between the present passage and 2 Sam. 7:1-2, where David thought it wrong to reside in a comfortable house while Yahweh's ark was "sitting in the midst of the curtains." Uriah's words about the *ark* almost reflect those of Ps. 132:3-5, and it is ironic that David has to be reminded of them.

Staying in booths might also mean, "dwelling in Succoth," a city mentioned in Josh. 13:27; Judg. 8:5; Ps. 60:6; etc., which is probably to be identified with Tell Deir ʿAllāh, a city situated on the Jabok River at a location strategically important for protecting against Aram and Ammon.[602] However, Tell Deir ʿAllā is rather far from Rabbah to serve as a base for operations against it, besides being in a valley (see Ps. 60:6), which would mean the army would have to climb out of the valley to begin their advance. Furthermore, Joab is already conducting operations against the city itself (v. 20).

600. McCarter, II, p. 280.

601. Herbert, *RBDSS*, p. 141.

602. M. M. Homan, "Booths or Succoth? A Response to Yigael Yadin," *JBL* 118 (1999) 691-95.

12-13 Following the MT verse division, JPS connects the phrase *and the next* with the following verse (v. 13) and translates: "The next day, David summoned him, and he ate and drank . . ."[603] However, it should be noted that a day starts with the sunset; see on 1 Sam. 20:5. Therefore the phrase *that day and the next* refers to that day and the same evening. So, Uriah *went out* of the palace after eating and drinking with the king on that night and slept *on his bed with his lord's servants.* With the JPS's translation, no information is given where Uriah spent the night of *that day.*

The phrase *ate and drank* is literally "ate before him and drank," A & B of AX&B, X being *before him.*[604]

14-15 *A letter* (*sēper*) can refer to any type of "document" such as a "letter," a "list," a "covenant"; see Ug. *spr.* It may take the form of a tablet or a book or a sheet of leather or papyrus, depending on the material on which the scripts are written; see the commentary on 1 Sam. 10:25.[605] The use of *sēper* for *letter* here could be another sign of antiquity of the language of 1–2 Samuel,[606] since in LBH the normal word for "letter" is *ʾiggeret.*[607] For ancient Hebrew epistolography, see Pardee, who notes that "letters in the Hebrew Bible are all embedded in narrative passages and lack the clearly formulaic feature of the Aramaic letters contained in the book of Ezra."[608]

The letter was probably sealed. Many seals, i.e., the dies that were impressed in clay, have been found in Israel, as well as many sealings (bullae) of clay that were applied to the documents, the papyrus letters themselves having decayed. It seems that both David and Joab could read and write (see also Judg. 8:14); it would have been too dangerous if they had had to depend on scribes when they wrote or read this letter.[609]

Alter gives an apt and reasonable observation:

603. Muraoka, "Philological Notes on the David-Bathsheba Story I," p. 297, holds that the verse division of the MT is wrong here.

604. See Tsumura, "Coordination Interrupted," pp. 117-32.

605. Tsumura, I, pp. 299-300. For the motif of the messenger carrying his own death warrant, see H. Gunkel, *Die Schriften des Alten Testaments in Auswahl* (Göttingen: Vandenhoeck & Ruprecht, 1921), 132.

606. See the commentary on 1 Sam. 16:20 in Tsumura, I, p. 431; also pp. 29-31.

607. See A. Hurvitz, "The Historical Quest for 'Ancient Israel' and the Linguistic Evidence of the Hebrew Bible: Some Methodological Observations," *VT* 47 (1997) 311-14.

608. D. Pardee, "An Overview of Ancient Hebrew Epistolography," *JBL* 97 (1978) 330.

609. A. Käser, "Then David Wrote a Letter (2 Sam. 11:14) — He Himself or Was It His Secretary? A Study of the Criteria for Handling the 'Semantic Causative,'" *TynB* 65 (2014) 21-35. In this case, it is reasonable to assume David's literacy as well as Joab's, also even Uriah's, since they must have written in the easily learnable alphabetic script. The ostracon found at Khirbet Qeiyafa, which was probably written by an ordinary man during the days of David, suggests that literacy was widespread in Israel around 1000 B.C. See A. R. Millard, "The Ostracon from the Days of David Found at Khirbet Qeiyafa," *TynB* 62 (2011) 1-13.

David is counting on the fact that Uriah as a loyal soldier will not dream of opening the letter. If he does not know of the adultery, he has in any case no personal motive to look at the letter. If he does know, he is accepting his fate with grim resignation, bitterly conscious that his wife has betrayed him and that the king is too powerful for him to contend with.[610]

4) Death of Uriah (11:16-21)

16 *As Joab kept watch over the city, he placed Uriah at the place where he knew that there were powerful men.*

17 *And the men of the city went out and fought with Joab and some of the people of David's servants fell,*[611] *and Uriah the Hittite also died.*

18 *And Joab sent (a messenger) and informed David of all the matters of the battle.*

19 *And he commanded the messenger, saying*
"When you finish telling all the matters of the battle to the king,
20 *if the king's anger rises and he says to you,*
'Why did you go near to the city to fight?
Didn't you know that they would shoot from the wall?
21 *Who struck down Abimelech son of Jerubbesheth?*[612]
Did not a woman throw an upper millstone on him
from the wall
and he died at Thebez?
Why did you approach the wall?'
you shall say,
'Your servant Uriah the Hittite is also dead.'"

16 Joab *placed* Uriah at the strategically most dangerous place.

18 In the ANE, more than one messenger was often sent.[613] But, in the Bible the solitary messenger was dominant, as is the case here (v. 19; also 2 Sam. 18:19-23, etc.).[614]

19 Joab tells the messenger not only what he should say, but also how to deal with the king. Similarly, in ch. 14, Joab will send the "wise" woman of Tekoa with instructions on what to say to David.

610. Alter, *The David Story*, p. 253.

611. The singular verb may be impersonal as *wy'mr* in v. 3 (see above). See Muraoka, "Philological Notes on the David-Bathsheba Story I," p. 299.

612. Alternatively, the K. *yrbšt* is to be read *y^{e}rubbōšet*, while the Q. would lead us to read *y^{e}rubba'al*, though it appears that the K., without ', should be read as *y^{e}rubbe'el.*

613. Note that two messengers are usually sent with a message in Ugaritic mythology: see, e.g., *DULAT*, p. 319.

614. Meier, *The Messenger in the Ancient Semitic World*, pp. 116-19.

20-21 Revell points out that David's anticipated speech constitutes an envelope structure, ABBA.[615] *Why did you . . .* (A), *Didn't you . . .* (B), *Did not . . .* (B), *Why did you . . .* (A).

Abimelech was son of Gideon, also known as Jerubbaal (Judg. 8:29-9:57). Here, the element "baal" in a name is changed to "bosheth" (*bōšet* "shame"), as can be seen elsewhere in Samuel (see on 4:4), so we have *son of Jerubbesheth.* Abimelech had told his armor-bearer to kill him "lest they say of me, 'a woman killed him'" (Judg. 9:54), but here such is said of him anyway.

For *an upper millstone* (Judg. 9:53), see also Deut. 24:6 (cf. BDB, p. 939: "as *riding* on the lower").

5) Report of Uriah's Death (11:22-25)

22 *And the messenger went and came and reported to David all that Joab had sent him to say.*

23 *And the messenger said to David,*
"Because the men prevailed over us,
they marched out toward us in the battlefield.
And then we were against them up to the entrance of the gate.
24 *And the archers shot at your servants*
from above the wall,
and some of the king's servants are dead;
and your servant Uriah the Hittite is also dead."
25 *And David said to the messenger,*
"Thus you shall say to Joab:
'Do not let this matter be evil in your eyes,
for the sword devours this way as well as that way.
Make your battle against the city stronger
and tear it down!'
and encourage him."

22 The viewpoint of the narrator[616] changes from the battlefield to Jerusalem where David was; hence *the messenger went and came.* See, "The messenger set out, and when he arrived he told David everything" (NIV).

23-24 The LXX has a long addition. Some say the MT of these two verses is "defective" and take the long addition as the original. Thus, McCarter makes an eclectic reconstruction of the text between the third line (*and some*

615. See E. J. Revell, "The Repetition of Introductions to Speech as a Feature of Biblical Hebrew," *VT* 47 (1997) 94 n. 7.

616. See Tsumura, I, pp. 54-55.

of the king's servants are dead;) and the fourth line of v. 24 (*and your servant Uriah the Hittite is also dead*):

> and some eighteen of the king's servants died." When the messenger finished telling the king all the details of the battle, David was furious with Joab. "Why did you go close to the city to fight?" he asked the messenger. "Didn't you know you would be assailed from the wall? Who slew Abimelech son of Jerubbaal? Didn't a woman drop an upper millstone on him from the wall when he died at Thebez? Why did you go close to the wall?"[617]

see McCarter, II, pp. 283-84. On the other hand, REB reconstructs v. 22 following the LXX, as follows:

> The messenger set out and, when he came to David, he made his report as Joab had instructed him. David, angry with Joab, said to the messenger, 'Why did you go so near the city during the fight? You must have known you would be struck down from the wall. Remember who killed Abimelech son of Jerubbesheth. Was it not a woman who threw down an upper millstone on him from the wall of Thebez and killed him? Why did you go near the wall?'

The shorter version, the MT, however, seems to be original and makes sense as it is, without the additional information.

As for *we were against them* (MT *wannihyeh ʿălêhem*), McCarter adopts LXX and translates "and when we drove them back" but there is no strong need to alter the MT. The messenger suggests that the battle first went to the advantage of the enemy, while later (*and then*), *we*, the Israelites, prevailed.

The verb of the K. *wyrʾw hmwrʾym* ("the archers shot") is a historical spelling, based on the root *yrʾ; the Q. *yōrû* is a phonetic spelling, which resulted from *sandhi* as follows:

> *yōrû* ← (*sandhi*) — *yōr*^{e}*û* ←(loss of the intervocalic *aleph*) — *yōr*^{e}*ʾû*
> cf. "the arrows rained heavily" (McCarter), based on the LXX^{L}.

25 *Let not this matter be evil in your eyes*, i.e., "Do not worry about this." The messenger would take it to mean "don't blame yourself"; Joab, however, would understand it as "don't think evil of me for the murder." David probably knows Joab would not have been happy about killing a good officer, so he is saying, "he might have been killed anyway." David excuses his own sin by directing attention toward a different matter.

617. McCarter, II, p. 278.

6) Bathsheba Becomes David's Wife (11:26-27)

26 *And Uriah's wife heard that her husband Uriah was dead and lamented for her husband.*

27 *And the mourning passed.*
And David sent and brought her to his house; and she became his wife and bore him a son.
And the matter that David did was evil in the eyes of the LORD.

26-27 For *lamented* (*wattispōd* *spd), see the comment on 1 Sam. 25:1.[618] The *mourning* (*'ēbel*) here probably lasted seven days, as in the case of Joseph's mourning for Jacob (Gen. 50:10) and in the ancient city of Ugarit, where the sacrifices were made on the first seven days after the king Niqmaddu died and was buried; see *KTU* 1.161.[619]

Note that in Hebrew the relative clause *that David did* (*'ăšer-'āśāh Dāwīd*) is inserted between the main clause *And the matter . . . was evil in the eyes of the* LORD (*wayyēra' haddābār . . . b^e'ênê YHWH*); see the comment on v. 2 above and 1 Sam. 2:29[620] and 2 Sam. 2:24. This statement, like those in 12:24 and 17:14, specifically states the Lord's attitude. Here it makes clear that the troubles that follow in David's family are God's judgement on him. The phrase echoes in the words of David in Ps. 51:4 as he prayed in repentance to God.

NRSV and JPS treat this final sentence as the beginning of the new paragraph. However, the following verse, 12:1, most probably constitutes a TRANSITION and the SETTING for the subsequent episode, with *movement* verbs ("sent" and "came") as well as the introductory phrase of utterance, i.e., "and he said,"[621] so it is better to take the verse as the TERMINUS of the preceding episode, constituting a link in the Ab/B pattern, preparing the reader for the very specific indictments of the oracle in 12:7-12.

b. "You Are the Man!" (12:1-15a)

David started his great sin by breaking the tenth commandment, then the seventh, then the sixth, while the Lord silently watched his behavior. Now, just as

618. Tsumura, I, p. 574.

619. D. T. Tsumura, "The Interpretation of the Ugaritic Funerary Text *KTU* 1.161," in *Official Cult and Popular Religion in the Ancient Near East: Papers of the First Colloquium on the Ancient Near East; the City and Its Life; Held at the Middle Eastern Culture Center in Japan (Mitaka, Tokyo), March 20-22, 1992*, ed. E. Matsushima (Heidelberg: C. Winter, 1993), pp. 40-55. See the commentary on 1 Sam. 31:13 in Tsumura, I, p. 655; also Gen. 50:10; Sir. 10:12.

620. Tsumura, I, pp. 166-67.

621. See Tsumura, I, pp. 50-53.

David in chapter 11 sent messengers to Bathsheba (v. 4), to Joab (v. 6), and again to Bathsheba (v. 27) in order to commit adultery, camouflage his wrong doings, commit murder, and finally make Bathsheba his wife, so here the Lord sends his messenger Nathan to David to confront him and condemn his great sin—the same prophet Nathan who had given David the promise of an eternal house in ch. 7. Here, the Lord accuses David of standing above God's law. Unlike in the Canaanite religio-political setting, where kings were often deified, the king of Israel had to obey the law of the Lord. As Samuel had warned the people of Israel, the king was also under God's judgment: "And if you act wickedly, both you and your king will be swept away!" (1 Sam. 12:25).[622] Although there are also accounts where the prophets in Mari were sent by their god Dagan as messengers to the king, they talked about repairing the temple, not about repairing the relationship of the people and king with their god.[623]

As in 2 Sam. 14:5-17 and 1 K. 20:39-43, the king is asked to act as a judge in a legal matter, only to find that he has passed judgment upon himself. Here the Lord sends his messenger, David's personal counselor (see the commentary on 7:3), to David so that he might realize his own personal and spiritual condition.

1) Nathan's Parable (12:1-6)

1 *And the Lord sent Nathan to David. And he came to him and said to him,*
"There were two men in the same[624] city,
one rich and one poor.
2 *The rich man[625] had a great many sheep and cattle,*
3 *but the poor man[626] had nothing*
except one little ewe-lamb which he had bought.
And he brought it up[627]
and it grew up together with him and his children.

622. See Tsumura, I, p. 330.

623. See A. Malamat, "Prophecy at Mari," in *"The Place Is Too Small for Us,"* ed. R. P. Gordon (SBTS 5; Winona Lake, Ind.: Eisenbrauns, 1995), pp. 50-73. Also Y. Kaufmann, *The Religion of Israel: From Its Beginnings to the Babylonian Exile* (Chicago: University of Chicago Press, 1960), p. 215 n. 1.

624. So JPS; lit. "one"; see "daughters of the same (lit. one) mother" (Ezek. 23:2).

625. If the noun is definite, the MT *lᵉʿāšîr* lacks *segol* (*e*) for *lamed, the rich man.*

626. MT *lārāš* "to/for the poor man." The spelling *rāš* is phonetic, without *aleph*; cf. *rāʾš* (v. 1). See Tsumura, "Vowel *sandhi* in Biblical Hebrew," pp. 575-88.

627. Or "tended it" (JPS); lit. "let it live, preserve it alive" (*HALOT*, p. 309). LXX seemingly translates it by two verbal phrases: "preserved it alive and sustained its life by nourishing and feeding it" (*periepoiēsato kai eksethrepsen autēn*); see T. Muraoka, "Philological Notes on the David-Bathsheba Story II," in *Sophia — Paideia: Sapienza e educazione (Sir 1,27); Miscellanea di studi offerti in onore del prof. Don Mario Cimosa*, ed. G. Bonney and R. Vicent (Rome: Liberia Ateneo Salesiano, 2012), 89.

It used to eat of his morsel
and drink of his cup
and lie in his bosom.
And it was like a daughter to him.
4 *And a visitor came to the rich man*[628]
and he was reluctant to take (an animal) from his sheep and from his cattle
to cook[629] *for the traveler who had come to him,*
and took the ewe-lamb of the poor man
and cooked it for the man who had come to him."
5 *And David got very angry with the man and said to Nathan,*
"As the LORD lives,
the man who did this deserves to die!
6 *As for the ewe-lamb, he should repay it fourfold,*
because he did this thing and because he had no compassion."

1 *And he came to him and said to him* is a TRANSITION sentence, being the SETTING for the following EVENT, with a *movement* verb and an introductory formula of utterance, "and he said." See the commentary on 11:27b.

3 *It used to eat . . . and drink . . . and lie*: these three verbs are impf., which express habit.[630] These three verbs were used in the same order by Uriah in 11:11.

4 That the Lord has special concern for the poor is a major theme in the Bible, and as his representative, the king and other judges were supposed to protect against the abuse of the powerful (Exod. 23:6; Lev. 19:15; Prov. 31:9; Isa. 3:14; etc.). The rich man *took* (*lqḥ) the poor man's lamb, just as David *took* Bathsheba (11:4). It was especially heinous because he had plenty of sheep of his own. While in 1 Sam. 8:14 the king was said to have the right to take people's property, he was also supposed to uphold the cause of the powerless and prevent abuse; see Ps. 72:2, 4, 12-14; also the Ugaritic Krt epic (*KTU* 1.16 VI 33-34, 45-47).

5 *David got very angry with the man.* Here, as Alter aptly comments,[631] "Nathan's rhetorical trap has now snapped shut. David, by his access of anger, condemns himself, and he is now the helpless target of denunciation that Nathan will unleash." David has a true concern for justice when he is not blinded by his own passion. (Compare his ready acceptance of Abigail's words in 1 Sam. 25:32-33.)

628. The MT *lᵉʾîš heʿāšîr* lacks *qameṣ* (*ā*) for *lamed*. This is explained as "a Massoretic error" (McCarter, II, p. 294; also Driver, p. 291; GKC §126x). The expected form is *lāʾîš heʿāšîr*. It is possible that the MT is spelled phonetically, like *rāš* (v. 3), which involves a resonant /L/: *lāʾîš* -→ *Lᵉʾîš* , as in the case of *leʿāšîr* → *Lᵉʿāšîr* (v. 2).

629. Lit. "make."

630. Driver, p. 291.

631. Alter, *The David Story*, p. 258.

For the oath formula *As the Lord lives,* see 1 Sam. 14:39.[632]

The expression *deserves to die* (*ben-māwet*) literally means "a son of death"; see 1 Sam. 20:31; 26:16; also 2 Sam. 19:28 ("men of death"). David's utterance is not so much giving information or legal opinion as expressing his strong emotion.

6 For *fourfold,* see Ex 22:1 [21:37], which states a stolen sheep must be repaid fourfold (see also Luke 19:8). McCarter takes this as "sevenfold," based on LXX^{BAMN}; cf. Prov. 6:31.

2) The Lord's Message to David (12:7-12)

7 *And Nathan said to David,*
"You are the man!
Thus says the Lord God of Israel:
'It was I who anointed you as a king over Israel,
and it was I who delivered you from the hand of Saul.
8 *And I gave you your master's house*
and your master's women into your bosom;
I gave you the house of Israel and Judah.
If this were too little,
I would have added to you accordingly.
9 *Why have you despised the word of the Lord*
by doing evil in his eyes?
Uriah the Hittite you have struck down with the sword;
his wife you have taken as your wife;
him you have killed with the sword of the Ammonites.
10 *Now, a sword shall never turn aside from your house,*
because you have despised me
and have taken the wife of Uriah the Hittite to be your wife.'
11 *Thus says the Lord,*
'I am going to raise up evil against you from your house.
And I will take your wives
and give them to your friend
before your eyes.
And he shall lie with your wives
before the eyes of this sun.
12 *For, you did (that) secretly,*
but I will do this thing in front of[633] *all Israel and the sun.'"*

632. Tsumura, I, p. 377.

633. Heb. *neged.* This particle expresses "more strongly than *lipnê* the idea of being *conspicuous before*" (Driver, p. 292).

This section has similarities with Nathan's oracle in chapter 7. In both, the Lord looks back on what he has done by grace for David. However, while in chapter 7 the Lord out of grace promised him an enduring house, here he announces that David for his own deeds will experience misery in his house, for David has *despised* the Lord (v. 10) and the word of the Lord (v. 9).

7b *You are the man!* (*'attāh hā'îš*) As Muraoka notes, the word order of this nominal clause (S-P) is pragmatically marked: "The person whom you have just condemned as deserving capital sentence is none other than you."[634]

Then the prophet Nathan conveys the Lord's message to David. The formula *Thus says the* Lord *God of Israel* introduces the solemn announcement of the God of Israel.

8 The passages in 16:21-22 and 1 K. 2:17-25 may suggest that marrying the wives of the previous king could be a sign of claiming the throne, though in the former Absalom's act in itself makes him odious to David, and in the latter Bathsheba does not seem to realize a problem. Also, Abner seems to have had no intention of becoming king himself (3:6-12). Whether David actually married Saul's wives is not certain—there is nothing in the account of Rizpah (ch. 21), or indeed anywhere else, to indicate it—but at least he was in a position to do so.[635]

9 This sin was against the Lord, as David should have known through *the word of the* Lord. Compare Ps. 51:4. *With the sword* is a general term for violence, as in 11:25, not a reference to the specific mode of death (see 11:24).

The expression *despised the word of the* Lord may be a euphemism, softening an original phrase, "despised the Lord" (so LXX^L, Theodotion).

In this verse, the Lord refers to himself in the 3 m.s.. Such alternation is often seen in Psalms and other poetic passages as Ps. 61:7-8.

The following sentence constitutes a tricolon, that is, a three-line parallelism:

Uriah the Hittite you have struck down with the sword; [A]
 his wife you have taken as your wife; [X]
him you have killed with the sword of the Ammonites. [B]

634. Muraoka, "Philological Notes on the David-Bathsheba Story II," p. 94.

635. J. D. Levenson and B. Halpern suggested that Saul's wife, Ahinoam daughter of Ahimaaz (1 Sam. 14:50), and David's wife Ahinoam, who is always referred to as being of Jezreel (27:3), are the same person ("The Political Import of David's Marriage," *JBL* 99 [1980] 513-14). Almost the only somewhat sensible grounds they give is that these two are the only women in the Bible with the name Ahinoam. Their theory must conclude that Ahinoam, presumably even more enamored of David than her daughter was, left her home with Saul to join David in the wilderness before he went to Ziklag (30:5; 2 Sam. 2:2; 3:2) and bore him a son. Even if the scenario were credible, it is hard to connect it with the present verse, as *wives* is plural.

Here, the first and the third line correspond to each other very well with a ballast variant *the sword of the Ammonites,* while the second line gives the real problem of David's deed. Thus, what God focuses on in this oracle as a whole is, as Janzen notes, not so much murder and adultery — "the adultery, in fact, is not even explicitly mentioned" — as "David's act of taking Bathsheba." David's rebellion against the Lord and his despising the Lord (v. 10) and his word (v. 9) led to this act of taking. "The oracle accuses David of doing what the rich man in Nathan's parable does: he takes when he should not, a matter that God interprets as David's usurpation of God's own role in their relationship."[636] This is probably the reason why David confesses his sin to be *against the LORD* (v. 13), and *only* against him (cf. Ps. 51:4).

10 David's family will be ravaged by the sword: Amnon (13:29), Absalom (18:15), and Adonijah (1 K. 2:25) all die by the sword. Thus David's words to Joab, "the sword devours one as well as another" (11:25), will come back to him. Note that the great principle in 1 Sam. 2:30, which the Lord God of Israel announced to Eli by the agency of the man of God, is still valid:

For those who honor me I will honor;
those who despise me will be humiliated.

11-12 Verse 11 seems to refer to Absalom's actions in 16:21-22.

Both in 2 Sam. 7 and here, "the house of David" is the principal theme. But while the former passage gives "a promise of continuing rule for David's house," this passage promises "trouble to arise from David's house."

The phrase *before your eyes* (*lᵉʿênệkā*) comes in the position of X of the AX&B pattern: in the Hebrew word order, "And I will take your wives before your eyes and give them to your friend." I translate the word *rēʿeykā,* as "your friend," following Driver, who takes the *yod* (*y*) as an etymological, not a plural, indicator.[637]

The word *šemeš* ("sun") is a *feminine* noun here, used idiomatically, though it is normally masculine; see also on 2:24 (above) as well as on 1 Sam. 20:19.[638] Muraoka suggests that when Nathan said *this sun* he indicated the sun by some gesture.[639]

636. D. Janzen, "The Condemnation of David's 'Taking' in 2 Samuel 12:1-14," *JBL* 131 (2012) 216.

637. Driver, p. 292; also J-M, §96Ce.

638. See Tsumura, I, pp. 512-13; "*šemeš* - sun," in *NIDOTTE*, 4, pp. 185-90.

639. Muraoka, "Philological Notes on the David-Bathsheba Story II," p. 95.

3) David's Repentance (12:13-15a)

13 *And David said to Nathan,*
"I have sinned against the Lord."
And Nathan said to David,
"The Lord also has taken away[640] *your sin;*
you shall not die.
14 *Nevertheless,*
since[641] *you have indeed insulted [the enemies of] the Lord*
with this thing,
the child who is born to you shall surely die."
15a *And Nathan went back to his house.*

13-14 David truly repents. However, the results of his actions remain.

13 Unlike Saul who in 1 Sam. 15:24 said simply *I have sinned!* David confesses his sin *against the Lord* (*ḥāṭā'tî lᵉYHWH*). The 1 c.s. pf. *ḥāṭā'tî* is a *performative perfect,* denoting "I am a sinner because I have sinned," rather than "I sinned" or "I have sinned." David is saying "I stand convinced of my sin against the Lord."[642] When a sinner confesses it is important for him to state against whom he has sinned. And his confession cannot be complete until he accepts that his sin is ultimately against the Lord and his commandments (see Ps. 51:4).

A sin must be atoned for by someone. Hence, Nathan's word *The Lord also has taken away your sin* (lit. "to cause your sin to pass over") implies that David's sin will be atoned for by the Lord himself. The perfect verb here is also to be taken as *performative* with Muraoka, that is, that Nathan's words are the means by which David is absolved of his sin.[643] McCarter translates "the Lord transferred your sin."[644] REB even paraphrases: "The Lord has laid on another the consequences of your sin." Certainly, David, the Lord's anointed, does not die now (see Lev. 20:10), for his sin was transferred to another person, his son. Hence, Nathan assures David with the promise: *you shall not die.* Yet, he has to face the consequences of his sin: that the child who had just been born would die.

14 The MT "you have insulted the enemies of the Lord" does not seem to fit the context here, and various solutions have been proposed. The Qumran manuscript, 4QSam[a], reads *'t dbr yhwh* "the word of the Lord";[645]

640. Lit. "to make to pass away"; see 24:10.

641. On the phrase *'epes kî,* see *HALOT,* p. 79; Muraoka, "Philological Notes on the David-Bathsheba Story II," pp. 96-97.

642. Muraoka, "Philological Notes on the David-Bathsheba Story II," 95-96.

643. Muraoka, "Philological Notes on the David-Bathsheba Story II," p. 96 n. 31.

644. McCarter, II, p. 301.

645. See Herbert, *RBDSS,* p. 147.

but BHS gives an incorrect form (*l[.]bd*). This is certainly a later adjustment. Some translations, such as AV, NASB, and NIV, take the verb *insult (ni'aṣtā)* as a causative Piel, and interpret it as "you have caused the enemies of the LORD to insult him." However, there is no support for taking this Pi. verb (*n'ṣ*) as causative.[646] GKC §52g gives examples of verbs with "the eager pursuit of an action" that "may also consist in *urging* and *causing* others to do the same." The phrase *ni'ēṣ ni'aṣtā* can be most naturally translated as *you have indeed insulted*, for the verb in piel means "to treat disrespectfully, discard" (*HALOT*, p. 658), never with a causative sense elsewhere.

Here as well as in 1 Sam. 25:22, the term *the enemies* was probably added euphemistically out of respect for God.[647] However, whether this euphemism was in the original text or was a later scribal exercise (so McCarter, Anderson, Stoebe,[648] etc.), and if the latter how late, or early, is a matter of speculation.[649] So, our translation *[the enemies of] the LORD*. NRSV, REB, ESV, etc. follow this interpretation. Compare Ps 74:10, 18, where the verb *n'ṣ* (Pi.) appears with "enemy" and its equivalents as its subject. Note that unlike here, "enemies" in 1 Sam. 20:16 is not a euphemistic addition.[650]

The death of Bathsheba's child is announced here. And David is to be bereaved of three more sons as well, Amnon, Absalom, and Adonijah, as the fourfold penalty decreed by David himself in v. 6.

EXCURSUS: "DAVID'S REPENTANCE IN PSALM 51"

Psalm 51 was composed on this occasion. The title of the psalm reads: "A Psalm of David, when Nathan the prophet went to him, after he had gone in to Bathsheba." There is no reason for dismissing such a description as unhistorical in view of the many pre-Davidic examples of hymns and psalms with detailed subscriptions in the ANE.[651] See also the commentary on 2 Sam. 22:1-2a (below).

646. Firth, p. 425, following Fokkelman, *Narrative Art and Poetry in the Books of Samuel*, I, p. 451, takes the piel as causative.

647. See M. J. Mulder, "Un euphémisme dans 2 Sam. XII 14?" *VT* 18 (1968) 109-10; also D. W. Parry, "The 'Word' or the 'Enemies' of the Lord? Revisiting the Euphemism in 2 Sam 12:14," in *Emanuel: Studies in Hebrew Bible, Septuagint and Dead Sea Scrolls in Honor of Emanuel Tov*, ed. S. M. Paul et al. (VTS 94; Leiden: E. J. Brill, 2003), pp. 367-78. See also Janzen, "The Condemnation of David's 'Taking,'" 217 n. 20.

648. McCarter, II, p. 296; Anderson, p. 159; Stoebe, II, p. 299.

649. Parry, "The 'Word' or the 'Enemies' of the Lord?" pp. 370-72.

650. Tsumura, I, p. 510.

651. See Tsumura, "Hymns and Songs with Titles and Subscriptions in the Ancient Near East," pp. 1-7 [Japanese with an English summary].

In this, his psalm of repentance, David asks first for mercy for the forgiveness of his personal sin (vv. 1-17) and then for the recovery of Zion, tainted by his sin, as the place of worship of the holy God (vv. 18-19).

> 1 Have mercy on me, O God, A
> according to your steadfast love;
> according to your abundant mercy
> blot out my transgressions.
> 2 Wash me thoroughly from my iniquity,
> and cleanse me from my sin!
> . . .
> 16 For you will not delight in sacrifice, or I would give it;
> you will not be pleased with a burnt offering.
> 17 The sacrifices of God are a broken spirit; Z
> a broken and contrite heart, O God, you will not despise.
>
> 18 Do good to Zion in your good pleasure; A'
> build up the walls of Jerusalem;
> 19 then will you delight in right sacrifices, Z'
> in burnt offerings and whole burnt offerings;
> then bulls will be offered on your altar.

Thus, in vv. 1-17, King David humbly comes before the merciful God begging for forgiveness of his personal sin; note the frequent use of the first-person singular forms, that is, the independent pronoun, pronominal suffixes, verbal forms ("me," "my," "I") in vv. 1-16:

vv. 1 (2×), 2 (4×), 3 (5×), 4 (2×), 5 (3×), 6 (1×), 7 (4×), 8 (1×), 9 (2×), 10 (2×), 11 (2×), 12 (2×), 13 (1×), 14 (3×), 15 (3×), 16 (1×).

While the last two verses, vv. 18-19, are often taken as a later, post-exilic, addition, the literary structure of the entire psalm rather supports its literary unity. In the first section, vv. 1-17, David confesses his own personal sin and makes supplication for forgiveness. Then, in the second section, vv. 18-19, David as king, the representative of his people, prays for the recovery of his kingdom and his royal city Jerusalem and for the recovery of worship of the Holy God at the holy city Zion. A king's sin does not stop on the personal level; it affects the entire society and kingdom spiritually. The first section and the second section correspond to each other in the pattern of a detailed statement (A . . . Z: vv. 1-17) followed by the *summary statement* (A'Z': vv. 18-19). Note that v. 1 (A: "Have mercy on me") // v. 18 (A': "Do good to Zion in your good pleasure") and vv. 16-17 (Z: "sacrifice - burnt offering") // v. 19 (Z': "sacrifices - burnt offerings").

As for the expression *build up the walls of Jerusalem*, it does not automatically point to the postexilic period. Repair or (re)building of the city walls was carried out not only by Nehemiah, but also by Solomon (1 K. 3:1) and Hezekiah (2 Chr. 32:5). In this psalm, David asks God to *build up the walls of Jerusalem.* Note that the term *walls* here is a metonymy for Jerusalem-Zion. He could have rebuilt them on his own authority. But he is asking God for the recovery of Zion, the place of worship for God's people.[652]

c. Death of David's Son and Birth of Solomon (12:15b-25)

15b *And the Lord struck the child whom Uriah's wife bore to David, and he was sick.*

16 *And David sought God on behalf of the boy.*

And David fasted, fasting and going in[653] *and spending the night and lying on the ground.*

17 *And the elders of his house stood by him*[654] *to raise him up from the ground, but he was not willing and would not eat*[655] *food with them.*

18 *On the seventh day the child died.*

And David's servants were afraid to tell him that the child was dead, for they said,

"While the child was alive,
we spoke to him
and he did not listen to our voice.
How then can we say to him that the child is dead?
He may do evil."[656]

19 *And David saw*[657] *that his servants were whispering together.*
And David realized that the child was dead.
And David said to his servants,
"Is the child dead?"
and they said,
"Yes, dead."

20 *And David arose from the ground and washed and anointed himself and changed his clothes*[658] *and entered the house of the Lord and worshipped;*

652. D. T. Tsumura, "The Unity of Psalm 51," *Exeg* 2 (1991) 35-48 [in Japanese].

653. inf. abs. and pf.

654. *'ālâw*; or "beside him."

655. *bārā'*; cf. *brh* in some MSS and 4QSam[a].

656. See "do *himself* harm" (NASB).

657. McCarter reads *noticed wyśkl* on the basis of LXX[BAMN]. But David would have *seen* them whispering.

658. MT (Q.) *śimlōtâw*; cf. K. *śmltw* [śimlōtô] "his cloak."

and he came to his house, and he requested and they set out food for him and he ate.

21 *And his servants said to him,*
"What is this thing that you have done?
In order that the child might stay alive
you fasted and wept;
but when the child died,
you arose and ate food."

22 *And he said,*
"While the child was still alive,
I fasted and wept,
for I thought,
'Who knows?
The LORD may be gracious to me,
that the child may live.'
23 *But now he is dead;*
why am I to fast?
Can I bring him back again?
I will go to him,
he will not come back to me."

24 *And David comforted his wife Bathsheba; he came to her and lay with*
her. She bore a son and named him Solomon. Now the LORD loved him
25 *and sent Nathan the prophet, and he*[659] *named him Jedidiah for the sake of the LORD.*

15b-23 The child would have been born rather early after David's marriage, but way too late for its being Uriah's child, so David must have openly announced it as his child as soon as possible.

When the child falls ill, David still hopes that the Lord might change his mind, and so petitions him with fasting, as Judg. 20:26; Ezra 8:23; Esth. 4:16; Ps. 35:13; etc. As fasting and uncleanliness were also part of ordinary mourning (1 Sam. 31:13; 2 Sam. 3:35; 14:2), his actions puzzle his servants, who wonder why he stopped mourning when the child died.

15b The child's mother is still called *Uriah's wife*, perhaps to stress David's crime, and perhaps because when the child was conceived she was still Uriah's wife.[660]

16 David *sought God* (*waybaqqēš . . . ʾet-hāʾĕlôhîm*; "entreated God") to spare his son's life. For this expression, see Deut. 4:29; Jer. 50:4; Hos. 3:5; 2 Chr. 11:16. Note that the Qumran text 4QSam[a] has *wybqš . . . mn* ("from").

659. I.e., Nathan.

660. Muraoka, "Philological Notes on the David-Bathsheba Story II," p. 99.

Some scholars see these acts as vestiges of a cult of the dead, a ritual descent to the underworld to bring his son back.[661] However, as others have pointed out, this assumption is unfounded,[662] and a non-Israelite practice is being read into the text; see also below on the commentary on v. 23. Besides, at this point, his son was still alive.

For *spending the night and lying* (*wᵉlān wᵉšākab*), LXX^{L}, OG and 4QSam^{a} reflect only the second verb, while LXX^{BMN} reads only the former. McCarter says one has to choose one of the two verbs as original,[663] though the longer form of MT with both verbs is highly probable.

The verbs *ûbāʾ wᵉlān wᵉšākab* are sometimes taken as habitual forms.[664] However, David did this only for these particular seven days, so it is strange to take the verbal form *weqtl* as customary action.[665] Stoebe takes the "perfect consecutives" as constituting conditional clauses, citing GKC, §159g.[666] However, I would take the series *weqtl . . . weqtl . . .* here as a procedural discourse, stating *HOW-it-was-done*,[667] translating:

> And David sought God on behalf of the boy. And David fasted
> (WHAT), fasting
> and going in and spending the night and lying on the ground (HOW).

The last two verbs are a hendiadys.[668]

18 The child's illness, hence David's fasting, lasted for seven days. The child seems to have been several days or weeks old when he became ill. Note that he is not given a name. *He may act evil,* that is, commit suicide.

20 For the word pair, "to wash" and "to anoint" (*swk), see Ezek. 16:9, *KTU* 1.3:II:38-41.[669]

661. T. J. Lewis, *Cults of the Dead in Ancient Israel and Ugarit* (HSM 39; Atlanta: Scholars Press, 1989), pp. 43-44; H. Nieh, "Ein unerkannter Text zur Nekromantie in Israel: Bemerkungen zum religionsgeschichtlichen Hintergrund von 2Sam 12, 16a," *UF* 23 (1991) 301-6.

662. K. Spronk, review of *Cults of the Dead in Ancient Israel and Ugarit*, by T. J. Lewis, *BO* 48 (1991) 237.

663. McCarter, II, p. 297.

664. As did, e.g., Anderson, p. 158.

665. Driver, p. 292, takes the pf. verbs as denoting repeated actions.

666. Stoebe, II, p. 299.

667. For a discourse-grammatical view of the *weqtl* form in Hebrew, see the commentary on 7:9b-16 above. For a detailed analysis of the LXX verbal forms in 12:16, see Muraoka, "Philological Notes on the David-Bathsheba Story II," p. 100, though he is concerned with the verbal aspects rather than the discourse-grammatical features of the verbal sequence.

668. Tsumura, "Tense and Aspect of Hebrew Verbs in 2 Samuel 7:8-16," p. 650.

669. See M. Dahood, "Ugaritic-Hebrew Parallel Pairs," in *RSP* 3, pp. 151-52.

Here, the narrative discourse changes from a slow flow in v. 19, expressed by three *wayqtls* (*noted . . . realized . . . said*), each followed by the stated subject[670] *David*, to a quick flow with ten *wayqtls*, only the first of which has the stated subject *David*: i.e., *arose . . . washed . . . anointed . . . changed . . . entered . . . worshipped . . . came . . . requested . . . (they set) . . . ate.* Muraoka nicely explains this change of narrative flow in the image of stage movement: "One could visualise David on a stage with the floodlight following every single movement of his as he moves round on the stage, although in this case David was lying still on the ground. The moment this gripping tension is gone, we are back to the familiar narrative style."[671]

The mention of "the house of the LORD" (*bêt YHWH*) here has been considered anachronistic by several scholars. However there is no reason to think that the author meant Solomon's temple; it was probably a tent shrine for the ark, which could be called a "house" like the *bt* of El in Ugarit (*KTU* 1.23:36), who is said to have lived in his "tent" or "tabernacle" with "seven rooms" or "eight compartments."[672] Note that Akk. *bītu* sometimes means "a tent."[673] And *bt* does not necessarily refer to a stone or brick building; it often means simply "dwelling-place."[674] See the commentary on 7:6 and 1 Sam. 1:7.[675]

21 For our translation *In order that the child might stay alive*, McCarter translates: "While the child was still alive," reading *bʿwd* with Wellhausen on the basis of LXX^L, Syr. and Targ.[676] NASB, NIV, JPS also translate "While the child was alive." However, the MT possibly purposely distinguishes the two expressions *baʿăbûr hayyeled ḥay* (here) and *b^{e}ʿôd hayyeled ḥay* (v. 22). While this verse expresses David's purpose, to try to keep the child alive, in the next he simply states the situation, i.e., *while the child was still alive.*

22 David's use of the expression *Who knows?* (*mî yôdēaʿ*) seems to function in the same way the prophetic *'ûlay* "perhaps" does in Amos 5:15, etc. See also the similar expressions in Joel 2:14 and Jonah 3:9. David had hoped that even in this situation the Lord would change his mind. It should be noted that his attitude toward the death of his beloved one is completely

670. For the stated subject of *wayqtl*, see Tsumura, I, p. 51; also Introduction, III.2 (above).

671. Muraoka, "Philological Notes on the David-Bathsheba Story II," p. 103.

672. *KTU* 1.3:V:26-27; see D. T. Tsumura, "The Ugaritic Drama of the Good Gods: A Philological Study" (PhD diss., Brandeis University, 1973), pp. 48, 65; *DULAT*, pp. 245-50.

673. See *AHw*, p. 133. See also Tsumura, I, pp. 114-15.

674. See *HALOT*, p. 124; see GN Bethel, which means "the house of God."

675. Tsumura, I, pp. 114-15.

676. McCarter, II, p. 298; also Stoebe, II, p. 300; Muraoka, "Philological Notes on the David-Bathsheba Story II," p. 103.

the opposite of that of the Canaanite cult of the dead. While in the latter family members intercede and appeal to their deities to "save" the soul of the dead, David, while the child was alive, sought God's mercy for his recovery, but, after his death, he entrusted the fate of the dead child completely to the hands of the sovereign and merciful God. David's behavior has nothing to do with a Canaanite cult of the dead, in which even the chief deity El had to depend on divination to heal the dying king Keret. Here, we may catch a glimpse of the fact that David was a *realistic* monotheist, trusting on the only God for his mercy.

23 *I will go to him.* When he dies. Compare Jacob's words in Gen. 37:35 and the common expressions "was gathered to his people" (Gen. 25:8, etc.) or "slept with his fathers" (1 K. 11:43, etc.). Lewis interprets this as a ritual descent to the underworld (see above), but as Emerton notes, this depends on a questionable translation of this verse, which depends on a questionable interpretation of Gen. 37:35, which in turn depends on the uncertain interpretation of *barṣ* in *CTA* 5.6.25 as "into the underworld."[677]

24-25 1 Chr. 3:5 suggests that Solomon was the fourth son of David by Bathsheba. This verse may skip over a number of years to introduce the most important child of the union. This is an example of the practice of carrying a narrative through to the thematic end, to the person or event that makes the narrative significant, even though it goes beyond the immediate time setting, and then going back and resuming the narrative, a principle of *dischronologization* in the narrative.[678] To write a history is to present a multidimensional reality in terms of a monodimensional form of language.[679]

24 This time David *came to her and lay with her*, while in 11:4 *she came to him and he lay with her.* In both cases it was David who took the initiative. However, while their first encounter was characterized by David's royal request to Uriah's wife Bathsheba and her forced consent, this time it was David's wish to comfort his wife Bathsheba. See the commentary on 11:4.

The birth of Solomon could be taken as a sign of divine forgiveness after the divine punishment, namely the death of the illegitimate child.

According to the Q., it was Bathsheba who named the baby; the K. has "he named." In 1 Sam. 1:20; 4:21 the mother named the child, but those were special circumstances.

677. J. A. Emerton, review of *Cults of the Dead in Ancient Israel*, by T. J. Lewis, *VT* 41 (1991) 384.

678. W. J. Martin, "'Dischronologized' Narrative in the Old Testament," in *Congress Volume Rome 1968*, ed. G. W. Anderson et al. (VTS 17; Leiden: E. J. Brill, 1969), 179-86.

679. On this topic, see Tsumura, I, p. 64.

For the name *Solomon* (*šᵉlōmōh*), which first appeared in 5:14, several etymologies have been suggested. T. N. D. Mettinger translates it as "his (the previous child's) substitute/replacement" and explains Solomon to be "a compensation for the child that died."[680] For another possibility, linking it with the Canaanite divine name *Šlm*, see the commentary on 3:3. Another translation is "his peace." McCarter takes it to mean David's peace (or the dead child's replacement),[681] but Bergen holds the literal meaning of the name is "His [Yahweh's] Restoration/Peace."[682] Solomon disappears from the stage until the struggle for royal succession in 1 K. 1. The narrator keeps silent about him — about where he was during the rebellion of Absalom, though one assumes he fled Jerusalem as part of David's household (15:16).

25 The name *Jedidiah* means "Beloved of the LORD" and appears only here; it can be compared with the Ugaritic phrase *ydd il* "Loved one of El."[683] The name is probably given to Solomon due to his future special relation to Yahweh as David's heir. Therefore, McCarter, Anderson, Stoebe, etc., hold that *Jedidiah* was possibly the throne name while on the other hand *Solomon* the private and personal name, since the former was given by the dynastic god through his prophet.[684] However, it is certainly strange that the public, throne name would appear only here, whereas the "private" name would appear 287 times in the OT. Firth, on the other hand, thinks that *Solomon* was a throne name, while *Jedidiah* a family nickname.[685] However, it would be strange for a family nickname to be given by a prophet. It may be that both names are official but *Solomon* became more popular than *Jedidiah* for some unknown reason.

The phrase *for the sake of the LORD* (*baʿăbûr YHWH*) has been translated variously: "because of the LORD" (RSV, NRSV); "at the instance of the LORD" (JPS); "because the LORD loved him" (NIV). McCarter translates it as "by the grace of," following de Boer, who cites the same Phoenician expression *bʿbr* DN in Karatepe inscriptions (*KAI* 26A I 8; II 6, 12; III 11).[686] However, when translating, it may be better to reserve the term "grace" for other Hebrew terms such as *ḥesed* or *ḥen.*

680. Mettinger, *King and Messiah*, p. 30 and n. 21.
681. See McCarter, II, p. 303.
682. Bergen, p. 376. For other possibilities, see *HALOT*, pp. 1540-41.
683. *DULAT*, p. 956.
684. McCarter, II, p. 303; Anderson, p. 165; Stoebe, II, p. 300.
685. Firth, p. 430.
686. McCarter, II, p. 304.

3 [B]. End of Israel-Ammon War (12:26-31)

26 *And Joab fought against Rabbah of the Ammonites and captured the royal city.*

27 *And Joab sent messengers to David, saying,*
"I have fought against Rabbah;
I have even captured the city of waters.
28 *And now, gather the rest of the people together*
and camp against the city and capture it,
lest I capture the city myself
and my name be called on it."

29 *And David gathered all the people together and went to Rabbah and fought against it and captured it*

30 *and took the crown of their king*[687] *from his head; its weight was a talent of gold. A precious stone was there. It was on David's head. As for the spoil of the city, he brought it out in great amounts.*

31 *As for*[688] *the people who were in it (=the city), he brought them out and put*[689] *them (to work) with saws, sharp iron instruments, and iron axes. He thus assigned them*[690] *to brickmaking. And thus he did to all the cities of the Ammonites.*

And David and all the people returned to Jerusalem.

The narrative, having finished the story of the birth of Solomon, returns to the siege of Rabbah, last mentioned in 11:25 (*the city*). The *city of waters* (12:27) was probably the section of the city that controlled the water supply. With no water, the surrender of the city itself would follow shortly. Therefore Joab calls David to come to the front so he can get credit for its capture.

This section concludes the long account of David's Ammonite-Aramean war that began in chapter 10 and was interrupted by the account of David's sin with Bathsheba, thus constituting the AXB pattern.[691] The parallel description in 1 Chr. 20:1-3 reflects the episode AB, without the interruption (X) of the David-Bathsheba affair.

687. McCarter, II, pp. 312-13, would read "Milcom" for the MT *malkām* "their king." O'Ceallaigh even read "their Molech" but this is somewhat dubious (G. C. O'Ceallaigh, "And So David Did to All the Cities of Ammon," VT 12 [1962] 185-89). "This proposal is somewhat dubious" (Mulder), cited in A. Cooper, "Divine Names and Epithets in the Ugaritic Texts," *RSP*, 3, p. 448.

688. Or "But."

689. McCarter, II, p. 311 translates "ripped [it]," based on 1 Chr. 20:3 and LXX^{L}.

690. Lit. "causing them to pass into."

691. See Introduction in Tsumura, I, pp. 60-64.

27 The term *saying* is lit. "and said." Note that "sending messengers" and "saying" are simultaneous actions.[692]

The phrase (*ʿîr hammāyim*; *tēn polin tōn hudatōn* [LXX]), probably refers to the part of the city with the water supply. Both *the city of waters* and *the royal city* (*ʿîr hamm^{e}lûkāh*) probably refer to the royal fortress of Rabbah, "which stood atop the steep hill overlooking and protecting the flowing spring fed by the Jabbok (Wadi Amman), which provided the city's water."[693] Compare the "City of David," which was the fortified citadel of larger Jerusalem (2 Sam. 6:10). The capture of Rabbah as a whole comes in v. 29.

28 Joab wants David to get credit for the capture.

30 The crown weighed *a talent*, about seventy-two and three-quarter pounds (33 kg); one might wonder if it is too heavy for a person to wear on the head. However, there are a few stone statues from Amman, from the late eighth and seventh centuries B.C. that show men, probably kings, wearing huge Egyptian-style crowns. These might be echoes of the tenth century ones.[694]

A precious stone was there; it was on . . . (*w^{e}'eben y^{e}qārāh watt^{e}hî ʿal . . .*; lit. "and a precious stone and it was on . . ."). Here, the *waw* (*w^{e}*) is an existential particle[695] rather than a conjunction "and." The parallel text in 1 Chr. 20:2 has "and in it was a precious stone," which is adopted here by NASB, NRSV. Also cf. "and it was set with precious stones — and it was placed on" (NIV). Or, it is possible it is another case of *casus pendens* transposed of the verbal phrase *wa+yqtl*: "As for a precious stone, it was on."[696]

31 David *put them with saws, sharp iron instruments, and iron axes.* In other words, "David is setting up work crews of captives for the economic exploitation of the conquered territory, evidently standard practice for victorious kings."[697] *Brickmaking* (*malkēn* [K.]; *malbēn* [Q.])[698] "the brickkiln") here is the work of the prisoners.

---

692. See Tsumura, I, pp. xii and 599-600.

693. McCarter, II, p. 312.

694. See the pictures of the Ammonite head with a huge crown, published by R. D. Barnett, "Four Sculptures from Amman," *Annual of the Department of Antiquities of Jordan* 1 (1951) 34; S. Horn, "The Crown of the King of the Ammonites," *AUSS* 11 (1973) 176; and F. Zayadine, "Note sur l'inscription de la statue d'Amman J. 1656," *Syria* 51 (1974) 131; also in the catalogue of the exhibition "La Voie royale," held in Paris in 1986 (*La Voie royale : 9000 ans d'art au royaume de Jordanie* [Paris: Musée du Luxembourg, 1986]). I thank A. Millard for pointing this out to me.

695. Gordon, *UT*, §19.977.

696. Tsumura, I, pp. 46-48.

697. See R. de Vaux, *The Early History of Israel*, trans. D. Smith (Philadelphia: Westminster, 1978), p. 326.

698. For a detailed discussion of this term, see Driver, pp. 294-97.

STORY OF ABSALOM'S REVOLT (13:1–20:26)

Chapters 13 to 20 show the *evil . . . from your house* (12:11) that Nathan announced to David, centering around the rebellion of his son Absalom. Absalom kills his brother Amnon to avenge the rape of his sister, but is eventually pardoned by David. Absalom then forms a conspiracy and declares himself king, but the rebellion is put down and Absalom is killed. In the aftermath there is an attempt by a group of Benjaminites to withdraw from Israel, but it also is put down. Even though it was the Lord who raised evil out of David's house, he did not do it by some external force, but by the natural qualities of David and his family.

Often in this section the narrator has to follow several simultaneous lines. Several times he connects two sections by backtracking and picks up a line by repeating the last statement in that line with expansion or variation. See 13:34a and 37; 15:37 and 16:15; 18:17b and 19:8b; 18:33 and 19:4; 19:24a and 25. The writer of Kings also uses this technique to keep track of reigns in Judah and Israel. This reflects the nature of narrative, which is by nature monodimensional, while in the actual world, events occur simultaneously, i.e., multidimensionally.[1]

This section has the following outline.

VI. "Story of Absalom's Revolt" (13:1–20:26)
- A. Absalom the Rebel (13:1–14:33)
  1. Amnon and Tamar (13:1-22)
  2. Absalom's Vengeance and Escape (13:23-39)
  3. Absalom's Return (14:1-33)
- B. Absalom's Rebellion (15:1–20:22)
  1. Absalom's Conspiracy (15:1-12)
  2. David's Escape from Jerusalem (15:13–16:14)
  3. Ahithophel and Hushai (16:15–17:23)
  4. David's Arrival at Mahanaim (17:24-29)
  5. Absalom's Death (18:1–19:8a)
  6. David's Return to Jerusalem (19:8b-43)
  7. Sheba's Revolt (20:1-22)
- C. David's Officials (20:23-26)

A. ABSALOM THE REBEL (13:1–14:33)

Even though the chief actors of the opening episode (13:1-22) are Tamar and Amnon, this section is principally concerned with Absalom, whose name is

1. See Tsumura, I, pp. 64, 409, 467, 476, 528, 548, 582, 615, etc.

mentioned at the start, as well as in v. 4 and vv. 20-22. Note that Tamar is introduced as Absalom's sister, not as David's daughter. Thus, chapters 13-14 ("Absalom the Rebel") serve as a prologue to "Absalom's Rebellion" in chapters 15-20.

As a prologue, the narrative of "Amnon and Tamar" (vv. 1-22) makes a perfect literary unit.

1. Amnon and Tamar (13:1-22)

This is an account of rape and incest — the brother-sister relationship between Tamar and Amnon is referred to a dozen times. This rape was an "outrageous thing" (Gen. 34:7; Deut. 22:21; Judg. 20:6; Jer. 29:23), which was "not done in Israel," and since it occurred in the royal family, it had implications for the whole nation.

a. Absalom's Sister Tamar (13:1-2)

1 *This is what happened afterward.*
Now, Absalom son of David had a beautiful sister whose name was Tamar.
And Amnon son of David loved[2] *her.*
2 *And Amnon was in such distress that he made himself sick because of Tamar his sister, for she was a virgin.*
And it seemed to Amnon that to do anything to her was beyond his power.

1 *Afterward* suggests that some time has passed since the end of chapter 12.

Tamar was Absalom's full sister, both of them being children of David and Maacah, which meant she was the half-sister of Amnon, David's eldest son. Tamar may have been named after David's ancestress; see Gen 38.[3]

2 For the expression *was in such distress* (lit. "it [3 m.s.; cf. 3 f.s. in 1 Sam. 30:6] was narrow for"), see the commentaries on 1 Sam. 13:6; 30:6.[4]

With the phrase *to make himself sick* compare Song 2:5; 5:8. The Hit. form is used only in this chapter (vv. 2, 5, 6). However, Amnon's "love" could better be described as "lust."

The expression *it seemed to Amnon that . . . was beyond his power* is lit. "it was too wonderful in the eyes of Amnon to do." They lived in different houses, and probably would not have met except in public.

2. I.e., "fell in love with her" (so Bergen); cf. "desired her" (Anderson).

3. See J. W. Flanagan, "Court History or Succession Document? A Study of 2 Samuel 9-20 and 1 Kings 1-2," *JBL* 91 (1972) 180.

4. See J-M, §152d; Tsumura, I, p. 339, 638-39.

b. Jonadab's Advice (13:3-7)

3 *Now, Amnon had a friend whose name was Jonadab, the son of Shimeah the brother of David; and Jonadab was a very shrewd man.*

4 *And he said to him,*
"Why are you low[5] like this, O son of the king,
morning after morning?
Won't you tell me?"
And Amnon said to him,
"I am in love with Tamar, the sister of my brother Absalom."

5 *And Jonadab said to him,*
"Lie down on your bed and pretend to be ill.
When your father comes to see you
say to him,
'Let my sister Tamar come
that she may give[6] me some bread.
And let her prepare the food in my sight
so that I may watch and eat from her hand.'"

6 *And Amnon lay down and pretended to be ill.*
And the king came to see him.
And Amnon said to the king,
"Let my sister Tamar come
that she may make a couple of dumplings in my sight
so that I may eat from her hand!"

7 *And David sent a messenger to Tamar at home to say,*
"Go to the house of your brother Amnon
and prepare food for him!"

3 *Jonadab* was Amnon's cousin, the son of *Shimeah* (*šimʿāh*; also v. 32 and 21:21 [Q.]; cf. *šimʿāʾ* in 1 Chr. 2:13; 20:7; *šimʿî* in 2 Sam. 21:21 [K.]; and *šammāh* in 1 Sam. 16:9; 17:13). *Shimeah* was Jesse's third son, so David's elder brother.

The term *ḥākām* is normally translated as "wise," "skillful," "clever," "experienced," or "pious." However, here, it is used in a negative sense as "shrewd" or "crafty." *Jonadab* later was wise enough to stay home when Amnon, his "friend," was assassinated by the command of Absalom (v. 32). He had a good name, though, "Yahweh is willing or generous." For the meaning of the root *ndb, see the commentary on 1 Sam. 2:8.[7]

5. Or "weak, poor"; "so depressed" (NASB).

6. Hi. *brh ("to eat"); lit. "feed."

7. Tsumura, I, p. 139 n. 30.

4 The repetitions of the *aleph* in the Hebrew *'et-tāmār 'ăḥôt 'abšālōm 'āḥî 'ănî 'ōhēb* (With Tamar, the sister of my brother Absalom I am in love), may indicate gasping sighs.

6-7 The word for the food (*lᵉbābôt*) is used only here. It is related to the word "heart" (*lēbāb*), hence to the verb "to hearten," "to give strength," so it was probably a food for the sick. But it is also related to the word *libbabtînî* for "you have captivated my heart" or "you have enchanted my heart" in Song 4:9. It is often translated "cakes," as in NASB, NRSV, JPS. But in 2 Sam. 13:8 she is said to do something (*wattəbaššēl* *bšl) to the food, and that word usually means "boil" (see 1 Sam. 2:13), so the food was probably some type of dumplings, that is, boiled dough-balls.[8] This is supported by the use of the verb "to pour" in v. 9.

One wonders what reason Amnon gave for wanting the *dumplings* to be made by Tamar. Could there have been some kind of superstition connecting the efficacy with who made them? It apparently never occurred to David to be suspicious, and Tamar, of course, would obey her father.

c. Tamar Goes to Amnon's House (13:8-14)

8 *And Tamar went to the house of her brother Amnon, where he was lying down, and took dough and kneaded*[9] *and made dumplings and boiled them in his sight*

9 *and took the pan*[10] *and poured them before him and he refused to eat.*
And Amnon said,
"Send out everyone from me!"[11]
And everyone went out from him.

10 *And Amnon said to Tamar,*
"Bring the food into the bedroom,
that I may eat from your hand."
And Tamar took the dumplings that she had made and brought them to her brother Amnon into the bedroom

11 *and brought them near to him to eat and he took hold of her and said to her,*
"Come, lie with me, my sister!"

12 *and she said to him,*
"No, my brother, do not violate me,
for such a thing is not done in Israel.

8. Also Anderson, p. 174.
9. K.: *wtlwš*; Q.: *wattālāš*. See 1 Sam. 28:24 where the same form as Q. appears.
10. Heb. *maśrēt*. For this *hapax legomenon*, see BDB, p. 602; *HALOT*, p. 641.
11. = Gen. 45:1; also Judg. 3:19.

Do not do this disgraceful thing!
13 *As for me, where can I take my reproach?*
As for you, you will be like one of the fools in Israel.
Now, speak to the king,
for he will not withhold me from you."

14 *But he would not listen to her and was stronger than she and violated her and lay with*[12] *her.*

8 If Tamar was going to make bread, there was not enough time for the dough (*bāṣēq*) to rise after kneading, for it would take several hours to rise! Thus, *dumplings*, rather than bread, seems more likely in the context.

The phrase *made dumplings and boiled them in his sight* is literally "made in his sight and boiled the dumplings" (*watt^e labbēb l^e'ênâw watt^e baššēl 'et-hall^e bībôt*), which is the AX&B pattern[13] with the phrase (X) *l^e'ênâw* ("in his sight") inserted between the two verbal phrases (A & B), i.e., *made* and *boiled*, modifying the total actions of making and boiling (the dumplings).

9 The verb *yṣq, "to pour" is usually used for liquids; e.g., for oil (Gen. 28:18; Exod. 29:7; 1 Sam. 10:1; etc.), for blood (Lev. 8:15; 9:9; etc.), and for water (2 K. 3:11; Isa. 44:3; Ezek. 24:3; etc.). It may be that the dumplings were poured from the cooking pan into a bowl together with the soup or broth. See "dished them out" (NASB); "set them out" (NRSV; also JPS); "served" (NIV; McCarter); cf. "set down" in 2 Sam. 15:24.

11 While she as his half-sister is regularly called his "sister," here he seems to use the word following the traditional terminology of love poetry; see Song 4:9, etc.

12 Note here the poetic nature with a parallelism of the AXB pattern, in which the first line (A) and the third (B) as a whole are modified by the second (X).[14] In this way, the element B, which is a restatement of the element A, is retarded by the literary, or rhetorical, insertion of X. Thus, the final key word *n^e bālāh* is emphasized as the concluding remark.

No, my brother, do not violate me,	(A)
for such a thing is not done in Israel.	(X)
Do not do this disgraceful thing!	(B)

For the expression *such a thing is not done in Israel*, see the similar language used in the case of Shechem's rape of Dinah in Gen. 34:7. The *disgraceful thing*

12. MT regularly takes *'ōt-*, instead of *'itt-*, after the verb *škb when referring to illicit intercourse: e.g., Gen. 34:2; Num. 5:13, 19; Ezek. 23:8. See Driver, p. 298; McCarter, II, p. 317.

13. Tsumura, "Coordination Interrupted," pp. 117-32.

14. See Tsumura, I, pp. 61-62.

(*n^e^bālāh*; cf. "wicked thing" [NIV]; "sacrilege" [McCarter]) is not simply a "foolish" (*nbl) thing. It is used especially of sexual misconduct such as rape (Judg. 20:6, 10), promiscuity (Deut. 22:21), adultery (Jer. 29:23) and homosexual assault (Judg. 19:23).[15]

13 Intercourse between brother and sister, even half-brother and half-sister, was forbidden in Lev. 18:9, and from the stress on the outrageousness it seems unlikely that the prohibition was not accepted also at this time. Perhaps Tamar is saying here that David would be willing to bend the rules, or perhaps she is just trying to escape.

d. Amnon Hates Tamar (13:15-18)

15 *And Amnon hated her with a very great hatred, for the hatred with which he hated her was greater than the love with which he had loved her.*
And Amnon said to her,
"Get up! Go!"
16 *and she said to him,*
"[No,] because this wrong in sending me away
is greater than the other which you have done to me. . ."
But he would not listen to her
17 *and called his servant who attended him and said,*
"Send this woman away from me to the outside
and lock the door behind her!"
18 *— Now she had on a long-sleeved gown, for in this way the virgin daughters of the king dressed themselves in robes. —*
And his attendant took her to the outside.
The door was thus locked behind her.

15 This hatred and contempt ("this woman," v. 17; see below) can be said to be an archetypal example of "blame the victim" mentality. The expression *hated her with a very great hatred* is literally "hated her a very great hatred" with a verb with an internal object, or "cognate accusative," which has been called *figura etymologica*.[16]

16 If a man seduced an unmarried or unbetrothed woman, he had to marry her, unless her father refused, and if he raped her, he was not permitted to divorce her (Exod. 22:16; Deut. 22:28-29). Having ruined her life, he had a responsibility toward her. Tamar seems to be protesting that Amnon's

15. See McCarter, II, p. 323; also Tsumura, I, p. 588 on 1 Sam. 25:25.

16. For the unusual syntax of a Niphal with an internal object, see Tsumura, "Niphal with an Internal Object in Hab 3, 9a," pp. 11-16.

action of sending her away is much worse than raping her. But, her word of protest was interrupted by his command to his servant (v. 17); see below on *aposiopesis.*

The MT *'al-'ôdōt* "because of" could have resulted from assimilation (distant, regressive, total assimilation) of *'al 'ôdōt,* as many MSS suggest.[17] The MT as it stands has been taken as "untranslateable" (Driver) or "unintelligible" (McCarter).[18] But this is an example of *aposiopesis,* the sentence stopped before the main clause begins; see 1 Sam. 1:22 ("[Not] until").[19] It is literally, "because of this wrong greater than the other which you have done to me to send me away." Note that as in 2 Sam. 2:24; 11:27; and 15:7 a relative clause is interrupting the nucleus of a main clause.

17 The Hebrew expression for *Send . . . and lock, šilḥû-nā' . . . ûg'ōl,* is not consistent, for the first verb is plural and the second, singular. McCarter takes this as "a simple error," since Amnon is speaking to one attending servant.[20] However, it might be that Amnon knew how wrong he was and was reluctant to order his servant to do the wrong of thrusting her out, and so used the plural imperative form for the first verb *send* to spread the responsibility around.

The expression *this woman* (*'et-zō't*; lit. "this" [f. sg.]) is used contemptuously like *zeh* "this fellow" (1 Sam. 10:27; 21:16; 1 K. 22:27; Isa. 6:10).[21]

18 McCarter, following Wellhausen, thinks that the text is smoother if the first and second halves of the verse are exchanged. Some modern translators, as NIV and REB, do this.[22] However, v. 18a was probably placed here intentionally as a *literary insertion* (AXB), with the intention of *slowing down* the flow of discourse from the command (A) to the action (B). One can picture Tamar's resistance as she was forced outside.[23]

The phrase *a long-sleeved gown* (*kᵉtōnet passîm*) besides here appears only in Gen. 37, describing Joseph's coat; cf. "a richly ornamented robe"

17. See Tsumura, "Scribal Errors or Phonetic Spellings?," p. 403; Tsumura, "Textual Corruptions, or Linguistic Phenomena?," pp. 140-41.

18. Driver, p. 298; McCarter, II, p. 318. Following the Lucianic recension of the LXX, G. Ridout reads *'al-'aḥî kî* and makes it correspond to v. 12 (*'al-'aḥî 'al-tᵉ'annēnî kî*). However, such a rhetorical analysis exhibits an inability to recognize the MT's rhetorics of *aposiopesis* and of the rhetorical insertion AXB pattern. See G. Ridout, "The Rape of Tamar: A Rhetorical Analysis of 2 Sam 13:1-22," in *Rhetorical Criticism: Essays in Honor of James Muilenburg,* ed. J. J. Jackson and M. Kessler (Pittsburgh: Pickwick Press, 1974), pp. 75-84.

19. Tsumura, I, p. 128.

20. McCarter, II, p. 318.

21. GKC §136b.

22. McCarter, II, p. 325; Anderson, p. 175; Bergen, p. 379, etc. But, Stoebe, II, pp. 319 and 321 keeps the MT as it is.

23. For the *AXB* pattern, see Tsumura, I, pp. 60-64.

(NIV); "an ornamented tunic" (JPS); or "a long robe with sleeves"; see McCarter for various views of its etymology. However, his etymology, *'epes, "extremity," based on the obscure place names in 1 Sam. 17:1 (Ephes-dammim) and 1 Chr. 11:13 (*bappas dammîm*), is not well-founded (see on 1 Sam. 17:1).[24] Tile decorations from the palace of Ramesses III (1198-1166) depict Asiatics wearing such long-sleeved garments.[25]

The verbal form *wᵉnāʿal* (*waw*+Qal, pf. 3 m.s.; *and locked*) is often said to be "incorrect" and read as *waw* cons. + impf[26] or as a resumptive infinitive absolute.[27] But, from the discourse-grammatical point of view, this text is a narrative-result discourse with the sequence of verbal forms *wayqtl* . . . *weqtl* like Judg. 3:23.[28] In other words, here, there is a shift from a narrative discourse to a result discourse in the sequence of *wayqtl* to *weqtl*; hence, the following explanation seems better:

> And his attendant took her to the outside (WHAT-happened: NARRATIVE).
> The door was thus locked behind her (RESULT: agent defocusing; lit. And he locked the door behind her).[29]

e. Absalom, the Brother of Tamar (13:19-22)

19 *And Tamar took ashes on her head; as for the long-sleeved gown on her, she tore it. And she put her hand on her head and went crying continually.*
20 *And her brother Absalom said to her,*
"Was your brother Amnon with you?
And now, my sister, be silent.
He is your brother.
Don't let your heart brood about this matter."
And Tamar lived in the house of her brother Absalom as a deserted woman.
21 *As for the king David, he heard all these things and became very angry.*

24. Tsumura, I, p. 438.

25. McCarter, II, pp. 325-26. See also Beni Hassan's wall picture and the woman of Lachish on Sennacherib's reliefs. However, as A. Millard pointed out to me, none depict a "virgin daughter of the king."

26. H. P. Smith, *A Critical and Exegetical Commentary on the Books of Samuel* (ICC; Edinburgh: T. & T. Clark, 1951), p. 330. See also Driver, p. 300; GKC, §112tt.

27. McCarter, II, p. 325.

28. On the discourse-grammatical view of *weqtl* form in Hebrew, see the commentary on 7:9b-16 above.

29. See Tsumura, "Tense and Aspect of Hebrew Verbs in II Samuel VII 8-16," p. 652; Tsumura, "Temporal Consistency" pp. 385-92.

22 *Absalom did not speak to Amnon either bad or good, for Absalom hated Amnon because he had violated his sister Tamar.*

19 Putting ashes (or dirt; *'ēper*) on one's head and tearing one's clothes were expressions of grief or humiliation (see on 1 Sam. 4:12),[30] as was covering the head with the hand(s) or a garment (Jer. 2:37; 2 Sam. 15:30; Esth. 6:12).

The expression *and went crying* (*wattēlek hālôk wᵉzāʿāqāh*) is lit. "and went continually and cried." Here *weqtl*, indicating reiteration,[31] follows an infinitive absolute as in Josh. 6:13. Elsewhere two infinitive absolutes are coordinated; e.g., Josh. 6:9; 1 Sam. 3:12; 6:12; 17:16; 2 Sam. 3:16; 5:10; 15:30.

20 *Don't let your heart brood about this matter*, perhaps because he was of the same rank as she or because it would be easier to hush up. However, Absalom himself, Tamar's full brother, did take it to heart.

The expression *Was . . . with you* in this context is a euphemism for a sexual intercourse; see Gen. 39:10. Tamar *lived in the house of her brother*. However, it is not easy to prove that here we have a fratriarchal family structure.

The phrase *as a deserted woman* (*wᵉšōmēmāh*) is lit. "and a desolate woman" (*waw*+participle). McCarter ignores *waw* as not being original.[32] Others take it as "an emphatic or epexegetical *waw*"; or *waw explicativum* (GKC, §§118p; 154aN). However, this phrase is probably to be taken as an X of the AXB pattern,[33] in which the phrase (X) is inserted into a verbal phrase "to live in the house of" (McCarter), thus interrupting the flow of discourse: *wattēšeb Tāmār wᵉšōmēmāh bêt 'Abšālôm 'āḥîhā*. The verb, *šāmem*, "be desolate" usually refers to the state of land being abandoned and neglected (Isa. 49:8; Jer. 12:11). For its use to describe a woman, see Isa. 54:1 ("For the sons of the desolate woman will be more than the sons of the married woman"). Tamar lives as one who has been rejected by her husband.

21 David became *very angry*, but he did not do anything. This sentence conveys how indecisive David was with regard to his sons, the source of much of the later problems. Heads of households have to deal justly among members of their household. After *very angry*, the LXX reads "but he would not punish his son Amnon, because he loved him, for he was his firstborn." McCarter and others claim that the 4QSam[a] supports this

30. Tsumura, I, p. 198; de Ward, "Mourning Customs in 1, 2, Samuel," p. 7.

31. Driver, p. 300.

32. McCarter, II, p. 319.

33. See above the commentary on v. 18.

and the MT lacks it because of haplography.[34] However, Herbert notes that this reconstruction of the Hebrew text of 4QSam[a] following the LXX is not necessarily correct.[35] It seems more natural that this was added later to the LXX to explain David's action, or rather lack of action.

22 In these three verses, the name *Absalom* appears four times, hinting that he will become the major character in the subsequent story. Thus, this repetition links the present and the following episodes, an example of the Ab/B pattern of "transitional techniques."[36]

2. Absalom's Vengeance and Escape (13:23-39)

Absalom avenges the violence to his sister by taking the life of his brother. The consequences were disastrous both publicly for Israel and privately for the royal family.

a. Absalom's Invitation to Amnon (13:23-27)

23 *And two full years passed. Absalom had sheepshearings in Baal-hazor, which is near Ephraim.*
And Absalom invited all the sons of the king.
24 *And Absalom came to the king and said,*
"Now, your servant is having sheepshearings.
May the king and his servants go with your servant."
25 *And the king said to Absalom,*
"No, my son.
We would not all go,
lest we should be burdensome to you!"
And he urged him but he would not go and blessed him.[37]
26 *And Absalom said,*
"If not, then at least let my brother Amnon go with us!"
And the king said to him,
"Why should he go with you?"
27 *But Absalom urged him, and he let Amnon and all the sons of the king go with him.*

34. McCarter, II, pp. 319-20.

35. Herbert, *RBDSS*, pp. 155-56.

36. See H. Van Dyke Parunak, "Transitional Techniques in the Bible," *JBL* 102 (1983) 525-48.

37. I.e., "said 'good-bye' to him."

As was seen in 1 Sam. 25, sheepshearing was a time of feasting.[38] Absalom *invited all the sons of the king*, and the next four verses give the details of how he issues the invitation. Probably Absalom invited David, guessing that he would decline, in order to lend color to the request for his brothers to come. If he had started out by asking for Amnon to come, it could have been suspicious.

The modern site of *Baal-hazor* is Jebel ʿAsur; for names with the pattern "Baal-GN," see *RSP*, 3, p. 358. The phrase *near Ephraim* could mean "near the border of Ephraim" (NIV).

25 The phrase *be burdensome to you* is lit. "be heavy on you" (Qal *kbd). McCarter translates "make things more difficult for you," following 4QSam[a] *nkbyd* (Hiph.). However, as Herbert notes, the MT reading is supported by LXX.

The term *urged* (*wayyiproṣ*) is a metathesis of *wypṣr* : *pṣr > prṣ ; also in v. 27, 1 Sam. 28:23; 2 K. 5:23. This is supported by *wypṣr* of 4QSam[a].

b. Murder of Amnon (13:28-33)

28 *And Absalom had commanded his servants, saying,*
"See, when Amnon's heart is merry with wine
and when I say to you: 'Strike Amnon!'
you shall kill him!
Don't be afraid.
Is it not I that command you?
Be strong, be brave!"[39]

29 *And the servants of Absalom did to Amnon just as Absalom had commanded.*
And all the sons of the king arose, and each rode on his mule and fled.

30 *While they were on the way, the report came to David, saying:*
"Absalom has struck down all the sons of the king;
not one of them is left."

31 *And the king arose and tore his clothes and lay down on the ground; and all his servants were standing by with clothes torn.*

32 *And Jonadab, the son of David's brother Shimeah, responded:*[40]
"Do not let my lord think
that all the young men, the king's sons have been killed.

38. J. C. Geoghegan, "Israelite Sheepshearing and David's Rise to Power," *Bib* 87 (2006) 55-63.

39. Lit. "become sons of might"; see "be valiant" (NASB); also the commentary on 2 Sam. 2:7.

40. Lit. "answered and said"; see Introduction of Tsumura, I.

For only Amnon is dead!
For according to Absalom's command[41] *this has been decided*
since the day when he violated his sister Tamar.
33 *So now, do not let my lord the king take the matter to heart,*
thinking that all the sons of the king are dead.
For only Amnon is dead."

29 The mule, not the ass or horse, seems to have been the riding animal of royalty in the time of David. Absalom even rides one into battle (18:9); see also 1 K. 1:33, 38, 44. Leviticus 19:19 commands not to breed two different kinds of animals, but it is possible these were imported. Their use seems to have been limited, for even Saul's grandson Mephibosheth used a donkey, not a mule (16:1;19:26).

32 One has to wonder why Amnon's "friend" (v. 3) did not advise him not to go. He himself stayed in Jerusalem.

McCarter translates *that all the young men, the king's sons have been killed* as "that the servants killed all the king's sons," taking "the young men" as the servants of Absalom. However, the expression here is "object-focused" and concerned with "whom" (PATIENT) rather than "who" (AGENT). Hence, *young men* is preceded by the object marker (*'ēt kol-hann^{e}'ārîm*) and placed before the verb, which is probably *impersonal* 3 m.pl.

c. Absalom Flees to Geshur (13:34-39)

34 *And Absalom fled.*
And the young man, the watchman, raised his eyes and saw many people coming from the road behind him by the side of the mountain.
35 *And Jonadab said to the king,*
"Here come the sons of the king!
According to the word of your servant, so it has happened."
36 *When he finished speaking, the sons of the king came, and they lifted their voices and wept; and the king and his servants also wept very bitterly.*
37 *As for Absalom, he fled and went to Talmai the son of Ammihud,*[42] *the king of Geshur.*

41. McCarter, II, p. 331, emends *'al-pî* ("command") to *'al-'ap* ("anger") on the basis of *'al-'ap YHWH* (2 K. 24:20; Jer. 52:3; cf. Jer. 32:31). However, *'al-pî* NP ("according to NP's command") is much more idiomatic; see Gen. 41:40; 45:21; Exod. 17:1; 38:21; Deut. 34:5; Josh. 19:50; 22:9; etc. McCarter's textual support is rather thin; Jer. 24:3, which he cites twice, has nothing to do with the present expression.

42. Q. However, the K. *'myḥwr* could be a hybrid name of the Hebrew *'my* "my kinsman" and the Egyptian DN "Horus." See Y. Muchiki, *Egyptian Proper Names and Loanwords in North-West Semitic* (SBLDS 173; Atlanta: Society of Biblical Literature, 1999), p. 218.

And he mourned for his son for a long time.

38 *As for Absalom, he fled and went to Geshur and was there for three years.*

39 *And King David's desire to go out against*[43] *Absalom was over, for he was comforted concerning Amnon's death.*

34 McCarter, following Driver, thinks the phrase *And Absalom fled* is the insertion of a marginal note into the wrong place.[44] But it may be to inform the audience that Absalom escaped right after Amnon's assassination; so Absalom had already left by the time the report reached David at Jerusalem.[45]

The phrase *from the road behind him* is literally "from the road (cstr) of 'behind him.'" While Driver believes this text cannot be right,[46] it may be that the phrase "behind him" is treated as a nominalized prepositional phrase, as in the phrase *that which was upon it* (*he'ālеyhā*) in 1 Sam. 9:24;[47] see "from the road to his rear" (JPS); "on the road west of him" (NIV).

37 Talmai was Absalom's maternal grandfather (3:3).

David *mourned for his son*, i.e., Amnon. Some like McCarter believe the son here is Absalom,[48] but what follows does not seem to imply that. On *Geshur*, see the commentary on 3:3.[49]

39 Driver claims that the Hebrew *watt^{e}kal Dāwīd hammelek lāṣē't 'el-'Abšālôm*, literally "the king David to go out toward (or against) Absalom finished," is "untranslatable," since "finished" is a feminine verb, and its subject cannot be the king.[50] The 4QSam^a text seems to support the reconstruction of "spirit" (*rwḥ*) before "the king," as McCarter, Firth, NIV, etc. do;[51] see "And the spirit of the king longed to go out to Absalom" (ESV). However, this construction is probably *brachylogy*, i.e., where a key term such as *nepeš* (fem. sg.), which means "soul, throat, desire,"[52] is omitted as unnecessary in Hebrew (see the Targum also).

Almost all modern translations take the text as referring to David's positive feeling toward Absalom: e.g., "King David was pining away for Absalom"

43. See *'l* in 2 MSS, Targ., LXX^L; cf. "to" (NASB, NIV), "yearning for" (NRSV). See the commentary on 2 Sam. 14:1 below.

44. Driver, pp. 303-4; McCarter, II, pp. 331-32.

45. See Tsumura, I, pp. 64, 409, etc.

46. Driver, p. 304.

47. Tsumura, I, p. 279,

48. McCarter, II, p. 332.

49. See Younger, *PHA*, pp. 204-13.

50. Driver, p. 305.

51. McCarter, II, p. 344; Bergen, pp. 386-87; Anderson, p. 184; Firth, p. 442.

52. Stoebe, II, p. 335, suggests the possibility of *nepeš* beside *rû^{a}ḥ*. On the *brachylogy*, see Tsumura, I, pp. 64-65.

(JPS); "the heart of King David longed to go out to Absalom" (NASB); "the spirit of the king longed to go to Absalom" (NIV); "the heart of the king went out, yearning for Absalom" (NRSV). However, as McCarter comments, "if David longed for Abishalom, Joab's ruse in 14:1ff. would not be necessary."[53] The sentence seems to mean, *King David's [desire] to go out against Absalom finished.* For the verb, "to be over" is the most natural rendering; the same Hebrew verb ("finished") appears just a few verse earlier (v. 36) with the same meaning.

3. Return of Absalom (14:1-33)

a. Wise Woman of Tekoa (14:1-20)

This section shows the convoluted process by which Absalom is finally recalled. Similarities have been noted between David's interview with the wise woman of Tekoa here and Joab's interview with the wise woman of Abel of Beth-maacah in 2 Sam. 20. McCarter points out that these two accounts are an *inclusio* to the account of Absalom's rebellion in chapters 15-19.[54] However, the present situation is more similar to ch. 12. In both incidents, a wise messenger, there a prophet, here a woman, tells a parable, or *mashal,* so that David may come to realize his own real problem. See the commentary on ch. 12.

The passage has some difficulties. The woman tells her story, delivers her real message clearly in v. 14, but in v. 15 goes back to her story. McCarter, therefore, accepts Budde's view that vv. 8-14 and 15-17 are to be reversed, against the MT and all versions. However, I believe that the present order of discourse in the MT and versions is the original and should be retained. From the literary structural point of view, vv. 4-7 (A) and vv. 15-17 (B) form a "framing" to her real message in vv. 8-14 (X). Thus, the interruption of the flow of dialogue by her message reflects the actual dialogue between the woman and the king and, as a result, it became an effective way of presenting this whole episode using the AXB pattern, with suspense and plot as well as tension and relief.[55]

53. McCarter, II, pp. 335 and 344.

54. See McCarter, II, pp. 350-51; and also see on 2 Sam. 20 and Nathan's parable in 12:1b-4.

55. On the AXB pattern, in which X interrupts the flow of discourse (A-B) for the sake of bringing suspense and plot to the narrative, see Tsumura, I, pp. 60-64.

1) David's Mind on Absalom (14:1)

1 *And Joab son of Zeruiah realized*[56] *that the king's mind was on Absalom.*

1 The initial verse brings together the three major characters in the story of Absalom's revolt—Joab, David, and Absalom.

The name *Joab* dominates the present chapter, appearing fifteen times. Thus, together with Absalom (see 13:1) and David, Joab is introduced as a major character in this prologue to the revolt in chs. 15-20. The phrase *son of Zeruiah* is not added here unpurposefully. We are continually reminded of the willfulness of the brothers.

NASB ("the king's heart was inclined toward") and NIV ("the king's heart longed for") take the preposition *'al* of *on Absalom* (*'al-'Abšālôm*) positively (i.e., not "against") and interpret the verse as a continuation of the last verse of the previous episode, which they understand as referring to David's favorable feeling toward Absalom. However, the Hebrew (lit. "the heart of the king [was] on Absalom") does not necessarily imply that his thoughts were positive. Since *King David's desire to go out against Absalom was over* (2 Sam. 13:39), David's mind was on his son Absalom, as NRSV and JPS render it. Thus, the term *lēb* (lit. "heart") refers to David's state of mind, rather than his emotion, hence translating *mind*. He was just thinking about the matter. Joab decides to push the king toward accepting him, though later he does not show himself to be particularly a partisan of Absalom.

2) Joab Sends a Wise Woman of Tekoa (14:2-3)

2 *And Joab sent (a messenger) to Tekoa and brought a wise woman from there and said to her,*

"Pretend to be a mourner
and dress in mourning clothes;
and do not anoint yourself with oil
and be like a woman
who[57] *for many days has been mourning for the dead.*
3 *And you shall come to the king*
and speak to him like this."
And Joab put the words into her mouth.

2 *Tekoa* is modern Khirbet Tequ', a village in the Judean hills about ten miles (16 km) south of Jerusalem, near Bethlehem, presumably Joab's home

56. Lit. "knew" (ESV, NIV); "came to know" = perceived (Driver, p. 305).

57. Heb. *zeh* here functions as a relative pronoun like Ug. *d*. See *DULAT*, pp. 254-59.

town (2:32). It is known as the hometown of Amos (Amos 1:1). Though it is not certain whether Tekoa was one of the centers of wisdom tradition in ancient Israel, Joab brought *a wise woman* from there. The speech of this wise woman of Tekoa can be compared with that of two other women in Samuel, Abigail in 1 Sam. 25:24-31[58] and the wise woman of Abel in 2 Sam. 20:16-19.[59]

3) Two Sons in the Field (A: 14:4-7)

4 *And when the woman of Tekoa spoke*[60] *to the king, she fell on her face to the ground and prostrated herself and said,*

"Help, O king!"

5 *And the king said to her,*

"What is your problem?"

And she said,

"Truly I am a widow,
and my husband is dead.

6 *Now,*[61] *your maidservant had two sons.*
And the two of them struggled with each other in the field,
but there was no one to tear them apart.[62]
And one struck down the other[63] *and killed him.*

7 *And now, the whole clan*[64] *has risen against your maidservant and said,*

'Give us the man who struck down his brother
so that we may kill him for the life of his brother
whom he slew
and eliminate the heir[65] *also!'*

So they would extinguish my coal that is left

58. Tsumura, I, pp. 586-91.

59. For the "Wise woman of Tekoa," see Lyke, *King David with the Wise Woman of Tekoa*, and my review of it for *Themelios* 24/3 (1999) 48-49. On "intertextuality," see Tsumura, I, pp. 22-23, and the Introduction (II.B) of this book.

60. So NASB; cf. "went" (NIV, Bergen) or "came" (NRSV, JPS, Anderson), following multiple MSS (MT), LXX, Syr, Vulg, Targ.

61. Brongers cites this *waw* as an example of the *explicative waw*; see Baker, "Further Examples of the *waw explicativum*," 136, "Postscript."

62. Heb. *maṣṣîl bênêhem*; lit. "deliverer between them."

63. The MT *wayyakkô hā'eḥād 'et-hā'eḥād*: "and he struck him down, the one the other." This "him" could be the "anticipatory pronominal suffix" (Rendsburg, *DAH*, p. 127). Or, it may be an old spelling, reflecting III-*w* (like Ugaritic *šnw*; see *DULAT*, pp. 834-35). McCarter, II, p. 338, following Thenius, Wellhausen, and others, reads *wyk* with LXX, Syr., Targ., Vulg.

64. Heb. *hammišpāḥāh*. Here, "clan," rather than "family." See v. 15 (below).

65. Heb. *yôrēš* = *zēra'* (e.g., 7:12).

and not leave[66] *for my husband any name*[67] *or remnant*
on the surface of the ground."

5-7 Like Nathan's "parable," this kind of parable is called a *mashal.*[68] In this *mashal* the woman appeals to the king to set aside the ordinary laws demanding the death of a murderer (Num. 35:31, etc.), not because of any extenuating circumstances in the killing, but for the good of the family. The woman emphasizes her widowhood and the fact that the culprit is now the only heir of her late husband.[69] Thus, she asks the king for exceptional treatment.

6 Lyke notes the theme of sibling rivalry between "two sons" — or, in his words, "the 'two sons' element of the topos of sibling rivalry" — in biblical and nonbiblical accounts of Cain and Abel, Shem and Japheth, Abraham and Nahor, Lot and Eliezer, Ishmael and Isaac, Jacob and Esau, and Jacob's sons. His explanation is full of speculation, based on later Jewish traditions. For the theme of "two men," see 2 Sam. 12:1. Bergen also seems to see too much in the similarities between the story of Cain and Abel and Joab's tale. He holds that the plot of the woman's *mashal* and Gen. 4 have "a remarkable similarity," without referring to their differences.[70]

It is true that the story of two sons *in the field* where one killed the other might remind the reader of the Bible of the story of Cain and Abel in Gen. 4:8 and that there are certain correspondences between the two stories:

"two sons" - "in the field"
"one struck down the other and killed"

However, the reason for such correspondences is due to the universal nature of sibling rivalry, especially when there are only two sons in the family. Such rivalry can be seen often in extrabiblical literatures also, both ancient and modern. It should also be noted that the idea that manslaughter was requited through blood revenge was accepted throughout the East Mediterranean.[71]

66. Lit. "set" or "establish."

67. See 1 Sam. 24:22 on "seed" and "name."

68. See also Hallo, "Proverbs Quoted in Epic," pp. 203-17, and 1 Sam. 24:14.

69. On the problem of childlessness, especially for a widow, see D. T. Tsumura, "The Problem of Childlessness in the Royal Epic of Ugarit," in *Monarchies and Socio-Religious Traditions in the Ancient Near East,* ed. T. Mikasa (Wiesbaden: Otto Harrassowitz, 1984), pp. 11-20; Tsumura, "The Family in the Historical Books," in *Family in the Bible: Exploring Customs, Culture, and Context,* ed. R. S. Hess and M. D. Carroll R. (Grand Rapids: Baker Academic, 2003), 59-79.

70. Bergen, p. 389. Furthermore, he tries to see too much connection between David's treatment of Absalom and the Lord's dealing with Cain; see Bergen, p. 393.

71. See Gordon, *CB,* p. 15.

However, there are differences. Cain's murder of Abel was planned, but in the woman's story it seems to have been a sudden quarrel. Absalom's case is more similar to Cain's murder in this aspect, though he and Amnon were not David's only sons.

The present story shows that even though Israel at the time was a centralized state, i.e., a kingdom, the kin group dealt with a case of domestic homicide; they are called "the clan," *hammišpāḥāh* in v. 7 and *hāʿām* in v. 15.

7 Apparently, Absalom was now considered *the heir*, at least in popular sentiment. The woman's plea contains the "subtle suggestion" that by destroying *the heir* the kinsmen would secure the inheritance for themselves.[72] This term would have certainly led David to associate the story of this woman with his own situation, for Absalom was his oldest surviving son and would have become his heir under a normal situation. Her relatives' desire to eliminate her only surviving son, *the heir* would have reminded David of his postponed reconciliation with his son Absalom. Therefore, it is the purpose of the woman to remind David that he as the Lord's anointed king should be concerned with his heir who would sit on his throne after him; see the commentary on 7:11b-16.

Coal here means "hope for the family." Note that an Old Babylonian expression for a man who has no family is one "whose brazier has gone out."[73] *Name or remnant* means "remaining posterity" on the surface of the earth, i.e., among the living.[74]

4) The King's Banished One (X: 14:8-14)

8 *And the king said to the woman,*
"Go to your house,
and I will give orders concerning you."
9 *And the woman of Tekoa said to the king,*
"On me and on my father's house, O my lord the king,
be the guilt,[75]
but may the king and his throne be innocent!"
10 *And the king said,*

72. On inheritance rights in ancient Israel, see E. W. Davies, "Inheritance Rights and the Hebrew Levirate Marriage. Part 1," *VT* 31 (1981) 138-44.

73. See *CAD*, B, p. 73.

74. H. C. Brichto, "Kin, Cult, Land and Afterlife — A Biblical Complex," *HUCA* 44 (1973) 34 n. 54.

75. Lit. "On me, O my lord the king, is the guilt and on the house of my father." According to the principle of *vertical grammar*, the phrase "and on my father's house" should be coordinated; thus the coordination is interrupted by the insertion of a NP ("the guilt"). For this phenomenon, see Tsumura, "Coordination Interrupted," pp. 117-32. See also Tsumura, I, pp. 55-59.

"'As for the one who has spoken to you,[76] *bring him*[77] *to me,*
and he will not touch you anymore."

11 *And she said,*
"May the king remember[78] *the* LORD *your God*
so that the avenger of blood may not[79] *destroy so much*[80]
and not exterminate my son."

And he said,
"As the LORD *lives,*
not one hair of your son shall fall to the ground."

12 *And the woman said,*
"Let your maidservant speak a word to my lord the king."

And he said,
"Speak!"

13 *And the woman said,*
"Why have you plotted this thing against the people of God?[81]
For by speaking[82] *this word*
the king has become as one who is guilty[83]
in that the king has not brought back his banished one.
14 *For*[84] *we will surely die*
just[85] *like water poured to the ground*
that cannot be gathered up;
but God will not take away life
and will devise plans so that the banished one will not remain banished.

8-14 The woman asks for an immediate ruling, so she can comment on it and deliver her message. She says what she came to say (vv. 13-14) and goes

76. Cf. "Who is the one who has been speaking to you?" (LXX[B]).

77. The MT *hăbēʾtô* ("bring [impv, fs] him") is a *sandhi* form from *hăbēʾtî-ô*; see Tsumura, "Vowel *sandhi* in Biblical Hebrew," p. 588.

78. Cf. "invoke" (NIV), "mention" (McCarter), like Akk. *zakāru*, "mention, call (the name of)." McCarter, II, p. 348, notes that "the woman is asking the king to utter Yahweh's name in a binding oath."

79. Lit. "from" (privative).

80. Lit. "from . . . excessively."

81. So also 4QSam[a]; cf. "Yahweh" in LXX[L].

82. Heb. *ûmiddabbēr*; *waw+min+**dbr (Pi. ptc). This *waw* is disjunctive, being proclitic to a nonverbal (participial) word, and it makes the following clause a subordinate one.

83. Heb. *kᵉʾāšēm*; lit. "as being guilty"; *kᵉ-* "as, like"; *ʾāšēm* participle, rather than pf., "being guilty"; see "for in speaking this word the king is as one who is guilty" (NASB); cf. "the king convicts himself" (NRSV).

84. The *speaker-oriented kî*; it explains the reason why I said so.

85. Lit. "and." Here, the *waw* is emphatic.

back to her act (vv. 15-17). Her speech in vv. 5–17 has an AXB structure. *This thing* in v. 15 would refer both to her real message in vv. 13-14 and to her family problem in vv. 5-7 (A). Wisely she finishes her dialogue with David (X: 8-14) by mentioning her own problem (B: 15-17), thus placing herself on the side of the needy and helpless, not in the position of an accuser of the king.

While the discourse structure (AXB) is possibly the narrator's literary technique to induce suspense, it is probable that David had already begun identifying this woman's problem with his own problem with Absalom and involved himself in it emotionally. Perhaps, he thought he would ask his own servant to deal with her problem and hence ordered her to go home (v. 8). She may have sensed that something was wrong with David's feeling. That was possibly why she admitted that she, not David, is guilty if anything bothered David (v. 9). Or, would she mean that she would be guilty if David's pardon was against Num. 35:31?

Then David mentions an ambiguous phrase "the one who has spoken to you" (v. 10), which may refer either to the one of her clan who asked for her surviving son or to the one who sent her to speak to the king (vv. 2-3). David may have already suspected Joab's device and so purposefully used this ambiguouse phrase on purpose. The woman however stays with her own clan problem by referring to "my son," while she uses a very sensitive term "the avenger of blood" (v. 11), which could refer to the king himself, who has probably already been very much concerned with his own son, Absalom. By saying the following words (v. 11b), David expresses his determination (note the oath formula: "As the Lord lives") toward his own lost son indirectly.

After another polite and humble entreaty (v. 12; cf. Abigail's words in 1 Sam. 25:24), this wise woman discloses her own real message to the king in vv. 13-14 and speaks directly about David's having not brought back his banished one, carefully without mentioning Absalom's name. After addressing the king both in the second person ("you") and in the third person ("the king's" and "his") in v. 13, the woman stands together with the king, before God, referring to herself and David by the *inclusive* "we," and assures David that God *will devise plans so that the banished one will not remain banished* (v. 14).

Now that the woman has accomplished her mission of delivering her real message to the king, she finished by referring to her own story, that of her two sons. McCarter considers that vv. 15-17 are "a carefully fashioned component of the imposture, hardly 'a gush of feminine loquacity' (cf. Hertzberg)."[86]

9 Exactly what *guilt* (*heʿāwōn*) she refers to is not clear. With v. 8 the woman's explanation of her problem is interrupted by the king with a command: "Go to your house!" This was truly a royal intervention to the

86. McCarter, II, pp. 345-46.

widow's plea and almost a promise that he would spare her son. One can take her words as meaning that she will take the guilt for the king's sparing a man-slayer. It is also possible that her self-imprecatory language[87] is an expression of thanks, similar to Abigail's in 1 Sam. 25:24: "With me myself, my lord, is the guilt!" at the beginning of her long petition. One may only surmise why David interrupted her words in v. 10. It may be that he has already sensed some relationship of her speech with his own painful experience.

11 The phrase *the avenger of blood* (*gōʾēl haddām*) refers to *the clan* (v. 15) and *the man* (v. 16). According to tribal custom, he had "the responsibility of avenging the death of a family member"; see Num. 35:9-29; Deut. 19:3-10. According to de Vaux, the use of the phrase "the avenger of blood" is used loosely here; here "the clan seeks the life of the woman's son not in vengeance for his brother's blood but to purge the clan of guilt."[88] On "the avenger of blood," see also on 2 Sam. 3:27.

As the Lord lives: on this *oath formula*, see the commentary on 1 Sam. 14:39.[89] As McCarter notes, this solemn royal oath "now protects the fictitious son of the Tekoite woman and also . . . his own son Abishalom."[90]

13 Note that here, after the polite and humble words in v. 12, the woman uses the second person, speaking to the king directly as she delivers her real message.[91]

The king is said here to have planned a device *against the people of God* for whom he is responsible as their representative. See below on *the inheritance of God* (v. 16).

14 The woman here stands with the king as a mortal; note that the first-person plural, *we* and *us*, in this verse is *inclusive*, i.e., the woman the speaker and the king the hearer. Thus, after speaking directly and frankly to the king in v. 13, she is beside him before God; see above.

The Hebrew phrase *nśʾ + *npš* means either to *take away life* or, the opposite, to "carry/bear life"; see "take away life" (NASB); cf. "and as water . . . cannot be gathered up, so he cannot take up his life again" (McCarter, following LXX).[92] However when the clause is combined with the following one as in the MT, the context requires a negative sense, "carry away life," for it is negated by "not."

In sequence to the preceding *yqtl*, "God" is the subject of *and will devise plans* (*wᵉḥāšab*; pf. 3 m.s.); cf. "you planned" (v. 13). Here the king-God

87. For the self-imprecatory oath, see the commentaries on 1 Sam. 3:17; 14:44; 20:13; etc., in Tsumura, I, pp. 182, 280, 508, etc.

88. McCarter, II, p. 348.

89. Tsumura, I, pp. 377-78.

90. McCarter, II, p. 348.

91. See above. On the history of the interpretation of this verse, see J. Hoftijzer, "David and the Tekoite Woman," *VT* 20 (1970) 429-34.

92. McCarter, II, p. 341.

relationship is clearly presupposed. The king was supposed to act as God would act, for he is simply a human agent of his divine king. But, king David is "guilty" here since he has not "planned [devices]" to bring back "his banished one," while God "will devise plans so that the banished one will not remain banished." Also note v. 13: *the people of God.*

5) The Woman's Concern about Her and Her Son (B: 14:15-17)

15 *Now, thus*[93] *I have come to tell this thing to the king my lord,*
for the clan[94] *have threatened me.*
And your maidservant thought,
'Let me speak to the king;
perhaps the king will perform
in the matter of his handmaid.
16 *For the king will listen (to me)*
to deliver his handmaid from the hand of the man
who is about to destroy[95] *me and my son together*
from the inheritance of God.'
17 *And your maidservant said,*
'May the word of my lord the king be the resolution.
For just as the angel of God is,
so my lord the king listens[96] *to good and evil.'*[97]
May the Lord *your God be with you!"*

15 Having accomplished the mission of delivering her real message to the king in vv. 13-14, the woman now finishes up her own interrupted episode, i.e., the story of her two sons. See above on the structure of the entire episode: "dialogue." As Anderson notes, the change from *maidservant* (*šipḥāh*) to *handmaid* (*'āmāh*) in this verse is probably for stylistic reasons.[98]

The *man who is about to destroy* the woman and her surviving son (v. 16) is certainly a member of this clan; see on v. 7 (*the whole clan*).

16 *For* may simply be an explanation of the previous utterance, i.e., the entreaty: "Let me speak"; the *speaker-oriented kî* ("For") explains the reason why the speaker, in this case *your maidservant* (for the first-person "I"), said that *the king will perform.*

93. Heb. *wᵉʿattāh ʾăšer*; lit. "Now, that."

94. Heb. *hāʿām*; lit. "people."

95. Heb. *lᵉhašmîd*; inf. cstr with a preposition *lᵉ*; cf. "who is seeking to eliminate" (McCarter, II, p. 339), following LXX (see Driver, p. 309) and 4QSamᶜ (see DJD 17, p. 259).

96. I.e., "to understand" or "to discern"; cf. 1 K. 3:9 (Driver, p. 309).

97. I.e., "everything," as a merismus; see 19:35.

98. Anderson, p. 189.

For *the inheritance of God* (*naḥălat ʾĕlōhîm*),[99] see the commentary on 1 Sam. 26:19.[100] The *inheritance* means either "the people" or "the land" of Israel. More specifically, it may mean "the family's landed property or its share in Yahweh's land."[101] Here, what the woman means is that her family will have no representative among the future generations of Israel if her son is killed. In Ps. 127:3, sons (or "children") are said to be "a heritage from the Lord" (ESV). See on "the people of God" in v. 13.

17 The Hebrew *limnûḥāh* is literally "a resting, resolution" (of the legal matter); see "be final" (McCarter, II, p. 339); cf. "be comforting" (NASB); "set me at rest" (NRSV); "bring me rest" (NIV).

For the expression *just as the angel of God is* (*kᵉmalʾak hāʾĕlōhîm*), which is "routine flattery," see also v. 20 and 19:27, as well as 1 Sam. 29:9.[102] The expression seems to reflect the view that the Israelite king "was the earthly representative of Yahweh and so his judicial pronouncements must have been divinely inspired."[103]

6) Your Servant Joab Commanded Me (14:18-20)

18 *And the king answered the woman,*
"Do not hide anything from me that I am going to ask you."
And the woman said,
"Let my lord the king speak."
19 *And the king said,*
"Is the hand of Joab with you in all this?"
And the woman answered,
"As your soul lives, my lord the king,
there is no way to turn to the right or to the left[104]
from everything that my lord the king has spoken.
For it was your servant Joab who commanded me,
and it was he who put all these things
into the mouth of your maidservant.

99. See T. J. Lewis, "The Ancestral Estate (נחלת אלהים) in 2 Samuel 14:16," *JBL* 110 (1991) 597-98. On the family in the Bible, see Tsumura, "The Family in the Historical Books," 59-79.

100. Tsumura, I, pp. 604-5.

101. Anderson, p. 189.

102. See Tsumura, I, p. 636.

103. K. Whitelam, *The Just King: Monarchical Judicial Authority in Ancient Israel* (JSOTSS 12; Sheffield: JSOT Press, 1979), p. 135; also B. S. Jackson, "Law in the Ninth Century: Jehoshaphat's 'Judicial Reform,'" in *Understanding of the History of Ancient Israel*, ed. H. G. M. Williamson (PBA 143; Oxford: Oxford University Press, 2007), p. 382 n. 76.

104. MT *ûlhaśmîl* is a *sandhi* spelling, without *aleph*; see Tsumura, "Vowel *sandhi* in Biblical Hebrew," 588.

20 *In order to change the course of the matter*[105]
your servant Joab has done this thing.[106]
But my lord is wise,
like the wisdom of the angel of God,
to know all that is in the earth."

As noted above, David must have noticed that the woman's problem was similar to his and he suspected that her coming to him had something to do with his treatment of his son Absalom, especially after listening to her message in vv. 13-14. He finally openly questions her.

19 The standard existential particle is *yēš*; = Ug. *iṯ*; Aram. *'itay*. This form *'im-'iš* (*there is no way*) is the only occurrence in the Bible. It can be explained as a "phonetic spelling"[107] of the standard form, i.e., an *assimilation* of /y/ to /'/ and of /ē/ to /i/: *'im yēš* → *'im 'iš.*

b. Absalom Returns to Jerusalem (14:21-24)

21 *And the king said to Joab,*
"Now, I hereby do this thing.
Go, bring back the young man Absalom!"
22 *And Joab fell on his face to the ground and prostrated himself and blessed the king.*
And Joab said,
"Today your servant knows
that I have found favor in your eyes, my lord the king,
because the king has performed in the matter of his[108] *servant."*
23 *And Joab arose and went to Geshur and brought Absalom to Jerusalem.*
24 *And the king said,*
"Let him go to his house;
My face he shall not see."
And Absalom went to his house; he did not see the king's face.

21 Heb. *'āśîtî* is a *performative perfect*, which denotes the speaker's instantaneous action: speech act, hence translating *I hereby do*; see "I do" (Driver,

105. Heb. *pᵉnê haddābār*; lit. "the face of the matter" or "the appearance of things" (NASB); "the course of affairs" (NRSV); "the present situation" (NIV).

106. The phrase *haddābār hazzeh* ("this thing") appears four times in this chapter: vv. 13, 15, 20, 21.

107. See Tsumura, "Scribal Errors or Phonetic Spellings?," pp. 390-411.

108. K.; cf. "your" (Q.)

p. 309), "I am acting" (McCarter, II, p. 341; cf. GKC, §106m); "I will surely do" (NASB); "I will do" (NIV, JPS).

24 David recalls him, but his forgiveness is incomplete, as we see here and as Absalom complains in v. 32. *My face he shall not see*: for the privilege of seeing the king's face, see on 2 Sam. 3:13.

c. David Receives Absalom (14:25-33)

25 *As for Absalom,*[109] *there was no one as handsome and highly praised as he in all Israel; from the sole of his foot to the top of his head there was no blemish in him.*

26 *And when he shaved his head — it was at the end of each year when he shaved it, for it was heavy on him — he would shave it and weigh the hair of his head at two hundred shekels by the king's weight.*

27 *And to Absalom there were born three sons and one daughter whose name was Tamar; she was a woman beautiful in appearance.*

28 *And Absalom lived in Jerusalem for two full years, but he did not see the king's face.*

29 *And Absalom sent a messenger to Joab in order to send him to the king, but he would not come to him, and he sent again a second time, but he would not come.*

30 *And he said to his servants,*
"See, Joab's property is next to mine,[110]
and he has barley there.
Go, and set it on fire!"
And the servants of Absalom set the property on fire.
31 *And Joab set out and came to Absalom in his house and said to him,*
"Why have your servants set my property on fire?"
32 *And Absalom said to Joab,*
"Look, I sent a messenger to you saying,
'Come here,'
so that I may send you to the king to say,
'Why have I come from Geshur?
It would be better for me if I were still there.
And now, let me see the king's face!
If there is iniquity in me, put me to death!'"

109. MT *ûk'abšālôm*; lit. "and like Absalom"; as a *casus pendens*. McCarter, II, p. 342, reconstructs *gm*, instead of MT's *wk*, based on 4QSam[c].

110. Heb. *'el-yādî*; lit. "to my hand."

33 *And Joab came to the king and told him, and he summoned Absalom, and he came to the king and prostrated himself on his face to the ground before the king.*

And the king kissed Absalom.

25-27 This long parenthetical note has been considered as "secondary" by a number of commentators. However, from a literary point of view, it prepares us for the next chapter, especially how Absalom "stole the hearts of the men of Israel" by his personal charms (15:6).

25 Absalom's *handsomeness* can be compared with that of Saul in 1 Sam. 9:2; see also David's handsomeness in 1 Sam. 17:42. The term *mûm* (*blemish*) is a *sandhi* spelling of *m*^{e}*'ûm* (only in Dan. 1:4 *mu'wm* [Q. *mûm*]; Job 31:7 *mu'ûm* [*sic* L.; mlt MSS Edd *m'ûm*]).[111]

26 The verbal sequence of this verse is rather complicated: i.e., prep+inf cstr ("in his shaving") — *w*^{e}*hāyāh* temp-ph *'ăšer* impf. ("to shave") *kî* pf. (*was heavy*) *w*^{e}+pf. ("to shave"). The most natural interpretation is to take the final *w*^{e}+pf. ("to shave") as being part of the main clause, as *w*^{e}*hāyāh* normally introduces a subordinate clause, often a temporal clause.[112] However, we then have "in his shaving . . . he would shave" in the main clause, which seems redundant. Hence, RSV and others take the final "to shave" as being within the parenthetical clause and translate, "And when he *cut* the hair of his head (for at the end of every year he used to *cut* it; when it was heavy on him, he *cut* it)" (RSV, NRSV, ESV); "for it was heavy on him so he cut it" (NASB); "for it would be heavy on him, that he would shave [it] —" (McCarter).[113] Nevertheless, such repetition is not impossible as a Hebrew expression, especially after an intervening parenthetical clause as in Lev. 16:1,[114] so it seems best to leave it in the main clause.

two hundred shekels, about five pounds (2.8 kg). The MT reading of *two hundred* is supported by 4QSam^{c}[115] against LXX^{L} and OL's "one hundred shekels" (McCarter).[116]

The phrase *the king's weight* (*'eben hammelek*; lit. "king's stone"), which is not mentioned elsewhere in the Bible, indicates that there was a royal stan-

111. See Tsumura, "Vowel *sandhi* in Biblical Hebrew," 585-86.

112. Driver, p. 310: "והיה can only be resumed by וגלחו."

113. Note that NIV, JPS, REB, NJB, etc. ignore the third occurrence. E.g., "Whenever he *cut* the hair of his head — he used to *cut* his hair once a year because it became too heavy for him—he would weigh it" (NIV); "When he *cut* his hair — he had to have it *cut* every year, for it grew too heavy for him — the hair of his head weighed" (JPS); (emphasis added on all).

114. See Driver, pp. 310.

115. See DJD 17, p. 260. Firth's 4QSam^{a} is wrong; see Firth, p. 443.

116. McCarter, II, p. 342.

dard at the Israelite court; a similar phrase can be found in Aram. *ʾbny mlkʾ* in Elephantine papyri and Akkadian *aban šarri*[117] or Sumerian NA_4.LUGAL ("king's stone").[118]

27 As the sons are unnamed and Absalom says he had no sons (18:18), these probably died young. His daughter was probably named for his sister.

Tamar (MT) appears here also in 4QSam[c]; cf. "Maacah" in LXX[LMN], OL(MS). "Maacah daughter of Abishalom" (or "Absalom") appears as the wife of Rehoboam and mother of King Abijam in 2 Chr. 11:20-21 and 1 K. 15:2. But it is most likely that Maacah the mother of Abijam, rather than being Absalom's daughter Tamar, is the daughter of Tamar, or perhaps of another daughter of Absalom, and Uriel of Gibeah (2 Chr. 13:2). The Absalom of 2 Chr. 11:20-21 does seem to be the son of David: Rehoboam's other named wives are the daughters of "Jerimoth the son of David" and of "Eliab the son of Jesse." In this context it is hard to think that just "Absalom" would refer to another Absalom. Since in the formal introduction to Abijam's reign Maacah is said to be the "daughter of Uriel of Gibeah" and one would expect Absalom's daughter to be rather older than Rehoboam, Maacah is probably Absalom's granddaughter, not his daughter. Similarly, given the generational and age differences, the "daughter of Eliab" that Rehoboam married is more likely to be Eliab's granddaughter than his daughter. Of course, it is still surprising that Rehoboam would marry the granddaughter of a flagrantly unfilial traitor.

28-32 Absalom *lived in Jerusalem* as he had before (ch. 13), even though he had property in Baal-hazor (13:23). As he apparently could not call on Joab himself, there may have been restrictions on his movements; cf. the restrictions on Shimei in 1 K. 2:36. The fact that Absalom was not allowed to *see the king's face* (vv. 28 and 32) shows that David was still angry with his conduct.

33 McCarter thinks that "the text of MT and LXX appears overcrowded, probably the result of a conflation of variants."[119] However, this "clumsy" repetition of verbal actions may be retardation as a sign of the TERMINUS of discourse.

And the king kissed Absalom as a sign of reconciliation, these words thus ending the section dealing with his banishment.

117. McCarter, II, p. 350.
118. *CAD*, A/1, p. 59.
119. McCarter, II, p. 343.

B. ABSALOM'S REBELLION (15:1–20:22)

This long section can be divided into six parts:

1. Absalom's conspiracy (15:1-12)
2. David's escape from Absalom and the people he met on the way (15:13–16:14)
3. The war council where the battle between Ahithophel and Hushai determines David's fate (16:15–17:23)
4. David's reception at Mahanaim (17:24-29)
5. The battle and the death of Absalom (18:1–19:8)
6. David's return to Jerusalem (19:9-43).

The narrator's final comment *And the king kissed Absalom* in the previous chapter (14:33) sounds neutral with regard to their degree of reconciliation. However, it seems that a root cause of Absalom's rebellion is his resentment toward his father, though the immediate cause is his ambition. From the divine perspective, all the calamities David experienced are the result of his own rebellion against God's commandments. Certainly, he has been losing his own people's support and respect. That is the main reason why Absalom is able to steal *the hearts of the men of Israel* (15:6).

The story moves first quickly, then very slowly. The outbreak of the premeditated revolt was determined and fast, narrated in six verses. On the other hand, the narration of David's departure from Jerusalem is a sustained tension of thirty-nine verses.

1. Absalom's Conspiracy (15:1-12)

1 *After this Absalom provided*[120] *for himself a chariot and horses, together with fifty men to run before him.*

2 *Absalom used to*[121] *get up early and stand beside the way to the gate. And when*[122] *anyone who had a suit was about to come to the king for judgment, Absalom would call him:*[123]

120. Lit. "made"; cf. "began to make use of" (McCarter, II, p. 354), reading the verb as imperfect, based on 4QSam[c].

121. Taking *waw*+pf. as indicating habitual actions. See Driver, p. 310.

122. There is no need to change the MT *wayhî* to *whyh* based on 4QSam[a], LXX[L] and OL, since the phrase usually introduces a temporal clause or phrase in the past tense.

123. Lit. "and called him and said"; see Tsumura, I, p. xii.

"What city are you from?"
and he would say,
"Your servant is from one of the tribes of Israel."
3 *And Absalom would say to him,*
"See, your case[124] *is good and straight,*
but you will have no hearing from the king."
4 *And Absalom would say,*
"Would that someone appoint me[125] *as a judge in the land!*
Then anyone who had a suit could come to me for judgment
and I would give him justice."[126]

5 *And whenever a man came near to prostrate himself to him, he would put out his hand and take hold of him and kiss him.*

6 *And in this way Absalom would deal with all Israel who came*[127] *to the king for judgment.*[128]

Thus Absalom stole the hearts of the men of Israel.

7 *Toward the end of "forty years" Absalom said to the king,*
"Let me go and fulfill in Hebron
the vow which I made to the LORD.
8 *For your servant made a vow*
when I was staying in Geshur in Aram, thus:
'If the LORD will indeed bring me back to Jerusalem,
I will serve the LORD.'"
9 *And the king said to him,*
"Go in peace."
And he arose and went to Hebron.
10 *And Absalom sent agents throughout the tribes of Israel, saying:*
"When you hear the sound of the horn,
you shall say: 'Absalom is king in IIebron!'"

11 *With Absalom went two hundred men from Jerusalem who were invited and went innocently; but they did not know anything.*

12 *And Absalom sent for Ahithophel the Gilonite, David's counselor, from his city of Giloh, while he was offering sacrifices.*

And the conspiracy was strong, and the people with Absalom increased continually.

124. Lit. "your word"; cf. "statements, arguments" (Driver, p. 310).

125. Or "If only I were appointed" (NIV, JPS); lit. "who will appoint me?" See Driver, p. 311.

126. Heb. *w*^{e}*hiṣdaqtîw*; lit. "do justice for him."

127. I.e., impf. verb.

128. MT: *lammišpāṭ*; also in v. 2; see the commentary on v. 4.

1-6 Despite the passage of three thousand years and a completely different political system, one can see that some things never change. It is easy to say "you are right" when you can ignore the other party in a law-suit or argument, and personal attention from someone high-up, in this case the handsome, accessible son of the king, is flattering.

Verses 1-6 are a SETTING and give the background information for the subsequent EVENT (7ff.). The verbal form *waw*+pf describes habitual actions.

1 It was the custom for the royal chariot to be escorted by a team of runners, who served as bodyguard for the king; see 1 Sam. 8:11. *A chariot and horses, together with fifty men to run before him.* In an Aramaic inscription of the eighth century B.C., Panamuwa was noted as an ardent military supporter of the Assyrian king Tiglathpileser III, running at the wheel of his lord's chariot.[129] Later Adonijah behaves similarly, exalting himself, "saying 'I will be king'" (1 K. 1:5). The phrase *fifty men* is probably the size of one military unit, since "fifty" and "hundred" are usually military units (e.g., 1 Sam. 29:2; 2 K. 1:9; 2 K. 11:4; also Arad 24:12).[130]

3 Absalom's statement *you will have no hearing from the king* is somewhat of an exaggeration, for the widow of Tekoa got a hearing, and if it were known that there was no chance of a hearing, people would not come.

4 *And Absalom would say* is an example of "repeated introduction to speech" in which "speech by one character, introduced with a finite form of the verb 'say' (*'mr*), is interrupted by a second introduction, also using a finite form of 'say.'"[131]

Absalom is here appealing to the tradition of the king as *judge* (Prov. 31:9; Isa. 11:3-5), which is bound closely with the concept of the Lord as judge (Ps. 96:10; Isa. 33:22), not to the judgeship of the previous era. Thus he is saying, "Oh that I were king!"; see 1 Sam. 8:5. This is in line with his chariot and runners in v. 1. Thus, Absalom is acting as an heir preparing for kingship. C. H. Gordon compares the author's treatment of the rebellion of Absalom in this "royal epic" with the rebellion of the crown prince Yassib in the Ugaritic Keret royal epic.[132] It is noteworthy that Yassib, like Absalom, claimed to be motivated by a lack of justice.

The two words *suit* and *judgment* appear as a pair in Mic. 7:9; Ps. 35:23; 2 Chr. 19:8. However, when compared with *lammišpāṭ* in vv. 2 and 6, *waw* (*û-*) could be taken as adverbial, and the phrase *rîb ûmišpāṭ* ("a dispute or

129. See Younger, *PHA*, p. 417.

130. See Aharoni, *AI*, p. 48.

131. See E. J. Revell, "The Repetition of Introductions to Speech as a Feature of Biblical Hebrew," pp. 96-97 n. 15. See the commentary on 1 Sam. 16:11 in Tsumura, I, p. 421.

132. Gordon, *CB*, p. 154.

cause" [ESV], "a complaint or case" [NIV]) might be translated as "a suit for justice" as if it constituted a construct chain (*rîb mišpāṭ*) or, as we adopt here, *a suit . . . for judgment.*[133]

5 This verse has four *weqtl* (i.e., *waw*+pf.) forms, which denote the customary actions of Absalom (see on 1 Sam. 1:4).[134] Thus, *And whenever a man came near* [*wᵉhāyāh*] *he would put out* [*wᵉšālaḥ*] *his hand and take hold of* [*wᵉheḥĕzîq*] *him and kiss* [*wᵉnāšaq*] *him.* Absalom represents himself as approachable and sympathetic.

6 *To steal the hearts of* has been explained as "the image of the distant heart (which) is a way of expressing loss of devotion";[135] for the Hebrew *lēb* (lit. "heart") which indicates "courage" and "devotion," see 1 Sam. 17:32. McCarter thinks the idiom probably means "to deceive" or "to dupe" as in Gen. 31:20.[136] However, looking at v. 13, *The hearts of the men of Israel have followed Absalom!* it would seem that here it means "to capture the affection of."

In chs. 15-18, "Israel" usually means "Absalom's side," while David's side is referred to as "David's servants" or "the army." Does the designation *Israel* here refer only to the northern tribes, or to both Israel and Judah? There are some scholars that favor the former position, but this is hard to reconcile with the text. There is nothing to suggest that Judah did not join. Absalom proclaimed himself king in Hebron and presumably raised enough men there to be a credible threat to David in Jerusalem; Hushai said Absalom could call men from Dan to Beersheba (17:11); and 19:11-14 imples that Judah did participate in the rebellion.

7 The majority of modern scholars accept "four years," following LXX^L, Syr, and Vul (see RSV, NIV, ESV, Anderson), or "forty days" (Ehrlich, Eissfeldt),[137] though the MT reading *"forty years"* (so NASB, JPS) is certainly the *lectio difficilior* and supported by the main LXX tradition. The phrase "forty years" cannot refer to the fortieth year of David's reign, that is its last year (5:4) since he seems to have stayed king after Absalom's death until his old age; see 1 K. 1:1f. McCarter suggests that the primitive reading of *'arbā'îm* could be *'rb'-m*, with enclitic *-m*, meaning "four years" (see also the commentary on 1 Sam. 6:19).[138] The four years would presumably have been

133. See "a legal dispute" (JPS); "just cause" (McCarter, p. 354); "eine richterliche Entscheidung" (Stoebe, p. 355).

134. Tsumura, I, pp. 112-13.

135. B. A. Levine, "The Semantics of Loss: Two Exercises in Biblical Hebrew Lexicography," in *Solving Riddles and Untying Knots: Biblical, Epigraphic, and Semitic Studies in Honor of Jonas C. Greenfield*, ed. Z. Zevit, S. Gitin, and M. Sokoloff (Winona Lake, Ind.: Eisenbrauns, 1995), pp. 145, 137-58.

136. McCarter, II, p. 356; Driver, p. 311.

137. See McCarter, II, p. 355.

138. Tsumura, I, pp. 226-27.

those since Absalom's return to Jerusalem or his reconciliation with David. Althann takes *šānāh wayyō'mer* as a hendiadys, taking *šānāh* as a verbal form ("to repeat"), and translates: "And at the end of forty days Absalom spoke insistently to the king."[139] However, his syntax and interpretation is a little forced.

The end of "forty years" (*miqqēṣ 'arbā'îm šānāh*) appears in Ezek. 29:13. This could be a formulaic phrase that signifies the end of a long period of wandering like that of the Israelites' forty years in the desert. Tentatively, I take the phrase to mean "toward the end of Absalom's waiting period."

Fulfill in Hebron the vow that I made to the LORD — McCarter translates this as "fulfill the vow I made to Yahweh-in-Hebron," seeing here a divine name, the local manifestation worshipped in Hebron of the national god, comparing it to "Dagon-in-Ashdod (1 Sam. 5:5)"[140] and expressions such as "Yahweh of Samaria" and "Yahweh of Teman" in the Kuntillet Ajrud inscriptions. However, the comparison is invalid. For one thing, the local deities are expressed not by "DN in GN," but by the construct chain, "DN of GN," both in the texts from Kuntillet Ajrud (*YHWH Šmrn* and *YHWH Tmn*) and in those from Ugarit ("Baal of Ugarit" [*b'l ugrt*], "Baal of Aleppo" [*b'l ḫlb*], etc.).[141] Also, his understanding of the Hebrew syntax here is somewhat forced. The phrase *in Hebron* modifies the main verbs "go and fulfill," not the subordinate "made," hence *fulfill in Hebron my vow*. Such an interruption of the nucleus of a sentence by the insertion of a relative clause is common; see the commentary on 2:24.[142] Similarly, in 1 Sam. 5:5 the phrase "in Ashdod" modifies the whole of "the threshold of Dagon"; it is not a modifier of "Dagon," so there is no reference to a "Dagon-in-Ashdod."

8 For the vow formula *If the LORD will indeed*, see the commentary on 1 Sam. 1:11.[143]

While the K. means "he will bring back," the Q. is "he will do again." The Q. should be taken as inf. abs. of *yšb (not *šwb), which is probably a by-form of *šwb (cf. *šwb as a by-form of *yšb in Ps. 23:6). Gordon takes this as an "unmistakable" Y-causative, infin.[144] Note also that Qal inf. abs. is used with a derived stem of a finite verb, here Hi, as sometimes happens;

139. R. Althann, "The Meaning of ארבעים שנה in 2 Sam 15,7," *Bib* 73 (1992) 248-52.

140. Stoebe, p. 356, takes the expression "Jahwe von Hebron" to be connected with the "Volksfrömmigkeit" in Gen. 13:18.

141. See *DULAT*, p. 209. For the phenomenon of local manifestations of Yahweh, see Tsumura, "Yahweh and His Asherah," pp. 1-15 (in Japanese).

142. See also Tsumura, I, p. 48, esp. n. 219.

143. Tsumura, I, pp. 117-18.

144. Gordon, *UT*, §9.38.

e.g., Gen. 26:11; Exod. 19:13; 1 Sam. 23:22; 2 Sam. 20:18. For *Geshur*, see the commentary on 3:3.

9 The expression *Go in peace* marks "a successful conclusion of negotiation or assurance that the request for a desired state of relationships has been granted";[145] see also the commentaries on 1 Sam. 1:17; 20:42.[146]

12 These sacrifices, while announced as payment of his vow, were apparently actually part of a coronation ceremony, formally asserting his kingship (v. 10; 16:16); see 1 K. 1:9-11; also 1 Sam. 11:14-15.

The element "tophel" of *Ahithophel* possibly means "foolishness." It is otherwise unknown among Hebrew names. McCarter suggests that this name is "a deliberate distortion satirizing the man's ill-used wisdom."[147] Compare the substitution of *bošet* for *baʿal* in Samuel.

The title *counselor* (*yôʿēṣ*) appears also in 1 Chr. 26:14; 27:32 and Isa. 1:26; 3:3; 9:6; etc. *Giloh* appears in a list of towns in the Judean hills in Josh. 15:51. It is located somewhere south and west of Hebron near Kh. Rabud (MR 151093).[148]

2. David's Escape from Jerusalem (15:13–16:14)

a. David Leaves the Palace (15:13-18)

15:13–16:14 David flees Jerusalem lest the city be destroyed. Psalm 3 is said to have been composed on this occasion. On the way he meets a loyal band of foreigners, the priests Abiathar and Zadok, his friend Hushai, Mephibosheth's servant Ziba, and the Benjaminite Shimei.

Scholars have noticed that there is a certain symmetry between the account of David's flight from Jerusalem to the Jordan (15:13–16:14) and that of his return (19:16[15]–20:3).[149]

13 *And a person came to David and reported,*
"The hearts of the men of Israel have followed Absalom!"
14 *And David said to all his servants who were with him in Jerusalem,*
"Arise and let us flee,
for we shall have no escape from Absalom.

145. Wiseman, "'Is It Peace?,'" p. 324.

146. Tsumura, I, pp. 122, 524-25.

147. McCarter, II, p. 357.

148. *ABD*, II, p. 1027.

149. See McCarter, II, pp. 374-77; D. M. Gunn, "From Jerusalem to the Jordan and Back: Symmetry in 2 Samuel XV-XX," *VT* 30 (1980) 109-113. See our analysis of the outline of 2 Samuel in the Introduction.

Go quickly,
lest he overtake us quickly and bring disaster upon us
and strike the city with the edge of the sword."
15 *And the servants of the king said to the king,*
"According to whatever my lord the king chooses,
here are your servants."
16 *And the king and all his household went out on foot.*
And the king left ten concubines to keep the house.
17 *And the king and all the people went out on foot, and they stopped at the last house.*
18 *All his servants were passing by him,*
that is, all the Cherethites and all the Pelethites.
And all the Gittites, six hundred men
who had come from Gath, on foot,
were passing on before the king.

14 The MT of *for we shall have no escape* is *kî lō'-tihyeh-llānû p^{e}lêṭāh*, taking *kî* as *speaker-oriented.*[150] McCarter reads *thy lnw plyth* ("Then we shall have an escape"), based on 4QSam^c. However, note that the MT reading that he gives is incorrect.[151]

16 The prepositional phrase *b^{e}raglâw* (*on foot;* lit. "in his legs/feet") modifies *went out,* not the immediately preceding NP as usually understood (e.g., "after him" [RSV]; "followed him" [NEB]).

The *concubines* are mentioned here in preparation for 16:21-22.

17-18 The LXX of these verses is much longer than the MT, which McCarter thinks has been shortened by haplography.[152] However, the prose text of MT in v. 18 is "poetic" and may be the original; see below.

17 Since *the last house* (*bêt hammerḥāq*) was located before David crossed the Kidron Valley (v. 23), it was probably the last one before going out the city gate.

18 This verse can be analyzed as poetic prose.[153]

All his servants were *passing by* him,
that is, all the Cherethites and all the Pelethites.
And all the Gittites, six hundred men
who had come from Gath, on foot,
were *passing on* before the king.

150. See Tsumura, I, pp. 48-49.
151. McCarter, II, p. 363.
152. See McCarter, II, pp. 363-64; also Driver, p. 311.
153. Tsumura, I, pp. 59-60.

The *waw* in the head of the second line can be taken as a *waw explicativum*,[154] hence *that is*. Since the grammar of parallelism works vertically[155] as well as horizontally, the phrase *on foot* could modify the participle *passing* rather than the verb *had come*.

The *Cherethites . . . Pelethites* are David's bodyguard (8:18). They have been identified as the "Cretans and Philistines."[156]

These *Gittites* (i.e., men from *Gath* [see on 1 Sam. 5:8[157]]; see on 2 Sam. 6:10) are not likely to be David's own men who had gone with him from Israel to Gath in 1 Sam. 27:2-6, since they had come *yesterday* (v. 20), that is recently, and furthermore, Ittai is a "foreigner."

Six hundred is apparently the standard size of regiments in Israel and Philistia.[158] These *Gittites* probably formed a military unit, following the Philistine practices, which David presumably learned while he was in Gath.

b. Ittai (15:19-22)

19 *And the king said to Ittai the Gittite,*
"Why will you also go with us?
Return and remain with the king,[159]
for you are a foreigner; you are also an exile.
[Go back] to your position!
20 *Yesterday you came;*
but today shall I make you wander to go with us,
while I am going wherever I am going?
Return and take your brothers back.
May grace and truth be with you."
21 *And Ittai answered the king:*
"As the LORD lives, and as my lord the king lives,
surely in the place where my lord the king is,
whether for death or for life,
there your servant shall be."
22 *And David said to Ittai,*
"Go and pass over."

154. See Baker, "Further Examples of the *wāw explicativum*," p. 131.

155. For the vertical grammar of parallelism, see Tsumura, "Vertical Grammar of Parallelism in Hebrew Poetry," pp. 167-81. See also Tsumura, I, pp. 55-60.

156. See A. Mazar, *Archaeology of the Land of the Bible, 10,000-586 B.C.E.* (ABRL; New York: Doubleday, 1992), p. 306.

157. Tsumura, I, pp. 209-10.

158. B. Mazar, "The Military Élite of King David," *VT* 13 (1963) 314.

159. See "the new king" (JPS); "King Absalom" (NIV).

And Ittai the Gittite, all his men and all the children who were with him passed by.

19 The name *Ittai* (*'Ittay*) can be compared with Hittite *atta-* and Hurrian *attai*, both meaning "father."[160] Garsiel hears the echo of the name *Ittai, the Gittite* in the fourfold repetition of the pronouns "you" (*'attāh*) and "with us" (*'ittānû*).[161] If the original form is *'atta(i)*, this wordplay is all the more effective. As Garsiel notes, the narrator seems to emphasize "the common fate of Itai [*sic*], David, and his loyal followers."

[Go back] to your position! Usually, *gam-gōleh 'attāh limqômekā* is taken to mean "you are an exile from your home." Driver takes *limqômekā* as "simply a copyist's error" for *mmqwmk*, following LXX and Vulg.[162] However, since the preposition *l* can mean "(away) from" as in Ugaritic,[163] such a translation is certainly possible for the MT text as it is. But I would like to suggest another possibility, though with much reservation, that is, to take *limqômekā* as an independent utterance, "Return to your [assigned duty] station!"

20 On *grace and truth*, see 2:6. See "and may the LORD show steadfast love and faithfulness to you" (ESV, NRSV). One can compare the scene in Ruth where Naomi bids farewell to Ruth and Orpah, but Ruth says she will remain with Naomi, wherever she goes.

21 For the oath formula *as the LORD lives*, see 1 Sam. 14:39.[164]

22 The two phrases *pass over* (*lēk wa'ăbōr*) and *passed by* (*wayya'ăbōr*) are based on the same Hebrew term, but from different viewpoints:[165] one, that of David, and the other, that of the narrator, hence different renderings.

c. David Crosses the Kidron (15:23)

23 *While all the country was weeping with a loud voice, all the people were passing by. While the king was crossing the Kidron Valley, all the people were passing over toward the way of the wilderness.*

160. See Laroche, *Ugaritica* V, p. 450; Gröndahl, *PTU*, p. 221; Huehnergard, *UVST*, p. 48.

161. M. Garsiel, "Word Play and Puns as a Rhetorical Device in the Book of Samuel," in *Puns and Pundits: Word Play in the Hebrew Bible and Ancient Near Eastern Literature*, ed. S. B. Noegel (Bethesda, Md.: CDL Press, 2000), pp. 191-92.

162. Driver, p. 313.

163. Gordon, *UT*, §10.1; *HALOT*, p. 508.

164. Tsumura, I, p. 377.

165. Tsumura, I, pp. 54-55.

23 The *Kidron Valley* runs just east of Jerusalem; the Mount of Olives (v. 30) is to the east of that. It was the traditional eastern boundary of Jerusalem (see 1 K. 2:36-37); so at this point David has left the city.

Now David himself was *crossing* (lit. "passing over") the valley. Note the discourse describing the evacuation of the city (vv. 14-23) has moved at a very slow TEMPO.[166]

d. Zadok with the Ark (15:24-29)

24 *There came also Zadok and all the Levites with him, carrying the ark of the covenant of God, and they set down the ark of God.*

And Abiathar offered sacrifices until all the people had finished passing over out of the city.

25 *And the king said to Zadok,*
"Take back the ark of God to the city.
If I find favor in the eyes of the LORD,
he will bring me back
and show it and its habitation[167] *to me.*
26 *But if he should say thus: 'I have no delight in you,'*
here I am,
let him do to me as it is good in his eyes."
27 *And the king said to Zadok the priest,*
"Are you a seer?
Return to the city in peace.
Your (pl.) two sons,
your (sg.) son Ahimaaz and Abiathar's son Jonathan,
shall be with you (pl.).
28 *Look! I will be waiting in the steppes of the wilderness*
until word comes from you (pl.) to inform me."

29 *And Zadok and Abiathar returned the ark of God to Jerusalem and stayed there.*

24-37 Though David leaves the city, by the providence of God he is able to set up a messenger system — Hushai, to Zadok and Abiathar, to their sons (via a maid, 17:17), to David (v. 36).

24 *Zadok* and *Abiathar* are David's two chief priests; see 20:25.

Some scholars take the reference to *the Levites* to be a secondary addi-

166. Tsumura, I, pp. 53-54.
167. Cf. "His habitation" (NASB); "its camping place" (McCarter, II, p. 371).

tion by the hand of "a late, possibly Deuteronomistic, editor."[168] However, the Levites existed during the preexilic days, and they are mentioned in 1 Sam. 6:15.[169] For the clause *wayya'al 'ebyātār* (lit. "and Abiathar lifted up"), NIV translates "Abiathar offered sacrifices," while the majority translate: "Abiathar came up" (NASB, NRSV, JPS, etc.). Since the verb *'lh (Hi.) is often used with the meaning "to offer up a sacrifice at the altar" (see *HALOT*, p. 830), Driver suggested the possibility that an object such as *'ōlōt* (6:17; 1 K. 3:15) has fallen out. However, one could take this as an example of *brachylogy*,[170] which omits the expected object of the verb as an idiomatic expression; note that the object "sacrifices" is omitted in 1 K. 12:32-33. Abiathar was most likely interceding for the safe departure of David and his people, though Bergen suggests the possibility of the usual "morning offerings (cf. Num. 28:2-4)."[171]

25 Heb. *nāweh* means "pasture" and "dwelling of flocks," but it is often used in poetry for the general sense of "abode." In prose the word occurs only in 7:8 and here.[172]

David does not use the ark as a charm, in contrast to the attitude in 1 Sam. 4:3. Perhaps one factor is that he realizes that the rebellion is partly the result of his sins (2 Sam. 12:10). He does not know how far the Lord intends to punish him. His symbols of mourning and penitence and acceptance of malice (16:10) are probably related to this. However, as he does consider the rebellion wrong, he is willing to use prayer and the human opportunities God gives him (vv. 28, 31, 34; see Neh. 4:9).

27 *And the king said to Zadok the priest* is an example of "repeated introduction to speech."[173]

Various emendations have been proposed for *hărô'eh 'attāh* ("Are you a seer?"): e.g., Hoftijzer,[174] who takes it as a "formulaic idiom" and emends it to "Pay attention!"; "Look, you return," based on LXX^{L}.[175] The most natural translation is a rhetorical question expecting the answer "No." So, *Are you a seer?* : i.e., "You are no seer!"; REB however takes it as a positive rhetorical question: "Are you not a seer?"

28 The K. *b'brwt* is the metathesis of the Q. *b^{e}'arbôt*, which means "steppes." A word with a resonant /r/ sometimes experiences metathesis

168. McCarter, II, p. 370.
169. Tsumura, I, p. 221.
170. See Tsumura, I, pp. 64-65.
171. Bergen, p. 405.
172. See Driver, pp. 315-16.
173. See above (v. 4).
174. J. Hoftijzer, "A Peculiar Question: A Note on 2 Sam. XV 27," *VT* 21 (1971) 608-9.
175. McCarter, II, p. 366; Driver, p. 316.

of /r/ and its contiguous consonant,[176] so the K. is the phonetic spelling of the "phonic" reality. The phrase, *the steppes of the wilderness* here (also 17:16), refers to the Jordan Valley, north of the Dead Sea. David and his group will stop on the west bank (see 16:14) and wait the news from Jerusalem (17:16).

e. David Goes Up the Mount of Olives (15:30-31)

30 *Now David was going up the Slope of Olives, weeping as he went. His head was covered; he was walking barefoot. And all the people who were with him each covered their head and went up, weeping as they went.*

31 *Then, David*[177] *was told:*

"Ahithophel is among the conspirators with Absalom."

And David said,

"Please make the counsel of Ahithophel foolish, O Lord!"

30 David starts going up the slope to the top of Mount of Olives. *The Slope of Olives* (*maʿălēh hazzêtîm*) may be an older name for the Mount of Olives, as McCarter suggests.[178] *His head was covered; he was walking barefoot.* These are the signs of mourning (Isa. 20:2; Mic. 1:8; Esth. 6:12).

31 The participation of Ahithophel, David's counselor (15:12), in the conspiracy was mentioned in v. 12. His counsel was greatly esteemed (16:23). In extremity one often utters short prayers, and David's is clearly answered in the next verse by the arrival of Hushai.

f. Hushai (15:32-37)

32 *Just as David was reaching the summit, where God was worshipped, there to meet him was Hushai the Archite with his coat torn and soil on his head.*

33 *And David said to him,*

"If you come over with me, you will be a burden to me.

34 *But if you return to the city, and say to Absalom:*

'Your servant I will be, O king!

I have been[179] *your father's servant in time past,*

176. See Tsumura, "Scribal Errors or Phonetic Spellings?," pp. 391-92.

177. Lit. "and David"; *casus pendens.* Two MT MSS and the Qumran text have the preposition *l* before "David."

178. McCarter, II, p. 371.

179. Heb. *wa'ănî.* This *waw* might be taken as emphatic.

But now I am[180] *your servant,'*
then you can ruin the counsel of Ahithophel for me.
35 *Are not Zadok and Abiathar the priests there with you?*
Whatever you hear from the house of the king
you shall report to Zadok and Abiathar the priests.
36 *Their two sons,*
Ahimaaz of Zadok and Jonathan of Abiathar,
are there with them.
You (pl.) shall send me by them everything you hear."
37 *And Hushai, the friend of David, entered the city.*
As for Absalom, he was entering Jerusalem.

32 *Just as David was reaching the summit.* At the place of worship Hushai was providentially sent by God to David. The name *Hushai* (*Ḥûšay*) is also known in Arad 57:2. The *Archite* clan of Benjamin is from the southwest of Bethel; see Josh. 16:2.

For the custom of mourning, *with his coat torn and dirt on his head*, see on 1 Sam. 4:12;[181] also 2 Sam. 1:2; 13:19; 13:31.

34 Based on a long LXX, McCarter restores "Your brothers departed, O king, after the departure of your father, and now" before the phrase *Your servant*. After the phrase *O king!* McCarter restores "Spare my life!," based on LXX.[182] But these restorations are not necessary, for such words would not have helped Hushai gain Absalom's trust.

37 *Friend* (*rēʿeh*) may be a title, like the Ugaritic *mdʿ* "the friend (of the king),"[183] as it is not the normal word for friend and it appears in the list of officials in 1 K. 4:5. However, David is called the friend of Hushai in 16:17, so it also expresses a relationship.

g. Ziba (16:1-4)

1 *Now David passed a little beyond the summit. There came Ziba, the steward of Mephibosheth, toward him, with a yoke of saddled donkeys on which were*
two hundred (loaves of) bread,
one hundred (bunches of) raisins,
one hundred (baskets of) summer fruit
and a skin of wine.

180. Heb. *wa'ănî.*
181. Tsumura, I, pp. 197-98.
182. McCarter, II, p. 367.
183. Gordon, *UT*, §19.1080.

2 *And the king said to Ziba,*
"Why do you have these things?"
And Ziba said,
"The donkeys are for the household of the king to ride,
and the bread[184] *and the summer fruit are for the young men to eat,*
and the wine is for the faint in the wilderness to drink."[185]
3 *And the king said,*
"But where is your master's son?"
And Ziba said to the king,
"He is staying in Jerusalem, for he said,
'Today the house of Israel will be returned[186] *to me*
with my father's kingdom.'"
4 *And the king said to Ziba,*
"Now all that belongs to Mephibosheth is yours."
And Ziba said,
"I prostrate myself![187]
May I find favor in your sight, O my lord, the king."

1 For *Ziba* and *Mephibosheth* see chapter 9.

It seems that riding animals like the mules the king's sons rode (13:29) or Shimei's donkey (1 K. 2:40) were normally pastured at some distance from the city, which is why all the king's household were on foot. Mephibosheth would have been one of the few who had daily need of riding animals and kept them in the city.

The phrase *a yoke of . . . donkeys* (*ṣemed ḥămōrîm*) often appears: e.g., *ṣmd ḥmrm* (Arad 3:4-5) "two donkeys."[188] Two loaded donkeys are normally driven by one man (see Judg. 19:3, 10). A pair of donkeys harnessed together can transport a heavier load than the same two animals loaded separately.[189] Aharoni notes that the concept of a "two mules' burden" appears in 2 Ki. 5:17.[190] For the ass-measure, see the commentary on 1 Sam. 16:20.[191]

The list of food here is similar to the list of food that Abigail brought

184. Following the Q. *wᵉhalleḥem*; cf. K. *wlhlḥm* ("and as for the bread"). In the light of Jer. 42:14, *wᵉlalleḥem* ← *wᵉ-lᵉ-halleḥem*, and 1 Chr. 23:29, *ûl(ᵉ)leḥem* ← *wᵉ-lᵉ-leḥem*, the K. might be read *ûl(ᵉ)-halleḥem.*

185. I.e., "for those who faint in the wilderness to drink" (ESV).

186. Lit. "they will return."

187. This verb is a *performative* perfect.

188. Y. Aharoni, *AI*, p. 18.

189. Malamat, "Military Rationing in Papyrus Anastasi I and the Bible," p. 119 n.1.

190. Aharoni, *AI*, 18.

191. Tsumura, I, pp. 30, 431; Tsumura, "*ḥamôr leḥem* (1 Sam XVI 20)," *VT* 42 (1992) 412-14.

David in 1 Sam. 25:18.[192] The ratio of bread to wine is similar to that in the Arad ostraca.[193]

A skin of wine (*nēbel yāyin*) contained about fourty-two to fifty-three quarts (40-50 l). There is a record that an Egyptian Kittiyîm, a unit of fifty or one hundred, was given a little more than this for a march of four days.[194] See also the commentary on 1 Sam. 1:24; 10:3; 25:18 (two skins of wine).[195]

3 *Your master's son.* i.e., "the [grand]son of your former master Saul" (see 9:9). *The house of Israel will be returned to me.* If there were divided feelings between the Israelites and the Judahites at that time, it is possible that Mephibosheth would have hoped that people would turn to him as the heir of the former king at this chaotic moment of the reign of David. It was hardly a practical scenario, however. Even Shimei did not suggest it (vv. 7-8). Mephibosheth in 19:24-27 claims that Ziba was lying here.[196] As the next section and chapter 20 show, there was still feeling against David among some Benjaminites, so David may have been very sensitive about Mephibosheth's position, and Ziba in his statement effectively used this.

4 David here gives what he had bestowed upon Mephibosheth to Ziba. This clearly shows that "human kings in Israel had the right to transfer the grants they had made" to other persons.[197]

h. Shimei (16:5-14)

5 *When King David came up to Bahurim, there came out from there a man of the clan of the house of Saul; his name was Shimei son of Gera. He came out cursing continually.*

6 *And he threw stones at David and at all the servants of King David. And all the people and all the warriors were at his right and left.*

7 *Thus said Shimei, cursing,*
"Get out, get out, O man of blood!
O worthless man!

192. Tsumura, I, pp. 583-84.

193. Aharoni, *AI*, 18

194. Aharoni, *AI*, 145.

195. Tsumura, I, pp. 129-32, 285, 583-84.

196. Cf. J. Schipper, "Why Do You Still Speak of Your Affairs?": Polyphony in Mephibosheth's Exchanges with David in 2 Samuel," *VT* 54 (2004) 344-51, who holds that Mephibosheth's speech both as reported in this chapter and in ch. 19 allows a "multiplicity of interpretations." He thinks that his exchanges with David "only add to the ambiguity of the situation and the complexity of his character."

197. See Gordon, *CB*, p. 241; see also the commentary on 1 Sam. 15:28 in Tsumura, I, p. 406.

8 *The LORD has returned to you*
all the blood of the house of Saul
in whose place you have ruled;
and the LORD has given the kingdom
into the hand of Absalom your son.
Now you are in trouble[198]
for you are a man of blood!"
9 *And Abishai, son of Zeruiah, said to the king,*
"Why should this dead dog curse my lord the king?
Let me go over and take his head off!"
10 *And the king said,*
"What is it to me and to you, O sons of Zeruiah,
that[199] *he curses?*
For[200] *the LORD said to him*
'Curse David!'
Who can say, 'Why have you done this?'"
11 *And David said to Abishai and to all his servants,*
"Even my son who came out of me seeks my life;
how much more[201] *now this Benjamite?*
Let him alone and let him curse,
for the LORD has told him.
12 *Perhaps the LORD will look at my eyes*
and the LORD will return good to me
in return for his cursing this day."
13 *And David and his men went on the way.*
— And Shimei was going along on the hillside to the side of him, while cursing, and cast stones from the side of him, while throwing dust. —
14 *And the king and all the people who were with him arrived weary,*[202] *and he refreshed himself there.*

5 *Shimei son of Gera* is apparently a prominent man (19:17) *of the clan* (*mišpāḥāh*) *of the house of Saul*; see 1 Sam. 10:21 on Saul's clan, Matri; also 1 Sam. 9:21.[203] *Bahurim* is a Benjaminite town on the north side of the Mount of Olives, though it did have inhabitants who supported David

198. Lit. "in your evil"; cf. "you are taken in your own evil" (NASB), "disaster has overtaken you" (NRSV).

199. K. *ky* (Q. *kh*); as a nominal clause.

200. Heb. *kî* as a *speaker-oriented* particle. David is explaining the reason why he said this.

201. See 2 Sam. 4:11.

202. LXX adds "at the Jordan," followed by ESV, JPS, and REB.

203. See Tsumura, I, pp. 277-78 and 297-98.

(17:18). See on 2 Sam. 3:16. Shimei acts very differently the next time he meets David (19:16).

7 *O man of blood* (*ʾîš haddāmîm*) is literally "the man of the blood"; cf. "murderer" (NRSV). Here and in the next phrase the definite noun is used as a vocative; cf. *a man of blood* (v. 8).

O worthless man (*ʾîš habbᵉlîyāʿal*) is literally "the man of *the* Beliyaal"; for *Beliyaal,* see the Excursus: "Daughter of Beliyaal" (1 Sam. 1:16).[204] McCarter takes these two phrases as hendiadic, translating "You bloodstained fiend of hell!" (lit. "man of blood and man of hell").[205] Anderson translates "*murderer and monster*."[206]

8 With the expression *all the blood of the house of Saul,* Shimei was probably blaming David for the deaths of Abner (3:26-27) and Ish-bosheth (ch. 4), and possibly for the deaths of Saul's sons and grandsons in 21:1-9 (if it had happened by then) or even that of Saul himself, though he is not necessarily accusing him of actual complicity in the deaths. Since the writer of Samuel goes to great lengths to absolve David from complicity, one can surmise that some of ill-feeling toward David because of the house of Saul remained even at the time the book of Samuel was written. In a context of cursing, however, the phrase and expression tend to become extreme and hyperbolic.

9 As in 1 Sam. 26:8, Abishai as always is ready to act; see also on 2:18. The phrase *dead dog* (*hakkeleb hammēt*) is a term of contempt or self-abasement; see on 9:8. Cursing a ruler is forbidden in Exod. 22:28.

10-11 The repetitive style of these two verses is due to the rhetorical and poetic nature of David's speech rather than a conflation of various texts. This is not a "Deuteronomistic anticipation of the execution of Shimei" in 1 K. 2:8, 44, as Veijola holds;[207] rather vv. 10-12 are similar to David's reply to Abishai's similar proposal in 1 Sam. 26:8-11.

10 *What is it to me and to you . . . ?* (*mah-llî wᵉlākem*) again appears in 19:22 as well as Judg. 11:12; 1 K. 17:18; 2 K. 3:13; 2 Chr. 35:21; cf. "What have I to do with you" (NASB; NRSV); "What do you . . . have against me?" (McCarter). David's point is that "it would be disastrous for him to take Abishai's advice."[208]

12 The expression *look at my eyes,* based on the Q. *bᵉʿênî* (K. *bᵉʿăwōnî* "my guilt"; cf. "my affliction" [NASB], "my distress" [NRSV]) means "to examine my heart/intention." This is an example of *Tiqqun sopherim* "the

204. Tsumura, I, p. 122-24.
205. McCarter, II, p. 373.
206. Anderson, p. 199.
207. Veijola, *Die ewige Dynastie,* p. 33.
208. McCarter, II, p. 374.

emendation of the scribes." David's idea that Shimei's actions might lead the Lord to have pity on him, is also expressed in Prov. 24:17-18, from the opposite perspective: "Do not rejoice when your enemy falls. . . lest the Lord see it and be displeased, and turn away his anger from him."

13 The *main line* of discourse (vv. 13a → 14) is interrupted by the embedded discourse: *And Shimei was going along* (v. 13b). The *weqtl* form (*w^{e}ʿippar*) after the *wayqtl* (narrative tense: WHAT; *cast stones*) is a PROCEDURAL (HOW) discourse, thus the translation *while throwing dust.*[209]

The phrase *to the side of him l^{e}ʿummātô* (lit. "to his parallel") probably indicates a slope above David, for it would be easy for Shimei to throw "dust" (or "lumps of dry earth" [BDB, p. 780]?) on David; see NASB; cf. "opposite him" (NRSV). The same phrase is translated here as *from the side of him (= David)* on its second occurrence. Note the preposition *l-* can mean "from" as well as "to."[210]

3. Ahithophel and Hushai (16:15–17:23)

a. Hushai Comes to Absalom (16:15-19)

15 *Now Absalom and all the people, the men of Israel, came to Jerusalem; Ahithophel was with him.*

16 *And when Hushai the Archite, David's friend, came to Absalom, Hushai said to Absalom,*
"Long live the king! Long live the king!"
17 *And Absalom said to Hushai,*
"Is this your loyalty to your friend?
Why did you not go with your friend?"
18 *And Hushai said to Absalom,*
"No!
But the one whom the LORD, this people,
and all the men of Israel have chosen,
to him[211] *I will belong and with him I will remain.*
19 *Moreover,*
whom should I serve?
Should I not (serve) before his son?
As I have served before your father,
so I will be before you."

209. Tsumura, "Tense and Aspect of Hebrew Verbs in II Samuel VII 8-16," p. 652.
210. See Gordon, *UT*, §10.1.
211. Q.; cf. K. *l'*.

15 Here we go back to 15:37, with the repetition of the notice of Absalom's arrival in Jerusalem.

16 *Long live the king!* literally, "May the king live!" is not just a prayer, but an acclamation submitting to royal authority. However, the referent here and in v. 18 and 17:7 might be considered ambiguous (Who is the king? Good for whom?). Compare David's words to Achish in 1 Sam. 29:8.

17 The term *loyalty* (*ḥesed*) or "loyal deed" literally means "kindness"; see the commentary on 2:5. For the term "friend," see the commentary on 15:37. Absalom uses the term twice here, perhaps sarcastically.

19 Hushai probably knows that professing a change of heart toward David would be difficult, so he doesn't try. In the present day his speech probably would have been along the line, "Whatever my feelings are toward your predecessor, you have now become our leader, and I will serve you for the good of the country."

The Hebrew term *haššēnît* for *moreover* might be compared with Amarna Akkadian *šamitam.* The abbreviated expression "Is not before his son?" (*hălô' lipnê bᵉnô*) is translated here as *Should I not (serve) before his son?*

b. Ahithophel's Advice (16:20–17:4)

Chapter 17 presents the climax of this section, the crucial battle between Ahithophel and Hushai before Absalom and the elders of Israel. The outcome of the military battle in the next chapter is determined here. Much of the account of David's departure was preparatory to this, in particular, the encounters with the priests and Hushai.

Ahithophel gives two pieces of advice to Absalom. The first is for Absalom to lie with David's concubines to proclaim a complete break with his father (16:21). The second is to pursue David immediately with twelve thousand soldiers (17:1-3).

In the war council, Ahithophel makes the very sound proposal to attack and kill David immediately. With no one else to turn to, he says, the whole country would embrace Absalom. If this "good counsel" (v. 14) had been followed, it is likely that David, whose large group was indeed *weary and exhausted* (16:14), would have been destroyed. However, Absalom decides to hear the opinion of Hushai also. He trusts him enough to hear him, but, sensibly, not enough to invite him to take part in the deliberations of the war council.

Hushai gives a vivid, time-consuming speech full of similes, making a proposal which is flattering to Absalom as leader of *all Israel,* but which will let David regroup and choose his own time and place of battle with his experienced, trained force. Hushai apparently then withdraws as the council considers the proposals. Hushai knows that if Ahithophel's advice is accepted there will be no time to lose, so even before he hears the results of the deliberations, he sends word to David that he should at least cross the Jordan River.

However, the council rejects Ahithophel's "good" counsel in favor of Hushai's counsel, and we are specifically told that this rejection was the work of the Lord (v. 14). The poor decision seals Absalom's doom. When Absalom does finally gather his army and go after David, David is already in Mahanaim in Gilead, with the forest of Ephraim between him and Absalom.

16:20 *And Absalom said to Ahithophel,*
"Give your (pl.) advice. What shall we do?"
21 *And Ahithophel said to Absalom,*
"Go in to your father's concubines,
whom he has left to keep the house,
and all Israel will hear
that you have made yourself odious to your father.
And the hands of all who are with you will be strengthened."
22 *And they pitched a tent for Absalom on the roof.*
And Absalom went in to his father's concubines in the sight of all Israel.
23 *Now the advice of Ahithophel, which he gave in those days, was as if one inquired of the word of God; so was all the advice of Ahithophel regarded both by David and by Absalom.*
17:1 *And Ahithophel said to Absalom,*
"Let me choose twelve thousand men
so that I may start pursuing David tonight
2 *and attack*[212] *him, while he is weary and exhausted.*[213]
Then I will terrify him,
and all the people who are with him will flee.
Then I will strike down only the king
3 *so that I may bring back all the people to you.*
When everyone returns, all the people will be at peace,
for it is that man whom you are seeking."
4 *And the matter was acceptable in the eyes of Absalom and all the elders of Israel.*

21 To *go in to your father's concubines* (15:16) may have been claiming the rights of a king (see on 12:8, also 1 K. 2:22), but in any case, David could hardly have a reconciliation with Absalom after this flagrant adultery, actually the rape of his wives. Absalom's followers would know that the die was cast, and

212. Lit. "come upon."
213. Lit. "weak of both hands."

the hands of all who are with you will be strengthened. This incident is clearly pointed to in 12:11. Was the *roof* (v. 22) the one from which David saw Bathsheba (11:2)?

For the expression *you have made yourself odious to*, see on 1 Sam. 13:4; 27:12; 2 Sam. 10:6. Compare "*you have made a complete break with your father*" (Anderson).

23 The high estimation of Ahithophel's advice suggests that Hushai has a difficult task before him, in which he can succeed only with the help of the Lord.

1-3 Ahithophel's counsel, as Bergen notes, incorporated "three hallmarks of classic military strategy: use of overwhelming force, the element of surprise, and a narrowly focused objective.[214] *Let me choose* (yqtl) *twelve thousand men - that I may start pursuing* (lit. "arise and pursue": *w yqtl* + *w yqtl*) - *and attack* (*w yqtl*) =(then)⇒ *I will terrify* (*weqtl*) *him — and all the people . . . will flee* (*weqtl*). *Then I will strike* (*weqtl*) *only the king - so that I may bring back* (*w yqtl*). Thus, in this chain of actions, the initial action in *yqtl* ("to choose") is succeeded by three *weqtl*, while all the others in *w yqtl* comprise *subordinate clauses*. The *inchoative* use of *qwm[215] supports the translation *start pursuing*; also "set out . . . in pursuit of" (NIV, JPS); "set out and pursue" (NRSV). See the commentary on 1 Sam. 17:48; 26:5.[216] One notes that in Ahithophel's proposal he himself is the leader in everything, from choosing the men to bringing the people back.

3 The syntax of this verse is rather complicated; the literal translation of the MT would be as follows:

> and I will bring back all the people to you,
> when the all returns the man whom you are seeking
> all the people will be at peace.

Scholars since Thenius have emended the Hebrew text's first line according to the LXX by reading *kallāh* ("bride") instead of MT *hakkōl* ("the all"), and translating: "as a bride comes back to her husband." Barthelemy and Ehrlich have objected to this emendation, because the text has *'îš* ("husband" or "man"), while the normal word for "bridegroom" is *ḥātān*.[217] However, here, probably the noun *hā'îš* ("the man") in the second line has been preposed to the word *'ăšer* for emphasis, hence the translation *for it is that*

214. Bergen, pp. 411-12.

215. See F. W. Dobbs-Allsopp, "Ingressive *qwm* in Biblical Hebrew," *ZAH* 8 (1995) 31-54.

216. Tsumura, I, pp. 464, 598, etc.

217. See Barthélemy's view and McCarter's objection to it; McCarter, II, p. 381.

man whom you are seeking. Moreover, it may be suggested that this clause, which is a noun clause used as an adverb, is inserted as a whole between the temporal phrase *when everyone returns* and the main clause *all the people will be at peace*.[218]

c. *Hushai's Advice (17:5-14)*

5 *And Absalom said,*
"Call[219] *Hushai the Archite also*
that we may hear what he, too, has to say."
6 *And Hushai came to Absalom.*
And Absalom said to him,
"This is what Ahithophel has said;
shall we do as he said?
If not, you tell us."
7 *And Hushai said to Absalom,*
"This time the advice that Ahithophel has given
is not good."
8 *And Hushai said,*
"You know your father and his men,
that they are warriors
and that they are embittered
like a bear robbed of her cubs in the field.
And your father is a man of war;
he will not spend the night with the people.
9 *Even now, he has hid himself in one of the pits,*
or in another place.
And when someone falls into them[220] *at first,*
whoever hears it will say,
'There has been a slaughter
among the people who follow Absalom.'
10 *And he, even a valiant one*
whose heart is like the heart of a lion,
will faint completely;

218. Tsumura, I, pp. 60-64.

219. The pl. verb "we may hear" does not make the sg. impv. "call" in MT an inferior reading in comparison with LXX, which has a pl. impv. (so Hoffner). Absalom orders someone (sg.) to summon Hushai so that he and members of the council ("we" pl.) could hear his advice.

220. I.e., "into the pits"; cf. "he falls on them at the first attack" (NASB); "some of our troops fall at the first attack" (NRSV).

for all Israel knows that your father is a warrior
and that those who are with him are valiant men.
11 *I truly advise you*
that all Israel be surely gathered to you,
from Dan to Beersheba,
in abundance as the sand that is by the sea;
and that you go into battle[221] *in person.*
12 *Then we shall come to him*
in one of the places where he may be found;
then we shall fall on him
as the dew falls on the ground;
and of him and of all the men who are with him,
not even one will be left.
13 *And if he withdraws into a city,*
then all Israel will bring ropes to that city,
and we shall drag it into the valley
until not even the smallest stone is found there."
14 *And Absalom and all the men of Israel said,*
"The advice of Hushai the Archite is better
than the advice of Ahithophel."
For the LORD had ordained to break the good advice of Ahithophel, in order that the LORD might bring disaster to Absalom.

5-14 These verses contain the longest speech in the story of Absalom's rebellion, and the episode serves as a dramatic turning point.[222] The incident was critical in the history of the united monarchy.[223] While Ahithophel's advice is straightforward and terse, that of Hushai is full of similes. The former is "an unembellished string of verbs":[224] *choose . . . start pursuing . . . attack . . . testify . . . strike . . . bring back.* It is not only terse and short in form, but advises terse and immediate action. On the other hand, the latter is nearly triple in length, suggesting a slowing down of the action.

5 The phrase *what he, too, has to say* (*mah-bᵉpîw gam-hûʾ*) is literally, "what is in his mouth, also he," *gam-hûʾ* being emphatic.

8-10 *And Hushai said* — This is an example of "repeated introduction to speech"; see the commentary on 15:4.

221. Cf. "among them" (McCarter), based on LXX^B.

222. For a structural analysis of Hushai's speech, see Bar-Efrat, "Some Observations on the Analysis of Structure in Biblical Narrative," pp. 170-71.

223. Bergen, p. 412.

224. S.-M. S. Park, "The Frustration of Wisdom: Wisdom, Counsel, and Divine Will in 2 Samuel 17:1-23," *JBL* 128 (2009) 458.

With the metaphor *like a bear robbed of her cubs in the field*, compare Hos. 13:8 and Prov. 17:12.

As Bar-Efrat has shown, Hushai's speech contains many phrases and terms that appear in the narrative of David's early years (e.g., "warriors" [2 Sam. 23:8], "embittered" [1 Sam. 22:2], "bear" [1 Sam. 17:36], and "a man of war" [1 Sam. 16:18]).[225]

11 While in v. 1-3 Ahithophel proposed that he himself do everything, Hushai recommends that Absalom himself lead all of Israel into battle. The verbal form *yāʿaṣtî* is a *performative* perfect, hence the translation *I advise*, rather than "I advised."

The expression *from Dan to Beersheba* is a merismatic expression for greater Israel; see 1 Sam. 3:20. The phrase implies that Judah as well as Israel was involved in the revolt; see on 2 Sam. 15:6.

For the metaphor *as the sand that is by the sea*, see 1 Sam. 13:5.

13 Cities were often attacked by pulling down their walls by means of *ropes* attached to grappling hooks. As they were usually built on high places, once their stones were dragged *into the valley*, they were hard to rebuild. For attacking a city to get one person who had fled there, see 1 Sam. 23:7-13 and 2 Sam. 20:14-22.

14 Thus, both the style and content of Hushai's advice convinced Absalom and his men. However, the choice of Hushai's advice by Absalom and *all the men of Israel*, presumably including some experienced fighting men, was divinely influenced, for the narrator comments that *the LORD had ordained to break* Ahithophel's advice. This was clearly an answer to David's prayer in 15:31 (*Please make the counsel of Ahithophel foolish, O LORD!*). But beyond that, his purpose was to destroy Absalom, thus defeating his rebellion.

d. Hushai Warns David (17:15-23)

15 *And Hushai said to the priests Zadok and Abiathar,*
"This is what Ahithophel advised Absalom
and the elders of Israel;
and this is what I myself have advised.
16 *And now, send quickly and tell David,*
'Do not spend the night
at the steppes of the wilderness,
but by all means cross over,
lest the king and all the people who are with him

225. S. Bar-Efrat, *Narrative Art in the Bible* (JSOTSS 70; Sheffield: Almond Press, 1989), pp. 231-32.

be swallowed up.'"

17 *Now Jonathan and Ahimaaz were waiting at En-rogel; a maidservant was to go and tell them, who in turn were to go and tell King David, for they were not to be seen entering the city.*

18 *And a boy saw them and told Absalom; so the two of them went quickly and came to the house of a man in Bahurim who had a well in his courtyard and went down into it.*

19 *And the woman took and spread a covering over the well*[226] *and scattered crushed (barley) on it so that nothing would be known.*

20 *And Absalom's servants came to the woman at the house and said,*
"Where are Ahimaaz and Jonathan?"
And the woman said to them,
"They have passed over the bank of the water."
And they searched but could not find them; so they returned to Jerusalem.

21 *After they had gone, they came up out of the well and went and told King David. They said to David,*
"Start crossing the water quickly,
for thus Ahithophel has advised against you."

22 *And David and all the people who were with him started crossing the Jordan; by daybreak not even one was lacking who had not crossed the Jordan.*

23 *As for Ahithophel, when he saw that his advice was not accepted, he saddled the donkey and went off to his house in his city and gave orders concerning his house and hanged himself. He died and was buried in the grave of his father.*

16 For the clause *lest the king . . . be swallowed up* (*pen y^ebulla' lammelek*), McCarter suggests the translation "disaster will befall the king," following Guillaume's view[227] that compares the verb *y^ebulla'* with Arabic *balaǵa*, which "refers to exertion."[228] However, the issue here is not so much whether the verbal etymology is *blʿ (I) "to swallow" or *blʿ (II) "to reach" as the interpretation of the preposition *la-* of *lammelek*. Though the meaning is clear, and while Driver would take *l* as the *nota accusativi*,[229] I would rather take it as a case for *ergativity* in Biblical Hebrew, where the "subject" of an intransitive verb, here in passive, is introduced by an *ergative* marker *l*. See the commentary on 1 Sam. 9:9.[230]

226. Lit. "surface of the well"; cf. "well's mouth" (NASB, NRSV), following other MSS.

227. A. Guillaume, "Short Notes," VT 12 (1962) 321.

228. McCarter, II, p. 388.

229. Driver, p. 324.

230. See Tsumura, I, p. 267 n. 25; p. 508 n. 46; G. R. Driver, "Hebrew Notes," *ZAW* 52 (1934) 52.

17 David had given instructions concerning *Jonathan and Ahimaaz* in 15:27. The spring *En-rogel,* known now as "Job's Well," is just south of where the Kidron Valley meets the Hinnom Valley. It was on the boundary between Judah and Benjamin (Josh. 15:7; 18:16). As it would be dangerous for the priests' sons, apparently known supporters of David (v. 18), to be seen in Jerusalem, a necessary link in the chain from Hushai to David is the female servant, probably a maid in the household of one of the priests, whose normal duties took her to the water.

Weqtl (*waw*+pf.) in the sentence *wᵉhālᵉkāh haššipḥāh wᵉhiggîdāh* is frequentative.[231] It usually represents a normal activity, as Absalom's in 15:2-5. However, as it must have been the first time the system was used, here it explains the procedure[232] by which communication was to be maintained between David and his friends in Jerusalem. Hence the translation, *a maidservant was to go and tell.*

18-20 This episode has been compared with the story of Rahab and the spies in Joshua 2. While Van Seters argues for Samuel's direct literary dependence, Gunn and McCarter take this as "a case of the influence of a traditional story pattern on the composition of an original *literary* work."[233]

18 For *Bahurim,* see also 16:5; see the commentary on 3:16.

19 The etymology and meaning of the rare term *rīpôt* (here, translated as *crushed* [*barley*]), which is found only here and in Prov. 27:22, are not clear; cf. "groats" (JPS). See *HALOT*, p. 1227. J. Naveh thinks it may be the same as the *dqyr* in Aramaic inscription #7-11 from Arad.[234]

20 The MT phrase *over the bank of the water* (*mîkal hammāyim*) has been explained variously. The "water" must be the Jordan, but the meaning of *mîkal* is not clear. McCarter translates the phrase as "in the direction of the watercourse," tentatively reading it as *miyyebal hammayim.* However, in the light of *klw "bank of a river," Ar. *kallā',*[235] the term *mîkal* probably has something to do with the riverbank.[236]

23 Ahithophel is wise enough to realize the rejection of his advice means the defeat of Absalom and his own ruin. Ahithophel's city is Giloh (15:12). He instructed the servants about what to do with his property; "put his household in order" (KJV).

231. GKC §112k n. 4; Driver, p. 324.

232. Tsumura, "Tense and Aspect of Hebrew Verbs in II Samuel VII 8-16," pp. 641-54; Tsumura, "Temporal Consistency and Narrative Cohesion in 2 Sam. 7:8-11," pp. 385-92. See also the commentary on 7:8-16 (above).

233. McCarter, II, pp. 388-89.

234. See J. Naveh, in Aharoni, *AI*, pp. 156-57.

235. See Beilla, *DOSA*, p. 246.

236. For various versions, see McCarter, II, p. 383; Driver, p. 325.

4. David Arrives at Mahanaim (17:24-29)

24 *David came to Mahanaim; on the other hand*[237] *Absalom crossed the Jordan with all the men of Israel with him.*

25 *As for Amasa, Absalom set him over the army in place of Joab. Amasa was the son of a man whose name was Ithra the Israelite, who went into Abigal, the daughter of Nahash and the sister of Zeruiah, the mother of Joab.*

26 *And Israel and Absalom camped in the land of Gilead.*

27 *Now when David had come to Mahanaim,*
Shobi the son of Nahash from Rabbah of the Ammonites,
Machir the son of Ammiel from Lo-debar,
and Barzillai the Gileadite from Rogelim
28 *brought*[238]
beds,[239] *basins, and pottery;*
wheat, barley, flour, and parched grain;
beans, lentils, and parched seed;[240]
29 *honey and curds, sheep, and cheese of the herd*
for David and for the people who were with him, to eat;
for they thought[241] *that the people would be hungry and weary and thirsty in the wilderness.*

24-29 The Transjordanian area around *Mahanaim*, a city in the deep canyon of the Jabbok River, was the seat of Ishbosheth's government in his long struggle with David; see the commentary on 2:8-9.[242] But now David finds here a haven and support for his struggle against his son Absalom.

24 As Hushai had suggested, Absalom gathers "all the men of Israel" and goes after David.

25 Amasa, David's nephew, son of his sister Abigal (see on 2:13), so Absalom's cousin, appears for the first time. His support was important for Absalom's revolt in the south. After the revolt, he was appointed over David's army (19:13).

Ithra (*yitrā'*) sounds like an Amaraic name with a determinative suffix -*ā'*. It appears in the shorter form *yeter* "Jether" in 1 Chr. 2:17.[243] For the MT

237. The word order of the verse is: *waw*+NP V(pf.) *waw*+NP V(pf.).

238. Heb. *higgîšû* "they brought in close" (v. 29).

239. Cf. "sleeping couches with embroidered covers" (McCarter, II, p. 392), based on LXX^B.

240. Cf. McCarter, II, p. 392, omits "and parched seed" "on authority of" LXX and Syr.; so NRSV, NIV.

241. Lit. "they said."

242. *SB*, p. 163; also see *CBA*, #109.

243. For this name, see M. Broshi and A. Yardeni, "On *netinim* and False Prophets," in Zevit, *Solving Riddles and Untying Knots*, p. 31.

the Israelite (*hayyiśrᵉʾēlî*), LXX^A has "the Ishmaelite," which is in keeping with *hayyišmᵉʿēʾlî* (1 Chr. 2:17).[244] The phrase "the Yisraelite" was possibly supplied by the narrator in order to make it clear that *Ithra* has an Israelite background, despite his Amaraic-sounding name. On the other hand, as Na'aman suggests, the gentilic *yiśrᵉʾēlî* might be a variant form of *ʾaśrᵉʾēlî* (an Asraelite), which indicates that Amasa son of *Ithra* was "a member of a neighbouring Manassite clan located north of Ephraim's tribal territory."[245] However, based on the fact that an interchange of initial /ya-/ (> /yi-/) and /ʾa-/ (> /ʾi-/) in Ugaritic appears, e.g., in *KTU* 1.14 I 8 (*itdb*) and 24 (*yitbd*);[246] II 43 (*yḥd*) and IV 21 (*aḥd*), etc.;[247] it may well be that *yiśrᵉʾēlî* is a variant form of *ʾiśrᵉʾēlî*, which means "an Isra'elite."

Ithra may have had a special type of marital relationship with his wife *Abigal*, as indicated by the verbal phrase *went in to* (*bāʾ ʾel-*). McCarter compares this marriage with "the *sadiqa* marriage of the ancient Arabs, according to the terms of which the woman remained with her children in her parents' home and received periodic visits from the man (Smith, Hertzberg)."[248] Samson's marriage to the Philistine woman in Timnah in Judg. 14 may also have been this type of marriage.

The spelling of *Abigal* (*ʾăbîgal*) might be explained as a case of a vowel *sandhi*[249] : ai → a, rather than the result of *contraction* of diphthong /ai/ to /a/, like in Eblaite, instead of the usual /ē/ (so McCarter).[250]

For Abigal's parentage see on 2:13.

27 *Shobi the son of Nahash from Rabbah of the Ammonites* apparently was the brother of Hanun, the king of Ammon (10:2). David probably had set him on the throne in place of his brother (12:30). It is remarkable he did not try to revolt at this time, so he must have had a good relationship with David.

Machir had sheltered Mephibosheth in his childhood in *Lo-debar* (9:4). *Burzillai* later accompanies David on his trip back to Jerusalem (19:31-39). The fact that these people came from a distance suggests that David had real support in the area of Gilead. Perhaps being neither Judahite nor Ephraimite they could appreciate more than others David's efforts at unification.

244. See Levenson and Halpern, "The Political Import of David's Marriages," p. 512. Also Anderson, p. 219.

245. N. Na'aman, "Amasa the Asrielite (2 Samuel 17,25)," *Semitica* 57 (2015) 177-83.

246. Tsumura, "The Problem of Childlessness in the Royal Epic of Ugarit," p. 16.

247. See Tsumura, "Prologue of the Keret Epic," *Studies in Literature and Linguistics: Linguistics* 9 (University of Tsukuba, 1984), p. 54 [in Japanese].

248. McCarter, II, p. 393.

249. See Tsumura, "Vowel *sandhi* in Biblical Hebrew," pp. 575-88.

250. On this form of the name, see Tsumura, I, p. 591 n. 81.

28-29 The items they brought are given in a list-like format; see the commentaries on 1 Sam. 6:17-18a.[251]

29 The items *honey and curds* (*d^{e}baš - ḥemʾāh*) also appear in Job 20:17 and in Isa. 7:15, 22 (in reverse order). Since a construct chain, A of B, sometimes appears as a word pair, A and B, McCarter translates *w^{e}ḥemʾāh w^{e}ṣōʾn* ("curds and flocks") as "the curd of the flocks" on the basis of Syr., like the immediately following phrase, *cheese of the herd* (*š^{e}pôt bāqār*), taking the two phrases as parallel.[252] The term *š^{e}pôt* designates "a foodstuff such as hard cheese or curd cheese made from cow's milk" (see *HALOT*, p. 1620).

5. Absalom's Death (18:1–19:8)

a. The King's Order (18:1-5)

1 *And David mustered the people who were with him and set over them commanders of thousands and commanders of hundreds.*

2 *And David sent the people out,*[253] *one third under the command of Joab, one third under the command of Abishai the son of Zeruiah, Joab's brother, and one third under the command of Ittai the Gittite.*

And the king said to the people,
"I myself will surely go out with you too."

3 *And the people said,*
"You should not go out
—for even if we indeed flee,
they will not pay attention to us;
and even if half of us die,
they will not pay attention to us —
but you are now worth ten thousand of us!
So now it is better
that you should be helping us from the city."

4 *And the king said to them,*
"Whatever seems best to you I will do."

And the king stood by the side of the gate, while all the people went out by hundreds and by thousands.

5 *And the king ordered Joab and Abishai and Ittai,*
"Deal gently for my sake with the young man Absalom."

251. Tsumura, I, pp. 223-24, etc.; see entry for "list formula" on p. 662 of the index.

252. McCarter, II, p. 394; Driver, p. 327.

253. For the verb *sent . . . out* (*wayšallaḥ*), a different reading *wyšlš* "divided into three" (McCarter, NRSV) has been suggested on the basis of LXX^L.

And all the people heard when the king ordered all the commanders concerning Absalom.

2-3 David's men, like Ahithophel (17:2-3), believe that the success or failure of the rebellion depends on whether David is killed.

2 A threefold division of an army appears also in Judg. 7:16; 9:43; 1 Sam. 11:11; and 13:17 as well as in Mari records.[254]

Abishai is already known to the audience, but the phrase *Joab's brother* is added to stress Joab's importance in the events.[255]

3 The particle *kî* in the phrase *but you are now* (*kî-ʿattāh*) means "but" after the negative expression *You should not go out*. The sentence *for even if . . . to us* may be taken as an insertion between these two clauses. Some scholars use the reading *ʾattā* found in two MSS (BHS) instead of *ʿattāh* and translate the phrase "But you are."

Here, the K. *laʿzîr* is generally taken as a simple misspelling that the Q. corrects with the normal grammatical form *laʿzôr* (Qal. inf. cstr.: "to help"). However, the K. seems to reflect the actual pronunciation, resulting from the distant assimilation of the *ô* to the preceding *mēʿîr*.[256]

4 For the expression *by the side of* (*ʾel-yad*), see the commentary on 1 Sam. 4:18.[257]

5 *Deal gently* is the impv. of *lʾṭ; see 1 Sam. 18:22; 2 Sam. 19:4. McCarter translates it as "Protect," in the light of *lwṭ "cover, veil." David seems to have made the request out of pure fatherly love, or perhaps with also a feeling of guilt toward him, for *the young man* (*naʿar*) is a term with an affectionate tone. But it seems unlikely that the narrator had an agenda of absolving David from involvement in Absalom's death, because unlike the case of Abner and Ishbosheth, hardly anyone would have criticized David even if he had not tried to save him.

b. Absalom Killed (18:6-17)

6 *And the people went out into the field against Israel, and the battle took place in the forest of Ephraim.*

7 *And the people of Israel were defeated there before the servants of David, and the slaughter there was great on that day, 20,000 men.*

254. See Tsumura, I, p. 311.

255. C. Conroy, *Absalom Absalom! Narrative and Language in 2 Sam 13-20* (AnBi 81; Rome: Pontifical Biblical Institute, 1978), p. 56; see McCarter, II, p. 404.

256. See Tsumura, "Scribal Errors or Phonetic Spellings," pp. 394-96, 401-9; also Tsumura, "Textual Corruptions, or Linguistic Phenomena?," p. 138.

257. Tsumura, I, p. 199.

8 *And the battle there spread over the face of all the country.*
And the forest devoured more people that day than the sword devoured.
9 *And Absalom appeared before the servants of David.*
While Absalom was riding on his mule, the mule went under the thick branches of a great oak.
And his head caught fast in the oak and he was set[258] *between heaven and earth,*[259] *while the mule that was under him went on.*
10 *And a certain man saw it and told Joab,*[260]
"I saw Absalom hanging in an oak."
11 *And Joab said to the man who had told him,*
"Now you saw him!
Why did you not strike him there to the ground?
I would have had
to give you ten pieces of silver
and one belt."
12 *And the man said to Joab,*
"Even if I were weighing a thousand shekels of silver
on my palm,
I would not lay my hand on the king's son,
for in our hearing[261] *the king commanded*
you and Abishai and Ittai,
'Protect for my sake the young man Absalom.'
13 *Otherwise I would have dealt treacherously with his life,*[262]
but nothing is hidden from the king,
though you may stand aloof."
14 *And Joab said,*
"It is not good for me to wait before you!"
and took three spears in his hand and thrust them into the heart of Absalom, while he was still alive in the midst of the oak.
15 *And ten young men, Joab's armor-bearers, surrounded and struck Absalom and killed him.*
16 *And Joab blew the trumpet.*
And the people returned from pursuing Israel, for Joab held them in check.
17 *And they took Absalom and cast him into the great pit in the forest and erected over him a very great heap of stones.*
As for all Israel, they fled, each to his own tent.

258. *ntn: Qal passive: lit. "it was given."
259. Cf. "in midair" (NIV).
260. Lit. "told . . . and said"; see Introduction in Tsumura, I, pp. xi-xii.
261. Lit. "in our ears."
262. Cf. "my life" (Q.).

6-8 The *forest of Ephraim* was actually not in the tribal territory of Ephraim, but east of the Jordan in Gilead.[263] Gilead was apparently known for its forests (Jer. 22:6). Here David's experienced army is at an advantage against even a much larger force of newly raised men, most of whom were apparently unable even to move around effectively in a forest.

7 *20,000 men* (*ʿeśrîm ʾālep*) may mean "20 units," since the term *ʾelep* can be a military unit. See 2 Sam. 6:1; also the commentary on 1 Sam. 4:2 and 6:19.[264]

8 The phrase *and the forest devoured more people . . . than* (literally "and the forest multiplied to eat the people than") means that more people perished in the forest.

9-10 The phrase *appeared before* (*qrʾ* [ni.] *lipnê*) is possibly the Ni. of *qrʾ "to call," which might mean "to appear" like the Ni. of *mṣʾ "to find," though the majority view is to take the verb as a by-form of *qrh* "to meet" and translate as "happened to meet" (NASB, NRSV, NIV); "encountered" (JPS). Compare "was far ahead of" (McCarter), on the basis of LXX^L.

As for *while Absalom was riding,* the participle *rōkēb* with a preceding subject suggests that this is a subordinate clause, providing background information for the following events: *the mule went . . . and his head caught fast . . . and he was set,* all in *wayqtl* form.

Mules were the normal mounts of the king's sons (13:29).

The term *thick branches* (*śôbek*) is a *hapax legomenon.* It may mean "the tangled branches" (JPS) in the light of Arabic *šabaka* "entangle, intertwine."

The Hebrew expression *his head caught fast* suggests simply that his head was caught in the branches of the tree.[265] However, from Josephus (*Ant.* 7.239) on, it has been popularly understood that the hair on which he prided himself (see 14:26) got tangled in the branches and caused his undoing. This understanding has led J. S. Ackerman to make the farfetched association of Absalom with the ram caught in a thicket in Abraham's trial (Gen 22:13).[266]

Brueggeman, who uses a literary and theological approach, thinks that the text here is "very difficult" and suggests that the "obscurity may reflect the reticence of the narrator or the inability of the tradition to express what in fact happened, because it is so dark and ominous."[267] But the Hebrew text here has no textual problem and there is no reason why Brueggemann should say

263. See *CBA,* #110. For a detailed topographical and ecological description of the area, see Hutton, "Over the River and Through the Woods," pp. 111-23.

264. Tsumura, I, pp. 189-90, 226-27.

265. See also Hutton, "Over the River and Through the Woods," p. 117.

266. Ackerman, "Knowing Good and Evil," p. 50.

267. W. Brueggemann, *First and Second Samuel* (Interpretation: A Bible Commentary for Teaching and Preaching; Louisville: John Knox, 1990), p. 318.

it is "a very difficult text." The term "head" in Hebrew (as in Japanese) could stand by synecdoche for "hair."[268] So, the explanation, "That obscurity may" is utter nonsense. If such is a "theological" comment, one can do so only by reading one's own ideas into the ancient text without a solid basis.

In v. 10 Absalom is described as "hanging," but it may be too much to see here a reference to the curse of Deut. 21:23 as Bergen does.[269]

11 For the MT *ten pieces of silver* (*ʿăśārāh kesep*), "fifty" pieces has been suggested based on LXX^L, Josephus, *Ant.* 7.240, and 4QSam^a. The last reads [*ḥm*]*šym*[270] which is taken as a Proto-Lucianic reading by DJD 17, p. 165. The term *silver* refers to a "shekel" weight of silver, not to coined money. *Ten pieces of silver* is equivalent of "ten shekels of silver."[271]

12 *Protect for my sake* (*šimrû-mî*); so NIV, NRSV, NASB; cf. "Be careful" (McCarter). McCarter takes the particle *-mî* as an *enclitic mem* like the Akkadian particle (*-mi*) for direct speech.[272] However, the MT form could reflect a phonetic spelling[273] in which the original form *šimrû-lî* ("protect for me") experienced the following phonetic change:

šimrû-lî → *šimruw-lî* → *šimruw-mî*

(The *m* in the final change is the result of partial assimilation of [l] to a bilabial [w]k.)

14 The narrator stresses repeatedly (vv. 5 and 12) that David had ordered all the troops to spare Absalom. Joab probably worries that Absalom, who had risen from disgrace once before, even using Joab, might be able to cause problems again.

The Hebrew term *šᵉbāṭîm* is translated variously: "spears," "javelins," "darts." But McCarter thinks if they were darts or the like, it would not take ten men to kill Absalom later. Therefore he takes it as a bunch of stout sticks Joab used to dislodge him from the tree. He also suggests Joab ordered a whole group to kill him so no one person could be blamed.[274]

268. Also Firth, 477. In Japanese, "to wash one's hair" is literally expressed as "to wash one's head" [*atama* "head" *wo arau* "to wash"].

269. Bergen, p. 421.

270. See DJD 17, pp. 163-65.

271. A. R. Millard, "Are There Anachronisms in the Books of Samuel?" in *Studies on the Text and Versions of the Hebrew Bible in Honour of Robert Gordon*, ed. G. Khan and D. Lipton (VTS 149; Leiden: E. J. Brill, 2012), pp. 39-48. See also F. H. Polak, "Conceptions of the Past and Sociocultural Grounding in the Books of Samuel," in *History, Memory, Hebrew Scriptures: A Festschrift for Ehud Ben Zvi*, ed. I. D. Wilson and D. V. Edelman (Winona Lake, Ind.: Eisenbrauns, 2015), p. 119.

272. For different views, see McCarter, II, p. 401.

273. See Tsumura, "Scribal Errors or Phonetic Spellings?" 401-9; Tsumura, "Textual Corruptions, or Linguistic Phenomena?" 138.

274. McCarter, II, p. 407.

17 It was the custom for *a very great heap of stones* to mark the burial place of an accursed man, as Achan in Josh. 7:26 and the defeated kings in Josh. 8:29; 10:27.

The expression *each to his own tent* (*’îš l^{e}’ōholâw*) is a cliché that means to leave military service either because the army is no longer needed and hence is discharged (Judg. 7:8; 20:8; 1 Sam. 13:2; 2 Sam. 20:1, 22) or as a result of flight upon defeat (1 Sam. 4:10; 2 Sam. 19:8; 2 K. 14:12).

x. Absalom's Pillar (18:18)

18 — *Now Absalom in his lifetime took*[275] *and set up for himself a pillar which is in the King's Valley, for he said,*
"I have no son to preserve my name."
And he named the pillar after his name.
And it is called Absalom's monument to this day —

The author contrasts the memorial pillar with his actual tomb, a big pile of rocks.

The preceding episode ended with v. 17b (*As for all Israel, they fled, each to his own tent*), while v. 19 initiates a new paragraph concerning the report of Absalom's death to David. Thus the present verse is a LINK between two episodes.

Gaster as well as Cassuto[276] compares the *pillar* (*maṣṣebet*) with "the stele of his family deity" (*skn . ilibh*) as in the Ugaritic cult of the dead.[277] However, a crucial difference is that while in the cult the stele is built by a descendant, Absalom set up his own pillar as a replacement for a descendant, not as a means for a descendant to care for his spirit. The *King's Valley* is "usually located at the confluence of the Kidron and the Valley of Hinnom, south of the City of David" (McCarter). The term *monument* is literally "hand"; see 1 Sam. 15:12 for *yad* as a stele that symbolizes victory, conquest, or ownership.[278]

The "Absalom's Tomb" now seen in the Kidron Valley in Jerusalem is a Hellenistic or Roman-period structure and there is no confirmation that it sits on Absalom's ancient gravesite.

The statement *I have no son to preserve my name* contradicts with the

275. For this use of the verb "to take" (*lqḥ), see 17:19.

276. U. Cassuto, "Daniel et son fils dans la tablette IID de Ras Shamra," *Revue des études juives* 105 (1939) 126-27.

277. See Rainey, "Institutions: Family, Civil, and Military," pp. 78-79; see also E. M. Bloch-Smith, "The Cult of the Dead in Judah: Interpreting the Material Remains," *JBL* 111 (1992) 221-22.

278. Tsumura, I, pp. 396-97.

note, *to Absalom there were born three sons,* in 2 Sam. 14:27. It may be that Absalom's three sons died young.[279]

c. Man of Tidings (18:19-23)

19 *When Ahimaaz son of Zadok said,*
"Let me run,
that I may bring the news to the king
that the Lord has delivered him justly
from the hand of his enemies,"
20 *Joab said to him,*
"You are not the man of tidings today.
You shall bring news another day;
but today you shall not bring news,
for[280] *the king's son is dead."*
21 *And Joab said to the Cushite,*
"Go, tell the king what you have seen."
And the Cushite[281] *bowed to Joab and ran.*
22 *And Ahimaaz the son of Zadok said once more to Joab,*
"Whatever happens,
let me also run after the Cushite."
And Joab said,
"Why are you going to run, my son,
while you have no reward for going?"
23 *(And he said,)*
"Whatever happens, I will run."
And he said to him,
"Run!"
And Ahimaaz ran by the way of the plain and passed the Cushite.

19 Verse 19 begins with a clause of *waw*+NP pf., which serves as a subordinate clause (*When*) to the main clause, which starts at v. 20.

279. Hutzli connects this passage with the religious custom of establishing a stele to remember the deceased and his deeds as well as to make him offerings. See J. Hutzli, "Role and Significance of Ancestors in the Books of Samuel," in Dietrich, *The Books of Samuel,* p. 430.

280. K. *'al*; cf. Q. *'al-kēn.*

281. Heb. *kûšî.* The expected normal form is *hakkûšî.* The form *kûšî* could have resulted from the phonetic adjustment with the preceding word *wayyištaḥû* ("and bowed"), which ends with a long vowel *û*; thus, *wayyištaḥû hakkûšî* —(intervocalic *h* dropped)→ *wayyištaḥû+akkûšî* —(vowel *sandhi*)→ *wayyištaḥû kûšî.* See Tsumura, "Scribal Errors or Phonetic Spellings?" 399-400. The LXX seems to treat the term in this passage as a PN *Chousi Badisas* (= Chousi Wanderer).

The phrase *has delivered . . . justly* (*špṭ*) literally means "has judged"; see also v. 31.

20 It is not clear why Joab did not want Ahimaaz to run. He apparently knows that the death of Absalom will not be good news for the king, something that had not occurred to Ahimaaz. Joab does not seem to be trying to hide anything: "Go tell the king what you have seen" (v. 21).

Bergen surmises that Joab was concerned for Ahimaaz's safety, for Joab remembered David's treatment of previous messengers.[282] But those who had announced Saul's and Ishbosheth's deaths also said they killed them. Perhaps, if rewards were given for good news, one might use less important members of a staff for bad news. But, as McCarter holds, "both Joab and the Cushite thought the news was good and wanted the king to think so too."[283]

21 A *Cushite* is a man from Cush to the south of Egypt. The Hebrew *Kûš* refers to various locations, e.g., Nubia and northern Sudan, Ethiopia (often *Haithiopia* in LXX, but see p. 263 n. 281; Esth. 1:1; 8:9), and somewhere in northern or possibly southeast Mesopotamia[284] (see Gen. 2:13). Here, the man was either a Nubian or an Ethiopian.

22 Ahimaaz use the expression *whatever happens* (*wîhî māh*) in both v. 22 and v. 23. He must have been so excited that he could not resist being the first to bring the good news to the king.

Various suggestions have been made for the MT *bᵉśôrāh mōṣēʾt* ("reward for going"): e.g., " reward for the news" (ESV); " reward for the tidings"(NRSV); "any news that will bring you a reward" (NIV); "no message *finding* or *attaining*, i.e., no message that will secure you a reward" (Driver[285]), etc. The most reasonable seems to be McCarter's "reward for going,"[286] reading the second term as *miṣṣēʾt*, lit. "from going forth," while taking the first as "reward" (so in 4:10), not the ordinary sense "news"; see also *HALOT*, p. 164: "messenger's reward."[287]

23 The expression *and he said*, does not appear in the MT, but is found in the LXX^{BA}, Syr., and Vulg. Though LXX^{LMN} specifies "Ahimaaz" as the subject, in the Hebrew dialogue pattern the subject is not necessary here; see Introduction on "dialogue pattern."

The plain (*hakkikkār*) refers to "the valley of the lower Jordan." While the Cushite went straight across the mountains from *the forest of Ephraim*,

282. Bergen, p. 423.

283. McCarter, II, p. 408.

284. Tsumura, "Rediscovery of the Ancient Near East and Its Implications for Genesis 1-2," p. 235.

285. Driver, p. 331.

286. McCarter, II, p. 409.

287. McCarter, II, pp. 402-3.

probably located toward the northern Gilead southward to Mahanaim, Ahimaaz took the longer but easier road and arrived sooner than the Cushite.[288]

d. David Informed of Absalom's Death (18:24-32)

24 *While David was sitting between the two gates, the watchman went up to the roof of the gate by the wall and lifted up his eyes and saw a man running alone.*

25 *And the watchman called and told the king.*
And the king said,
"If he is alone, there must be news in his mouth."
And he came nearer and nearer.
26 *And the watchman saw another man running.*
And the watchman called to the gatekeeper,[289]
"Behold, another man running alone!"
And the king said,
"This one also must be bringing news."
27 *And the watchman said,*
"I see that the running style of the first one
is like the running style of Ahimaaz son of Zadok."
And the king said,
"This is a good man,
and he must be coming with good news."
28 *And Ahimaaz called to the king,*[290]
"Peace!"
and prostrated himself to the king with his face to the ground and said,
"Blessed be the LORD your God,
who delivered up the men who raised their hand
against my lord the king!"
29 *And the king said,*
"Is the young man Absalom all right?"
And Ahimaaz said,
"I saw a great tumult
when Joab sent the king's servant,
your servant.
I don't know what it was."

288. Driver, pp. 331–32; McCarter, II, p. 409. Hutton, "Over the River and Through the Woods," pp. 105-27.

289. Lit. "called to . . . and said"; see Tsumura, I. p. xii.

290. Lit. "called and said to."

30 *And the king said,*
"Turn aside
and stand here."
And he turned aside and stood still.
31 *Then the Cushite came.*
And the Cushite said,
"May my lord the king receive good news,
for the LORD *has delivered you justly this day,*
from the hand of all who rose against you."
32 *And the king said to the Cushite,*
"Is the young man Absalom all right?"
And the Cushite said,
"May the enemies of my lord the king
and all who rise against you for evil
be like that young man!"

24 The *two gates* are the outer gate and the inner gate of the city's gate complex.

25 A man running alone would be a messenger; a group would probably be men fleeing.

27 David's comment which associates *a good man* with *good news* reminds us of 1 K. 1:42 ("you are a worthy man and surely you bring good news"). The "good(ness)" often has a connotation of political loyalty.[291]

29 Ahimaaz must have known Absalom was dead, else he would have just said he did not know anything and would not have brought up the *great tumult*. Furthermore, as S. A. Meier notes, "the ignorance of Ahimaaz would be a key narrative feature, yet up to the delivery of Ahimaaz' message, no clue to the reader of such ignorance ever occurs."[292]

31-32 While the Cushite reports his news as *good*, David is mainly concerned about Absalom's safely. For the phrase *delivered you justly*, see the commentary on v. 19.

The phrase *all who rose against* is a common counterpart of the paired word "enemies" (v. 32). The Cushite here repeats an oath purposely in an indirect way, knowing that his "good" tiding was bad to David who was very much concerned about the life of Absalom.

291. See McCarter, I, p. 322.

292. Meier, *The Messenger in the Ancient Semitic World*, p. 169 n. 16. In pp. 168-79 he deals with deceptive messengers.

e. David Mourns for Absalom (18:33–19:8)

18:33 [MT 19:1] *[here]And the king was deeply moved and went up to the chamber over the gate and wept. And as he walked, he spoke thus:*

"My son Absalom,
my son, my son, Absalom!
I wish I had been the one to die instead of you,
Absalom, my son, my son!"

19:1 [MT 2] *And it was told Joab,*
"The king is now weeping;
he mourns for Absalom."

2 *And the victory that day became mourning for all the people, for the people heard that day,*
"The king is in pain concerning his son."

3 *And the people stole into the city that day, as people do who are humiliated when they flee in battle.*

4 *As for the king he covered his face.*
And the king cried out with a loud voice,
"O my son Absalom,
O Absalom, my son, my son!"

5 *And Joab entered the house to the king and said,*
"Today you have covered with shame
the faces of all your servants,
who today have saved your life,
the lives of your sons and daughters
and the lives of your wives and the lives of your concubines,
6 *by loving those who hate you*
and by hating those who love you.
For you have made it clear[293] *today*
that princes and servants are nothing to you;
for I know today
that if[294] *Absalom were alive and all of us were dead today,*
then you would be pleased.
7 *And now, arise, go out, and speak to the hearts of your servants,*
for I swear by the Lord,
if you do not go out,
not a man will stay with you this night.
This will be worse for you

293. Lit. "you have declared."
294. Following MT (Q.); also 4QSam[a].

than all the evil that has come upon you
from your youth until now."
8 *And the king arose and sat in the gate.*
Now all the people were told,
"See, the king is sitting in the gate!"
And all the people came before the king.
As for Israel, they had fled, each to his own tent.

18:33–19:8 David lets his own grief overcome his kingly responsibilities, and even his gratitude to God for his salvation. The conflict between David as king and David as father is a theme throughout the story of Absalom's rebellion, actually from chapter 13, as well as 1 K. 1:6.

David, *deeply moved* (lit. "trembling with emotion";[295] *rgz: "be agitated"), went up to *the chamber over the gate* (*ʿălîyat haššaʿar*) to mourn for his son Absalom. In this regard, de Ward notes that in the ancient Near East the funeral rites were usually performed beside the corpse or at the grave, but "one stage in mourning, cultic or national or personal, might be passed on roofs."[296] For example, in accordance with Ugaritic funerary practice, King Keret went up to the roof to make sacrifice to the god El; see *KTU* 1.14 II 20-27. However, one cannot say that this is what is involved here. There is no mention of David's performing any rite; he is simply convulsed with emotion. He probably went to the gate chamber because it was the nearest place he could be private. Furthermore, the place he went to is described as a "chamber," as opposed to "the roof of the gate by the wall" in 18:24.

David's lament is highly elevated poetry, a four-line parallelism with the repetition of *my son* (5×) and *Absalom* (3×) and a chiastic structure. The first line is expanded in the second with the additional phrase "my son," which is chiastically repeated in the fourth line. The formal structure emphasizes the degree of David's anguish.[297]

1 This verse is v. 2 in the MT. The verbal form of *he mourns* (*wayyit'abbēl*; lit. "and he mourned") is unusual after a participle. Many modern English translations follow Syr., Targ., and MT (2 MSS)[298] and translate "mourning."

5 Joab as always is very pragmatic and follows his own judgment. His words are basically true, though somewhat exaggerated in order to shock.

Because David has *covered his face* (v. 4) with grief he has *covered with shame the faces* of his loyal servants (v. 5). His joy is their joy; his sorrow is

295. See *HALOT*, p. 1183.
296. De Ward, "Mourning Customs in 1, 2, Samuel," p. 4.
297. Anderson, p. 226.
298. See *BHS* apparatus.

their sorrow. When he sorrows at their actions, he is rejecting them. Joab's words also accuse David of violating the covenant between a king and his subjects — the love of loyalty should be repaid with the love of loyalty. Olyan discusses this in terms of a vassal-suzerain relationship.[299] Hobbs however believes that the metaphor is rather drawn from the patron-client relationship, which was a "more immediate social metaphor than political interactions between kings."[300] However, the relationship here is not that between kings or between patron and client, but the "king-subject" relationship. 1 Sam. 10:25 and 2 Sam. 5:3 seem to imply a covenant.

7 The Hebrew term *nišbaʿtî* for *I swear* is a perfect verb which has a *performative* meaning; see the commentary on 1 Sam. 3:14.[301]

8 At these words, David puts his emotions under control. He makes his peace with his men, behaving as king, sitting in the gate. Kings and elders often are described as sitting at the gate (1 K. 22:10; Jer. 39:3; Deut. 25:7; Ruth 4:11); at the excavations at Dan, a stone object that appears to be a canopy base was found within the Iron Age gate.

Now David has to work on reuniting the country.

6. David's Return to Jerusalem (19:9-43)

The whole country finally agrees they should bring David back, but even this creates problems as it shows up the division between Judah and the rest of Israel. Israel, in this chapter referring to the northern tribes, had spoken with David about his return to Jerusalem, but David has to make a special appeal to Judah. So a Judean contingent comes and accompanies David back, apparently without consultation with the other tribes. At the Jordan David speaks with people connected with his journey in the other direction — Shimei, Ziba, Ziba's master Mephibosheth, and Barzillai, who had welcomed the king in Mahanaim. However, Israel and Judah bicker over the ceremony of David's triumphal return to his capital.

299. Olyan, "Honor, Shame, and Covenant Relations in Ancient Israel and Its Environment," pp. 209-11.

300. T. R. Hobbs, "Reflections on Honor, Shame, and Covenant Relations," *JBL* 116 (1997) 502; see N. P. Lemche, "Kings and Clients: On Loyalty between the Ruler and the Ruled in Ancient 'Israel,'" *Semeia* 66 (1995) 119-32.

301. Tsumura, I, p. 180.

a. Israel's Tribes and Judah (19:9-15)

9 *And all the people were disputing each other in all the tribes of Israel, saying*
"It was the king who delivered us
from the hand of our enemies;
it was he who saved us from the hand of the Philistines.
But now he has fled out of the land
from the side of Absalom.[302]
10 *As for Absalom, whom we anointed over us,*
he is dead in battle.
Now, why are you silent about bringing the king back?"
11 *As for King David, he sent (a messenger) to Zadok and Abiathar the priests, saying*
"Speak to the elders of Judah,
'Why are you the last
to bring the king back to his house,
while the word of all Israel has come to the king,
even to his house?
12 *You are my kin;*
you are my bone and flesh.
Why should you be the last
to bring back the king?'
13 *And to Amasa you shall say*[303]*:*
'Are you not my bone and flesh?
May God do so to me, and more,
if you will not be the army commander
before me
from now on, in place of Joab.'"
14 *Thus the hearts of all the men of Judah were turned as one man.*
And they sent (messengers) to the king, (saying)
"Return, you and all your servants."
15 *And the king returned and came as far as the Jordan.*
As for Judah, they came to Gilgal to go to meet the king and to bring the king across the Jordan.

9 In the following narrative the various groups are competing for the "position in a hierarchy of honor" in a king-people relationship; see above on v. 5.

302. For the textual problem of this phrase *mēʿal ʾabšālôm*, see A. Ravasco, "A Paleographical Note on 2 Sam 19:10 in 4QSam[a]," *RQ* 26 (2014) 461-66.

303. The Hebrew *tōmᵉrû* for *you shall say* is a *phonetic spelling* without *aleph*. See Tsumura, I, pp. 9-10.

For *the tribes of Israel,* see the commentary on 2 Sam. 7:7.

10 There is no explicit mention of Absalom's anointing in the account, but he was probably anointed at the time of the sacrifices during the coronation ceremony at Hebron (15:10-12). David had also been anointed in Hebron, by Judah (2:4) and then by all Israel (5:3). After the phrase, *bringing the king back?* McCarter restores "When the things all Israel was saying reached the king," on the basis of "LXX, OL, and, as space considerations require, 4QSam^a."[304] However, Herbert does not see any "substantial suspicion of deviation" from the MT in 4QSam^a.[305]

11-12 Verses 11a and 12b constitute an envelope structure, in which the phrases "Why are you" and "Why should you" are an *inclusio,* or a frame.[306]

11 Judah, where the revolt began (15:10), was slower in reclaiming David as its king than was Israel. It may be that the Judahites had been divided into pro-and anti-David groups during Absalom's revolt, while the people of Israel had been united.

12 For the phrase *bone and flesh,* which means "my kin" or "my kinsmen" (*DCH,* p. 174), see 2 Sam. 5:1, where the northern tribes use it of David.

13 For *Amasa,* see on 2 Sam. 17:25. To demote the victorious loyal general in favor of the soundly defeated rebel general (17:25) seems shocking. Perhaps David pointed out to Joab that he had disobeyed his specific order about Absalom (18:5). He might have added that if Joab claimed it had been necessary to kill Absalom, he, David, also was doing what was necessary to unite the nation.

For *the army commander,* see 1 Sam. 12:9.[307] For the oath formula *may God do so to me, and more, if,* see on 1 Sam. 3:17.[308]

14 The MT form *wayyaṭ* (*were turned*) is lit. "he turned the hearts of." "He" can stand for David or Amasa, and NRSV translates: "Amasa swayed the hearts." But it seems the agent of the verb "to turn" has been defocused and hence 3 m.s. of the verb is used impersonally[309]: "one turned the hearts of," which means "the hearts of . . . were turned," like Lev. 1:5, *wᵉšāḥaṭ 'et-ben habbāqār lipnê-YHWH* "The bull shall be slaughtered before the LORD"; (NRSV); lit. "and he slaughtered the bull." So there is no need to emend the MT as McCarter does.[310]

304. McCarter, II, p. 415; DJD 17, p. 169.

305. Herbert, *RBDSS,* p. 176. Also see Ravasco, "A Paleographical Note on 2 Sam 19:10 in 4QSam^a," pp. 461-66.

306. Revell, "The Repetition of Introductions to Speech as a Feature of Biblical Hebrew," p. 94 n. 7.

307. Tsumura, I, p. 322.

308. Tsumura, I, p. 182.

309. See Tsumura, I, pp. 132, 134, 253-54.

310. McCarter, II, p. 416.

15 Gilgal was an important cultic center near Jericho and the Jordan River (Josh. 4:19, 5:10; 1 Sam. 10:8, 11:14, 13:12, 15:21), but its location is uncertain. See the commentary on 1 Sam. 7:16.[311]

x. TRANSITION (19:16-18a)

16 *And Shimei the son of Gera, the Benjamite, who was from Bahurim, hurried and came down with the men of Judah to meet King David;*

17 *and there were a thousand men of Benjamin with him.*

As for Ziba, the steward of the house of Saul, and his fifteen sons and his twenty servants with him, they rushed down to the Jordan in the sight of[312] *the king.*

18a *A crossing was set up in order to bring over the king's household and to do what was good in his sight.*

16 For *Shimei,* see the commentary on 2 Sam. 16:5-13.

17 The Hebrew *wᵉṣālᵉḥû* for *they rushed* is *waw*+pf.[313] McCarter translates "waded through," reading it as *waw*+impf. (*wyṣlḥw*) on the basis of LXX^B; for its meaning, McCarter refers to Aramaic *ṣalleḥ,* "cleave, split; penetrate, pass through." Wellhausen tries to solve the problem by assuming a dittography of *waw*: i.e., *'tw wṣlḥw.* However, the MT as it stands could be treated as a case of topicalization. *As for Ziba . . ., they rushed*: a *casus pendens,* the TOPIC being preposed to *waw*+pf. (*weqtl*): see 2 Sam. 19:40, 20:12.[314]

18 It is hard to decide whether this verse is TERMINUS for the preceding episode or SETTING of the following. It is probably a HINGE connecting the quick movements by Ziba and Shimei with the following discussion between David and the *sons of Zeruiah* concerning the fate of Shimei.[315]

A crossing was set up (*wᵉʿābᵉrāh hāʿăbārāh*): certainly, this is not an EVENT that carries the narrative forward. The verb *ʿābᵉrāh* is 3 f.s. pf., which is taken here as middle, intransitive, though translated as passive; cf. BDB, p. 717; "and did the work," based on LXX;[316] "Then they kept crossing the ford" (NASB); "while the crossing was taking place" (NRSV) — also cf. the verbal root *mṣ'.

311. Tsumura, I, p. 241.

312. Lit. "before."

313. See R. E. Longacre, "Weqatal Forms in Biblical Hebrew Prose," pp. 77-78; Tsumura, "Tense and Aspect of Hebrew Verbs in II Samuel VII 8-16," pp. 641-54.

314. Tsumura, I, pp. 46-48.

315. For a general discussion of discourse grammar, see Tsumura, I, pp. 49-52.

316. McCarter, II, p. 416.

The Hebrew *laʿăbîr* (*to bring over*) is a *sandhi* spelling after an intervocalic /h/ dropped;[317] thus,

laʿăbîr ← (*sandhi* spelling) — *l^eaʿăbîr*
← (intervocalic *h* dropped) — *l^ehaʿăbîr* (prep. *l^e* + Hi. inf. cstr. of *ʿbr*)

b. Shimei (19:18b-23)

18b *As for Shimei the son of Gera, he fell down before the king as he was about to cross the Jordan*

19 *and said to the king,*
"May my lord not consider me guilty,
nor remember what your servant did wrong
on the day when my lord the king went out of Jerusalem,
so that the king may not bear it in his heart!
20 *For your servant knows*
that I myself sinned;
so, here I have come today,
as the first of all the house of Joseph
to come down to meet my lord the king."
21 *And Abishai son of Zeruiah answered,*
"Should not Shimei be put to death for this?
For he cursed the LORD*'s anointed."*
22 *And David said,*
"What is it to me and to you (pl.), O sons of Zeruiah,
that you should become an adversary to me today?
Should anyone be put to death in Israel today?
For do I not know
that today I am king over Israel?"
23 *And the king said to Shimei,*
"You shall not die."
And the king swore to him.

18b-23 Now that the Lord has repaid David with good for his patience under Shimei's cursing (16:12), Abishai thinks there is no reason not to give him the death he deserves. However, David wants this to be a day of rejoicing, not retribution. He apparently did not forgive him from the heart, however (see 1 K. 2:8-9, 36-46).

317. See GKC, §53q; also Tsumura, "Vowel *sandhi* in Biblical Hebrew," *ZAW* 109 (1997) 575-88.

20 *The house of Joseph* here refers to all the northern tribes in contrast to "the house of Judah," as Benjamin was Joseph's brother, not his son.

21 For the phrase *the LORD's anointed* (*m*^{e}*šîaḥ YHWH*), see on 1 Sam. 24:6,[318] 2 Sam. 1:14. For Abishai's earlier attitude toward Saul, "the Lord's anointed," see 1 Sam. 26:8-9.[319] Has he learned from David, or is he being inconsistent?

22 For the expression *What is it to me and to you*, see the commentary on 16:10.

For the term *adversary* (*śāṭān*), see 1 Sam. 29:4,[320] where the Philistine rulers worried about David's becoming "an adversary" to them in the battle. McCarter takes the passage, *today I am king over Israel*, together with 1 Sam. 11:13-15, as suggesting that "a coronation was accompanied by a general amnesty."[321]

c. Mephibosheth (19:24-30)

24 *As for Mephibosheth the (grand)son of Saul, he came down to meet the king. He had not taken care of his feet, nor trimmed his beard; and he had not washed his clothes from the day the king left until the day he came home safely.*

25 *When he came from Jerusalem to meet the king, the king said to him,*
"Why did you not go with me, Mephibosheth?"
26 *And he said,*
"O my lord, the king, my servant deceived me;
for your servant said,
'I will saddle a donkey for myself
that I may get on it
and go with the king,'
because your servant is lame.
27 *And he has slandered your servant to my lord the king.*
But my lord the king is like the angel of God;
so do what is good in your sight.
28 *For all the house of my father were nothing but dead men to my lord the king,*
but you set your servant among those who ate at your table.
What further right do I have
even[322] *to shout anymore to the king?"*

318. Tsumura, I, p. 567.
319. Tsumura, I, p. 600.
320. Tsumura, I, p. 635.
321. McCarter, II, p. 421.
322. The emphatic *waw*; lit. "and by crying."

29 *And the king said to him,*
"Why do you still speak of your affairs?
Now I declare:
'You and Zibah shall divide the land.'"
30 *And Mephibosheth said to the king,*
"Let him even take it all,
after my lord the king comes back to his house safely."

24-30 Mephibosheth claims that in 16:3 Ziba was lying when he said Mephibosheth had chosen to stay in Jerusalem. The narrator does not state directly which is telling the truth — after all, he may not have had direct information — but v. 24 suggests that he believes Mephibosheth. In a city facing invasion, when even the king's household was grateful for two donkeys (16:1-2), it is not surprising that Mephibosheth was stuck in Jerusalem when his own donkeys were taken by Ziba.

24 The verb *yārad* should be translated as *came down* (so NRSV, NASB, JPS) rather than "went down" (NIV), since the narrative setting is still near the Jordan and the narrator's viewpoint is there. The "down" suggests that Mephibosheth came from Jerusalem (see on v. 25).

For "son" or "grandson," see the commentary on 9:7.

25 This is a partial repetition of v. 24a after an explanation. Discourse grammatically, v. 24 as a whole is a SETTING for the subsequent dialogue, with the first EVENT (*wayqtl* "the king said to him").

Mephibosheth *came from Jerusalem* (*bā' yᵉrûšālaim*). When used adverbially, the term "Jerusalem" can mean either "to Jerusalem" or "from Jerusalem," and some translations and McCarter[323] translate "Mephibosheth came to Jerusalem." However, the use of the verb "came" (*bā'*) rather suggests that the narrator's viewpoint is still the same, and near the Jordan. So, Mephibosheth came down (v. 24) *from* Jerusalem (from Jerusalem to the Jordan River is "down" from the capital both literally and figuratively) to meet the king.

26 For the verbal phrase *get on it and go* (or "ride on it and go"), see the commentary on 1 Sam. 25:42.[324]

27 The expression *like the angel of God* is "routine flattery"; see on 2 Sam. 14:17.

28 The expression *the house of my father* here refers to the house of Saul; 9:3.

The phrase *was nothing but dead men* (lit. "men of death" *'anšê-māwet*) means "deserved nothing but death" (NIV). See 2 Sam. 12:5.

For *those who ate at your table*, see 2 Sam. 9:7.

323. McCarter, II, p. 421.
324. Tsumura, I, p. 594.

29 The Hebrew verb *ʾāmartî* is perfect, which is here *performative* as in Judg. 2:3; Isa. 22:4; 36:5 ("I now challenge"); Ps. 31:14 [15] ("I trust" // "I say"); 75:4 [5]; 82:6; 119:57 ("I promise"); 140:6 [7]; 142:5 [6]; Job 32:10; Song 7:8 [9]; Eccl. 6:3. So, the translation *Now I declare*: lit. "I said"; cf. "I have decided" (NASB, NRSV); "I decide" (GKC, §106i).

It is difficult to decide which David believes here. His verdict (*you and Zibah shall divide the land*) suggests that he is not sure, but McCarter thinks he believes Mephibosheth, but is grateful for Ziba's help.[325]

d. Barzillai (19:31-40)

31 *As for Barzillai the Gileadite, he came down from Rogelim.*
He went on to the Jordan with the king to escort him through the Jordan valley.
32 *— Barzillai was very old, being eighty years old; and he had sustained the king while he was staying at Mahanaim, for he was a very great man —*
33 *And the king said to Barzillai,*
"You cross over with me,
and I will sustain you in Jerusalem with me."
34 *And Barzillai said to the king,*
"How many days of years will I have yet to live
that I should go up with the king to Jerusalem?
35 *Today I am eighty years old.*
Can I distinguish between good and bad?
Or can your servant taste what I eat or what I drink?
Or can I still listen to the voice of singing men
and singing women?
Why should your servant still become a burden
to my lord the king?
36 *For a little bit further your servant will go on to the Jordan*
with the king.
Why should the king recompense me with such a reward?
37 *Please let your servant return,*
that I may die in my own city,
near[326] *the grave of my father and my mother.*
But here is your servant Chimham;
let him cross over with my lord the king;
and do for him what is good in your sight."

325. McCarter, II, p. 422.
326. Lit. "with."

38 *And the king said,*
"Chimham shall cross over with me;
I myself will do for him what is good in your sight;
and all that you desire of me I will do for you."
39 *And all the people crossed over the Jordan.*
As for the king, when he crossed over, he kissed Barzillai and blessed him, and he returned to his place.
40 *And the king went on to Gilgal, and Chimham went on with him.*
As for all the people of Judah, they and also half of the people of Israel accompanied[327] *the king.*

31 *Barzillai* had helped David in Mahanaim (17:27). He is an old man for whom dying in the family home is more important than the pleasures of the capital.

The verb (*ʿbr*) here means "to go on to (someplace)" or "to go along" (McCarter) rather than "to cross over," for Barzillai himself did not cross over the Jordan River, despite the king's request in v. 34; see 39-40.

The K. *bayyardēn* (lit. "in-the-Jordan"; cf. Q. *hayyardēn* "the Jordan"), preceded by the object marker (*ʾet*), may mean "the Jordan valley" (lit. "the in-the-Jordan"). It is probably a *nominalization* of a prepositional phrase like *habbaddîm* (Ex 25:14) "the in-the-hands" as "the handles" (see Gordon, *UT*, §19.1072, p. 408) as well as *heʿālêhā* (1 Sam. 9:24), lit. "the upon-it," "that which was upon it." Compare "over the Jordan" (NASB; NRSV); "from the Jordan" (McCarter).

32 The prepositional phrase *bᵉšîbātô* (*while he was staying*) literally means "in his staying." Morphologically, *šîbāto* is the feminine infinitive *šîbāh* II (a *hapax legomenon*; see *HALOT*, p. 1477) with a suffix, from the root *šwb* ("to return"), but semantically it is based on the root *yšb* ("to dwell"), just like *wᵉšabtî* ("and I will dwell"; Ps. 23:6). The term probably derives originally from a *biconsonantal* root *šb*, the common base of *yšb* and *šwb*.

37 *Chimham* is probably Barzillai's son or grandson and one of the sons of Barzillai commended by David to Solomon (1 K. 2:7). David never forgot Barzillai's help. The meaning of the name has been explained on the basis of Arabic *kamiha*, "change complexion, become pale" (Noth).[328] Note also, according to Ezra 2:61, a man who may have been a priest took a wife from the daughters of Barzillai the Gileadite, and was called by their name.

327. The K. *wyʿbrw* (*accompanied*) indicates a *casus pendens* or *topicalization*, preposed of *wayqtl*; the Q. *heʿĕbîrû* ("they accompanied") is a later grammatical normalization. See v. 17 (above) and 20:12 for the *waw*+pf. (*weqtl*) pattern; 1 Sam. 14:19 and 2 Sam. 20:14 for the *wayqtl* pattern.

328. McCarter, II, p. 422.

39 For *crossed over* (*'br*), see v. 31, where it is translated as "to go on to (someplace)." Compare "stayed behind" (McCarter), based on LXX^{LMN}.[329]

40 *Chimham* here appears in the variant spelling *kimhān*, as a result of dissimilation.

e. Men of Israel (19:41-43)

41 *Then all the men of Israel came*[330] *to the king.*
And they said to the king,
"Why have our kindred the men of Judah stolen you away,
and brought the king and his household over the Jordan,
and all the men of David with him?"
42 *And all the men of Judah answered the men of Israel,*
"Because the king is a close relative to me.
Why then are you (sg.) angry about this matter?
Have we eaten at all at the king's expense?
Or has anything been taken for us?"
43 *And the men of Israel answered the men of Judah:*
"I have ten shares in the king;
yea, in David I have more than you (sg.).
Why then did you despise me?
Did I not speak the first words about bringing back my king?"
And the words of the men of Judah were more severe than the words of the men of Israel.

41-43 Apparently, David left Mahanaim and came to the Jordan without leaving time for the northern tribes to come and accompany him. They resent this, being the larger group and considering themselves more loyal to David (vv. 9-11) than Judah, whom they accuse of "privatizing" the king. The men of Judah retort that David did not favor his own tribe with grants (unlike Saul in 1 Sam. 22:7). In making Jerusalem his capital and bringing the ark there, David seems to have made effort to be not a Judahite king ruling Israel, but an Israelite king. However, he was not able to overcome the division. The singular first- and second-person pronouns in vv. 42-43 suggest the acrimony of the debate.

42-43 There were differences in the attitudes toward David between the men of Judah and the men of Israel. To the former, King David was a man of their own who became king. On the other hand, to the latter, he was a man

329. McCarter, II, p. 418.
330. Hebrew is ptc.

chosen by God and accepted by them as king (5:1-4), and as he was king of all Israel, each tribe had an equal share.

42 The expression "to eat at the king's expense" means "to obtain any advantage from our tribal connexion with David."[331] For the difficult expression *has anything been taken for us?* (*niśśēʾt niśśāʾ lānû*; NASB), three views are listed by Driver:[332] (1) "Has anything been carried away by us?"; (2) "Has he been carried away by us?"; (3) "Has anything been carried away by us as a *portion*?" McCarter rather translates "Has he given us a gift? Has he brought us a present?" based on LXX^{L}.[333] We accept the first (1) position, without emending the MT, taking the form *nsʾt* as an infinitive absolute.[334]

43 For *yea, in David I have more than you,* McCarter suggests, "And furthermore we, not you, are firstborn!" based on the LXX and the OL, reading *bkwr* instead of *bdwd.*[335] However, the phrase *yea, in David* should be kept as original since direct speech often is made up of parallelisms,[336] here in chiasms:

"I have ten shares in the king;
Yea, in David I have more than you."

Since both lines talk about their relationship with *King David* (v. 19; here, *the king // David*), the term *wᵉgam* means "and even" for intensification rather than meaning "and also"; see also v. 30.[337] In other words, both lines say they have the priority with regard to David.

And the words of the men of Judah were more severe than the words of the men of Israel: this rivalry between Israel and Judah for priority in bringing David back leads up to Sheba's revolt in the following chapter.

7. Sheba's Revolt (20:1-22)

Sheba's revolt is directly connected with the split within the country in the previous paragraph. It does not seem to have gained support outside of his

331. See Driver, pp. 338-39.

332. Driver, pp. 338-39.

333. McCarter, II, pp. 418-19. For "gift," see the commentary on 1 Sam. 9:7 (Tsumura, I, p. 269).

334. For the most recent treatment of *infinitive absolute,* see S. N. Callaham, *Modality and the Biblical Hebrew Infinitive Absolute* (AKM 71; Wiesbaden: Otto Harrassowitz, 2010); G. Hatav, "The Infinitive Absolute and Topicalization of Events in Biblical Hebrew," in Moshavi, *Advances in Biblical Hebrew Linguistics*, pp. 207-32.

335. McCarter, II, p. 419.

336. See also the commentary on 20:1. For poetic prose, see Tsumura, I, pp. 59-60. Straight narrative can be sometimes analyzed as being made up of parallelisms, and ordinary conversations can also be often analyzed as parallelistic, due to their oral and aural features.

337. *HALOT*, p. 196; *DULAT*, p. 300.

own clan (v. 14), but even after this, the feeling that the king was not treating them well seems to have lingered among the northern tribes, increased under Solomon (who did not require Judah to supply him with food in the list in 1 K. 4:7-19), and finally ended up causing the nation to split in two (1 K. 12).

a. Sheba Son of Bichri (20:1-2)

1 *There happened to be a worthless fellow whose name was Sheba son of Bichri, a Benjaminite.*

And he blew the trumpet and said,

"No portion is there for us in David;
no share for us in the son of Jesse.
Everyone to his own tent, O Israel!"

2 *And all the men of Israel withdrew from David and followed Sheba son of Bichri.*

But the men of Judah remained close to their king, from the Jordan up to Jerusalem.

1-2 Sheba seems to say, "If we don't have ten shares, we have none." For *worthless fellow* (*'îš b^elîya'al*), see the Excursus in Tsumura, I, pp. 122-24. Saul (1 Sam. 13:3) and Absalom (2 Sam. 15:10) also announced their rebellions by a *trumpet*; see also 2:28; 6:15; 18:16. Sheba's words constitute a poem with a three-line parallelism.[338]

Portion (*ḥēleq*) and *share* (*naḥălāh*) are a word pair in the OT as in Gen. 31:14; Deut. 10:9; 12:12; 14:27; 32:9; Job 20:29; 27:13; 31:2; etc. *David . . . son of Jesse* is an example of the *breakup* of "A son of B" into parallel lines.[339] *Everyone to his own tent* is a summons to resume the old tribal independence. This rallying cry is repeated over forty years later during the reign of Rehoboam (1 K. 12:16).

x. David's Ten Concubines (20:3)

3 *And David came to his house at Jerusalem.*

And the king took the ten women, the concubines whom he had left to keep the

338. M. O'Connor, "War and Rebel Chants in the Former Prophets," in *Fortunate the Eyes That See: Essays in Honor of David Noel Freedman in Celebration of His Seventieth Birthday*, ed. A. B. Beck et al. (Grand Rapids: Eerdmans, 1995), pp. 330-34.

339. See S. Gevirtz, *Patterns in the Early Poetry of Israel* (SAOC 32; Chicago: University of Chicago Press, 1963, 1973), p. 50; also Tsumura, "Vertical Grammar of Parallelism in Hebrew Poetry," *JBL* 128 (2009) 179-81.

house, and put them in a guarded house and provided for them, but he did not go in to them.[340] *So they were shut up until the day of their death, as life-long widows.*

3 The *ten concubines* are those that David had left to keep the house and Absalom had sexual relations with (15:16; 16:22).

The phrase *'almᵉnût ḥayyût,* literally "widowhood of livingness" (BDB, p. 313), refers to *life-long widows*; cf. "living as widows" (NASB, NIV); "living as if in widowhood" (NRSV, ESV); "widows in the prime of life" (NEB); "living as if they were widows until the day of their death" (REB). The term probably refers to widows who stay unmarried for the rest of their life.

b. Joab Kills Amasa (20:4-14)

4 *And the king said to Amasa,*
"Call out the men of Judah to me in three days;
and be present here yourself!"

5 *And Amasa went to call out (the men of) Judah, but he delayed beyond the set time that he had appointed him.*

6 *And David said to Abishai,*
"Now Sheba son of Bichri will do us more harm
than Absalom.
As for you, take your lord's servants and pursue him.
Perhaps he has found for himself fortified cities
and escaped[341] *from our sight."*[342]

7 *And Joab's men went out after him, along with the Cherethites and the Pelethites and all the mighty men.*

And they went out from Jerusalem to pursue Sheba the son of Bichri.

8 *While they were at the large stone that is in Gibeon, Amasa came before them. Now Joab was dressed in his military attire, and over it was a belt of a sword in its sheath fastened at his waist.*[343] *When he went forward, it fell out.*

340. *Them* appears three times, in m.pl. instead of f.pl.

341. As for *and escaped* (*wᵉhiṣṣîl*), it is to be taken as a simple *waw* followed by a perfect verb rather than as a *waw consecutive* + perfect.

342. *Perhaps he has found for himself* [*pen-māṣā' lô*] . . . *and escaped*: usually the particle *pēn* is followed by an imperfect verb; the only exceptions are 2 K. 2:16 and here. The imperfect of *mṣ'* never appears after this particle. Cf. "lest he find for himself fortified cities" (NASB); "or he will find fortified cities for himself" (NRSV).

343. *A sword in its sheath fastened at his waist* —literally reads "a sword fastened at his waist in its sheath" (*ḥereb mᵉṣummedet 'al-motnâw bᵉta'rāh*). Though a strange expression, it possibly is the AXB pattern, in which "fastened at his waist" is inserted between the noun "sword" and the modifying phrase "in its sheath." For this pattern, see Tsumura, I, pp. 60-64.

9 *And Joab said to Amasa,*
"Is it well with you, my brother?"
And Joab's right hand took hold of Amasa's beard to kiss him.
10 *But Amasa did not notice the sword that was in Joab's hand.*
And he struck him in the belly with it.
And his inward parts poured out on the ground.
Though he did not strike him again, he died.
As for Joab and his brother Abishai, they pursued Sheba the son of Bichri.
11 *But a man of Joab's young men stood by him (Asama) and said,*
"Whoever favors Joab,
whoever is for David,
let him follow Joab,"
12 *while Amasa was wallowing in his blood in the middle of the approach road.*

And the man saw that all the people stood by, and he moved Amasa away from the highway into the field and threw a garment over him, as he saw that all who came by him stood by.

13 *As he was removed from the highway, all the men passed on after Joab to pursue Sheba the son of Bichri,*

14 *who had gone through all the tribes of Israel, to Abel, even to Beth-maacah,*[344] *and through the midst of all the Beerites, who assembled*[345] *and followed him too.*

4-22 The rebellion of Sheba is the close of the story of Absalom's revolt in 13:1-20:26. The killing of Amasa shows how ruthless Joab could be with a rival; compare his revenge on Abner in 3:27.

4 David had made *Amasa* commander in 19:13, replacing Joab. *Three days* is a rather short time if he was supposed to muster fighting men from all over Judah.

5 The Hebrew spellings of the word for *delayed*, both the K. *wayyêḥar* and Q. *wayyôḥer*, are the phonetically written variants without the consonant *aleph* of the root *'ḥr "to delay, tarry"; see another phonetic spelling in

344. Here the directive *he* is attached only to *Abel*, but functions as X of the AX&B pattern; hence literally "to *Abel and Beth-maacah*"; see LXXB "to Abel *and* to Beth-maacah" (McCarter, II, p. 428); "to Abel even to Beth-maacah" (NASB); cf. "to Abel of Beth-maacah" (NRSV, JPS, ESV, McCarter); "Abel Beth Maacah" (NIV). The *waw* "and" here is a *waw explicativum*. See Erlandsson, cited by Baker, "Further Examples of the *wāw explicativum*," p. 135.

345. As for *they assembled*, the K. *wyqlhw* reflects a *metathesis* of the normal form as preserved in the Q. *wayyiqqāhălû*. The K. however reflects a *phonetic spelling*. See Tsumura, "Scribal Errors or Phonetic Spellings?" 390-411; Tsumura, "Textual Corruptions, or Linguistic Phenomena?," p. 138. Anderson's translation "treated him with contempt" (Anderson, p. 241, but see p. 231: "assembled") is unnecessary.

wattōḥez (v. 9) from root *'ḥz "to take, seize."[346] No one can deny that these spellings with the omission of *aleph* are for phonetic reasons rather than the result of a scribal error.

K. *wayyêḥar* and Q. *wayyôḥer* ←(*aleph* dropped)

K. *wayye'ĕḥar* and Q. *wayyō'ḥer*

6 *Now Sheba son of Bichri will do us more harm than Absalom*: David fears that his kingdom is dangerously fragile. However, he seems to have overestimated Sheba's strength. In v. 2 *all the men of Israel withdrew . . . and followed Sheba*, but apparently just to the extent of returning home, though of course David could not predict how they would act. In the event, though, everyone except the Bichrites, the members of Shiba's own clan, seems to have acted neutral (v. 14).

When David ordered Abishai to take over, could he have been predicting what would happen between Amasa and Joab? First Kings 2:5 shows that he blamed Joab for what ensued, but perhaps here David just felt the military situation was too urgent to entrust the leadership to anyone except one of the sons of Zeruiah. *Your lord's servants* refers to David's standing army, as does "the servants of David" in 18:7.

The phrase *escaped from our sight* is literally "take away our eye." McCarter, following Ewald, takes the verb as a denominative of *ṣēl* "shadow" and translates it as "cast a shadow over," based on LXX in the light of a possible *Vorlage*.[347] Though attractive, this elaborate emendation is based on an unnatural treatment of Semitic idioms involving body terms. The phrase "to take away one's eye" is most probably an idiom meaning "to be stealthy," similar to the Japanese idiom "to steal someone's eye" (*hitono-me-wo-nusumu)*.

7 *And Joab's men went out after him*: This probably means the members of David's army normally directly commanded by Joab. As Joab shows up in the next verse, McCarter translates "Abishai called out after him (i.e., Sheba) Joab," partly based on LXX^{L}.[348] But this is not necessary in view of the fact that Abishai and Joab seem normally to have worked in consort (3:30; 10:9-10; 18:2; also cf. 1 Chr. 18:12 and the heading to Ps. 60).

For *the Cherethites and the Pelethites,* see the commentary on 2 Sam. 8:18; 15:18.

8-10 We are not told why Amasa was in Gibeon, not in Judah. The sword conspicuously falls out of Joab's belt, but when he takes Amasa's beard with his right hand, with his left hand he either picks it up again or gets out a hidden sword (see the story of Ehud in Judg. 3:15-23). Compare Joab's simi-

346. See Tsumura, "Scribal Errors or Phonetic Spellings?," pp. 390-411; also Tsumura, "Textual Corruptions, or Linguistic Phenomena?," p. 136.

347. McCarter, II, p. 426. See Driver, p. 342.

348. McCarter, II, pp. 426-27.

lar murder of Abner in 3:27. *Brother* may refer to the fact that they were first cousins (see commentary on 2:13).

8 *The large stone* either refers to "the great high place" at Gibeon where Solomon offers sacrifices in 1 K. 3:4 (so Pritchard), or to the large stone set up as an altar by Saul after the battle of Michmash Pass (1 Sam. 14:33) (so Blenkinshopp[349]).

His military attire (so NASB) is literally "his garment (and) his attire" (*middô lᵉbūšô*) which Driver explains as a "strange combination"[350] but probably is to be taken as a *hendiadys*. Note BHS, in its revised edition, has *lᵉbūšô* (his *attire*) instead of *lᵉbūšû.*[351]

10 The *sword* was *in Joab's hand*, i.e., in his left hand; see above. *Pursued* is a singular verb in Hebrew, though the subject is "Joab and Abishai," and the men of v. 7 presumably went as well. Revell notes that "a verb following a compound subject is singular where the narrator wishes to draw attention to the status of the singular component [here Joab] of the compound as principal actor."[352] Similarly, see 2 K. 4:7; Esth. 4:16.

11-13 The *people* who are addressed and who stopped are probably the "men of Judah" of v. 4 who had come with Amasa from Judah to Gibeon.

12 For the *approach road* (also v. 13), see the commentary on 1 Sam. 6:12.[353]

The main line of the narrative is *And the man saw . . . and he moved . . . and threw*, in the light of the sequence of *wayqtl* + stated subject . . . *wayqtl . . . wayqtl.*

The phrase *all who came by him*, which is the subject, is preposed before *weqtl* (*wᵉʿāmād*) as a case of *extraposition* or *topicalization*; see on 2 Sam. 19:40 [MT 41].[354]

14 The phrase *all the men of Israel* in v. 2 is a hyperbole. The present section shows that there was no organized "revolt" by Sheba; only the "Beerites" followed him, as he went *through all the tribes of Israel . . . and through all the Beerites.*

The first place name mentioned, *Abel*, has a directive *he* attached (see also vv. 15, 18). The main candidate for the site of Abel is Tell Abil el-Qamḥ (MR 204296), four and one-third miles (7 km) west-northwest of Dan.[355]

349. See McCarter, II, p. 429.

350. See Driver, pp. 343-44 for various interpretations.

351. For various attempts to explain this unusual expression, see McCarter, II, p. 427.

352. Revell, "Concord with Compound Subjects and Related Uses of Pronouns," pp. 76-77.

353. Tsumura, I, p. 220.

354. For other cases of "unusual topicalization" see Introduction of Tsumura, I, pp. 46-48.

355. *ABD*, I, p. 10; *SB*, p. 163; *CBA*, #111.

See 1 K. 15:20; 2 K. 15:29. In my view, *and all the Beerites* (*w^ekol-habbērîm*) is best understood as connected with *all the tribes of Israel,* as the Masoretic punctuation shows. Thus, *to Abel, even to Beth-maacah* is an element (X) inserted between the two regions (rather than peoples) (A and B) in the AX&B pattern. See NIV: "and through the entire region of the Berites." Actually, Sheba went through two regions and finally reached Abel, even Beth-maacah.

As for *Beerites* (*bērîm*), *bērî* (sing.) is the name of a descendant of Asher (1 Chr. 7:36). It may be that *bērîm* is a phonetic spelling of a *sandhi* form.[356] It should be noted that the name *b^{e}'ērî* is borne by a Hittite, Esau's father-in-law (Gen. 26:34) and as well as by Hosea's father (Hos. 1:1). The association of the name with northern Israel fits the narrative very well. Compare "Bichrites" (NRSV, ESV, McCarter), based on LXX^B.

c. Death of Sheba (20:15-22)

15 *And they came and besieged him in Abel of Beth-maacah and heaped up an earthwork against the city, and thus it stood against the rampart. And all the people who were with Joab were attacking the wall.*

16 *And a wise woman called from the city,*
"Listen! Listen!
Please tell Joab,
'Come here
that I may speak to you.'"
17 *And he came near her.*
And the woman said,
"Are you Joab?"
And he said,
"I am."
And she said to him,
"Listen to the words of your maidservant."
And he said,
"I am listening."
18 *And she said,*
"Formerly they indeed used to say,
'Let them surely inquire[357] *at Abel';*
thus they finished the matter.

356. For vowel *sandhi,* see Tsumura, "Vowel *sandhi* in Biblical Hebrew," pp. 575-88.

357. Inf. abs. in Qal together with Pi. verb (also Josh. 24:10), with other verbal stems; see Driver, p. 347; GKC, §113w.

19 *I am of those who are peaceable and faithful in Israel.*[358]
You are seeking to destroy a mother city in Israel.
Why will you swallow up the inheritance of the LORD?"
20 *And Joab answered,*
"Far be it, far be it from me
that I should swallow up or destroy!
21 *Such is not the case.*
But a man from the hill country of Ephraim
whose name is Sheba the son of Bichri
has lifted up his hand against King David.[359]
Give up only him,
and I will go away from the city."
And the woman said to Joab,
"Soon his head will be thrown to you over the wall."
22 *And the woman came to all the people with her wisdom, and they cut off the head of Sheba the son of Bichri and threw it to Joab, and he blew the trumpet, and they dispersed from the city, each to his tent.*
As for Joab, he returned to Jerusalem to the king.

15 *Abel of Beth-maacah* is Abil el-Qamḥ, which is modern Tel Avel Bet Maakha,[360] located twelve and one-half miles (20 km) north of Lake Huleh, just east of Tel Dan.

The subject of the verb *came and besieged him* is not specified until the second half of the verse, i.e., *all the people who were with Joab.* Discourse grammatically, such an agent defocusing together with the plural subjects here signals a SETTING or TRANSITION to the main line discourse, that is, the prolonged dialogue between the wise woman and Joab in vv. 16-21. *And they came* — a new stage of the narrative begins with this ambiguous phrase; besides, the plural unspecified subject "they" of a movement verb "to come" indicates a transition from the previous stage despite the *wayqtl* form.[361]

An earthwork (*sōlᵉlāh*) is an earthen assault ramp built against the wall to get near its top so the soldiers may get inside; also 2 K. 19:32; Isa. 37:33; Jer. 6:6; Ezek. 4:2; etc. For the verb *heaped up* (*špk*), see Akk. *šapāku* "to heap up (for military purposes)";[362] cf. "cast up a mound against the city" (NASB); "threw up a siege-ramp against the city" (NRSV).

358. Lit. "peaceable and faithful of Israel" (construct chain); see McCarter, II, pp. 428-29, 430.

359. Literally, "in the king, in David."

360. *SB*, p. 163.

361. See Introduction (VI) to Tsumura, I, pp. 49-55.

362. *CAD*, Š/1 (1989), pp. 413-14.

The participle *attacking* (*mašḥîtîm*), literally "making a pit" (see BDB, p. 1008) is a denominative from *šaḥat* "pit" (so Ewald). McCarter tentatively adopts the translation of "intending," based on LXX^L and Targ, reading *mḥšbym.*[363] They were undermining the walls, or more generally, attacking the walls. However, there is no mention of "rams," only "an earthwork" and "the rampart." The practices described here are not necessarily following the Assyrian-style siege techniques.[364]

16-19 This speech of the wise woman can be compared with those by Abigail in 1 Sam. 25:24-31 and the wise woman of Tekoa in 2 Sam. 14:4ff. The woman says that Abel was famous from of old for the wisdom of its inhabitants, and hence a proverb arose that advised people to consult them in any difficult problems.

Listen! Listen! (v. 16): Such repetition adds urgency to a request;[365] see also in Judg. 19:23.

18 The term *finished* (*hētammû*) means "settle a matter" (NRSV); "ended the dispute" (NASB).

19 *A mother city* (*'îr wᵉ'ēm*) is literally "a city and a mother" (so JPS), which is a *hendiadys*, referring to a metropolis. It is a city with associated (daughter) villages (Judg. 1:27).

For *the inheritance of the* Lord (*naḥălat YHWH*), see the commentary on 1 Sam. 26:19.[366] The phrase refers to Israel as the covenant people as well as Israel as the promised land.

20 *Far be it, far be it* (*ḥālîlāh ḥālîlāh lî*) — the reduplication of *far be it* is for emphasis; such repetition reinforces a disclaimer.[367]

21 The *hill country of Ephraim* here includes Benjaminite territory.

22 *Joab . . . returned to Jerusalem to the king.* Apparently, David did not punish Joab for the murder of Amasa, as he was commander at the end of David's reign (1 K. 1:19), but he did not forgive him either (1 K. 2:5-6).

C. DAVID'S OFFICERS (20:23-26)

23 *Now Joab was over all the army of Israel;*
Benaiah the son of Jehoiadah
was over the Cherethites[368] *and the Pelethites;*

363. McCarter, II, p. 428.

364. Millard, "Are There Anachronisms in the Books of Samuel?," pp. 39-48.

365. See Revell, "The Repetition of Introductions to Speech," p. 94 n. 9.

366. Tsumura, I, pp. 604-5.

367. Revell, "The Repetition of Introductions to Speech," 94 n. 9.

368. Following the Q. *hakkᵉrētî*; note that the K. *hakkᵉrî* refers to the Carians; see *HALOT*, p. 497.

24 *Adoram*[369] *was in charge of the forced labor;*
Jehoshaphat son of Ahilud was the recorder;
25 *Sheva was scribe;*
Zadok and Abiathar were priests;
26 *Ira the Jairite also was a priest for David.*

23-26 This list is very similar to the list in 8:16-18 and the one of Solomon's officials in 1 K. 4:1-6. The posts and officials overlap to a large degree, but the order is different, and the one in this chapter does not start out with the king, unlike the others.

It is usually surmised that the list in 2 Sam. 8:16-18 is from the early years of David's reign, and the list in the present passage is from the later years, since the former is presented earlier in the book and also since Adoram, who continued in office under Solomon, is only in the latter.

23 For *Benaiah* as well as *the Cherethites and the Pelethites*, see on 8:18.

24 An official *in charge of the forced labor* is not mentioned in ch. 8, so as just noted, this list may reflect the situation toward the end of David's reign. The office is probably listed after the bodyguards as a military office because it supervised mostly captured peoples, at least at first. *Adoram* was eventually stoned to death at the time of Rehoboam by the northern tribes (1 K. 12:18). He is probably the same person as Adoniram in 1 K. 4:6.

During their sojourn in Egypt, the Israelites were themselves under *the forced labor* (Heb. *mas*). The corvée apparently became a state-organized institution in Israel sometime during David's reign (see 12:31). Thus, David had appointed a high-ranking officer to be in charge of the corvée system.[370] Also see 1 K. 4:6; 5:28.

For *the recorder* (*mazkîr*), see the commentary on 8:16.

25 For *Sheva* (Q. *Šᵉwāʾ*; cf. K. *Šēyāʾ*), see the commentary on 8:17.

For *Zadok and Abiathar*, see on 8:15-18; cf. *Zadok son of Ahitub and Ahimelech son of Abiathar* (8:17). Both appear frequently as David's agents in chs. 15-19.

26 Jair was the eponymous ancestor of the inhabitants of a region called Havvoth-jair, "the village of Jair," in Gilead.[371] *A priest for David* (*kōhēn lᵉdāwīd*) may have been similar to a private chaplain or advisor, probably the same office as Solomon's "priest and king's friend" (see the commentary on 8:18).

369. Cf. "Adoniram" (NIV; McCarter, II, p. 433), based on MT (MS), LXX^{BAMN}, and Syr. See 1 K. 4:6 ("Adoniram son of Abda — in charge of forced labor").

370. Avigad and Sass, *Corpus of West Semitic Stamp Seals*, p. 28. Also see T. N. D. Mettinger, *Solomonic State Officials: The Civil and Sacral Legitimation of the Israelite Kings* (CB: Old Testament Series 5; Lund: C. W. K. Gleerup, 1971), pp. 128-39.

371. See Num. 32:41; Deut. 3:14; Josh. 13:30; 1 K. 4:13; 1 Chr. 2:22, 23; McCarter, II, p. 434.

VI. EPILOGUE (21:1–24:25)

Those who take 2 Samuel basically as a Succession Narrative (SN) treat the last four chapters, chs. 21-24, as an appendix and hold that the main narrative flows from 2 Sam. 20 to 1 K. 1. However, these four chapters themselves are a tightly organized literary unit and form the epilogue of the entire book, i.e., 1–2 Samuel, corresponding to the prologue (1 Sam. 1-7). The poems in the prologue and the epilogue, that is, the Song of Hannah (1 Sam. 2:1-10) and David's Song (2 Sam. 22) and Last Words (23:1-7), constitute an *inclusio* of the entire narrative. Thus the overall structure of 1–2 Samuel as a whole strengthens and focuses on the main themes of the entire book, that is, the monarchy, the Davidic kingdom and the royal throne of David.[1]

- I. Prologue (1 Sam. 1:1–7:17): "Story of Samuel"
  - A. Rise of Samuel as Prophet (1:1–3:21)
  - X. "Story of the Ark of God" (4:1–7:1)[2]
  - B. Judgeship of Samuel (7:2-17)
- II. Transition to the Monarchy (1 Sam. 8:1-22)
- III. "Story of Saul" (1 Sam. 9:1–15:35)
- IV. "Story of Saul and David" (1 Sam. 16:1–31:13)
- V. "Story of King David" (2 Sam. 1:1–20:26)
- VI. Epilogue (2 Sam. 21:1–24:25)
  - A. Famine and the Death of Saul's Sons (21:1-14)
  - B. Philistine War (21:15-22)
  - X. Song of David (22:1-51) = Ps. 18
  - X'. Last Words of David (23:1-7)
  - B'. David's Heroes (23:8-39)
  - A'. Census and the Lord's Anger (24:1-25)

It should be noted that the AXB pattern[3] appears both in the Prologue and in the Epilogue.[4] The Epilogue is a chiastic arrangement: two poems (X and

1. See Introduction of Tsumura, I, pp. 67-68.

2. In the first volume, *The First Book of Samuel*, p. 66, I designated this section as "B," and the next as "C," but since it is an embedded discourse, it is better designated as "X," an inserted episode of the AXB pattern.

3. The literary structure is designated as A-B-C-C'-B'-A' by other scholars such as Anderson, p. 248; W. Dietrich, *Samuel*, vol. 1, p. 5*. But the C/C' are poetic, while the others are narrative, hence it seems we have here the AXB pattern rather than the chiastic pattern ABA. See Tsumura, I, pp. 60-64.

4. In my *The First Book of Samuel*, p. 67, I took 2 Sam. 21-24 as constituting a concentric structure, the ABCBA pattern. But, I now revise it as a complex AXB pattern, i.e., ABXX'B'A'.

X') are in the center, framed by two lists with narrative,[5] B and B',[6] which are framed by the first and last sections, which are both narratives with the theme of death as the result of God's anger.[7]

The narratives are not placed in chronological order, however, for the first poem (ch. 22 = Ps. 18) is probably from the earlier part of David's life, possibly even before he became king, and the second (23:1-7) from the last days of his life. On the other hand, the narrative sections (A, B, E and F) seem to be sequential. The last section (ch. 24) is climactic, describing the events leading to the purchase of the land upon which Solomon would build the temple. Thus, I analyze the literary structure here as a kind of the AXB pattern, i.e., ABXX'B'A',[8] where the two poems in chs. 22 (X) and 23 (X'), are inserted into the narrative flow of A-B-B'-A'.

A. FAMINE FOR THREE YEARS (21:1-14)

1. Saul against the Gibeonites (21:1)

1 *And there was a famine in the days of David for three years, year after year.*
And David sought the LORD's face.
And the LORD said,
"Due to Saul and his bloody house,
and because he put the Gibeonites to death."

The first section of Epilogue[9] pushes us back to sometime before the previous chapter, probably to the early part of Davidic monarchy, but no earlier than chapter 9. See the commentary on that chapter.

1 A *famine* had afflicted Israel *for three years* because of Saul's attempt to exterminate the Gibeonites, who were protected by an oath sworn in the time of Joshua (Josh 9:3-27). There is no other direct mention of the incident in the Bible, but it may be in the background of 2 Sam. 4:2-3 (see commen-

5. For the relation between list and narrative, see Tsumura, I, pp. 222-24; Tsumura, "List and Narrative in I Samuel 6,17-18a," pp. 353-69.

6. See H. H. Klement, *2 Samuel 21-24: Context, Structure and Meaning in the Samuel Conclusion* (European University Studies; Frankfurt: Peter Lang, 2000).

7. See Bergen, p. 442, who analyzes the six sections into three chiastic pairs: A B C C' B' A'.

8. See "C. Literary Insertion: AXB Pattern," in Tsumura, I, pp. 60-64, et passim.

9. For a recent survey and a detailed literary-critical study of this episode see S. Chavel, "Compository and Creativity in 2 Samuel 21:1-14," *JBL* 122 (2003) 23-52; see p. 24, no. 4, for various interpretations with detailed bibliographical notes.

tary).[10] The famine was an expression of divine wrath against King Saul's violation of the treaty. This incident illustrates how serious the consequences may be when the leader of God's people offends God's righteousness. But we don't know why God did not punish Saul at the time. Generally speaking, leaders' failures must be sorted out by their successors, if the justice is to prevail.

Regarding the present incident, C. H. Gordon calls our attention to the fact that "the fitness (physical and moral) and deportment of kings were serious matters, for they were believed to bring on a corresponding state of land and people." While in *Odyssey* 19:109-14 "a faultless king who fears the gods and rules his mighty men justly, brings on fertility of earth, trees, cattle and sea," in *Oedipus Rex* "Sophocles tells of the blight on Theban grain, cattle and women in travail, because of the King's sin."[11]

According to Malamat and Fensham,[12] the incident is to be taken as a case of punishment for treaty violations in the ancient Near East. Looking at Hittite texts such as the so-called plague prayers of the fourteenth century Hittite king Mursili II, Malamat identifies "a common doctrine of causality" in both Israelite and Hittite literatures according to which "a national disaster (famine, plague, etc.) might arise from a past violation of a treaty oath."

The act of seeking *the LORD's face* is to ask the Lord's special favor, as one might seek an audience with a king in times of trouble.

Due to Saul and his bloody house (*'el-šā'ûl wᵉ'el-bêt haddāmîm*) is an incomplete sentence, not a "confused wording" (Budde),[13] and is literally "to Saul and to the house of the blood." It is presumably uttered in response to such a question as, "Why did this famine occur?" See the commentary on 1 Sam. 1:22 for the phenomenon of aposiopesis, i.e., the device of suddenly breaking off in mid-speech.[14] The Hebrew expression *his bloody house* means "bloodguilt on his house" (see NRSV; also McCarter) or "the bloodguilt of his house" (JPS), not simply "bloodshed of his house."

2. David and the Gibeonites (21:2-6)

2 *And the king called the Gibeonites and spoke to them.*
— *Now*[15] *the Gibeonites were not of the sons of Israel but of the remnant of*

10. For various speculations concerning this incident, see McCarter, II, p. 441.

11. Gordon, *CB*, p. 242.

12. A. Malamat, "Doctrines of Causality in Biblical and Hittite Historiography. A Parallel," *VT* 5 (1955) 1-12; F. C. Fensham, "The Treaty between Israel and the Gibeonites," *BA* 27 (1964) 96-100.

13. See Chavel, "Compository and Creativity," 26, no. 10.

14. Tsumura, I, p. 128.

15. The disjunctive *waw* here introduces parenthetical clauses.

the Amorites. Although the sons of Israel had sworn to them, Saul had sought to strike them out in his zeal for the sons of Israel and Judah —

3 *And David said to the Gibeonites,*
"What shall I do for you?
How can I make atonement
that you may bless the inheritance of the LORD?"
4 *And the Gibeonites said to him,*
"We have nothing[16] *to do with silver or gold*
with regard to Saul or his house.
It is not for us[17] *to put anyone to death in Israel."*
And he said,
"Whatever you say I will do for you."
5 *And they said to the king,*
"As for the man who[18] *consumed us*[19]
and who planned to exterminate us[20]
from remaining in any territory of Israel,
6 *let seven men from among his sons be given*[21] *to us,*
and we will hang them before the LORD
in Gibeah of Saul, the chosen of the LORD."
And the king said,
"I will give them."

2 *The remnant of the Amorites* refers to the pre-Israelite inhabitants of the land. Though the Israelites *had sworn to,* i.e., made an alliance with, the Gibeonites, Saul had conducted bloodshed against them *in his zeal for* his people of *Israel and Judah.* A king should not do such an unlawful thing against God's will even in his zeal for the covenant people of God. In other words, his "bloody [from bloodshed] house" bore "bloodguilt" for this violence.

16. Lit., "there is not to us," following the Q. reading *'ên-lānû,* instead of the K. *'yn-ly* ("I have nothing").

17. Or "we have no right to put anyone to death in Israel" (see NIV).

18. McCarter, II, p. 438, reads the extant letters of v. 5 in 4QSam[a] as *'yš '[šr]* "a man who," but Herbert and DJD now read *h]'yš 'š[r* "the man who," which is the same as the MT (also LXX[B]); see Herbert, *RBDSS,* p. 182; DJD 17, p. 177. Herbert reads [h] "since, if it were lacking, we would expect to see the tail of the final ך of the preceding word." (p. 183).

19. For *the man who consumed us,* McCarter suggests the translation "set himself against us and persecuted us," based on the LXX[B]. However, according to Herbert, *RBDSS,* p. 183, the reconstruction suggested by McCarter would not fit in the lacunae of 4QSam[a]. See Introduction.

20. MT: *wa'ăšer dimmāh-lānû nišmadnû;* literally, "and who devised against us (and) we were exterminated."

21. The Q. *yuttan* is the older *qal passive,* while the K. *yntn* is Ni.

3 For the expression *make atonement* (*kpr, Pi.), see the commentary on 1 Sam. 3:14.[22] David admits here that he is the one who should make compensation, as the leader of his people, for the difficult situation his predecessor had left him.

The Hebrew of *you may bless* (lit. "you, bless!") is the imperative, which is used "instead of the more normal voluntative, for the purpose of expressing with somewhat greater force the intention of the previous verb."[23]

For *the inheritance of the LORD* (*naḥălat YHWH*), see 2 Sam. 14:16; 20:19; see especially the commentary on 1 Sam. 26:19.[24]

4 The Gibeonites have no interest either in monetary compensation from the house of Saul or in putting *anyone to death in Israel.* The latter seems to contradict v. 6, but Brichto explains this as meaning the death of any random Israelite as compensation for the Gibeonite slaughter.[25]

6 *Seven men* is a symbolic number of Saul's descendants. In order that God be *entreated* (v. 14), these seven sons were to be hanged *before the LORD*. This of course was against the command "nor shall children be put to death because of their fathers" (Deut. 24:16). Were these seven accomplices of Saul's act? The text does not suggests that, and furthermore, as David must have been at least in his late teens when Merab married (1 Sam. 18:19) and was no more than thirty when Saul died (2 Sam. 5:4), even Merab's oldest son could scarcely have been ten when Saul died. See also commentary on ch. 9.

The meaning of the term *hang* (so NASB) is uncertain; see Num. 25:4; cf. "impale" (NRSV, JPS); "crucify" (McCarter); "to be killed and exposed" (NIV).[26] Such exposure of the corpse was probably "part of the punishment for a treaty violation elsewhere in the ancient Near East."[27]

For the phrase *Gibeah of Saul, the chosen of the LORD* (*bᵉgibʿat Šāʾûl bᵉḥîr YHWH*), McCarter suggests reading it as "(to Yahweh-)in-Gibeon on the mountain of Yahweh," following Wellhausen and explaining that *bhr "on the mountain" was misread as *bᵉḥîr* "the chosen one."[28] However, such a scribal error (i.e., *h* for *ḥ*) occurs less likely than has been asserted.[29] Also there is no support for his hypothesis that this refers to "the Gibeonite Yahweh, the local manifestation of the national god"; see the commentary on McCarter's view of "Yahweh-in-Hebron" in 2 Sam. 15:7 and my criticism of his view. See 1 Sam. 11:4 on the phrase "Gibeah of Saul."

22. Tsumura, I, p. 180.
23. Driver, p. 350.
24. Tsumura, I, pp. 604-5.
25. H. C. Brichto, "Kin, Cult, Land and Afterlife," p. 37.
26. For various interpretations of this term, see McCarter, II, p. 442; Driver, p. 351.
27. Fensham, "The Treaty between Israel and the Gibeonites," pp. 96-100.
28. McCarter, II, p. 438.
29. See Tsumura, "Scribal Errors or Phonetic Spellings?," pp. 390-411.

3. The Death and Exposure of Saul's Sons (21:7-11)

7 *But the king spared Mephibosheth, son of Jonathan son of Saul, because of the oath of the* LORD *that was between them, between David and Jonathan son of Saul.*

8 *And the king took the two sons of Rizpah the daughter of Aiah, whom she bore to Saul, Armoni and Mephibosheth, and the five sons of Merab*[30] *the daughter of Saul, whom she bore to Adriel son of Barzillai the Meholathite,*

9 *and gave them into the hands of the Gibeonites and they hanged them on the mountain before the* LORD.

And the seven of them fell together. They[31] *were put to death in the days of harvest on the first (days), that is, at the beginning of barley harvest.*[32]

10 *And Rizpah the daughter of Aiah took sackcloth and spread it for herself on the rock, from the beginning of the harvest until rain*[33] *fell on them from the sky; and she did not allow the birds of the sky to rest on them by day, or the beasts of the field by night.*

11 *And it was told David what Rizpah the daughter of Aiah, the concubine of Saul, had done.*

7 It is often asserted that David found out about Mephibosheth only after this incident, so originally ch. 9 was placed after this incident and this verse was inserted when the material was separated.[34] However, this is unnecessary; see the commentary on ch. 9. *Mephibosheth, son of Jonathan* here should be distinguished from *Mephibosheth* in v. 8 who is the son of Saul; see on 4:4. Both in ch. 9 and here David remembered his *oath* to his friend Jonathan and his descendants (1 Sam. 20:14-16).

8 *Rizpah* is mentioned in 2 Sam. 3:7 as Saul's concubine. Merab's marriage to Adriel was mentioned in 1 Sam. 18:19.

For *the five sons of Merab* the Leningrad Codex reads "the five sons of Michal," but we know that Michal was childless (see 2 Sam. 6:23) and furthermore that Adriel was the husband of her sister Merab (1 Sam. 18:19).[35] So "Michal" is

30. See LXX^{LN} and MT(MSS). But, BHS has "Michal," following the majority of the MT texts.

31. As for *They*, the K. *hēm* is a *phonetic spelling*, without the final *mater lectionis*; cf. Q. *hēmmāh*.

32. The K. *bārī(')šōnîm t^{e}ḥillat q^{e}ṣîr ś^e'ōrîm*, which means *on the first* (days), i.e., *at the beginning of barley harvest*, is a *phonetic spelling* of *bārī(')šōnîm bitḥillat q^{e}ṣîr ś^e'ōrîm*, which occurred as a result of *external sandhi*, i.e., a phonetic adjustment at a word boundary. See Tsumura, "Scribal Errors or Phonetic Spellings?" 401-3.

33. Literally "water."

34. McCarter, II, p. 442-43.

35. For the textual problem, see S. D. Walters, "Childless Michal, Mother of Five," in

likely a scribal error, substituting a more familiar name for a less familiar name. For *Adriel . . . the Meholathite*, see the commentary on 1 Sam. 18:19.[36]

9 The translation *the seven of them* (also NASB, NRSV, McCarter) is based on the Q. *šᵉbaʿtām*; the K. *šibaʿtāyim* is either a dual of "seven," i.e., "fourteen," or adverbial "seven times."

The *beginning of barley harvest* was in April. McCarter suggests taking *harvest on the first (days)* as "Ziv" on the basis of *zeion* in LXX^L which he thinks is "a Hellenized transliteration of the month name *zw*, 'Ziv,'" but this is farfetched.[37]

10 *Until rain fell on them*, possibly implies that "the rain should have fallen upon them." Perhaps it had been decided that they would not be buried until the rains fell (and the famine stopped). That would suggest that when David heard what Rizpah was doing (v. 11) he buried them earlier than planned, and then God responded (v. 14), probably by rain.

There was great horror of leaving bodies unburied to be eaten by animals or birds (1 Sam. 17:44, 46; Ps. 79:2); Deuteronomy 21:22-23 says that the bodies of those who are hung should be buried that day (see Josh. 8:29). C. H. Gordon notes that "the disgrace of the unburied corpse left to be devoured by dogs and carrion-eating birds" appears also in Homer.[38] This was famously the fate of Ahab and Jezebel (1 K. 21:23-24; 22:38; 2 K. 9:10, 36).

11 *what* (*'et 'ăšer*) with the particle *'et* is grammatically the object, but semantically it is the subject of the passive verb *was told*. For other examples in which a noun with *'et* is the subject of verb, see on 1 Sam. 20:13.[39]

4. God's Wrath Ends (21:12-14)

12 *And David went and took the bones of Saul and the bones of Jonathan his son from the citizens*[40] *of Jabesh-gilead, who had stolen them from the open square of Beth-shan, where the Philistines had hung*[41] *them on the day when the Philistines struck down Saul on Gilboa.*

The Tablet and the Scroll. Near Eastern Studies in Honor of William W. Hallo, ed. M. Cohen, D. Snell, and D. Weisberg (Bethesda, Maryland: CDL Press, 1993), pp. 290-96; R. P. Hays, "A Problematic Spouse: A Text-Critical Examination of Merab's Place in 1 Samuel 18:17-19 and 2 Samuel 21:8," *ZAW* 129 (2017) 220-33.

36. Tsumura, I, pp. 486-84.

37. McCarter, II, p. 439.

38. Gordon, *CB*, p. 268.

39. Tsumura, I, p. 508 n. 46. See W-O, §10.3.c.

40. Lit. "lords"; cf. "men" (NASB); "people" (NRSV); cf. "men" in 2 Sam. 2:5.

41. The K. *tālûm* (*had hung*) is a *sandhi* spelling of *tᵉlāʾûm* (i.e., without the *aleph*). See Tsumura, "Scribal Errors or Phonetic Spellings?" 399. The Q. *tᵉlāʾûm* is most probably a later standardization of the spelling.

13 *And he brought up the bones of Saul and the bones of Jonathan his son*
from there; and they gathered the bones of those who had been hanged
14 *and buried the bones of Saul and Jonathan his son in the land of Benja-*
min in Zela, in the grave of Kish his father; they did all that the king commanded.
And God responded to the plea[42] *for the land after that.*

12 For *the bones of Saul and the bones of Jonathan*, see 1 Sam. 31:12-13, where the men of Jabesh burned the bodies of Saul and Jonathan and his two other sons and buried their bones. McCarter thinks that as the bodies were burned, it could have been no more than ashes that David recovered. However, even after lengthy burning of a body, the bones remain.[43] For *Jabesh-gilead*, see on 1 Sam. 11:1; 31:11-13;[44] and 2 Sam. 2:4.

MT *Bêt-šan* is a phonetic spelling of the normal *Bêt-š^{e}ʾan*, in which the intervocalic /ʾ/ lost its consonantal value and the resultant contiguous vowels, ^{e}+*a*, become *a* as the result of vowel *sandhi*. The spelling without {ʾ} appears only in 1–2 Samuel. For Beth-shan, see the commentary on 1 Sam. 31:10.[45]

14 Saul was apparently from Gibeon (1 Sam. 11:4), but his family could have originally come from the Benjaminite town of Zela, which is also known as Zela Ha-eleph (Josh 18:28). The town was probably the modern Khirbet es-Salah, less than three miles (5 km) to the south of Gibeon;[46] see also on 1 Sam. 9:2.[47] Presumably they buried in this same grave the bones of the seven who were hanged that they had gathered (v. 13), as well as those of Saul's two other sons who died at Gilboa. For Saul's usual place of residence, see "Gibeah" in 1 Sam. 10:10.[48]

Note here that proper burial was considered essential for the welfare of the dead and the living, as illustrated by the Ugaritic funerary text *KTU* 1.161, in which a sevenfold sacrificial ritual was performed after the burial, presumably for seven days, for the welfare (*šlm*) of the newly enthroned king Amurapi and his family as well as for his kingdom.[49]

42. Lit. "was entreated."

43. McCarter, p. 443. However, in Japan, even after cremation there are bones among the ashes. It is normal for the family to put these bones into the funeral urn after cremation — I have done it myself; the ashes are then poured in.

44. Tsumura, I, pp. 304, 655-56.

45. Tsumura, I, p. 654. For the phenomenon of *sandhi*, see Tsumura, "Scribal Errors or Phonetic Spellings?" 399; Tsumura, "Vowel *sandhi* in Biblical Hebrew," p. 585.

46. See K. van der Toorn, "Saul and the Rise of Israelite State Religion," *VT* 43 (1993) 520.

47. Tsumura, I, p. 263.

48. Tsumura, I, p. 292.

49. See Tsumura, "The Interpretation of the Ugaritic Funerary Text *KTU* 1.161," pp. 40-55.

God "was entreated" (*ʿtr): or "God was pleaded with" (*HALOT*, p. 905) implies that God heard and responded. The expression also appears at 24:25. In both instances, God's anger was finally appeased by David's conduct — here by burying the bones, and in ch. 24 by the sacrifices at the designated place.

B. THE PHILISTINE WARS (21:15-22)

15 *And there was again a war between the Philistines and Israel.*[50]
And David went down together with his servants and they fought against the Philistines.
And David became weary.
16 *As for Ishbi-benob,*[51] *who was among the descendants of the giant, the weight of whose spear was three hundred shekels of bronze and who was girded with a new (sword), he said that he would strike David.*
17 *And Abishai the son of Zeruiah helped him and struck the Philistine and killed him.*
Then the men of David swore to him, saying
"You shall not go out again with us to battle,
so that you may not extinguish the lamp of Israel."
18 *After this there was war again with the Philistines at Gob; then Sibbecai the Hushathite struck down Saph, who was among the descendants of the giant.*
19 *And there was war with the Philistines again at Gob, and Elhanan the son of Jaare-oregim, the Bethlehemite, struck down Goliath the Gittite, the shaft of whose spear was like a weaver's beam.*
20 *And there was again war at Gath, where there was a man of great size; his fingers on each hand and his toes on each foot were six each, thus making twenty-four in number. He too was a descendant of the giant.*[52]
21 *And he defied Israel.*
And Jonathan the son of Shimei, David's brother, struck him down.
22 *These four were born to the giant in Gath.*
And they fell by the hand of David and by the hand of his servants.

50. Lit. "a war of the Philistines with Israel."

51. As for *Ishbi-benob* (Heb. *yišbî b^{e}nōb* as the Q.), the K. *yišbô b^{e}nōb* may be reflecting a phonetic reality resulting from a partial assimilation of the semivowel /i/ to /u/ in the context where the bilabial consonant /b/ appears both in the preceding and the subsequent positions. Cf. "Dod son of Joash" (McCarter), restoring "the displaced marginal plus that stands before v. 11 in LXX^{L} and after v. 11 in LXX^{BA}." (McCarter, II, pp. 447-48)

52. Lit. "born to the giant" (NASB); "descended from the giants" (NRSV).

There was again a war (v. 15) suggests that this is an excerpt from some writing about David's wars. It is an account of four fights of David's men with Philistine giants.

16 *The giant* (Heb. *rāpāh*) has usually been understood as referring to the Rephaim, the "legendary giants of the past" (Gen. 14:5; 15:20; Deut. 2:10-11, 20; 3:13; Josh. 12:4; 13:12; 17:15; etc.). It is certainly understandable that the giants were explained as the *descendants* of Rapi'u, the giant ancestor, on the popular level; in fact, giants are sons of giants, just as gods were sons of gods (*bn ilm*) in Hebrew and Ugaritic.[53]

The meaning of the Hebrew term *qên* (here translated *spear*) is uncertain. Some suggestions are "spear" (so RSV; LXX), "bronze spearhead" (NIV), or "lance" (*HALOT*, p. 1097), and "helmet," reading *qwbʿw* (McCarter and others).[54] Translations of *ḥădāšāh*, include "a new sword" (RSV, ESV), "a new (sword)" (NIV), "new weapons" (NRSV) and "new armor" (JPS, McCarter). Compare "a club, mace" (LXX^{B}).[55] In any case, both are weapons of some type.

17 On *Abishai*, see the commentary on 1 Sam. 26:6[56] and 2 Sam. 2:18.

The expression *the lamp of Israel* (*nēr Yiśrā'ēl*) appears only here; for a similar idea about the importance of the king, see 18:3. But, here, it explains David not so much as a military leader as a symbolic figure of a leader of the covenant people Israel. David was certainly Yahweh's anointed king and, as D. G. Firth holds, "the lamp symbolism (*nēr*) is important for the Davidic monarchy (1 K. 11:36; 15:4; 2 K. 8:19; 2 Chr. 21:7)."[57]

18 The geographical name *Gob* has been interpreted variously. McCarter[58] takes it as "Gezer," as in 1 Chr. 20:4; cf. "Gath" (LXX^{B}). However, Na'aman identifies the recently excavated Khirbet Qeiyafa on the northern side of the valley of Elah as the biblical Gob.[59] The city was already destroyed in the early ninth century, so this identification would support the antiquity of the story of David, if the identification is correct.

53. In Ugaritic, however, the term *rpum* refers to the deified ancestors of the dynasty who were of an earlier generation rather than the recently deceased ancestors, who were referred to as *mlkm*; see *KTU* 1.161 (Tsumura, "The Interpretation of the Ugaritic Funerary Text *KTU* 1.161"). It is used as a divine name *Rpu*, the "eponymous deity of the group of deified ancestors" in 1.108 (*DULAT*, pp. 742-43). See also J. N. Ford, "The 'Living Rephaim' of Ugarit: Quick or Defunct?" *UF* 24 (1992) 73-101.

54. McCarter, II, p. 448.

55. For various translations, see McCarter II, p. 448.

56. Tsumura, I, pp. 599-600.

57. Firth, p. 510.

58. McCarter, II, p. 448.

59. See N. Na'aman, "In Search of the Ancient Name of Khirbet Qeiyafa," *JHS* 8 (2008) article 21.

For *Sibbecai*, see on 2 Sam. 23:27. *The Hushathite* means he was from the village of Hushah (1 Chr. 4:4), which is the modern Husan in the Judaean hills; it is located a few miles (a few km) southwest of Bethlehem. In 1 Chr. 20:4 *Saph* appears as "Sippai," which could be a longer form of the same name.

19 *Elhanan. . . struck down Goliath the Gittite.* Since in 1 Sam. 17 David killed Goliath *from Gath* (v. 4; "Gittite" means someone from Gath), this statement has caused endless controversy.[60] Suggestions of the relation between these two passages range from saying that the phrase "Lahmi the brother of" has fallen out of the text before "Goliath" in this chapter (see the parallel passage in 1 Chr. 20:5) to saying that the deed of Elhanan was later attributed to David.[61] Other suggestions are that the name "Goliath" became attached to David's anonymous victim or, as I tend to hold, that the passages refer to two different men called Goliath by the Israelites.

The name *Goliath* (*golyāt*) (see on 1 Sam. 17:4)[62] has been traced by Albright and others back to the non-Semitic Anatolian name *Walwatta*, an older form of the Lydian name *Alyattes*. Recently, similar personal names, *Alwt* [Hebrew script, *aleph-lamed-vav-tav*] and *Wlt*, have been identified in the "Goliath Inscription," the earliest known inscription from the Philistine Gath, Tell eṣ-Ṣâfī, which dates from the tenth to mid-ninth century B.C.[63] While the *Alyattes* = Goliath etymology has been considered doubtful by some, the PNs *Alwt* and *Wlt* as well as *golyāt* are most probably non-Semitic Indo-European names. And *Alwt* and the Carian PN *w/uliat* (cf. Hittite *walliwalli* "powerful") might explain the etymology of Goliath, as suggested by H. C. Merchert.[64]

Though no direct relation of the inscription with David's story should be proposed, one possibility is that the Philistine counterpart of the Hebrew name *golyāt* was a well-known PN in Philistine Gath. It is possible that the name and its variants became a common name used by the Israelites to refer to a Philistine giant, just as "the descendant of Rapha" means *the descendants of giant* (vv. 16, 18). For the originally non-Semitic proper name *Achish* (1 Sam. 21:10, 27:2) that may have become a title for a Philistine ruler, see the commentary on 1 Sam. 21:10.[65]

60. See Japhet, pp. 368-69.

61. Many hold that "the tradition attributing the slaying of Goliath to Elhanan is older than that which credits the deed to David" (McCarter, II, p. 450).

62. Tsumura, I, p. 440.

63. A. M. Maeir et al., "A Late Iron Age I/ Early Iron Age II Old Canaanite Inscription from Tell eṣ-Ṣâfī/ Gath, Israel: Palaeography, Dating, and Historical-Cultural Significance," *BASOR* 351 (2008) 39-71.

64. Maeir et al., "A Late Iron Age I / Early Iron Age II Old Canaanite Inscription from Tell eṣ-Ṣâfī / Gath, Israel," 58.

65. Tsumura, I, pp. 535-36.

For *the shaft of (his) spear* (lit. "the wood of his spear"), see on 1 Sam. 17:7.[66] Korpel notes the same usage of "wood" for the shaft of a spear in Baal's seven wooden shafts of his lightning-spears (*ʿṣ brq*) in *KTU* 1.101:4.[67] For the expression *like a weaver's beam*, see on 1 Sam. 17:7.[68]

21 Jonathan may be the Jonathan listed as one of David's thirty mighty men (23:32). *Shimei* was David's third eldest brother. His name is given in various forms in 1 Sam. 16:9; 17:13; 2 Sam. 13:3; and 1 Chr. 2:13.

22 *These four*, which is used with the particle *ʾet*, serves as the subject of a passive verb, reflecting grammatical ergativity.[69]

For *the giant in Gath*, see on v. 16. McCarter translates it as "Rapha-in-Gath," taking Rapha as a divine name of a chthonic character.[70]

X. THE SONG OF DAVID (22:1-51 = Ps. 18)

Chapters 22 and 23 both are songs of David, the first with a title alluding to the beginning of his reign, and the second alluding to its end. The "Song of David" in ch. 22 is essentially the same psalm as Ps. 18. However, in the Hebrew text of the two passages there are many differences in spelling, etc., though few of them come across in translation. Most of these differences can be understood when one realizes that the Book of Psalms, which was regularly used in worship throughout history, uses "standard" Hebrew spelling, while the spelling in the Samuel passage tends to avoid using consonant letters for long vowels and is much more phonetic in character (e.g., 2 Sam. 22:8, 27, 36, 40, 46, etc.), due to the fact that as a poem included within a narrative, it was written as it was meant to be heard, that is, aurally.

For example, in vv. 1-2, 2 Sam. 22 has defective spellings, while the corresponding verses of Ps. 18 has full spellings: e.g.

defective spelling	*full spelling*
אֹתוֹ (2 Sam. 22:1)	אוֹתוֹ (Ps. 18 title)
וּמְצֻדָתִי (2 Sam. 22:2)	וּמְצוּדָתִי (Ps. 18:3)

As another example, the term *waʿănōtᵉkā* in v. 36, which has troubled many scholars, is often emended to mean "your help" in the light of 4QSam[a]

66. Tsumura, I, pp. 443-44.

67. M. C. A. Korpel, *A Rift in the Clouds: Ugaritic and Hebrew Descriptions of the Divine* (UBL 8; Münster: Ugarit-Verlag, 1990), p. 498 n. 461.

68. Tsumura, I, pp. 443-44.

69. See Tsumura, I, p. 508 n. 46; also W-O, §10.3.c.

70. McCarter, II, p. 451. On the relationship between the biblical Rephaim and Ugaritic *rpum*, see the various works cited in *DULAT*, 742-43.

(*w'zrtk*), even though LXX^{B} and LXX^{L} support the MT against 4QSam^{a}.[71] However, it is possible to explain *wa'ănōtᵉkā* as a phonetic variant of the corresponding *wᵉ'anwatkā* in Ps. 18:35, which is from *'nw ("to oppress").[72]

These two psalms are usually explained as two versions of a single original composition,[73] one being used by the writer of Samuel, and the other by the collector of Book 1 of the Psalms.

There are in general two theories on the relation between 2 Sam. 22 and Ps. 18.

1. One is that David wrote all his psalms in fairly standard spellings, basically as they are now in the Book of Psalms, and they existed as a collection. When the Books of Samuel were written, the author took Ps. 18 and wrote it either from memory or dictation using phonetic spelling.
2. The second is that the original collection of David's psalms used phonetic spellings, the "standard" spelling of the court for several generations, and the author of Samuel copied Ps. 18 as it was written. Later, the spelling of all of the psalms in the book of Psalms was "modernized" for use in the choir.

As for the nonspelling differences, perhaps the Samuel version is as David first wrote it, but the Psalm version reflects changes that were made for various reasons either by David himself or by the choirmasters. For example, 2 Sam. 22 starts off with a series of nouns, "Lord, my rock and my fortress." It is most natural to take these as attributive statements, "The Lord is my rock and my fortress, my deliverer." But it is not until we get to the second-person verb (*you save me*) at the end of v. 3 that we realize that all those nouns are vocative (O Lord, my rock), not attributive (O Lord, you are *my rock*).[74] Perhaps for this reason in Ps. 18 the song was changed by adding "I love you, O Lord, my strength" at the start and deleting "you save me from violence," so the nouns are clearly attributive from the beginning *The Lord is my rock*, and the listener does not have to do a reanalysis upon hearing *you save me from violence*.

The song is often said to have many similarities to Canaanite mythology, and it has even been asserted that the language, especially that of vv. 8-20, was

71. See Herbert, *RBDSS*, p. 187.

72. Tsumura, "Scribal Errors or Phonetic Spellings?," p. 394.

73. E.g., T. Young, "Psalm 18 and 2 Samuel 22: Two Versions of the Same Song," in *Seeking Out the Wisdom of the Ancients: Essays Offered to Honor Michael V. Fox on the Occasion of His Sixty-Fifth Birthday*, ed. R. L. Troxel, K. G. Friebel, and D. R. Magary (Winona Lake, Ind.: Eisenbrauns, 2005), pp. 53-69.

74. Most translations, as Vulg., KJV, RSV, NIV, ESV, take these nouns as attributive nouns, not vocatives. But JPS translates them as vocatives.

adapted from the myths of the storm god Baal.[75] However, that view is too simplistic, and the similarities have been overemphasized. The song rather describes the Lord's control over the universe and the forces of nature, using a rich selection of imagery and metaphor from the ancient Near Eastern literature; see below.[76]

1. 22:1-2a

1 *And David spoke to the* LORD *the words of this song when the* LORD *delivered him from the hand of all his enemies, especially*[77] *from the hand of Saul.*
2a *And he said,*

This is the heading of the song. It is essentially the same as that of Ps. 18. Psalm 18 is one of thirteen psalms (3; 7; 18 [=2 Sam. 22]; 34; 51; 52; 54; 56; 57; 59; 60; 63; and 142) that identify themselves as connected with events in the life of David. The heading of the psalm starts off, "To the choirmaster. Of David, the servant of the LORD, who spoke to the LORD."

And David spoke— This "speaking" is an act of recitation or singing. The term *song* (*šîrāh*) here is a feminine noun; also in Exod. 15:1; Deut. 31:19, 21, 22, 30; 32:44.

The term *when* is literally "in the day." This does not refer to one particular incident in David's life, though, since the text is concerned with deliverance from "all his enemies."

The term *hand* (twice) here is literally "palm" (*kap*), for which the psalm heading has the synonymous variant "hand" (*yad*) in the phrase *the hand of Saul.* Both *kap* and *yad* have the meaning of "power" in this context.

An elaborate title followed by the phrase *And he said* can be found also in second millennium Egyptian songs as the Great Hymn to Osiris (*CS* 1.26) and The Great Hymn to Aten (*CS* 1.28).[78] A literary tradition of songs and hymns with titles, which give information about the occasion, the singer, and musical notices such as instruments and modes, has been attested since the third millennium B.C. in the ancient Near East. One noticeable example is the "Nikkal hymn from Ugarit" (RS 15.30+15.49+17.387) of mid-second

75. For example, see P. C. Craigie, *Ugarit and the Old Testament* (Grand Rapids: Eerdmans, 1983), p. 88; Craigie, *Psalms 1-50* (WBC 19; Waco, Tex.: Word, 1983), p. 174.

76. D. T. Tsumura, *Creation and Destruction: A Reappraisal of the* Chaoskampf *Theory in the Old Testament* (Winona Lake, Ind.: Eisenbrauns, 2005), pp. 149-51.

77. The particle *w*, here translated as *especially*," is an emphatic *waw*; GKC, § 154a n. 1b; Anderson, pp. 262-63.

78. See also Tsumura, "Hymns and Songs with Titles and Subscriptions in the Ancient Near East," p. 2 [Japanese with an English summary].

millennium B.C., a Hurrian hymn with Akkadian musical notation, that gives the name of a historical king, Ammurapi.[79] Other examples showing that kings or other royal family members participated in musical activities are also known from the pre-Davidic ANE. "Theban king Intef II waxes lyrical in his very personal praise of the goddess Hathor, in his exuberant hymn, engraved on one of the stelae at his tomb."[80]

This song deals with battle. Its first part (vv. 2-31) describes the fight in terms of the actions of the Lord; the next section (vv. 33-49) deals with the fight against enemies in terms of what David did, thanks to the Lord who equipped him for battle (v. 40).

2. 22:2b-4

2b *O Lord, my rock and my fortress,*
and my deliverer,
3 *God, who is my rock, in whom I take refuge,*
my shield and the horn of my salvation,
my stronghold and my refuge,
my savior, you save me from violence![81]
4 *As the one who is worthy to be praised I call upon the Lord;*
from[82] *my enemies I am saved.*

2b LXX^L and Syr. follow Ps. 18:1 in beginning this verse with a *monocolon*, "I love you, Lord, my strength!"

O Lord (cf. "The Lord is"; so NIV, ESV, REB) is followed by nine titles or epithets of Yahweh in the vocative. These vocatives are in keeping with the

79. Tsumura, "Hymns and Songs with Titles and Subscriptions," 2-7; see also N. Wyatt, "The Religion of Ugarit: An Overview," in *HUS*, p. 580.

80. K. A. Kitchen, *On the Reliability of the Old Testament* (Grand Rapids: Eerdmans, 2003), p. 105. Cf. B. S. Childs, "Psalm Titles and Midrashic Exegesis," *JSS* 16 (1971) 137-50; A. M. Cooper, "The Life and Times of King David According to the Book of Psalms," in *The Poet and the Historian: Essays in Literary and Historical Biblical Criticism*, ed. R. E. Friedman (HSS 26; Chico: Scholars Press, 1983), pp. 117-31.

81. Ps. 18:2 has
The Lord is my rock and my fortress,
and my deliverer,
my God, who is my rock, in whom I take refuge,
my shield and the horn of my salvation,
my stronghold.

82. Note that Ps 18:3 has the unassimilated form *min-'ōyᵉbay* ; the Samuel text reflects *phonetic reality*.

second-person verb *you save me* (v. 3). In Ps. 18, which lacks the verb "you save me (from violence)," at the end of the verse, the syntax is "The Lord is my rock. . ., and the horn of my savior, my stronghold." Besides in the parallel text Ps. 18:2, the same expression *my rock and my fortress* appears also in Pss. 31:3; 71:3.

The phrase *my deliverer* is literally "deliverer of me, to me"; the "to me" is added for emphasis, but Ps. 18:2 lacks it.

3 *God, who is my rock* (*'ĕlōhê ṣûrî*; lit. "God of my rock"), that is, "God who is my strength"; cf. "my God, my rock" in Ps. 18:2 (*'ēlî ṣûrî*), hence, as a hendiadys "my divine crag" (McCarter). In this psalm the LXX avoids a literal translation of *ṣûr* "rock" and translates *boēthos mou* "my helper"; in other places, the LXX sometimes translates it as "strength" (e.g., Ps. 73:26).[83] The description of God as "a rock" that offers refuge and safety is frequent in the Bible; see on 1 Sam. 2:2.[84]

The term *horn* in the phrase *the horn of my salvation* signifies here strength rather than dignity as in 1 Sam. 2:1, 10. Compare "my mighty champion" (JPS); "my . . . sure defender" (REB). The word pair, *stronghold* and *refuge*, also appears in Ps. 59:16 [17].

The end of v. 3, *and my refuge, my savior, you save me from violence!* is lacking in Ps. 18:2. McCarter, deleting *mšʿy* "my savior" as a conflation, rereads *mōšīʿî mēḥāmās tōšīʿēnî* ("my savior, you save me from violence") as *mḥmsym yšʿny* ("from violent men he saves me") since there is no other second-person verb in the first twenty-five lines of the poem.[85] But with all the vocatives (see on v. 2b), a second-person verb *you save me* (*tōšīʿēnî*) is not to be wondered at. It might be possible to translate the verb as "he saves me," taking the verb as a *taqtul*- 3 m.sg. form (see Gordon, *UT*, p. 74) as in 1 Sam. 17:21. However, *taqtul*- is usually a 3 m.pl. or du. form.

4 The word *mᵉhullāl*, translated here as *the one who is worthy to be praised*, and *YHWH* are appositional; the verb *'eqrā'* ("I call upon") interrupts the adjacency of two nominal phrases, thus constituting the AXB pattern: i.e., *mᵉhullāl 'eqrā' YHWH*. McCarter emends the text to *mᵉhôlāl* "treated as a fool, derided" in the light of Ps. 102:8, where "enemies" (*'ôyᵉbāy*) and "those who deride me" (*mᵉhôlālay*) appear in parallelism, in order that the colon may be "semantically and structurally equivalent" to the beginning of v. 7. But there is no support for his reading from ancient versions.

The verbs *'eqrā'* and *'iwwāšēaʿ* in this verse have been translated variously: e.g., "I called" (JPS), "call" (ESV), "shall call" (REB)" and "I was"

83. McCarter, II, p. 455.
84. Tsumura, I, pp. 143-44.
85. McCarter, II, pp. 455-56.

"I am," or "I shall be" saved. The tense of a *yqtl*-verb in poetical texts can be either past or nonpast; it is decided from the context. Since, as explained below, it seems we should take vv. 5-7 with the change of verbal forms from *yqtl*s to *qtl*s as referring to David's past experience, the *yqtl*s in v. 4 should be taken as his present conviction.

3. 22:5-7

5 *For*[86] *the waves of death encompassed me;*
the torrents of destruction overwhelmed me.
6 *The cords of Sheol surrounded me;*
the snares of death confronted me.
7 *In my distress I called upon the* LORD,
and to my God I called.
And he heard my voice from his temple,
and my cry for help was in his ears.

5-6 These verses can be compared with Ps. 116:3:

the waves of death (v. 5)	*the cords of death* (Ps. 18:4; 116:3)
the torrents of destruction	
the cords of Sheol (v. 6)	*the terrors of Sheol* (Ps. 116:3)
the snares of death	
in my distress (v. 7)	*distress and sorrow* (Ps. 116:3)

While Ps. 116:3 is a tricolon, the present text consists of three bicola, each corresponding to one line of the tricolon of Ps. 116. Jonah 2:5-6a uses a similar structure.

5 For the phrase *the waves of death* (*mišbᵉrê-māwet*), Ps. 18:4 has *ḥeblê-māwet* "the cords of death."

The phrase *torrents of destruction* (*naḥălê bᵉlîya'al*) is literally "the torrents of Beliyaal (i.e., "worthlessness")"; only here in the OT is this term paired with *death* (*māwet*); cf. "hell" (McCarter).[87] See on 1 Sam. 1:16 and Excursus in *The First Book of Samuel*;[88] also 2 Sam. 16:7; 20:1.

6 *Sheol* normally refers the place of the dead. But here it is used as a synonym for death. The etymology of the term (i.e., "a place of inquiry"[89])

86. Ps. 18:4 lacks "for."
87. McCarter, II, p. 465. For "Beliyaal," see Tsumura, I, pp. 122-24.
88. Tsumura, I, pp. 121-24.
89. See Excursus in Tsumura, I, pp. 617-18, esp. n. 12.

is still hotly debated,[90] but it probably refers to a place where the living *asks* (*š'l) about the whereabouts or fate of the dead in order to facilitate a reunion. In 1–2 Samuel it appears only twice, here and in 1 Sam. 2:6, both poetic texts. In fact, in the entire Bible the term appears only in poetic texts or in idiomatic phrases such as "to go down to Sheol" (e.g., Gen. 37:35), which means "to die."

The Hebrew term *sabbūnî* for *surrounded* is a shorter phonetic spelling of the corresponding term *sᵉbābûnî* (Ps. 18:5).[91]

In vv. 5-6, the two sets of word pairs constitute a chiastic order AB// BA: *death - destruction // Sheol - death.* All four lines say in prose, "I was facing death."

7 For the sequence in Samuel of *I called* (*'eqrā'*) . . . *I called* (*'eqrā'*) followed by *and he heard* (*wayyišma'*), Ps. 18:6 has *I called* (*'eqrā'*) . . . *I cried for help* (*'ăšawwēa'*). *He heard* (*yišma'*) without *waw* consecutive. The parallelism of these verbal forms may support the hypothesis that in poetic texts the tense of the so-called imperfect verbs may be past, regardless of *waw*.

As is usual, *heard* does not simply mean a passive "hearing"; it implies an attentive listening and, usually, a positive response. This is the point at which the situation changes. *Temple* probably refers to God's heavenly temple, from which he comes down in v. 10; see Ps. 11:4; Micah 1:2-3.

4. 22:8-16

8 *And the earth trembled and quaked;*
the foundations of the heavens shook
and trembled, because he was angry.[92]
9 *Smoke went up from his nostrils;*
and fire from his mouth devoured;
glowing coals flamed forth from him.[93]

10 *He spread open the heavens*[94] *and came down;*
and thick darkness was under his feet.

90. See *HALOT*, pp. 1368-69.

91. Tsumura, "Scribal Errors or Phonetic Spellings?," p. 394 n. 19.

92. Lit. "it (="an anger") burned to him," i.e., "he was angry"; see "you are angry" (*ḥārāh lᵉkā*) in Gen. 4:6; 2 Sam. 19:42. This is an example of *brachylogy*, i.e., the ellipsis of the subject of an idiom; see Tsumura, I, pp. 64-65.

93. Or "by it," referring to the mouth of the Lord.

94. Cf. "bowed" (NASB, NRSV); "bent" (JPS); "parted" (NIV). See D. T. Tsumura, "*šmym*- Heaven, sky, firmament, air," in *NIDOTTE*, pp. 160-66, on "heavens" and this verb.

11 *And he rode on a cherub*[95] *and flew;*
and he appeared[96] *on the wings of the wind.*
12 *And he made the darkness around him his canopies,*
the sieve of the waters, the thick clouds of the skies.
13 *From the brightness before him*
coals of fire flamed forth.
14 *The* LORD *thundered from heaven;*
and the Most High uttered his voice.
15 *And he sent out arrows, and scattered them;*
lightning, and routed them.
16 *And the sources of the sea appeared;*
the foundations of the world were laid bare
at the rebuke of the LORD,
at the blast of the breath[97] *of his nostrils.*

8-16 The action of the Lord is described in vivid metaphor. What is the metaphor used? The phenomenon that would cover most of the description is a volcano, which causes earthquake, smoke, fire, fiery coals, and ash clouds. However, there are no volcanoes nearby. There are volcanoes near the southern end of the Red Sea, but they were not active three thousand years ago.

Earthquake imagery (earthquakes were known, see Amos 1:1) is often associated with the Lord (Isa. 5:25; 24:18), but earthquakes do not cause clouds.

I believe it is best to take these as storm images; describing battle in terms of storm is common both in the Bible and other Near Eastern literature.[98] In this song, the Lord is depicted as a mighty warrior riding in a chariot drawn by the wind or a cherub. David is probably thinking mainly of actual fighting, though he may have been thinking of some instances of spiritual battle also.

8 The trembling of *the earth* is here said to be due to Yahweh's *anger* as in Isa. 13:13; Jer. 10:10; Nah. 1:5. But it also accompanies his approach (Judg. 5:4; Ps. 68:8; 77:18) or results from his uttering his voice (Joel 3:16). The phrase *the foundations of the heavens* (*môs^{e}dôt haššāmayim*) is a unique expression, which is replaced by its variant phrase "the foundations of the mountains" (*môs^{e}dê hârîm*) in Ps. 18:7; the latter also appears in Deut. 32:22. Compare *the foundations of the world* in v. 16.

95. The *cherub* (*k^{e}rûb*) is "a winged sphinx"; see on 1 Sam. 4:4 in Tsumura, I, p. 192; also 2 Sam. 6:2.

96. McCarter, II, p. 457, reads "he swooped" (cf. NIV: "he soared"), reading *wyd'* with Syr., Vulg., and Targ., as in Ps. 18:10.

97. With an adverbial *min* (lit. "from").

98. See Tsumura, *Creation and Destruction*, pp. 182-95.

Here the sequence of verbs, *trembled* (*wattigʿaš*) . . . *quaked* (*wattirʿaš*) . . . *shook* (*yirgāzû*) . . . *trembled* (*wayyitgāʿăšû*), is *wayqtl* . . . *wayqtl* . . . *yqtl* . . . *wayqtl*. It should be noted that the third verb (*yqtl*) is past tense without *waw*; see above (v. 4).

Q. *wayyitgāʿaš* (*trembled:* 3 m.s.) does not match the subject *the earth* (f.s). K. *wtgʿš* should be vocalized either as *wattigʿaš* (Qal, impf., 3 f.s.), as in Ps 18:7, or *wattiggāʿaš* < *wattitgāʿaš* (Hit. impf., 3 f.s.) like *wayyitgāʿăšû* "and (they) trembled" of the third colon of the same verse.[99]

9 When he was *angry*, *smoke* went up from Yahweh's *nostrils* as it did from the nostrils of Leviathan in Job 41:20 (MT v. 12). The imagery here is probably that of a thunderstorm.

10-11 In Ps. 68:33 the Lord is metaphorically described as "the rider of the ancient highest heavens" (*rōkēb bišmê šᵉmê-qedem*), who employs a cloud chariot to fly *on the wings of the wind* (v. 11; Ps. 104:3; Isa. 19:1). See the Ugaritic epithet of Baal as "the Rider of the clouds" (*rkb ʿrpt*) in *KTU* 1.2 IV 8, etc.[100] The Lord is fighting against David's enemies.

12[101] Verse 12 and Ps. 18:11 differ slightly; the former is a bicolon, while the latter a tricolon.[102]

wayyāšet ḥōšek sᵉbîbōtâw sukkôt
ḥašrat-mayim ʿābê šᵉḥāqîm

And he made the darkness around him his canopies,
the sieve of the waters, the thick clouds of the skies.

Ps. 18:11 (MT 12)
yāšet ḥōšek
sitrô sᵉbîbôtâw sukkātô
ḥeškat-mayim ʿābê šᵉḥāqîm

He made the darkness his covering,
around him his canopy,
the darkness of waters, the thick clouds of the skies.

99. See Tsumura, "Scribal Errors or Phonetic Spellings?," pp. 394-95.

100. *DULAT*, p. 740; also see A. Rahmouni, *Divine Epithets in the Ugaritic Alphabetic Texts* (Leiden: E. J. Brill, 2008), pp. 288-91.

101. For vv. 12-19, see M. Weinfeld, "Divine Intervention in War in Ancient Israel and in the Ancient Near East," in *History, Historiography and Interpretation: Studies in Biblical and Cuneiform Literatures*, ed. H. Tadmor and M. Weinfeld (Jerusalem: Magnes Press, 1983), pp. 136-40.

102. Tsumura, "Vertical Grammar of Parallelism in Hebrew Poetry," p. 175.

Comparing the first line in the Samuel passage and the first two lines of the psalm passage, it seems that one could say that the colon (or line) of Samuel is expanded into a bicolon in the psalm, with the addition of the parallel term, "his covering." Here, the grammatical relation between "he made the darkness" and "around him" is horizontal in Samuel, while in the psalm it is vertical with the structure AX // BX'. The phrases A ("he made the darkness") and B ("around him") have a vertical grammatical relationship, while on the other hand X' ("his canopy") is simply a restatement of X ("his covering").[103] The phrase *wayyāšet* (*and he made*) in Samuel is impf. with *waw consecutive*, while on the other hand *yāšet (he made)* in the psalm could be an old *yqtl* preterite; see below on v. 14.

The phrase *ḥašrat-mayim* is here translated as *the sieve of the waters*, following McCarter, who explains it based on Postbiblical Hebrew *ḥašar* "sift, distill through as sieve." He holds that "this cosmic structure is the celestial rain cloud" which was, he assumes, called a sieve "because rain falls to earth from it in small drops."[104] See "a mass of waters" (NASB); cf. *ḥeškat-mayim* "the darkness of waters" in the psalm.

The phrase *thick clouds of the skies* (*ʿābê šeḥāqîm*; also Ps. 18:11) has been taken as a gloss,[105] but the structures of the two parallel passages rather support its existence in its original contexts, as noted above. The basic meaning of the two parallel passages is almost the same:

2 Sam. 22:12 And he made the darkness around him, namely the sieves of the waters,
namely the thick clouds of the skies, (to be) *his* canopies.
Ps. 18:11 He made the darkness around him, namely the darkness of waters,
namely the thick clouds of the skies,
(to be) his covering, namely his canopy.

See below on v. 39, where the parallelism is a tricolon, while the corresponding Ps. 18:38 has a bicolon.

13 Here, *coals of fire* (*gaḥălê ʾēš*), an imagery of flashing lightning and hail, is added to the rain-cloud imagery; cf. "fiery coals" (JPS); "bolts of lightning" (NIV).

14 The mode of theophany is the thunderstorm, as is often in older biblical poetry.[106] The verb *thundered* (*yarʿēm*), which is a *yqtl*-form, is an

103. See Tsumura, "Vertical Grammar of Parallelism in Hebrew Poetry," pp. 167-81; also Tsumura, "Textual Corruptions, or Linguistic Phenomena?," pp. 141-42.

104. McCarter, II, p. 466.

105. E.g., McCarter, II, pp. 453, 457.

106. See Cross, *Canaanite Myth and Hebrew Epic*, pp. 156-63.

old preterite. It appears in 2 Sam. 22 only here and in v. 16, while the parallel passages in Ps. 18 have *wayqtl* (*wayyarʿēm*; *wayyiggālû*); see on v. 12.

Thundered and *uttered his voice* are a paired expression. On the Lord's thundering, see on 1 Sam. 7:10.[107] For the voice of the storm god Baal as thunder, see *KTU* 1.5 V 8-9 (*UT* 51:5:70-71). The same idiomatic expression is attested in Amos 1:2;[108] Ps. 29:3-9; 46:6; etc.[109]

15 This verse is a good example of poetic parallelism exhibiting "verticality" in Biblical Hebrew parallelism."[110] It has the parallelistic structure a-b-x // b'-x':

And he sent out arrows, and scattered them;
// lightning, and routed them.

wayqtl - NP(O) - *wayqtl*
// NP(O) - *wayqtl*

The first VP (*sent out*) governs both NP(O)s, not only *arrows* in the first line but also *lightning* in the second line, so *he sent out* and *lightning* are vertical-grammatically related to each other; see also vv. 23 and 41 below.

Instead of *bārāq* "lightning," Ps. 18:14 has the variant form *ûbᵉrāqîm rāb*, which has been translated as "and he shot out lightnings" etc., by taking *rāb* as a verbal form. However, the verse in the Samuel text is a good example of a parallelism with vertical grammar, and the variant text in the psalm should be analyzed similarly with a NP at the beginning of the line, not a sentence; hence, "And lightning flashes in abundance" or the like, taking *rāb* adverbially.

For the term *routed* (K. *wyhmm*; Q. *wayyāhōm*; or "confused"), see 1 Sam. 7:10. McCarter takes the two "them"s of this verse to refer to the previous nouns "arrows" and "lightning bolts" respectively since the "enemies" do not appear until v. 18, and translates this verb as "made them rumble."[111]

16 Based on *the sources of the sea* (*ʾăpīqê yām*), the variant phrase "the sources of water" (*ʾăpîqê mayim*) in Ps. 18:15 is often translated as "the channels of the sea" (e.g., NRSV, JPS and NIV), the first *mem* being taken as enclitic to the preceding construct noun: thus (*ʾăpîqê-m ym*).[112] See the Ugaritic expression, *apq thmtm* "the springs of two oceans" (*DULAT*, p. 91).

107. Tsumura, I, pp. 236-37.

108. See D. T. Tsumura, "Amos 1:2a," *Exeg* 8 (1997) 89-92.

109. Weinfeld, "Divine Intervention in War," pp. 141f.

110. Tsumura, "Vertical Grammar of Parallelism in Hebrew Poetry," 178; Tsumura, "Verticality in Biblical Hebrew Parallelism," pp. 189-206.

111. McCarter, II, pp. 453 & 67.

112. McCarter, II, p. 457.

For the phrase *the foundations of the world* (*mōsᵉdôt tēbēl*), see Isa 24:18; Mic. 6:2; Ps. 82:5; etc., also the Ugaritic expression *msdt arṣ* in *KTU* 1.4 I 40, and 1 Sam. 2:8b "the pillars of the earth."

The phrase *at the rebuke of the* LORD has the variant "at your rebuke, O LORD!" in Ps 18:15; see Pss 76:6; 104:7.

On the phrase *at the blast of the breath,* Block comments that "this poet perceives the *rûaḥ* as divine breath with which the world is controlled and the forces in opposition to Yahweh are defeated."[113]

5. 22:17-20

17 *He sent (his hand) from on high (and) took me;*
he drew me out of mighty waters.
18 *He delivered me from my strong enemy,*
from those who hated me,
for they were too strong for me.
19 *They confronted me in the day of my calamity;*
and the LORD *became a support for me.*
20 *And he brought me forth*[114] *into a broad place;*
he rescued me, because he delighted in me.

17 *Mighty waters* (*mayim rabbîm*) goes back to the imagery of v. 5. The expression is sometimes taken as referring to a *Chaoskampf* (battle with chaos) through which the Lord supposedly established order as the result of his victory. However, the Bible does not suggest there was any battle in connection with creation.[115] This and other similar expressions are meta-

113. D. I. Block, "Empowered by the Spirit of God: The Holy Spirit in the Historiographic Writings of the Old Testament," *Southern Baptist Journal of Theology* 1 (1997) 44.

114. *Wayyōṣē'* . . . *'ōtî* ; cf. *wayyôṣî'ēnî* (Ps. 18:19).

115. One should distinguish the following terminology: (1) *Chaoskampf* — a divine battle resulting in creation, known only in the battle against the sea monster Tiamat in which the storm god Marduk won the victory against Tiamat and eventually "created" the cosmos out of the dead corpse of Tiamat, as reflected in *Enuma elish*; (2) *theomachy* — a battle between two deities such as the Canaanite storm god Baal and the sea god Yamm without a creation motif; (3) *divine battle* — the battle where a god fights on behalf of his people against spiritual or historical enemies, with a destruction motif. See D. T. Tsumura, "The 'Chaoskampf' Motif in Ugaritic and Hebrew Literatures," in *Le Royaume d'Ougarit de la Crète à l'Euphrate: Nouveaux axes de Recherche,* ed. J.-M. Michaud (Proche-Orient et Littérature Ougaritique 2; Sherbrooke: GGC, 2007), pp. 473-499; and Tsumura, "Chaos and *Chaoskampf* in the Bible: Is 'Chaos' a Suitable Term to Describe Creation or Conflict in the Bible?" in *Conversations on Canaan and the Bible: Creation, Chaos, Monotheism, Yahwism,* ed. R. S. Watson and A. H. W. Curtis (Berlin: Walter de Gruyter, forthcoming).

phors describing the psalmist's difficult situation in the languages of storm and flood.[116] Passages like this describe the destruction of enemies for the sake of deliverance or protection of those who trust in God: e.g., Ps. 46:1-4; 74:12-14; Hab. 3:8.[117]

The phrase *sent (his hand)* is a *brachylogy* of the key term "his hand."[118]

18 Here, for the first time the psalmist's enemy is mentioned directly. The term *enemy* (sg.) is in parallel with *those who hated* (pl.). This word pair appears also in v. 41.

20 *A broad place* is the opposite of a place that is "narrow," an idiom meaning "to be greatly distressed" (lit. "the matter is narrow for") in 1 Sam. 30:6; 2 Sam. 13:2; Ps. 4:1; etc. See Ps. 31:8, "You have set my feet in a broad place." Compare Dahood and Tromp, who understand the phrase as "the broad domain," which they take as "a designation of the netherworld,"[119] but this is unnecessary and certainly does not fit the present context.

6. 22:21-25

21 *The LORD rewarded me according to my righteousness;*
according to the cleanness of my hands he recompensed me.
22 *For I have kept the ways of the LORD;*
I have not acted wickedly, that is, without my God.
23 *For all his ordinances were before me;*
his statutes, I did not turn away from them.[120]
24 *I was*[121] *blameless toward him;*
I kept myself from my iniquity.
25 *And the LORD recompensed me according to my righteousness,*
according to my cleanness[122] *before his eyes.*

116. Tsumura, *Creation and Destruction*, pp. 184-87.

117. See Tsumura, *Creation and Destruction*, ch. 9, "A Creation Motif in Psalm 46?" (pp. 156-63) and ch. 10, "A Destruction Motif in Habakkuk 3" (pp. 164-81). For the destruction motif in Ps. 74:12-14, see D. T. Tsumura, "The Creation Motif in Psalm 74:12-14? A Reappraisal of the Theory of the Dragon Myth," *JBL* 134 (2015) 547-55.

118. For the *brachylogy*, see Tsumura, I, pp. 64-65.

119. M. J. Dahood, *Psalms I* (AB 16; Garden City, N.Y.: Doubleday, 1965), p. 111; N. J. Tromp, *Primitive Conceptions of Death and the Nether World in the Old Testament* (Rome: Pontifical Biblical Institute, 1969), p. 47.

120. Lit. "from it" (3 f.s.).

121. Or "I have been."

122. Ps. 18:24 has "the cleanness of my hands" (*kᵉbōr yāday*) as in 2 Sam. 22:21.

21 The verb *rewarded* is imperfect; but it is an old *yqtl* that is a preterite or past tense. Similarly, the phrase *he recompensed me* (*yāšîb lî*; lit. "he returned . . . to me") is preterite. The bicolon constitutes a chiasmus.

22 McCarter translates the Hebrew *wᵉlōʾ rāšaʿtî mēʾĕlōhāy* (lit. "I had not acted wickedly from my god") as "strayed wickedly from my god." He notes similar constructions involving *min-* with other verbs in GKC §119xy and especially 119ff.[123] However, the construction is rather to be explained simply as the privative use of the preposition *min*, hence *without*. This bicolon is a good example of a *synonymous parallelism*, where the two lines describe two sides of the same coin.

23 The parallelism should be understood vertically as in vv. 15 and 41. Thus,

> *For all his ordinances were before me,*
> *and his statutes, I did not turn away from them.*

It can be paraphrased as, "For all his ordinances and his statutes were before me; I did not turn away from them." The grammatical structure of the bicolon is: NP(S) – prepPh // NP(S); VP(*ʾāsûr* "turn away" [S+Vi]) – prepPh.

McCarter reads *mimmennāh* as "from me," emending the text following LXX^L and Ps. 18:22,[124] which, however, has a different grammatical structure:

> For all his rules were before me,
> and his statutes I did not put away from me. (ESV)

There, NP(S) – prepPh // NP(O) – VP(*ʾāsîr* "put away" [S+Vt]) – prepPh.

The second line is simply an example of *inversion* of the word order of V-O. In Ps. 18 "statutes" is the object of the transitive verb "put away," but in 2 Samuel it cannot be the object of the intransitive verb "turn away."

24 The term *tāmîm* "blameless" appears four times in this poem: also in vv. 26, 31, 33. Here and in v. 26, David's concern is his own blamelessness, while in vv. 31 and 33, it denotes the "perfect" *way*, i.e., the blameless state of divine conduct.[125]

25 This verse repeats the phrase *recompensed me* and the word pair *cleanness* and *righteousness* of v. 21b. Thus, it and v. 21 constitute a chiastic *inclusio*, delimiting the section vv. 21-25.

Compared to v. 21, the element *lᵉneged ʿênâw* (*before his eyes* or "in his sight") is new, replacing "of my hands," while all the other phrases and ex-

123. McCarter, II, p. 468.
124. McCarter, II, p. 458.
125. For various interpretations, see *HALOT*, pp. 1749-50.

pressions are the same or similar. Psalm 18:24 repeats "the cleanness of my hands" here.

7. 22:26-33

26 *Toward*[126] *the kind you show yourself kind;*
toward the blameless man[127] *you show yourself blameless.*
27 *Toward the pure you show yourself pure;*
toward the crooked you show yourself perverse.
28 *A humble people you deliver;*
but with your eyes on the haughty you bring them down.
29 *For you are my lamp, O* LORD*;*
the LORD *lightens my darkness.*
30 *For by you I can run over a barricade;*[128]
by my God I can leap over a wall.
31 *As for God, his way is blameless;*
the utterance of the LORD *is refined.*
He is a shield to all who take refuge in him.
32 *For who is God besides*[129] *the* LORD*?*
And who is the rock besides our God?
33 *God is the one who strengthens me with power;*
and he certainly[130] *shows his way to the blameless.*

26-27 These two verses form a quadracolon, i.e., a four-line parallelism, all of the form "With the X (man) you show yourself X (or X')." (The addition of "man" in the second line seems to be for line length.) "You show yourself X" is a verbal form derived from the adjective X.

26 Though McCarter refers to "the textual confusion in this verse,"[131] the MT makes good sense with a proper understanding of the structure of the poetic parallelism.

The verb *you show yourself kind* (*tithassād*) is a denominative verb from *ḥesed*; see 2 Sam. 2:5 on this term.

The phrase *the blameless man* (*gibbôr tāmîm*) is literally "a blameless warrior," but *gibbôr* may no longer have a military sense. Like *gibbôr* in

126. See Ugaritic *'m*.
127. Cf. *g^ebar tāmîm* (Ps. 18:25).
128. NIV, note; or "wall" (*HALOT*, p. 177).
129. Lit. "from without"; cf. "except" (*zûlātî*) in Ps. 18:31; see Josh. 22:19; Isa. 43:11; 44:6, 8; 45:21.
130. Taking *wayqtl* as pf. of assurance or certainty.
131. See McCarter, II, p. 458, for his highly speculative explanation.

1 Sam. 9:1, it probably simply refers to a high member of society (see Ruth 2:1).[132]

27 The Hebrew term *tittappāl* (*you show yourself perverse*) here differs from *titpattāl* in Ps. 18:26. While the Psalm preserves the regular Hithpael form, the Samuel text is the result of several phonetic changes.[133]

tittappāl <-(metathesis)- tippattāl <-(assimilation)- titpattāl

28 This verse restates the theme of the Song of Hannah at the beginning of Samuel (1 Sam. 2:7-8): God controls human destiny, humbling the proud, but raising the humble. This is certainly one of the book's main themes.

The phrase *w*^{e}*'et-'am 'ānî* (*A humble people* [you deliver]) is *kî-'attāh 'am-'ānî* ("For you [deliver] a humble people") in Ps. 18:27. In Samuel the initial part is *waw* plus the object marker, while in the latter it is *ki* plus the independent pronoun *attāh* as the subject. Nevertheless the basic grammar and meaning are the same in the two passages.

Similarly, in the second half of this verse, MT Samuel *w*^{e}*'ênêkā 'al-rāmîm* (*with your eyes on the haughty*) and *w*^{e}*'ênayim rāmôt* ("the haughty eyes") in Ps. 18:27 are both grammatically and semantically the same. That is, the verb *tašpîl*, which appears in both texts, means *you bring down*.

30 "*šwr(?)*" "wall" is literally "bull." Millard has personally suggested that the meaning here is indeed "bull," and it is related to the bull-leaping of Minoan Crete, which is depicted on the fresco of the Great Palace at Knossos.

31 The meaning of the term *ṣ*^{e}*rûpāh* (*refined*) is uncertain, but presumably has something to do with silver in the light of Akkadian *ṣarpu* "refined (said of silver)"; "silver."[134]

32 This also is close to 1 Sam. 2:2 in Hannah's song, extolling the Lord as a rock and the one and only God. It also reflects back to the beginning of the song (vv. 2-3), where God is called a *refuge*.

For the expression *who is God besides the* L*ORD*? see 1 Sam. 2:2. This is the "monotheistic formula," which Eichrodt thinks appears in other literature first in the seventh century.[135] McCarter also speculates that the present passage is an expansion of Isa. 45:5. On the other hand, D. N. Freedman holds a tenth-century date for Hannah's song,[136] and the present psalm could be very

132. See R. L. Hubbard, Jr., *The Book of Ruth* (NICOT; Grand Rapids: Eerdmans, 1988), p. 133.

133. Tsumura, "Scribal Errors or Phonetic Spellings?," p. 396.

134. *CAD*, Ṣ, p. 113.

135. W. Eichrodt, *Theology of the Old Testament*, vol. I (OTL; London: SCM Press, 1961), p. 221; McCarter, II, p. 469.

136. D. N. Freedman, "Psalm 113 and the Song of Hannah," *EI* 14 (1978) 56*-69*. See Tsumura, I, p. 135 n. 2.

old like that. Here too, as in Hannah's prayer, Yahweh's incomparability and his uniqueness are juxtaposed, though implicitly.[137]

For God as *the rock*, see on v. 3. Here, the "rock" is in parallel with "God" (*ʾēl*); see Hab. 1:12 (YHWH// "the rock"). Also, the phrase "the LORD our God" is here broken up into two parallel phrases.[138]

33 The Hebrew *māʿuzzî ḥāyil* has been variously translated: "my strong fortress," or "the one who arms me with strength." McCarter translates "who girded me," following Ps. 18:32 (*ham'azzᵉrēnî ḥāyil*) as well as 4QSam[a];[139] see on 1 Sam. 2:4.[140] However, the text should be translated as *the one who strengthens me with power*, taking the verbal form as a Piel participle with an object suffix; see LXX[B], for which McCarter reads *mʿzzny* as the *Vorlage*.

The meaning of the MT form *wayyattēr*, translated here as *he certainly shows*, is uncertain. It has been taken as the assimilation of the consonant /n/ to the following /t/ of the verb *ntr, Hi ("to leap away"; see *HALOT*, p. 736). See *DULAT*, p. 652: *ntr* "to jump, leap." However, such a meaning does not fit the context. McCarter explains the term as a defective spelling of *wayyetaʾer* from *tʾr ("and he traced") and translates "and mapped out" in the light of Isa. 44:13 and Num. 34:7, 8, 10.[141] However, he ignores the vowel points of the MT spelling. Instead, purely morphologically, it could be a *sandhi* spelling from *ʾtr, Pi *wayyᵉʾattēr*. But, now, we can only guess its meaning. Compare Ps. 18:32 "and he made (*wayyittēn*) my way (*darkî*) blameless" (so *HALOT*, p. 734).[142]

Taken together with v. 31, the second half of v. 33 means "God, whose way is blameless, certainly shows his way to the blameless." This is in keeping with v. 26b, which states that God shows himself blameless to the blameless. Compare "God, whose way is blameless, makes my way blameless" in Ps. 18:30a, 32b.

8. 22:34-43

34 *Setting my feet, like hinds,*
yea on the heights he makes me stand.
35 *He trains my hands for battle;*
my arms bend a bow of bronze.
36 *You have given me the shield of your salvation;*

137. Labuschagne, *The Incomparability of Yahweh in the Old Testament*.

138. See Melamed, "Break-up of Stereotype Phrases as an Artistic Device in Biblical Poetry," pp. 115-53.

139. McCarter, II, p. 459.

140. Tsumura, I, p. 145.

141. McCarter, II, p. 459.

142. Cf. "richtig *wayyittēn*" (Delitzsch, 112).

your chastisement has made me great.
37 *You have enlarged my steps under me;*
my ankles have not slipped.
38 *I pursued my enemies and destroyed them;*[143]
I did not turn back until they were consumed.
39 *I consumed them and smashed them;*
they did not rise[144]
but fell under my feet.
40 *You girded me with strength for battle;*
you subdued under me those who rose against me.
41 *You made my enemies turn their backs to me,*
those who hated me, and I destroyed[145] *them.*
42 *They looked for help, but there was none to save;*
at the LORD, *but he did not answer them.*
43 *I beat them fine like the dust of the earth;*
like the mire of the streets I crushed and stamped on them.

34 The phrase *setting my feet, like hinds* appears in Hab. 3:19 also.

The phrase *yea on the heights* (*w*e*'al bāmôtay*) modifies both *setting* and *stand*, thus being *double-duty*; *waw* of the second colon can be ignored in translation. For this expression, see also 2 Sam. 1:19, 25.

35 Based on Ugaritic and Arabic cognates, McCarter translates this verb (*nḥt) as "he shaped."[146] However, the meaning *bend* (lit. "cause to descend" = "press down") fits in the practice of the idiomatic expression "to bend a bow" (*drk "to tread [a bow]") in order to shoot an arrow; see Pss. 7:12; 11:2; 58:7; 64:3; etc.[147] A *bow of bronze* (*qešet-n*e*ḥûšāh*) is probably a bow reinforced with bronze, which would be difficult to draw, but powerful and very durable. Note that "bronze" is a symbol of unbreakability in Jer. 1:18; Mic. 4:13; Job 6:12; 40:18; etc. *A bow of bronze* also appears together with "an iron weapon" in Job 20:24.

36 After *your salvation*, Ps. 18:35 has the additional colon, "and your right hand supported me" (*wîmîn*e*ka' tis'ādēnî*).

Your chastisement (*'anwatka*; lit. "oppression," from the root *'nw) is often translated as "help" by emending the text based on 4QSam[a]; cf. "gen-

143. *wā'ašmîdēm*; cf. *w*e*'aśśîgēm* "and overtook them" (Ps. 18:37).

144. *w*e*lō' y*e*qûmûn*; cf. "they were not able to rise" *w*e*lō'-yūk*e*lû qûm* (Ps. 18:38).

145. For the verb *ṣmt "to destroy, wipe out, defeat" in Ugaritic, see *KTU* 1.2 IV 9, 1.3 II 8; and *DULAT*, 786-87.

146. McCarter, II, pp. 459, 470.

147. Tsumura, I, p. 380 n. 100. On the topics of *brachylogy* and *idiom*, see Tsumura, I, pp. 64-65; Tsumura, "Literary Insertion (AXB Pattern) in Biblical Hebrew," pp. 473-75; Tsumura, "Niphal with an Internal Object in Hab 3, 9a," p. 14 n. 10.

tleness" (ESV), "you stoop down" (NIV). However, the difference between *waʿănōt*^{e}*kā* in this text and *w*^{eʿ}*anwatkā* in Ps. 18:35 can be explained as follows:[148]

w^{eʿ}*anwatkā* = *w*^{eʿ}*anuatkā* -(contraction)→ *w*^{eʿ}*anōt*^{e}*kā* -(shwa rule)→ *waʿănōt*^{e}*kā*

37 The Hebrew form *taḥtēnî* (*under me*) with -n- (cf. *taḥtāy* in Ps. 18:36) occurs only in this poem (also in vv. 40, 48), though in Ugaritic and Phoenician prepositions sometimes appear with an -n- form.[149]

39 McCarter thinks that *I consumed them* (*wāʾăkallēm*) reflects the LXX of the end of v. 38: "until I finished them." However, the phrase here should be taken as a word pair: "consume and smash"; in Ugaritic these two verbs, *kly* and *mḫṣ*, appear also as a word pair.[150]

The expression *not rise . . . and fell* is a transposition of the common *A not B* pattern; see Amos 5:2. The verse can be analyzed as a tricolon: 8-5-8,

wāʾăkallēm wāʾemḥāṣēm
w^{e}*lōʾ y*^{e}*qûmûn*
wayyip^{e}*lû taḥat raglāy*

while Ps 18:38 is a bicolon: 8-7

ʾemḥāṣēm w^{e}*lōʾ-yūklû qûm*
yipp^{e}*lû taḥat raglāy.*

See on v. 12 above where the parallelism is a bicolon, while Ps. 18:11 is a tricolon.

40 The term *wattazrēnî* (*you girded me*) is a *sandhi* spelling[151] of the corresponding term *watt*^{eʾ}*azz*^{e}*rēnî* in Ps. 18:39. Thus,

watt^{eʾ}*azz*^{e}*rēnî* — (loss of intervolalic *aleph*)→ *watt*^{e}*azz*^{e}*rēnî*
— (vowel *sandhi*)→ *wattazz*^{e}*rēnî*
— (restructuring)→ *wattazrēnî*

In other words, the term *watt*^{eʾ}*azzerēnî* first experienced the loss of an intervocalic *aleph*; then, vowel *sandhi* occurred between [^{e}] and [*a*]. Finally the phonetic structure was slightly modified to become *wattazrēnî.*

148. See Tsumura, "Scribal Errors or Phonetic Spellings?," p. 394.

149. See Gordon, *UT*, §12.9; S. Segert, *A Basic Grammar of the Ugaritic Language: With Selected Texts and Glossary* (Berkeley: University of California Press, 1984), §51.26; Bordreuil and Pardee, *A Manual of Ugaritic*, p. 40. For the Phoenician form *thtn*, see *KAI* 24.14; 14.9.

150. *DULAT*, pp. 540-41; see *KTU* 1.4 II 24-25; 1.5 I 1; 1.19 IV 34; etc.

151. See Tsumura, "Scribal Errors or Phonetic Spellings?" 396-97; also Tsumura, "Textual Corruptions, or Linguistic Phenomena?," p. 139.

Therefore the text should not be explained as a scribal error or a misspelling, i.e., scribal omission of the *aleph*, but rather as an example of internal vowel *sandhi*.

The phrase *those who rose against me* (*qāmay*) is a parallel term of *my enemies* (*'ōyᵉbay*) in vv. 38 and 41. For this word pair, see also on v. 49.

41 Here, vertical grammar (see on v. 15) is at work; *those who hated me*, like its paired expression *my enemies*, is the object of the verb *made* in the first line. Hence, the meaning is: "You made my enemies, i.e., those who hated me, turn their backs to me, and I destroyed them."

One could take the second line as an example of topicalization before a *wayqtl* construction,[152] "as for those who hated me, I destroyed them." However, vertical grammar explains poetic parallelism better than prose grammar, which is basically horizontal.

42 Normally the verbal root *š'h means "to gaze." In view of Ps. 18:41, which has *šw' "to cry out for help," and of the verbal root *yš', which means "to help, save," one may reasonably suggest that the term *yiš'û* (*š'h) of this verse is originally from a biconsonantal verb *š' and means *they looked for help.*

The phrase *at the Lord* (*'l YHWH*) — also 4QSamᵃ — in the second line *vertically* modifies *They looked for help* in the first line, while the clause *but he did not answer them* in the second line is a further specification of *but there was none to save* in the first. In other words, according to the *vertical grammar* of parallelism,[153] the bicolon as a whole means: "They looked at the Lord for help, but there was none to save them, and the Lord did not answer them."

43 The expression *the dust of the earth* (*'ăpar-'āreṣ*) appears also in Amos 2:7 and Job 14:19; the word pair constitutes a construct chain; cf. LXXᴸ and Syr. The phrase *kᵉ'āpār 'al-pᵉnê-rûaḥ* "like the dust before the wind" in Ps. 18:42 is similar to *like the dust of the earth* as a metaphorical expression for fineness.

9. 22:44-46

44 *You delivered me from the contentions of my people;*
you kept me as the head of the nations;
people whom I had not known served me.
45 *Foreigners came cringing to me;*
as soon as they heard,[154] *they obeyed me.*
46 *Foreigners lost heart;*
they came trembling out of their fortresses.

152. See Tsumura, I, p. 47.
153. Tsumura, "Vertical Grammar of Parallelism in Hebrew Poetry," pp. 167-81.
154. Lit. "to the hearing of ear."

44 The variants between the Samuel passage and Ps. 18:43, i.e., *my people* (*ʿammî*) - "the people" (*ʿām*) and *you kept me* (*tišmᵉrēnî*) - "you have set/ made me" (*tᵉśîmēnî*), are not evidence of scribal errors, but features of slightly variant versions of the same poem.

45 Note that the colons v. 45a and v. 45b are inverted with variations in Ps. 18:44.

46 The MT of *came trembling* (*wᵉyaḥgᵉrû*) is a *metathesis* of *wᵉyaḥrᵉgû* (so Ps. 18:45), which is from the verbal root *ḥrg "quake." Such metathesis often occurs when the verbal root includes the consonant /r/.[155] Hence, both forms are acceptable, and either could have existed in the original texts.

The Hebrew *misgeret* (*sgr "to shut") refers to a place such as a "prison" (*HALOT*) or *fortress.* McCarter takes the phrase as "their collars" (lit. "their rims"), as in Ps. 142:8 where *masger* means "neck stock, collar" like *sugar*, from the Assyrian *sigaru*. However, *misgeret* is better taken as a term for a place such as a "prison" or *fortress*, for the verbal root is most likely *ḥrg rather than *ḥgr ("to gird oneself").

10. 22:47-49

47. *The LORD lives! Blessed be my rock;*
exalted be the God of my salvation, a rock!
48 *The God, the one who executes vengeance for me,*
the one who brings down[156] *peoples under me.*
49 *He is the one who brings me out from my enemies;*
above[157] *my adversaries you lift me high;*
from the violent man you deliver me.

47-49 This is the close of the second half, summarizing what the Lord has done and repeating the key-word *rock* (also v. 3).

47 For the oath formula *the LORD lives,* see 1 Sam. 14:39.[158]

The Hebrew expression *ʾĕlōhê ṣûr yišʿî* (lit. "God rock of my salvation") follows the AXB pattern, in which the construct chain *God of my salvation* is interrupted by the insertion of X.[159] For the phrase *God of my salvation,*

155. See Tsumura, "Scribal Errors or Phonetic Spellings?," p. 392; Tsumura, "Textual Corruptions, or Linguistic Phenomena?" 138.

156. *môrîd:* m.sg. participle; cf. *wayyadbēr* "and subdues" (Ps. 18:47).

157. Lit. "from."

158. Tsumura, I, p. 377.

159. Tsumura, I, pp. 60-64.

see the parallel text Ps. 18:46 and many other texts that read "God of (my, our, your, etc.) salvation." The phrase *God of my salvation, a rock* is perfectly adequate as a restatement of *my rock* in the first line. No emendation of the construct form *'ĕlōhe* to *'ĕlōhay* is necessary.

The translation "God, the rock of my salvation" (lit. "God of the rock of my salvation") is also possible in the light of the expressions such as "the rock of my/our salvation" (*ṣûr yᵉšû'ātî* in Ps. 89:26; *ṣûr yiš'ēnû* in 95:1), and "the Rock of his salvation" (*ṣûr yᵉšū'ātô* in Deut. 32:15); also "the rock of my strength" (Ps 62:7). In this case, the first construct chain ("God of the rock") is taken as *apposition* (see above in v. 3): "God, [who is] the rock of my salvation." Note that a construct chain AB is sometimes broken up, with A and B distributed in two parallel colons: A of B ==> A//B.[160] For example, the construct chain "coals of fire" (A of B; vv. 13-14) is broken up and "fire" (B) and "coals" (A) are distributed into two parallel lines in v. 9. However, B is not appositive to A in A//B.

49 In this tricolon, *my enemies* in the first line and *my adversaries* in the second are a popular word pair that closely connects the first two lines. On the other hand, while the first line is in the third person, both the second and the third are in the second person. Thus, the second line serves as a *hinge*, tightly connecting the first and the third lines.

For *you deliver me* (*taṣṣîlēnî*), McCarter translates "you protected me," reading *tnṣrny* with LXX^{L} and 4QSam^{a}, but his reading [t]nṣrny of 4QSam^{a} is rejected by Herbert and corrected in DJD 17 to]*tṣrny*.[161]

11. 22:50-51

50 *Therefore I will extol you, O Lord, among the nations;*
to your name I will sing praises.
51 *He is the one who magnifies the salvation of his king,*
the one who does lovingkindness to his anointed,
to David and to his seed forever.

50-51 The song concludes with a reference to ch. 7 and to the last verse of the Song of Hannah (1 Sam. 2:10).

50 The particle *'al-kēn* (*therefore*), which usually appears in prose rather than in poetry (only 13 times in the Psalms out of 161 times in the OT), here introduces a chiastic bicolon:

160. See most recently Tsumura, "Vertical Grammar of Parallelism in Hebrew Poetry," pp. 179-80.

161. Herbert, *RBDSS*, p. 190; DJD 17, pp. 181, 186.

Therefore
I will extol you, O LORD, among the nations;
to your name I will sing praise.

51 The translation *the one who magnifies* follows the K. *mgdyl,* not the Q. *migdôl,* which means "tower." See also the Q. *magdîl* in Ps. 18:50.

For *lovingkindness* (*ḥesed*), see 2 Sam. 2:5; cf. "steadfast love" (RSV); "unfailing kindness" (NIV). JPS translates the idiom *'śh *ḥesed* (lit. "to do lovingkindness") as "deals graciously."

Some hold that the verse as a whole is an addition intended to give the psalm closer application to the context identified in v. 1, while others think that only v. 51c (*to David and to his seed forever*) is secondary. Since the terminology such as *'ōśeh ḥesed, zar'ô, and 'ad-'ôlām* is "that of Nathan's oracle and related passages," McCarter suggests two possibilities: (1) v. 51 is original and stemmed from circles at the Jerusalem court; (2) v. 51 (or at least v. 51c) is an addition based on Nathan's oracle in order to associate the psalm of a northern (Israelite) origin with the house of David.[162] The first possibility is more likely, in view of the fact that Nathan the prophet of the Lord (7:4-7) was also David's counselor (7:2-3) at the Jerusalem court. Verse 51 reminds us of the Lord's promise to David and his "house" (*dynasty*) of his *seed (heir)* and eternal *throne* in 7:12-16.

Thus, this song of victory (X) by David marks the center of the concluding section of the Books of Samuel, with a praise to the Lord who *magnifies the salvation of his king,* and *who does lovingkindness to his anointed,* namely, *to David and to his seed forever,* and is situated in the middle of the Epilogue (ABXX'B'A') with the other poetic text, David's Last Words (X': 23:1-7).

X'. THE LAST WORDS OF DAVID (23:1-7)

The "Last Words of David" is a psalm praising God for establishing his house as the ruler; it reflects back to the promise in ch. 7. Also, like the wisdom psalms, it contrasts the just ruler and worthless men.

It consists of five parts:[163]

1. Title: *These are the last words of David,* and identification of David (v. 1).[164]
2. Introduction (vv. 2-3a)

162. McCarter, II, pp. 472-73.

163. See G. del Olmo Lete, "David's Farewell Oracle (2 Samuel XXIII, 1-7): A Literary Analysis," *VT* 34 (1984) 414-37.

164. See Tsumura, "Hymns and Songs with Titles and Subscriptions in the Ancient Near East," pp. 1-7 [Japanese with an English summary].

3. Description of the righteous ruler (vv. 3b-4) - like the light of the morning at sunrise
4. David's comment (v. 5)
5. Description of worthless men (vv. 6-7) - like uprooted thorns

McCarter sees here a motif of "the king under the image of sun," a widespread motif in the royal ideologies of the ancient Near East. He cites solar imagery and terminology from Egyptian and Hittite materials as well as biblical passages such as Ps. 84:12; Mal. 3:20.[165]

Not a few scholars regard David as the author of the psalm "from at least v. 3b onwards."[166] McCarter tentatively dates it to the early monarchical period, "perhaps to the time of David," since he can find no "late" vocabulary here and the opening of this poem is parallel to the Balaam oracles (Num. 23), which are "widely recognized as very ancient."[167] He also cannot find any trace of the later Deuteronomistic language.

The elaborate title in v. 1, as noted below, resembles those in some Egyptian poetry. It may be, as already noted above (see the commentaries on 5:6-10 and 8:16), that David had learned the Egyptian literary practices indirectly from the Jebusite court in Jerusalem, which had a close relationship with Egypt during the Amarna age.

The general idea of David's poem is: if my successors are guided by righteous principles of government, my dynasty, under the blessing of God, will be established and prosper.[168] This theme is carried on throughout the books of 1-2 Kings.

1 *And*[169] *these are the last words of David.*
The oracle of David the son of Jesse,
the oracle of the man who was raised by the Exalted One,
the anointed of the God of Jacob,
the minstrel of the songs of Israel:
2 *The spirit of the LORD speaks through me;*
his word is on my tongue.
3 *The God of Israel has spoken;*
to me the rock of Israel has said:
"As for one who rules over men righteously,

165. McCarter, II, p. 484.

166. Hertzberg, p. 400. See G. A. Rendsburg, "The Northern Origin of 'The Last Words of David' (2 Sam 23,1-7)," *Bib* 69 (1988) 115 n. 15.

167. McCarter, II, p. 486.

168. Driver, pp. 361–62.

169. MT has *waw.* It is supported by 4QSam[a], LXX; see Hoffner.

who rules in the fear of God,
4 *he is like the light of a morning when the sun rises,*
(of) a morning when there are no clouds;
(he is like) shafts of sunshine, after rain,
on the grass from the earth."
5 *Is not my house like this*[170] *with God?*
For he has made the eternal covenant with me,
which is ordered and secured in all things;
as for[171] *all my salvation and all my desire,*
will he not indeed make them grow?
6 *As for the worthless, all of them*[172] *are like*[173] *uprooted thorns,*
for they cannot be taken with the hand.
7 *But the man who strikes them*
should be equipped with the blade and shaft of a spear;
with fire they will be completely burned on the spot.

1 This long title is similar to that of some Egyptian poems; e.g., "The Great Cairo Hymn of Praise to Amun-Re" and "The Great Hymn to the Aten."[174] The formula *the oracle of . . . the oracle of the man* appears also in Num. 24:3-4, 15-16; see also Prov. 30:1 and Ps. 36:1. Only in these four contexts is this formula used in connection with human speakers. G. Rendsburg thinks this usage is of northern, i.e., Israelian, origin.[175]

The phrase *hqym ʿāl* translated here with a noun *by the Exalted One* (or "Most High" [NIV]) can also be translated with an adverb "on high" (RSV, JPS, ESV). Unlike *ʿlw* ("against them") in 1 Sam. 2:10, the term here has no final *w.*[176] McCarter reads *hqym ʾl* based on 4QSam^a and LXX^L, and translates it as "God established" "in view of the frequent interchange of the prepositions *ʾl* and *ʿl* in Samuel (22:42; etc.)."[177] NRSV translates similarly as "God exalted." However, it should be noted that in the MT this interchange of the initial *aleph* and *ayin* is mostly limited to the cases of the prepositions *ʾl* and

170. So, T. N. D. Mettinger, "'The Last Words of David': A Study of Structure and Meaning in II Samuel 23:1-7," *Svensk exegetisk Årsbok* 41/42 (1976/1977) 153-54.

171. *topicalization,* introduced by *kî.*

172. Possibly, either the *conflation* or *metaplasm* of two suffixes: *-hem* and *-am*; see McCarter, II, p. 478, for de Boer's view.

173. See BHS [corrected]; based on a misprinted edition of BHS, McCarter discusses "MT" *b-* as a confused spelling; however, in fact, the MT Leningrad has *k-* ; Tadahiro Matsumoto called my attention to this.

174. *CS*, I, pp. 37, 45.

175. Rendsburg, "The Northern Origin," 115.

176. Tsumura, I, p. 140 n. 36.

177. McCarter, II, p. 477.

ʿl, and not for the noun "god." This "raising" refers to the divine inauguration of the kingship of David, *the anointed of the God of Jacob*.

The phrase *n^{e}ʿîm z^{e}mîrôt Yiśrāʾēl*, lit. "the sweet one of the *z^{e}mîrôt* of Israel," has been interpreted in two ways, depending on the meaning of *z^{e}mîrôt*.

Traditionally, *z^{e}mîrôt* has been taken to come from *dmr (I) "to sing, play a musical instrument," and the phrase has been interpreted musically and translated as "the sweet psalmist of Israel" (KJV, RSV, NASB); "the favorite of the songs of Israel" (JPS); "Israel's singer of songs" (NIV).

However, recently some have interpreted *z^{e}mîrôt* in the light of *dmr (II) "to protect," and translated the phrase as "the favorite of the Strong One of Israel" (NRSV); "the darling of the stronghold of Israel" (McCarter). The latter reads *z^{e}mîrôt Yiśrāʾēl* as *zimrat Israel*, a divine epithet that is in parallel to *the God of Jacob*. He sees the same verbal root in *ʿozzî w^{e}zimrāt yāh* (Exod. 15:2; Isa. 12:2; and Ps. 118:14) which he translates "my strength and my stronghold."

Nevertheless, the MT here reads *z^{e}mîrôt*, not *zimrat*, and hence is most naturally translated as "songs." Furthermore, in Ugaritic the word *nʿm* "good," a cognate of *n^{e}ʿîm*, "sweet," is used to mean "minstrel," that is a "good-voiced person," so *n^{e}ʿîm z^{e}mîrôt Yiśrāʾēl* most naturally means *the minstrel of the songs of Israel*.[178] See also the commentary on 2 Sam. 1:26.

It should not be surprising to see a man of war as a musician in the ancient world. For example, Achilles is represented as entertaining himself with his lyre (*Iliad* 9:185-86).[179]

2 The sentence *the spirit of the* LORD *speaks through me* (*bî*), which is in parallel with *his word is on my tongue*, shows that David represents himself as a prophet (see Matt. 22:43; Acts 1:16; 2:30; 4:25; Heb. 4:7) rather than simply as a poet who was thought to be divinely inspired.[180]

3 For *the rock* as a designation of God, see on 1 Sam. 2:2[181] and 2 Sam. 22:2.

The king who *rules over men righteously* is one who *rules in the fear of God*, according to the divine statutes. In other words, the king who fears God would rule over people *righteously* in the same way as the righteous God would rule the people. For *the fear of God* (*yirʾat ʾĕlōhîm*), see Prov. 1:7; 9:10; etc.

178. See D. T. Tsumura, "Ugaritic Contributions to Hebrew Lexicography," *Studies in Language and Literature* 1 (Institute of Literature and Linguistics, U of Tsukuba, 1976), 101-5 [Japanese]; see also Lewis, *Cults of the Dead in Ancient Israel and Ugarit* (Atlanta: Scholars Press, 1989), p. 52.

179. Gordon, *CB*, p. 225.

180. The minstrel is described as "divine" in the *Odyssey*; see Gordon, *CB*, p. 121 n. 1, and p. 224. See W-O, p. 173; O'Connor, "War and Rebel Chants in the Former Prophets," pp. 322-23.

181. Tsumura, I, pp. 143-44.

4 The *he* is the just ruler of the previous verse, not God (see "For the LORD God is a sun and shield" in Ps 84:11). David is talking neither of God nor of himself; he is referring to the future messiah, the *offspring* (or *heir*) of David; see 2 Sam. 7:16. Revelation 3:14 (also 1:5) seems to identify the "faithful and trusted" witness of Ps. 89:36-37 as Jesus Christ.[182]

RSV, ESV, etc. see here three metaphorical expressions, "like the morning light" - "like the sun" - "like rain." Likewise, Mettinger takes the verse as "a triple simile," while de Boer sees here three proverbs. Smith holds that v. 4 compares the king both to the sun as it dawns and to the rain as it causes grass to grow, just as Hos. 6:3 compares Yahweh to both the sun and the rain.[183]

However, the parallelism rather supports the following fairly literal translation:

he is like the light of a morning when the sun rises,
(of) a morning when there are no clouds;[184]
(he is like) shafts of sunshine after rain
on the grass from the earth.

Here, *the shafts of sunshine* (*minnōgah*) is literally "some of the brightness" with a partitive *min*.[185] "Light" (*'ôr*) and "brightness" (*nōgah*) are a word pair seen in Isa. 60:3, 19; Amos 5:20; Hab. 3:4,[186] 11; etc. The parallelism and the word pair suggest rather that only *one* metaphor is involved, the solar metaphor: *like the light // (like) the shafts of sunshine*.

The phrase *after rain* (X: lit. "from rain") is better taken as inserted into the phrase *(like) the shafts of sunshine on the grass* (McCarter), thus constituting the AXB pattern.[187] Hence, the metaphor involves the light of the rising sun in the morning that is shining bright on the grass after rain. Note that there is no verb such as "spring up" in the Hebrew text. Thus, what is described poetically in vv. 3b-4 is this: the righteous king, to whom David refers here, would rule his people righteously *like the sun shines over all*.

182. See the commentary on 2 Sam. 7 and its relationship with Ps. 89, esp. vv. 36-37. Also see Introduction: Themes and Theology of 2 Samuel.

183. M. S. Smith, "The Near Eastern Background of Solar Language for Yahweh," *JBL* 109 (1990) 36: "In the Iron Age, the Israelite king was described, like Yahweh, in solar metaphor, sometimes in combination with rain imagery." Hoffner also sees here references to the sun and the rain.

184. Cf. "a morning too bright for clouds" (McCarter, II, pp. 477-78: lit. "a morning without clouds from (= because of) brightness."

185. For the partitive *min*, see J-M, §133e.

186. For the Janus parallelism in this verse, see D. T. Tsumura, "Janus Parallelism in Hab. III 4," *VT* 54 (2004) 124-28 [reprinted in *VT* 63 (2013) 113-16].

187. See Tsumura, I, pp. 60-64.

5 The *eternal covenant* (*bᵉrît ʿôlām*) here refers to the covenant God made with David in ch. 7, which is referred to also in Ps. 89:19-37; 132:11; Isa. 55:3; Jer. 33:17; 2 Chr. 13:5; 21:7; etc. For discussion of "eternal covenant," see the commentary on ch. 7.

The phrase *ordered and secured* (*ʿărûkāh . . . šᵉmūrāh*) is, according to Driver, "an expression borrowed probably from legal terminology, and intended to describe the *bryt* [covenant] as one of which the terms are fully and duly set forth . . . , and which is secured by proper precautions against surreptitious alteration or injury."[188] *All my salvation and all my desire* expresses David's confidence in his covenant God, who will certainly let them *grow*.

6 This verse describes *the worthless* (*bᵉlîyaʿal*). The etymology of this word is hotly debated. The term can also mean "the destructive ones."[189] In this poem, *the worthless* is structurally contrasted with the *one who rules over men righteously, who rules in the fear of God* (v. 3). Also, the metaphor describing them here *like thorns* is contrasted with the metaphors describing the ruler *like the light // (like) the shafts of sunshine* (v. 4).

The phrase *qôṣ mūnād* has been traditionally taken as meaning "scattered thorns" (LXX) based on the root *ndd* (Hoph. ptc.) "move." See *HALOT* on *ndd* I and *qôṣ* II. McCarter, however, suggests the root *nwd* whose basic meaning is "move out of place," and translates *uprooted thorns*; see Isa. 17:11; 1 K. 14:15.[190] The term can be traced back to the original biconsonantal *nd; either root would suggest the impermanent state of dead thorns.

7 Since *thorns* cannot be touched directly by hand, the people handing them are *equipped with* (*yimmālēʾ*) a long tool. The verb is literally "to be filled"; see also "arms himself with" (RSV, ESV, JPS) in the light of 2 K. 9:24. The translation "uses" (NRSV, NIV) is not specific enough to convey the nuance of the Hebrew verb, however. McCarter reads *ʾm lʾ* "if not, unless, except," based on the LXX^{L}.[191]

Here, the metaphor functions as follows:

the worthless men — like *uprooted thorns*
  they cannot be taken with the hand;
the man who strikes the worthless men
  should be equipped with . . . a spear;
with fire they (both *the worthless* and *uprooted thorns*) *will be completely burned on the spot.*

188. Driver, p. 360.
189. For a detailed discussion of this term, see Tsumura, I, pp. 122-24.
190. McCarter, II, p. 483.
191. McCarter, II, p. 479.

The phrase *the blade and shaft of a spear* (*barzel wᵉʿēṣ ḥănît*) (lit. "iron and wood of a spear") refers merismatically to the whole of a spear; it does not mean "either an iron or a wooden tool." For the phrase *shaft of a spear*, see 1 Sam. 17:7 and 2 Sam. 21:19.[192]

The phrase *on the spot* (*baššābet*) is literally "in the sitting."[193] For the image of thorns burning, see Isa. 9:18; 10:17; Heb. 6:8.

B'. DAVID'S HEROES (23:8-39)

This list of "David's mighty men" begins formally with the title *These are the names of* and ends with the total number, *thirty-seven in all* (v. 39). For lists, see on 1 Sam. 6:17-18.[194] The list is divided into two groups, "the three," that is, Josheb-basshebeth, Eleazar, and Shammah (vv. 8-12), and "the thirty" (18-39). Thirty-three men are mentioned as being among "the thirty." It is generally accepted that Joab, who is not listed, is assumed, making thirty-four men. These thirty-four men plus "the three" make up the "thirty-seven" of v. 39.

This section is paralleled in 1 Chr. 11:10-41a; vv. 41b-47 give additional names. It does not give a total number corresponding to the "thirty-seven" of the Samuel passage, however.

1. David's Three (23:8-12)

8 *These are the names of the warriors whom David had:*
Josheb-basshebeth a Tahchemonite,
the head of the captains;
he was (called) Adino the Eznite,
because of eight hundred slain by him at one time.
9 *Next to him was Eleazar the son of Dodo the son of Ahohi;*
he was among the three warriors with David.
When they defied the Philistines who were gathered there to battle,
the men of Israel withdrew.[195]
10 *It was he who arose and struck the Philistines until his hand was weary and clung to the sword.*

192. See Tsumura, I, p. 441 n. 43.

193. For various interpretations of this term, see S. Naéh, "A New Suggestion Regarding 2 Samuel XXIII 7," *VT* 46 (1996) 260-65.

194. Tsumura, I, pp. 221-23.

195. Lit. "went up."

And the LORD *brought about a great victory that day; the people went back after him only to strip (the slain).*

11 *Next to him was Shammah the son of Agee the Ararite.*

And the Philistines were gathered into a troop.

And a plot of ground was there which was full of lentils, but the people fled from the Philistines.

12 *And he took his stand in the midst of the plot, defended it and struck the Philistines.*

And the LORD *brought about a great victory.*

8 At the top of David's heroes are listed the triad of officers, Josheb-basshebeth, Eleazar and Shammah. None of them are dramatis personae in the stories in 1–2 Samuel.[196]

Josheb-basshebeth (*yōšeb-baššebet*) seems to be a popular etymologization, rather than "deformation" (*HALOT*, p. 445), of the formal "Jashobeam" (*yāšob'ām*) in 1 Chr. 11:11, which follows the typical Semitic name pattern impf. verb + *'ām* (e.g., *Jeroboam yārob'ām*). Probably, both names for him circulated among the Israelites. *Tahchemonite* (*taḥkᵉmōnî*) here is a noun using the *taqtilān*-type, while the corresponding name in 1 Chr. 11:11 "the Hachmonite" (*ben-ḥakmônî*) uses the *qatilān*-type noun gentilic formation. According to 1 Chr. 27:2-3 he was in charge of David's military division for the first month.

The term *the captains* (lit. "the three"; *haššālīšî*) has been interpreted variously: e.g., "the chief warriors who stood immediately next to the king and the commander of the army" (Thenius); "officers of the third rank, below the king and commander of the army" (Mastin, Na'aman); "the third man in the chariot." Schley argued that the term refers to "a special group of warriors whose original distinction had been that they had fought in three-man squads."[197] Margalith compares it with Ugaritic *ṯlṯ* "a metal, probably 'bronze, copper'" (*UT* §19.2691), which he thinks means also "armoured."[198] According to him, the third-ranking officials are called "telestai" in Pylos in Greece, which is the original hometown of the Philistines. They are possibly "reminiscent of the *šlyš*, the knights of David (1 Chr. 12:19) and Ahab (2 Ki. 7:17); they were charioteers and wore heavy armour, like the *šlyšm* of Pharaoh (Exod. 14:7)."[199] See "Triad" (a different Hebrew word) in v. 18 below.

196. See the commentary on v. 18 and Gordon, *CB*, p. 17. See also N. Na'aman, "The List of David's Officers (*šālîšîm*)," *VT* 38 (1988) 71-79.

197. D. G. Schley, "The *šālîšîm*: Officers or Special Three-man Squads?" *VT* 40 (1990) 326.

198. O. Margalith, "A Note on *šālîšîm*," *VT* 42 (1992) 266.

199. O. Margalith, "Where Did the Philistines Come From?" *ZAW* 107 (1995) 107-8.

The Hebrew text of Adino the Eznite is *ʿădînô hʿṣnw* (K.); *ʿădînô hāʿeṣnî* (Q.). It is probably an otherwise unknown name *Adino the Eznite* (so JPS). It is possible that the heroic action of Josheb-basshebeth, his name itself a popular etymology of Jashobeam as noted above, resembled the heroism of a certain *Adino the Eznite* who was well known to the audience of 2 Samuel. But in any case, it is phonologically impossible to posit a case of textual corruption from *ʿôrēr ʾet-ḥănîtô* (1 Chr. 11:11) to *ʿădînô hāʿeṣnî.*[200] Note that the K. seems to reflect a phonetic assimilation of *-nî* (Q.) to - *nô*.

9 The Hebrew of *the son of Dodo, ben-ddy* (K.) is a phonetic spelling that results from the assimilation of the final *-î* of *ben-dōdô ben-ʾăḥōḥî*. For *the son of Ahohi*, compare "the Ahohite" in 1 Chr. 11:12. Aho(a)h was the name of a son of Benjamin's oldest son Bela (1 Chr. 8:4). Another of the thirty, Zalmon (Ilia) was also an Ahohite (v. 28; 1 Chr. 11:29).

"He was among": The Hebrew spelling (K.) *bšlšh gbrym* reads *bišlōšāh haggibbōrîm* (lit. "in three warriors") in the Q; the K. is probably a phonetic spelling reflecting the actual pronunciation [*bišlōšāgibbōrîm*], rather than being a haplography.[201]

11-12 Third hero was *Shammah the son of Agee the Ararite*. He was defending the plot, or rather the *lentils* in it, against theft. Compare the Philistines robbing the threshing floors in 1 Sam. 23:1. In view of the parallel spelling *hāʾrārî* in v. 33, the term *the Ararite* (*hārārî*) is a *sandhi* form of *hāʾărārî*, i.e., "the Ararite" (JPS).

The difficult Hebrew phrase *laḥayyāh* (v. 11) probably means *into a troop*; see v. 13. Some like *HALOT*, p. 525, take it as a geographical name, a corruption of the more difficult form *leḥyāh*, and translate the phrase "at Lehi," as in Judg. 15:14, 17, etc. However, it should probably be taken as a variant form of *laḥawwāh*; in fact, the form with a directive *he* would be *leḥîyāh*.

x. Water from the Well of Bethlehem (23:13-17)

13 *And three of the thirty chiefs went down and came to David*
at harvest time[202] *to the cave of Adullam, while the troop of the Philistines was camping in the Valley of Rephaim.*
14 *David was then in the stronghold; the garrison of the*
Philistines was then at Bethlehem.
15 *And David had a strong desire and said,*

200. For a detailed discussion of the textual problems, see McCarter, II, pp. 489-90.

201. See Tsumura, "Scribal Errors or Phonetic Spellings?," pp. 400-401; also Tsumura, "Textual Corruptions, or Linguistic Phenomena?," p. 140.

202. Lit. "to harvest time."

"Who would give me water to drink
from the well of Bethlehem which is in the gate?"
16 *And the three warriors broke through the camp of the*
Philistines, and drew water from the well of Bethlehem which
was in the gate, and took it and brought it to David. But he
would not drink it and poured it out to the LORD.
17 *And he said,*
"Far be it from me, O LORD, that I should do this.
Is it not the blood of the men who went at the risk of their
lives?"
Therefore he would not drink it.
These things the three warriors did.

13-17 This episode may have occurred during the time David was fleeing Saul, or during one of the Philistine attacks in 2 Sam. 5:17-25. The taste of the water in different localities varies, and of course, the water one grew up drinking tastes best. One can guess that David was more homesick than thirsty. His words are not a command. It probably did not occur to him that someone might actually act on them. This episode shows the love his men had for their leader and his regard for them. Garsiel holds that this "water retrieval" mission was during the battles at the Valley of Rephaim (see 2 Sam. 5:17-25). But the reference to *the cave of Adullam* in v. 13 suggests the earlier occasion. Also, the text does not suggest that it was "primarily a reconnaissance mission."[203] On *Valley of Rephaim*, see the commentary on 2 Sam. 5:17.

13 These three men were apparently not the above "three," but rather members of the "thirty" mentioned below. The translation *three of the thirty chiefs* is based on Q. *šelōšāh mēhaššelōšîm rō'š* and supported by the context. Evidently K. *šlšym mēhaššelōšîm rō'š* experienced a *dittography*; *šelôšāh minhaššelôšîm rō'š* (1 Chr. 11:15 follows the Q). The influence of Egyptian institutions here on the early Israelite monarchy has been noted, since a group of *thirty* men can be identified as the king's bodyguard in the Egyptian court in a Theban inscription about the coronation of Ramesses II.[204]

It was *at harvest time*, hence it was hot and dry and rain was not expected. For *the cave of Adullam*, see on 1 Sam. 22:1.[205]

203. M. Garsiel, "The Water Retrieval Mission of David's Three Warriors and Its Relationship to the Battle of the Valley of Refaim," in *Teshurot LaAvishur: Studies in the Bible and the Ancient Near East, in Hebrew and Semitic Languages; Festschrift Presented to Prof. Yitzhak Avishur on the Occasion of His 65th Birthday,* ed. M. Heltzer and M. Malul (Tel Aviv: Archaeological Center Publications, 2004), p. 58*.

204. See McCarter, II, pp. 496-97.

205. Tsumura, I, p. 538.

The word *troop* (*ḥayyat*) is a variant form of *ḥawwat*, the construct of *ḥawwāh* ("army, troop").

14 *David was then in . . .* and *the garrison . . . was then* are circumstantial clauses like "The Canaanites were then in" (Gen. 12:6; also 13:7) with exactly the same grammatical construction: *wᵉ* – N. - *'āz* – Adv.

15 The expression *in the gate* means inside of the complex structure of the city-gate, not "by the gate" (NASB; NRSV).

16 For the water libation, see on 1 Sam. 7:6.[206]

17 For the idiom *far be it from me, O LORD*, see on 1 Sam. 2:30.[207] David may be offering this water in acknowledgment that he should not have made such a remark, but in that case it seems he would have made some other sacrifice also. It seems rather that he is saying this water is too precious for him to drink. *Is it not the blood of. . .?* is often translated as "Shall I drink the blood of" (NASB, RSV, ESV, etc.) in the light of 1 Chr. 11:19 "Shall I drink the blood of these men *who went* at the risk of their lives?" But, our text is an example of *aposiopesis.*[208] The preposition *be* (at the risk of) is the *beth pretii:* "at the cost of their lives"; see 1 K. 2:23.[209]

2. The Thirty: The First Two—Abishai and Benaiah (23:18-23)

Verses 18-39 is the list of David's "thirty men." They are Abishai, Benaiah, and the men listed in 24-39. Most of the first dozen and a large part of the remainder are Judahites, so the group was probably formed early in David's career. It has thirty-four names in it, probably representing thirty-five men (see on v. 32). Probably those of "the thirty" who died in battle like Asahel (v. 24; 2:18-23) and Uriah (v. 39; 11:17) were replaced by others. Some of the names appear as officers in 1 Chr. 27, and most appear in the list in 1 Chr. 11:20-47, which is an expansion of this, but is not labeled as being a list of "the thirty" (compare v. 24 here and 1 Chr. 11:26).

18 *Now Abishai, the brother of Joab, the son of Zeruiah, was chief of the thirty. And he swung*[210] *his spear against three hundred and killed them; he won a name beside the Three.*[211]

206. Tsumura, I, p. 234.

207. Tsumura, I, p. 168.

208. For *aposiopesis*, see the commentaries on 2 Sam. 13:16 (above) and Tsumura, I, pp. 119, 128.

209. Driver, p. 367.

210. Lit. "to awake, to set in motion" (*'wr: *HALOT*, p. 802).

211. Lit. "to him (is) the name in the Three."

19 *Is it that he was honored more than the thirty? And he became their commander; but to the Three he did not attain.*[212]

20 *Now Benaiah the son of Jehoiada was a valiant man with great deeds from Kabzeel. He struck down two (sons) of Ariel of Moab. He also went down and struck down a lion in the middle of a pit on the day of snow.*

21 *And he struck down an Egyptian, a huge man. In the hand of the Egyptian was a spear. And he went down to him with a staff and snatched the spear from the hand of the Egyptian and killed him with his own spear.*

22 *These things Benaiah the son of Jehoiada did; he had a name beside the three warriors.*

23 *More than the thirty he was honored; but to the Three he did not attain. And David appointed him over his bodyguard.*

18 The term *thirty* is literally "the third" (K. *hšlšy*) or "the three" (Q. *haš̌ᵉlōšāh*).[213] It can possibly be explained as a phonetic spelling, the result of consonatal *sandhi* (m + w → w): thus

> *haš̌ᵉlōšîm+wᵉhû'* "the thirty. And he" →
> *haššelōšîwehû'* → *haš̌ᵉlōšî wᵉhû'*: *hšlšy* (K.)

Note that two Hebrew manuscripts and the Syriac version have "thirty," which is followed by NASB, NRSV, ESV; Driver.[214] See also 1 Chr. 11:25.

19 *Is it that* (*hăkî*) is a neutral interrogative; see BDB, p. 472; cf. "He was most honored of the thirty" (NASB); "He was the most renowned of the Thirty" (NRSV). There is a Hebrew manuscript that has the reading of *the thirty* (*hšlšym*), against the Leningrad Codex "the three"; see above on v. 18.

20 *Benaiah* was captain of the Cherethites and Pelethites, the royal bodyguard; see 2 Sam. 8:18; 20:23. He replaced Joab as the army commander under Solomon; see 1 K. 2:35. Zeron holds that Benaiah is treated as special in this list, so it was "probably published during the reign of Solomon when Benaiah was commander of the army."[215] According to 1 Chr. 27:5-6, his father Jehoiada was chief priest. The passage says Benaiah's son was in charge of his division; perhaps his other duties prevented him from the normal care of his division.

The phrase *a valiant man* (lit. "the son of a man of ") is based on the Q. *ben-'îš-ḥayil* (so 1 Chr. 11:22). The phrase refers to a special class of citizen, i.e., "wealthy landowner who is competent, apt for military service and

212. Lit. "but to the three he did not come."
213. See Gordon, *CB*, p. 17.
214. Driver, p. 367.
215. See McCarter, II, p. 496.

brave" (*HALOT*, p. 312). Talmon[216] takes this expression as "a conflation of two synonymous readings" — *ben-ḥayil* and *'îš-ḥayil*. But this example should be compared with *ben-'îš gēr* "the son of a sojourner" in 2 Sam. 1:13, while *a Benjamite* (*ben-'îš yᵉmînî*) in 1 Sam. 9:1 should be compared with *ben-'îš miṣrî* ("the son of an Egyptian man" in Lev. 24:10) and *ben-'îš 'eprātî* ("the son of an Ephrathite" in 1 Sam. 17:12). NRSV and ESV suggest another reading, "the son of Ishhai." However, the K. *ben-'îš-ḥay* is a form resulting from "consonantal *sandhi*"[217] between the two consonants [l] and [r]. In other words, as the result of *sandhi*, [r] absorbed [l] at the word boundary.

ben-'îš-ḥayil rab- → *ben-'îš-ḥayilrab-* → *ben-'îš-ḥay rab-*

Hence, the K. reflects a phonetic spelling and no other reading is necessary.

Kabzeel is a town in the extreme south of Judah, near Arad and Beersheba; see Josh. 15:21; 1 Chr. 11:22.

21 The Hebrew K. *'ăšer mar'eh* "one who has a sight," that is, *a huge man*, is preferable to the Q. *'îš mar'eh* "a man of appearance," that is, "a handsome man" (NRSV, ESV). In fact, the K. is the more difficult, and hence probably the more original, reading. The final /r/ was likely absorbed by the following /m/ as a result of *consonantal sandhi* at the word boundary.[218]

3. The Rest of the Thirty (23:24-39)

24 *Asahel the brother of Joab was among the thirty.*
Elhanan the son of Dodo of Bethlehem
25 *Shammah the Harodite*
Elika the Harodite
26 *Helez the Paltite*
Ira the son of Ikkesh the Tekoite
27 *Abiezer the Anathothite*
Mebunnai the Hushathite
28 *Zalmon the Ahohite*
Mahrai the Netophathite
29 *Heled the son of Baanah the Netophathite*
Ittai the son of Ribai of Gibeah of the Benjaminites

216. S. Talmon, "Double Readings in the Masoretic Text," *Textus* 1 (1960) 166.

217. Tsumura, "Scribal Errors or Phonetic Spellings?" 401; Tsumura, "Textual Corruptions, or Linguistic Phenomena?" 139-40.

218. See Tsumura, "Scribal Errors or Phonetic Spellings?" 401; Tsumura, "Textual Corruptions, or Linguistic Phenomena?" 140.

30 *Benaiah a Pirathonite*
Hiddai of the brooks of Gaash
31 *Abi-albon the Arbathite*
Azmaveth the Barhumite
32 *Eliahba the Shaalbonite*
(and) Jonathan, the sons of Jashen
33 *Shammah the Hararite*
Ahiam the son of Sharar the Ararite
34 *Eliphelet the son of Ahasbai, the son of the Maacathite*
Eliam the son of Ahithophel the Gilonite
35 *Hezro the Carmelite*
Paarai the Arbite
36 *Igal the son of Nathan of Zobah*
Bani the Gadite
37 *Zelek the Ammonite*
Naharai the Beerothite
the armor bearers of Joab the son of Zeruiah
38 *Ira the Ithrite*
Gareb the Ithrite
39 *Uriah the Hittite*

total 37

24 For *Asahel*, see on 2 Sam. 2:18. He was in charge of David's military division for the fourth month; and his son Zebadiah after him (1 Chr. 27:7). This is probably mentioned because he died very early.

Elhanan is described as the slayer of "Goliath" in 2 Sam. 21:19 (see commentary).

25 *Shammah* and *Elika* are from Harod, which is probably modern Khirbet el-Haredan (?), a few miles (km) southeast of Jerusalem, rather than the Spring of Harod near Jezreel (Judg. 7:1).[219]

26 A *Paltite* is probably either a member of the Calebite clan descended from Pelet (1 Chr. 2:47) or an inhabitant of Beth-pelet, a town in the extreme southern district of Judah near Beersheba (Josh. 15:27).

Ira was from Tekoa and in charge of David's military division for the sixth month in 1 Chr. 27:9. For Tekoa, see on 2 Sam. 14:2.

27 *Abiezer* was from Anathoth and in charge of David's military division for the ninth month, according to 1 Chr. 27:12. Anathoth has been identified with Ras el-Kharrubeh, near the modern village of Anata, three miles (4.8 km) north-northeast of Jerusalem. It was the birthplace of the prophet

219. See McCarter, II, p. 497.

Jeremiah (Jer. 1:1) and a priestly city in Benjamin, the place to which Abiathar was banished by Solomon (1 K. 2:26).

For *Mebunnai*, LXX^{LMN} supports the reading of "Sibbecai" *sibbᵉkay*, as in 2 Sam. 21:18 and 1 Chr. 11:29. McCarter posits that the MT form resulted from two "graphic errors": confusion of *kap* and *nun*; and confusion of *samek* and *mem.*[220] Husha is identified as modern Husan, southwest of Bethlehem.

28 Here for Zalmon the Ahohite, 1 Chr. 11:29 has Ilai the Ahohite.

Mahrai was in charge of David's military division for the tenth month, according to 1 Chr. 27:13. He and *Heled* are from Netophah, which is usually identified as the modern site Khirbet Bedd Faluh between Bethlehem and Tekoa, but most recently as Umm Tuba, in the southern hills of Jerusalem.[221]

29 The MT *ḥēleb* reads "Heleb" (so NASB, JPS, NRSV, ESV). McCarter reads it as "Heldai" (*ḥelday*) like 1 Chr. 27:15, explaining that the MT arose "by graphic confusion of *dy* and *b*." But the MT could be a phonetic spelling resulting from a regressive total assimilation from *ḥēled ben-baʿănāh* (so 1 Chr. 11:30): *ḥēled ben* → *ḥēleb ben.*[222] In 1 Chr. 27:15 Heled is described as being in charge of David's military division for the twelfth month.

For *Gibeah of the Benjaminites*, the home of Saul, see on 1 Sam. 9:1-2.[223]

30 *Benaiah* the Pirathonite was in charge of David's military division for the eleventh month according to 1 Chr. 27:14. Pirathon was the hometown of the minor judge Abdon; Judg. 12:13-15. McCarter identifies it as an Ephraimite town, "perhaps" Farʿâtā, ca. five miles (8 km) southwest of Shechem.[224]

Hiddai appears as "Hurai" in 1 Chr. 11:32, Mount Gaash (Josh. 24:30 = Judg. 2:9) lies south of Timnath-heres, which is about fifteen miles (24 km) southwest of Shechem. *Hiddai* appears also as a Phoenician PN, which is a "hypocoristicon or affection-name."[225]

31 McCarter proposes that the original reading of *Abi-albon the Arbathite* (*ʾăbî-ʿalbôn hāʿarbātî*), is "Abial the Beth-arabathite" in the light of Abiel the Arbathite *ʾăbîʾēl hāʿarbātî* in 1 Chr. 11:32.[226] However, LXX *Abiēl huios tou Arabōthitou* suggests the normal form *ʾăbîʾēl ben hāʿarbāti*, of which the MT's *ăbî-ʿalbôn hāʿarbāti* could be a phonetic variant. Hence, the LXX and the MT preserve variant names of the same person.

220. McCarter, II, p. 492.

221. http://www.mfa.gov.il/MFA/Israel+beyond+politics/Royal-seal-impressions-discovered-23-Feb-2009.aspx.

222. See Tsumura, "Scribal Errors or Phonetic Spellings?" 403.

223. Tsumura, I, pp. 262-64.

224. McCarter, II, p. 498.

225. Avigad and Sass, *Corpus of West Semitic Stamp Seals*, p. 496, No. 738.

226. McCarter, II, p. 492.

Azmaveth means "death is strong." A person with the same name was in charge of David's storehouses; see 1 Chr. 27:25. It also appears as a place name in Benjamin: Ezra 2:24; Neh 7:28; 12:29. In the Ugaritic mythological texts, the expression *mt ʿz* "Mot is strong" appears several times: *KTU* 1.6 VI 17, 18, 20. No direct relation should be posited between Ugaritic myths and the Hebrew personal name, however. The expression "as strong as death" reflects general human experience; see Song 8:6.[227]

Barhumite (*barḥūmî*) is probably a variant name of "Bahrumite," which was changed by metathesis: *baḥrūmî —> barḥūmî.* The Chronicler's "Baharumite" (*baḥărûmî*) is another variant form of "Bahrumite." Both names are simultaneously current, like "Gezrite" (= of Gezer), which has two phonetic variant forms: *gizrî* (1 Sam. 27:8 [Q.]) and the metathesized form *girzî* (K.).[228] *Barhumite* and "Bahrumite" are both probably connected with the village of Bahurim on Jerusalem's east outskirts; see on 2 Sam. 3:16.

32-33 The translation of vv. 32-33 given here is the most natural, but it should be noted that those verses have been translated a number of ways; see also 1 Chr. 11:34-35.

A *Shaalbonite* (*haššaʿalbōnî*) is one who is from the city Shaalbim (Judg. 1:35; 1 K. 4:9) or its dialectal variant Shaalbin (Josh. 19:42). Shaalbon may be "a dialect by-form" of Shaalbim; see *HALOT*, p. 1612. It has been identified with *Selbit/Tell-Šaʿalʾwīm*, three miles (4.5 km) northwest of *Ayyalōn* and eight miles (6.5 km) north of Beth-shemesh.

1 Chr. 11:34 has "the sons of Hashem" followed by the gentilic *the Gizonite. Jashen* could be an assimilated form of *Hashen, a possible dialictal variant of *Hashem.* Thus:

bᵉnê hāšēm: bᵉnê hāšēn → bᵉnê yāšēn

Thus, the correspondence of the names is as follows:

2 Sam. 23:32-33a	*1 Chr. 11:33b-34*
Eliahba the Shaalbonite,	Eliahba the Shaalbonite,
the sons of Jashen,	the sons of Hashem the Gizonite,
Jonathan, Shammah the Hararite	Jonathan the son of Shagee the Hararite

The sons of Jashen, using only the patronymic, is unique in this list of personal names. The Hebrew order is "Eliahba the Shaalbonite, the sons of Jashen, Jonathan" (2 Sam. 23:32). The phrase *the sons of Jashen* probably refers to two men, or twins (the "sons" could be a dual construct), and is inserted between

227. *HALOT*, p. 810 on *Azmavet.*
228. Tsumura, "Scribal Errors or Phonetic Spellings?" 392.

two names *Eliahba* and *Jonathan*[229] following the AXB pattern, hence meaning *Eliahba the Shaalbonite and Jonathan, the sons of Jashen.*

The phrase *the Hararite* (*hahărārî*) is a definite article *ha* + *hărārî*, a noun which itself could be a *sandhi* form of *hā'ărārî*, i.e., "the Ararite"; see on v. 11.

The Ararite (*hā'rārî*) is a historical spelling with the consonant *aleph*: cf. "Hararite" (NRSV, NIV). McCarter reads "the Urite," based on LXX^{B}.[230]

34 *The Maacathite* is not to be associated with the northern Aramean kingdom of Maacah (2 Sam. 10:6) or with Beth-maacah near Dan (20:14-15). According to 1 Chr. 4:19, "Eshtemoa the Maacathite" belonged to a Judahite clan near Hebron.

Whether this *Eliam* should be identified with Bathsheba's father (see 2 Sam. 11:3) is not certain. For *Ahithophel the Gilonite*, see 2 Sam. 15:12.

35-36 *Hezro* (K. *ḥeṣrô*), as in 1 Chr. 11:37, is a contracted form of *ḥeṣraw*, which could be a variant of *ḥeṣray* (Q.).

For *the Carmelite*, see 1 Sam. 15:12, 25:2, 27:3. Carmel is located south of Hebron in Judah.

The following discrepancy,

2 Sam. 23:35b-36	*1 Chr. 11:37b-38*
Paarai the Arbite,	Naarai the son of Ezbai,
Igal the son of Nathan of Zobah,	Joel the brother of Nathan,
Bani the Gadite,	Mibhar the son of Hagri,

may reflect two different oral traditions. It is impossible to determine the original names.

37 The K. takes both *Zelek the Ammonite* and *Naharai the Beerothite* as *the armor bearers* (pl.) *of Joab*, while the Q. (also 1 Chr. 11:39) takes only *Naharai* as the "armor bearer" (sg.).

The *Beerothite* is written here with the full spelling *b*^{e}*'ērōtî*, while 1 Chr. 11:39 has a shorter *sandhi* spelling:

bērōtî <-(*sandhi*)[231]- *b*^{e}*ērōtî* <-(loss of intervocalic *aleph*)- *b*^{e}*'ērōtî.*

For the *Beerothite*, see on 2 Sam. 4:2.

38 *The Ithrite* (also 1 Chr. 11:40). They were the chief indigenous clan of Kiriath-jearim; see 1 Chr. 2:53.

39 For *Uriah the Hittite*, see on 2 Sam. 11:3.

total (*kōl*) *37*:

For comparison, see the list of defeated kings in Josh. 12 with total (v. 24). For examples of lists with the total (sum), see Ugaritic economic texts such

229. See Tsumura, "Coordination Interrupted," pp. 117-32; also Tsumura, I, pp. 60-64.

230. McCarter, II, p. 493.

231. Tsumura, "Vowel *sandhi* in Biblical Hebrew," pp. 575-88.

as *KTU* 4.63, 69, 71-72, 100, etc. with the Sumerian ŠU.NIGÍN ("total, sum"), or 4.173 with the Ugaritic *tgmr* ("total").[232]

The above list has only thirty-six names by my analysis and that of most scholars. As mentioned above, the most obvious solution is to include Joab as having been so obvious he was left out.[233] On the other hand, McCarter would find the thirty-seventh name in some name that has been taken as an appellative, such as "Adino the Eznite" (v. 8). But, as he holds, it is futile to make any guess "because we do not know the condition of the text at the time the editor made his computation."[234]

A'. CENSUS AND THE LORD'S ANGER (24:1-25)

The Lord's anger and David's sin lead to a plague, but this in turn leads to the purchase of a threshing floor in Jerusalem to offer burnt offerings to the Lord. This site will become the location of Solomon's temple, and so this event became the preparation for building the earthly palace of the heavenly king. The Books of Samuel thus end anticipating the building that David himself had desired but had not been allowed to accomplish (2 Sam. 7).

The placement of this episode seems to be climactic rather than chronological.

1. David's Census (24:1-9)

a. David and Joab (24:1-4a)

1 *Now again the anger of the LORD burned against Israel*
and stirred David up against them to say "Go, count Israel and Judah."
2 *And the king said to Joab, the commander of the army, who was with him,*[235]
"Go through all the tribes of Israel,
from Dan to Beersheba,

232. See *DULAT*, pp. 861-62. For the Akkadian term for "sum, total," see *CAD*, N/1, pp. 293-94. Also see Tsumura, "List and Narrative in I Samuel 6,17-18a," pp. 353-69; also Tsumura, I, p. 222.

233. See, e.g., K. Elliger, "Die dreissig Helden Davids," *Palästinajahrbuch* 31 (1935) 36.

234. McCarter, II, p. 499.

235. For *to Joab, the commander of the army, who was with him,* the LXX^{L} has "to Joab and the commanders of the army" and hence NRSV translates "who were with him." The LXX^{L} reading of the plural "commanders" is probably the result of adjustment to v. 4a. Since Joab is one of the commanders, the MT reading should be retained.

and register the people
so that I may know the number of the people."

3 *And Joab said to the king,*
"May the LORD your God add to the people
a hundred times as many as they are
while the eyes of my lord the king still see.
As for my lord the king,
why does he delight in this thing?"

4a *But the word of the king prevailed against Joab and against the commanders of the army.*

1-4a This verse at the beginning of a new episode is the SETTING for the following EVENT (vv. 2ff.), because the verb (lit. "to add, do again"), though in the *wayqtl* form, is followed by the impersonal subject *the anger of the LORD* (see Introduction). The EVENT starts in v. 2 with *And the king said* and consists of a dialogue between David and Joab. Verse 4a is the TERMINUS, again with the *wayqtl* form followed by the impersonal subject *the word of the king.*

1 We are told nothing of why the *anger of the LORD burned against Israel* or what the previous incident ("again") refers to. This *anger* incited David to count the number of soldiers (v. 9). While the text does not explain explicitly why his counting resulted in the Lord's punishment, David's counting was an offense serious enough to bring about a disaster. One possible answer is that David as the human representative of the divine king may have shown a lack of faith and obedience to his sovereign master. Often, sinners are not aware of their sinfulness immediately, as David in the Bathsheba incident in 2 Sam. 11-12; see also Lev. 5:1-6. For the "psychology" of divine wrath, see Ezek. 5:13, "My anger shall spend itself, and I will vent my fury on them and satisfy myself."[236]

There are two possibilities for the subject of the verb *stirred:* namely *the anger* (see "it incited" [NASB]) and *the LORD* (see "he incited" [NRSV; ESV; Anderson; Bergen]). In the light of the discourse grammar that supports the principle that "every *wayqtl* followed by a stated subject initiates a new discourse unit,"[237] the most natural translation, however, is "the anger (m.sg.; lit. "nose") of the LORD burned against Israel and stirred David up." This syntax, taking the same agent as the subject of both verbs, may be supported by the Chronicler's rendering in 1 Chr. 21:1, which reads: "Then Satan stood against Israel and incited David to number Israel" (ESV; also NIV, JPS, etc.). It seems

236. C. H. Gordon, *CB*, pp. 270-71 notes the common theme of divine "wrath" in Homer and the Bible.

237. See Introduction, III.1.

that the author simply introduces Satan as the Lord's agent for punishing David because of the unknown "evil" of David.

However, it is not necessary to think that the Chronicler simply reinterprets the Lord's action as Satan's.[238] Japhet holds the term *śāṭān* in 1 Chr. 21:1 serves "as a common noun, similar to 1 K. 11:14, 23, 25, or Ps. 109:6, and refers to 'an adversary,' who acts against Israel by inciting the king to take the wrong action."[239] Our passage, 2 Sam. 24:1, also states that it was not the Lord but *the anger of the LORD* that *stirred David up*. As far as its syntactical understanding is concerned, Japhet's view seems convincing, though she takes the term *śāṭān* as a common noun despite the fact that the term is without an article.

The inf. phrase *lēʾmōr* here means "to say" in a literal sense; it is not being used as a direct speech marker ("saying").

3 By numbering the people for military purposes (v. 9), David was apparently showing lack of trust in the Lord to supply the necessary men when needed. Or, it may be that the issue is David's dependence on human rather than divine force. It's also possible that the protocol for David's census violates the requirements of Exod 30:12, as noted below. We do not know exactly why Joab opposed it.

b. Registration (24:4b-9)

4b *And Joab and the commanders of the army went out from before*[240] *the king to register the people of Israel.*

5 *And they crossed the Jordan and camped in Aroer, on the right side of the city that is in the middle of the valley of Gad, and (came) to Jazer.*

6 *And they came to Gilead and to the land of Tahtim-hodshi; and they came to Dan-jaan and around to Sidon.*

7 *And they came to the fortress of Tyre and to all the cities of the Hivites and Canaanites; and they went out to the Negeb of Judah at Beersheba.*

8 *And they went through all the land; and they came back to Jerusalem at the end of nine months and twenty days.*

9 *And Joab gave the number of the registration of the people to the king; and there were in Israel eight hundred thousand soldiers who drew the sword; and the men of Judah were five hundred thousand men.*

238. See R. E. Stokes, "The Devil Made David Do It . . . Or *Did* He? The Nature, Identity, and Literary Origins of the *Satan* in 1 Chronicles 21:1," *JBL* 128 (2009) 91-106.

239. Japhet, p. 375.

240. Lit. "before"; here the context requires the translation *from before*.

The census here lists only men who are eligible for military activities, while a census list in Ugarit (*KTU* 4.102) lists women, children, or young people by household. It is possible, as Greenwood recently suggested, that David conducted this census "to assign *corveé* labor" for preparing for the construction of a temple for the Lord but it proved to have been premature and too early.[241] This is, however, a pure speculation, although the ending point at the threshfloor could support this.

4b Verse 4b is the TRANSITION to a new stage, which is indicated by the movement verb *went out.* At the same time it is the SETTING to the following EVENT, Joab and his men's travel (*they crossed . . . camped . . . came . . . came . . . came . . . went out* in vv. 5-7; *they went through . . . came back* in v. 8) to various places *to register the people of Israel.*

5-8 The details of the census trip are not certain, but it seems the men begin at Aroer, a city on the Arnon River on the border with Moab, go north through Gilead and Bashan, and then go north-northwest to Dan. From there they go to the coast, to the *fortress of Tyre*, then go south to Beersheba, then return to Jerusalem.[242] It takes nine months and twenty days. The territory covers the entire area under the direct control of Davidic monarchy.

Jazer is a stronghold facing the kingdom of the Ammonites; see Josh. 21:39; 1 Chr. 6:81; etc.[243] The land of *Tahtim-hodshi*, though obscure, suggests the Bashan area in the light of LXX^{B} *Thabasōn. Jaan* (*yʿn*) could be a metathesis of the name Ijon (*ʿyn*), which Rainey identifies with Tell ed-Dibbin in Marj ʻAyyun, about 10 miles (16 km) north of Dan.[244]

7 The *fortress of Tyre* probably is not the city of Tyre, but the Israelite fortress of Usu a little to the south of Tyre, known from Egyptian and Assyrian inscriptions.[245] The phrase *all the cities of the Hivites and Canaanites* does suggest that they were the pre-Israelite population that had maintained their social and political integrity up to that point. No information is given here about those cities; see Judg. 1:27-36.

Beersheba was a local administrative center during the united monarchy. It is near the junction of the Hebron wadi from the hill country and the Beersheba wadi from the east.[246] It marks the jumping-off-point for travel through the barren Negev to the south.

241. See K. R. Greenwood, "Labor Pains: The Relationship Between David's Census and *Corvée* Labor," *BBR* 20 (2010) 467-78.

242. See *CBA*, #106.

243. See *ABD*, III, pp. 650-51.

244. *SB*, p. 163.

245. *SB*, pp. 163-64. It has been suggested that the "fortified city" in Ps. 60:9 and 108:10 refers to this Usu; see *SB*, p. 161.

246. *SB*, p. 40.

9 The EVENT, Joab's reporting *the number of the registration of the people to the king,* is finally mentioned. Then, the summary is given as the TERMINUS: there were a total of 1,300,000 soldiers in Israel and Judah. 1 Chr. 21:5 gives different numbers: 1,100,000 in Israel, 470,000 in Judah.

2. David's Guilt (24:10-14)

a. "I Have Sinned" (24:10-11a)

10 *And David's heart struck him after he had numbered the people.*
And David said to the Lord,
"I have sinned greatly in what I have done.
But now, O Lord,
please take away the guilt of your servant,
for I have acted very foolishly."
11a *And David arose in the morning.*

10 The verb *struck*, impf. with a *waw*-consecutive, has an impersonal subject (*David's heart*). The verse 10a is hence a SETTING for the following EVENT of David's confession and supplication. David's verbal action (*David said to the Lord*), is followed by the TERMINUS of this short episode: *And David arose in the morning.* The last sentence functions also as a TRANSITION, with a movement verb *arose*, to the following episode of "David and Gad."

McCarter notes the unusual use of *after* (*'aḥărê-kēn* "afterward") here and supplies "because" after it. Miscall would keep the MT as it is and explains that the "unusual" usage here and in 21:14 indicates "the open, uncertain relation with the preceding event(s)."[247]

I have sinned — this is a genuine confession of sin against God. What he has done presumably offended God, and David is aware of it. Though the text does not specify what his sin was, one possibility is that he did not fulfill the requirement of the law in Exod. 30:12 that he take a *ransom* (*kōper*), the "half-shekel tax," from them to give to the Lord when he numbered them:

> When you take the census of the people of Israel, then each shall give a ransom for his life to the LORD when you number them, that there be no plague among them when you number them. (ESV)

11a This half verse is usually translated with 11b as follows:

247. P. Miscall, "2 Samuel 24: A Meditation on Wrath, Guilt, and the King," *Shofar* 11 (1993) 71.

And when David arose in the morning, the word of the LORD came (RSV).

However, v. 11a should be a main clause according to Hebrew syntax, while v. 11b is a disjunctive clause with *the word of the LORD* being topicalized. As noted above, it is better to hold that the current episode closes with v. 11a and a new episode begins with v. 11b.

b. David and Gad (24:11b-14)

11b *Now, the word of the LORD came to the prophet Gad, David's seer, saying,*

12 *"Go and speak to David,*
'Thus says the LORD:
Three things I am offering to you.
Choose one of them for yourself
so that I may do it to you.'"
13 *And Gad came to David and told him:*[248]
"Shall seven years of famine come to you in your land?
Or for three months will you flee before your foes
who pursue you?
Or shall there be three days' pestilence in your land?
Now consider and see
what answer I shall return to the one who sent me."
14 *And David said to Gad,*
"I am in great distress.
Let us fall into the hand of the LORD,
for his mercies are great;
into the hand of man let me not fall!"

V. 11b and v. 12 function as a SETTING with a nominal sentence (with a *casus pendens* of the impersonal noun *word*) to the following EVENT (a dialogue between Gad and David) in vv. 13-14.

11b The term *seer* (*ḥōzēh*) could be an older (or "dialectal") designation for a prophet; see 1 Sam. 9:9 on "seer" (*rō'ēh*).[249]

12 The 3 m.pl. pronoun *them* refers here to the fem. pl. noun "three" (*šālōš*). This has been explained as an example of "gender neutralization"

248. Lit. "and told him and said to him"; see Introduction of Tsumura, I, p. xii.
249. Tsumura, I, p. 270.

which is a characteristic of the spoken Hebrew dialect; see also 1 Sam. 9:20; 2 Sam. 1:24.[250]

The phrase *thus says the Lord* is the prophetic "messenger formula" used by the prophet of the Lord (also 7:5, 8; 12:7, 11) who is confident that what he conveys is not his personal opinion. For this formula, see the comment on 1 Sam. 2:27.[251]

13 In the Ugaritic epic of King Keret, famine struck the land because of the king's sin, just as Israel was punished for David's sin. Homer also states that the well-being of a land depends on the conduct of its sovereign.[252] See also 2 Sam. 21:1.

Seven years of famine was an important theme in the ancient Near East — see Gen. 41:30, and 2 K. 8:1. It can also be found in a Ugaritic myth and ritual text (*KTU* 1.23)[253] as well as the Aqhat Epic. First Chronicles 21:12 gives "three years of famine," instead of *seven years of famine.* It is commonly said that the Chronicle passage preserves the original reading, "in view of the pattern 'three years', 'three months' and 'three days', in descending order."[254] It seems that while the Books of Samuel reflect the epic style that adopts the perfect number "seven" to describe a severe famine (cf. Gen. 41),[255] the Chronicler is more realistic in describing the length of famines in general (see Isa. 37:30; 2 K. 19:29). Probably even two years of famine would cause real suffering.

Famine, sword, and pestilence is a well-known trio of disasters (Jer. 14:12; 18:21; Ezek. 5:17; etc.). Probably the number of people who would die in each of these disasters would be approximately equal (pestilence kills faster than a famine): i.e., "seven" (or three) years of famine = three months of enemies' pursuit = three days of pestilence. One might wonder why the gracious God demanded this much as a recompense for David's sin (v. 10). One thing is certain; he is also the holy God who demands that a human king as his representative be faithful to his commands as he acts as the vice-regent of the Sovereign King.

14 David apparently does not even consider choosing the famine. He considers that falling into the hand of the merciful Lord is much better than falling *into the hand of man.* David was confident in God's mercy in the midst of his punishment, while on the other hand human enemies are sinful and

250. See Rendsburg, *DAH*, p. 44.

251. Tsumura, I, p. 165.

252. Gordon, *CB*, p. 151.

253. Tsumura, "The Ugaritic Drama of the Good Gods"; Tsumura, "Kings and Cults in Ancient Ugarit," pp. 215-38. See also Tsumura, "Revisiting the 'Seven' Good Gods of Fertility in Ugarit," pp. 629-41.

254. See Japhet, p. 380.

255. For the use of number seven in the epic literatures, see Tsumura, I, pp. 420-21.

cruel without any compassion. Though *the hand of the LORD* is a destroying agent of God, the Lord himself is both holy and merciful.

3. The Lord's Anger (24:15-25)

a. Three Days' Pestilence (24:15-19)

15 *And the LORD sent a pestilence in Israel from the morning until the appointed time; and seventy thousand men of the people died, from Dan to Beersheba.*

16 *And the angel sent his hand toward Jerusalem to destroy it.*

And the LORD relented concerning the calamity and said to the angel who was destroying the people,

"It is enough!
Now relax your hand!"

The angel of the LORD was then by the threshing floor of Araunah[256] *the Jebusite.*

17 *And David said to the LORD when he saw the angel who was striking the people:*

"Behold, it is I who have sinned!
It is I who have done wrong!
As for these sheep, what have they done?
Please let your hand be against me
and against my father's house!"

18 *And Gad came to David that day and said to him,*

"Go up and erect an altar to the LORD
on the threshing floor of Araunah the Jebusite."

19 *And David went up according to the word of Gad, as the LORD commanded.*

256. The K., *h'wrnh*, of the name *Araunah* results from *metathesis* :
hā'ăwarnāh ← *hā'ărawnāh* (Q.);
cf. K. *'rnyh* (v. 18): *'ărōnyāh* ← *'ărōnāh* ← *'ărawnāh*.

The Ugaritic equivalent of *'ărawnāh* could be the PN *arwn* (*KTU* 4.783:1), which may be analyzed as *arw* "lion" (*KTU* 6.62:2; see *UT* §19.2356) + *-n*. However, B. Mazar takes it as a Hurrian name or title that means "the lord." He even suggests that it was the title of the last ruler of the Jebusites. See B. Mazar, "King David's Scribe and the High Officialdom of the United Monarchy of Israel," pp. 136-37; B. Mazar, *Biblical Israel: State and People* (Jerusalem: Magnes Press, 1992), p. 93. But the identification is unlikely because of the difference of the vowel and the consonant order; cf. Hurrian *iwrn* (see *UT*, §19.116; also *i-wi-ir-ni* in a syllabic spelling, which is identified with Ug. *ma-al-ku* "king" in *Ug.* V 130:III:13'; see Huehnergard, *UVST*, p. 27), the suffix *-n* corresponds to the definite article *h-*.

15 The *hand* of the Lord brought a pestilence and, as the result, *seventy thousand men* died in the whole country (*from Dan to Beersheba*). These people were sacrificed in order to appease God's anger toward David. First Chronicles 22:8 possibly refers to this incident when it says that David shed "much blood" before the Lord and hence could not build a house for the name of the Lord.

16 The *angel of the Lord* here is God's agent who brings destruction or judgment in the form of *pestilence*. First Chronicles 21:16 does not have an equivalent to the MT of 24:16-17, but it does appear in 4QSam[a].[257]

For *Jebusites*, see on 2 Sam. 5:6.

17 David sees his people as *sheep*, thus identifying himself as their shepherd, as do Hammurbi and other ancient rulers. The phrase *my father's house* means my extended family; see on 1 Sam. 17:25.[258]

It may be appropriate to think of David's feeling for his people here in this chapter and his concern with the recovery of Zion after his repentance in Ps. 51:18-19.[259]

> Do good to Zion in your good pleasure;
> build up the walls of Jerusalem;
> then will you delight in right sacrifices,
> in burnt offerings and whole burnt offerings;
> then bulls will be offered on your altar.

When David as the representative of his people (his sheep) committed that terrible sin against God, the entire country suffered the disaster not only spiritually but also politically. Hence, after repenting his great sin on the personal level in vv. 1-17, David prayed for the recovery of the place of worship for the entire people in vv. 18-19 of this psalm.

In the same way, in 2 Sam. 24, due to the king's offence to his God, his people, i.e., his *sheep* would suffer due to God's judgment. Thus, the internal scheming among David's children impacted the day-to-day lives of ordinary Israelites. Certainly Absalom's rebellion (chs. 15-19) and Sheba's revolt (ch. 20) were the outcome of his great sin. Moreover, Adonijah's self-coronation (1 K. 1:5-53) obviously divided the nation's leadership into factions. Thus, the offence of the leader involves judgment on his people. But, why ought they

257. Herbert, *RBDSS*, p. 195. See also A. Rofé, "4QSam[a] in the Light of Historico-literary Criticism: The Case of 2 Sam 24 and 1 Chr 21," in *Biblische und Judaistische Studien: Festschrift für Paolo Sacchi*, ed. A. Vivian (Judentum und Umwelt 29; Frankfurt am Main: Peter Lang, 1990), pp. 109-19.

258. Tsumura, I, p. 454.

259. See the Excursus in 2 Sam. 12 (above) on David's repentance in Ps 51.

suffer? We are not totally informed of why in the biblical context. However, it may be due to the character of the holy God who cannot compromise with the misconduct of the leader, the representative of the group. We know that, according to the ancient religious tradition, the welfare of the country deeply depends on the health of the king. See the case of the Ugaritic King Keret's serious illness, as the result of his failure to fulfill his vows to a goddess. In that case, the entire country languished from drought and famine, "in keeping with the notion that a land reflected the moral and physical state of its king."[260] According to the biblical tradition, the welfare of the country deeply depends on the moral and spiritual relationship with God of the leader of the covenant people.

Here in 2 Sam. 24 it is not David's supplication (as in Ps. 51:18) but the Lord's initiative that commanded through the prophet Gad to *erect an altar to the LORD*, so that David and his people may propitiate the anger of the Lord. So, it was not by chance that *the angel of the LORD* was by the threshing floor of Araunah (v. 16). Rather, the Lord guided David mercifully to the very place of worship, where his son Solomon eventually builds the temple for the Lord. The temple is thus the place where the sinful people are invited by God's mercy to worship and have fellowship with God.

b. David and Araunah (24:20-25)

20 *And Araunah looked down and saw the king and his servants crossing over toward him.*

And Araunah went out and prostrated himself before the king with his face to the ground.

21 *And Araunah said,*
"Why has my lord the king come to his servant?"
And David said,
"To buy the threshing floor from you
in order to build an altar to the LORD,
so that the plague may be restrained from the people."
22 *And Araunah said to David,*
"Let my lord the king take and offer up
what is good in his sight;
Look, the oxen for the burnt offering
and the threshing-sledges and the yokes of the oxen
for the wood.
23 *Everything, O king, Araunah gives to the king."*

260. Gordon, *PLMU*, p. 36.

And Araunah said to the king,
"May the LORD your God accept you favorably."
24 *And the king said to Araunah,*
"No, but I will surely buy them from you for a price;
I will not offer burnt offerings to the LORD my God
without payment."
And David bought the threshing floor and the oxen for fifty shekels of silver.
25 *And David built there an altar to the LORD and offered burnt offerings and peace offerings.*
And the LORD was entreated for the land.
And the plague was restrained from Israel.

20 This verse (v. 20) is a SETTING for the following dialogue (vv. 21-24). It consists of two subparagraphs, both of which begin with a *wayqtl* followed by a stated subject (here *Araunah*), the former with verbs of perception and the latter with verbs of movement.

Araunah looked down. Threshing floors were usually on a high place so the wind could blow the chaff away. The site of the temple (Temple Mount) is the top of the hill to the north of the City of David, about 450 yards (400 m) uphill from it.

23 *Araunah gives,* i.e., "I give," is a performative perfect,[261] thus Araunah by announcing his giving carries it out.[262]

24 For the biblical emphasis on paying the full price in the purchase of land, see Abraham's purchase of a field (Gen. 23:3-16).[263] David feels that as he is the one who sinned and it is for the sake of the nation, he should pay for the place of sacrifice.

25 What the author does not mention here, probably because everyone knew it, is that this threshing floor is the site upon which Solomon would build the temple to the Lord (2 Chr. 3:1). Thus, it is a fitting end to the story of David.

For the phrase *was entreated for the land,* see also 21:14.

The Books of Samuel end here without further development of David's plan and desire to build the temple for the Lord. First Chronicles 22:7-10 explains why the Lord did not permit David to fulfill his desire to build the

261. E. Talstra, "Text Grammar and Hebrew Bible II: Syntax and Semantics," *BO* 39 (1982) 26-38, cited by Y. Endo, *The Verbal System of Classical Hebrew in the Joseph Story: An Approach from Discourse Analysis* (SSN 32; Assen: Van Gorcum, 1996), §2.5.2.2.

262. For this verse, see B. A. Levine, "'The Lord Your God Accept You' (2 Samuel 24:23): The Altar Erected by David on the Threshing Floor of Araunah," *EI* 24 (Avraham Malamat Volume; 1993) 122-29.

263. See R. Westbrook, *Property and the Family in Biblical Law* (JSOTSS 113; Sheffield: JSOT Press, 1991).

house for the name of the Lord. It was Solomon, son of David, who actually built the earthly temple. The next book, 1 Kings, first deals with the establishment of Solomon's throne after succession troubles (chs. 1-2) and then with his building of the temple with the help of Hiram king of Tyre (5:1-6:38).

Thus, the main themes of the books of Samuel are the establishment of monarchy and kingship in Israel (1 Samuel) and the confirmation of David's throne and his heir (2 Samuel). As noted above, the climax of the books is the chapter on the Davidic covenant in 2 Sam. 7. Here, 1–2 Samuel end with God's merciful intervention to guide David and his people to the place of worship to be reconciled with God. It is the faithfulness of the Lord that led and fulfilled the whole plan of salvation through the human agencies used by his divine purpose. This plan and purpose were finally fulfilled in the life and death of his son Jesus Christ, the Messiah (see Matt. 1:1).

Index of Subjects

Index of Modern Authors

Index of Scripture and Other Ancient Sources

20:8 262
20:10 207
20:15-16 111
20:26 50, 195
20:34 111

Ruth
2:1 315
2:20 85
4:5 73
4:11 269
4:13-17 152

1 Samuel
1:3 100, 112
1:4 136, 232
1:5 17
1:7 129, 197
1:9 129
1:11 233
1:16 245, 305
1:17 234
1:20 198
1:22 208, 291
1:24 165, 243
1:28 61
2:1 304
2:2 143, 304, 315, 325
2:3 142
2:4 316
2:6 306
2:7-8 315
2:8 204
2:8b 311
2:10 321, 324
2:12-17 141
2:13 205
2:18 118
2:22 130
2:27 345
2:29 71, 185
2:30 190, 332
3:3 112, 129
3:12 210
3:14 269, 293
3:15 129
3:16-18:61 13
3:17 76, 85, 222, 271
3:19 133
3:20 252
4:1-7:2 113
4:2 154, 260
4:3 79, 107, 239
4:4 112, 180, 307
4:10 262
4:11 104
4:12 241
4:12-17 47
4:18 94, 258
4:21 198
5:5 144, 233
5:8 236
6:3 130
6:7 109, 112
6:9 97
6:12 210, 284
6:15 239
6:17 169
6:17-18 119, 257, 328
6:18b 116
6:19 84, 115, 260, 232
6:21 112
7:1 105, 111-12
7:2 112
7:6 332
7:10 310
7:16 17, 272
8:5 231
8:8 87, 116
8:11 231
8:11-17 173, 178
8:14 187
8:22 62
9-12 17
9:1 164, 315, 334
9:1-2 336
9:2 106, 296
9:3 68
9:9 253, 344
9:12 54
9:16 93, 132
9:18 81
9:20 16, 345
9:21 244
9:24 157, 214, 277
9:47 54
10:1 206
10:3 243
10:5 114, 155
10:8 16-17, 272
10:10 106, 296
10:12b 145
10:21 244
10:22 61
10:25 92-93, 181, 269
10:26 99
10:27 208
11 167
11:1 62, 168, 296
11:1-12:25 167
11:4 293, 296
11:8 62
11:11 258
11:13-15 274
11:14 272
11:14-15 234
11:15 17, 92
12:1 162
12:9 172, 271
12:11 4
12:25 186
13 17
13:1 11
13:2 106, 262
13:3 280
13:4 169
13:5 252
13:6 203
13:8 16
13:9 17
13:12 272
13:14 132
13:17 258
14:3 158-59
14:18 107, 109, 180
14:19 277
14:24 50
14:30 91
14:33 284
14:37 61
14:39 91, 222, 237, 320
14:40 222
14:48 49
14:50 189
15:1 162
15:2 49
15:4 62
15:6 64
15:10 128
15:11 115
15:12 262, 338
15:20 47
15:21 272
15:24 191
15:28 76
15:32 162

68:8 307
68:33 308
69:18 150
71:3 304
71:22 114
73:26 304
74:10 192
74:12-14 312
74:18 192
75:4 276
76:6 311
77:18 307
78:49 146
79:2 295
82:5 311
82:6 276
84:11 326
84:12 323
86:8-10 143
89 108
89:1 121
89:3 120
89:4 18
89:19 121
89:19-37 327
89:20-38 123
89:26 321
89:28 120
89:34 120
89:36 122, 138
89:36-37 326
90:10 94
95:1 321
96:10 231
102:8 304
103:4 150
104:3 308
104:7 311
106:10 150
107:2 150
109:6 341
116:3 305
118:14 325
119:57 276
120:5 126
122:5 126
127:3 224
132 9, 18, 107
132:3-5 180
132:7 107
132:11 123, 327
140:6 276
142:5 276
142:8 320
149:1 114
150 114

Proverbs
1:7 325
4:27 69
6:31 188
9:10 325
17:12 252
25:22 85
27:11 76
27:22 254
30:1 324
30:15 11
30:18 11
30:21 11
31:9 187, 231
31:21 58

Ecclesiastes
6:3 276
9:4 76
11:2 11

Song of Solomon
2:5 119, 203
4:9 205-6
5:8 203
6:8 73
7:8 276
8:6 337

Isaiah
1:11 57
1:26 234
3:3 234
3:14 187
3:20 48
4:2 18
5:25 307
6:9 129
6:10 208
7:15 257
7:22 257
9:6 234
9:7 18
9:18 328
10:17 328
11:1 18
11:3-5 231
12:2 325
13:13 307
17:11 327
19:1 308
20:2 240
20:4 168
22:4 276
24:5 122
24:18 307, 311
28:21 104
33:5 157
33:22 231
36:5 276
37:30 345
37:33 286
38:5 129
43:11 314
44:3 206
44:6 314
44:8 314
44:13 316
44:15 136
45:5 315
45:21 314
49:8 210
54:1 210
55:3 122-23, 327
60:3 326
60:19 326
61:8 122

Jeremiah
1:18 317
2:37 210
6:6 286
9:3 76
9:24 157
10:10 125, 307
12:11 210
14:12 345
15:21 150
18:21 345
22:6 260
23:5 18
24:3 213
28:13 129
29:23 203, 207
31:11 150
32:31 213
32:40 122
33:15 18
33:17 123, 327

Index of Foreign Words

mišk^{e}nôt, 107
mišpāḥāh, 217, 219, 244
mišpāṭ, 230, 231, 232
mišpāṭ ûṣdāqāh, 157, 158
*n'ṣ, 192
*nbl, 207
n^{e}bālāh, 206, 207
nēbel yāyin, 243
neged, 188
nōgah, 326
*ngʿ, 97
*nd, 327
*ndb, 204
*ndd, 327
*nwd, 327
nāweh, 239
*nwḥ, 133, 134
naḥălāh, 280
naḥălê b^{e}lîyaʿal, 305
naḥălat 'ĕlōhîm, 224
naḥălat YHWH, 287, 293
*nḥt, 317
*nṭh, 69
nākôn, 114
nēkār, 50
*nʿm, 59
nāʿîm, 59, 325
neʿîmīm, 57, 58
naʿar, 48, 165, 258
n^{e}ʿārîm, 68, 213
nepeš, 94, 214
nēṣer, 18
*nqy, 82
*nqy + *min*, 82
nēr, 298
nēr Yiśrā'ēl, 298
*nś' + *npš*, 222
nāśôg, 53
*ntn, 259
*ntr, 316
*sgr, 320
sugar, 320
*swk, 196
*swr, 69, 96
*swt, 96
sōl^{e}lāh, 286
*spd, 50, 84, 185
ʿebed, 162
*ʿbr, 277, 278
ʿad hayyôm hazzeh, 144
ʿad-m^{e}'ōd, 68
*ʿdn, 59
ʿad-ʿôlām, 80, 140, 141, 148, 322
ʿāwōn, 75, 245, 221
*ʿwr, 332
ʿiwwēr, 99, 145
ʿîr, 61
ʿîr hammāyim, 201
ʿîr hamm^{e}lûkāh, 201
ʿîr w^{e}'ēm, 287
ʿal, 17, 65, 83, 86, 115, 166, 201, 208, 216, 263, 281, 317, 319
ʿal-'ap, 213
ʿal-habbayit, 158
ʿal-kēn, 17, 99, 142, 143, 144, 145, 263, 321
ʿal-pî, 213
ʿal-haṣṣābā', 157
*ʿlh, 239
ʿlz, 55
heʿālêhā, 277
heʿāleyhā, 214
ʿām, 139, 140, 219, 223, 320, 329
ʿim, 114
*ʿnh, 137
*ʿnw, 301, 317
ʿānî, 315
k^{e}ʿāpār, 319
ʿăpar-'āreṣ, 319
ʿeṣʿādāh, 48
ʿăṣê 'ărāzîm, 100
ʿăṣê b^{e}rôšîm, 113
*ʿqr, 154
*ʿśh, 162
*ʿśh *ḥesed*, 322
ʿāśāh ṭôbāh, 64
*ʿtr, 297
*pdh, 17, 91, 147, 149, 150
*pdh + *l^{e}*, 91
*pdh + *min*, 91
pīlegeš, 75
pelek, 80, 82
pēn, 281
pisséaḥ, 99, 145, 166
*pṣr, 212
*pqd, 75
*pqd + *'t*-NP + *'l*-NP, 75
*prṣ, 104, 212
k^{e}pereṣ, 104
pārāš, 49, 154
ṣō'n, 257
ṣ^{e}bî, 54
ṣûr, 304, 320, 321
ṣūrîm, 68
ṣelṣ^{e}lîm, 114
ṣemed, 242
ṣemaḥ, 18
*ṣmt, 317
ṣinnôr, 97, 98, 99
ṣ^{e}ʿārāh, 105
ṣāraʿat, 82
*qwm, 249
qām, 319
hqym ʿāl, 324
*qyn, 51, 52, 84
qên, 298
qînāh, 51, 52, 84
qôṣ II, 327
*qr', 260
*qrh, 260
qešet, 52, 317
rô'eh, 239, 344
rō'š keleb, 76
rī'šōnîm, 160
rāb, 310
*rgz, 137, 268
*rwḥ, 214
rûaḥ, 214, 311, 319
*rwm, 55
rîb, 232
rîb ûmišpāṭ, 231
*rkb, 112
rekeb, 49, 154
rēʿeh, 241
rāpāh, 298
rīpôt, 254
śôbek, 260
śāṭān, 274, 341
śmḥ, 55
*š'l, 306
š'l b-, 61
*šb, 277
*šōbēṭ, 130
šēbeṭ, 130
šibṭê Yiśrā'ēl, 130
š^{e}bāṭîm, 261
šābāṣ, 49
*šbt, 134
*šwb, 233, 277
šwb + *dbr*, 76
*šwʿ, 319
*šwr, 315
šaḥat, 287
šîbāh, 277
šîrāh, 302
*škb, 206
*škn, 126, 137
šulḥānî, 166
šeleṭ, 155